Women: Images and Realities

W9-BWZ-807

WOMEN
IMAGES AND REALITIES

A Multicultural Anthology

Amy Kesselman

State University of New York, New Paltz

Lily D. McNair

The University of Georgia

Nancy Schniedewind

State University of New York, New Paltz

Mayfield Publishing Company
Mountain View, California
London • Toronto

Library of Congress Cataloging-in-Publication Data

Women : images and realities : a multicultural anthology / [edited by]
  Amy Kesselman, Lily D. McNair, Nancy Schniedewind.
      p.   cm.
  Includes bibliographical references.
  ISBN 1-55934-117-3
    1. Feminism—United States. 2. Women—United States—Psychology.
  3. Women—United States—Social conditions. I. Kesselman, Amy Vita
  II. McNair, Lily D. III. Schniedewind, Nancy
  HQ1421.W653 1994
  305.42'0973—dc20   94–17291
                                              CIP

Manufactured in the United States of America
10 9 8 7 6 5 4 3 2 1

Mayfield Publishing Company
1280 Villa Street
Mountain View, California 94041

Sponsoring editor, Franklin C. Graham; *production editor,* Lynn Rabin Bauer; *manuscript editor,* Betsy Dilernia; *text and cover designer,* Joan Greenfield; *manufacturing manager,* Martha Branch; *photographs:* Parts I–IV and VI–VIII by Virginia Blaisdell; Part V © 1993 Illene Perlman, Impact Visuals. The text was set in 9.5/12 Plantin Light by G&S Typesetters, Inc. and printed on 50# Ecolocote by Malloy Lithographing.

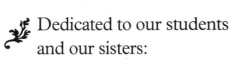 Dedicated to our students
and our sisters:
Laura Kesselman Devlin (1938–1981)
Naomi McNair
Carol Schniedewind

Contents

PART VI
THE CONSEQUENCES OF SEXISM: CURRENT ISSUES   273

Preface

This book grew out of our experiences as teachers of introductory women's studies and psychology of women courses. Dissatisfied with the available texts, we spent many years foraging among journals and anthologies to bring our students a view of feminism that reflected their diverse experience and spoke in a language that was accessible and compelling. While we wanted to include some of the fruits of feminist research, we felt it most important that students' first encounter with women's studies be one that engaged them and evoked the flash of recognition and connection that has drawn women to feminism. To this end, *Women: Images and Realities* includes a great many first person and fictional accounts of women's experiences. In order to address issues that emerge from discussions of the lives of women with diverse backgrounds, we not only included pieces about a variety of female experiences, but also, in Part V, directly address some of the systems of domination that interact with gender in women's lives.

The introductory women's studies course at State University of New York at New Paltz, called Women: Images and Realities, provided both the inspiration and the structure for this anthology. Since it was first offered in 1974, the course has developed to reflect the responses of the thousands of students who have taken it. Instructors found that students were more adept at analyzing social structures after they had discussed ideas about gender and its effect on individual women's lives. We have therefore structured the book to move from the more visible manifestations of sexism in our culture to the forms of discrimination that are embedded in social institutions.

We are all academics: a historian, a clinical psychologist, and an educator. Amy has written about women workers during World War II and is currently researching the history of women's liberation. Lily's research focuses on women's issues in addictive behaviors, especially stress-related alcohol use and African-American women's experiences in psychotherapy. Nancy's work is in the areas of multicultural education, feminist pedagogy, and cooperative learning.

Our interest in women's studies and feminism, however, is not merely academic; we are all deeply committed to feminist social change. We have tried, in *Women:*

Images and Realities, to stimulate an intellectual interest in women's studies by presenting a wide variety of women's studies topics. In addition, by demonstrating the ways that women have been able to make significant changes in our society and culture, we hope to encourage a political commitment to creating a just and generous world.

ACKNOWLEDGMENTS

This book has truly been a collaborative effort. Our cooperative working arrangements and consensual decision making, characteristic of feminist process, have been both stimulating and arduous.

Many people have made invaluable contributions to this book. Stephanie Brown, Lisa DeBoer, Lori Gross, Lena Hatchett, and Candace Watson were able and dedicated research assistants. We appreciate the ideas and perspectives that Johnella Butler and Elisa Davila contributed to the early stages of this project. Stacey Yap offered many valuable resources on Asian-American women. Rayna Green and Paula Gunn Allen provided helpful suggestions regarding a number of the selections. Virginia Blaisdell's critical eye improved several parts of this manuscript and we are extremely grateful for the use of her photographs. Thanks for the ongoing contributions of David Porter and George Roberts, and our friends and colleagues Lee Anne Bell, Eudora Chikwendu, Alison Nash, and Rickie Solinger.

Pat Clarke, the program assistant at the women's studies program at SUNY, New Paltz, has helped in innumerable and invaluable ways over the years. We also appreciate the clerical assistance of Adam Cody, Ceal Donato, Lorraine Fazio, and Lynn Johnson. The State University of New York, College at New Paltz has supported this book through several grants under its program for research and creative projects. We appreciate support from the School of Education's program for released time for research.

Franklin Graham, sponsoring editor at Mayfield Publishing Company, and Andrea Sarros, editorial assistant, have been encouraging throughout the process of completing this book. Lynn Rabin Bauer, production editor, saw the manuscript through its final stages with patience and flexibility. We also thank our copy editor, Betsy Dilernia, for her thoughtful attention to detail. The helpful comments of reviewers who read earlier drafts of the manuscript have been incorporated into the text. Finally, we thank all the contributors, especially those who wrote or revised articles for this volume.

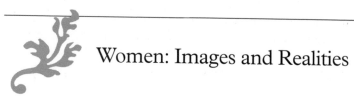

Women: Images and Realities

Introduction

In *Women: Images and Realities: A Multicultural Anthology,* you will enter the lives of many different women. By exploring their experiences and ideas, you will learn more about yourself and what it means to be female in the United States today. You will hear the voices of women of different racial, cultural, and socioeconomic backgrounds who have made various choices in their lives. Because the selections reflect a wide variety of female experience, some parts of this book will resonate with your own experience, while others will not. We hope the book will help you understand what women have in common as well as the different ways that the experience of being female is shaped by race, class, and culture.

The structure of this book was inspired by the consciousness-raising process that has been a central part of contemporary feminism. The goal of consciousness raising is to use insights from personal experience to enhance a political critique of the position of women in society. Echoing this process, the book moves back and forth between personal experience and social realities, illuminating the way sexism in society affects women's lives. We hope the selections in this book will stimulate your thinking about your own life.

ORGANIZATION AND USE OF THIS BOOK

Women: Images and Realities is divided into eight parts. We begin by introducing the subject of women's studies, an approach to knowledge that emerged as part of the contemporary feminist movement. Because a feminist perspective provides the groundwork for women's studies, Part I explores the meaning of feminism and women's studies for different groups of women. As the project of feminism is to change the position of women in society, this part includes a brief examination of women from a cross-cultural perspective. This perspective enables us to approach the study of women in the United States today with an understanding that the social position of women and men varies across cultures and has changed over time.

Part II presents prevailing ideas about what it means to be female in our society and describes the way we learn and internalize these ideas. Part III explores the effects of these ideas on women's attitudes toward our bodies and our sexuality. Because this anthology is designed to let you make connections between your personal life and social realities, it moves from a focus on individual experience in Parts II and III to an examination of the social institutions that shape women's lives in Part IV. Articles in this part demonstrate the ways that the subordination of women is deeply embedded in social institutions such as the legal system, the workplace, the family, and the health care system.

While all the parts in *Women: Images and Realities* include accounts of female experience in a variety of cultural contexts, Part V directly addresses the ways women have been divided from each other. It examines the ways that racial and class inequities in our society have often separated women, and explores the interplay between institutional discrimination and relationships among different groups of women. Part VI discusses several issues that women in the United States face today. It focuses on discrimination against women growing older, the struggle to control our reproductive lives, and various forms of violence against women. While these issues have always been a part of women's lives, they have only recently been discussed publicly as a result of the efforts of the feminist movement.

While the first six parts focus on the ways women have been constrained by our society and culture, the last two parts consider methods of improving women's lives. Part VII examines women's individual efforts to shape their own lives, and Part VIII explores ways that women have worked together to make social and political change. By reminding us of the rich tradition of female resistance both inside and outside an organized feminist movement, the selections in Parts VII and VIII provide inspiration and hope.

We have tried to create a rich brew—a mixture of short stories, poems, autobiographical accounts, and journal excerpts, as well as analytical and descriptive essays from a variety of disciplines. We hope this mixture will engage you intellectually and emotionally. Introductions to sections provide a framework that places the selections in the broader context of the part. While most of the material is current, some articles provide a historical perspective. Those written in the early years of the contemporary feminist movement are important because they laid the conceptual groundwork for future research and analysis.

While there are theoretical insights in *Women: Images and Realities,* the book does not provide a theoretical introduction to women's studies in the various disciplines. Theory is discussed in those women's studies courses that explore feminist issues and particular disciplines in depth. Here, you will hear the voices of a wide variety of women, some prominent feminist writers and some students like yourself. Because the emotions provoked by this material can sometimes be unsettling, you may find it useful to discuss your responses outside of class as well as in the classroom. These discussions might take place with friends, family members, or a counselor, depending on the intensity of your personal connection with the issues.

This book may raise specific questions for African-American, Asian-American, Latina, Native American, and Jewish women. Women of color are struggling against both sexism in minority communities and the particular ways sexism and racism interact in their lives. The different priorities and emphases that emerge from various cultural and racial contexts enrich the feminist perspective. The focus of *Women:*

Images and Realities is on the struggle of American women for freedom. The feminist movement in the U.S., however, is part of a global women's movement that has raised significant questions for women in the U.S. While some of the issues raised by the global feminist movement are touched on briefly in this book, they are explored more fully in other women's studies courses and texts.

Men who have taken women's studies courses have often found it intellectually and emotionally challenging to be in a course focused on women, taught by women, and usually comprised of a majority of female students. By listening to women's experiences and sharing their own experiences of being male in a sexist society, men can both benefit from and contribute to a women's studies course.

Many students will use this book in the introductory women's studies course, an interdisciplinary course that familiarizes students with the field of women's studies and the feminist perspective that shapes women's studies scholarship. In such a course, you may also be asked to read *The New Our Bodies, Ourselves,* written by the women of the Boston Women's Health Book Collective (Simon & Schuster, 1992). Even if the book is not assigned in your course, it is an excellent complement to *Women: Images and Realities,* and we recommend it.

HOW WE SEE FEMINISM

Because *Women: Images and Realities* is informed by a feminist perspective, we want to describe what feminism means to us. We see sexism as a central fact of all women's lives, even though it wears many different faces. The life of a single mother struggling to support her family on the wages she earns doing domestic work is very different from the life of a woman struggling to succeed in a scientific establishment dominated by men. But both must survive in a world in which women are paid less than men on all levels, both live in a society in which one woman is raped every three minutes, and both face the possibility of losing their jobs if they resist their employer's sexual advances. Feminism is a social movement whose goal is to eliminate the oppression of women in all its forms. This means making major social, economic, political, and cultural changes in our society—changes so fundamental and numerous that the task sometimes seems overwhelming. Yet feminists have succeeded in making changes that were unthinkable just 50 years ago—and such accomplishments give us hope and courage.

One of the most important ideas contemporary feminism has generated is that "the personal is political"—what happens in our private lives reflects the power relations in our society. This book examines the inequities both in women's personal lives and in the world. The belief in our right to determine the course of our lives empowers us to expand our choices: to develop relationships based on equality and mutual respect, to choose when and if we have children, to work toward career goals that are meaningful to us.

Because of the connection between personal and political life, our ability to control our own lives is limited by the environment in which we live. We cannot, for example, choose when and if we have children unless safe, effective, and legal birth control and abortion are available. Feminism is more than an individual lifestyle. It involves <u>a commitment to social change</u>, which can take a variety of forms. It might mean working to make your campus safer for women; forming a support group for women in your school, department, or office to discuss the conditions of your lives and ways to improve them; organizing a forum about sexual harassment at your workplace or on your campus; or organizing a cooperative child-care center in your community. Feminism means making changes wherever you are.

THE AUTHORS: THREE FEMINIST JOURNEYS

Because this book affirms the differences among us, we want to tell you who we are and what feminism means to each of us.

Amy   Growing up Jewish in New York City in the 1950s, I always felt different from the boys and girls whose images I confronted in grade school textbooks. The blond children and white picket fences represented normalcy to me, while my apartment building and multiethnic neighborhood seemed deviant. I went to a large city college in which men dominated the intellectual and cultural life, and I struggled to be taken seriously in and out of the classroom. The movements of the 1960s for civil rights and peace in Vietnam gave direction and meaning to my life, but I found that even as we worked toward a fairer world, women were treated in demeaning ways. In the late 1960s when feminism was a foreign word to most people, I began talking with other women about my experiences and participated in the birth of the women's liberation movement.

Feminism saved my life. It replaced the self-hatred of being female in a woman-hating culture with the power of anger at injustice. It replaced isolation with a sense of connection and identification with other women. It replaced despair with a vision of a world in which everyone is able to develop fully in loving connection with one another. But feminism did not liberate me. I am still vulnerable to rape, sexual harassment, discrimination, and unremitting degradation by the media and other woman-hating institutions. Ultimately, I see feminism as a political movement. Its power to change the world depends on its ability to mobilize women to challenge the power relations of the institutions in our society.

Lily   I grew up in a rural community on the outskirts of a major military installation in New Jersey. My childhood memories are filled with images of other children who, like me, were of mixed racial backgrounds. Most had mothers who were Asian (Japanese, Korean, or Filipino) and fathers who were African American. This setting made it impossible for me to ignore the effects of race and class on the lives of people around me. I began to realize that the world was unfair and that this unfairness shaped the lives of most of the people I knew.

My parents taught me, very early, that I was a black child in a racist society. There were times when I didn't quite understand why they attached so much significance to this fact, but I gradually learned about the world from their history. My mother talked about her experiences as a Japanese girl-child during World War II, and as a "war bride" in the Deep South of the 1950s. Bitter toward a society that treated him as less than a person because of his black skin, my father promised me that one day I would understand what he meant.

When I went away to an Ivy League college, I saw inequities both within the structure of the institution (such as hiring and tenure practices) and within the student body. Blacks and women were still viewed as unwanted, unqualified newcomers to this formerly all-white, all-male bastion. Fortunately, the African-American community provided me with peers and a black, female mentor who helped strengthen my commitment to fighting racial, sexual, and class oppression.

For me, feminism is a natural extension of my experiences as an African-American-Asian woman. Feminism provides me with a framework for looking at and understanding power relationships in our society. I recognize that I must be aware of the realities of oppression because this knowledge forces me to challenge racism and sexism. A feminist perspective is consistent with my view of a more just society—one in which differences among people can be appreciated and celebrated, not dismissed. Feminism is a positive force in my personal life as well. It enables me to develop relationships based on equality, cooperation, and an affirmation of the strengths of women and men.

Nancy Growing up as a white female in a semirural New England community, I was not aware of the price I was paying for being female. I did not wonder why I hated science. No one called my attention to how few females appeared in my textbooks or discussed the ways that the absence of role models inhibits learning and stunts expectations. I never wondered why no one encouraged me to become a scientist despite my aptitude for science. Though I knew I loved sports, I never connected my failure to take myself seriously as an athlete with the fact that the high school athletic budget and programs for boys' sports were extensive, while those for girls were nonexistent.

I was also unaware of the privileges I received by being white. I didn't realize that because we were white, my family was able to move to our town and find housing, thereby benefiting from better public schools. I didn't wonder why there were only two African-American families in our town. I never thought about the comfort of being in the racial majority in my school and how my sense of being "normal" enhanced my ability to learn. I didn't ask why I had the privilege of going home to play when my African-American classmates went home to help their mothers do the laundry they took in to support their families.

I saw my life as my own. Even throughout my masters degree program, I failed to see patterns of discrimination and privilege. I thought the sexual harassment I experienced was my own problem, not part of a pattern experienced by millions of women. There were no women's studies courses in the late 1960s, and it was only through long talks with friends and co-workers that I opened my eyes to sexism. Subsequently, I read much of what the burgeoning women's movement was producing. Looking back at my life, I saw how I had been affected by gender, race, and class, and I looked to the future with a renewed commitment to work for change.

Feminism offers me the support, values, and ideas for living an authentic life. It provides me a way of understanding women's experiences and a vision of a more just and humane future. Feminism contributes to my role as an educator by helping me understand how sexism limits both men's and women's educational potential. Feminist values inspire a more equitable and empowering educational vision and practice. Feminism reaffirms for me the values of cooperation and care, strengthening my female friendships. As a family member, feminism gives me the consciousness and strength to make family relationships more equitable. Finally, feminism sustains my faith in women's collective power to transform individual lives and social institutions.

As our own stories demonstrate, the experience of integrating feminism into one's life can be challenging and exhilarating. We hope this book makes you feel stronger and better able to make choices in your own life and participate in the process of creating a more just and generous world.

PART I

What Is Women's Studies?

What *is* women's studies? You will probably hear this question often when you tell people you are taking women's studies courses. The question itself tells you something about the answer; some faculty members and students still see women's studies as marginal to the main business of the university. Yet to countless others, women's studies is an important and exciting experience, one that introduces new ways of seeing both the world and oneself. Women's studies scholars and teachers place women at center stage in the learning process, challenging both the content and the form of education. A basic tenet of women's studies is that women's experiences and contributions are significant to understanding our world. A women's studies approach to education emphasizes an interactive learning process in which all students are intellectually and emotionally engaged.

These goals of women's studies contradict the realities of schooling in America that many girls and women encounter. Education has often been a bittersweet experience for women. We expect that knowledge of our world can be empowering. For many women, particularly those who have been the victims of racial or ethnic discrimination, education promises access to resources and opportunities. But U.S. educational institutions have too often been limiting, rather than empowering, for women. The practices of educational institutions frequently encourage girls and women to pursue occupations in traditionally "female" areas rather than in traditionally "male" domains, such as mathematics and the sciences. Schools and teachers tend to reward girls who are compliant and passive rather than assertive and inquisitive. Men have historically exercised authority in institutions of higher learning, determining "valid" areas of inquiry and "legitimate" methods of analysis and research. The world that students encounter in college classrooms can be one where women play marginal roles, while men occupy center stage. The dominant message is that human experience equals male experience.

Out of the conviction that women are worth learning about and that understanding women's experiences helps us understand how to change the condition of women, women's studies was born. Women's studies courses first appeared in the 1970s and quickly spread across the country. By 1989, there were women's studies programs in over 500 colleges in the United States. In the past 20 years, thousands of books and articles about women have been published, challenging old assumptions and charting new territory. Today, women's studies conferences, workshops, journals, and research institutes flourish.

A women's studies perspective contests the male-centered bias of scholarship. The nature of this challenge, however, has changed as the field of women's studies has developed. Initially, women scholars endeavored to compensate for the absence of women in the literature of various academic areas by researching women's achievements. It quickly became apparent, however, that the basic concepts of many academic disciplines excluded women. In order for women to be at the center of human experience rather than an anomalous footnote, the basic assumptions that structure academic knowledge have to be challenged. In the field of history, for example, historical subject matter was traditionally limited to the public arena such as political parties, wars, and the economy. The domestic world, where many women spent a great deal of their time, was considered trivial or irrelevant; and the relationship between the domestic and public worlds was ignored. In literature, the very definition of what constitutes great literature or "the canon" was based on standards generated by white male authors. As women's studies research develops, it is transforming the terrain of human knowledge. When women are placed at the center of inquiry, everything changes, as if a kaleidoscope has been turned. Even the boundaries that separate the disciplines begin to appear arbitrary when we seek to answer questions about women's lives.

As feminist scholars began to chart female experience, they sometimes found the available vocabulary inadequate and confusing. As a result, feminist scholarship has generated several new words and has endowed familiar words with new meaning. The word "gender," for example, used to pertain only to grammar but has come to mean the socially constructed behaviors and characteristics that are associated with each sex. While gender is a social category, the word "sex" describes the physiological identities of women and men. The distinction between sex and gender enables us to see that the particular expectations for women and men in our culture are neither immutable nor universal.

The word "sexism" appeared because the available phrase, "sex discrimination," did not adequately describe the pervasive bias against women in our culture. Sexism has therefore come to mean behaviors, attitudes, and institutions based on assumption of male superiority. The word "patriarchy" refers to "power of the fathers" and is used by feminists in two ways: to describe a society in which older men are in positions of power and to describe a male-dominated society.

Women's studies theory and courses are inspired by the ideas of feminism. "Feminism" refers to the belief that women have been historically subordinate to men, and a commitment to working for freedom for women in all aspects of social life. While feminist beliefs, values, and practices are continually evolving, reflecting new ideas, movements, and historical research, it is clear that similar values have informed the lives and work of many different groups of women, even when they may not have identified their beliefs as "feminist." Paula Gunn Allen, a Native American writer, pointed out that roots of contemporary feminism can be found in many Native American cultures.[1] Some of these societies were gynarchies—governed by women—which were egalitarian, pacifist, and spiritually based. These values and practices are comparable to those of present-day feminism such as cooperation and respect for human freedom. As we understand the varied ways that women have worked toward self-determination in different contexts and cultures throughout history, the definition of feminism becomes broader and richer.

The word "feminism" originated in France and was introduced into this country in the early 1900s after efforts to expand women's political rights had been flourishing throughout the world for many decades.[2] The women who first identified them-

---

[1] Paula Gunn Allen, *The Sacred Hoop: Recovering the Feminine in American Indian Traditions* (Boston: Beacon Press, 1986), p. 213.
[2] Nancy Cott, *The Grounding of Modern Feminism* (New Haven, CT: Yale University Press, 1987), p. 14.

selves as feminist in the early twentieth century believed that the "emancipation of women" required changes in the relations between women and men and between women and the family, as well as between women and the state. At a 1914 meeting entitled "What Is Feminism?" Mary Jenny Howe stated: "We want simply to be ourselves, . . . not just our little female selves but our whole big human selves."[3]

For many women, the goal of freedom for women was inextricably linked with the end of all forms of domination. Women of color in particular saw the connections between sexual and racial oppression. Anna Cooper, an African-American woman, pointed out in her address to the World's Congress of Representative Women in 1896:

> Not till . . . race, color, sex and condition are seen as accidents, and not the substance of life . . . not till then is woman's lesson taught and woman's cause won—not the white woman's, nor the black woman's nor the red woman's but the cause of every man and every woman who has writhed silently under a mighty wrong. Woman's wrongs are thus indissolubly linked with all undefended woe, and the acquirement of her "rights" will mean the final triumph of all right over might. . . .[4]

U.S. historians often refer to the movement that began in the nineteenth century and culminated with the Nineteenth Amendment, granting women the right to vote, as the first wave of feminism. The legal, educational, and political achievements of the movement were considerable, despite the fact that it faced enormous opposition to every demand. Yet the organizations that led the movement did not speak for all women and often refused to seriously consider the concerns of African-American and immigrant women. The history of the suffrage movement demonstrates how race and class divisions can prevent a movement from working effectively to achieve freedom for all women.

In the decades after women won the right to vote in 1920, the organized women's rights movement dissipated and the word "feminism" fell into disuse and ill repute. In the 1960s, a new generation revived the fight for what they now called "women's liberation" and a vision of a world free of domination and subordination. This movement struck a responsive chord in thousands of women. The feminist movement grew rapidly throughout the 1970s, permeating every aspect of social, political, and cultural life. The new feminist movement has argued that reproductive rights are essential for women's freedom. It has criticized the disadvantaged position of women in the workplace and the subordination of women in the family, pointing out the connection between the place of women in the labor force and the family. By declaring that "the personal is political," contemporary feminists have brought into the open subjects that had only previously been discussed in whispers, such as sexuality, rape, incestuous sexual abuse, and domestic violence. For feminists, all of these struggles are inextricably connected, and changes in all of them are necessary to attain freedom for women.

---

[3] Quoted in Cott, p. 39.
[4] Anna Cooper in May Wright Sewell, *World's Congress of Representative Women* (Chicago, 1983), quoted in Elsa Barkley Brown, "Womanist Consciousness: Maggie Lena Walker and the Independent Order of St. Luke," *Signs*, Vol. 14 (3), 614.

Feminism is continually developing a more multicultural and inclusive perspective, mirroring the lives of women in all races, ethnic groups, and classes. Feminists of varied races and ethnicities are generating theory and practice that address their particular experiences and consciousness, broadening and deepening the scope of feminist analysis.

Black feminist thought, for example, reflects the unique position of African-American women in American society. As eloquently expressed by Alice Walker, black feminism, or "womanism," draws on the historical strength of black women in their families and communities and the rich African-American tradition of resistance and survival. Black feminists have also emphasized the concept of "multiple consciousness": that the distinct systems of racism, sexism, and class oppression interact simultaneously in the lives of women of color in the United States. They have also suggested an Afrocentric rather than a Eurocentric perspective on the history of women, allowing for an appreciation of the powerful roles that women played in some African societies.

Jewish feminists have also reclaimed their tradition of Jewish female resistance and have reexamined insulting stereotypes like "pushy Jewish mother" and "Jewish American Princess" to express the legitimacy of female assertiveness. They have revived Rabbi Hillel's question, "If I am not for myself, who will be? If I am only for myself, what am I?" to explore both the meaning of anti-Semitism for Jewish women and the importance of the connections between different groups of suppressed people. Reflecting on this project, Melanie Kaye/Kantrowitz has pointed out that "What is best in people is a sturdy connection between respect for the self and respect for the other: reaching in and out at the same time."[5]

Asian and Latina feminists have pointed out the tensions between immigrant and U.S. cultures, and the concurrent need to affirm their cultural heritage and reject its sexism. Traditional Japanese culture, for instance, expects women to be docile and to put family honor ahead of their own needs. One's self is inextricably tied to one's family; to break away is often viewed as an act of betrayal. Asian-American feminists have also confronted the myths about Asian women's sexuality, myths that have emerged from an interplay between Western stereotypes of Asian women and the expectations of women in Asian cultures. Latina feminists have demonstrated the need to negotiate a path between the sometimes conflicting demands of the Latino community's expectations and female self-determination. Feminism for Latina women, and women of other oppressed groups, means simultaneously working with Latino men against their common oppression and challenging sexist or "macho" attitudes and behavior.

Contemporary American Indian feminists carry many of the traditional values and practices of woman-centered Native American cultures into the present. In addition, Native American women's history and their vision of connectedness to the earth, along with a legacy of responsibility toward the environment, are emerging as important concerns for many feminists.

---

[5]Melanie Kaye/Kantrowitz, "To Be a Radical Jew in the Late Twentieth Century," *Sinister Wisdom*, Vol. 29–30 (1986), p. 280.

The ideas and concerns of different groups of women are expanding the boundaries of feminism, contributing to multicultural feminist theory and practice aimed at liberating all people. As this feminism continues to develop, we acknowledge and incorporate the struggles of women who have worked for equality and freedom for women, though they may not have called themselves "feminists."

The atmosphere of a women's studies classroom is often different from that of most academic classrooms. Women's studies emerged as an academic discipline from women asking questions about their own experiences, and this process remains a central part of a women's studies education. Women's studies instructors usually encourage students to ask questions of the material, and to bring their own experiences to bear. The values of feminism, including a critique of all forms of domination, an emphasis on cooperation, and a belief in the integration of theory and practice, have shaped an approach to teaching called "feminist pedagogy," which makes the women's studies classroom an interactive learning environment.

The essays in Part I emphasize women's personal experiences as they gain deeper awareness and understanding of the value of a women's studies education. The first four selections are about women taking an active stance in their lives and their education. Articles 5–9 focus more specifically on the role of women's studies in the education of young women today. The part closes with a biological and an anthropological examination of the social construction of gender.

Speaking up for themselves is an essential first step for women in taking an active role in their education. In the first selection, bell hooks writes from the context of the Southern black community in which she grew up, where "talking back" as a girl was an act of daring. It often takes such courage for women to speak up for themselves in educational settings, where male-oriented norms, curricula, and classroom processes often silence women's voices.

Adrienne Rich, feminist author and poet, wrote the next selection as an address to a primarily white, female graduating college class in 1977. Its message, about the importance of women "claiming an education" that is meaningful to them, continues to be relevant today in any educational setting. The tradition of female activity and assertiveness is reflected in Pulitzer Prize-winning author and poet Alice Walker's definition of "womanist." Drawing on the history and culture of women of color, Walker appreciates and celebrates the resourcefulness and resiliency of women. These and other aspects of women's experience are also at the heart of teaching and learning in women's studies.

Women's studies courses are different from what students experience in many other educational settings. Taly Rutenberg compares women's studies to more traditional approaches to education and analyzes the many sources of learning for students in women's studies. Through its commitment to challenging gender bias, validating women's personal experience, valuing diversity, and effecting change, women's studies offers a unique learning experience.

The next five articles are voices of a women's studies teacher and former students. These women, of varied racial and ethnic backgrounds, explore the meaning and value of a women's studies education for their own lives, both personally and politically.

Because women's studies validates the potential for change in society, it challenges the assumptions that women's inferior status is natural, biologically determined, and consistent throughout history. An important tool of feminist thought has been the concept of social construction. Rather than seeing human behavior as a reflection of innate tendencies or characteristics, feminist scholars have analyzed the ways that social and cultural norms, institutions, values, and power relationships shape human behavior and attitudes.

Ruth Hubbard explores the ways in which biological interpretations of women's behavior reinforce socially constructed ideas about what are acceptable and appropriate aspects of their lives. Meredith Brown points out in the final article that cross-cultural studies reveal wide variations in the ways cultures distribute power and resources between women and men, and how those cultures define femininity and masculinity. Such knowledge demonstrates that our own system of gender relations, rather than being "natural," is socially constructed and therefore can be changed. It is through women's studies that students explore the potential for such change.

 1

Talking Back

BELL HOOKS

In the world of the southern black community I grew up in, "back talk" and "talking back" meant speaking as an equal to an authority figure. It meant daring to disagree and sometimes it just meant having an opinion. In the "old school," children were meant to be seen and not heard. My great-grandparents, grandparents, and parents were all from the old school. To make yourself heard if you were a child was to invite punishment, the back-hand lick, the slap across the face that would catch you unaware, or the feel of switches stinging your arms and legs.

To speak then when one was not spoken to was a courageous act—an act of risk and daring. And yet it was hard not to speak in warm rooms where heated discussions began at the crack of dawn, women's voices filling the air, giving orders, making threats, fussing. Black men may have excelled in the art of poetic preaching in the male-dominated church, but in the church of the home, where the everyday rules of how to live and how to act were established, it was black women who preached. There, black women spoke in a language so rich, so poetic, that it felt to me like being shut off from life, smothered to death if one were not allowed to participate.

It was in that world of woman talk (the men were often silent, often absent) that was born in me the craving to speak, to have a voice, and not just any voice but one that could be identified as belonging to me. To make my voice, I had to speak, to hear myself talk—and talk I did—darting in and out of grown folks' conversations and dialogues, answering questions that were not directed at me, endlessly asking questions, making speeches. Needless to say, the punishments for these acts of speech seemed endless. They were intended to silence me—the child—and more particularly the girl child. Had I been a boy, they might have encouraged me to speak believing that I might someday be called to preach. There was no "calling" for talking girls, no legitimized rewarded speech. The punishments I received for "talking back" were intended to suppress all possibility that I would create my own speech. That speech was to be suppressed so that the "right speech of womanhood" would emerge.

Within feminist circles, silence is often seen as the sexist "right speech of womanhood"—the sign of woman's submission to patriarchal authority. This emphasis on woman's silence may be an accurate remembering of what has taken place in the households of women from WASP backgrounds in the United States, but in black communities (and diverse ethnic communities), women have not been silent. Their voices can be heard. Certainly for black women, our struggle has not been to emerge from silence into speech but to change the nature and direction of our speech, to make a speech that compels listeners, one that is heard.

Our speech, "the right speech of womanhood," was often the soliloquy, the talking into thin air, the talking to ears that do not hear you—the talk that is simply not listened to. Unlike the black male preacher whose speech was to be heard, who was to be listened to, whose words were to be remembered, the voices of black women—giving orders, making threats, fussing—could be tuned out, could become a kind of background music, audible but not acknowledged as significant speech. Dialogue—the sharing of speech and recognition—took place not between mother and child or mother and male authority figure but among black women. I can remember watching fascinated as our mother talked with her mother, sisters, and women friends. The intimacy and intensity of their speech—the satisfaction they received from talking to one another, the pleasure, the joy. It was in this world of woman speech, loud talk, angry words, women with tongues quick and sharp, tender sweet tongues, touching our world with their words, that I made speech my birthright—and the right to voice, to authorship, a privilege I would not be denied. It was in that world and because of it that I came to dream of writing, to write.

Writing was a way to capture speech, to hold onto it, keep it close. And so I wrote down bits and pieces of conversations, confessing in cheap diaries that soon fell apart from too much handling, expressing the intensity of my sorrow, the anguish of speech—for I was always saying the wrong thing, asking the wrong questions. I could not confine my speech to the necessary corners and concerns of life. I hid these writings under my bed, in pillow stuffings, among faded underwear. When my sisters found and read them, they ridiculed and mocked me—poking fun. I felt violated, ashamed, as if the secret parts of my self had been exposed, brought into the open, and hung like newly clean laundry, out in the air for everyone to see. The fear of exposure, the fear that one's deepest emotions and innermost thoughts will be dismissed as mere nonsense, felt by so many young girls keeping diaries, holding

and hiding speech, seems to me now one of the barriers that women have always needed and still need to destroy so that we are no longer pushed into secrecy or silence.

Despite my feelings of violation, of exposure, I continued to speak and write, choosing my hiding places well, learning to destroy work when no safe place could be found. I was never taught absolute silence, I was taught that it was important to speak but to talk a talk that was in itself a silence. Taught to speak and yet beware of the betrayal of too much heard speech, I experienced intense confusion and deep anxiety in my efforts to speak and write. Reciting poems at Sunday afternoon church service might be rewarded. Writing a poem (when one's time could be "better" spent sweeping, ironing, learning to cook) was luxurious activity, indulged in at the expense of others. Questioning authority, raising issues that were not deemed appropriate subjects brought pain, punishments—like telling mama I wanted to die before her because I could not live without her—that was crazy talk, crazy speech, the kind that would lead you to end up in a mental institution. "Little girl," I would be told, "if you don't stop all this crazy talk and crazy acting you are going to end up right out there at Western State."

Madness, not just physical abuse, was the punishment for too much talk if you were female. Yet even as this fear of madness haunted me, hanging over my writing like a monstrous shadow, I could not stop the words, making thought, writing speech. For this terrible madness which I feared, which I was sure was the destiny of daring women born to intense speech (after all, the authorities emphasized this point daily), was not as threatening as imposed silence, as suppressed speech.

Safety and sanity were to be sacrificed if I was to experience defiant speech. Though I risked them both, deep-seated fears and anxieties characterized my childhood days. I would speak but I would not ride a bike, play hardball, or hold the gray kitten. Writing about the ways we are traumatized in our growing-up years, psychoanalyst Alice Miller makes the point in *For Your Own Good* that it is not clear why childhood wounds become for some folk an opportunity to grow, to move forward rather than backward in the process of self-realization. Certainly, when I reflect on the trials of my growing-up years, the many punishments, I can see now that in resistance I learned to be vigilant in the nourishment of my spirit, to be tough, to courageously protect that spirit from forces that would break it.

While punishing me, my parents often spoke about the necessity of breaking my spirit. Now when I ponder the silences, the voices that are not heard, the voices of those wounded and/or oppressed individuals who do not speak or write, I contemplate the acts of persecution, torture—the terrorism that breaks spirits, that makes creativity impossible. I write these words to bear witness to the primacy of resistance struggle in any situation of domination (even within family life); to the strength and power that emerges from sustained resistance and the profound conviction that these forces can be healing, can protect us from dehumanization and despair.

These early trials, wherein I learned to stand my ground, to keep my spirit intact, came vividly to mind after I published *Ain't I A Woman* and the book was sharply and harshly criticized. While I had expected a climate of critical dialogue, I was not expecting a critical avalanche that had the power in its intensity to crush the spirit, to push one into silence. Since that time, I have heard stories about black women, about women of color, who write and publish (even when the work is quite successful) having nervous breakdowns, being made mad because they cannot bear the harsh responses of family, friends, and unknown critics, or becoming silent, unproductive. Surely, the absence of a humane critical response has tremendous impact on the writer from any oppressed, colonized group who endeavors to speak. For us, true speaking is not solely an expression of creative power; it is an act of resistance, a political gesture that challenges politics of domination that would render us nameless and voiceless. As such, it is a courageous act—as such, it represents a threat. To those who wield oppressive power, that which is threatening must necessarily be wiped out, annihilated, silenced.

Recently, efforts by black women writers to call attention to our work serve to highlight both our presence and absence. Whenever I peruse women's bookstores, I am struck not by the rapidly growing body of feminist writing by black women, but by the paucity of available published material. Those of us who write and are published remain few in number. The context of silence is varied and multi-dimensional. Most obvious are the ways racism, sexism, and class exploitation act to suppress and silence. Less obvious are the inner struggles, the efforts made to gain the necessary confidence to write, to re-write, to fully develop craft and skill—and the extent to which such efforts fail.

Although I have wanted writing to be my lifework since childhood, it has been difficult for me to claim "writer" as part of that which identifies and shapes my everyday reality. Even after publishing books, I would often speak of wanting to be a writer as though these works did not exist. And though I would be told, "you are a writer," I was not yet ready to fully affirm this truth. Part of myself was still held captive by domineering forces of history, of familial life that had charted a map of silence, of right speech. I had not completely let go of the fear of saying the wrong thing, of being punished. Somewhere in the deep recesses of my mind, I believed I could avoid both responsibility and punishment if I did not declare myself a writer.

One of the many reasons I chose to write using the pseudonym bell hooks, a family name (mother to Sarah Oldham, grandmother to Rosa Bell Oldham, great-grandmother to me), was to construct a writer-identity that would challenge and subdue all impulses leading me away from speech into silence. I was a young girl buying bubble gum at the corner store when I first really heard the full name bell hooks. I had just "talked back" to a grown person. Even now I can recall the surprised look, the mocking tones that informed me I must be kin to bell hooks—a sharp-tongued woman, a woman who spoke her mind, a woman who was not afraid to talk back. I claimed this legacy of defiance, of will, of courage, affirming my link to female ancestors who were bold and daring in their speech. Unlike my bold and daring mother and grandmother, who were not supportive of talking back, even though they were assertive and powerful in their speech, bell hooks as I discovered, claimed, and invented her was my ally, my support.

That initial act of talking back outside the home was empowering. It was the first of many acts of defiant speech that would make it possible for me to emerge as an independent thinker and writer. In retrospect, "talking back" became for me a rite of initiation, testing my courage, strengthening my commitment, preparing me for the days ahead—the days when writing, rejection notices, periods of silence, publication, ongoing development seem impossible but necessary.

Moving from silence into speech is for the oppressed, the colonized, the exploited, and those who stand and struggle side by side a gesture of defiance that heals, that makes new life and new growth possible. It is that act of speech, of "talking back," that is no mere gesture of empty words, that is the expression of our movement from object to subject—the liberated voice.   [1989]

 2

Claiming an Education

ADRIENNE RICH

For this convocation, I planned to separate my remarks into two parts: some thoughts about you, the women students here, and some thoughts about us who teach in a women's college. But ultimately, those two parts are indivisible. If university education means anything beyond the processing of human beings into expected roles, through credit hours, tests, and grades (and I believe that in a women's college especially it *might* mean much more), it implies an ethical and intellectual contract between teacher and students. This contract must remain intuitive, dynamic, unwritten; but we must turn to it again and again if learning is to be reclaimed from the depersonalizing and cheapening pressures of the present-day academic scene.

The first thing I want to say to you who are students is that you cannot afford to think of yourselves as being here to *receive* an education; you will do much better to think of yourselves as being here to *claim* one. One of the dictionary definitions of the verb "to claim" is: to take as the rightful owner; to assert in the face of possible contradiction. "To receive" is to come into possession of; to act as receptacle or container for; to accept as authoritative or true. The difference is that between acting and being acted-upon, and for women it can literally mean the difference between life and death.

One of the devastating weaknesses of university learning, of the store of knowledge and opinion that

has been handed down through academic training, has been its almost total erasure of women's experience and thought from the curriculum, and its exclusion of women as members of the academic community. Today, with increasing numbers of women students in nearly every branch of higher learning, we still see very few women students in nearly every branch of higher learning, we still see very few women in the upper levels of faculty and administration in most institutions. Douglass College itself is a women's college in a university administered overwhelmingly by men, who in turn are answerable to the state legislature, again composed predominantly of men. But the most significant fact for you is that what you learn here (and I mean not only at Douglass but any college in any university) is how *men* have perceived and organized their experience, their history, their ideas of social relationships, good and evil, sickness and health, etc. When you read or hear about "great issues," "major texts," "the mainstream of Western thought," you are hearing about what men, above all white men, in their male subjectivity, have decided is important.

Black and other minority peoples have for some time recognized that their racial and ethnic experience was not accounted for in the studies broadly labeled human; and that even the sciences can be racist. For many reasons, it has been more difficult for women to comprehend our exclusion, and to realize that even the sciences can be sexist. For one thing, it is only within the last hundred years that higher education has grudgingly been opened up to women at all, even to white, middle-class women. And many of us have found ourselves pouring eagerly over books with titles like: *The Descent of Man; Man and His Symbols; Irrational Man; The Phenomenon of Man; The Future of Man; Man and the Machine; From Man to Man; May Man Prevail?; Man, Science and Society; One-Dimensional Man*—books to describe a "human" reality that does not include over one-half the human species.

Less than a decade ago, with the rebirth of a feminist movement in this country, women students and teachers in a number of universities, began to demand and set up women's studies courses—to *claim* a woman-directed education. And, despite the inevitable accusations of "unscholarly," "group therapy," "faddism," etc., despite backlash and budget cuts, women's studies are still growing, offering to more and more women a new intellectual grasp on their lives, new understanding of our history, a fresh vision of the human experience, and also a critical basis for evaluating what they hear and read in other courses, and in the society at large.

But my talk is not really about women's studies, much as I believe in their scholarly, scientific, and human necessity. While I think that any Douglass student has everything to gain by investigating and enrolling in women's studies courses, I want to suggest that there is a more essential experience that you owe yourselves, one which courses in women's studies can greatly enrich, but which finally depends on you, in all your interactions with yourself and your world. This is the experience of *taking responsibility toward yourselves*. Our upbringing as women has so often told us that this should come second to our relationships and responsibilities to other people. We have been offered ethical models of the self-denying wife and mother; intellectual models of the brilliant but slapdash dilettante who never commits herself to anything the whole way, or the intelligent woman who denies her intelligence in order to seem more "feminine," or who sits in passive silence even when she disagrees inwardly with everything that is being said around her.

Responsibility to yourself means refusing to let others do your thinking, talking, and naming for you; it means learning to respect and use your own brains and instincts, hence, grappling with hard work. It means that you do not treat your body as a commodity with which to purchase superficial intimacy or economic security; for our bodies and minds are inseparable in this life, and when we allow our bodies to be treated as objects, our minds are in mortal danger. It means insisting that those to whom you give your friendship and love are able to respect your mind. It means being able to say, with Charlotte Bronte's Jane Eyre: "I have an inward treasure born with me, which can keep me alive if all the extraneous delights should be withheld or offered only at a price I cannot afford to give."

Responsibility to yourself means that you don't fall for shallow and easy solutions—predigested books and ideas, weekend encounters guaranteed to change your life, taking "gut" courses instead of ones you know will challenge you, bluffing at school

and life instead of doing solid work, marrying early as an escape from real decisions, getting pregnant as an evasion of already existing problems. It means that you refuse to sell your talents and aspirations short, simply to avoid conflict and confrontation. And this, in turn, means resisting the forces in society which say that women should be nice, play safe, have low professional expectations, drown in love and forget about work, live through others, and stay in the places assigned to us. It means that we insist on a life of meaningful work, insist that work be as meaningful as love and friendship in our lives. It means, therefore, the courage to be "different"; not to be continuously available to others when we need time for ourselves and our work; to be able to demand of others—parents, friends, roommates, teachers, lovers, husbands, children—that they respect our sense of purpose and our integrity as persons. Women everywhere are finding the courage to do this, more and more, and we are finding that courage both in our study of women in the past who possessed it, and in each other as we look to other women for comradeship, community, and challenge. The difference between a life lived actively, and a life of passive drifting and dispersal of energies, is an immense difference. Once we begin to feel committed to our lives, responsible to ourselves, we can never again be satisfied with the old, passive way.

I have said that the contract on the student's part involves that you demand to be taken seriously so that you can also go on taking yourself seriously. This means seeking out criticism, recognizing that the most affirming thing anyone can do for you is demand that you push yourself further, show you the range of what you *can* do. It means rejecting attitudes of "take-it-easy," "why-be-so-serious," "why-worry-you'll-probably-get-married-anyway." It means assuming your share of responsibility for what happens in the classroom, because that affects the quality of your daily life here. It means that the student sees herself engaged with her teachers in an active, ongoing struggle for a real education. But for her to do this, her teachers must be committed to the belief that women's minds and experience are intrinsically valuable and indispensable to any civilization worthy of the name; that there is no more exhilarating and intellectually fertile place in the academic world today than a women's college—*if* both students and teachers in large enough numbers are trying to fulfill this contract. The contract is really a pledge of mutual seriousness about women, about language, ideas, methods, and values. It is our shared commitment toward a world in which the inborn potentialities of so many women's minds will no longer be wasted, raveled-away, paralyzed, or denied.   [1977]

❦ 3

Womanism

ALICE WALKER

Womanist   **1.** From *womanish.* (Opp. of "girlish," i.e., frivolous, irresponsible, not serious.) A black feminist or feminist of color. From the black folk expression of mothers to female children, "You acting womanish," i.e., like a woman. Usually referring to outrageous, audacious, courageous or *willful* behavior. Wanting to know more and in greater depth than is considered "good" for one. Interested in grown-up doings. Acting grown up. Being grown up. Interchangeable with another black folk expression: "You trying to be grown." Responsible. In charge. *Serious.*

* * *

2. *Also:* A woman who loves other women, sexually and/or nonsexually. Appreciates and prefers women's culture, women's emotional flexibility (values tears as natural counterbalance of laughter), and women's strength. Sometimes loves individual men, sexually and/or nonsexually. Committed to survival and wholeness of entire people, male *and* female. Not a separatist, except periodically, for health. Traditionally universalist, as in: "Mama, why are we brown, pink, and yellow, and our cousins are white, beige, and black?" Ans.: "Well, you know the colored race is just like a flower garden, with every color flower represented." Traditionally capable, as in: "Mama, I'm walking to Canada and I'm taking you and a bunch of other slaves with me." Reply: "It wouldn't be the first time."

* * *

3. Loves music. Loves dance. Loves the moon. *Loves* the Spirit. Loves love and food and roundness. Loves struggle. *Loves* the Folk. Loves herself. *Regardless.*

* * *

4. Womanist is to feminist as purple to lavender.
                                    [1983]

❦ 4

Learning Women's Studies

TALY RUTENBERG

We are all familiar with the cliché of the professor, pointer in hand, stoically drilling information into the heads of students who appear as bored as he does. In this scenario, the three components of education—the student, the teacher and the material—are not interacting. The result is an alien and alienating educational experience. One of the unique and inspiring features of women's studies is that it is a discipline which inherently appreciates and encourages the interrelationship between these components of learning. Women students have to strain not to identify, as course content is intimately linked to our experience. Instructors are often enthusiastically engaged in teaching because women's studies is an evolving and personally relevant discipline. And women's studies content is engaging because it is not an isolated study, it is intimately connected with the women's movement which is a dynamic and politically volatile social force. Appropriately, the principles of the movement are evident in the content and method of teaching women's studies. Feminist process (e.g., politicizing the personal, interacting cooperatively), manifested academically as women's studies, creates the potential for what I call a fulfilling learning experience.

In the minds of students, the university is no longer merely a sanctuary of knowledge. We have limited use for theories which are disseminated in an intellectual vacuum and whose application is restricted to the academic setting. We expect a college education to be intellectually stimulating as well as practical. In order for students to have a meaningful learning experience, we must be educated in ways which not only stimulate our creative conceptual faculties but which facilitate the application of creative thought to circumstances in the outside world.

We know that no theory or critique has a purely intellectual foundation: we are emotional as well as intellectual beings. To be wholly effective, education must be approached with an appreciation of the totality of our natures.

Finally, students need to be trained and encouraged to think beyond our fore-scholars. We should not merely be indoctrinated with their truths; rather, we should be invited to think through theories and methods with respect to our present cultural disposition and social circumstances. I believe that a "fulfilling learning experience" develops a student's creative intellectual faculties and encourages her to see the relationship between her intellect, her personal life and society.

THE LEARNING EXPERIENCE IN WOMEN'S STUDIES

How does women's studies, in contrast to the traditional disciplines and even other non-traditional disciplines, offer students a fulfilling learning experience? I believe the answer lies in women's studies' connection to the ideals of the women's movement, which, manifested in the classroom, can increase the potential for a meaningful and relevant learning experience.

The most significant difference between women's studies and other disciplines is that women's studies emerged from a political and social movement outside the walls of the university. As a result, its concerns are not strictly academic and its legitimacy is dependent on its acceptance by the feminist community as well as by the standards of the academy. Women's studies is responsible to the goals of the women's movement, goals which include a critique of these traditional "standards of academia."

In fact, women's studies arose partly as a critique of the traditional disciplines because they do not accommodate the experiences of women in their theories or methods. Women's studies is concerned with the patriarchal biases inherent in the traditional disciplines and works to challenge them. Part of learning women's studies, therefore, is learning how to analyze basic assumptions underlying traditionally accepted theories. Women's studies, then, teaches

us to identify and critique different perspectives, not to feed them back to our instructors "in our own words." Along with the critique of patriarchal myths, women's studies works to develop new, more viable theories which are drawn from the experiences of women and other oppressed groups. Creativity and imagination are inherent in this process. Because the struggle against hierarchical stratification is embedded in the ideals of the women's movement, students are encouraged to use their creative resources to construct new theories.

The movement's emphasis on cooperation instead of competition is embodied in women's studies and serves to enrich a student's learning experience. The goal of feminist scholarship is not to form conclusions about all women; rather, feminist theory attempts to reflect the diversity of women's lives. To do this effectively, we must talk to each other while we develop and rework our theories. Feminist scholarship is collective in both form and content. As such, women's studies students are encouraged to learn from each other; our individual and collective insights and stories become our scholarship.

Women's studies is relevant to those who are concerned with political and social reform because it prepares us to recognize and confront the tensions we will encounter in our feminist struggles outside the university. The relationship between women's studies and the university at large can be used as an example. As women's studies represents the interest of the women's movement, the university generally represents the interest of segments of a more traditional society. These two sets of interests often conflict. Throughout its short history, the very survival of women's studies has often been threatened because the university does not consider it a "legitimate" study. As a result, women's studies programs often have difficulties securing a permanent budget, tenured positions or departmental status. Such marginality is an instant lesson in politics. By virtue of her connection to a vulnerable discipline, a women's studies student is forced to confront tensions similar to those she will encounter in the struggle against injustice outside the university.

Women's studies is relevant to students because it validates personal experience within the context of academia. Throughout modern history, women have occupied the familial and expressive role. The personal nature of this sphere has been devalued by society at large and ignored in traditional scholarship. Women's studies, on the other hand, clearly values personal experience and integrates it into scholarship and classroom experience. Although some large lecture courses are held within women's studies, usually as introductory classes, most women's studies courses are conducted in the small seminar format or include a discussion group. This format creates an intimate setting where students can feel comfortable responding personally as well as intellectually to the ideas being discussed. Sexist myths, which women often internalize on a deep personal level, can only be challenged in a setting which facilitates the expression of both the intellectual and emotional realm. The women's studies classroom can be a place to identify feelings of oppression, express these feelings openly and constructively redirect them toward change. Although women's studies delves intellectually into conflicts once they are identified, the identification process is inherently linked to a visceral experience. Contrary to the traditional disciplines, women's studies has a firm commitment to subjective knowledge and learning.

CAREERS AND THE DISCIPLINES

Because students expect their education to have some practical application, it is important to examine how the traditional disciplines and women's studies approach this aspect of education. It is important to note that few disciplines actually "prepare" one for later work. We are all too familiar with the decreasing practical worth of the BA degree. But if students want to succeed in the traditional career world, the traditional disciplines do have an advantage over the non-traditional disciplines; the qualities one must have to "succeed" in the traditional disciplines are similar to those required to "succeed" in the traditional career world. The traditional disciplines characteristically stress competition, specialization and a myopic devotion to their specific field. In our society, professional and financial success is rewarded to those with exactly these characteristics.

In contrast, women's studies provides us with a perspective on the traditional academic world and its corollary in the outside world so that we may be conscious in approaching these worlds. And women's studies helps us to see alternatives: an education which encourages students to think beyond tradition and to incorporate their emotions into this process benefits students who wish to create or engage in feminist work. "Feminist work" cannot be described in terms of a specific occupation or career because it is an approach to working. That is, in choosing work, one must consider individual needs and talents as well as the needs of the larger community. One must also consider how to structure one's work so that it does not contradict or undermine its primary function. This approach to work parallels the women's studies approach to education in that it appreciates the relationship between the individual, the community and her work. Feminist work, like a feminist education, does not thrive in a competitive and hierarchical climate. Women's studies, then, in terms both of ideology and structure, can help a student formulate and engage in work which is innovative and personally relevant as well as useful to the community.

Students who seek a discipline which offers more than a version of knowledge and a methodology based on the truths of the dominant culture have few options in the university today. Women's studies, however, rooted in a vital social movement, offers students a very different experience than do the more traditional disciplines. Through its commitment to challenge gender bias, incorporate the totality of women's experience into scholarship and to effect change, women's studies offers students a unique opportunity to develop critical thinking skills, learn from personal experiences and feelings and to engage in creating a more just world. [1983]

 5

Have You Ever Heard of Asian-American Feminists?

STACEY G. H. YAP

I can say that I stumbled into women's studies accidentally. I had no intention in my younger days to choose this area. It's true that there were few to no courses offered in women's studies in the early 1970s when I first arrived at college on the East Coast, and it's also true that I stereotyped women's liberation as a group of white women gone mad! I didn't see myself identifying with "them" even if I had seen courses offered in the women's studies area then. It was only when I went to graduate school and unintentionally selected a course about "men and women in corporations" that I was first introduced to the research in women's studies without ever knowing it. And from then on, my life was transformed.

Today I am a faculty member and chair of the women's studies (minor) program in my college, and teaching a course in women's studies, I cannot help thinking how much my life has changed from an undergraduate business major to a women's studies/sociology college teacher. My students must wonder about the irony of any Asian (American) teacher teaching them about women's studies and the American women's movement. The unexpected role that I play in influencing my students' lives will probably help them remember how much common ground we share even though we are ethnically different. What will transform my life and my students' lives is the complete element of surprise that women's studies can offer. It is the story of our lives, our mothers' and our grandmothers' lives, and the conditions and experiences we women have gone through and are going through now. Feminist scholars have researched experiences in great detail and told stories of our lives that have never been told before in colorful and powerful language.

What is more surprising are the uncharted territories women's studies offers, and what is not documented. Particularly, since I look and speak differently from my students, women's studies presents an opportunity for my women students to ask me more questions about me: How do I feel about American white men? What do I think about American black women? Do I think that the socialization process they learn is different in the Asian context? What is different about mother-daughter relationships among whites and those that are written by Chinese Americans like Amy Tan and Maxine Hong Kingston? The fact that Asian-American women are not represented in the mainstream of women's studies literature made my students and

myself more intense in our search to wonder about their absence. As a feminist, I acknowledge their absence but do not feel upset nor angry by their lack of recognition. This neglected treatment by white American women who dominated this field in producing women's anthologies for women's studies courses is understandable. I try to remedy this by teaching my students and my friends about Asian-American women and their experiences. I center my research in the "unearthing" of Asian women's experiences. Whether they are Asian-born women or American-born Asian women, I recognize that their experiences have helped shape the history, politics, and literature of this country.

Women's studies has taught me that women must be studied on their own terms and not judged by male-defined standards. Similarly, Asian women must be allowed to speak for themselves because, while we share a great deal with other women, our experiences are unique, and women of other backgrounds can't speak for us. Asian women come to feminism in a variety of ways. Some of us stumbled into politics through fighting against unfair wage practices, and others protested against the Vietnam war. Including Asian women's experiences in women's studies courses is important, for we, like most women around the world, do not passively or silently accept the oppression we share with all women.

[1992]

 6

Women's Studies as a Growth Process

DANISTA HUNTE

I remember trying to fit Introduction to Women's Studies into my schedule for five semesters and feeling frustrated each time that chemistry or some other requirement took precedence. Finally, first semester senior year, I was able to fit it into my schedule. After three years at Vassar College, I thought my feminist development was far beyond the introductory level and there would not be much for me to learn from the class. I was wrong. My politics were challenged daily. It seemed that everything that was changing and developing could be linked to a reading or discussion in women's studies. I learned life lessons that take some people all of their lives to learn. The most important lesson was that the many parts of myself—black, female, feminist, Caribbean, pro-choice, working class, etc.—could coexist as one healthy individual. I gained a better understanding of how our society consistently seeks to "divide and conquer" or to squash any possible coalition among oppressed individuals. I confronted a lot of the anger I felt toward white society. I do not know whether I will ever resolve that anger, but identifying its source and understanding the way in which it can stifle my own growth and development are valuable lessons. I gained a better understanding of the environment and the culture in which my mother was raised and in turn how she raised me. I realized how difficult it is to be someone's mother, and I appreciate my mother even more. Although I left some class sessions feeling confused and schizophrenic, by the end of first semester I felt empowered and confident that I could handle anything.

On the first day of class, I counted the number of women of color in the class. There were two of us. I had a reputation of being a vocal student, and nothing less was expected of me in this class. I also knew that I would be the official spokeswoman of color and the voice of all black women on campus. Initially I resented having to occupy the "speaker" role, and I was even angry at the other sister in class who never spoke in concert with me. As a matter of fact she never spoke at all, which may tell another tale altogether. There was no support or comfort upon which to depend.

These feelings were not new. For the three years prior to women's studies, my being was fueled by anger and the thrill of battle. I craved the opportunities for combat with the administration of the college. I enjoyed sitting on committees with faculty and feeling confident about what I had to contribute or debating with a white man who presumed to know "who I was and what my life was about" based upon his proficiency in two Africana studies courses! These encounters excited me and made me feel powerful; however, by the time I had reached

senior year, I was *tired* and did not want to fight anymore. After reading Audre Lorde's "The Uses of Anger: Women Responding to Racism" in *Sister Outsider,* those feelings of anger and resentment began to subside. Through Lorde's writings I identified some of the reasons for the anger I was feeling about the class, my experiences at Vassar College, and toward myself. Lorde warns black women not to let our justified anger eat away at our compassion to love ourselves and others. She advocates that black women must find ways in which to channel their anger into *healthy* and *productive* actions that will hopefully transform our situations. Anger should not be denied, but explored and used to produce something positive that will move the individual forward.

Introduction to Women's Studies was painful, but I learned a lot. There is *much* work to be done on the part of all women, and especially by women of color. The class offered very little feminist theory by African-American women, Hispanic women, Asian women, or Native American women, which angered me. From my own personal readings I had found a wealth of writings by women of color on issues of motherhood and parenting, male domination, and the portrayal of women in film, etc. There are time constraints when developing a syllabus. However, when the theoretical and critical analyses that comprise the syllabus are written by white feminists, this conveys only one perspective. This imbalance facilitates the myth that black women do not theorize or are not capable of critically analyzing their own situations or of offering criticism of their society. We as black women need to pursue fields in which we can create and command our own destinies and have an impact upon our lives and the lives of our sisters.

Lorde says that, "for survival, Black children in america must be raised to be warriors."[1] Unfortunately, that often means we grow up justifiably paranoid and untrusting of anyone who is not like us. Women's studies rejuvenated my spirit and reassured me that people can grow and things can

---

[1] Audre Lorde, "Man Child: A Black Lesbian Feminist's Response," *Sister Outsider* (Freedom, CA: The Crossing Press, 1984), p. 75.

change. As a result of the class, I try not to build walls around myself and I want to be more inclusive in my politics. Each new experience, whether categorized as "good" or "bad," facilitates growth. I look upon my experience in Introduction to Women's Studies as a growth process—and, for the record, it was "good." [1991]

 7

Finding My Latina Identity Through Women's Studies

LUANA FERREIRA

Taking a women's studies course entitled Women: Images and Realities helped me to become the person that I am today. It enabled me share both my experience as a woman and my experience of Latino culture with other women and understand more fully the position of women in society.

When I lived in the Dominican Republic, I'd see the same scene over and over, especially around the holidays: women were in the kitchen cooking and setting the table while the men were in the living room discussing sports or politics. My grandmother always told me that once a woman learned how to do house chores, she was ready for marriage, and that a woman should always depend on a man because a woman will always need the *strength* of a man. At this point in my life I was beginning to feel frustrated and anxious. I asked myself why at the age of 17 I still was not engaged, or in a relationship, and what would happen if I never got married.

Once I arrived in the United States and enrolled in college, I began to see male-female relationships differently. I saw that women were indeed more career-oriented and independent. However, as a college student, I thought that the women's movement, womanism, and feminism were a little too radical for me. The word "feminist" to me meant "man hater."

The course taught me a great deal about women in the United States and around the world. I could not believe how much I had been missing out! I must admit that I was biased in choosing the teacher. Looking in the catalogue, I saw three different names, but one stood out: Delgado. Since I am Latina, the idea of having a teacher I can relate to pleased me. Professor Linda Delgado, a proud Puerto Rican woman, taught me how to detach myself from traditional ideas about women without losing my cultural values and awareness. At the same time, having a Latina teacher for this course has helped me to become more involved in my community. I learned about sexism in religion and in the labor force, and I became more aware of issues such as rape, abortion, and sexual harassment.

In my traditional family, my parents always taught me "where a woman's place in society is." According to them, rape victims deserve to get raped because of the way they were dressed, pregnancy is a punishment for the irresponsibility of a woman, virginity is a proof of purity and decency and is the best wedding gift to a man, a spouse can be found through one's cooking, and so forth. I can go on forever with these myths and taboos.

The course made me realize that clothing should not determine the reputation of a woman, that women have the right to make their own decisions about sex, and that both men and women should be concerned about pregnancy. I also learned that one should learn to do chores for survival, not to please someone else. I have become more secure about myself. I am able to make my own decisions because I am using my own judgment, *not* doing what my parents expect or what society dictates. I am also more firm in my decisions. Before, if I were involved in a discussion with a male, I always worried that if I opened my mouth he would lose interest in me. I cannot believe that I used to think this way! I operated on the assumption that if I were too articulate or too much of an activist, I would lose the relationship of my dreams. I thank my teacher and the course for making me understand that standing up for your rights and for what you believe in will raise your self-confidence and self-esteem. Now I find myself having interesting discussions with many colleagues, males and females, and I am more open with my female friends.

Today I am happy to say that I am a woman

striving for a career. I am very involved in my community, and I am not afraid to state my beliefs and ideas. Now I know that being a feminist, far from being a man hater, is rather fighting for equal rights, struggling against discrimination, and educating one's self and others about women's issues.   [1992]

8

What Women's Studies Has Meant to Me

LUCITA WOODIS

I had no understanding of what women's studies meant when I first looked through the spring catalogue at the University of New Mexico, but it sounded intriguing. So I went to the Women's Studies Center on campus and asked lots of questions: What is women's studies? What can I gain from a course like this? Can I use the information from women's studies courses outside the university? Can I use this for a certain area of my life?

Well, my questions were answered in such a positive way that the very same day, I stepped into the Women's Center and signed up as a women's studies minor.

Now that I've been introduced to the curriculum, I believe that women's studies means empowerment for women. We as women want equality in our lives—in areas such as the workplace, where we want to have acknowledged that people should be paid on the basis of their experience, not their sex; that regardless of sex, we are human. As women, we need respect for making our choices and decisions. We need power and control—not power over others, but shared power with other human beings who work together cooperatively. This is especially meaningful to me as a woman of color, a Native American artist who grew up on the Navajo Reservation.

I have never experienced a more close, supportive, nurturing, and expressive multicultural group of women as I did in the Women in Contemporary Society class at the University of New Mexico. Our bond as women enabled us to break through the barriers of race, creed, and color to interact as human beings and discover a common ground. In our class discussions, we were able to express our intolerance at being victims of pornography and sexual abuse, knowing that with every issue there has been some change for the better. We saw how we as women have bonded together through self-help groups, have opened up shelters for battered women, and in a sense have been saying that we do have power—power to overcome these intolerable abuses and survive as powerful women into the 1990s.

The knowledge I gained through the course came from the classroom, my classmates, and my professor, Deborah Klein. Ms. Klein was very avid in our discussions and presentations, as we bonded together through our openness. She helped the class evolve to an intimate level. With no remorse or self-consciousness, we created an atmosphere of acceptance, shared a great deal of ourselves, and enhanced each other's lives. As a sister to women of color, I experienced support, nurturing, and the embrace of other women as we expressed our experiences openly and individually.

I used part of my class experience to take the group on a journey about the meaning of sexual abuse in a woman's life, particularly in mine. I chose to present my journey as a narrative. I told my story with the visual images of my artwork, as well as with my words. My goal was to convey to others that confronting one's self can be a positive path toward strength, confidence, and the ability to be true to one's self.

Exploring women's issues has truly been a journey for me, a spiritual journey filled with healing and cleansing and enlightenment. My explorations have lead me toward harmony and balance and enable me to feel peaceful, calm, and serene.

As a Native American (Navajo), I can only stress that women are powerful. We are a maternal society, the bearers of children. We are patient yet very strong in our decision making. I can say I have benefited from the women's studies program and won't be silent long. I will be verbally expressive as well as visually expressive, because that is who I am—an artist. I share a very intimate part of myself through my art. I will always be a Native first, as I am from a traditional family, and I'm proud to know my clan through my ancestors. Yet I can also say that I'm from the Navajo Nation *and* part of the larger women's experience in our society.

Today, I understand that I am not alone. I am important. I am not a second-class citizen, I am a capable, strong, and independent Native American Navajo woman. I will always carry my culture and traditions in my heart whether on the Reservation or in the outside world. Through my spirit, I will carry a message visually and verbally that to survive and heal from abuse is to come full-circle to contentment, that we are all part of a larger whole.

Nishtínígíí shit beehozin   (Navajo)
I know who I am   (English)   [1992]

9

Why Women's Studies?

DEBORAH HALSTEAD LENNON

Whenever I tell people I am majoring in women's studies, the response is usually along the lines of, "Whatever are you going to *do* with *that?*" I know they are expecting me to respond by specifying some kind of practical job application for the degree. I could say, "I'm going to be a personnel consultant, increasing morale and productivity through understanding and meeting the needs of the work force." But that's not why I enrolled in the program.

I returned to school as a women's studies major at the age of 31. My intended purpose was to validate the perspective I had developed from my life experiences. I have found that—and so much more. Women's studies shows us women's lives and their art of living, how women's contributions to society are so intricately woven into the fabric of their daily lives that they go unrecognized because they are so familiar. It has ended my isolation by showing me that other women have had similar experiences. Through nurturing my growth and self-esteem, I have regained my voice and learned how to use it. Women's studies has united me with women and oppressed peoples from all over the world.

Women's studies has enabled me to discuss issues such as birth control, abortion, rape, and domestic violence with my children. Addressing these and other issues as part of my coursework greatly decreased the apprehension parents and children often experience when approaching these topics. My daughter is now a year younger than I was when these became issues in my life. I am now able to look forward to her teenage years with confidence that when these things touch her life, as they almost surely will in some form, she will not feel the confusion and devastation that I endured. The reason for this confidence is twofold: She has an awareness and understanding that precede her experience, enabling her to avoid some situations that ignorance may have otherwise drawn her into; and she knows how to network and form a supportive community with other women.

Women's studies has been, for me, a metamorphosis; it teaches a way of being, a different mode of perception that pervades our very essence. Now when I hear of a woman in an abusive situation, I can see the factors that keep her trapped: housing, earning potential, child care, fear. I also see how our society perpetuates women's fears through promoting the idea that women are defenseless without a male companion. Women's studies teaches us to crack the shell of fear so that we may spread our wings and fly. What do I *do* with *that?* I help other women (and men) be strong and secure in who they are, in following their dreams. Some of us will do this as lawyers, as teachers, as wives and mothers . . . the possibilities are endless.

Welcome to the beginning of *your* journey. You will find your beauty in your strength, and your wings will take you wherever you want to go.

[1992]

10

Rethinking Women's Biology

RUTH HUBBARD

Women's biology is a social construct and a political concept, not a scientific one, and I mean that in at least three ways. The first can be summed up in

Simone de Beauvoir's dictum "One isn't born a woman, one becomes a woman." This does not mean that the environment shapes us, but that the concept, woman (or man), is a socially constructed one that little girls (or boys) try to fit as we grow up. Some of us are better at it than others, but we all try, and our efforts have biological as well as social consequences (a false dichotomy because our biological and social attributes are related dialectically). How active we are, what clothes we wear, what games we play, what we eat and how much, what kinds of schools we go to, what work we do, all affect our biology as well as our social being in ways we cannot sort out. So, one isn't born a woman (or man), one becomes one.

The concept of women's biology is socially constructed, and political, in a second way because it is not simply women's description of our experience of our biology. We have seen that women's biology has been described by physicians and scientists who, for historical reasons, have been mostly economically privileged, university-educated men with strong personal and political interests in describing women in ways that make it appear "natural" for us to fulfill roles that are important for their well-being, personally and as a group. Self-serving descriptions of women's biology date back at least to Aristotle. But if we dismiss the early descriptions as ideological, so are the descriptions scientists have offered that characterize women as weak, overemotional, and at the mercy of our raging hormones, and that construct our entire being around the functions of our reproductive organs. No one has suggested that men are just walking testicles, but again and again women have been looked on as though they were walking ovaries and wombs.

In the nineteenth century, when women tried to get access to higher education, scientists initially claimed we could not be educated because our brains are too small. When that claim became untenable, they granted that we could be educated the same as men but questioned whether we should be, whether it was good for us. They based their concerns on the claim that girls need to devote much energy to establishing the proper functioning of their ovaries and womb and that if they divert this energy to their brains by studying, their reproductive organs will shrivel, they will become sterile, and the race will die out.

This logic was steeped in race and class prejudice. The notion that women's reproductive organs need careful nurturing was used to justify excluding upper-class girls and young women from higher education but not to spare the working-class, poor, or black women who were laboring in the factories and homes of the upper class. If anything, these women were said to breed too much. In fact, their ability to have many children despite the fact that they worked so hard was taken as evidence that they were less highly evolved than upper-class women; for them breeding was "natural," as for animals.

Finally, and perhaps most importantly, our concept of ourselves is socially constructed and political because our society's interpretation of what is and is not normal and natural affects what we do. It therefore affects our biological structure and functioning because . . . what we do and how our bodies and minds function are connected dialectically. Thus norms are self-fulfilling prophecies that do not merely describe how we are but prescribe how we should be.

BODY BUILD AND STRENGTH

Let us consider a few examples. We can begin with a few obvious ones, such as height, weight, and strength. Women and men are physically not very different. There are enormous overlaps between women and men for all traits that are not directly involved with procreation.

For example, there is about a two-foot spread in height among people in the United States, but a difference of only three to five inches between the average heights of women and men. When we say men are taller than women, what we really mean is that the abstraction *average (or mean) height* is a few inches greater for men than women. Overall, women and men are about the same height, with many women as tall as, or taller than, lots of men. The impression that women are shorter than men is enhanced by our social convention that when women and men pair off, it is considered preferable for the man to be taller than the woman. In some countries, such as Bali, differences in height and, indeed, overall body build are much smaller than in the United States.

Clearly, height is affected by social factors, such as diet. In the early part of this century, English working-class men were significantly shorter, on average, than men from the upper class, and this difference in height was due to differences not just in the adequacy but in the composition of their diets—proportions of carbohydrates, proteins, fats, vitamins. In the United States we are familiar with a similar phenomenon when comparing the heights of immigrants and their U.S.-born children. We have tended to think that the U.S.-born children are taller than their immigrant parents because they get a better diet. But now that we are learning more about the health hazards of the typical U.S. diet, with its excessive fat and protein content, we should probably defer value judgments and just acknowledge that the diets are different.

Sex differences in height probably also arise from the differences in growth patterns between girls and boys. Until early adolescence, girls, on average, are taller than boys, but girls' growth rates tend to decrease after they begin to menstruate, whereas boys continue to grow throughout their teens. It is generally assumed that this difference is due to the fact that the increase in estrogen levels after the onset of menstruation tends to slow the growth of girls' long bones. But the age of onset of menstruation, hence of increased estrogen secretion, depends on a number of social factors, such as diet, exercise and stress. For example, female swimming champions, who, because of their intense, early training, tend to begin to menstruate later than most girls, tend also to be taller than average. We might therefore expect factors that delay the onset of menstruation to decrease the difference in average height between women and men, those that hasten the onset of menstruation to increase it.

It is probably not that simple because the factors that affect the onset of menstruation may also affect height in other ways. All I want to suggest is that height, in part, is a social variable and that differences in the average height of women and men vary with the social environment.

Weight clearly has considerable social components. Different societies have different standards of beauty for women, and many of these involve differences in desirable weight. Today we call the women in Rubens's paintings fat and consider Twiggy anorexic. In our society changes in style not just of clothing but of body shape are generated, at least in part, because entire industries depend on our not liking the way we look so that we will buy the products that promise to change it. To some extent this is true also for men: Padded shoulders are not that different from padded bras. But there is more pressure on women to look "right," and what is "right" changes frequently and sometimes quite drastically. At present, U.S. women are obsessed by concerns about their weight to the point where girls and young women deliberately eat less than they need for healthy growth and development.

Although we may inherit a tendency toward a particular body shape, most women's weight can change considerably in response to our diets, levels of physical activity, and other patterns of living. These also affect physical fitness and strength. When women begin to exercise or engage in weight training and body building, we often notice surprisingly great changes in strength in response to even quite moderate training. Here again, what is striking is the variation among women (and among men).

People ask whether there are "natural" limits to women's strength and therefore "natural" differences in strength between women and men. In Europe and the United States women and men are far more similar in lower body strength than in the strength of our upper bodies. This fact is not surprising when we consider the different ways girls and boys are encouraged to move and play from early childhood on. We tend to use our legs much more similarly than our arms. Both girls and boys tend to run a lot, and hopscotch and skipping rope are considered girls' games. But when it comes to carrying loads, playing baseball, and wrestling and other contact sports, all of which strengthen the arms and upper body, girls are expected to participate much less than boys are. In general, male/female comparisons are made between physically more highly trained men and less trained women so that so-called sex differences at least in part reflect this difference in activity levels. More and less active men also differ in strength, and so do more and less active women.

If we compare the records of male and female marathon runners, we find that in 1963, when women were first permitted to run the Boston marathon, their record was 1 hour 20 minutes slower than the men's record. Twenty years later, Joan Benoit won in 2 hours, 22 minutes, and 43 seconds, a record that was only about fifteen minutes slower than the record of that year's male winner. And she

ran the course in over an hour less time than the female winner in 1963. The dramatic improvement
women runners made in those twenty years clearly
came with practice but no doubt also required
changes in their expectations of what they could
achieve. Men's records have improved by less than
fifteen minutes during the entire time since modern
marathon competitions began in 1908. Again the
question: Are there "natural" limits and "natural"
differences between women and men? Only time
and opportunities to train and to participate in athletic events will tell. Note that in the 1988 Olympics,
the woman who won the hundred-meter sprint took
less than one minute longer than the male winner,
and he set a new world record. This feat is especially
remarkable because women are said to compare
with men much more favorably in long runs than in
sprints.

WORK

The stratification of the work force is often explained as though it reflected inherent biological differences between women and men. Women have
been disqualified from construction and other relatively well-paid heavy labor because they are said to
be too weak for it. But the most prestigious men's
jobs and those that pay most, in general, do not require physical strength, while much of women's traditional, unpaid or underpaid work involves strenuous physical labor. Nurses must sometimes lift
heavy, immobilized people, and housework frequently involves carrying and pushing heavy, awkward loads. In many cultures women are responsible for providing the firewood and water, which
usually means carrying heavy loads for long distances, often with small children tied to their chests
or backs. In the United States, where men are expected to carry the heaviest loads, most men have
"bad backs," which is why occupational health advocates argue that loads that are considered too
heavy for women should be rated too heavy for
everyone.

At present, there is an overemphasis on the reproductive hazards of employment for women and
an underemphasis on comparable hazards for men,
to the detriment of women, men, and children.
Women have been barred from some higher-paying
jobs unless they could prove they were sterile, while

men in those very jobs, and in others, continue to be
exposed to preventable chemical and radiation hazards. Women, too, continue to be exposed to reproductive hazards in traditional women's work, such as
nursing and housework, and as x-ray technicians,
beauticians, and hairdressers.

In other words, biological differences between
women and men are used to rationalize the stratification of the labor force by sex; they do not explain
it. One can readily find women or men who qualify
for every kind of paid work, except that of sperm
donor and what has come to be called surrogate
mother. If society instead stratifies the work force
into women's and men's jobs, it does so for economic, social, and political reasons. Such stratification is not mandated by biology.

MENSTRUATION

Let us leave these biosocial examples and look at
menstruation, which most people would consider
purely biological. A good way to begin is by asking,
What is a normal woman's normal menstrual pattern? The standard answer is: a twenty-eight day
cycle with five days of menstruation that begins at
age twelve or thirteen and ends at about fifty. Yet
that pattern does not reflect most women's actual
experience. Until recently, we have had little information about the normal range of variation in age of
onset, frequency, regularity, discomfort, and cessation of menstruation. Little information has been
shared among women, and there has been almost
no research on our routine experiences. Women
have learned about menstruation mostly from their
mothers or other female relatives or, if they had
problems, from physicians—most of them men,
who learn what they know from textbooks written
by other men or from their "clinical experience,"
which means from women with problems.

In recent years, women's health activists and
feminist medical and social scientists have finally
begun to give us a sense of the variety of women's
normal experiences of menstruation. We are also
beginning to learn about the experiences in other
times and cultures. Rose Frisch has shown that, during the last century, the age of onset of menstruation
has gone down and the age of cessation has gone up
in both Europe and the United States. From this
change and from studies of the menstrual patterns

of athletes, she has concluded that nutrition and exercise strongly affect these parameters, probably by influencing the amounts of stored body fat. She suggests that women need to accumulate a threshold amount of fat in order to establish the hormonal cycles that regulate menstruation. As European and American diets have become richer in fats, girls reach the critical level earlier, and older women maintain it longer. Participation in vigorous sports affects menstrual patterns because athletes convert more of the food they eat into muscle (protein) and store less of it as fat.

Anthropologists observing the !Kung, a group of foragers living in the Kalahari desert in southern Africa, have noted that their menstrual and reproductive histories are quite different from what we in the West think of as "normal." !Kung women and men collect their food, and as is true in most foraging societies, women provide most of it which involves a good deal of walking and carrying. The !Kung diet is plentiful and nutritionally adequate but very different from ours because it is relatively high in complex carbohydrates and plant proteins but low in animal proteins and fats.

Presumably because of their high activity levels and their diet young !Kung women do not begin to menstruate until they are about eighteen years old, by which time they already tend to be heterosexually active. Like girls in the West, they tend not to ovulate during their first few cycles. They therefore experience their first pregnancy when they are about nineteen and have a first child at perhaps twenty. They nurse that child for two or three years but quite differently from the way many of us do. They suckle their babies as often as the infant wants to nurse, which can be several times an hour, albeit briefly. Melvin Konner and Carol Worthman have postulated that because of the frequent nursing, !Kung women tend not to menstruate or ovulate for almost the entire time they suckle their children. This experience contrasts with that of Western women, who tend to resume menstruation within a year after a birth, even when they nurse their children for several years, because they let them suck much less frequently and tend to supplement their diet with other foods. Thus, Western babies suckle less intensely and frequently than !Kung babies do.

!Kung women tend to wean a child sometime during its third year. By this time they may be pregnant, without having resumed menstruation, or they may menstruate and ovulate a few times before they become pregnant again. This pattern repeats until the women reach menopause, which they tend to do in their late thirties or early forties.

The menstrual and reproductive experience of !Kung women therefore is entirely different from what we take to be "normal." They have a shorter reproductive span, during which they tend to bear no more than four or five children, quite without contraception, and they experience few menstruations. But when the !Kung move into towns and live more as we do, their menstrual and reproductive patterns change to the ones we are used to seeing. So the difference between their experience and ours is not genetic.

Clearly it is meaningless to specify norms for even such a normal, biological function as menstruation without considering how women live. For !Kung women it is normal to menstruate rarely and have few children without using birth control. For us it is normal to menstruate every twenty-eight or so days and to get pregnant within a year after a birth, if we are heterosexually active without using birth control. Thus, even such biological events as menstruation and fecundity are strongly influenced by sociocultural factors.

WOMEN'S BIOLOGY IN CONTEXT

How had we best take these influences into consideration? Clearly we need to think about women's biology in its social context and consider how it interacts with culture. We need to get information directly from women and not rely on so-called experts, who are often male and whose knowledge tends to be based on the experience of "patients"—that is, of women with problems. Only when women have the opportunity to share experiences and when scientists collect the experiences of women of different ages and from different classes, races, and cultural groups can we get a sense of the texture and variety of women's biology.

We need to pay attention to the obvious contradictions between stereotypic descriptions of women's biology and the realities of women's lives. For example, women's reputed "maternal instinct" needs to be looked at in light of some women's desperate efforts to avoid having children, while society persuades or forces them to have children against their wills. Similarly, descriptions of women's frailty, passivity, and weakness need to be juxtaposed with the reality of women as providers and workers who in most societies, including our own, tend to work harder and for longer hours than most men.

Women's work histories are often obscured by the fact that work has been defined so that it excludes much of their daily work load. Indeed, whereas most of what men do is called work, much of what women do has been interpreted as the natural manifestation of our biology. How often do we hear people say, "My mother didn't work when I was growing up"? If she didn't work, how did we manage to grow up? Even women usually refer to what we do as work only when we get paid for it, implying that what we do at home and in our neighborhoods and communities is not work. This misrepresentation of work sets up the vicious circle whereby women are thought to be less good workers in the workplace when we have family and community obligations and less good housewives and mothers when we work outside the home.

No question, we are biological organisms like other animals, and women and men have different procreative structures and functions. But to try to find the biological basis of our social roles or to sort people by sex when it comes to strength, ability to do math, or other intellectual or social attributes is a political exercise, not a scientific one.

THE MEANING OF DIFFERENCE

That said, I want to stress that we need have no ideological investment in whether women and men exhibit biological differences, aside from the obvious ones involved with procreation. I have argued that we cannot know whether such biological differences exist because biology and society (or environment) are interdependent and cannot be sorted out. And in any gender-dichotomized society, the fact that we are born biologically female or male means that our environments will be different: We will live different lives. Because our biology and how we live are dialectically related and build on one another, we cannot vary gender and hold the environment constant. Therefore, the scientific methodology of sex-

differences research is intrinsically flawed if scientists try to use it to sort effects of biology and society. Scientists can catalog similarities and differences between women and men but cannot establish their causes.

There are other problems with research on differences. One is that it is in the nature of scientific research that if we are interested in differences, we will go on looking until we find them. And if we do not find any, we will assume that our instruments were wrong or that we looked in the wrong place or at the wrong things. Another problem is that most characteristics vary continuously in the population rather than placing us into neat groups. To compare groups, however defined, we must use such concepts as the "average," "mean," or "median" in order to characterize each group by a single number. Yet these constructed, or reified, numbers obscure the diversity that exists within the groups (say, among women and among men) as well as the overlaps between them. That is why statisticians have invented the concept of the standard deviation from the mean to reflect the spread of the actual numbers around the reified average. This problem is obvious when we think about research into differences between blacks and whites. Just to do it, we have to agree on social definitions of who will count as black and who as white because after several centuries of mixing, the biological characteristic, skin color, varies continuously. Research comparing blacks and whites must first generate the group differences it pretends to catalog or analyze.

Differences, be they biological or psychological, become scientifically interesting only when they parallel differences in power. We do not frame scientific questions about differences between tall people and short people, although folk wisdom suggests there may be some. Nor do we, in this society, pursue differences between blue-eyed, blond people and dark-haired, dark-eyed ones. Yet the latter were scientifically interesting differences under the Nazis.

Sex differences are interesting in sexist societies that value one group more highly than the other. Because the overlaps are so large for all the characteristics that are not directly involved with procreation, it is easy to find women and men to perform any task we value. The existence of average sex differences is irrelevant to the way we organize society. To achieve an egalitarian division of labor requires political will and action, not changes in our biology. There is enough variability among us to let us construct a society in which people of both sexes contribute to whatever activities are considered socially useful and are rewarded according to their talents and abilities. [1990]

🌿 11

Cross-cultural Studies of Women: Moving from the Exotic and Erotic to Center Stage

MEREDITH L. BROWN

When I took my first anthropology course, over 20 years ago, anthropology seemed to me to be the study of the exotic, obscure, and irrelevant. Fieldwork in other cultures seemed to be exercises in pursuing trivia. Ethnographies, the written descriptions of the results of this fieldwork, seemed an unending litany of facts about what people wore, ate, produced, and celebrated. The portrayal of women seemed to focus on the exotic and erotic. This was particularly true in popular representations, for example, of naked women in *National Geographic*. But the academic discipline seemed little better. Women were most likely to be featured in contexts designed to be stimulating to the male reader. For example, in the definition of different forms of marriage, polygyny was often defined as the marriage of one man to several women, while polyandry was when several men shared one woman. The male centered nature of such definitions is clear, as is the implied sexual intrigue. The bias of such reporting, while not transparent to most of us at the time, meant that we could find few points of connection with women of other cultures. I certainly made no connections between anthropological material and social and political analyses of "my" world. I found no support for my budding

feminist political views in looking cross-culturally, nor did I expect to be able to make such connections. Other cultures were clearly not relevant to modern life and politics.

After a generation of research in women's studies and anthropology, and the women's movement itself, the anthropological contribution to understanding women's roles and status in society is much clearer. This article examines selected examples of cross-cultural research and its meaning for women's studies. It will focus on those theories that attempt to explain the origins of patriarchy through reference to cross-cultural data.

At the simplest level, cross-cultural studies have provided examples of cultural variations of gender-related factors that we tend to assume are constants based on our experience in modern, Western culture. We tend to think of our own gender relations, roles, or hierarchies as "natural." We assume that what we know to be true in our own culture is true for all cultures at all times. Looking cross-culturally sometimes surprises us, as we find that these roles and relations may be structured differently. This can provide inspiring examples for potential change, or, at least, a veto of the idea that these traits are naturally mandated universals. Finding exceptions to the "rules" that we have been raised to believe provides some vision of how we might reconceive social roles.

This type of research, finding exceptions to western rules for behavior, predates the second wave of the women's movement and the development of modern women's studies as an academic field in the 1970s. Anthropologists have been busily vetoing supposed "universals" posited by psychologists and sociologists since at least the turn of the century. Included among these cross-cultural tests of universals in the early part of the twentieth century were many examples of cross-cultural exceptions to Western gender roles. Among the more famous of the anthropologists pursuing this kind of cross-cultural test was Margaret Mead.

Mead's *Sex and Temperament in Three Primitive Societies* (1935), for example, suggests that those personality traits that we perceive as "feminine" and "masculine" are not so identified by all cultures in the world. In the three groups she examined, it appeared that aspects of temperament that we associate with the feminine, such as passivity, nurturance, or preoccupation with physical appearance, were variously labeled as masculine, or neither masculine nor feminine, or both masculine and feminine in different cultures. Among the Tchambuli, for example, women were in control economically, while men spent great amounts of time in self-adornment. The conclusion that such traits are culturally rather than biologically constructed is apparent from such research. This conclusion was supported by numerous other ethnographies, which revealed the wide variety of ways that humans organize gender relations.

In general, aside from the functions of reproduction, it seems that gender roles are so highly variable across cultures that little can be said absolutely about universals. Where in some cultures men are the weavers, others insist that textile arts are the woman's province. Women are variously healers, political leaders, spiritual leaders, and artists in other cultures. However, one universal must be noted here.

All societies do have a division of labor according to gender. And they all see such a division as natural; that is, all cultures argue that the distinctions between men and women that exist in their own cultures are "natural." In addition, these roles are supported in the culture's systems of symbolism, mythology, and religion. For example, where women have positions as religious and political leaders, stories of how the world was created feature women in central roles (Sanday, 1981). Beyond the stories of formalized religion, everyday folk sayings and stories support the social distinctions between the genders found in that society.

Perhaps the grandest and most complicated cross-cultural test deals with the question, "Is patriarchy universal?" Is it written by nature that there will always be a power differential between men and women and that women will always be at the short end of the relationship? There have been several answers to this question. Feminist research conducted in the 1960s and 1970s began to question the universality of patriarchy. Several cultural examples seem to suggest that some cultures maintain egalitarian gender relations. Among the most cited of examples were the !Kung of the Kalahari Desert. There, the relations between men and women

seemed marked by an absence of a power differential. In fact, social relations in general among these people, and among other people who gather and hunt (rather than farm) for a living, are generally egalitarian. In these small, basically cooperative groups, there was no form of government. There were no leaders with power to make other people do what they decided; any leadership was without the power to force others. Thus, women and men were not subject to the rules, or whims, of others. Instead, all people had some power over their own lives, within the constraints of the social group as a whole. While differences in the definition of gender roles existed, there was generally no stigma attached to the roles of either gender, nor were the boundaries between masculine and feminine roles and personalities rigid. Since there was no ownership of property (beyond personal), no one could maintain a position of power on the basis of wealth, much less conceive of human relations in terms of issues of ownership. Men did not "own" women or children, and people were not dependent on others because of lack of economic resources. Both men and women produced, women producing more of the staples and basic calories of the group through gathering (Draper, 1975).

Then we have the example of the Iroquois. Here, there were institutionalized relations of power, hierarchy, and government. But women in this culture seemed to be in the center of things. They maintained decision-making positions, owned the land, and were spiritually central in the culture. Inheritance and kinship were determined matrilineally (through women) (Brown, 1975).

Finding and discussing such examples made us look at our own biases and reexamine other research previously conducted. We discovered that anthropologists had, for years, frequently failed to see differences in gender relations in other cultures because of their own biases. Examining the culture of the Montagnais-Naskapi, Leacock (1980) found that a culture that was previously identified as patriarchal was not. She found evidence that the culture was matrilineal and that, in fact, originally appeared to be egalitarian. In evidence from the initial European contact with these people, it is transparent that the Jesuit missionary, LeJeune, found them to be too woman-centered for his Western tastes. "Women have great power. . . . A man may promise you something and if he does not keep his promise, he thinks he is sufficiently excused when he tells you that his wife did not wish him to do it" (quoted in Leacock, 1980, p. 27). While evidence existed well into the twentieth century that gender relations among the Montagnais-Naskapi were not merely primitive duplicates of the Western norms, Western anthropologists had repeatedly seen them as patriarchal and patrilineal, apparently reporting what they expected to see as a natural course of events. We have learned from revaluations such as this one to what extent our vision is distorted by our own cultural background. Sometimes, anthropological studies tell us more about our own culture than the culture being studied. The studies are, after all, written by members of our own culture, who carry with them all the cultural assumptions that they have learned to take for granted.

The above reexaminations of cultural evidence have made us wonder if initial researchers were biased by their own assumptions so as to see the elements of modern, Western patriarchy everywhere they looked. While the bias is clear, our conclusions are not. Unfortunately, feminist anthropologists are not in consensus on the issue of whether or not patriarchy is universal. Many claim that despite the fact that some cultures are more egalitarian than our own, all cultures exhibit evidence of patriarchy (Friedl, 1975; Ortner, 1974; Rosaldo, 1974). The disagreement is based both in issues of interpretation of the data that exist and in the lack of data available. While small-scale primitive societies today may be more egalitarian than our own, there are no cultures on the face of the earth today who are untouched by patriarchal Western values. Thus, what some anthropologists see as evidence of patriarchy, others claim to be merely evidence of a long history of contact with the West. Ethnographic data alone are unlikely to resolve this issue one way or another.

This leads us to the issue of whether or not there are cultures in which the power relations between men and women found in our own culture are reversed. Classical anthropologists in the nineteenth century believed that human social organization was originally matriarchal, that is, that women had power over men in the same way that men today have power over women. Much popular culture

(e.g., myths concerning the Amazons) builds upon this vision, but we see little evidence of matriarchy in the cultural record, present or historical. What is certainly clear is that missionaries and anthropologists who first encountered cultures in which gender relations were relatively egalitarian were convinced that these cultures were matriarchies. Seeing, for the first time, cultures that did not oppress women, they were astounded by the independence, skills, achievements, and respect held by women, and concluded that they must be in power in that culture. Such was likely the reaction of LeJeune (above). Thus, it seems likely that matriarchy was a myth born of the colonial experience. While feminists remain split on the issue of whether or not there have been egalitarian cultures, there is virtually no academic support for the idea of a true matriarchy. This is not to deny that many cultures, however, have strong women-centered elements.

Examples of the variation in gender roles and gender hierarchy do much to separate biology and culture. This lies at the base of the distinction made in feminist research between the terms "sex" and "gender." Biology may determine sex, or those characteristics associated with male and female, but culture determines how the masculine and feminine are defined and structured. And, increasingly, what we initially perceived to be biologically given, seems now to be clearly culturally learned.

REFERENCES CITED AND RESOURCES FOR FURTHER RESEARCH

Brown, Judith K. (1975) "Iroquois women: an ethnohistoric note." In Rayna R. Reiter, ed. *Towards an Anthropology of Women.* Monthly Review Press.

Draper, Patricia (1975) "!Kung women: contrasts in sexual egalitarianism in foraging and sedentary contexts." In Rayna R. Reiter, ed. *Towards an Anthropology of Women.* Monthly Review Press.

Duley, Margot I., and Mary I. Edwards (1986) *The Cross-Cultural Study of Women.* The Feminist Press.

Engels, Frederick (1972) *The Origin of the Family, Private Property and the State.* International Publishers.

Friedl, Ernestine (1975) *Women and Men: An Anthropologist's View.* Holt, Rinehart and Winston.

Gough, Kathleen (1975) "The origin of the family." In Rayna R. Reiter, ed. *Towards an Anthropology of Women.* Monthly Review Press.

Leacock, Eleanor B. (1980) "Montagnais women and the Jesuit program for colonization." In Mona Etienne and Eleanor Leacock, eds. *Women and Colonization.* Praeger.

Mead, Margaret (1935) *Sex and Temperament in Three Primitive Societies.* William Morrow.

Morgan, Sandra (1989) *Gender and Anthropology: Critical*

Reviews for Research and Teaching. American Anthropological Association.

Ortner, Sherry B. (1974) "Is female to male as nature is to culture?" In Michelle Zimbalist Rosaldo and Louise Lamphere, eds. *Women, Culture and Society.* Stanford University.

Rosaldo, Michelle Zimbalist (1974) "Woman, culture and society: a theoretical overview." In Michelle Zimbalist Rosaldo and Louise Lamphere, eds. *Women, Culture and Society.* Stanford University.

Rubin, Gayle (1975) "The traffic in women: notes on the political economy of sex." In Rayna R. Reiter, ed. *Towards an Anthropology of Women.* Monthly Review Press.

Sacks, Karen (1975) "Engels revisited: women, the organization of production and private property." In Rayna R. Reiter, ed. *Towards an Anthropology of Women.* Monthly Review Press.

Sanday, Peggy Reeves (1974) "Female status in the public domain." In Michelle Zimbalist Rosaldo and Louise Lamphere, eds. *Women, Culture and Society.* Stanford University.

Sanday, Peggy Reeves (1981) *Female Power and Male Dominance: On the Origins of Sexual Inequality.* Cambridge University.   [1992]

PART II

Becoming a Woman in Our Society

Ideas about what it means to be a woman permeate all cultures, shaping the ways women are perceived and treated. Although these ideas vary from one culture to another, they are presented as if they were ordained by either God or nature. In Part II, we explore the notion of "femininity" as a social construct: a prevailing set of ideas, myths, stereotypes, norms, and standards that affect the lives of all women in a variety of ways. Disentangling "nature" from "culture" has been a central task of women throughout history who struggle to free themselves from constricting images and expectations.

Western concepts of femininity include a combination of ideas about female good and evil that feminists have identified as the madonna/whore dichotomy. Female virtue has traditionally been presented as pure, selfless, and maternal, while female evil has been presented as deceitful, dangerous, and sinful. In the fairy tales, for example, the "virtuous" woman lives happily ever after, not because of her own efforts but because she is rescued by a male figure who recognizes her innate qualities. On the other hand, "evil" women, such as the Queen in *Snow White and the Seven Dwarfs,* lust after power and are punished in the end. In a society that is racist as well as sexist, it is frequently white women who appear pure and selfless while women of racial and ethnic minorities are seen as deviant. Thus, we often hear of the African-American woman's "domineering" nature; the exotic sensuality of the Asian-American woman; the Chicana's stereotype as evil, sexually uncontrollable, and betrayer of her race; and the status-conscious Jewish-American woman.

Though specific to different racial and ethnic groups, these images reflect the negative half of the madonna/whore and good-girl/bad-girl stereotypes that have historically defined standards of behavior for all women. One learns early on—from family, peers, educational institutions, and the media—what are acceptable behaviors, attitudes, and values. For females, this means that from infancy on, young girls are bombarded with messages about what "good" girls do and, even more insistently, what they don't do.

In the United States, ideas about femininity have been inextricably linked with ideas about race and class. In the nineteenth century, for example, urban, white middle-class women were told it was "woman's nature" to be frail and delicate while slave women worked alongside men. Sojourner Truth, in her famous speech, pointed out these contradictions in the ideology of femininity.

Consider the many ways that American society communicates the expectations of females and males from the moment of birth. Gender markers in the form of the color of clothing immediately differentiate female infants from male infants. Pink gowns with frills and bows convey a feminine gentleness, purity, and fragility, while blue sleepers decorated with animals, trains, and sports scenes portray boys as strong, active, and vigorous. In "A Work of Artifice," Marge Piercy compares the cultivation of femininity to that of the bonsai tree, whose growth is stunted for decorative purposes.

As we explore the experience of being female, we call attention to the ways in which society has limited and trapped women through myths and stereotypes. We see that our self-perceptions are often distorted, reflecting cultural values about women rather than realistic appraisals of our worth. All too often, these self-images take the form of diminished notions of ability and strength, and exaggerated ideas of inferiority and weakness. Ultimately, many girls and women begin to question themselves and feel powerless, whether they are in the classroom, at work, or in relationships with others. As Folami Harris-Gray points out, many African-American women sacrificed their own needs and power for those of their men in the name of civil rights for all. To begin to value oneself beyond these limiting boundaries and expectations can be an arduous task when the majority of society's messages are saying otherwise.

Prevailing norms of behavior also influence how the behavior of women is judged. Women have traditionally been defined in relation to male standards and needs. Man is seen as strong, woman weak, and this type of dichotomy is essential for perpetuating the superiority of males. Woman has historically been viewed as man's subordinate, someone different from and inferior to him. "Masculine" traits are socially desirable and valued, while "feminine" ones are not—setting up another dichotomy that influences the ways the behavior of women and men is judged. Naomi Weisstein details the ways psychologists have lent a mantle of scientific authority to these ideas by promoting the concept of a "female essence" and ignoring the powerful influence of social context on human behavior.

There are few cultural institutions and practices that do not promote and reinforce the stereotyping of women. Through language, for example, we are subjected to maleness being the standard (consider the words "mankind," "chairman," "policeman," "postman," and so on). Only recently has nonsexist language become more widely used, providing an opportunity for gender-inclusive communication. In the second section of this part, the selections focus on family and cultural norms, educational experiences, nonverbal communication, and the media, which have all had powerful effects on the way women and girls see themselves and their world. The dynamics of the classroom, for example, reinforce existing power relationships between males and females. These patterns are so pervasive that we don't usually notice them. Lee Anne Bell's study of elementary school girls shows how success in school can be a source of conflict for girls who are well aware of the negative stereotypes about "smart girls." The girls in this study had difficulty accepting their own achievements in the competitive environment of the classroom. Myra and David Sadker's research highlights specific ways in which classroom interactions affect girls and boys differently. For example, teachers call on female students less frequently than on male students, discouraging females' classroom participation and eroding their intellectual self-confidence.

When women are bombarded with messages of male superiority, they inevitably feel powerless and insignificant. By becoming more conscious of this process of becoming a woman, we can begin to challenge and change those norms, practices, and institutions that have restricted girls' and women's fullest expressions of themselves.

Dominant Ideas About Women

What does it mean to be a woman in our society? While at first glance it may appear that ideas about femininity are somewhat fixed, closer examination reveals that these ideas vary according to class, ethnic group, and race, and have been manipulated to serve the needs of those in power. Perhaps no one has made this point more powerfully than Sojourner Truth, an eloquent African-American lecturer, in her famous speech before the Women's Rights Convention in Ohio in 1850. Truth had been a slave in New York state until 1827 when she ran away (one year before New York freed its slaves) and became active in the antislavery and women's rights movements. Over a century later, in her extremely influential book *The Feminine Mystique,* Betty Friedan exposed the myths and realities of the happy middle-class housewife. Friedan and Marge Piercy, in her poem "A Work of Artifice," both voice the dissatisfaction of college-educated women with the decorative, supportive roles that were glorified in the media during the 1950s and 1960s. By equating the fragile beauty of the bonsai with traditional expectations of femininity, Piercy suggests that women pay a high price for complying with social norms.

Images of femininity often interact with specific stereotypes. In their selections, Gloria Anzaldua, Maureen Ismay, and Susan Schnur confront myths about Chicanas, African-American women, and Jewish women. Another widely held misconception is that women with disabilities do not have sexual lives. Debra Kent challenges this assumption and describes her own sexual exploration.

The theories of "experts" on women's nature, personality, and behavior often mirror prevalent biases and assumptions about femininity. Naomi Weisstein's classic article, a critical analysis of the field of psychology, pinpoints the ways that psychologists fail to accurately explain the behavior of women. Although written over 20 years ago, her critique continues to have relevance now and has generated much new research by and about women. While her article focuses on psychology, it also has implications for social scientists in general, who are concerned with examining social groups and social phenomena. Weisstein shows us that scientists are imperfect, and that dominant ideas about women can negatively affect the validity of the conclusions drawn about us.

🌿 12

"Ar'n't I a Woman?"

· *Reminiscences by Frances D. Gage of Sojourner Truth.*

Sojourner Truth was born into slavery in Ulster County, New York in about 1797 (the exact date of her birth is uncertain). After her escape from slavery she became involved in several of the religious and political movements of her day. Changing her name from Isabella to Sojourner Truth, she traveled widely, speaking eloquently against slavery, for women's rights and about her vision of a kind and loving God. She died in Battle Creek, Michigan in 1883.

At the 1851 Women's Rights Convention in Akron, Ohio, Sojourner Truth gave a stirring speech pointing out the contradictions in arguments against women's rights. Twelve years later, Frances Gage, who had been chairing the meeting, recorded her memories of the convention, including an account of Sojourner Truth's speech. While there is some controversy about whether Gage's version accurately reflects Sojourner's original words, there is general agreement in the contemporary press about most of the central ideas of the speech.[1] We have dropped the dialect Gage used to record Sojourner Truth's words.

The second day the work waxed warm. Methodist, Baptist, Episcopal, Presbyterian, and Universalist ministers came in to hear and discuss the resolutions presented. One claimed superior rights and privileges for man, on the ground of "superior intellect"; another, because of the "manhood of Christ; if God had desired the equality of woman, He would have given some token of His will through the birth, life, and death of the Saviour." Another gave us a theological view of the "sin of our first mother."

There were very few women in those days who dared to "speak in meeting"; and the august teachers of the people were seemingly getting the better of us, while the boys in the galleries, and the sneerers among the pews, were hugely enjoying the discomfiture, as they supposed, of the "strong-minded." Some of the tender-skinned friends were on the point of losing dignity, and the atmosphere betokened a storm. When, slowly from her seat in the corner rose Sojourner Truth, who, till now, had scarcely lifted her head. "Don't let her speak!"

---

[1] For a discussion of other versions of the speech see Carleton Mabee with Susan Mabee Newhouse, *Sojourner Truth: Slave, Prophet, Legend* (New York: N.Y.U. Press, 1993), pp. 67–82. Mabee argues that the refrain "a'rn't I a woman" was invented by Frances Gage.

gasped half a dozen in my ear. She moved slowly and solemnly to the front, laid her old bonnet at her feet, and turned her great speaking eyes to me. There was a hissing sound of disapprobation above and below. I rose and announced "Sojourner Truth," and begged the audience to keep silence for a few moments. The tumult subsided at once, and every eye was fixed on this almost Amazon form, which stood nearly six feet high, head erect, and eyes piercing the upper air like one in a dream. At her first word there was a profound hush. She spoke in deep tones, which, though not loud, reached every ear in the house, and away through the throng at the doors and windows.

"Well, children, where there is so much racket there must be something out of kilter. I think that 'twixt the Negroes of the South and the women at the north all talking about rights, the white men will be in a fix pretty soon. But what's all this here talking about?

"That man over there says that women need to be helped into carriages, and lifted over ditches and to have the best place everywhere. Nobody ever helps me into carriages, or over mudpuddles, or gives me any best place!" And raising herself to her full height, and her voice to a pitch like rolling thunder, she asked, "And ar'n't I a woman? I could work as much and eat as much as a man—when I could get it—and bear the lash as well! And ar'n't I a woman? I have borne thirteen children, and seen them almost all sold off to slavery, and when I cried out with my mother's grief, none but Jesus heard me! And ar'n't I a woman?

"Then they talk about this thing in the head; what this they call it?" ("Intellect" whispered some one near.) "That's it, honey. What's that got to do with women's rights or Negroes? If my cup won't hold but a pint, and your holds a quart, wouldn't you be mean not to let me have my little half-measure full?" And she pointed her significant finger, and sent a keen glance at the minister who had made the argument. The cheering was long and loud.

"Then that little man in black there, he says women can't have as much rights as men, 'cause Christ wasn't a woman! Where did your Christ come from?" Rolling thunder couldn't have stilled that crowd, as did those deep, wonderful tones, as she stood there with outstretched arms and eyes of fire. Raising her voice still louder, she repeated, "Where did your Christ come from? From God and a woman! Man had nothing to do with him." Oh, what a rebuke that was to that little man.

Turning again to another objector, she took up the defense of Mother Eve, I cannot follow her through it all. It was pointed, and witty and solemn; eliciting at almost every sentence deafening applause; and she ended by asserting: "If the first woman God ever made was strong enough to turn the world upside down all alone, these women together" (and she glanced her eye over the platform) "ought to be able to turn it back, and get it right side up again! And now they are asking to do it, the men better let them. Obliged to you for hearing me, and now old Sojourner has got nothing more to say."

Amid roars of applause, she returned to her corner, leaving more than one of us with streaming eyes, and hearts beating with gratitude. She had taken us up in her strong arms and carried us safely over the slough of difficulty turning the whole tide in our favor.   [1863]

🌿 13

The Problem That Has No Name

BETTY FRIEDAN

Gradually I came to realize that the problem that has no name was shared by countless women in America. As a magazine writer I often interviewed women about problems with their children, or their marriages, or their houses, or their communities. But after a while I began to recognize the telltale signs of this other problem. I saw the same signs in suburban ranchhouses and split-levels on Long Island and in New Jersey and Westchester County; in colonial houses in a small Massachusetts town; on patios in Memphis; in suburban and city apartments; in living rooms in the Midwest. Sometimes I sensed the problem, not as a reporter, but as a suburban housewife, for during this time I was also bringing up my own three children in Rockland County, New York. I heard echoes of the problem in college dormitories and semi-private maternity wards, at PTA meetings and luncheons of the League of Women Voters, at suburban cocktail parties, in station wagons waiting for trains, and in snatches of conversation overheard at Schrafft's. The groping words I heard from other women, on quiet afternoons when children were at school or on quiet evenings when husbands worked late, I think I understood first as a woman long before I understood their larger social and psychological implications.

Just what was this problem that has no name? What were the words women used when they tried to express it? Sometimes a woman would say "I feel empty somehow . . . incomplete." Or she would say, "I feel as if I don't exist." Sometimes she blotted out the feeling with a tranquilizer. Sometimes she thought the problem was with her husband, or her children, or that what she really needed was to redecorate her house, or move to a better neighborhood, or have an affair, or another baby. Sometimes, she went to a doctor with symptoms she could hardly describe: "A tired feeling. . . . I get so angry with the children it scares me. . . . I feel like crying without any reason." (A Cleveland doctor called it "the housewife's syndrome.") A number of women told me about great bleeding blisters that break out on their hands and arms. "I call it the housewife's blight," said a family doctor in Pennsylvania. "I see it so often lately in these young women with four, five and six children who bury themselves in their dishpans. But it isn't caused by detergent and it isn't cured by cortisone."

Sometimes a woman would tell me that the feeling gets so strong she runs out of the house and walks through the streets. Or she stays inside her house and cries. Or her children tell her a joke, and she doesn't laugh because she doesn't hear it. I talked to women who had spent years on the analyst's couch, working out their "adjustment to the feminine role," their blocks to "fulfillment as a wife and mother." But the desperate tone in these women's voices, and the look in their eyes, was the same as the tone and the look of other women, who were sure they had no problem, even though they did have a strange feeling of desperation. //

A mother of four who left college at nineteen to get married told me:

> I've tried everything women are supposed to do—hobbies, gardening, pickling, canning, being very social with my neighbors, joining committees, running PTA teas. I can do it all, and I like it, but it doesn't leave you anything to think about—any feeling of who you are. I never had any career ambitions. All I wanted was to get married and have four children. I love the kids and Bob and my home. There's no problem you can even put a name to. But I'm desperate. I begin to feel I have no personality. I'm a server of food and putter-on of pants and a bedmaker, somebody who can be called on when you want something. But who am I?

A twenty-three-year-old mother in blue jeans said:

> I ask myself why I'm so dissatisfied. I've got my health, fine children, a lovely new home, enough money. My husband has a real future as an electronics engineer. He doesn't have any of these feelings. He says maybe I need a vacation, let's go to New York for a weekend. But that isn't it. I always had this idea we should do everything together. I can't sit down and read a book alone. If the children are napping and I have one hour to myself I just walk through the house waiting for them to wake up. I don't make a move until I know where the rest of the crowd is going. It's as if ever since you were a little girl, there's always been somebody or something that will take care of your life: your parents, or college, or falling in love, or having a child, or moving to a new house. Then you wake up one morning and there's nothing to look forward to.

A young wife in a Long Island development said:

> I seem to sleep so much. I don't know why I should be so tired. This house isn't nearly so hard to clean as the cold-water flat we had when I was working. The children are at school all day. It's not the work. I just don't feel alive."

In 1960, the problem that has no name burst like a boil through the image of the happy American housewife. In the television commercials the pretty housewives still beamed over their foaming dishpans and *Time*'s cover story on "The Suburban Wife, an American Phenomenon" protested: "Having too good a time . . . to believe that they should be unhappy." But the actual unhappiness of the American housewife was suddenly being reported—from the *New York Times* and *Newsweek* to *Good Housekeeping* and CBS Television ("The Trapped Housewife"), although almost everybody who talked about it found some superficial reason to dismiss it. It was attributed to incompetent appliance repairmen (*New York Times*), or the distances children must be chauffeured in the suburbs (*Time*), or too much PTA (*Redbook*). Some said it was the old problem—education: more and more women had education, which naturally made them unhappy in their role as housewives. "The road from Freud to Frigidaire, from Sophocles to Spock, has turned out to be a bumpy one," reported the *New York Times* (June 28, 1960). "Many young women—certainly not all—whose education plunged them into a world of ideas feel stifled in their homes. They find their routine lives out of joint with their training. Like shut-ins, they feel left out. In the last year, the problem of the educated housewife has provided the meat of dozens of speeches made by troubled presidents of women's colleges who maintain, in the face of complaints, that sixteen years of academic training is realistic preparation for wifehood and motherhood."

There was much sympathy for the educated housewife. ("Like a two-headed schizophrenic . . . once she wrote a paper on the Graveyard poets; now she writes notes to the milkman. Once she determined the boiling point of sulfuric acid; now she determines her boiling point with the overdue repairman. . . . The housewife often is reduced to screams and tears. . . . No one, it seems, is appreciative, least of all herself, of the kind of person she becomes in the process of turning from poetess into shrew.")

Home economists suggested more realistic preparation for housewives, such as high-school workshops in home appliances. College educators suggested more discussion groups on home management and the family, to prepare women for the adjustment to domestic life. A spate of articles appeared in the mass magazines offering "Fifty-eight Ways to Make Your Marriage More Exciting." No month went by without a new book by a psychiatrist or sexologist offering technical advice on finding greater fulfillment through sex.

A male humorist joked in *Harper's Bazaar* (July, 1960) that the problem could be solved by taking away women's right to vote. ("In the pre-19th Amendment era, the American woman was placid, sheltered and sure of her role in American society. She left all the political decisions to her husband and he, in turn, left all the family decisions to her. Today a woman has to make both the family *and* the political decisions, and it's too much for her.")

A number of educators suggested seriously that women no longer be admitted to the four-year colleges and universities: in the growing college crisis, the education which girls could not use as housewives was more urgently needed than ever by boys to do the work of the atomic age.

The problem was also dismissed with drastic solutions no one could take seriously. (A woman writer proposed in *Harper's* that women be drafted for compulsory service as nurses' aides and baby-sitters.) And it was smoothed over with the age-old panaceas: "love is their answer," "the only answer is inner help," "the secret of completeness—children," "a private means of intellectual fulfillment," "to cure this toothache of the spirit—the simple formula of handing one's self and one's will over to God."

The problem was dismissed by telling the housewife she doesn't realize how lucky she is—her own boss, no time clock, no junior executive gunning for her job. What if she isn't happy—does she think men are happy in this world? Does she really, secretly, still want to be a man? Doesn't she know yet how lucky she is to be a woman?

The problem was also, and finally, dismissed by shrugging that there are no solutions: this is what being a woman means, and what is wrong with American women that they can't accept their role gracefully? As *Newsweek* put it (March 7, 1960):

She is dissatisfied with a lot that women of other lands can only dream of. Her discontent is deep, pervasive, and impervious to the superficial reme-

dies which are offered at every hand. . . . An army of professional explorers have already charted the major sources of trouble. . . . From the beginning of time, the female cycle has defined and confined woman's role. As Freud was credited with saying: "Anatomy is destiny." Though no group of women has ever pushed these natural restrictions as far as the American wife, it seems that she still cannot accept them with good grace. . . . A young mother with a beautiful family, charm, talent and brains is apt to dismiss her role apologetically. "What do I do?" you hear her say. "Why nothing. I'm just a housewife." A good education, it seems, has given this paragon among women an understanding of the value of everything except her own worth. . . .

And so she must accept the fact that "American women's unhappiness is merely the most recently won of women's rights," and adjust and say with the happy housewife found by *Newsweek:* "We ought to salute the wonderful freedom we all have and be proud of our lives today. I have had college and I've worked, but being a housewife is the most rewarding and satisfying role. . . . My mother was never included in my father's business affairs . . . she couldn't get out of the house and away from us children. But I am an equal to my husband; I can go along with him on business trips and to social business affairs."

The alternative offered was a choice that few women would contemplate. In the sympathetic words of the *New York Times:* "All admit to being deeply frustrated at times by the lack of privacy, the physical burden, the routine of family life, the confinement of it. However, none would give up her home and family if she had the choice to make again." *Redbook* commented: "Few women would want to thumb their noses at husbands, children and community and go off on their own. Those who do may be talented individuals, but they rarely are successful women."

The year American women's discontent boiled over, it was also reported (*Look*) that the more than 21,000,000 American women who are single, widowed, or divorced do not cease even after fifty their frenzied, desperate search for a man. And the search begins early—for seventy per cent of all American women now marry before they are twenty-four.

A pretty twenty-five-year-old secretary took thirty-five different jobs in six months in the futile hope of finding a husband. Women are moving from one political club to another, taking evening courses in accounting or sailing, learning to play golf or ski, joining a number of churches in succession, going to bars alone, in their ceaseless search for a man.

Of the growing thousands of women currently getting private psychiatric help in the United States, the married ones were reported dissatisfied with their marriages, the unmarried ones suffering from anxiety and, finally, depression. Strangely, a number of psychiatrists stated that, in their experience, unmarried women patients were happier than married ones. So the door of all those pretty suburban houses opened a crack to permit a glimpse of uncounted thousands of American housewives who suffered alone from a problem that suddenly everyone was talking about, and beginning to take for granted, as one of those unreal problems in American life that can never be solved—like the hydrogen bomb. By 1962 the plight of the trapped American housewife had become a national parlor game. Whole issues of magazines, newspaper columns, books learned and frivolous, educational conferences and television panels were devoted to the problem.

Even so, most men, and some women, still did not know that this problem was real. But those who had faced it honestly knew that all the superficial remedies, the sympathetic advice, the scolding words and the cheering words were somehow drowning the problem in unreality. A bitter laugh was beginning to be heard from American women. They were admired, envied, pitied, theorized over until they were sick of it, offered drastic solutions or silly choices that no one could take seriously. They got all kinds of advice from the growing armies of marriage and child-guidance counselors, psychotherapists, and armchair psychologists, on how to adjust to their role as housewives. No other road to fulfillment was offered to American women in the middle of the twentieth century. Most adjusted to their role and suffered or ignored the problem that has no name. It can be less painful, for a woman, not to hear the strange, dissatisfied voice stirring within her.

[1964]

 14

A Work of Artifice

MARGE PIERCY

The bonsai tree
in the attractive pot
could have grown eighty feet tall
on the side of a mountain
till split by lightning.
But a gardener
carefully pruned it.
It is nine inches high.
Every day as he
whittles back the branches
the gardener croons,
It is your nature
to be small and cozy,
domestic and weak;
how lucky, little tree,
to have a pot to grow in.
With living creatures
one must begin very early
to dwarf their growth:
the bound feet,
the crippled brain,
the hair in curlers,
the hands you
love to touch.

[1973]

15

Cultural Tyranny

GLORIA ANZALDUA

Culture forms our beliefs. We perceive the version of reality that it communicates. Dominant paradigms, predefined concepts that exist as unquestionable, unchallengeable, are transmitted to us through the culture. Culture is made by those in power—men. Males make the rules and laws;

women transmit them. How many times have I heard mothers and mothers-in-law tell their sons to beat their wives for not obeying them, for being *hociconas* (big mouths), for being *callajeras* (going to visit and gossip with neighbors), for expecting their husbands to help with the rearing of children and the housework, for wanting to be something other than housewives?

The culture expects women to show greater acceptance of, and commitment to, the value system than men. The culture and the Church insist that women are subservient to males. If a woman rebels she is a *mujer mala*. If a woman doesn't renounce herself in favor of the male, she is selfish. If a woman remains a *virgen* until she marries, she is a good woman. For a woman of my culture there used to be only three directions she could turn: to the Church as a nun, to the streets as a prostitute, or to the home as a mother. Today some of us have a fourth choice: entering the world by way of education and career and becoming self-autonomous persons. A very few of us. As a working class people our chief activity is to put food in our mouths, a roof over our heads and clothes on our backs. Educating our children is out of reach for most of us. Educated or not, the onus is still on woman to be a wife/mother—only the nun can escape motherhood. Women are made to feel total failures if they don't marry and have children. *"¿Y cuándo te casas, Gloria? Se te va a pasar el tren." Y yo les digo, "Pos si me caso, no va ser con un hombre." Se quedan calladitas. Sí, soy hija de la Chingada.* I've always been her daughter. *No 'tés chingando.*

Humans fear the supernatural, both the undivine (the animal impulses such as sexuality, the unconscious, the unknown, the alien) and the divine (the superhuman, the god in us). Culture and religion seek to protect us from these two forces. The female, by virtue of creating entities of flesh and blood in her stomach (she bleeds every month but does not die), by virtue of being in tune with nature's cycles, is feared. Because, according to Christianity and most other major religions, woman is carnal, animal, and closer to the undivine, she must be protected. Protected from herself. Woman is the stranger, the other. She is man's recognized night-

marish pieces, his Shadow-Beast. The sight of her sends him into a frenzy of anger and fear.

La gorra, el rebozo, la mantilla are symbols of my culture's "protection" of women. Culture (read males) professes to protect women. Actually it keeps women in rigidly defined roles. It keeps the girlchild from other men—don't poach on my preserves, only I can touch my child's body. Our mothers taught us well, *"Los hombres nomás quieren una cosa";* men aren't to be trusted, they are selfish and are like children. Mothers made sure we didn't walk into a room of brothers or fathers or uncles in nightgowns or shorts. We were never alone with men, not even those of our own family.

Through our mothers, the culture gave us mixed messages: *No voy a dejar que ningún pelado desgraciado maltrate a mis hijos.* And in the next breath it would say, *La mujer tiene que hacer lo que le diga el hombre.* Which was it to be—strong, or submissive, rebellious or conforming?

Tribal rights over those of the individual ensured the survival of the tribe and were necessary then, and, as in the case of all indigenous peoples in the world who are still fighting off intentional, premeditated murder (genocide), they are still necessary.

Much of what the culture condemns focuses on kinship relationships. The welfare of the family, the community, and the tribe is more important than the welfare of the individual. The individual exists first as kin—as sister, as father, as *padrino*—and last as self.

In my culture, selfishness is condemned, especially in women; humility and selflessness, the absence of selfishness, is considered a virtue. In the past, acting humble with members outside the family ensured that you would make no one *envidioso* (envious); therefore he or she would not use witchcraft against you. If you get above yourself, you're an *envidiosa*. If you don't behave like everyone else, *la gente* will say that you think you're better than others, *que te crees grande.* With ambition (condemned in the Mexican culture and valued in the Anglo) comes envy. *Respeto* carries with it a set of rules so that social categories and hierarchies will be kept in order: respect is reserved for *la abuela, papá, el patrón,* those with power in the community. Women are at the bottom of the ladder one rung above the deviants. The Chicano, *mexicano,* and some Indian cultures have no tolerance for deviance. Deviance is whatever is condemned by the community. Most societies try to get rid of their deviants. Most cultures have burned and beaten their homosexuals and others who deviate from the sexual common. The queer are the mirror reflecting the heterosexual tribe's fear: being different, being other and therefore lesser, therefore sub-human, inhuman, non-human.   [1987]

🌿 16

Frailty Is Not My Name

MAUREEN ISMAY

Frailty is not my name
                    yet,
On the other hand,
I'm not a big strong, black woman
iron hard and carrying
all the sorrows of the world on my back.

My breasts large and hard as boxes
My eyes big and bulging
My skin, black and shiny and greasy

I'm not big and strong
and keeping a man underneath my tail
able to take all that garbage
                    'Here dawg take that'

          I'm no mythology
          shaking the earth
          and freaking out the leaves.

I'm not a strong black woman
admirable and brawd

ten children at my breast
all at the same time
while cooking and cleaning
and singing and fixing up
my man . . .
with beads in my hair
and camel on my skin.

On the other hand
          Don't call me frailty!   [1988]

🌿 17

Blazes of Truth

SUSAN SCHNUR

When I was 12 years old, my parents sent me off to Camp Ramah in the Poconos. That June, I was a dull kid in an undershirt from Trenton, New Jersey, outfitted in lime-green, mix-and-match irregulars from E.J. Korvette's. By the end of August, though—exposed as I was, for two months, to suburban Philadelphia's finest pre-adolescent fashion cognoscenti—I had contracted that dread disease: "*JAP*itis."

Symptoms included not only the perfection of an elaborate, all-day triple-sink procedure for dyeing white-wool bobby socks to the requisite shade of dirty white (we called it oyster), but also my sudden, ignominious realization that the discount "Beatlemania" record my mother had bought for me the previous spring was not, after all, sung by the real group.

I'm not even sure that the term *JAP* existed yet back then (I don't think it did), but, in any case, by October I was—more or less—cured. I put the general themes of entitlement, of materialism, of canonized motifs (in those days, Lord and Taylor was the label of choice rather than Bloomingdale's) at the back of my mental medicine chest for the next two decades.

It wasn't until six months ago, actually—while teaching a course at Colgate University called "Contemporary Issues of Jewish Existence"—that I again gave the subject of *JAP*s a moment's pause.

A unit on *JAP*s was decidedly *not* on my course syllabus (I taught the standards: Holocaust—Faith—Immigration—Assimilation—Varieties of Religious Experience—Humor—Israel—Women). But my students, as it turned out, were obsessed with *JAP*s.

Week after week, in personal journals that they

were keeping for me, they talked *JAP*s: the stereotypes, dating them, hating them, not *being* them, *JAP* graffiti, *JAP* competitiveness, *JAP*s who gave them the willies back home in Scarsdale over spring break.

I had been raised on moron jokes; *they* had been raised on *JAP* jokes. ("What does a *JAP* do with her asshole in the morning? Dresses him up and sends him to work.")

Little by little, I came to realize that the *JAP* theme was by no means a one-note samba. It was kaleidoscopic and self-revealing; the students plugged it into a whole range of Jewish issues. I began to encourage them to look at their throwaway *JAP* comments with a measure of scrutiny.

The first, and most striking, ostinato in the students' journals was the dissociative one. As one Jewish student framed it, "There are so many *JAP*s in this class, it makes me sick." (An astonishing number of students were desperate to let me know this.)

Since over one-third of the class was not Jewish (the enrollment was 30), and since there was no one in the class that I would have identified sartorially as a *JAP*, this was an interesting fillip.

"That's funny," I started commenting back in these students' journals. "The other students think *you're* a *JAP*."

Eventually, one Jewish student wrote, "Maybe when I talk about *JAP*s and that whole negative thing, it's a way for me to get 'permission' to assimilate."

Another wondered why he feels "like every *JAP* on campus somehow implicates me. That's a very 'minority culture' reflex, isn't it? Why am I so hung up on how everyone else perceives Jews?"

Some students perceived the *JAP* phenomenon, interestingly, as a developmental phase in American Judaism—a phase in which one parades both one's success and one's entitlement. "When my best girlfriend from childhood was bat mitzvahed," wrote one student after reading *A Bintel Brief* and *World of Our Fathers*, "her grandmother gave her a '*JAP*-in-training' diamond-chip necklace. It's like the grandmother was saying, 'When I was your age, I had to sew plackets in a Lower East Side sweatshop. So you girls be *JAP*s. Take whatever you can and be proud of it.'"

A Black student mentioned—during a talk about the socialization of Jewish women—that Jewish women, like their Black counterparts, are encouraged to be extremely competent, but then are double-bound with the message that their competence must *only* be used for frivolous purposes. (Like Goldie Hawn, in *Private Benjamin*, scolding her upholsterer with impressive assertiveness: "I specifically said—the ottoman in mushroom!", or informing her superior officer that she refused to go to Guam because "my hair will frizz.") "Minority women are warned not to be a real threat to anyone," the student explained, "That's how *JAP*s evolve."

Another theme of the students touched on their perception that Jews are sometimes discriminated against not because they are *less* endowed than others, but because they are more endowed (smarter, richer, more "connected"). *JAP*s, then, become, in the words of an Irish Catholic student who was doing readings on theology and the theme of chosenness, "the 'chosen of the chosen.' Unlike Irish Catholics who have been discriminated against because we seem 'un-chosen'," she mused, "people hate *JAP*s because they seem to have everything: money, confidence, style."

Of course, it's probably unnecessary for me to point out that the most prolific *JAP* references had to do with that venerable old feud—the Jewish War-Between-The-Sexes.

One pre-law Jewish male in the class (who was under a lot of pressure and had developed colitis during that semester) stated point-blank that he did not date Jewish women. I was shocked by the number of 20-year-old, seemingly fully-assimilated Jewish males who were right up there with Alexander Portnoy on this subject.

Several students responded to his comment in their journals. "He's angry at *JAP*s," one woman wrote, "because they get to be needy and dependent, whereas the expectations on him are really high."

Another student related the experience of two friends of hers at SUNY Binghamton: "Someone spray-painted the word *JAP* on their dormitory door," she recounted. "But now I wonder—which one of the girls was being called a *JAP*? The one with the dozen Benetton sweaters, or the one who'd gotten 750 on her L-SATs?" The question being, of course, which is ultimately more threatening: the demanding woman or the self-sufficient one?

An Hispanic woman in the class talked about what she called "the dialectic of prejudice"—that is, the contradictory nature of racist or sexist slurs as being, in itself, a diagnostic of irrational bias. "A *JAP* is portrayed as both frigid and nymphomaniacal," she wrote. "She's put down both because of her haughty strut that says, 'I'm independent,' and because of her *kvetching* that says, 'I'm dependent.'"

A twist on this theme was provided by a Jewish woman who commented, "Whatever Jewish men call us—cold, hot, leech, bitch—it's all the same thing: They're afraid they can't live up to our standards."

A psych major in the class took a different tack.

"It's not that the Jewish male really believes Jewish women are terrible, rather that he simply wants majority culture males to believe it. It's like when territorial animals urinate on a tree," she explained. "It's a minority male's possessive instinct. Like a sign that says, 'Robert Redfords—stay away!'"

Finally, several Jewish students framed their relations with one another in the context of Jewish family systems. "Lashing out at Jewish women—calling them all *JAP*s or refusing to marry them—is a way to get back at the entire high-expectation, high-pressure Jewish family," stated one student in response to a film I showed in class called "Parenting and Ethnicity." "You can lash out by becoming an academic failure," he went on, "or you can become a doctor—which is less self-destructive—and then simply refuse to marry a Jewish woman."

JAP: The New Antisemitic Code Word

FRANCINE KLAGSBRUN

Isn't it odd that the term *JAP,* referring to a spoiled, self-indulgent woman, should be so widely used at a time when women are working outside their homes in unprecedented numbers, struggling to balance their home lives and their work lives to give as much of themselves as they can to everybody—their husbands, their kids, their bosses?

Jewish women, like women throughout society, are trying to find their own paths, their own voices. And, along with other changes that have taken place, they have been finding themselves Jewishly. And yet we hear the term *JAP* being used, perhaps almost more now than ever before. Why?

The new-found, or rather newly-accepted, drive of women for achievement in many arenas threatens many men. What better put-down of the strong woman than to label her a "Princess"? She is not being attacked as a competitor—that would be too close to home. No—she's called a princess, and that label diminishes her, negating her ambition and her success.

One may note, and rightly so, that there *are* materialistic Jewish women—and men too. But are Jews the only people guilty of excesses in spending? Why should the word "Jewish" be used pejoratively to describe behavior we don't approve of?

I think the answer is that there is an underlying antisemitic message in that label. Loudness is somehow "Jewish." Vulgarity is somehow "Jewish." All the old stereotypes of Jews come into play in the use of the term *JAP.* In this day, polite Christian society would not *openly* make anti-Jewish slurs. But *JAP* is O.K. *JAP* is a kind of code word. It's a way of symbolically winking, poking with an elbow, and saying, "well you know how Jews are—so materialistic and pushy."

What is interesting is that this code word can be used in connection with *women*—the Jewish American *Princess*—and nobody protests its intrinsic antisemitism.   [1980]

Towards the end of the term, a feminist friend pointed out to me something I had not considered: that the characterizations of *JAP*s and Yuppies are often identical—the difference being, of course, that a Yuppie designation is still generally taken as neutral or even positive, whereas there is hardly one of us left—I don't think—who would compete for the label of *JAP.*

All in all, I trust that the larger lessons in all of these *JAP* ruminations have not been lost on my students. For example: Why has it become socially sanctioned to use a *Jewish* designation (*JAP*) for a description that fits as many Christians as Jews? Or why—along the same lines—is it okay to use a *female* designation (again, *JAP*) for a description that fits as many men as women? Or, sensing what we now sense, shouldn't we refuse any truck altogether with the term *JAP?*   [1987]

18

In Search of Liberation

DEBRA KENT

When I joined a women's consciousness-raising group a few years ago, I'm not quite sure what I expected—to discover some bond of understanding with other women, perhaps, to feel myself part of the growing sisterhood of the liberation movement. But through session after session, I listened in amazement and awe as the others delivered outraged accounts of their exploitation at the hands of bosses, boyfriends, and passersby. They were tired of being regarded as sex objects by male chauvinist pigs. All their lives, they lamented, they had been programmed for the confining roles of wife and mother, roles in which their own needs were submerged by those of the men they served.

I had to admit that their indignation was justified. But it was impossible for me to confess my own reaction to their tales of horror, which was a very real sense of envy. Society had provided a place for them as women, however restricting that place might be, and they knew it.

Totally blind since birth, I was seldom encouraged to say, "When I grow up I'll get married and have babies." Instead, my intellectual growth was nurtured. I very definitely received the unspoken message that I would need the independence of a profession, as I could not count on having the support of a husband.

For myself and for other disabled women, sex discrimination is a secondary issue—in life and in the job market. To the prospective employer, a visible handicap may immediately connote incompetence, and whether the applicant is male or female may never come under consideration at all. In fact, the connotations that disability holds for the public seem, in many ways, to negate sexuality altogether. In a culture where men are expected to demonstrate strength and dominance, the disabled man is regarded as weak and ineffectual. But in social situations he may have an advantage over the disabled woman.

Our culture allows the man to be the aggressor. If he can bolster himself against the fear of rejection, he can make overtures toward starting a relationship. At least he doesn't have to sit home waiting for the telephone to ring.

According to the stereotype, women are helpless creatures to be cuddled and protected. The disabled woman, however, is often merely seen as helpless. A man may fear that she will be so oppressively dependent upon him that a relationship with her may strike him as a terrifying prospect. To prove him wrong she may strive for self-sufficiency, only to have him say that she's too aggressive and unfeminine.

People may pity the disabled woman for her handicap, or admire her for her strength in overcoming it, but she is too unlike other females to be whistled at on the street. Somehow she is perceived as a nonsexual being. If men don't make passes at girls who wear glasses, what chance does a blind girl have, or one in a wheelchair, or a woman with spastic hands?

American culture still pictures the ideal woman: slender, blonde, blue-eyed, and physically perfect. Of course, there is plenty of leeway, and not every man is worried about these cultural stereotypes when choosing a mate. But as long as a woman remains a status symbol to the man who "possesses" her, the living proof of his prowess, the woman with a disability will be at a severe disadvantage. The man who is not completely secure will be afraid to show her off with pride because she is too different.

The worst period for most disabled men and women is probably adolescence, when conformity to the group's norms is all-important. Then, even overweight or a bad case of acne is enough to brand one as a pariah. Things may become easier later on, as emphasis on outward appearances gradually yields to concern with qualities as well. But it is hard to shake off the sense of being an outcast.

Even when she establishes a healthy relationship with a man, the disabled woman may sometimes find herself wondering, "Why does he want me unless there is something wrong with him? If someone else comes along, won't he leave me for her?"

But why, I ask myself, should it ever make a difference to society whether people with disabilities are ever accepted intact––as human beings with minds, feelings, and sexuality? Though we have become more vocal in recent years, we still constitute a very small minority.

Yet the Beautiful People—the slender, fair, and perfect ones—form a minority that may be even smaller. Between these two groups are the average, ordinary citizens: Men who are too short, women who are too tall, people who are too fat or too thin, people with big noses, protruding ears, receding hairlines, and bad complexions. Millions of people go through life feeling self-conscious or downright inadequate, fearing that others will reject them for these physical flaws. Perhaps the struggle of disabled people is really everyone's battle against the binding rules of conformity, the struggle for the right to be an individual.

As I sat in that consciousness-raising group, I realized that disabled women have a long and arduous fight ahead. Somehow we must learn to perceive ourselves as attractive and desirable. Our struggle is not unlike the striving for self-acceptance of the millions of nonhandicapped who also fall short of the Beautiful People image.

Our liberation will be a victory for everyone.

[1987]

✤ 19

Coming of Age

FOLAMI HARRIS-GRAY

I come from a generation of women who were raised by women. These women supported their families financially and emotionally. They provided, in the absence or intermittent presence of men, the only semblance of family life. I come from a tradition of mothers and aunts who were fathers for children, grandmothers and sisters who were mothers. Yet these women sacrificed their considerable personal power to men. These women pawned their lives in the hope that liberation would come through black men's freedom. And they believed that their sacrifice of self would release their daughters from the burden of gender oppression; that their sons would see women's suffering and, out of love for their women-mothers, be just in their dealings with all women. In other words, I come from women who offered themselves on the altars of better tomorrows.

The generation of women who raised me didn't seem to have a vocabulary for articulating their oppression in a way that clearly isolated it from the oppressions of race and class—or so it seemed to my young female ears. They did not speak openly of their condition in terms of men's behaviors. This happened in hushed tones within the circle of intimates. As a result, protest against the exploitation of women by men was muted by the more vociferous opposition to economic and racial inequality.

In silence the mothers of my youth took the beatings, suffered through the drunken rapes, endured the tyranny of unending, stultifying housework and survived the emotional exhaustion of nurturing children alone. They even turned over their paychecks to the lustful pursuits of parasitic lovers. Most tragically, without voice, my mothers grew to expect nothing in return—no material tokens, no social supports, no appreciation for the work they donated in the home, no sexual gratification, no dreams, not even a quiet space of their own. If you expect nothing, you can't be disappointed when nothing happens. Or so they pretended.

The generation of women who raised me willed themselves to expect nothing from men in order to calm the enormous rage they held. They often turned this rage inward and destroyed their precious selves. They sacrificed themselves for the children, for a better future, for a peaceful life. For a peaceful life, they joined in their own destruction; and they tried to teach their daughters this acquired skill lest their sons fail to treat them justly, lest their daughters, too, find themselves with a rage too powerful for even them to acknowledge.

This is the generation of women who raised me in a small place called Jamaica in the 1950s and 1960s. I don't presume to speak for all women of my generation nor to generalize the experiences of my mothers to all women of their generation. The feminine identity is defined by class, culture, and sociopolitical realities and as such will differ from time to time and place to place. Yet I know the experience of my mothers is not so isolated or unique a perspective to be outside our collective "herstory."

There is a disturbing continuity about the oppression that imprisoned my mothers within my sisters' lives. There is an alarming continuity in the ability of my brothers to recreate the same oppressive spaces that stunted my mothers' growth and made mockery of their womanhood. I see this oppression in the lives of many women of my generation who lose themselves in this same labyrinth of male privilege. We happen upon these tortuous structures so unsuspectingly.

At the age of 16, I was beckoned into the universe of female adulthood. I came to understand the meaning of being seen but not heard, a condition which I thought was visited only on the most uninteresting of children. I came of age wrestling with the paradox: How can one possess voice and reason and dignity and yet not be heard or acknowledged? Lacking the power to be heard, we were disregarded and utterly disrespected. Young men, not fully adult, felt empowered to disregard female feelings, to forcefully penetrate female bodies and laugh at our protest as a joke of minor importance. Such a menacing oppression continues today as my children come of age. How many female voices does it take to be heard, and in what language are we understood?

In spite of this continuity, there was discontinuity. The thread of oppression frayed in places so that I also came into womanhood when New York state legalized abortion for women of age and the first black woman was elected to Congress. There were still issues of consent to be resolved for some women, but men had come to acknowledge the necessity of reproductive choice for women. This was a momentous development for women. It affirmed the power of the collective voice and made it possible for us to exercise greater control over how our bodies could be used.

In places like Jamaica, Latin America, Africa, and black communities throughout America, issues of race and class complicated the liberalization of reproductive freedom for women. In those places we knew too well the duplicity of motives in concessions such as these. The legalization and liberalization of reproductive choice was therefore suspect. It was perceived to be a tool for the genocide of people from the periphery at a time when our labor had become superfluous. It was anathema to a male identity defined by sexual prowess and progeny. While it liberated women from unwanted pregnancies, it also made it easier for males to abdicate responsibility for paternity and support. Was this development some strange coincidental meeting of white male interests and female needs? Was it to be wrestled back later when male interests changed?

Hidden agendas notwithstanding, the legalization of abortion and liberalization of reproductive health care had the effect of fanning a smoldering female hope on these shores and of giving rise to voices elsewhere. It bolstered our determination to struggle openly as women, even if our voices were not always heard or understood. It encouraged us to talk to ourselves and seek comfort in our own murmurings.

It was a hopeful time as I assumed womanhood, for myself and the sisters around me. We were pregnant with anticipation about the changes possible in the political and personal arenas. There were Angela Davis, Shirley Chisholm, and ERA. There was optimism about the prospects for intellectual growth, greater access to meaningful employment, wider options for shaping our life spaces.

We looked forward to improvements in our relationships with black men. Men, after all, were also benefiting from these newly won freedoms.

We struggled with them for economic and racial equality locally as well as globally. And we believed the aspirations they expressed in the socialist and black nationalist rhetoric to be genuine and whole. We also looked forward to strengthening our relationships as women, as sisters, and as lovers.

We ran headlong into careers, social activism, and parenting with every expectation for equity in the distribution of domestic responsibilities. We expected fairness in the workplace and equality within our emotional spaces. Our optimism soared like Icarus, and our confidence in the rightness of our cause grew. There was such a sense of urgency—we had so much to say after all, so much to undo.

But like Icarus, we flew too near the male-god, Power. We wanted it close by but were not prepared to worship at its feet. The proximity made us forget that we were, after all, still without real wings or real power—vulnerable, dependent on the good will of the sons of man who kiss Power's feet. And so, of age, I find myself with my sisters in the waxy sea of exceeding male standards in workplaces designed for nonparenting males. We still carry the brunt of nurturing children through an increasingly complex growth process or watch their need for guidance and emotional support go unmet. We still sustain relationships fraught with conflicting gender expectations or remain without male companionship if we are heterosexual. And throughout this all, we try to rebuild our wings destroyed by the sons of men. Such a troublesome continuity of oppression across generations of women, generations of change.

[1992]

🌿 20

Kinder, Kuche, Kirche: Psychology Constructs the Female

NAOMI WEISSTEIN

Edited by Virginia Blaisdell

The central assumption for most psychologists of human personality has been that human behavior rests on an individual and inner dynamic, perhaps fixed in infancy, perhaps fixed by genitalia, perhaps simply arranged in a rather immovable cognitive network. However, the evidence is collecting that what people do and who they believe themselves to be will in general be a function of what people around them expect and what the overall situation in which they are acting implies that they are.

How are women characterized in our culture, and in psychology? They are considered inconsistent, emotionally unstable, lacking in a strong conscience or superego, weaker than men, nurturant rather than productive, intuitive rather than intelligent, and, if they are "normal," suited to the home and the family. In short, the list adds up to a typical stereotype of minority group inferiority (Hacker, 1951): if they know their place, which is in the home, they are really quite lovable, happy, childlike, affectionate creatures.

What I will show, however, is there isn't the tiniest shred of evidence that these fantasies of servitude and childish dependence have anything to do with women's true potential. I will show that the idea that the nature of human possibility rests on the accidents of individual development or on the fundamentalist myth of sex organ causality has strangled and deflected psychology so that it is relatively useless in describing, explaining or predicting humans and their behavior, and worse than useless in contributing to a vision that could truly liberate us—men as well as women.

I want to stress that this failure is not limited to studies about women. Rather, the kind of psychology that has addressed itself to how people act and who they are has failed to understand the basics of why people act the way they do and certainly failed to understand what might make them act differently.

THEORY WITHOUT EVIDENCE

If we inspect the literature of personality, it is immediately obvious that the bulk of it is written by clinicians and psychiatrists and that the major support for their theories is "years of intensive clinical experience." This is a tradition started by Freud. His "insights" occurred during the course of his work with his patients. Now, there is nothing wrong with such an approach to theory *formulation;* a person is free to make up theories with any inspiration that works: But one is not free to claim *validity* for a theory until it has been tested and confirmed.

Theories are treated in no such tentative way in ordinary clinical practice. Consider Freud. What he thought constituted evidence violated the most minimal conditions of scientific rigor. In *The Sexual Enlightenment of Children* (1963), the classic document that is supposed to demonstrate empirically the existence of a castration complex and its connection to a phobia, Freud based his analysis not on the little boy who had the phobia, but on the reports of the father of the little boy, himself in therapy and a devotee of Freudian theory.

But certainly, you may object, "years of intensive clinical experience" is the only reliable measure in a discipline that rests for its findings on insight, sensitivity and intuition. The problem with insight, sensitivity and intuition is that they tend to confirm the biases one started out with. Years of intensive clinical experience is not the same thing as empirical evidence.

In addition, with judgments of human behavior, it is so difficult to tie down precisely just what behavior is going on, let alone what behavior should be expected, that one must test again and again the reliability of judgments. How many judges, blind, will agree in their observations? Can they replicate their own judgments at some later time?

As a graduate student at Harvard some years ago, I was a member of a seminar that was asked to identify which of two piles of a clinical test—the TAT— had been written by males and which by females. Only four students out of twenty identified the piles correctly, and this was after one and a half months of intensively studying the differences between men and women. Since this result is below chance—that is, this result would occur by chance about four out of thousand times—we may conclude that there is finally a consistency here; students *are* judging knowledgeably within the context of psychological teaching about the differences between men and women. The teachings themselves are simply erroneous.

THE SOCIAL CONTEXT

It has become increasingly clear that in order to understand why people do what they do, and certainly in order to change what people do, psychologists must turn away from the theory of the causal nature of the inner dynamic and look to the social context within which individuals live.

In a series of brilliant experiments, Rosenthal and his co-workers (Rosenthal and Jacobson, 1968; Rosenthal, 1966) have shown that if one group of experimenters has one hypothesis about what it expects to find, and another group of experimenters has the opposite hypothesis, both groups will obtain results in accord with their hypotheses. This is not due to mishandling of data by biased experimenters. Rather, somehow, *the bias of the experimenter creates a changed environment in which subjects actually act differently.*

This is true even with animal subjects. In two separate studies (Rosenthal and Fode, 1960; Rosenthal and Lawson, 1961), those experimenters who were told that rats learning mazes had been especially bred for brightness obtained better learning from their rats than did experimenters believing their rats to have been bred for dullness. In a later study, Rosenthal and Jacobson (1968) extended their analysis to the natural classroom situation. Here, they tested a group of students and reported to the teachers that some among the students tested "showed great promise." Actually, the students so named had been selected on a random basis. Some time later the experimenters retested the group of students. Those students whose teachers had been told that they were "promising" showed real and dramatic increases in their IQs as compared to the rest of the students. Something in the conduct of the teachers toward those whom the teachers believed to be the "bright" students made those students brighter, even though the people administering the second IQ test did not have the same bias.

Thus, even in carefully controlled experiments, and with no outward or conscious difference in behavior, the hypotheses we start with will influence enormously the behavior of another organism.

More important, the Rosenthal experiments point quite clearly to the influence of social expectation. In some extremely important ways, people are what you expect them to be, or at least they behave as you expect them to behave.

There is another series of brilliant social psychological experiments that point to the overwhelming effect of social context. These are the obedience experiments of Stanley Milgram (1965a) in which subjects are asked to obey the orders of unknown experimenters—orders that carry with them the distinct possibility that the subject is killing somebody.

In Milgram's experiments, subjects are told that they are administering a learning experiment and that they are to deal out shocks each time the other "subject" (in reality, a confederate of the experimenter) answers incorrectly. The equipment appears to provide graduated shocks ranging upwards from 15 through 450 volts. For each of four consecutive voltages there are verbal descriptions such as "mild shock," "danger, severe shock," and, finally, for the 435 and 450 volt increments, a red XXX marked over the switches. Each time the confederate answers incorrectly, the subject is supposed to increase the voltage. As the voltage increases, the confederate begins to cry in pain; he demands that the experiment stop; finally, he refuses to answer at all. When he stops responding, the experimenter instructs the subject to continue increasing the voltage; for each shock administered, the confederate shrieks in agony.

Under these conditions, how many of the subjects would administer a shock that they believed to be possibly lethal? No individual differences between subjects as shown on personality tests predicted which ones would continue to obey and which ones would break off the experiment. When forty psychiatrists were asked to predict how many of a group of 100 subjects would go on to give the lethal shock, their predictions were exponentially lower than the actual percentages; most expected only one-tenth of one percent of the subjects to obey to the end. In reality, 62.5% of the subjects obeyed to the end.

But even though *psychiatrists* have no idea how people will behave in this situation, and even though individual differences do not predict which subjects will obey and which will not, it *is* easy to predict when subjects will be obedient and when they will be defiant. All the experimenter has to do is change the social situation. In a variant of the experiment, Milgram (1965b) had, in addition to the "victim," two confederates posing as subjects. These worked along with the real subject in administering electric shocks. When these two confederates refused to go on with the experiment, only 10% of the subjects continued to the maximum voltage.

Finally, an ingenious experiment by Schachter and Singer (1962) showed that subjects injected with adrenalin, which produces a state of physiological arousal very similar to that which occurs when subjects are extremely afraid, became euphoric when they were in a room with an experimenter's confederate who was acting euphoric. When they were placed in a room with a confederate who was acting extremely angry, the subjects became extremely angry.

To summarize: if subjects under quite innocuous and non-coercive social conditions can be made to kill other subjects and under other types of social conditions will positively refuse to do so; if subjects can react to a state of physiological fear by becoming euphoric because there is somebody else around who is euphoric, or angry because there is somebody else around who is angry; if students become intelligent because teachers expect them to be intelligent and rats run mazes better because experimenters are told the rats are bright, then it is obvious that a study of human behavior requires, first and foremost, a study of the social contexts within which people move and the expectations about how they will behave.

CONCLUSION

In a review of the intellectual differences between little boys and little girls, Eleanor Maccoby (1966) has shown that there are no intellectual differences until about high school, or, if there are, girls are slightly ahead of boys. At high school, girls begin to do worse on a few intellectual tasks, such as arithmetic reasoning, and beyond high school the achievement of women, now measured in terms of productivity and accomplishment, drops off even more rapidly.

It is no use to talk about women being different but equal. All of the tests I can think of have a "good" outcome and a "bad" outcome. Women usually end up at the "bad" outcome. In light of social expectations about women, what is surprising is not that women end up where society expects they will. What is surprising is that little girls don't get the message until high school that they are supposed to be stupid. And what is even more remarkable is that some women resist this message even after high school, college and graduate school.

I don't know what immutable differences exist between men and women apart from differences in their genitals. Perhaps there are some other unchangeable differences; probably there are a number of irrelevant differences. But it is clear that until *social expectations* for men and women are equal—until we provide equal respect for both men and women—our answers to this question will simply reflect our prejudices.

REFERENCES

Freud, S., *The Sexual Enlightenment of Children*. Collier Books Edition, 1963.

Hacker, H. M., "Women as a Minority Group," *Social Forces,* 1951, *30,* 60–69.

Maccoby, Eleanor E., "Sex Differences in Intellectual Functioning," in Maccoby (ed.), *The Development of Sex Differences*. Stanford University Press, 1966, 25–55.

Milgram, S., "Some Conditions of Obedience and Disobedience to Authority," *Human Relations,* 1965a, *18,* 57–76.

Milgram, S., "Liberating Effects of Group Pressure," *Journal of Personality and Social Psychology,* 1965b, *I,* 127–134.

Rosenthal, R., "On the Social Psychology of the Psychological Experiment: The Experimenter's Hypothesis as Unintended Determinant of Experimental Results," *American Scientist,* 1963, *51,* 268–283.

Rosenthal, R., *Experimenter Effects in Behavioral Research.* New York: Appleton-Century-Crofts, 1966.

Rosenthal, R., & Fode, K. L., "The Effect of Experimenter Bias on the Performance of the Albino Rat." Unpublished manuscript, Harvard University, 1960.

Rosenthal, R., & Jacobson, L., *Pygmalion in the Classroom: Teacher Expectation and Pupil's Intellectual Development.* New York, Holt, Rinehart & Winston, 1968.

Rosenthal, R., & Lawson, R., "A Longitudinal Study of the Effects of Experimenter Bias on the Operant Learning of Laboratory Rats." Unpublished manuscript, Harvard University, 1961.

Schachter, S., & Singer, J. E., "Cognitive, Social and Physiological Determinants of Emotional State," *Psychological Review,* 1962, *69,* 379–399.   [1992]

Learning Sexism

We learn about sexism in a variety of overt and subtle ways. Ideas about what it means to be female are communicated through the language we use; media portrayals of women; direct messages from family, friends, and teachers; and many other sources. This section begins with two women's descriptions of how family expectations, peer norms, and cultural traditions affected them and influenced their ideas of what it meant to be a girl. Murielle Minard's poem, "The Gift," describes a doll given to a girl on her seventh birthday. Beautiful and perfect, the fragile doll symbolizes femininity. In Helena María Viramontes's "Growing," Naomi, an adolescent Chicana, reflects on the ways girls are treated in her community. During a rousing game of stickball, she breaks away from the stultifying expectations of "being a girl" and, in doing so, realizes just how limiting being a woman will be for her and Lucía, her younger sister.

Schooling is also a powerful socializing force. In a variety of ways, such as classroom interaction patterns and teachers' expectations of students, female students learn more than academic material in the classroom. Lee Anne Bell describes dilemmas that interfere with girls' success in school, and highlights the strategies girls use to deal with the individualistic, competitive atmosphere of the classroom. While the article by Myra Sadker and David Sadker was written in the 1980s, the classroom dynamics it describes are still prevalent today.

Accepted patterns of interpersonal and nonverbal communication reinforce traditional power relationships between females and males. The ways in which women and men address one another, disclose personal information, and even look at each other during conversations communicate messages about differences in status and power. Nancy Henley and Jo Freeman's piece, written in 1979, was instrumental in calling attention to subtle and powerful patterns of sexism in male-female communication. Observe the interpersonal behaviors in your environment to determine which of the patterns the authors point out still exist today.

One of the most influential purveyors of social norms is the media. The norms projected by television shape our views of what it means to be female—sometimes in overt, and sometimes in very subtle, ways. Sally Steenland discusses images of women portrayed on television shows that aired in the 1980s. Although many of these shows are no longer being broadcast, the televised images of women today are very similar to those of 10 years ago. Karin Schwartz addresses the "invisibility" of lesbians in the media, a consequence of the interaction between sexism and homophobia. The lyrics of many contemporary songs are even more explicit in their portrayal of women in demeaning ways, often reducing us to sex objects and caricatures of passivity and dependency. What messages about women are evident in the music you listen to, the television you watch, and the magazines you read?

This part closes with a fictional exploration of what might happen if society abandoned all traditional sex-role stereotypes and expectations of girls and boys. In "X: A Fabulous Child's Story," Lois Gould tells the story of Baby X, a child whose sex is unspecified as part of a social experiment. This account highlights the many seemingly insignificant ways children and adults learn sexism.

❧ 21

The Gift

MURIELLE MINARD

On my seventh birthday
A beloved uncle
Gave me a doll.
She was a beautiful creature
With blue eyes
That opened and shut,
Golden curls
And a blue velvet dress.

Once a week,
On Sunday afternoon,
My mother would sit me
In a chair
And place the doll in my arms.
I was not to disturb its perfection
In any way,
I would sit there
Transfixed
By its loveliness
And mindful
Of my mother's wishes.

After a time
She would take the doll from me,
Rewrap it carefully
In tissue,
Put it back into its own
Long, gray box
And place it
High on the closet shelf,
Safe from harm.

To this doll
Nothing must happen.

[1984]

❧ 22

Growing

HELENA MARÍA VIRAMONTES

The two walked down First Street hand in reluctant hand. The smaller of the two wore a thick, red sweater with a desperately loose button swinging like a pendulum. She carried her crayons, swinging her arm while humming *Jesus loves little boys and girls* to the speeding echo of the Saturday morning traffic and was totally oblivious to her older sister's wrath.

"My eye!" Naomi ground out the words from between her teeth. She turned to her youngest sister who seemed unconcerned and quite delighted at the prospect of another adventure. "Chaperone," she said with great disdain. "My EYE!" Lucía was chosen by Apá to be Naomi's chaperone and this infuriated her so much that she dragged her along impatiently, pulling and jerking at almost every step. She was 14, almost going on 15 and she thought the idea of having to be watched by a young snot like Lucía was insulting to her maturity. She flicked her hair over her shoulder. "Goddamnit," she said finally, making sure that the words were low enough so that neither God nor Lucía would hear them.

There seemed to be no way out of this custom either. Her arguments were always the same and always turned into pleas. This morning was no different. Amá, Naomi said, exasperated but determined not to back out of this one, Amá, América is different. Here girls don't need chaperones. Mothers trust their daughters. As usual Amá turned to the kitchen sink or the ice box, shrugged her shoulders and said: You have to ask your father. Naomi's nostrils flexed in fury as she said, But Amá, it's so embarrassing.

I'm too old for that; I am an adult. And as usual, Apá felt different and in his house, she had absolutely no other choice but to drag Lucía to a sock hop or church carnival or anywhere Apá was sure she would be found around boys. Lucía came along as a spy, a gnat, a pain in the neck.

Well, Naomi debated with herself; it wasn't Lucía's fault, really. She suddenly felt sympathy for the humming little girl who scrambled to keep up with her as they crossed the freeway overpass. She stopped and tugged Lucía's shorts up, and although her shoelaces were tied, Naomi retied them. No, it wasn't her fault after all, Naomi thought, and she patted her sister's soft light brown and almost blondish hair, it was Apá's. She slowed her pace as they continued their journey to Fierro's house. It was Apá who refused to trust her and she could not understand what she had done to make him so distrustful. *Tú eres mujer,* he thundered, and that was the end of any argument, any questions, and the matter was closed because he said those three words as if they were a condemnation from the heavens and so she couldn't be trusted. Naomi tightened her grasp with the thought, shaking her head in disbelief.

"Really," she said out loud.

"Wait up. Wait," Lucía said, rushing behind her. "Well would you hurry. Would you?" Naomi reconsidered: Lucía did have some fault in the matter after all, and she became irritated at once at Lucía's smile and the way her chaperone had of taking and holding her hand. As they passed El Gallo, Lucía began fussing, grabbing onto her older sister's waist for reassurance and hung onto it.

"Stop it. Would you stop it?" She unglued her sister's grasp and continued pulling her along. "What's wrong with you?" she asked Lucía. I'll tell you what's wrong with you, she thought, as they waited at the corner of an intersection for the light to change: You have a big mouth. That's it. If it wasn't for Lucía's willingness to provide information, she would not have been grounded for three months. Three months, 12 Saturday nights, and two church bazaars later, Naomi still hadn't forgiven her youngest sister. When they crossed the street, a homely young man with a face full of acne honked at her tight purple pedal pushers. The two were startled by the honk.

"Go to hell," she yelled at the man in the blue and white chevy. She indignantly continued her walk.

"Don't be mad, baby," he said, his car crawling across the street, then speeding off leaving tracks on the pavement, "You make me ache," he yelled, and he was gone.

"GO TO HELL, Goddamn you!" she screamed at the top of her lungs forgetting for a moment that Lucía told everything to Apá. What a big mouth her youngest sister had, for christsakes. Three months.

Naomi stewed in anger when she thought of the Salesian Carnival and how she first made eye contact with a Letterman Senior whose eyes, she remembered with a soft smile, sparkled like crystals of brown sugar. She sighed as she recalled the excitement she experienced when she first became aware that he was following them from booth to booth. Joe's hair was greased back to a perfect sculptured ducktail and his dimples were deep. When he finally handed her a stuffed rabbit he had won pitching dimes, she knew she wanted him.

As they continued walking, Lucía waved to the Fruit Man. He slipped his teeth off and again, she was bewildered.

"Would you hurry up!" Naomi ordered Lucía as she had the night at the Carnival. Joe walked beside them and he took out a whole roll of tickets, trying to convince her to leave her youngest sister on the ferris wheel. "You could watch her from behind the gym," he had told her, and his eyes smiled pleasure. "Come on," he said, "have a little fun." They waited in the ferris wheel line of people. Finally:

"Stay on the ride," she instructed Lucía, making sure her sweater was buttoned. "And when it stops again, just give the man another ticket, okay?" Lucía said okay, excited at the prospect of highs and lows and her stomach wheezing in between. After Naomi saw her go up for the first time, she waved to her, then slipped away into the darkness and joined the other hungry couples behind the gym. Occasionally, she would open her eyes to see the lights of the ferris wheel spinning in the air with dizzy speed.

When Naomi returned to the ferris wheel, her hair undone, her lips still tingling from his newly stubbled cheeks, Lucía walked off and vomited. Lucía vomited the popcorn, a hot dog, some chocolate raisins, and a candied apple, and all Naomi knew was that she was definitely in trouble.

"It was the ferris wheel," Lucía said to Apá. "The wheel going like this over and over again." She circled her arms in the air and vomited again at the thought of it.

"Where was your sister?" Apá had asked, his voice rising.

"I don't know," Lucía replied, and Naomi knew she had just committed a major offense, and that Joe would never wait until her prison sentence was completed.

"Owww," Lucía said. "You're pulling too hard."

"You're a slow poke, that's why," Naomi snarled back. They crossed the street and passed the rows of junk yards and the shells of cars which looked like abandoned skull heads. They passed Señora Nuñez's neat, wooden house and Naomi saw her peeking through the curtains of her window. They passed the "TU y YO," the one-room dirt pit of a liquor store where the men bought their beers and sat outside on the curb drinking quietly. When they reached Fourth Street, Naomi spotted the neighborhood kids playing stickball with a broomstick and a ball. Naomi recognized them right away and Tina waved to her from the pitcher's mound.

"Wanna play?" Lourdes yelled from center field. "Come on, have some fun."

"Can't." Naomi replied. "I can't." Kids, kids, she thought. My, my. It wasn't more than a few years ago that she played baseball with Eloy and the rest of them. But she was in high school now, too old now, and it was unbecoming of her. She was an adult.

"I'm tired," Lucía said. "I wanna ice cream."

"You got money?"

"No."

"Then shut up."

Lucía sat on the curb, hot and tired, and she began removing her sweater. Naomi decided to sit down next to her for a few minutes and watch the game. Anyway, she wasn't really in that much of a hurry to get to Fierro's. A few minutes wouldn't make much of a difference to someone who spent most of his time listening to the radio.

She counted them by names. They were all there. Fifteen of them and their ages varied just as much as their clothes. Pants, skirts, shorts were always too big and had to be tugged up constantly, and shirt sleeves rolled and unrolled, or socks mismatched with shoes that didn't fit. But the way they dressed presented no obstacle for scoring or yelling foul and she enjoyed the zealous abandonment with which they played. She knew that the only decision these kids possibly made was what to play next, and she wished to be younger.

Chano's team was up. The teams were oddly numbered. Chano had nine on his team because everybody wanted to be in a winning team. It was an unwritten law of stickball that anyone who wanted to play joined whatever team they preferred. Tina's team had the family faithful 6. Of course numbers determined nothing. Naomi remembered once playing with Eloy and three of her cousins against ten kids, and still winning by three points.

Chano was at bat and everybody fanned out far and wide. He was a power hitter and Tina's team prepared for him. They couldn't afford a homerun now because Piri was on second, legs apart, waiting to rush home and score a crucial point. And Piri wanted to score it at all costs. It was important for him because his father sat outside the liquor store with a couple of his uncles and a couple of malt liquors watching the game.

"Steal the base!" his father yelled, "Run, menso!" But Piri hesitated. He was too afraid to take the risk. Tina pitched and Chano swung, missed, strike one.

"Batter, batter, swing!" Naomi yelled from the curb. She stood up to watch the action better.

"I wanna ice cream," Lucía said.

"Come on, Chano!" Piri yelled, bending his knees and resting his hands on them like a true baseball player. He spat, clapped his hands. "Come on."

"Ah, shut up, sissy." This came from Lourdes, Tina's younger sister. Naomi smiled at the rivals. "Can't you see you're making the pitcher nervous?" and she pushed him hard between the shoulder blades, then returned to her position in the outfield, holding her hand over her eyes to shield them from the sun. "Strike the batter out," she screamed at the top of her lungs. "Come on, strike the menso out!" Tina delivered another pitch, but not before going through the motions of a professional preparing for the perfect pitch. Naomi knew she was a much better pitcher than Tina. Strike two. Maybe not, and

Lourdes let out such a taunting grito of joy that Piri's father called her a dog.

Chano was angry now, nervous and upset. He put his bat down, spat in his hands and rubbed them together, wiped the sides of his jeans, kicked the dirt for perfect footing.

"Get on with the game!" Naomi shouted impatiently. Chano swung a couple of times to test his swing. He swung so hard he caused Juan, Tina's brother and devoted catcher, to jump back.

"Hey baboso, watch out," he said. "You almost hit my coco." And he pointed to his forehead.

"Well, don't be so stupid," Chano replied, positioning himself once again. "Next time back off when I come to bat."

"Baboso," Juan repeated.

"Say it to my face," Chano said, breaking his stand and turning to Juan "say it again so I could break this bat over your head."

"Ah, come on, Kiki," the shortstop yelled, "I gotta go home pretty soon."

"Let up," Tina demanded.

"Shut up marrana," Piri said, turning to his father to make sure he heard. "Tinasana, cola de marrana, Tinasana, cola de marrano." Tina became so infuriated that she threw the ball directly to his stomach. Piri folded over in pain.

"No! No!" Sylvia yelled. "Don't get off the base or she'll tag you out!"

"It's a trick!" Miguel yelled from behind home plate.

"That's what you get!" This came from Lourdes. Piri did not move, and for a moment Naomi felt sorry for him, but giggled at the scene anyway.

"I heard the ice cream man." Lucía said.

"You're all right, Tina," Naomi yelled, laughing, "You're A-O-K." And with that compliment, Tina bowed, proud of her performance until everyone began shouting, "STOP WASTING TIME!" Tina was prepared. She pitched and Chano made the connection quick, hard, the ball rising high and flying over her head, Piri's, Lourdes', Naomi's and Lucía's, and landed inside the Chinese Cemetery.

"DON'T JUST STAND THERE!" Tina screamed at Lourdes, "Go get it, stupid!" After Lourdes broke out of her trance, she ran to the tall, chain-link fence which surrounded the cemetery,

jumped on the fence and crawled up like a scrambling spider, her dress tearing with a rip roar.

"We saw your calzones, we saw your calzones," Lucía sang.

"Go! Lourdes, go!" Naomi jumped up and down in excitement, feeling like a player who although benched in the sidelines, was dying to get out there and help her team win. The kids blended into one huge noise, like an untuned orchestra, screaming and shouting Get the Ball, Run in Piri, Go Lourdes, Go throw the ball Chano pick up your feet throw the ballrunrunrunrunthrow the ball. "THROW the ball to me!!" Naomi waved and waved her arms. For that moment she forgot all about 'growing up,' her period, her breasts that bounced with glee. All she wanted was an out on home base. To hell with being benched. "Throw it to me," she yelled.

In the meantime, Lourdes searched frantically for the ball, tip-toeing across the graves saying Excuse me, please excuse me, excuse me, until she found the ball peacefully buried behind a huge gray marble stone, and she yelled to no one in particular, CATCH IT, SOMEONE CATCH IT! She threw the ball up and over the fence and it landed near Lucía. Lucía was about the reach for the ball when Naomi picked it off the ground and threw it straight to Tina. Tina caught the ball, dropped it, picked it up, and was about to throw the ball to Juan at homeplate, when she realized that Juan had picked up the homeplate and ran, zig-zagging across the street while Piri and Chano ran after him. Chano was a much faster runner, but Piri insisted that he be the first to touch the base.

"I gotta touch it first," he kept repeating between pantings, "I gotta."

The kids on both teams grew wild with anger and encouragement. Seeing an opportunity, Tina ran as fast as her stocky legs could take her. Because Chano slowed down to let Piri touch the base first, Tina was able to reach him, and with one quick blow, she thundered OUT! She threw one last desperate throw to Juan so that he could tag Piri out, but she threw it so hard that it struck Piri right in the back of his head, and the blow forced him to stumble just within reach of Juan and homeplate.

"You're out!" Tina said, out of breath. "O-U-T, out."

"No fair!" Piri immediately screamed. "NO FAIR!!" He stomped his feet in rage like Rumpelstiltskin. "You marrana, you marrana."

"Don't be such a baby," Piri's father said. "Take it like a man," he said as he opened another malt liquor with a can opener. But Piri continued stomping and screaming until his shouts were buried by the honk of an oncoming car and the kids obediently opened up like the red sea to let the car pass.

Naomi felt like a victor. She had helped, once again. Delighted, she giggled, laughed, laughed harder, suppressed her laughter into chuckles, then laughed again. Lucía sat quietly, to her surprise, and her eyes were heavy with sleep. She wiped them, looked at Naomi. "Vamos" Naomi said, offering her hand. By the end of the block, she lifted Lucía and laid her head on her shoulder. As Lucía fell asleep, Naomi wondered why things were always so complicated when you became older. Funny how the old want to be young and the young want to be old. Now that she was older, her obligations became heavier both at home and at school. There were too many demands on her, and no one showed her how to fulfill them, and wasn't it crazy? She cradled Lucía gently, kissed her cheek. They were almost at Fierro's now, and reading to him was just one more thing she dreaded doing, and one more thing she had no control over: it was another one of Apá's thunderous commands.

When she was Lucía's age, she hunted for lizards and played stickball with her cousins until her body began to bleed at 12, and Eloy saw her in a different light. Under the house, he sucked her swelling nipples and became jealous. He no longer wanted to throw rocks at the cars on the freeway with her and she began to act different because everyone began treating her different and wasn't it crazy? She could no longer be herself and her father could no longer trust her because she was a woman. Fierro's gate hung on a hinge and she was almost afraid it would fall off when she opened it. She felt Lucía's warm, deep, breath on her neck and it tickled her momentarily. Enjoy, she whispered to Lucía, enjoy being a young girl, because you will never enjoy being a woman.   [1983]

 23

Something's Wrong Here and It's Not Me: Challenging the Dilemmas That Block Girls' Success

LEE ANNE BELL

"I bet all you do is study. You probably never have fun."
"I was just lucky. I'm sure yours was just as good."

These quotes are taken from a discussion with a group of third and fourth grade girls in Project REACH, a project designed to explore internal barriers to girls' achievement.[1] Two students were comparing their achievement on a project for which one of them has received an award. In the initial role play of this incident, the girl who did not win was envious and responded by teasing the other girl. The other girl, in an attempt to minimize the differences between them, downplayed her achievement. This taunt and the response to it encapsulate a core dilemma girls experience in school, the perceived disjunction between achievement and affiliation.

Something *is* wrong here. Each girl ends up feeling bad about herself. The "winner" at best feels uncomfortable and at worst undeserving. The "loser" feels inadequate, jealous and guilty for her reaction. Yet, this discomfort with competitive achievement situations is not uncommon among girls (Dweck, et al., 1978; Horner, 1972; Nicholls, 1975; Stein & Bailey, 1973.) Suggested interventions often seek to raise female aspirations and self-esteem (Kerr, 1983; Wilson, 1982) but whether intentional or not, present the problem as something *in* girls that needs to be fixed.

Girls who exhibit outstanding academic ability, intense commitment to their chosen interests, leadership and critical judgment are at risk in public schools today (Callahan, 1980; Rodenstein, Pfleger & Colangelo, 1977). By fourth grade, they begin to lose self-confidence, become extremely self-critical, and often lower their effort and aspirations in order to conform to gender stereotyped social expectations (Entwisle & Baker, 1983; Robinson-Awana, Kehle & Jenson, 1986). Underachievement among girls with high potential begins to emerge by fourth or fifth grade and becomes widespread by junior high school (Fitzpatrick, 1978; Olshen & Matthews, 1987; Callahan, 1980). As girls pull back from achieving to their fullest they drastically reduce their options for the future.

Project REACH sought to understand the core dilemmas girls experience in school from the perspective of the girls themselves. We identified a pool of high potential girls in one urban elementary school. From this pool, we randomly selected a group of 26 girls within racial/ethnic and economic categories which matched the diversity of the district as a whole (15% Hispanic, 28% Black, 57% White, 39% eligible for free or reduced lunch). Thirteen were in third and fourth grade and thirteen in fifth and sixth grade.[2] We met weekly for one hour with each group for fourteen weeks to explore achievement-related issues identified in educational and psychological literature as problematic for females. The dilemmas posed in this paper came from discussions with this diverse group of eight to eleven year old girls.

DILEMMA #1: SMART VS. SOCIAL

The segment of dialogue quoted at the beginning of this article illustrates one core dilemma girls experience, the perception that achievement and affiliation are mutually exclusive. We asked the girls to examine the science contest situation more closely and think of alternatives that would enable both girls to feel good about themselves *and* get what they want; to feel good about achieving *and* get the friendship and support they value. The girls eagerly engaged in a discussion which yielded the following options: "tear the trophy in half," "give it to the teacher," "leave it in school," "give half to the other girls," "give the trophy away, it's just a piece of metal." All of the suggested options sacrificed achievement in order to preserve the relationship.

We reiterated our challenge to the group to find a solution that would affirm both girls. They struggled and seemed stuck until Hadley, a fourth grader, offered:

When they [the judges] pick, probably a lot of people *could* have gotten first place, but they can only pick one. She wasn't there [to hear the judging process], she could have won too.

The sense of breakthrough was palpable. Immediately several new solutions emerged. All aimed at restructuring the situation to allow many people to do creative, high quality projects by working together cooperatively. The problem was externalized onto the system of judging rather than internalized as defects in individual girls. By expanding the problem to the larger context, in this case the competitive structure of the situation, the girls broke through the either/or dilemma and generated new options for confronting competitive situations. This process was used to examine additional dilemmas presented below.

DILEMMA #2: SILENCE VS. BRAGGING

Success is a loaded experience for females that incorporates a myriad of conflicting feelings, values and cultural messages about femininity. Girls receive contradictory messages about success from a competitively-oriented society that on the one hand claims females can be and do anything, but on the other promotes the belief that females should be "feminine" (e.g., passive and protected from risk) (Chodorow, 1974). The literature on achievement often claims that females avoid success because it conflicts with the feminine role (Horner, 1972), but discussions with Project REACH girls revealed just how complicated this issue is. The girls expressed pride in success but did not want to achieve it at the expense of others. Their responses support Sassen's (1980) assertion that females don't fear success itself so much as the social isolation with which they associate success.

This theme of hiding success for fear of seeming to put oneself above others was prevalent among all the girls in our sample regardless of grade. The student who won the science prize grappled with the dilemma in the following way:[3]

Jane: (after receiving a compliment on her prize): Well, I don't feel that great when you say that to me because I feel like everybody's equal and everybody should have gotten a prize no matter what they did. I think Chris should've gotten it.

Myra: OK, Jane, tell the group why you didn't say "I feel good about winning this prize."

Jane: Well, because I feel like um, like everybody's looking at me and um saying "Oh, she shouldn't have won that prize, I should have won," and everybody's gonna be mad at me because, um, I won and they didn't.

Myra: Is there any situation that you could think of where you won an honor that you were deserving of and feel good about it?

Jane: If other people won also.

While Jane feels uncomfortable about acknowledging her success publicly, she does feel good about her accomplishment.

Myra: When you said you didn't want to accept a compliment and thought other people should win, did you also really think you deserved it deep down? Just within yourself, not worrying about other people?

Jane: Yeah, I thought I deserved it but I didn't want to say it because then other people might think I was bragging.

Betsy: Jane, when you got the part of [a lead in the school play] and people said like congratulations and stuff, what did you do?

Jane: Well, I tried not to talk about it too much. I talked about it sometimes but you know, like with Tommy. You know I always eat with Melissa, Linda and Tommy. Well, um, he really wanted that part so I tried not to talk about it cuz I didn't want to make anyone feel bad.

The literature on achievement motivation indicates that girls are more likely to attribute success to external causes such as luck, timing or the help of others while boys are more likely to take credit for success by attributing it to ability or effort (Dweck, et al., 1978; Maehr & Nicholls, 1980). Our research found that girls learn to muffle acknowledgement of their successes in order to avoid the appearance of "bragging."

The term "bragging" was brought up so repeatedly by girls in both groups that we began to see it as symbolizing a core issue. This issue has at least two aspects. First, girls do not like to place themselves above others, partly because they fear ostracism but also because they value social solidarity. Second, girls may see more clearly the actual conditions that govern success in a competitive system.

Black and Hispanic children evidence similar conflicts with success (Lindstrom & Van Sant, 1986). Marginality provides insight into the unspoken norms governing social situations, norms that are often invisible to those who benefit from and thus have no reason to question the status quo

(Miller, 1986). As members of subordinate groups, perhaps girls and minority boys experience a value conflict that the dominant group does not. Part of the difficulty they have in taking credit for success may be the result of perceptive insight into a competitive system that mystifies the conditions for success. That is, although the system purports that individual effort alone is necessary, in fact, social class, race, status and opportunity have a great deal to do with actual achievement.

To the extent that girls do not become conscious of the conflicting values embedded in their reaction to success, they internalize the problem. Their ambivalence about success can lead to failure to own their achievements, an unwillingness to take risks in order to achieve, and ultimately an avoidance of success situations. When girls learn to publicly affirm their achievements and at the same time take seriously their aversion to competitive structures, they can then consider more than an either/or option to this dilemma.

DILEMMA #3: FAILURE VS. PERFECTION

Girls also receive conflicting messages about failure. The literature suggests that girls are more likely to internalize failure while boys are more likely to externalize it (Frieze, 1980). Boys' ability to more easily accept and learn from failure is attributed to their wider experience with competitive, team sports and the greater amount of critical, academic feedback they receive from teachers (Sadker & Sadker, 1982). The failure dilemma for girls is further confounded by race since many teachers give less attention and hold lower expectations for Black students (Rubovitz & Maehr, 1973); reward nonacademic, custodial behaviors in Black girls (Scott-Jones & Clark, 1986; Grant, 1984) and give Black girls fewer opportunities to respond in the classroom than they do boys and White girls (Irvine, 1986).

We asked each of our girls to tell about a time when she did poorly or failed. Many described athletic or academic situations. One fourth grader, gives this representative example:

Alexis: I was at baseball and we were losing the game. I was the last person to bat and I had to not get out. And I got out and they all said, "You're no good."

Evy: How did that make you feel?
Alexis: Like a basket case!

The result of doing poorly or failing was embarrassment and humiliation. We asked, "When you make a mistake or fail like everyone does, what do you do to make yourself feel better?" Their responses were to withdraw from the situation and to express or avoid feelings. None focused on ways to improve their performance or challenge the dynamics of the situation itself.

Anika: I lie to myself and say I don't care.
Judith: I turn my head away from everyone till everyone stops laughing. When they try to act nice, I'll be cheered up by them.
Rosa: I call my friend up and talk for two or three hours.
Celeste: I write something on notes then I hide them away in my treasure box.

We asked them to consider how they might respond differently. They struggled to move beyond the all or nothing dilemma of performing with perfection or withdrawing, but no other alternatives emerged until we suggested the possibility of asserting their feelings and ideas for change within the situation itself. We described a formula used in assertiveness training for learning to make an assertive statement:
"I feel ———— when you ———— because ————." The girls rehearsed this statement in response to the failure situations they had recounted previously:

Kamillah: I feel angry when you say that I can't act because I study a lot and I learn my lines.
Amy: I feel insulted when you say I should give up on math because it's not fair. I could just work harder and I could try to do it.

DILEMMA #4: MEDIA "BEAUTY" VS. MARGINALITY

The girls were extremely self-conscious about how they looked on the videotapes. This led us to explore the role physical appearance plays in girls' attitudes toward success. We asked them to list the media messages females receive about how we should look in order to be successful. The following list (a composite of both groups) was generated:

tall
thin
beautiful
pretty
long, wavy hair
dainty personality
matching clothes
look neat and in place, even with babies
blonde
rich
skinny
popular
fur coats
nice figure
accessories (extra stuff)
blue-eyed
long hair
good looking
famous
wear makeup
nice smile
clothes and dress for every occasion

berbie!

We then displayed a collection of pictures we had assembled on three walls of the room. These pictures included girls and women of all sizes, shapes, races, ages, and social classes doing a variety of interesting things. We asked the girls to examine the pictures and make a list of all the ways in which they contradicted the media messages. Their new list said: "You can be successful and look . . .

fat
old
poor
dressy
handicapped
wrinkly
many different ways
lots of different shades and colors
skinny
black
rich
Spanish
not rich
beautiful or not beautiful
doing different things
young
white
sloppy
in the middle

tough
boyish or feminine
old, young, and in-between

The girls discussed the differences between the two lists and then worked together on a definition of beauty that would include all the females in the pictures:

> Beauty is . . . doing your own thing
> having lots of interests
> believing in yourself
> looking how you want to . . .

Through this activity the girls challenged the "Success = Beauty" dilemma and created new options for themselves. This proved to be a powerful session having a lasting impact as evidenced by their continual references to it. At the beginning of this session one third grade Black girl whispered to me, "I really want to be white. I told my parents and that's what I want." At the end of the session we asked each girl to write an essay entitled: "Ways in which I am beautiful." This girl then wrote, "I am beautiful because I am proud of my race, I'm smart and I have pretty brown eyes." Another girl who had initially stated that she wanted to look like Vanna White, a stereotypic blonde, blue-eyed television game show hostess, later wrote, "I am beautiful because I'm good in school, I'm Puerto Rican and Dominican, and I'm good at sports."

DILEMMA #5: PASSIVE VS. AGGRESSIVE

Research indicates that boys, especially White boys, demand and receive more attention from teachers than girls (Grant, 1984; Irvine, 1986). Our girls expressed annoyance with the greater attention boys receive and with their method of getting this attention.

Judith: Sometimes, when the boys are uh with us they always misbehave and make the teachers scream and I hate it. I hate to hear people scream.

In addition to giving boys more attention, teachers often reward passivity and punish assertiveness in girls as well (Sadker & Sadker, 1982).

For our girls the alternatives to competing with boys for teacher attention were either to withdraw and be passive ("I just won't raise my hand anymore") or fight back ("I'll punch him out"). In this dilemma, clear racial differences emerged, with White and Hispanic girls more likely to withdraw and Black girls more likely to fight back. Either way, boys' behavior defines the situation and the girls are left to react.

The consequences are often negative for girls. Those girls who withdraw in response to boys' behavior lose opportunities to respond in class, to verbally explore their ideas, to actively shape the classroom, and to meet their own needs and desires. Those girls who fight back also receive more teacher disapproval and punishment for their assertiveness. This dilemma is especially damaging for Black girls whose resistance becomes a source of teacher hostility and disciplinary action.

We explored this dilemma by asking the girls to describe various situations in school that bothered them and develop alternative responses. Those girls who tended to withdraw or avoid expressing their needs were encouraged to respond actively. Those girls who tended to fight back in self-defeating or ineffective ways practiced asserting themselves more effectively, assertively rather than aggressively.

An interesting outcome of one discussion was observed in one fourth grade classroom following this session. The teacher was working with a small reading group and, as we had noticed repeatedly in our classroom observations, boys dominated the group by raising their hands more, calling out for the teacher's attention and misbehaving. One of our girls, small for her age and usually quiet, turned to a boy next to her who was pounding the table to get the teacher's attention and said, "When you do that it annoys me. Please control yourself. I want a chance to answer the question."

Group support for such endeavors is crucial. Students, especially girls, who respond assertively to authority figures run a high risk of punishment. Group support may increase the likelihood of being taken seriously.

Until adults change, however, girls are caught in the bind of conforming or being punished. Educators and counselors concerned about girls' achievement must work to challenge and change adult attitudes, behaviors and classroom structures that block girls' potential. Without such changes girls' resistance will continue to be met with individual and structural, conscious and unconscious barriers that undermine their attempts to participate fully and successfully in all areas of school.

CONCLUSION

Discussing dilemmas about achievement in a supportive environment with others can be a powerful form of consciousness raising for girls. The group context counteracts isolation by showing us that the problems we experience as "mine alone" are in fact shared by many others.

Group discussion and support also provide a way to analyze the social messages and behaviors that reinforce feelings of inadequacy and fears about achievement. Girls can help each other understand and critique the situations that create achievement-related conflicts and explore alternatives that would allow for achievement and connection to others. By defining the problem collectively, girls can then brainstorm ways to change the situation. Finally, females of all ages can organize to implement changes in the oppressive structures and situations that devalue female capacities and choices. Like consciousness raising for adults, these groups help their participants to stop asking "What's wrong with me?" and instead learn to say "What's wrong out there and what can we do collectively to change it for the better?"[4]

NOTES

1. The research for Project REACH was conducted during the 1987–88 school year. Methods included ethnographic observations in classrooms, interviews with teachers and fourteen one hour sessions with third/fourth and fifth/sixth grade groups. This article draws upon only one portion of the data collected, the transcripts of the videotapes of the sessions with the girls.
2. The pool from which the sample girls were drawn was established in cooperation with already established procedures of the gifted/talented program in the district. These procedures focused on academic ability and included IQ scores and parent and teacher nomination. Additional methods to identify athletic, artistic, creative and social ability were added to the criteria used by the district in developing the pool from which our sample was drawn.
3. Fictitious names were used for all the girls quoted in this article.
4. The Coopersmith Self-Esteem Inventory was administered as a pre/post test but these data have not yet been analyzed. Anecdotal comments from the principal, teachers and parents suggest that the program had a positive effect in raising the confidence of the girls in the sample group. We have also received letters from parents requesting that their daughters be allowed to continue with the program.

REFERENCES

Callahan. C. (1980). The gifted girl: An anomaly? *Roeper Review*. Vol. 2, No. 3, Feb–Mar.

Chodorow, N. (1974). Family structure and feminine personality. In M. Rosaldo and L. Lamphere (Eds.). *Women, Culture and Society*. Stanford, CA: Stanford University Press.

Dweck, C., Davidson, W., Nelson, S., and Enna, B. (1978). Sex differences in learned helplessness: II. The contingencies of evaluative feedback in the classroom and III. An experimental analysis. *Developmental Psychology*. Vol. 14, No. 3, 268–276.

Entwisle, D., and Baker, D. (1983). Gender and young children's expectations for performance in arithmetic. *Developmental Psychology*, 19, 200–209.

Fitzpatrick, J. (1978). Academic achievement, other-directedness and attitudes toward women's roles in bright adolescent females. *Journal of Educational Psychology*. Vol. 70, No. 4, 650–654.

Frieze, I. (1980). Beliefs about success and failure in the classroom. In J. H. McMillen (Ed.), *The social psychology of school learning*. New York: Academic Press.

Grant, L. (1984). Black females' "place" in desegregated classrooms. *Sociology of Education*. Vol. 57 (April): 98–111.

Horner, M. (1972). Toward an understanding of achievement-related conflicts in women. *Journal of Social Issues*. Vol. 28, 157–175.

Irvine, J. (1986). Teacher-student interactions: Effects of student race, sex and grade level. *Journal of Educational Psychology*. Vol. 78, No. 1, 14–21.

Kerr, B. (1983). Raising the career aspirations of gifted girls. *Vocational Guidance Quarterly*. Vol. 32, 37–43.

Lindstrom, R., and Van Sant, S. (1986). Special issues in working with gifted minority adolescents. *Journal of Counseling and Development*. Vol. 64, May, 583–586.

Maehr, M. and Nicholls, J. (1980). Culture and achievement motivation: A second look. In N. Warren (Ed.), *Studies in Cross-Cultural Psychology Vol. 2*. New York: Academic Press.

Miller, J. B. (1986). *Toward a New Psychology of Women*. Boston: Beacon Press.

Nicholls, J. (1975). Causal attributions and other achievement-related cognitions: Effects of task outcomes, attainment value and sex. *Journal of Personality and Social Psychology*. Vol. 31, 379–389.

Olshen, S., and Matthews, D. (1987). The disappearance of giftedness in girls: An intervention strategy. *Roeper Review*. Vol. 9, No. 4, 251–254.

Robinson-Awana, P., Kehle, T., and Jenson, W. (1986). But what about smart girls? Adolescent self-esteem and sex role perceptions as a function of academic achievement. *Journal of Educational Psychology*. Vol. 78, No. 3, 179–183.

Rodenstein, J., Pfleger, L., and Colangelo, N. (1977). Career development of gifted women. *The Gifted Child Quarterly*, 21, 340–347.

Rubovitz, P. and Maehr, M. (1973). Pygmalion, black and white. *Journal of Personality and Social Psychology*. Vol. 25, 210–218.

Sadker, M., and Sadker, D. (1982). *Sex Equity Handbook for Schools*. New York: Longman.

Sassen, G. (1980). Success anxiety in women: A constructivist interpretation of its sources and significance. *Harvard Educational Review*, 50, 13–25.

Scott-Jones, D., and Clark, M. (March, 1986). The school experience of black girls: The interaction of gender, race and socioeconomic status. *Phi Delta Kappan*, 520–526.

Stein, A., and Bailey, N. (1973). The socialization of achievement orientation in females. *Psychological Bulletin, 80*, 345–366.

Wilson, S. (1982). A new decade: The gifted and career choice. *Vocational Guidance Quarterly, 31*, 53–59. [1992]

🌿 24

Sexism in the Schoolroom of the '80s

MYRA SADKER and DAVID SADKER

If a boy calls out in class, he gets teacher attention, especially intellectual attention. If a girl calls out in class, she is told to raise her hand before speaking. Teachers praise boys more than girls, give boys more academic help and are more likely to accept boys' comments during classroom discussions. These are only a few examples of how teachers favor boys. Through this advantage boys increase their chances for better education and possibly higher pay and quicker promotions. Although many believe that classroom sexism disappeared in the early '70s, it hasn't.

Education is not a spectator sport. Numerous researchers, most recently John Goodlad, former dean of education at the University of California at Los Angeles and author of *A Place Called School*, have shown that when students participate in classroom discussion they hold more positive attitudes toward school, and that positive attitudes enhance learning. It is no coincidence that girls are more passive in the classroom and score lower than boys on SATs.

Most teachers claim that girls participate and are called on in class as often as boys. But a three-year study we recently completed found that this is not true; vocally, boys clearly dominate the classroom. When we showed teachers and administrators a film of a classroom discussion and asked who was talking more, the teachers overwhelmingly said the girls were. But in reality, the boys in the film were out-talking the girls at a ratio of three to one. Even educators who are active in feminist issues were unable to spot the sex bias until they counted and coded

who was talking and who was just watching. Stereotypes of garrulous and gossipy women are so strong that teachers fail to see this communications gender gap even when it is right before their eyes.

Field researchers in our study observed students in more than a hundred fourth-, sixth- and eighth-grade classes in four states and the District of Columbia. The teachers and students were male and female, black and white, from urban, suburban and rural communities. Half of the classrooms covered language arts and English—subjects in which girls traditionally have excelled; the other half covered math and science—traditionally male domains.

We found that at all grade levels, in all communities and in all subject areas, boys dominated classroom communication. They participated in more interactions than girls did and their participation became greater as the year went on.

Our research contradicted the tractional assumption that girls dominate classroom discussion in reading while boys are dominant in math. We found that whether the subject was language arts and English or math and science, boys got more than their fair share of teacher attention.

Some critics claim that if teachers talk more to male students, it is simply because boys are more assertive in grabbing their attention—a classic case of the squeaky wheel getting the educational oil. In fact, our research shows that boys are more assertive in the classroom. While girls sit patiently with their hands raised, boys literally grab teacher attention. They are eight times more likely than girls to call out answers. However, male assertiveness is not the whole answer.

Teachers behave differently, depending on whether boys or girls call out answers during discussions. When boys call out comments without raising their hands, teachers accept their answers. However, when girls call out, teachers reprimand this "inappropriate" behavior with messages such as, "In this class we don't shout out answers, we raise our hands." The message is subtle but powerful: Boys should be academically assertive and grab teacher attention; girls should act like ladies and keep quiet.

Teachers in our study revealed an interaction pattern that we called a "mind sex." After calling on a student, they tended to keep calling on students of the same sex. While this pattern applied to both sexes, it was far more pronounced among boys and allowed them more than their fair share of airtime.

It may be that when teachers call on someone, they continue thinking of that sex. Another explanation may be found in the seating patterns of elementary, secondary and even postsecondary classrooms. In approximately half of the classrooms in our study, male and female students sat in separate parts of the room. Sometimes the teacher created this segregation, but more often, the students segregated themselves. A teacher's tendency to interact with same-sex students may be a simple matter of where each sex sits. For example, a teacher calls on a female student, looks around the same area and then continues questioning the students around this girl, all of whom are female. When the teacher refocuses to a section of the classroom where boys are seated, boys receive the series of questions. And because boys are more assertive, the teacher may interact with their section longer.

Girls are often shortchanged in quality as well as in quantity of teacher attention. In 1975 psychologists Lisa Serbin and K. Daniel O'Leary, then at the State University of New York at Stony Brook, studied classroom interaction at the preschool level and found that teachers gave boys more attention, praised them more often and were at least twice as likely to have extended conversations with them. Serbin and O'Leary also found that teachers were twice as likely to give male students detailed instructions on how to do things for themselves. With female students, teachers were more likely to do it for them instead. The result was that boys learned to become independent, girls learned to become dependent.

Instructors at the other end of the educational spectrum also exhibit this same "let me do it for you" behavior toward female students. Constantina Safilios-Rothschild, a sociologist with the Population Council in New York, studied sex desegregation at the Coast Guard Academy and found that the instructors were giving detailed instructions on how to accomplish tasks to male students, but were doing the jobs and operating the equipment for the female students.

Years of experience have shown that the best way to learn something is to do it yourself; classroom chivalry is not only misplaced, it is detrimental. It is also important to give students specific and direct feedback about the quality of their work and answers. During classroom discussion, teachers in our study reacted to boys' answers with dynamic, precise and effective responses, while they often gave girls bland and diffuse reactions.

Teachers' reactions were classified in four categories: praise ("Good answer"); criticism ("That answer is wrong"); help and remediation ("Try again—but check your long division"); or acceptance without any evaluation or assistance ("OK" "Uh-huh").

Despite caricatures of school as a harsh and punitive place, fewer than 5 percent of the teachers' reactions were criticisms, even of the mildest sort. But praise didn't happen often either; it made up slightly more than 10 percent of teachers' reactions. More than 50 percent of teachers' responses fell into the "OK" category.

Teachers distributed these four reactions differently among boys than among girls. Here are some of the typical patterns.

Teacher: "What's the capital of Maryland? Joel?"
Joel: "Baltimore."
Teacher: "That's good. But Baltimore isn't the capital. The capital is also the location of the U.S. Naval Academy. Joel, do you want to try again?"
Joel: "Annapolis."
Teacher: "Excellent. Anne, what's the capital of Maine?"
Anne: "Portland."
Teacher: "Judy, do you want to try?"
Judy: "Augusta."
Teacher: "OK."

In this snapshot of a classroom discussion, Joel was told when his answer was wrong (criticism); was helped to discover the correct answer (remediation); and was praised when he offered the correct response. When Anne was wrong, the teacher, rather than staying with her, moved to Judy, who received only simple acceptance for her correct answer. Joel received the more specific teacher reaction and benefited from a longer, more precise and intense educational interaction.

Too often, girls remain in the dark about the quality of their answers. Teachers rarely tell them if their answers are excellent, need to be improved

Sexism and racism are so embedded in curriculum material that it requires a conscious effort to create a classroom climate that is truly inclusive. The questions below have been helpful to instructors in examining their texts and lectures. How have teachers' choices of materials and patterns of classroom interaction affected you?

Checklist for Inclusive Teaching

MERCILEE JENKINS

TEXTS, LECTURES, AND COURSE CONTENT

1. Are you and your texts' language sex-neutral, using words with relation to both sexes whenever this is the author's intent? If your texts use the masculine generic, do you point this out in the classroom?
2. Is content addressed equitably to men, to women, people of color?
3. Do you and your texts portray equitably the activities, achievements, concerns, and experiences of women and people of color? If your texts do not, do you provide supplemental materials? Do you bring omissions to the attention of your students?
4. Do your and your texts present the careers, roles, interests, and abilities of women and people of color without stereotyping? If there are stereotypes in your texts, do you point this out?
5. Do you and your texts' examples and illustrations (both verbal and graphic) represent an equitable balance in terms of gender and race? If your texts do not, do you point this out?
6. Do your texts and lectures reflect values that are free of sex and race bias, and if not, do you discuss your/their biases and values with your students?
7. Do your texts incorporate new research and theory generated by feminist and ethnic scholarship? If not, do you point out areas in which feminist and ethnic studies are modifying perceived ideas? Do you provide additional bibliographic references for

or are just plain wrong. Unfortunately, acceptance, the imprecise response packing the least educational punch, gets the most equitable sex distribution in classrooms. Active students receiving precise feedback are more likely to achieve academically. And they are more likely to be boys. Consider the following:

• Although girls start school ahead of boys in reading and basic computation, by the time they graduate from high school, boys have higher SAT scores in both areas.

• By high school, some girls become less committed to careers, although their grades and achievement-test scores may be as good as boys'. Many girls' interests turn to marriage or stereotypically

female jobs. Part of the reason may be that some women feel that men disapprove of their using their intelligence.

• Girls are less likely to take math and science courses and to participate in special or gifted programs in these subjects, even if they have a talent for them. They are also more likely to believe that they are incapable of pursuing math and science in college and to avoid the subjects.

• Girls are more likely to attribute failure to internal factors, such as ability, rather than to external factors, such as luck.

The sexist communication game is played at work, as well as at school. As reported in numerous studies it goes like this:

students who want to pursue these issues? When you order books for the library, do they reflect these issues?

8. Do your exams and assignments for papers, projects, etc. allow and encourage students to explore the nature, roles, status, contributions and experience of women and people of color?

9. Do your texts and materials make it clear that not everyone is heterosexual?

CLASSROOM INTERACTIONS

1. Are you conscious of sex- or race-related expectations you may hold about student performance?

2. How do you react to uses of language (accent, dialect, etc.) that depart from standard English or that are different from your own? Do you discount the speaker's intelligence and information?

3. What is the number of males versus females or of various cultural and racial groups called on to answer questions? Which students do you call by name? Why?

4. Which of these categories of students participate in class more frequently through answering questions or making comments? Is the number disproportional enough that you should encourage some students to participate more frequently?

5. Do interruptions occur when an individual is talking? If so, who does the interrupting? If one group of students is dominating classroom interaction, what do you do about it?

6. Is your verbal response to students positive? Aversive? Encouraging? Is it the same for all students? If not, what is the reason? (Valid reasons occur from time to time for reacting or responding to a particular student in a highly specific manner.)

7. Do you tend to face or address one section of the classroom more than others? Do you establish eye contact with certain students more than others? What are the gestures, postures, facial expressions, etc. used and are they different for men, women, people of color?

• Men speak more often and frequently interrupt women.

• Listeners recall more from male speakers than from female speakers, even when both use a similar speaking style and cover identical content.

• Women participate less actively in conversation. They do more smiling and gazing; they are more often the passive bystanders in professional and social conversations among peers.

• Women often transform declarative statements into tentative comments. This is accomplished by using qualifiers ("kind of" or "I guess") and by adding tag questions ("This is a good movie, isn't it?"). These tentative patterns weaken impact and signal a lack of power and influence.

Sexist treatment in the classroom encourages formation of patterns such as these, which give men more dominance and power than women in the working world. But there is a light at the end of the educational tunnel. Classroom biases are not etched in stone, and training can eliminate these patterns. Sixty teachers in our study received four days of training to establish equity in classroom interactions. These trained teachers succeeded in eliminating classroom bias. Although our training focused on equality, it improved overall teaching effectiveness as well. Classes taught by these trained teachers had a higher level of intellectual discussion and contained more effective and precise teacher responses for all students.

There is an urgent need to remove sexism from the classroom and give women the same educational encouragement and support that men receive. When women are treated equally in the classroom, they will be more likely to achieve equality in the workplace.   [1985]

🌿 25

The Sexual Politics of Interpersonal Behavior

NANCY HENLEY and JO FREEMAN

Social interaction is the battlefield where the daily war between the sexes is fought. It is here that women are constantly reminded where their "place" is and that they are put back in their place, should they venture out. Thus, social interaction serves as the most common means of social control employed against women. By being continually reminded of their inferior status in their interactions with others, and continually compelled to acknowledge that status in their own patterns of behavior, women learn to internalize society's definition of them as inferior so thoroughly that they are often unaware of what their status is. Inferiority becomes habitual, and the inferior place assumes the familiarity—and even desirability—of home.

Different sorts of cues in social interaction aid this enforcement of one's social definition, particularly the verbal message, the nonverbal message transmitted within a social relationship, and the nonverbal message transmitted by the environment. Our educational system emphasizes the verbal messages and teaches us next to nothing about how we interpret and react to the nonverbal ones. Just how important nonverbal messages are, however, is shown by the finding of Argyle et al.[1] that nonverbal cues have over four times the impact of verbal ones when both verbal and nonverbal cues are used. Even more important for women, Argyle found that female subjects were more responsive to nonverbal cues (compared with verbal ones) than male subjects. If women are to understand how the subtle forces of social control work in their lives, they must

learn as much as possible about how nonverbal cues affect people, and particularly about how they perpetuate the power and superior status enjoyed by men.

Even if a woman encounters no one else directly in her day, visual status reminders are a ubiquitous part of her environment. As she moves through the day, she absorbs many variations of the same status theme, whether or not she is aware of it: male bosses dictate while female secretaries bend over their steno pads; male doctors operate while female nurses assist; restaurants are populated with waitresses serving men; magazine and billboard ads remind the woman that home maintenance and child care are her foremost responsibilities and that being a sex object for male voyeurs is her greatest asset. If she is married, her mail reminds her that she is a mere "Mrs." appended to her husband's name. When she is introduced to others or fills out a form, the first thing she must do is divulge her marital status acknowledging the social rule that the most important information anyone can know about her is her legal relationship to a man.

These environmental cues set the stage on which the power relationships of the sexes are acted out, and the assigned status of each sex is reinforced. Though studies have been made of the several means by which status inequalities are communicated in interpersonal behavior, they do not usually deal with power relationships between men and women. Goffman has pointed to many characteristics associated with status:

> Between status equals we may expect to find interaction guided by symmetrical familiarity. Between superordinate and subordinate we may expect to find asymmetrical relations, the superordinate having the right to exercise certain familiarities which the subordinate is not allowed to reciprocate. Thus, in the research hospital, doctors tended to call nurses by their first names, while nurses responded with "polite" or "formal" address. Similarly, in American business organizations the boss may thoughtfully ask the elevator man how his children are, but this entrance into another's life may be blocked to the elevator man, who can appreciate the concern but not return it. Perhaps the clearest form of this is found in the psychiatrist-patient relation, where the psychiatrist has a right to touch on aspects of the patient's life that the patient might not

even allow himself to touch upon, while of course this privilege is not reciprocated.

Rules of demeanor, like rules of deference, can be symmetrical or asymmetrical. Between social equals, symmetrical rules of demeanor seem often to be prescribed. Between unequals many variations can be found. For example, at staff meetings on the psychiatric units of the hospital, medical doctors had the privilege of swearing, changing the topic of conversation, and sitting in undignified positions; attendants, on the other hand, had the right to attend staff meetings and to ask questions during them . . . but were implicitly expected to conduct themselves with greater circumspection than was required of doctors. . . . Similarly, doctors had the right to saunter into the nurses' station, lounge on the station's dispensing counter, and engage in joking with the nurses; other ranks participated in this informal interaction with doctors, but only after doctors had initiated it.[2]

A status variable widely studied by Brown and others[3] is the use of terms of address. In languages that have both familiar and polite forms of the second person singular ("you"), asymmetrical use of the two forms invariably indicates a status difference, and it always follows the same pattern. The person using the familiar form is always the superior to the person using the polite form. In English, the only major European language not to have dual forms of address, status differences are similarly indicated by the right of first-naming; the status superior can first-name the inferior in situations where the inferior must use the superior's title and last name. An inferior who breaks this rule by inappropriately using a superior's first name is considered insolent.[4]

According to Brown, the pattern evident in the use of forms of address applies to a very wide range of interpersonal behavior and invariably has two other components: (1) whatever form is used by a superior in situations of status inequality can be used reciprocally by intimates, and whatever form is used by an inferior is the socially prescribed usage for nonintimates; (2) initiation or increase of intimacy is the right of the superior. To use the example of naming again to illustrate the first component, friends use first names with each other, while strangers use titles and last names (though "instant" intimacy is considered proper in some cultures, such as our own, among status equals in informal settings). As an example of the second component, status superiors, such as professors, specifically tell status inferiors, such as students, when they can use the first name, and often rebuff them if they assume such a right unilaterally.

Although Brown did not apply these patterns to status differences between the sexes, their relevance is readily seen. The social rules say that all moves to greater intimacy are a male prerogative: It is boys who are supposed to call girls for dates, men who are supposed to propose marriage to women, and males who are supposed to initiate sexual activity with females. Females who make "advances" are considered improper, forward, aggressive, brassy, or otherwise "unladylike." By initiating intimacy they have stepped out of their place and usurped a status prerogative. The value of such a prerogative is that it is a form of power. Between the sexes, as in other human interaction, the one who has the right to initiate greater intimacy has more control over the relationship. Superior status brings with it not only greater prestige and greater privileges, but greater power.

These advantages are exemplified in many of the various means of communicating status. Like the doctors in Goffman's research hospital, men are allowed such privileges as swearing and sitting in undignified positions, but women are denied them. Though the male privilege of swearing is curtailed in mixed company, the body movement permitted to women is circumscribed even in all-women groups. It is considered unladylike for a woman to use her body too forcefully, to sprawl, to stand with her legs widely spread, to sit with her feet up, or to cross the ankle of one leg over the knee of the other. Many of these positions are ones of strength or dominance. The more "feminine" a woman's clothes are, the more circumscribed the use of her body. Depending on her clothes, she may be expected to sit with her knees together, not to sit crosslegged, or not even to bend over. Though these taboos seem to have lessened in recent years, how much so is unknown, and there are recurring social pressures for a "return to femininity," while etiquette arbiters assert that women must retain feminine posture no matter what their clothing.

Prior to the 1920s women's clothes were designed to be confining and cumbersome. The dress reform movement, which disposed of corsets and long skirts, was considered by many to have more significance for female emancipation than women's suffrage.[5] Today women's clothes are designed to be revealing, but women are expected to restrict their body movements to avoid revealing too much. Furthermore, because women's clothes are contrived to reveal women's physical features, rather than being loose like men's, women must resort to purses instead of pockets to carry their belongings. These "conveniences" have become, in a time of blurred sex distinctions, one of the surest signs of sex, and thus have developed the character of stigma, a sign of woman's shame, as when they are used by comics to ridicule both women and transvestites.

Women in our society are expected to reveal not only more of their bodies than men but also more of themselves. Female socialization encourages greater expression of emotion than does that of the male. Whereas men are expected to be stolid and impassive, and not to disclose their feelings beyond certain limits, women are expected to express their *selves*. Such self-expression can disclose a lot of oneself, and, as Jourard and Lasakow[6] found, females are more self-disclosing to others than males are. This puts them at an immediate disadvantage.

The inverse relationship between disclosure and power has been reported by other studies in addition to Goffman's earlier cited investigation into a research hospital. Slobin, Miller, and Porter[7] stated that individuals in a business organization are "more self-disclosing to their immediate superior than to their immediate subordinates." Self-disclosure is a means of enhancing another's power. When one has greater access to information about another person, one has a resource the other person does not have. Thus not only does power give status, but status gives power. And those possessing neither must contribute to the power and status of others continuously.

Another factor adding to women's vulnerability is that they are socialized to *care* more than men—especially about personal relationships. This puts them at a disadvantage, as Ross articulated in what he called the "Law of Personal Exploitation": "In any sentimental relation the one who cares less can exploit the one who cares more."[8] The same idea was put more broadly by Waller and Hill as the "Principle of Least Interest": "That person is able to dictate the conditions of association whose interest in the continuation of the affair is least."[9] In other words, women's caring, like their openness, gives them less power in a relationship.

One way of indicating acceptance of one's place and deference to those of superior status is by following the rules of "personal space." Sommer has observed that dominant animals and human beings have a larger envelope of inviolability surrounding them—i.e., are approached less closely—than those of a lower status.[10] Willis made a study of the initial speaking distance set by an approaching person as a function of the speaker's relationship.[11] His finding that women were approached more closely than men—i.e., their personal space was smaller or more likely to be breached—is consistent with their lower status.

Touching is one of the closer invasions of one's personal space, and in our low-contact culture it implies privileged access to another person. People who accidently touch other people generally take great pains to apologize; people forced into close proximity, as in a crowded elevator, often go to extreme lengths to avoid touching. Even the figurative meanings of the word convey a notion of access to privileged areas—e.g., to one's emotions (one is "touched" by a sad story), or to one's purse (one is "touched" for ten dollars). In addition, the act of touching can be a subtle physical threat.

Remembering the patterns that Brown found in terms of address, consider the interactions between pairs of persons of different status, and picture who would be more likely to touch the other (put an arm around the shoulder or a hand on the back, tap the chest, hold the arm, or the like: teacher and student; master and servant; policeman and accused; doctor and patient; minister and parishioner; adviser and advisee; foreman and worker; businessman and secretary. As with first-naming, it is considered presumptuous for a person of low status to initiate touch with a person of higher status.

There has been little investigation of touching by social scientists, but the few studies made so far indicate that females are touched more than males are. Goldberg and Lewis[12] and Lewis[13] report that from six months on, girl babies are touched more than boy babies. The data reported in Jourard[14] and Jourard and Rubin[15] show that sons and fathers tend to refrain from touching each other and that "when it comes to physical contact within the family, it is the daughters who are the favored ones."[16] An examination of the number of different regions in which subjects were touched showed that mothers and fathers touch their daughters in more regions that they do their sons; that daughters touch their fathers in more regions than sons do; that males touch their opposite-sex friends in more regions than females do. Overall, women's mean total "being-touched" score was higher than men's.

Jourard and Rubin take the view that "touching is equated with sexual interest, either consciously, or at a less-conscious level,"[17] but it would seem that there is a sex difference in the interpretation of touch. Lewis reflects this when he writes, "In general, for men in our culture, proximity (touching) is restricted to the opposite sex and its function is primarily sexual in nature."[18] Waitresses, secretaries, and women students are quite used to being touched by their male superordinates, but they are expected not the "misinterpret" such gestures. However, women who touch men are often interpreted as conveying sexual intent, as they have often found out when their intentions were quite otherwise. Such different interpretations are consistent with the status patterns found earlier. If touching indicates either power or intimacy, and women are deemed by men to be status inferiors, touching by women will be perceived as a gesture of intimacy, since it would be inconceivable for them to be exercising power.

A study by Henley puts forward this hypothesis.[19] Observations of incidents of touch in public urban places were made by a white male research assistant, naive to the uses of his data. Age, sex, and approximate socioeconomic status were recorded, and the results indicated that higher-status persons do touch lower-status persons significantly more. In particular, men touched women more, even when all other variables were held constant. When the settings of the observations were differentially examined, the pattern showed up primarily in the outdoor setting, with indoor interaction being more evenly spread over sex combinations. Henley has also reported observations of greater touching by higher status persons (including males) in the popular culture media;

and a questionnaire study in which both females and males indicated greater expectancies of being touched by higher status persons, and of touching lower status and female ones, than vice versa.[20]

The other nonverbal cues by which status is indicated have likewise not been adequately researched—for humans. But O'Connor argues that many of the gestures of dominance and submission that have been noted in the primates are equally present in humans.[21] They are used to maintain and reinforce the status hierarchy by reassuring those of higher status that those of lower status accept their place in the human pecking order.

The most studied nonverbal communication among humans is probably eye contact, and here too one finds a sex difference. It has repeatedly been found that women look more at another in a dyad than men do.[22] Exline, Gray, and Schuette suggest that "willingness to engage in mutual visual interaction is more characteristic of those who are oriented towards inclusive and affectionate interpersonal relations,"[23] but Rubin concludes that while "gazing may serve as a vehicle of emotional expression for women, [it] in addition may allow women to obtain cues from their male partners concerning the appropriateness of their behavior."[24] This interpretation is supported by Efran and Broughton's data showing that even male subjects "maintain more eye contact with individuals toward whom they have developed higher expectancies for social approval."[25]

Another possible reason why women gaze more at men is that men talk more,[26] and there is a tendency for the listener to look more at the speaker than vice versa.[27]

It is especially illuminating to look at the power relationships established and maintained by the manipulation of eye contact. The mutual glance can be seen as a sign of union, but when intensified into a stare it may become a way of doing battle.[28] Research reported by Ellsworth, Carlsmith, and Henson supports the notion that the stare can be interpreted as an aggressive gesture. These authors write, "Staring at humans can elicit the same sort of responses that are common in primates; that is, staring can act like a primate threat display."[29]

Though women engage in mutual visual interaction in its intimate form to a high degree, they may back down when looking becomes a gesture of dominance. O'Connor[30] points out, "The direct stare or glare is a common human gesture of dominance. Women use the gesture as well as men, but often in modified form. While looking directly at a man, a woman usually has her head slightly tilted, implying the beginning of a presenting gesture or enough submission to render the stare ambivalent if not actually submissive."*

The idea that the averted glance is a gesture of submission is supported by the research of Hutt and Ounsted into the characteristic gaze aversion of autistic children. They remark that "these children were never attacked [by peers] despite the fact that to a naive observer they appeared to be easy targets; this indicated that their gaze aversion had some signalling function similar to 'facing away' in the kittiwake or 'head-flagging' in the herring gull—behavior patterns which Tinbergen has termed 'appeasement postures.' In other words, gaze aversion inhibited any aggressive or threat behavior on the part of other conspecifics."[31]

Gestures of dominance and submission can be verbal as well as nonverbal. In fact, the sheer use of verbalization is a form of dominance because it can quite literally render someone speechless by preventing one from "getting a word in edgewise." As noted earlier, contrary to popular myth, men do talk more than women, both in single-sex and in mixed-sex groups. Within a group a major means of asserting dominance is to interrupt. Those who want to dominate others interrupt more; those speaking will not permit themselves to be interrupted by their inferiors, but they will give way to those they consider their superiors. Zimmerman and West found in a sample of 11 natural conversations between women and men that 46 of the 48 interruptions were by males.[32]

Other characteristics of persons in inferior status positions are the tendencies to hesitate and apologize, often offered as submissive gestures in the face of threats or potential threats. If staring directly, pointing, and touching can be subtle nonverbal threats, the corresponding gestures of submission seem to be lowering the eyes from another's gaze, falling silent (or not speaking at all) when interrupted or pointed at, and cuddling to the touch. Many of these nonverbal gestures of submission are familiar. They are the traits our society assigns as desirable secondary characteristics of the female role. Girls who have properly learned to be "feminine" have learned to lower their eyes, remain silent, back down, and cuddle at the appropriate times. There is even a word for this syndrome that is applied only to females: coy.

In verbal communication one finds a similar pattern of differences between the sexes. As mentioned earlier, men have the privilege of swearing, and hence access to a vocabulary not customarily available to women. On the surface this seems like an innocuous limitation, until one realizes the psychological function of swearing: it is one of the most harmless and effective ways of expressing anger. The alternatives are to express one's feelings with physical violence or to suppress them and by so doing turn one's anger in on oneself. The former is prohibited to both sexes (to different degrees) but the latter is decisively encouraged in women. The result is that women are "intropunitive"; they punish themselves for their own anger rather than somehow dissipating it. Since anger turned inward is commonly viewed as the basis for depression, we should not be surprised that depression is considerably more common in women than in men, and in fact is the most prevalent form of "mental illness" among women. Obviously, the causes of female depression are complex.[33]

Swearing is only the most obvious sex difference in language. Key has noted that sex differences are to be found in phonological, semantic, and grammatical aspects of language as well as in word use.[34] In one example, Austin has commented that "in our culture little boys tend to be nasal . . . and little girls, oral," but that in the "final stages" of courtship the voices of both men and women are low and nasal.[35] The pattern cited by Brown,[36] in which the form appropriately used by status superiors is used between status equals in intimate situations, is again visible: in the intimate situation the female adopts the vocal style of the male.

---

*"Presenting" is the term for the submissive gesture seen in primates, of presenting the rump to a dominant animal; O'Connor also points out that it is a human female submissive gesture as well, seen, for example, in the can-can.

In situations where intimacy is not a possible interpretation, it is not power but abnormality that is the usual interpretation. Female voices are expected to be soft and quiet—even when men are using loud voices. Yet it is only the "lady" whose speech is refined. Women who do not fit this stereotype are often called loud—a word commonly applied derogatorily to other minority groups or out-groups.[37] One of the most popular derogatory terms for women is "shrill," which, after all, simply means loud (out of place) and high-pitched (female).

In language, as in touch and most other aspects of interpersonal behavior, status differences between the sexes mean that the same traits are differently interpreted when displayed by each sex. A man's behavior toward a woman might be interpreted as an expression of either power or intimacy, depending on the situation. When the same behavior is engaged in by a woman and directed toward a man, it is interpreted only as a gesture of intimacy—and intimacy between the sexes is always seen as sexual in nature. Because our society's values say that women should not have power over men, women's nonverbal communication is rarely interpreted as an expression of power. If the situation precludes a sexual interpretation, women's assumption of the male prerogative is dismissed as deviant (castrating, domineering, unfeminine, or the like).*

Of course, if women do not wish to be classified either as deviant or as perpetually sexy, then they must persist in playing the proper role by following the interpersonal behavior pattern prescribed for them. Followed repeatedly, these patterns function as a means of control. What is merely habitual is often seen as desirable. The more men and women interact in the way they have been trained to from birth without considering the meaning of what they do, the more they become dulled to the significance of their actions. Just as outsiders observing a new

society are more aware of the status differences of that society than its members are, so those who play the sexual politics of interpersonal behavior are usually not conscious of what they do. Instead they continue to wonder that feminists make such a mountain out of such a "trivial" molehill.

NOTES

1. M. Argyle, V. Salter, H. Nicholson, M. Williams, and P. Burgess, "The Communication of Inferior and Superior Attitudes by Verbal and Non-verbal Signals," *British Journal of Social and Clinical Psychology,* 9 (1970), 222–31.
2. Goffman, "The Nature of Deference and Demeanor," *American Anthropologist,* 58 (1956), 473–502.
3. R. Brown, *Social Psychology* (Glencoe, Ill.: Free Press, 1965). See also R. Brown and M. Ford, "Address in American English," *Journal of Abnormal and Social Psychology,* 62 (1961), 375–85; R. Brown and A. Gilman, "The Pronouns of Power and Solidarity," in T. A. Sebeak, ed., *Style in Language* (Cambridge, Mass.: M.I.T. Press, 1960).
4. Brown, *Social Psychology,* pp. 92–97.
5. W. L. O'Neill, *Everyone Was Brave: The Rise and Fall of Feminism* (Chicago: Quadrangle, 1969), p. 270.
6. S. M. Jourard and P. Lasakow, "Some Factors in Self-Disclosure," *Journal of Abnormal and Social Psychology,* 56 (1958), 91–98.
7. D. I. Slobin, S. H. Miller, and L. W. Porter, "Forms of Address and Social Relations in a Business Organization," *Journal of Personality and Social Psychology,* 8 (1968), 289–93.
8. E. A. Ross, *Principles of Sociology* (New York: Century, 1921), p. 136.
9. W. W. Waller and R. Hill, *The Family: A Dynamic Interpretation* (New York: Dryden, 1951), p. 191.
10. R. Sommer, *Personal Space* (Englewood Cliffs, N.J.: Prentice-Hall, 1969), Chap. 2.
11. F. N. Willis, Jr., "Initial Speaking Distance as a Function of the Speakers' Relationship," *Psychonomic Science,* 5 (1966), 221–22.
12. S. Goldberg and M. Lewis, "Play Behavior in the Year-old Infant: Early Sex Differences," *Child Development,* 40 (1969), 21–31.
13. M. Lewis, "Parents and Children: Sex-role Development," *School Review,* 80 (1972), 229–40.
14. S. M. Jourard, "An Exploratory Study of Body Accessibility," *British Journal of Social and Clinical Psychology,* 5 (1966), 221–31.
15. S. M. Jourard and J. E. Rubin, "Self-Disclosure and Touching: A Study of Two Modes of Interpersonal Encounter and Their Interrelation," *Journal of Humanistic Psychology,* 8 (1968), 39–48.
16. Jourard, "Exploratory Study," p. 224.
17. Jourard and Rubin, "Self-Disclosure and Touching," p. 47.
18. Lewis, "Parents and Children," p. 237.
19. N. Henley, "The Politics of Touch," American Psychological Association, 1970. In P. Brown ed., *Radical Psychology* (New York: Harper & Row, 1973).

---

*We are not suggesting that just because certain gestures associated with males are responded to as powerful, women should automically adopt them. Rather than accepting male values without question, individual women will want to consider what they wish to express and how, and will determine whether to adopt particular gestures or to insist that their own be responded to appropriately meanwhile.

20. N. Henley, *Body Politics: Sex, Power and Nonverbal Communication* (Englewood Cliffs, N.J.: Prentice-Hall, 1977).

21. L. O'Connor, "Male Dominance: The Nitty Gritty of Oppression," *It Ain't Me Babe*, 1 (1970), 9.

22. R. Exline, "Explorations in the Process of Person Perception: Visual Interaction in Relation to Competition, Sex, and Need for Affiliation," *Journal of Personality*, 31 (1963), 1–20; R. Exline, D. Gray, and D. Schutte, "Visual Behavior in a Dyad as Affected by Interview Control and Sex of Respondent," *Journal of Personality and Social Psychology*, 1, (1965), 201–09; and Z. Rubin, "Measurement of Romantic Love," *Journal of Personality and Social Psychology*, 16 (1970), 265–73.

23. Exline, Gray, and Schuette, "Visual Behavior in a Dyad," p. 207.

24. Rubin, "Measurement of Romantic Love," p. 272.

25. J. S. Efran and A. Broughton, "Effect of Expectancies for Social Approval on Visual Behavior," *Journal of Personality and Social Psychology*, 4 (1966), p. 103.

26. M. Argyle, M. Lalljee, and M. Cook, "The Effects of Visibility on Interaction in a Dyad," *Human Relations*, 21 (1968), 3–17.

27. Exline, Gray, and Schuette, "Visual Behavior in a Dyad."

28. Exline, "Explorations in the Process of Person Perception."

29. P. C. Ellsworth, J. M. Carlsmith, and A. Henson. "The Stare as a Stimulus to Flight in Human Subjects: A Series of Field Experiments," *Journal of Personality and Social Psychology*, 21 (1972), p. 310.

30. O'Connor, "Male Dominance."

31. C. Hutt and C. Ounsted. "The Biological Significance of Gaze Aversion with Particular Reference to the Syndrome of Infantile Autism," *Behavioral Science*, 11 (1966), p. 154.

32. D. Zimmerman and C. West, "Sex Roles, Interruptions and Silences in Conversation," in B. Thorne and N. Henley, *Language and Sex* (Rowley, Mass.: Newbury House, 1975).

33. For more on this see P. B. Bart, "Depression in Middle-aged Women," in V. Gornick and B. K. Moran, *Woman in Sexist Society* (New York: Basic Books, 1971); and P. Chesler, *Women and Madness* (New York: Doubleday, 1972).

34. See also M. R. Key, *Male/Female Language* (Metuchen, N.J.: Scarecrow, 1975); R. Lakoff, *Language and Woman's Place* (New York: Harper & Row, 1975); C. Miller and K. Swift, *Words and Women* (New York: Doubleday, 1976); B. Thorne and N. Henley, *Language and Sex: Difference and Dominance* (Rowley, Mass.: Newbury House, 1975).

35. W. M. Austin, "Some Social Aspects of Paralanguage." *Canadian Journal of Linguistics*, 11 (1965), pp. 34, 37.

36. Brown, *Social Psychology*.

37. Austin, "Some Social Aspects of Paralanguage," p. 38.
[1979]

26

Ten Years in Prime Time: An Analysis of the Image of Women on Entertainment Television from 1979 to 1988

SALLY STEENLAND

PROFILE OF WOMEN ON TV DURING THE DECADE

Listed below are specific profiles of women on TV from 1979 to 1987, compared to profiles of real-life women. In most cases, data from the 1988 new fall TV shows are not included, since the statistics are not comparable. The data from 1988 represent a handful of new programs, while the data from 1979 to 1987 represent the top 25 Nielsen-rated shows of each year.

• **The percentage of working women on TV increased dramatically, as did the percentage of working mothers.**

In 1979, about 60% of adult female characters were in the TV work force. Almost three-quarters of them were single; a bit more than 10% were single mothers and fewer than 5% were married with children.

In 1987, over 75% of TV's female characters were employed. In a sharp decline from earlier years, only one-quarter of them were single. About 15% were single mothers, a slight increase from previous years; while almost 20% were married with children, a big jump.

The role of the homemaker, already declining on TV, grew even more slight, from 13% of female characters in 1979 to only 5% in 1987.

In reality, 56% of all women are in the labor force. Twenty-five percent of working women have never been married; 10% are single mothers; and 30% are married with children. Twenty-five percent of all women are homemakers.

• **The percentage of black women on TV almost tripled, although other minority races showed no increases.**

In 1979, black female characters accounted for only 8% of all women on TV; 92% were white.

In 1987, however, 22% of all women on TV were black, 75% were white and 2% were Hispanic; none were Asian or other women of color.

In reality, 77% of women in the U.S. are white, 12.5% are black, 7.5% are Hispanic, and 3% are Asian and other women of color.

- **Working class women on TV declined in number, while affluent females expanded greatly, shrinking the middle class.**

In 1979, over 10% of all female characters on TV were working class. Almost 70% were middle class, while 20% were affluent. In 1984, those proportions changed, so that only 2% of female characters were working class and less than half (42%) were middle class. That year, 56% of all women on TV were affluent, many of them millionaires.

In 1987, those percentages changed again. Working class female characters increased slightly to 5%, while the middle class grew to 66%. The percentage of affluent women on TV shrank to 29%.

In reality, two-thirds of women have yearly incomes of $15,000 or less, and only 1% have incomes above $50,000. Twenty-one percent of families earn less than $15,000 a year, 56% earn between $15,000 and $50,000, and 22% earn more than $50,000.

- **Women on TV grew older.**

In 1979, almost two-thirds of women on TV were between the ages of 20 and 40, while only 14% were over 40.

Those numbers have shifted significantly during the 80s. In 1987, fewer than half of female characters were between 20 and 40, while 22% were older than 40.

In reality, one-third of all females are between 20 and 40 years old, and 39% are over 40.

- **The percentage of TV women working in clerical and service jobs declined, while the percentage working in professional careers increased.**

In 1979, over 40% of working women on TV were employed in clerical or service jobs. The same percentage worked in professional jobs.

However, by 1987, only 23% worked in clerical or service jobs, while over half had professional careers, many working as corporate executives or entrepreneurs.

In reality, the figures are almost exactly reversed. Forty-seven percent of women are in clerical and service occupations, while only 24% work in professional or managerial jobs.

THE CHANGING PICTURE OF WORK AND FAMILY

Ten years ago, almost three-quarters of all working women on TV were young and single. Working mothers were hard to find, and harder still to locate were older women on the screen.

By the late 80s, the TV picture had shifted, so that in 1987 single working women on TV were outnumbered almost two-to-one by working mothers, and older women in the work force increased their numbers as well.

During those intervening years, TV programs began to reflect the changes of real-life Americans: record numbers of mothers with jobs, working parents balancing job and family responsibilities, and the splitting of homes by divorce.

At the same time, TV programs distorted those changes, so that the images reflected back to viewers were, for the most part, unrealistic and ideal. Viewers watched programs in which single women were millionaires, practically all women had rewarding professional careers, and working parents juggled their family obligations with ease.

Single working mothers like Alice, Kate and Allie, Carla on "Cheers," and Ann Romano on "One Day at a Time," who worked to support their families, were matched in the 80s by the single mothers on prime time soaps, such as Pam on "Dallas," Fallon on "Dynasty," and others who had no financial worries at all. Most of these single mothers worked either as entrepreneurs or in high-level executive positions, for which they had little experience; but they were extremely successful nonetheless.

Married women with children began to go to work on TV during the 80s. In 1979, hardly any married mothers in top-rated programs had jobs. Most were homemakers, like Caroline on "Little House on the Prairie" and Marion on "Happy Days." But with "The Cosby Show," "Family Ties," "Growing Pains," and "Alf," nuclear families with two working parents became the norm. By 1987, the only homemakers left on the screen on top-rated shows were Mary on "227" and Norma on "The Wonder Years," a show set in 1968. However, because of TV's upscaling, most TV working mothers had jobs as lawyers, architects and reporters, unlike their real-life counterparts, who were more likely to work as secretaries, factory workers and sales clerks.

AN ABUNDANCE OF AFFLUENCE

Although TV as a medium has always been reluctant to air stories about characters who are poor or economically struggling, the 1980s was a decade in which not only working class characters became practically extinct, but also middle class characters were overshadowed by those who were wealthy. Near the end of the decade, that trend appeared to be reversing, as the middle class made a solid comeback and working class characters began to reappear on the screen, although their numbers were smaller than in 1979.

The female characters on "Dallas," "Dynasty," "Falcon Crest," and "Knots Landing" accounted for most of this wealth, as did Jennifer, a journalist/detective on "Hart to Hart" and Victoria, an executive on "Hotel." In fact, the female characters on the prime time soaps created a new occupational category for women little before seen on TV, that of leisure class. Neither employed in the work force nor busy in the home, these women, such as Lucy and Sue Ellen on "Dallas," shopped, visited and went to lunch.

As the decade progressed, however, being a member of the leisure class went out of style for most wealthy female characters under age 40; and almost all of them got jobs. Despite their lack of training, education or previous work experience, though, they were all instant successes. Lucy became a successful model and Sue Ellen a manufacturer of lingerie. Pam ran an exercise business, then a clothing boutique and finally became a corporate oil executive.

These female millionaires were joined by those in the upper middle class, so that by 1984 affluent women on TV accounted for over half of all females on the screen. Middle class female characters on popular shows shrank to an all-time low and the working class was practically obliterated.

Working-class characters began the decade with reasonably strong representation. The waitresses on "Alice," Florence on "The Jeffersons," Elaine on "Taxi," Daisy on "The Dukes of Hazzard," and Jo on "Facts of Life" all appeared in top-rated programs in the early 80s. However, they were overshadowed by the popularity of programs with wealthy characters. As the 80s progressed, all of TV seemed to upscale itself, so that even conventional situation comedies, like "Family Ties," "Growing Pains" and "The Golden Girls" contained a sheen of affluence. Missing from these programs were any characters with economic struggles.

However, in the fall of 1988 a new situation comedy, "Roseanne," premiered, featuring a blue collar family with a factory-worker mother. The early ratings success of that program could mean the production of other shows like it in future seasons.

THE CLUSTERING OF RACE

In 1979, practically all of TV's female characters were white. In fact, only one of the 25 top-rated programs contained any black female characters at all. That show was "The Jeffersons," and its characters, Louise, her maid Florence, her neighbor Helen, and Helen's daughter Jenny, were the only minority females on popular shows that season.

For the next few seasons viewers saw little increase in black female characters, while Hispanic and Asian women were almost invisible on the screen.

In 1983, several new shows that contained minority female characters became popular. Soon-Lee was Corporal Klinger's wife on "AfterMASH," Julie worked at the information desk on "Hotel," and Tootie was a student at a boarding school on "Facts of Life."

Two years later, the number of minority female characters jumped again as "Dynasty," "Miami Vice," "The Cosby Show," and "227" added more minority females to nighttime programs.

On "Dynasty," Dominique, a black singer, rivaled Alexis in elegance and glamour; while on "Miami Vice," Trudy and Gina worked as undercover cops on dangerous stake-outs. On "The Cosby Show," attorney Clair Huxtable and her daughters introduced for the first time on weekly TV an affluent black nuclear family where the parents had professional careers. Much lower on the economic spectrum were the women of "227"—Mary, her daughter Brenda, and her friends Rose, Sondra, and Pearl, who sat on the front stoop of their apartment each week and shared neighborhood news.

By 1987, these black female characters had been joined by Darlene on "Head of the Class," Thelma, Casietta and Amelia on "Amen," Whitley, Jaleesa, Millie, Stevie and Lettie on "A Different World," and Althea on "In the Heat of the Night."

For the most part, black women on TV in the 80s played roles on black situation comedies, such as "The Jeffersons," "Amen," "227," "A Different World," and "The Cosby Show." They were less frequently seen on white situation comedies and were almost totally invisible on hour-long dramas. Shows like "Hotel," "Miami Vice" and "Dynasty," which included recurring black female roles, were the exception.

Ironically, of the scores of police shows, action/ adventure programs, prime time soap operas, and other dramas whose locations were cities with large minority populations, almost all contained female casts which were exclusively white.

And when TV did portray minority females in either situation comedies or dramas, those characters were almost always black. A decade of top-rated TV programs reveals only one Asian and two Hispanic recurring female characters: Soon-Lee on "AfterMASH," Gina on "Miami Vice," and Maria on "Head of the Class."

HIGH POINTS OF THE DECADE FOR WOMEN ON TV

More Working Mothers

In the 1980s, TV discovered the two-income family. Working mothers, previously a rare species on the screen, increased in number, especially on popular situation comedies, such as "The Cosby Show," "Growing Pains" and "Family Ties."

Newly Defined Families

Reflecting the increased diversity of families in the real world, TV family structures also became more varied during the 80s. On shows like "The Hogan Family," "Who's the Boss?," "My Sister Sam," and "Our House," households were headed by single mothers, single fathers, sisters, aunts, and grandparents, as well as by the traditional team of mom and dad.

Increased Visibility of Older Women

Long relegated to minor, eccentric roles, older female characters on TV began to develop a positive image in the 1980s. Jessica Fletcher was a clever sleuth with amazing deductive ability on "Murder, She Wrote," and "The Golden Girls" faced age discrimination, midlife sexuality and a host of other important issues with frankness and wit.

Strong Black Female Characters

At the beginning on the 1980s the only black women on TV were the female characters on "The Jeffersons." Almost 10 years later, they have been followed by attorney Clair Huxtable and her daughters on "The Cosby Show," four female college students and their dorm mother on "A Different World," five apartment neighbors on "227," a deacon's daughter and church volunteers on "Amen," an undercover cop on "Miami Vice," waitresses and a mortician on "Frank's Place," a college theater major on "Facts of Life," and a brilliant high school student on "Head of the Class."

More Female Buddy Shows

Three new TV shows in the 80s mirrored an important reality in women's lives: female friendship. Previously portrayed almost exclusively as competitors, dizzy comrades or male adjuncts, women were more often seen as friends. Female friendship blossomed in the workplace on "Cagney and Lacey," between two single mothers on "Kate and Allie," and among older women on "The Golden Girls."

Return of the Working Class Heroine

At the beginning of the 80s was "Alice" and at the end "Roseanne," although TV was a barren land for working class women during most of the years in between. Even so, a number of strong characters prevailed. Florence the maid on "The Jeffersons," Carla the waitress on "Cheers," Jo the student on "Facts of Life," and "Laverne and Shirley"—as well as "Alice" and "Roseanne"—brought much-needed economic diversity to the screen.

Authentic Female Cops

After years of portraying sexily dressed, ornamental female detectives, TV finally discovered the formula for realism and created in the 80s roles in which women cops were competent workers instead of decorative sex objects. Chris Cagney, Mary Beth Lacey, and Officer Lucy Bates on "Hill Street Blues" were brave, ambitious and respected by their male colleagues.

The Mainstreaming of Women's Issues

Television introduced women's issues to its network programs in the 1980s. On TV movies, viewers saw sexual harassment on "Fun and Games," sex discrimination on "Games Mother Never Taught You," bank tellers on strike over low wages on "A Matter of Sex," and blue collar work on "The $5.20 An Hour Dream." At the same time, weekly TV programs began incorporating women's issues into their plots, so that issues such as child care, unequal wages, juggling job and family, and sexual bias in the workplace have become more commonplace on entertainment programs.

Contributions of Women Behind the Camera

As women writers, producers and directors gained power during the 80s, their vision has been detected in the shows they produce and direct and in the scripts they write. Women such as Terry Louise Fisher of "LA Law" and "Cagney and Lacey," Diane English of "My Sister Sam" and "Murphy Brown," the Carsey-Werner production team, Susan Harris of "The Golden Girls," and Roseanne Barr of "Roseanne" have injected a new perspective—one which develops characters and treats issues from a woman's point of view—into the male-dominated television industry.

LOW POINTS OF THE DECADE FOR WOMEN ON TV

An Avalanche of Wealth

In a mirror of the political climate, women on TV became rich during the 80s. The extreme point occurred at the middle of the decade when wealthy women far outnumbered those who were middle class. Working class women on TV were hard to find, and the poor were invisible.

Racial Segregation

Despite the increase of black female characters on TV during the 80s, almost all appeared on black situation comedies such as "Amen," "227," "The Cosby Show," and "A Different World." Black women were almost nonexistent on TV dramas which contained mostly all-white female casts, despite their urban settings.

Narrow Definition of Minorities

Judged by its characters and programs, TV seems to define minority as black. Although the number of black female characters increased almost three-fold during the 80s, there was virtually no increase in the numbers of other minority female characters. Despite shows set in Texas, California, New York and Boston, almost no Asian, Hispanic or other women of color were cast as regular female characters during the 80s.

Sexist Humor

During the 80s, TV began to move away from the treatment of women as sex objects. Despite this improvement, lewd comments about women's bodies and jokes about plain-looking and heavy women were far too common. In addition, programs still tried to get easy laughs using sexist humor. One of the worst examples occurred in a 1988 episode of "Mr. Belvedere" in which a college fraternity party was held for the ugliest girls on campus.

Violence Against Women

Although women on TV grew more assertive and self-reliant during the decade, a continuing theme of too many programs was "woman-as-victim." Every season women have been drugged, kidnapped, tortured and murdered, often in graphic, gruesome detail. Even when not physically injured, women have been portrayed as helpless and frightened, standing by and waiting for men to come to their rescue.

CONCLUSION

The 1980s mark a decade of progress for women on television. Their portrayals have become more diverse and, for the most part, more true-to-life. TV programmers have discovered the realities of work, and so employment has become the norm for a critical mass of women on TV, as it has long been for

Lesbian Invisibility in the Media

KARIN SCHWARTZ

The friendliest thing one can say about the media's coverage of lesbians and their issues is that there isn't any. Straight women dominate what thoughtful coverage of women's issues there is, and gay men dominate most of the media attention paid to homosexuality. What little coverage of lesbians exists is sensationalistic, defamatory or both.

The "lesbian story" that received the most play in 1990 was ex-tennis pro Margaret Court's comment that Martina Navratilova's homosexuality sets a bad example for younger players. In comments reported by the *Associated Press* (7/11/90) shortly after Navratilova won her ninth Wimbledon tournament, Court stated that "some players don't even go to the changing rooms because of the problem [homosexuality]." Drawing on the stereotype of lesbians as predators and child molesters, Court implied that if she had a daughter on the tennis circuit, she would feel the need to protect her from the advances of other female players.

Many newspapers that carried the *AP* story edited out statements from the Gay & Lesbian Alliance Against Defamation (GLAAD) charging that Court's statements were fueled by ignorance and bigotry. Television news programs often ran Court's statements without any comment or rebuttal.

Similarly, the "lesbian story" of 1989 was actress Zsa Zsa Gabor's statement that she did not want to go to jail for fear of encountering lesbians. Again, the statement was widely reported; again, only a portion of the reports attempted to place the comments in the context of a homophobic society.

Even on the infrequent occasions when the media chooses to report on the lives of gay people, it tends to focus exclusively on gay men. This translates into news articles, features and television specials about the "gay community" that do not mention or quote a single lesbian (*Parenting* magazine's ground-breaking profile of a gay couple (4/90) and a New York *Daily News* magazine cover story about gay cops (6/24/90), for example); sitcoms and television dramas whose sole recurring gay characters are male (recently ABC's "Hooperman," CBS's "Doctor, Doctor" and ABC's "thirtysomething"); and numerous radio and television talk-show panels about gay issues in which gay men are expected to represent both gay and lesbian perspectives.

The exception proves the rule: The only recurring lesbian character to appear on national television during the last three years was nurse practitioner Marilyn McGrath on the ABC series "Heartbeat," which was cancelled after being targeted by the religious right.

[1991]

women in the real world. Working mothers, older women, more black female characters—all add up to a better picture at the end of the decade than the beginning, despite TV's preoccupation with wealth.

Our hope is that this trend toward diversity increases in upcoming seasons and that authentic female characters become the rule rather than the exception.

As one decade closes and another begins, current TV programs lack any unifying characteristics or common themes. Programmers appear uncertain of future direction, perhaps reflecting the mood of the country. TV's infatuation with wealth has diminished, but no strong trend has yet replaced the glamorous characters of the early 80s.

As the coming seasons unfold, it will be crucial to monitor TV programs to determine whether women's hard-won gains are continued. For, although these gains have been significant, in some ways they are fragile, as several of this season's new shows prove.

Rather than fall back on clichés and outdated stereotypes, television must keep pace with the lives of women today, in all economic brackets. TV must then, with talent and sensitivity, mirror back to viewers those lives and their stories, so that we recognize the characters on the screen not only as entertaining diversion, but as authentic parts of ourselves.   [1988]

 27

X: A Fabulous Child's Story

LOIS GOULD

Once upon a time, a baby named X was born. This baby was named X so that nobody could tell whether it was a boy or a girl. Its parents could tell, of course, but they couldn't tell anybody else. They couldn't even tell Baby X, at first.

You see, it was all part of a very important Secret Scientific Xperiment, known officially as Project Baby X. The smartest scientists had set up this Xperiment at a cost of Xactly 23 billion dollars and 72 cents, which might seem like a lot for just one baby, even a very important Xperimental baby. But when you remember the prices of things like strained carrots and stuffed bunnies, and popcorn for the movies and booster shots for camp, let alone 28 shiny quarters from the tooth fairy, you begin to see how it adds up.

Also, long before Baby X was born, all those scientists had to be paid to work out the details of the Xperiment, and to write the *Official Instruction Manual* for Baby X's parents and, most important of all, to find the right set of parents to bring up Baby X. These parents had to be selected very carefully. Thousands of volunteers had to take thousands of tests and answer thousands of tricky questions. Almost everybody failed because, it turned out, almost everybody really wanted either a baby boy or a baby girl, and not Baby X at all. Also, almost everybody was afraid that a Baby X would be a lot more trouble than a boy or a girl. (They were probably right, the scientists admitted, but Baby X needed parents who wouldn't *mind* the Xtra trouble.)

There were families with grandparents named Milton and Agatha, who didn't see why the baby couldn't be named Milton or Agatha instead of X, even if it *was* an X. There were families with aunts who insisted on knitting tiny dresses and uncles who insisted on sending tiny baseball mitts. Worst of all, there were families that already had other children who couldn't be trusted to keep the secret. Certainly not if they knew the secret was worth 23 billion dollars and 72 cents—and all you had to do was take one little peek at Baby X in the bathtub to know if it was a boy or a girl.

But, finally, the scientists found the Joneses, who really wanted to raise an X more than any other kind of baby—no matter how much trouble it would be. Ms. and Mr. Jones had to promise they would take equal turns caring X, and feeding it, and singing it lullabies. And they had to promise never to hire any baby-sitters. The government scientists knew perfectly well that a baby-sitter would probably peek at X in the bathtub, too.

The day the Joneses brought their baby home, lots of friends and relatives came over to see it. None of them knew about the secret Xperiment, though. So the first thing they asked was what kind of a baby X was. When the Joneses smiled and said, "It's an X!" nobody knew what to say. They couldn't say, "Look at her cute little dimples!" And they couldn't say, "Look at his husky little biceps!" And they couldn't even say just plain "kitchy-coo." In fact, they all thought the Joneses were playing some kind of rude joke.

But, of course, the Joneses were not joking. "It's an X" was absolutely all they would say. And that made the friends and relatives very angry. The relatives all felt embarrassed about having an X in the family. "People will think there's something wrong with it!" some of them whispered. "There *is* something wrong with it!" others whispered back.

"Nonsense!" the Joneses told them all cheerfully. "What could possibly be wrong with this perfectly adorable X?"

Nobody could answer that, except Baby X, who had just finished its bottle. Baby X's answer was a loud, satisfied burp.

Clearly, nothing at all was wrong. Nevertheless, none of the relatives felt comfortable about buying a present for a Baby X. The cousins who sent the baby a tiny football helmet would not come and visit any more. And the neighbors who sent a pink-flowered romper suit pulled their shades down when the Joneses passed their house.

The *Official Instruction Manual* had warned the new parents that this would happen, so they didn't fret about it. Besides, they were too busy with Baby X and the hundreds of different Xercises for treating it properly.

Ms. and Mr. Jones had to be Xtra careful about how they played with little X. They knew that if they kept bouncing it up in the air and saying how *strong* and *active* it was, they'd be treating it more like a boy than an X. But if all they did was cuddle it and kiss it and tell it how *sweet* and *dainty* it was, they'd be treating it more like a girl than an X.

On page 1,654 of the *Official Instruction Manual,* the scientists prescribed: "plenty of bouncing and plenty of cuddling, *both.* X ought to be strong and sweet and active. Forget about *dainty* altogether."

Meanwhile, the Joneses were worrying about other problems. Toys, for instance. And clothes. On his first shopping trip, Mr. Jones told the store clerk, "I need some clothes and toys for my new baby." The clerk smiled and said, "Well, now, is it a boy or a girl?" "It's an X," Mr. Jones said, smiling back. But the clerk got all red in the face and said huffily, "In *that* case, I'm afraid I can't help you, sir." So Mr. Jones wandered helplessly up and down the aisles trying to find what X needed. But everything in the store was piled up in sections marked "Boys" or "Girls." There were "Boys' Pajamas" and "Girls' Underwear" and "Boys' Fire Engines" and "Girls' Housekeeping Sets." Mr. Jones went home without buying anything for X. That night he and Ms. Jones consulted page 2,326 of the *Official Instruction Manual.* "Buy plenty of everything!" it said firmly.

So they bought plenty of sturdy blue pajamas in the Boys' Department and cheerful flowered underwear in the Girls' Department. And they bought all kinds of toys. A boy doll that made pee-pee and cried, "Pa-pa." And a girl doll that talked in three languages and said, "I am the Pres-i-dent of Gen-er-al Mo-tors." They also bought a storybook about a brave princess who rescued a handsome prince from his ivory tower, and another one about a sister and brother who grew up to be a baseball star and a ballet star, and you had to guess which was which.

The head scientists of Project Baby X checked all their purchases and told them to keep up the good work. They also reminded the Joneses to see page 4,629 of the *Manual,* where it said, "Never make Baby X feel *embarrassed* or *ashamed* about what it wants to play with. And if X gets dirty climbing rocks, never say 'Nice little Xes don't get dirty climbing rocks.'"

Likewise, it said, "If X falls down and cries, never say 'Brave little Xes don't cry.' Because, of course, nice little Xes *do* get dirty, and brave little Xes *do* cry. No matter how dirty X gets, or how hard it cries, don't worry. It's all part of the Xperiment."

Whenever the Joneses pushed Baby X's stroller in the park, smiling strangers would come over and coo: "Is that a boy or a girl?" The Joneses would smile back and say, "It's an X." The strangers would stop smiling then, and often snarl something nasty—as if the Joneses had snarled at *them.*

By the time X grew big enough to play with other children, the Joneses' troubles had grown bigger, too. Once a little girl grabbed X's shovel in the sandbox, and zonked X on the head with it. "Now, now, Tracy," the little girl's mother began to scold, "little girls mustn't hit little—" and she turned to ask X, "Are you a little boy or a little girl, dear?"

Mr. Jones, who was sitting near the sandbox, held his breath and crossed his fingers.

X smiled politely at the lady, even though X's head had never been zonked so hard in its life. "I'm a little X," X replied.

"You're a *what?*" the lady exclaimed angrily. "You're a little b-r-a-t, you mean!"

"But little girls mustn't hit little Xes, either!" said X, retrieving the shovel with another polite smile. "What good does hitting do, anyway?"

X's father, who was still holding his breath, finally let it out, uncrossed his fingers, and grinned back at X.

And at their next secret Project Baby X meeting, the scientists grinned, too. Baby X was doing fine.

But then it was time for X to start school. The

Joneses were really worried about this, because school was even more full of rules for boys and girls, and there were no rules for Xes. The teacher would tell boys to form one line, and girls to form another line. There would be boys' games and girls' games, and boys' secrets and girls' secrets. The school library would have a list of recommended books for girls, and a different list of recommended books for boys. There would even be a bathroom marked BOYS and another one marked GIRLS. Pretty soon boys and girls would hardly talk to each other. What would happen to poor little X?

The Joneses spent weeks consulting their *Instruction Manual* (there were 249½ pages of advice under "First Day of School"), and attending urgent special conferences with the smart scientists of Project Baby X.

The scientists had to make sure that X's mother had taught X how to throw and catch a ball properly, and that X's father had been sure to teach X what to serve at a doll's tea party. X had to know how to shoot marbles and how to jump rope and, most of all, what to say when the Other Children asked whether X was a Boy or a Girl.

Finally, X was ready. The Joneses helped X button on a nice new pair of red-and-white checked overalls, and sharpened six pencils for X's nice new pencilbox, and marked X's name clearly on all the books in its nice new bookbag. X brushed its teeth and combed its hair, which just about covered its ears, and remembered to put a napkin in its lunchbox.

The Joneses had asked X's teacher if the class could line up alphabetically, instead of forming separate lines for boys and girls. And they had asked if X could use the principal's bathroom, because it wasn't marked anything except BATHROOM. X's teacher promised to take care of all those problems. But nobody could help X with the biggest problem of all—Other Children.

Nobody in X's class had ever known an X before. What would they think? How would X make friends?

You couldn't tell what X was by studying its clothes—overalls don't even button right-to-left, like girls' clothes, or left-to-right, like boys' clothes. And you couldn't guess whether X had a girl's short haircut or a boy's long haircut. And it was very hard to tell by the games X liked to play. Either X played

ball very well for a girl or played house very well for a boy.

Some of the children tried to find out by asking X tricky questions, like "Who's your favorite sports star?" That was easy. X had two favorite sports stars: a girl jockey named Robyn Smith and a boy archery champion named Robin Hood. Then they asked, "What's your favorite TV program?" And that was even easier. X's favorite TV program was "Lassie," which stars a girl dog played by a boy dog.

When X said that its favorite toy was a doll, everyone decided that X must be a girl. But then X said that the doll was really a robot, and that X had computerized it, and that it was programmed to bake fudge brownies and then clean up the kitchen. After X told them that, the other children gave up guessing what X was. All they knew was they'd sure like to see X's doll.

After school, X wanted to play with the other children. "How about shooting some baskets in the gym?" X asked the girls. But all they did was make faces and giggle behind X's back.

"How about weaving some baskets in the arts and crafts room?" X asked the boys. But they all made faces and giggled behind X's back, too.

That night, Ms. and Mr. Jones asked X how things had gone at school. X told them sadly that the lessons were okay, but otherwise school was a horrible place for an X. It seemed as if the Other Children would never want an X for a friend.

Once more, the Joneses reached for the *Instruction Manual.* Under "Other Children," they found the following message: "What did you Xpect? *Other Children* have to obey all the silly boy-girl rules, because their parents taught them to. Lucky X—you don't have to stick to the rules at all! All you have to do is be yourself. P.S. We're not saying it'll be easy."

X liked being itself. But X cried a lot that night, partly because it felt afraid. So X's father held X tight, and cuddled it, and couldn't help crying a little, too. And X's mother cheered them both up by reading an Xciting story about an enchanted prince called Sleeping Handsome, who woke up when Princess Charming kissed him.

The next morning, they all felt much better, and little X went back to school with a brave smile and a clean pair of red-and-white checked overalls. There was a seven-letter-word spelling bee in class that day. And a seven-lap boys' relay race in the gym. And a seven-layer-cake baking contest in the girls' kitchen corner. X won the spelling bee. X also won the relay race. And X almost won the baking contest, except it forgot to light the oven. Which only proves that nobody's perfect.

One of the Other Children noticed something else, too. He said: "Winning or losing doesn't seem to count to X. X seems to have fun being good at boys' skills *and* girls' skills."

"Come to think of it," said another one of the Other Children, "maybe X is having twice as much fun as we are!"

So after school that day, the girl who beat X at the baking contest gave X a big slice of her prizewinning cake. And the boy X beat in the relay race asked X to race him home.

From then on, some really funny things began to happen. Susie, who sat next to X in class, suddenly refused to wear pink dresses to school any more. She insisted on wearing red-and-white checked overalls—just like X's. Overalls, she told her parents, were much better for climbing monkey bars.

Then Jim, the class football nut, started wheeling his little sister's doll carriage around the football field. He'd put on his entire football uniform, except for the helmet. Then he'd put the helmet *in* the carriage, lovingly tucked under an old set of shoulder pads. Then he'd start jogging around the field, pushing the carriage and singing "Rockabye Baby" to his football helmet. He told his family that X did the same thing, so it must be okay. After all, X was now the team's star quarterback.

Susie's parents were horrified by her behavior, and Jim's parents were worried sick about him. But the worst came when the twins, Joe and Peggy, decided to share everything with each other. Peggy used Joe's hockey skates, and his microscope, and took half his newspaper route. Joe used Peggy's needlepoint kit, and her cookbooks, and took two of her three baby-sitting jobs. Peggy started running the lawn mower, and Joe started running the vacuum cleaner.

Their parents weren't one bit pleased with Peggy's wonderful biology experiments, or with Joe's terrific needlepoint pillows. They didn't care that Peggy mowed the lawn better, and that Joe vacuumed the carpet better. In fact, they were furious. It's all that little X's fault, they agreed. Just because

X doesn't know what it is, or what it's supposed to be, it wants to get everybody *else* mixed up, too!

Peggy and Joe were forbidden to play with X any more. So was Susie, and then Jim, and then *all* the Other Children. But it was too late; the Other Children stayed mixed up and happy and free, and refused to go back to the way they'd been before X.

Finally, Joe and Peggy's parents decided to call an emergency meeting of the school's Parents' Association, to discuss "The X Problem." They sent a report to the principal stating that X was a "disruptive influence." They demanded immediate action. The Joneses, they said, should be *forced* to tell whether X was a boy or a girl. And then X should be *forced* to behave like whichever it was. If the Joneses refused to tell, the Parents' Association said, then X must take an Xamination. The school psychiatrist must Xamine it physically and mentally, and issue a full report. If X's test showed it was a boy, it would have to obey all the boys' rules. If it proved to be a girl, X would have to obey all the girls' rules.

And if X turned out to be some kind of mixed-up misfit, then X should be Xpelled from the school. Immediately!

The principal was very upset. Disruptive influence? Mixed-up misfit? But X was an Xcellent student. All the teachers said it was a delight to have X in their classes. X was president of the student council. X had won first prize in the talent show, and second prize in the art show, and honorable mention in the science fair, and six athletic events on field day, including the potato race.

Nevertheless, insisted the Parents' Association, X is a Problem Child. X is the Biggest Problem Child we have ever seen!

So the principal reluctantly notified X's parents that numerous complaints about X's behavior had come to the school's attention. And that after the psychiatrist's Xamination, the school would decide what to do about X.

The Joneses reported this at once to the scientists, who referred them to page 85,759 of the *Instruction Manual.* "Sooner or later," it said, "X will have to be Xamined by a psychiatrist. This may be the only way any of us will know for sure whether X is mixed up—or whether everyone else is."

The night before X was to be Xamined, the Joneses tried not to let X see how worried they were. "What if—?" Mr. Jones would say. And Ms. Jones would reply, "No use worrying." Then a few minutes later, Ms. Jones would say, "What if—?" and Mr. Jones would reply, "No use worrying."

X just smiled at them both, and hugged them hard and didn't say much of anything. X was thinking, What if—? And then X thought: No use worrying.

At Xactly 9 o'clock the next day, X reported to the school psychiatrist's office. The principal, along with a committee from the Parents' Association, X's teacher, X's classmates, and Ms. and Mr. Jones, waited in the hall outside. Nobody knew the details of the tests X was to be given, but everybody knew they'd be *very* hard, and that they'd reveal Xactly what everyone wanted to know about X, but were afraid to ask.

It was terribly quiet in the hall. Almost spooky. Once in a while, they would hear a strange noise inside the room. There were buzzes. And a beep or two. And several bells. An occasional light would flash under the door. The Joneses thought it was a white light, but the principal thought it was blue. Two or three children swore it was either yellow or green. And the Parents' Committee missed it completely.

Through it all, you could hear the psychiatrist's low voice, asking hundreds of questions, and X's higher voice, answering hundred of answers.

The whole thing took so long that everyone knew it must be the most complete Xamination anyone had ever had to take. Poor X, the Joneses thought. Serves X right, the Parents' Committee thought. I wouldn't like to be in X's overalls right now, the children thought.

At last, the door opened. Everyone crowded around to hear the results. X didn't look any different; in fact, X was smiling. But the psychiatrist looked terrible. He looked as if he was crying! "What happened?" everyone began shouting. Had X done something disgraceful? "I wouldn't be a bit surprised!" muttered Peggy and Joe's parents. "Did X flunk the *whole* test?" cried Susie's parents. "Or just the most important part?" yelled Jim's parents.

"Oh, dear," sighed Mr. Jones.

"Oh, dear," sighed Ms. Jones.

"*Sssh,*" ssshed the principal. "The psychiatrist is trying to speak."

Wiping his eyes and clearing his throat, the psy-chiatrist began, in a hoarse whisper. "In my opinion," he whispered—you could tell he must be very upset—"in my opinion, young X here—"

"Yes? Yes?" shouted a parent impatiently.

"*Sssh!*" ssshed the principal.

"Young *Sssh* here, I mean young X," said the doctor, frowning, "is just about—"

"Just about *what?* Let's have it!" shouted another parent. " . . . just about the *least* mixed-up child I've ever Xamined!" said the psychiatrist.

"Yay for X!" yelled one of the children. And then the others began yelling, too. Clapping and cheering and jumping up and down.

"*SSSH!*" SSShed the principal, but nobody did.

The Parents' Committee was angry and bewildered. How *could* X have passed the whole Xamination? Didn't X have an *identity* problem? Wasn't X mixed up at *all?* Wasn't X *any* kind of a misfit? How could it *not* be, when it didn't even *know* what it was? And why was the psychiatrist crying?

Actually, he had stopped crying and was smiling politely through his tears. "Don't you see?" he said. "I'm crying because it's wonderful! X has absolutely no identity problem! X isn't one bit mixed-up! As for being a misfit—ridiculous! X knows perfectly well what it is! Don't you, X?" The doctor winked. X winked back.

"But what *is* X?" shrieked Peggy and Joe's parents. "*We* still want to know what it is!"

"Ah, yes," said the doctor, winking again. "Well, don't worry. You'll all know one of these days. And you won't need me to tell you."

"What? What does he mean?" some of the parents grumbled suspiciously.

Susie and Peggy and Joe all answered at once. "He means that by the time X's sex matters, it won't be a secret any more!"

With that, the doctor began to push through the crowd toward X's parents. "How do you do," he said, somewhat stiffly. And then he reached out to hug them both. "If I ever have an X of my own," he whispered, "I sure hope you'll lend me your instruction manual."

Needless to say, the Joneses were very happy. The Project Baby X scientists were rather pleased, too. So were Susie, Jim, Peggy, Joe, and all the Other Children. The Parents' Association wasn't, but they had promised to accept the psychiatrist's report, and not make any more trouble. They even invited Ms. and Mr. Jones to become honorary members, which they did.

Later that day, all X's friends put on their red-and-white checked overalls and went over to see X. They found X in the back yard, playing with a very tiny baby that none of them had ever seen before. The baby was wearing very tiny red-and-white checked overalls.

"How do you like our new baby?" X asked the Other Children proudly.

"It's got cute dimples," said Jim.

"It's got husky biceps, too," said Susie.

"What kind of baby is it?" asked Joe and Peggy.

X frowned at them. "Can't you tell?" Then X broke into a big, mischievous grin. *"It's a Y!"*

[1972]

PART III

Gender and Women's Bodies

Just as the psychological experience of being female affects our self-perceptions, it also shapes our perception of our bodies and our sexuality. Although current attitudes about women's bodies are changing, reflecting a greater appreciation of athleticism, strength, and health, most of us still find fault with our bodies and appearance. Reproductive and sexual functions continue to define women's bodies, and the advertising world establishes standards of beauty that exclude most women, particularly those of us who are not white, Anglo-Saxon, and thin. When we strive to fit these standards, we often neglect and devalue our own uniqueness. For women of color, white definitions of female beauty are less powerful now than they were 20 years ago, but they continue to predominate in the media.

The traditional view of a woman's body as primarily ornamental and reproductive is so pervasive in our society that we often judge ourselves by these unrealistic norms. Along the way, we compare ourselves harshly and critically to "classic beauties," subject ourselves to beauty aids and procedures to achieve the "right look," and more frequently than not, end up feeling dissatisfied with ourselves.

The selections in the first section of Part III illuminate the ways in which cultural norms regarding beauty and bodies affect women. Some of the authors in this section challenge these rigid norms and joyously proclaim pride in the way they look. Inés Hernandez-Avila appreciates her natural beauty and prefers it to the unrealistic images portrayed in fashion magazines. Lucille Clifton pays homage to her African-American hair and large hips, which depart from the standard conceptions of beauty.

Expressions of female sexuality are closely related to how we view ourselves and our bodies. In the next section, we examine the ways gender socialization and sexism affect our sexual experiences. Male-defined attitudes about women's sexuality have created myths and stereotypes that have harmed women by generating false and unrealistic expectations of our sexual behavior. The sexual revolution of the 1960s signaled a loosening of restrictions on sexual behavior for both men and women. However, as Virginia Reath points out, the double standard for male and female sexuality has persisted throughout history and prevents women from fully experiencing our sexuality. Although the cultural climate in the United States is currently more conducive to accepting women's sexuality, we continue to see male sexuality described in positive terms, while the descriptors for female sexuality are usually negative. For example, a sexually active man who has several partners is "virile," but a woman who has several partners is described as "easy" or "promiscuous." When a woman's sexual activities are socially approved, it is expected that she will not be "too aggressive" in bed and will not enjoy herself "too much."

Additional proscriptions further limit the range of sexual expression available to women. In her essay, Sharon Thompson, a young African-American woman, describes her decision to be celibate. Her journey of self-discovery led her to confront a basic assumption about sexuality in our society—that one is supposed to be sexually involved with others. Lisa DeBoer reflects on the complexity of defining one's sexual identity and focuses on the restrictive expectations of a homophobic society. These women and others are purposeful, active participants in their sexual lives.

Taboos about women's sexuality, shaped by cultural ideology and mythology, directly affect a woman's experience of her own sexuality. It is not unusual to hear women discuss ambivalent feelings about their sexual desires and relationships, or to question whether or not "something is wrong" because they do not experience sex the way they think they "should." As we explore these different issues, we introduce the feminist perspective, which asserts that for women living in a sexist culture, sexuality encompasses both pleasure and danger. Previously, women's rights to sexual pleasure were denied or restricted. In some cultures, they still are, especially regarding practices such as masturbation. A feminist approach to sexuality acknowledges sexual expression as one way in which we can experience ourselves, as an avenue through which we have a right to explore our own feelings, needs, and desires. Feminists believe that women should make their own sexual choices, ranging from celibacy to monogamy to lesbianism. On the other hand, because of the danger of AIDS and other sexually transmitted infections, along with the possibility of unwanted pregnancy, our rights to sexual pleasure must be balanced with the responsibility of taking care of ourselves. Zoe Leonard confronts this reality in "Safe Sex Is Real Sex," in which she makes a convincing case for equating safe sex with satisfying sex.

Our attitudes about beauty, our bodies, and sexuality develop early in life. The unrealistic expectations created by a society that objectifies women can restrict our choices and limit our growth. As the selections that follow reveal, understanding how gender socialization and sexism create harmful stereotypes and expectations can help us claim our own standards for personal beauty and sexuality.

The Female Body

"The beauty myth," as Naomi Wolf calls it in her book by that name, has a powerful effect on all women. It consists of the belief that women must possess an immutable quality called "beauty" in order to be successful and attractive to men. Our culture is permeated by the conviction that beauty is the central measure of women's worth. In fact, standards of beauty vary greatly from culture to culture and have changed radically over time. In our culture, prevailing notions of beauty emphasize being young, thin, white, and Anglo-Saxon. In "Changing Landscapes," Wendy Chapkis challenges these ideals, and describes the different forms of female beauty by comparing them to the infinite changes in nature's panorama. Nellie Wong, Aishe Berger, and Vicki Sears describe their reactions to stereotyped expectations of beauty for Asian-American, Jewish, and Native American women. As the selections in this section demonstrate, these standards create anguish and confusion for most women, and particularly for women of color, who are outside the prevailing "norms" of beauty.

Ideals of physical beauty often have negative effects on a woman's self-image and physical health. The increasing rates of eating disorders are just one example of the unhealthy consequences of rigid standards of beauty. In the poem "Time to Eat," Donna Marquardt captures the intensity of a woman's experience of anorexia, portraying the ever-present connection between beauty norms and the pressure to conform to them. The obsession with thinness has devastating effects on many women, as shown by July Siebecker. As Linda Delgado points out, however, such notions of female beauty are not universal; Latino culture, she argues, prizes women of fuller proportions.

When women begin to challenge social scripts for physical beauty, they can begin to see the beauty within themselves and define beauty in a more meaningful way. This section concludes with two pieces that reflect contemporary women's new personal standards of beauty. While both of these selections are written by African-American women, they contain important messages for women of all racial and ethnic backgrounds who are challenging traditional standards of beauty.

 28

Changing Landscapes

WENDY CHAPKIS

"Mommy, why do you have a moustache?" asks the child in the Removatron Hair Removal ad. "Be-

cause sometimes even nature makes mistakes . . . unwanted facial hair can be embarrassing . . . put an end to those embarrassing questions . . . you'll be glad you did."

The moustached woman—like all women who fail to conform—is not only Other she is Error; flawed both in her failure to be a normal male and in her inability to appear as a normal female. Though this judgement is intrinsically impersonal, it is rarely experienced that way. Each woman is somehow made to feel an intensely private shame for her "personal failure." She is alone in the crowd pushing toward the cosmetics counter, the plastic surgeon, the beauty specialist. "Epilator 2700" reminds those in the industry how lucrative this belief can be:

> Hair removal is no doubt one of the fastest growing profit specialties in the beauty world today. It is estimated that 85% to 90% of all women have unwanted facial or body hair. Many of these people go to great lengths to solve this often embarrassing beauty problem.

We are like foreigners attempting to assimilate into a hostile culture, our bodies continually threatening to betray our difference. Each of us who seeks the rights of citizenship through acceptable femininity shares a secret with all who attempt to pass: my undisguised self is unacceptable, I am not what I seem. To successfully pass is to be momentarily wrapped in the protective cover of conformity. To fail is to experience the vulnerability of the outsider.

Despite the fact that each woman knows her own belabored transformation from female to feminine is artificial, she harbors the secret conviction that it should be effortless. A "real woman" would be naturally feminine while she is only in disguise. To the uninitiated—men—the image must maintain its mystery, hence the tools of transformation are to be hidden away as carefully as the "flaws" they are used to remedy.

Consider the difference between the public display of the masculine straight razor and shaving soap and the carefully concealed tweezer or depilatory secreted away in a woman's cosmetics case. For the removal of body hair, there is no female counterpart to the reassuring image of father, face lathered and razor in hand, daily reminding his family and himself of his manhood in the morning ritual of shaving. Advertisements make almost heroic the act of a manly He shaving away thick stubble while an admiring She looks lustfully on. Imagine a similar cultural celebration of a woman plucking her eyebrows, shaving her armpits or waxing her upper lip. All advertisements for products to de-hair the female show only the aftereffects; "before" scenes apparently would be too shocking.

Even more public acts of femininity, like applying make-up, tend to rely on an underlying message of female inadequacy. There is a problem to be corrected, a basic improvement to be made:

Problems: My eyes look pale and washed out. My nose is too wide at the bottom. Can you show me what to do so my lips don't look so thin? How can I soften the line of my pointy chin?
Solution: Merle Norman personalized skin care and make-up.

Women begin early in life with this sense that we aren't quite right. During childhood the identification of woman as other and less lays the groundwork for all forms of inequality. But appearance is the first, constant commentary. As a woman comes to accept her physical "difference" as evidence of personal failure, she also learns to share society's belief that hostility is her due. This experience of inadequacy means that no woman is allowed to say or to believe "I am beautiful."

In a women's writing workshop, we are given the following assignment: "Look at the woman on your left. Study her for a moment and then jot down one word that comes to mind as you look at her. Give her the paper. Now each of us will write for three minutes about that word."

My word is "golden"; my neighbor's is "apple." The interesting thing about the drill is not how well each of us can write, the choice of metaphors and nice turns of phrase. It is the content that is gripping. Not one of the descriptive words passed along is remotely critical. We are all careful of the responsibility not to wound each other by offering up words like "fat," "stringy," or even "glasses" or "gray." We all pass on words of power, pleasure or beauty. But what we have done with those words. . . .

"Golden," I write, "goldy locks, gold plated, the Midas Touch, all that glitters is not. . . ." My neighbor takes "apple" and writes "shiney and pretty to look at but watch out for the worms. Sleeping Beauty and the poison apple. . . ." Not one of us could take the word and proclaim, "I am good. I am deserving of this praise."

The rise of the second wave of feminism in the United States was heralded by demonstrations at the Miss America pageant in 1968. A Freedom Trash Can was provided by picketers into which women could throw bras, girdles, wigs, curlers. This challenge to commercial codes of beauty and privatized shame earned feminists the media tag "Bra Burners."

A few years later, my eight year old sister wrote a school essay about me: "Wendy is a feminist. When I grow up, I am going to be just like her except I'll dress better." Now, more than a decade gone by, I think her prophetic—only these days I dress better too. Despite my updated wardrobe (my flannels and jeans now share closet space with leather pants, a dress or two and fluorescent pink T-shirts), I am no less concerned about the politics of appearance. Today my twenty year old sister looks uncomfortably down at our hairy legs: "I don't have any problems with equal rights, sexual preference or fighting racism in the movement. But, hey Wendy, why is it we still can't shave?"

Ten or fifteen years ago we weren't allowed to display body hair and believe ourselves to be acceptable and sexual. And apparently we still aren't. A long decade after resolutions were passed against the sexual objectification of women's bodies and in favor of abolishing artificial gender distinctions, we are turning again to one another with doubts and confusions.

We know we fail as women to be "feminine enough" (by choice we reassuringly remind one another) and we fear we fail as feminists because we are still concerned about whether we are "attractive" (let alone to whom). Even more disturbing, we are beginning to suspect that while a genderless sisterhood may have made for wholesome family relations, it may not be the stuff of erotic fantasy.

Much of our joy in doing battle with sexism has been replaced with grim determination. Perhaps this is the inevitable result of ten years in which we changed faster than the world around us. In the early days of the movement, the call to resist gender stereotyping in appearance promised empowerment: we would create our own images of womanhood not measured against the feminine ideal. Those heady days of militant rejection have stretched into the long haul. The standards by which we are judged and self-critically judge ourselves remain much the same.

Though feminism has changed the way women view the world and themselves, it often feels as if the world has turned feminism into a new kind of lip gloss. The daring insistence of early feminists that a woman is beautiful just as she naturally appears has been rewritten in a commercial translation as the Natural Look. The horrible irony of this is, of course, that only a handful of women have the Natural Look naturally. Most of us have flaws that must be disguised if we are to resemble the beautiful models setting the standard—a fact the beauty industry is banking on.

No question that it was liberating to free hips from the binding of the girdle, breasts from the confines of a push-up bra, faces from the mask of heavy make-up. But the current ideal beauty remains a narrow-hipped, high-breasted woman with flawless skin. While the standards show little more flexibility and variety than in the past, women are now supposed to attain them without visible artifice.

This insistence on natural beauty has created two new categories of "attractive" women: the child-woman made popular by American film star Brooke Shields, and the over-forty physically fit midlife beauty (Jane Fonda, Raquel Welch and company). These women, though a generation apart, embody a cultural fantasy of unaffected (free from artifice) and unchanging (forever young) beauty.

A girl at the edge of puberty has a naturally hairless body that demands no shaving, waxing or chemicals to feel smooth. She has the soft, wrinkle-free skin of childhood older women can only regain with surgery and careful application of creams and cosmetics. Skin her slightly older acne stricken sisters struggle to recapture with make-up and astringents. Her body is naturally small, supple and nothing if not youthful.

The over-forty beauty shares with the child-woman the promise of eternal youth. To be beautiful, they seem to say, is to look a constant twenty whether biologically twelve or forty-five. Now that foundation garments and heavy make-up (which provided the illusion of youth) have fallen out of fashion, older women must literally remake their bodies in the pursuit of beauty. Scientific skin care, cosmetic surgery and fitness programs promise to minimize the visible changes of living.

Thus, despite the fact that the "baby boom"

generation is reaching midlife, beauty remains adolescent. Even with the growing visibility of older
women, their most striking quality is their apparent
youth.

As columnist Ellen Goodman notes, these
women do not so much challenge our ideas about
beauty as they:

> raise the threshold of self-hate faster than the age
> span . . . those of us who failed to look like Brooke
> Shields at seventeen can now fail to look like Victo-
> ria Principal at thirty-three and like Linda Evans at
> forty-one and like Sophia Loren at fifty. When Glo-
> ria Steinem turned fifty this year she updated her
> famous line from forty. She said, "This is what fifty
> looks like." With due apologies to the cult of midlife
> beauty, allow me two words: "Not necessarily."[1]

The midlife beauties would most likely agree. It
apparently takes hard work and concerted effort to
maintain beauty over forty; several of these women
are making a fortune on the sales of books outlining
exactly that position. Clearly the appeal of Jane Fonda's *Workout*, Linda Evans' *Beauty and Exercise
Book* and Raquel Welch's *Total Beauty and Fitness
Program* lies in the promise that they can get you in
shape—*their* shape. The over-forty beauties' insistence on energetic exercise seems to suggest that the
older body, left to itself, is lazy, undisciplined and
out of control. "Skin repair" advertisements echo
this message:

> . . . over time your skin gets lazier and lazier. And it
> doesn't produce new cells as fast or as frequently as
> it once did . . . Buf Puf Gentle promotes the rebirth
> of your skin . . . Age-controlling cream by Estee
> Lauder . . . encourages all skin to do what young
> skin does on its own.

The woman who "lets herself go" and shows her
age clearly only has herself and her lack of discipline
to blame:

> The ugly truth is we all age . . . No need to panic . . .
> La Prairie Cellular Skincare Preparations . . . ease
> the visible signs of aging. The over-forty look is over
> . . . you can actually feel your dull, tired-looking skin
> respond to Radiant Action. The fact is, from this
> moment on beautiful skin is simply a matter of Dis-
> cipline . . . rewarding you with skin that is sleek . . .
> Skin that has been disciplined. There are no mira-
> cles. There is only Discipline.

The acknowledged queen of physically fit midlife beauty, Jane Fonda, is a remarkably disciplined
woman. She is an accomplished actress, film pro-
ducer, political activist, businesswoman, mother,
partner and fitness fanatic. She is also a woman with
a history of twenty-three years of bulimia—of compulsive eating and induced vomiting. With characteristic courage, Fonda went public with her painful
history:

> Society says we have to be thin, and while most of
> us don't have much control over our lives, we can
> control our weight, either by starving to death or by
> eating all we want and not showing the effects . . . I
> loved to eat, but I wanted to be wonderfully thin. It
> didn't take long for me to become a serious bu-
> limic—bingeing and purging fifteen to twenty times
> a day! . . . bulimia was my secret "vice." No one was
> supposed to find out about it, and because I was
> supposed to be so strong and perfect, I couldn't ad-
> mit to myself that I had weaknesses and a serious
> disease.[2]

In her attempt to maintain a perpetually thin and
youthful beauty, Fonda was faced with the choice of
starving to death (stay pretty, die young) or control
(not showing the effects of eating, of aging). If bulimia was Jane Fonda's secret vice, fitness is her public virtue. And yet the objective of both is remarkably similar—live but don't change. Maintain an
attractive appearance through the disciplined exercise of control over the body.

This is not to say that there is nothing to choose
between working out and throwing up. Obviously
fitness—unlike bulimia—has positive and particular value for women. Physical strength can undoubtedly increase a woman's sense of personal power,
just as building muscular "definition" can be a
means of literally attaining a more distinct sense of
self. This is especially true for those people—older
women very much included—who have experienced a lack of social and physical identity. Stephen
Greco suggests a similar appeal among gay men for
body building:

> With bulk and definition, gay amateur body-
> building can compensate for the powerlessness and
> invisibility some say are ours as "marginal" mem-
> bers of society . . . the point is not merely the clarity
> of muscle groups under the skin, or a child's idea of
> the look of powerfulness, but the existential clarity

that comes from the individual articulating for himself his presence in the world. That's power.[3]

But is it? Taking control of the kind of body image to be presented to the world *can* be empowering—though it then seems a bit feeble to choose the shape that is currently most fashionable. Perhaps more to the point is the exhilarating experience of pushing past previous limits. This can build confidence that might enable a woman to do the same in a social or political context. It can, but it doesn't necessarily work that way.

After all, fitness training is an intensely individual process. You are your only obstacle at the weight machine and no one else can help push those pounds. But the workout metaphor is a less useful guide to attaining power in the workplace, home or community where collective effort is essential. Fitness imagery does speak, though, to a world in recession. Bite the bullet and go for the burn.

It, in fact, may well be the recession climate that makes so attractive the idea of getting in shape: the exercise of control over the body compensating for a basic sense of a life out of control; a body that says "that's power" substituting for real authority. If this is the case, fitness may not represent a revolution in female beauty standards as much as it does the latest in beauty fashion. One that reflects increased expectations and equally high insecurity among women. And it echoes the very old promise that beauty is the answer to both. . . .

Women and men both learn fear of and disdain for the mortal body and seek to escape its limits. Men, asserting independence from the body, identify themselves as soul or mind. The physical is then projected onto women. In a fascinating article on the "somatophobia" inherent in the philosophy of Plato, Elizabeth Spellman notes the

> . . . mixture of fear, awe, and disgust in men's attitudes toward the physical world, the body, the woman. Men have purchased one-way tickets to Transcendence in their attempt to deny, or conquer and control, the raging Immanence they see in themselves and project onto women.[4]

While men are busy conquering and controlling nature and woman, women are obsessed with controlling their own bodies. Man believes he survives through his enduring achievements. Woman is her mortal body. A man's relationship to his body, then,

appears to be less fraught with tension than a woman's. The male mind can afford to be a much more lenient master over the body, indulging in the appetites of the flesh. A man may sweat, scar and age; none of these indications of physicality and mortality are seen to define the male self. Indeed, those men who take an unseemly interest in the body are described as womanly and presumed to be homosexual. For a man to recognize the male body as Beauty is to be forced to recognize physical change and mortality; in effect condemning himself and his fellows to death.

Concern over control of the flesh (dieting, sexual self-control, disciplining the body against the signs of age) is a particularly feminine obsession. Though woman is identified with body she never can be confidently convinced she is mistress over it. Graying, wrinkling, gaining weight, all represent reminders that the one area of female identity and authority is only marginally governable. The body continually becomes Other until it finally ceases to exist at all; a particularly disturbing proposition for those reduced to no more than their bodies.

For a woman, then, her traditional—if entirely unreliable—ticket to success in life and transcendence beyond it is the mortal body. The woman who is awarded the title of Beauty momentarily escapes into the eternal ideal. Yet she knows, as each woman must, that she has been or will be seen as ugly in her lifetime. To be beautiful is to exist in a moment framed by expectation and fear. We thus deny ourselves pleasures in the special challenges and changing appearances of childhood, youth, maturity and old age in pursuit of a picture perfect moment.

The photographic metaphor is apt. The world of beautiful images photographed for fashion spreads and for the movie and TV screen is not only impossibly perfect but entirely static. One of the appeals of such programs as the internationally popular "Dynasty" is its continual perfect moment. The life of the Carringtons represents the ultimate expression of Beauty and Success as a state to be attained. And these people unquestionably have *arrived*. Even the sanitized tragedies that befall them are meant as proof that Real Beauty and True Success endure. Problems which would disfigure, defeat or destroy lesser creatures leave the stars fundamentally unaltered. So too is age used as evidence of success, not as a threat to it. The midlife trio of

Linda Evans, Joan Collins and Diane Carroll (all over forty) prove week after week that Real Beauty defies the changes of time.

In reality, though, the female body is a constantly changing landscape. From the budding breasts of adolescence, through the rounded belly of pregnancy and generous curves of maturity, to the smooth chest of mastectomy and deep creases of old age, our bodies weather and reshape. To call beauty only the still life of unchanging "perfection" is no praise for creatures so lively and diverse as womankind.

NOTES

1. Goodman, Ellen, "The Beauty Sales Pitch," *Boston Globe,* October 11, 1984.
2. Janos, Leo, "Jane Fonda, Finding Her Golden Pond," *Cosmopolitan,* January 1985, p. 170.
3. Greco, Stephen, "Strong Bodies Gay Ways," *The Advocate,* July 7, 1983, p. 22.
4. Spellman, Elizabeth V., "Woman as Body: Ancient and Contemporary Views," *Feminist Studies,* Vol. 8, no. 1, Spring 1982, p. 109.   [1986]

29

When I Was Growing Up

NELLIE WONG

I know now that once I longed to be white.
How? you ask.
Let me tell you the ways.

when I was growing up, people told me
I was dark and I believed my own darkness
in the mirror, in my soul, my own narrow vision

when I was growing up, my sisters
with fair skin got praised
for their beauty, and in the dark
I fell further, crushed between high walls

when I was growing up, I read magazines
and saw movies, blonde movie stars, white
skin,
sensuous lips and to be elevated, to become
a woman, a desirable woman, I began to wear
imaginary pale skin

when I was growing up, I was proud
of my English, my grammar, my spelling
fitting into the group of smart children

smart Chinese children, fitting in,
belonging, getting in line

when I was growing up and went to high
school,
I discovered the rich white girls, a few yellow
girls,
their imported cotton dresses, their cashmere
sweaters,
their curly hair and I thought that I too should
have
what these lucky girls had

when I was growing up, I hungered
for American food, American styles,
coded: white and even to me, a child
born of Chinese parents, being Chinese
was feeling foreign, was limiting,
was unAmerican

when I was growing up and a white man
wanted
to take me out, I thought I was special,
an exotic gardenia, anxious to fit
the stereotype of an oriental chick

when I was growing up, I felt ashamed
of some yellow men, their small bones,
their frail bodies, their spitting
on the streets, their coughing,
their lying in sunless rooms,
shooting themselves in the arms

when I was growing up, people would ask
if I were Filipino, Polynesian, Portuguese.
They named all colors except white, the shell
of my soul, but not my dark, rough skin

when I was growing up, I felt
dirty. I thought that god
made white people clean
and no matter how much I bathed,
I could not change, I could not shed
my skin in the gray water

when I was growing up, I swore
I would run away to purple mountains,
houses by the sea with nothing over
my head, with space to breathe,
uncongested with yellow people in an area
called Chinatown, in an area I later learned
was a ghetto, one of many hearts
of Asian America

I know now that once I longed to be white.
How many more ways? you ask.
Haven't I told you enough?   [1981]

 30

To Other Women
Who Were Ugly Once

INÉS HERNANDEZ-AVILA

Do you remember how we used to panic
when Cosmo, Vogue and Mademoiselle
    ladies
        would Glamour-us
        out of existence
                so ultra bright
                would be their smile
                so lovely their
                complexion
    their confianza[a] based on
    someone else's fashion
    and their mascara'd mascaras[b]
        hiding the cascaras[c]
        that hide their ser?[d]

I would always become cold inside
                mata*onda*[e] to compete
        to need
        to dress right
        speak right
        laugh in just the
        right places
        dance in just
        the right way

My resistance to this type of
    existence
    grows stronger every day
Y al cabo ahora se
    que se vale
    preferir natural luz[f]

              to neon.

---

[a]Confidence. [b]Masks. [c]Shells. [d]Being. [e]Dampener: *onda* is a "trip" in the positive sense—to *matar onda* is to kill, to frustrate the "trip"—to dishearten. [f]And now anyway I know that it is worthy to prefer natural light.

 31

Nose Is a Country . . . I Am
the Second Generation

AISHE BERGER

for Emma Eckstein

Emma Eckstein was a socialist and a writer before she became a patient of Freud's. He diagnosed her as an hysteric because she was prone to emotional outbursts and masturbated frequently. Freud turned Emma over to his colleague Dr. Fleiss, who believed operating on the nose would inhibit sexual desire. Fleiss broke Emma's nose and left a large wad of gauze inside her nasal passage. This "error" wasn't discovered until years later, long after Emma's physical and emotional health was ruined and she was left an invalid.

"Such a nice girl, you have the map of Israel all over your face."
          —Woman in fruitstore when I was thirteen

I. Rhinoplasty

Nose that hangs on my face like a locket
with a history inside   you kiss
on our once a week date like lovers
in their mid forties
or maybe just my mother who is a lover
in her mid forties who had a nose job
in her mid twenties
the bump
the bumpy roads that troubled my father
the trouble with my father
who liked *zoftig*[1] women
all sides moldable
no bumps on the nose
map of Israel   on the face
map of Israel   on the map
a place on the edge of a deep blue
romantic sea   on the map
a place that keeps shuffling its feet
backward   shrinking
like her nose under gauze
under wraps
under hemorrhage that accidentally

---

[1]Plump.

happened when the doctor left
the operating room and didn't
return till the anesthesia was already
loosening to sound
like an avalanche
in preparation
her nose bleeding under that
temporary wrap
a change in the landscape
my mother passes me down
this nation
this unruly semitic landmass on my face

My teeth were always
complimented for their four years
of braces
the rumblings of my jaw as my face
continentally drifted and my nose
grew
not like my mother's which is
like a border with its bone gates
levelled neutral
a passive face my mother's
bumpless smile

II. Hemorrhage

I think of Emma Eckstein
whose cartilage
was hammered out of her   the ancient
steppes on her face   the long view
of the world flooded
with large quantities of blood

Emma Eckstein who took her hands lovingly
inside her
who perhaps merely rubbed her legs together
in her seat and orgasmed
told she is hysterical
she wants too much in the final analysis
in the final analysis
the nose is inextricably linked
to the clitoris and the need to take hands
to yourself lovingly
is abnormal

Which was then a fresh new word
abnormal
the desire to treat oneself with kindness

Take your hands and put them on your lap

Take your nose and put it on inside out

On the ancient steps
up Emma Eckstein's nose
a man named Fleiss committed

strange unnatural acts in the name of
Psycho therapy
which was then a fresh new word

Emma
Levelled
Neutral
a passive face
a bumpless smile
her hands
jerk
at the thought
of herself
the hammer
reinforced
the hammer

III. Assimilation into the modern world

and the gauze
under my own eyes
black and blue staying
in my house for a week
like sitting *shiva*[2]
fourteen years old
the most important days of my life

My mother promises me
a profile
like Greta Garbo

She used to tell me
my best friend Hilary
was prettier than me

The little Yeshiva boys yelled
that I took all their air up
when I walked down the hall

---

[2] Practice of mourning the death of a relative by sitting in the house for a week.

Then the boys at camp said
they'd kiss me if they could
ever find my lips

My dermatologist pierces
my ears
when I'm ten and advises me
to wear big earrings
it will distract people away
from my face

At eight I learn the word *rhinoplasty*
and it becomes a goal in my future
like becoming the first woman president
or flying to the moon

I am the second generation

Nose is a country where little wooden puppets
tell lies
where paintings of Shylock
are in every hotel lobby
Nose is a country where women have to
walk with their heads down
Where I await my new
modern look
assimilated
deconstructed

IV. Bridges

The body doesn't let go
of bridges

they expose me to the world after seven days
I expect to be noseless   erased
but I am there   long and sloped
like a mountain after a fierce rain

I am there
the body knows

Mine stopped breathing at the crucial moment
the moment where they smash
bridges
the moment where the enemy
takes over

This time they couldn't finish
what they started
a part of me   revolted

against the gas   they had to
revive me before the last
bone was broken

The suspension of my long
winding bridge where my Jewish soul
still wanders over
the slightly altered terrain

the body knows

My desert nose my sweet ripe nose
   my kosher nose
my zoftig nose my mountain nose
   my gentle nose
my moon of nose my sea of nose
   my heart pumping
lungs stretching fire of nose
   my full bodied
wine of nose   my acres of *sheyne*
   sheyne meydele[3]
nose

that you kiss at night

Nose that I put my loving hands on.   [1986]

 32

Homage to My Hair

LUCILLE CLIFTON

when i feel her jump up and dance
i hear the music! my God
i'm talking about my nappy hair!
she is a challenge to your hand
black man,
she is as tasty on your tongue as good greens
black man,
she can touch your mind
with her electric fingers and
the grayer she do get, good God,
the blacker she do be!   [1987]

---

[3] Pretty, pretty girl.

🌿 33

Bra One

VICKI SEARS

I should have been a first-born son. Only I wasn't. Paper dolls, black patent-leather shoes, and dresses have been my downfall. And that's where things are so hard with Mom and me. Seems like it's always been bad because I'm not the frilly girl she wanted. It's not only that I act like a boy. I've just never been right with Mom. Maybe my little sister will do it for her, but it's hard to tell since she's only three. I hope she does, though, because it would take a lot of sweat off me. I mean, I think I was born preferring overalls and sneakers. Mom has had a hard time trying to jam me into dresses. And being a bookworm rather than a shopper doesn't help.

The whole thing makes me so sad I can barely think, but lately I've been wondering if it isn't that something's deep-down wrong with me. Like maybe Mom has a hard time seeing me because I remind her of my father's sister that she hates. Or maybe I'm too dark like my Dad rather than being like Mom, all soft pinks and creamy colors. We don't look anything alike. Could be that bothers her. Then the last thing is, well, it's probably a mortal sin to say and I'm going to be struck dead as soon as I do, but maybe she never really wanted to be a mother—she just got PG and that was that. Nothing I know is for certain except that whatever's wrong shows up most when there's clothes buying to do. Like last week.

Mother, a strange saleswoman, and my fourteen-year-old self were jammed into a tight pee-yellow rectangle. Instinctively I knew things were going to be as pagan as any ritual I'd ever heard about in voodoo, gypsy magic, witchcraft, or from my aunt, the medicine woman. That's the one Mom hates. The purpose of the rite was the first caging of my breasts.

Barely an hour before my feet had been skimming the earth as I sprinted from base to base in the softball field dust. Teammates yelled, "Watch the fat Injun run!" Everything else was wonderfully free. My down-to-the-butt braids sailed behind my ears and flapped on my chunky cheeks. Both arms pumped for speed. Sweat dripped from my face in the afternoon heat. Each short leg yelled out its power as it thudded and sprang on the ground. My breasts bounced. The nipples jumped up in excitement when I stole a base. They felt good rubbing against my shirt. I laughed as I ran. All in all, they were quite nice parts of myself. I noticed them with curious pleasure on other girls. I even felt pride in thinking that boys didn't get them.

In the midst of this pleasure, my mother arrived, surrounded by the armor of her dark-blue Chevy. She'd said she would pick me up to go shopping. It was never an activity I enjoyed, especially when being taken away from baseball. She had said nothing about buying a bra. Now we were in a cramped cube. *They* were lined up on one side looking at my body as though they owned it.

From her bench-sitting throne, Mother had her right leg slung over her left. She was shaking an irritated foot. The saleswoman stood at ready attention with her yellow tape measure. I was in a corner, back to the mirror.

"For Christ's sake, take your blouse off," ordered my mother.

I turned from her to the saleslady, then back. I fixed an expression of pleading on my face, but it went unread. Her foot thrashed up and down. The saleswoman looked resigned. I was defeated.

Reluctantly my hands went to my neck to pull up the T-shirt. My fingers began a slow climb, scooping folds of material up until the shirt was in my hands. Then, swiftly as any avenging righteousness, my mother suddenly snatched the shirt over my head. I was naked! My bosom, guarded by instantly crossed arms, flushed a reddened brown with my face. My eyes stung with blinked-back tears as Mom said, "We haven't got all day."

I longed for the softball field. Ached to run, jump, grass-roll, and tree-shimmy. Against my will, she was dragging me into a world of long dresses and obligatory dances. I could see it coming as I watched my mother's satisfied smile stating to the salesclerk, "She needs a bra, doesn't she?"

The woman nodded gloomily, advancing toward me with her tape measure, her black-numbered power insignia. Her sincerity did not inspire happiness.

Without words, she stuck one tape end under my arm, pushing it upward at the same time. It rested, half-risen, with my hand firmly clamped on my right breast. The woman leaned her body into mine as she struggled to measure my chubby personage. I turned my face away from her perfumed hair and the slick of beige make-up. Her cheek slid on my chin. I tried not to breathe. I heard my heart. Then, both of her arms around me, she wanted to join the measuring ends. My hands still cupped my bare buds. Mother let out a giant sigh, speeding her foot-quaking. I dropped my hands.

The salesclerk quickly took my depth and width, jotting numbers on her pad. She walked out, leaving me naked and not knowing what was going to happen next. I stood there uncertainly. I looked at Mom puffing her cigarette with annoyance.

I began to count the dots of nails in the wood of the dressing room walls. I imagined how many times the walls had been painted. Longed for my jackknife to seek the hidden layers. I thought about how important it seemed to Mom to buy me a bra when it was so unimportant to me. Turning toward Mom, I asked, "What happens next?"

She blew smoke through her nose with, "You're going to get a bra."

My question seemed bigger to me than her response. I asked, "How is it done?"

"For Christ's sake. It's just done. She will come in, and you'll get one. I don't know why you can't just accept things. Stop being so dramatic!"

I grew quiet. It was high drama. Mother and I were shopping without my sister. That was unusual. And, she wore a satisfied grin while sharing some secret with her new confidant, the salesclerk. Just as I was wondering if I *was* being overly dramatic, the saleswoman arrived.

"Well," she exclaimed, "we have several lovely styles here meant for young ladies." She proffered the bras.

One had lace leaping loftily from a solid white cotton cup. I knew it would creep to my throat. There was another firm white mass guarded by wires surrounding the cup. I thought, "Jesus. My boobs don't need that much armor." My mind reeked with the idea of living life in curled metal. No one would ever be able to lean against me. The third

option was black lace even to the straps. All I could think of was Patricia Neal in a movie I'd seen on the TV late show, *The Fountainhead*. Somehow I knew there was no way my wearing such a bra would cause the screen to darken and relight, as it did with her and Gary Cooper, Patricia stretching happily—obviously braless—in bed the next morning. I looked at mother with astonishment, but she was already holding out the final selection. It was dead-white, with a seam across the front, large clasps in the back, and heavy, sturdy straps. Functional and strong, like the blood-oxford shoes my mother's very British mother always wore. Like those shoes, it would last forever no matter what I wanted. I was about to ask for a compromise when the saleswoman said, "Bend over sweetheart."

"What?"

"Bend over for the fit," she stated.

As my fingertips touched my toes, I heard an under-the-breath mutter of, "Judas Priest!" It was Mom's favorite curse. I raised my eyes to see her furious foot flailing the air. "Oh shit," I thought as I dangled, "she's going to cream me for whatever mistake I've made."

Instead, the saleslady said, "Not quite so far, dear."

She pulled me to a slightly less bent posture. "You see, there's a right way and a wrong way to put on brassieres. You must lean forward with the bottom of the bra against your chest, snap up the back, and then drop your breasts into the cups. Then you adjust the straps here at the clips for support." She snaked the straps through a metal maze, pulling my breasts up. When done, she stepped back, patted my breasts underneath, and said, "What a lovely uplift you have!"

There were my breasts as I had never seen them, poking straight out of my body! They hadn't been there before. They were foreigners. I wanted to bend over to hide them. I knew I would be teased because I'd seen it happen to other girls, and mine were bigger than anybody's ever were. They weren't buds at all. They were full-fledged breasts! Then I thought about Patricia Neal and began to smile. Hers had certainly been nice. Maybe I'd get a boyfriend. Then I'd get babies if he touched my breasts. A mixture of excitement and fear was settling in when the clerk said, "Well, you certainly do have a . . . ah, well-endowed bosom. Perhaps you need this model instead."

From some unseen source she pulled forth a final horror. It boasted a wide back brace with two cups dangling on either end. Each cup was margined with metal hooks and teeth. They glared as she said, "This is a front-snapping model. It's very easy to put on and take off. It's probably better suited for such an athletic young lady."

It made no sense to me. All I could see was metal brackets nibbling at my breasts. I'd just found them, and now they were going to be mangled by some medieval torture instrument.

"Try that one on," ordered my mother.

"But Mom!"

She stopped my protest with a tapped foot and exhaled smoke. No dragon could have done better.

I slipped my arms into the holster, bent down to sag my breasts into the cups, and began to snap up. The bra covered half my stomach. It seemed as though there were thirty hooks. Finally harnessed, I looked at the monstrosity in the mirror. It was as awful as I'd anticipated. It was something my step-grandmother would wear. I had to get out of this one. I looked at my mother. I looked at the salesclerk. Both were pleased. I tried to move. It was restrictive. I thought, "This bra is Mom's plot to bind me from head to toe." At any moment I feared a girdle would appear. I was going to completely disappear. I knew that I had to rip out of there or I'd go home in a front-snapping bra. I said, "I gotta see if I can still play softball."

"Fine," Mom said, "but get on with it. You're really too old to be playing baseball anyway."

I filled my lungs as unobtrusively as possible, took a batting stance, and swung at an imaginary ball. At least five of the hooks undid themselves.

"See!" I exclaimed, "this one's gonna bust in no time."

Mom looked disgusted. The clerk was astounded. I snatched up the practical bra with, "This one's the sturdiest, Mom."

I hated it, but it was a victory over the front binder. Besides, I counted on her impatience.

"All right," Mom declared, "give her four of those. Now let's get out of here."

I sighed. I had done enough work for an eon. "What're we doing now, Mom?" I asked. I hoped to go home to put this ordeal behind me.

Calmly she said, "We're going to the maternity shop to find you some tops." [1990]

🌿 34

Time to Eat

DONNA MARQUARDT

I

Moving with a speed I cannot check,
the car hurtles down the black deserted road
towards an unfamiliar destination.
Immense cautioning roadsigns appear at every
    curve,
warnings that I am too close to turn back.
In school bathroom toilet stalls girls
smoke their first illegal cigarettes,
rites of passage to the world.
They major in beauty, and makeup,
a *Seventeen* magazine their textbook,
taking care to master the tools
of a trade necessary for survival.
Hungry, groping adolescent male hands
touch virgin bodies as clandestine kisses
are stolen in corners of dim high school hallways.
Mother says "sex is dirty."
"Boys are out for one thing."
Maybe she's right;
I don't know.
She tells me nothing;
I am so afraid;
she wants me to be perfect.
I am her firstborn daughter.
Brown-eyed, blond, curly-haired cooing baby,
I grow in her image and have her face.
She pinned her lost dreams on me
like crisp cotton diapers and pink lacy dresses.
Immortalized in bronze,
my baby shoes were placed atop the piano
harbingers of the greatness
I am expected to achieve.

I grew learning the lesson that legends
are hard to live by.
With budding breasts and spreading hips
bursting the protective garment of childhood,
I am left naked and exposed.
I soon will arrive
at this strange place for which I am not ready.
Stomping the brakes to no avail,
feeling powerless and out of control, I cannot stop.
From somewhere deep inside me a voice speaks
      softly.
"To stall the car, simply let it run out of fuel."

II

Refusing food, my flesh falls away.
Day by day I grow smaller and thinner,
Alice in a carnival funhouse wonderland.
My world becomes narrower.
Daily devotions of arduous exercise, weights and
      scales
assure my redemption through perfection and
      control.
Reborn, emerging purged and purified
under the light of eternal childhood,
I am my own power; I am my own strength.
Only once have I surrendered to temptation
gorging for a week on the forbidden fruit.
The tape measure showed the evidence
of the fall from grace.
Like Hester Prynne I am sentenced to wear
my sins on my body for everyone to see,
two days penance of fasting becoming
the only hope of absolution.

III

At the dinner table battleground,
Mother and I face each other in endless daily
      combat.
Like a military general she orders me to eat.
Stabbing at the enemy food on my plate,
raising it to my mouth in surrender,
the sour taste of defeat poisons my lips and tongue.
Rebellious prisoner of war on a hunger strike
I have become a problem to the victor.
Helpless she takes me to a Haitian shrink.
Tap, tap, tap,
he knocks on my brain with his witch doctor chants
of hypnotic incantations.

"Go away; you cannot come into my body temple
or perfection religion."

IV

Shivering in the cold wind, no flesh to warm me
I walk on the deserted playground
under an overcast, forbidding sky.
Lonely and sad I do not want to play here
      anymore.
All of my friends have grown-up and gone home.
Like castles in the sandbox pelted by
a torrent of sudden summer rain,
I have watched my idols crumble.
Like a broken seesaw off center,
my life is unbalanced and askew.
It is time to stop the games and put away the toys.
They are for children.
I too must go home.
I am hungry.
It is time to eat.   [1982]

❧ 35

Women's Oppression and the Obsession with Thinness

JULY SIEBECKER

Large numbers of women in the U.S. are engaged in a constant battle against our own flesh. Our society tells most of us that we need to change our physical selves in order to be happy, healthy, successful, accepted, and loved. We are too fat, we're told, and when shown the images of beautiful young women on fashion magazine covers, we must agree because all but 5% of us will never have the body shape of those fashion models. We feel immense pressure to conform, to remodel our bodies with an endless string of diet plans and exercise regimens, or hide ourselves in shame and self-loathing. Most of us would see this war against our bodies as a personal issue, but in fact it is a social problem with distinct political ramifications. It affects more than our self-esteem. It helps keep women in an inferior place in our society and is harmful to us socially, psychologically, and physically.

The American obsession with thinness is an issue I have had personal cause to study, as I grew up fat and suffered from a compulsive eating disorder for which I began treatment in my second year of college. While in therapy, I started questioning the directives I got from society, telling me that my success in life was greatly influenced by the size of my hips. I also began to suspect that my problem was not as uncommon as I had thought. I discovered that while not every woman had an eating disorder, *no* woman I knew was happy with her body or appearance. I spoke with many women about this issue and found that those whose backgrounds were similar to mine—white, middle-class, urban or suburban—were most likely to have had similar experiences. The Latina and African-American women I spoke with had the benefit of countervailing norms of beauty in their cultures, but all heard messages telling them they should look a different way than they do and could relate to what I was dealing with on some level.

My experience served as an entry point into feminism for me because I began to see that there is a tremendous gap between the myths and the realities of women's lives. We are all being told that this image is available to all if only we work hard enough and are "good" enough (meaning self-deprivational enough), but rarely do any of us achieve this image. The disparity between what we look like and how we are supposed to look erodes our self-esteem, as we try unsuccessfully to gain approval from our male-dominated society and feel unable to live the lives we want to until we reduce ourselves.

We are assured by the media and the diet industry that anyone can have the perfect body if she tries hard enough. This is a false and deceptive message because it is, in fact, not normal for most women's body types.[1] Millions of women are so caught up in the mythology of the perfect woman that we don't even know what is normal for our bodies. The phenomenon of the flat stomach is simply not anatomically appropriate for most women. In reality, we're not all meant to be one size. According to the research of Dr. David Garner, a specialist in eating disorders at the Clark Institute of Psychiatry, Toronto, each of us has a genetically predetermined "set point" of weight, just as we all have different heights, and our bodies will work to keep us at that size. The reason that 95–98% of all dieters gain back the weight we lose is because our bodies are trying to get back to our set points.[2] So the idea that one's size is a matter of willpower, which contributes to the negative stereotype of fat people as lazy and gluttonous, simply isn't true. If we all had the same rate of exercise and type of diet, some of us would be smaller and some of us would be larger—and very few of us would look the way society presently tells us that we should.

A look at the way we speak about weight makes clear the disapproval society feels for fat people. We categorize people who are not thin as deviant rather than simply being at different places in a continuum of body sizes. We use the words "overweight" or "out of shape" in our kinder moods; "fat" or "obese" in our more blunt moments. All are laden with value judgments. "Obese" is supposedly a bit more objective (though there is a distressingly wide range of definitions for it in the literature on health and size issues), but "fat" has such negative connotations that it is almost impossible to use without conferring an insult upon its recipient. We use "overweight" to talk about someone who isn't thin, but not "overheight" to refer to someone who is tall. Which weight is it that we're talking about, then, when we declare that we are over it? We have an ideal image for the adult female that is so deeply engraved in our minds that we see any deviation from it as unattractive and bad.

It is my observation that while both men and women suffer from discrimination because of body size, it is much more severe for women because in our culture a woman's worth is more tied to appearance. When we see that our bodies and sexuality are viewed and treated as commodities, we begin in subtle ways to think of ourselves as objects. Our role

[1] Garner and Garfinkel, *Handbook for the Treatment of Eating Disorders* (New York: The Guilford Press, 1985), p. 516.

[2] K. Chernin, *The Obsession: Reflections on the Tyranny of Slenderness* (New York: Harper & Row, 1981), p. 30.

models in the media are often shown in pieces; a set of legs here, a torso or just a pair of lips there, implying that we are the sum of our body parts and must be prepared to withstand intense scrutiny part by part for approval, rather than whole, unique individuals, complete with flaws. This leads us to believe that in order to have a successful life, we must fashion ourselves into perfect objects; only then will we be capable of earning the approval and affection of men. We are encouraged to think that if we don't end up in monogamous, heterosexual relationships, we will lead loveless, lonely, sad lives. And we know that if we are fat, we will be scorned and punished by society.

Women pursue the image of beauty for two reasons: because we are told that we need to for our health, and to avoid being social outcasts. While the first reason is what we speak openly about and hear the most public arguments for, I would assert that it is the second that more often truly compels us. Hence, we can be in fine health but miserable if we don't look the way we think we should in a bathing suit, but are delighted when an illness has caused us to temporarily lose a few pounds. We feel that if we fail to conform to the ectomorphic image, we will suffer both personally and socially. We are absolutely right in this assumption.

Fat women's lives are plagued by discrimination and derision because of their "deviance." We are viewed as unfeminine and are treated with a distinct lack of respect, as if we were animals or things rather than human beings with thoughts, feelings, and abilities. We experience ridicule in public and are shown only in negative or "character" roles in the media. Our sexuality is considered a humorous subject by definition at best, and perverse or disgusting at worst. We are told endlessly by well-meaning friends and relatives that we would be pretty if only we took off some weight, thus communicating that we are not and cannot be pretty now, and that until we become thin we are not entitled to participate in many facets of ordinary life. When applying to colleges that require interviews, we are turned away more often than thin women with lower SAT scores. When entering the work force, it is harder for us to get jobs or be promoted. Both socially and economically, fat women are punished and discriminated against for looking different; we are robbed of

our personhood, our dignity, our sexuality, our opportunities, our self-esteem, and our power.[3]

The stigma against fat women is reinforced by the pronouncement of the medical world that it is impossible to be both heavy and healthy. In fact, scientific findings about the relationship between health and weight are by no means clear, but until very recently, the media focused exclusively on studies that support the condemnation against fleshiness. For example, we have heard much about the strain put on the heart by gaining weight, but not that losing weight can present the same health risk. An American Cancer Society study showed that a 10% gain *or loss* of body weight puts a strain on the heart.[4] We are not adequately informed that it is yo-yo dieting (a series of unhealthy crash or "fad" diets in which the dieter loses and regains weight a number of times) that is the major cause of permanent weight gain. The body interprets the act of dieting as starvation and will put on more weight—and specifically more fat—than was originally lost in an attempt to defend itself.[5]

We are also not informed about the positive medical facts about fat. For instance, the findings of the 30-year Framingham Study indicated that "life expectancy was worst among the leanest in the populations, and in many instances best among the fattest."[6] In another study, Dr. Reubin Andres, Clinical Director of the National Institute on Aging, reviewed the mortality data on cancer, diabetes, and hypertension, all of which are supposed to be caused by obesity. He logically assumed that if this was the truth, then the mortality data would show fatter people dying earlier of these conditions. However, he found the *opposite* to be true; thinner people were the ones with higher mortality rates due to these illnesses.[7] These are just a few examples show-

[3]M. Millman, *Such a Pretty Face: Being Fat in America* (New York: W. W. Norton, 1980). See Millman for a comprehensive and moving study of what it is like to be a large woman in a size-biased society.
[4]K. Chernin, *The Obsession: Reflections on the Tyranny of Slenderness*, p. 41.
[5]Garner and Garfinkel, *Handbook for the Treatment of Eating Disorders*, pp. 532–533.
[6]R. Seid, *Never Too Thin: Why Women Are at War with Their Bodies* (New York: Prentice-Hall, 1989), p. 1.
[7]Ibid.

ing that we are not receiving the whole picture when it comes to health and fat.

The other side of this coin is that we are not adequately informed of the health risks of dieting or being underweight. These include "chronic fatigue, irritability, tension, inability to concentrate" as well as symptoms we may know more of, such as anemia and other vitamin deficiencies, dizziness, and headaches.[8] Rapid weight loss can actually release toxins into the body, instead of flushing them out.[9] While the medical industry is now beginning to warn about the dangers of yo-yo dieting, these warnings go unheeded by the majority of American women, who hear a louder and more wish-fulfilling message from the $32 billion diet industry telling us that physical perfection *is* quickly and easily attainable.[10] Clearly, the bias against fat women cannot be accounted for by health concerns; it is a socially induced fear. It must be understood as a product of our society's inability to accept diversity and as a manifestation of sexism.

Eating disorders, which involve both physical and mental health issues, are on the rise in our country. Thirty years ago, they were almost entirely unheard of, while today, they are being called "the sociocultural epidemic of our time."[11] There are three documented forms of eating disorders: bulimia, characterized by bouts of binge eating followed by purging through means such as vomiting or laxative abuse; compulsive eating, which involves binges but not purges; and anorexia nervosa, which involves binges, purges, self-starvation, and often compulsive exercising. All three share a similar fear and loathing of fat, involve similar obsessions with weight, appearance, and control, and afflict mainly women. These disorders have been regarded as bizarre psychological phenomena that affect a minority of emotionally disturbed young women. The problem has thus been isolated from the experiences of other women and marginalized into a psychological category. This has in effect thrown up a smokescreen between the clinically diagnosed eating disorder sufferer and the rest of women in society. If this smokescreen came down, what women would see is that, while we do not all actually have eating disorders, we are not so different from those sufferers. As psychologist Noelle Caskey comments: "In taking their fear of fat to life-threatening extremes, anorexics are simply obeying society's dictates in a more drastic manner than the rest of us."[12]

Symptoms associated with eating disorders are common in less severe forms in the general female population. Studies show, for example, that, like anorexics, large numbers of women whose weight was normal or were underweight, according to the Metropolitan Life Insurance Company tables, consider themselves overweight.[13] If the thriving businesses in liposuction, intestinal bypass surgery, gastric stapling, and jaw-wiring weren't enough to convince us that women are intensely afraid of being overweight (another eating disorder symptom), we should also note the 1980 *Cosmopolitan* survey that found that women are more afraid of becoming fat than they are of *dying*.[14] Eating disorders can be seen as part of a continuum of obsession that affects the vast majority of American women on some level. Even if a woman feels happy with her body as she is, if she is large, she will still be discriminated against in subtle or overt ways, and if she is thin, she will hear urgent messages to stay that way.

Besides eating disorders, there is an even more direct way in which the obsession with thinness hurts women psychologically. Women are socialized to be other-oriented, and deprivation of self is seen as virtuous for us. In her traditional (and encouraged) role as wife and mother, a woman becomes the caretaker of others and is considered good for not giving to herself, for being self-sacrificing, for spending all her time in the service of others. This trait of self-abnegation is a staple for the sex-role

---

[8] K. Chernin, *The Obsession: Reflections on the Tyranny of Slenderness*, p. 41.
[9] C. Solimini, "Body Pollution (Toxins Caused By Rapid Weight Loss)," *Weight Watchers Magazine*, v. 18 (April 1985), p. 62.
[10] C. Hemenway, "The Weighty Issue of Size," *Smith Commentary* (Northampton, MA: Smith College).
[11] E. Szekely, *Never Too Thin* (Toronto: The Women's Press, 1988), p. 12.

[12] N. Caskey, "Interpreting Anorexia Nervosa" in *The Female Body in Western Culture*, ed. S. Suleiman (Cambridge: Harvard University Press, 1986), p. 178.
[13] Garner and Garfinkel, *Handbook for the Treatment of Eating Disorders*, p. 392.
[14] M. MacKenzie, "The Politics of Body Size: Fear of Fat" (Berkeley: The Pacifica Tape Library, 1980).

stereotype of the good woman and also figures strongly into women's conflicts with food, size, and power. For example, when a woman is dieting and announces she was "good," she means she has deprived herself of something she wanted in order to be more appealing. In this way, we surrender the right to have our own needs and desires, and to have them seen as valid as those of men.

These issues demonstrate the pervasiveness of the complex knot of size, power, and sexism. The power relations between women and men are critical to understanding the fear of fat women. Today, in an age and a society where women are beginning to assert our right to equal power, the kind of body that we are told pleases men is a thin one. The womanly qualities of the adult female anatomy are discouraged in favor of the adolescent male's. Lithe, lean, and narrow-hipped, this image says more than androgyny; it says that power and acceptability don't come in overtly female packaging. Women are made to feel guilty for taking up a lot of space with our bodies, for being large, expansive, mature-looking, and for giving to ourselves and nurturing ourselves. These two ideologies are ultimately aimed at keeping women from getting figuratively and literally "too big for our britches." The bottom line is this: If a woman wants to succeed in a man's world, she must not threaten his hold on the power, and that means not appearing too mature, strong, powerful—sticking to little britches, to put it metaphorically. Ultimately, our bodies are a feminist battleground.

One would think that such a wide-reaching problem would be at the forefront of feminist concern over the position of women; after all, how much more basic an issue is there than how we relate to our bodies, and how they are perceived by society? Yet women do not band together to put an end to this situation. Instead, we accept the judgment against our flesh and are often the harshest judges of ourselves and each other. Why would we do this? Why, when faced with a situation of oppression that should be obvious to us, would we continue to condone and internalize it, continue to argue for our own oppression behind cries of concern for health?

I believe some reasons for this are: the strength of the stigma against large women, the power of the messages equating femininity with thinness, the cli-

mate of competition for male approval that is fostered within many different areas of society, and the absence of positive alternatives to conforming to the image of thinness. Having been instilled with the belief that we are not good enough as we are, women do not want to hear that diets don't work well and that our fear of fat oppresses us because it would mean having to accept the idea that we aren't able to solve our problems by losing weight. This would be giving up the dream of perfection that we are told is within our reach and is our true road to happiness. We have been sold a package, paid for in confidence and self-esteem, and we want to see our investment turn a profit.

So what alternatives are there to selling ourselves out? Comprehensive answers to such a complex problem would require at least another article, but some general ideas for personal and political action can at least get us started. If this issue were added to the feminist agenda, there are a number of possible ways to organize for change. We could petition the National Institutes of Health to include the obsession with thinness in its Women's Health Initiative project, and in particular press for a critical examination of the diet industry. We could also charge that more responsible research on women and issues of weight and diet be done. We can also challenge the diet industry itself, denounce its messages and tactics as harmful to women. We could put pressure on the fashion industry to create more clothing for women of all sizes and to have their models reflect the diversity of women who might be buying those fashions. We could organize campaigns to demand that a greater number of fat women be portrayed in positive roles in the media.

On the personal level, we need to stop fixating on weight. As Rita Freedman says in *Beauty Bound,* we need to "get off the scales and get on with our lives."[15] We need to educate ourselves and others that our current standards of beauty are inappropriate for 95% of the women trying to achieve them, and that these standards are unhealthy and ultimately oppress us. We should accept more diverse standards of beauty that are inclusive of many ages, shapes, races, and ethnicities. We mustn't let fashion

---

[15] R. Freedman, *Beauty Bound* (Lexington, MA: D.C. Heath, 1986), p. 170.

run our lives. If our clothes don't fit, we should change *them,* not ourselves. We need to reject the idea of self-deprivation as a virtue, to recognize that it is unhealthy to our physical and mental well-being and is a way to keep us complicitous in our own oppression. We should recognize and accept the idea that we are entitled to the things we want and not be ashamed of taking up space. We need to recognize that trying to be healthy and trying to be happy are two different projects. We should eat well, exercise, try to eliminate stress, and accept the size that our bodies are when we're following this lifestyle.

Most of all, we must recognize that we have a right to be treated as equals, a right not to spend all our lives worrying about approval from men, a right to feed and nurture ourselves, a right to all the power that comes with our mature women's bodies, whatever size they are. These are rights worth fighting for.   [1993]

🌿 36

Arroz Con Pollo vs. Slim-Fast

LINDA DELGADO

To many white American women, thinness and tallness are essential parts of beauty. Yet in Spanish, the words *delgada* and *flaca* have a different connotation. Both words mean thin. *Delgada* connotes thin and weak, while *flaca* connotes thin as in skinny. Neither is very flattering. In fact, the question that usually follows after someone notices you are looking rather *delgada* is whether you have been ill.

Weight problems, aside from their health implications, are not seen as important in Latino culture as they are in mainstream American culture. There is a ceremonial importance to food and many rituals assigned to the sharing of food with others. Recently during a warm-up exercise in a new class, students were asked to introduce themselves by identifying with a particular food. A young Dominican woman said she was like *arroz con pollo* (rice with chicken). Her reason for picking this dish was that rice with chicken symbolized warmth, love, and acceptance.

It is a dish made for new neighbors, new in-laws, and new friends to celebrate important events. It means welcome and good luck.

The breaking of bread with family, friends, and strangers is part of Latino hospitality. "*Mi casa, su casa*" is an unaltered tradition. When you visit my aunt's house, for example, go there hungry! The variety and amounts of food are quite extraordinary. I get full just looking at the table! Not only must you partake of everything there, you must also keep in mind that there are at least three or four desserts to follow. On special occasions, such as Easter, Christmas, and Mother's Day, everyone has a signature dish, and part of the celebration is sharing these delicacies. Failure to eat the right amount will cause personal distress to the hostess. What did she do wrong? At my aunt's house, usually my grandmother will ask if you have been sick or if your children have been giving you a hard time. There must be some explanation why you have not eaten your share of food. By "your share of food" they mean enough to feed a small army! The word "diet" or "calories" is never mentioned. For the current generations, these messages can be confusing.

Putting weight on your bones, as my grandmother explains it, is necessary for many reasons. First of all, how else can you carry the burdens of being a woman? You have to eat in order to have the strength to deal with a husband and/or children (regardless of the fact that, at present, you may be 11 years old). You have to eat to have the strength to deal with *lo que Dios te mande,* whatever God sends you because *uno nunca sabe lo de mañana, so uno tiene que aprobechar lo de hoy,* we never know what tomorrow may bring, so we have to enjoy what we have today. Living in New York, you also have to eat in order to deal with the cold, wintry weather. There is always a good reason for a second or third helping of food. In the film *Acting Our Age,* an African-American woman about the age of 65 expresses her concern for the next generation of young women. She says, "Now that black women are being used as models and thought of as beautiful, they will pick up the same false notions about beauty as white women." I think this is also true for Latinas in the United States.

One of my childhood memories was an episode involving my grandmother when I was in the fifth grade. She picked me up at school and told my mother we were going shopping. Well, we did, but first she had someplace to take me. For as long as I could remember, I was a tall and very skinny child. That day, my grandmother and I took a bus ride into Manhattan to a nutrition clinic. She swore I was undernourished and that something was wrong. The doctor said I was healthy and of a good weight. My grandmother was quite surprised and, in fact, didn't believe him.

Having a "good set of hips" means not only that you can carry a child well but also that you can manage whatever your husband has in store for you. "You have to eat in order to have strength." So, from the time you are an infant, chubbiness is applauded as healthy. As you grow older, mental and physical well-being are assessed by your outer appearance. Thin is not sexy. It is unhealthy, unappealing, and sad. My grandmother told me that I didn't look strong enough to carry my bookbag and asked how was I going to carry whatever God sent my way. I learned early in life to expect to bear something! That was part of the gender-role experience.

Interestingly, flabbiness is not acceptable, either. Flabbiness is a sign of laziness and overindulgence. Formal exercise is not part of the Latino culture for women, while men often play softball, handball, or paddle ball. It is generally accepted that women who are flabby and out of shape must not be taking care of their homes, themselves, or their children. They must be watching *novelas*. Women's exercise happens in the course of cleaning, cooking, and caring for children.

In the dating game, life gets really confusing for young Latinas. If women look too much like the models, they will be considered the kind of women men play with but don't necessarily marry. A man brings a woman who is a size 10 or 12 home to mother and a family dinner, but a woman who is size 5 or 6, you have to keep away from your brother! A 16-year-old Puerto Rican student recently told me that her boyfriend wanted her to put on some weight before the summer. She said that he was not pleased at the fact that other men were watching her on the beach last summer. The other side of the problem was that her mother had taught her that if she gained weight, she would not have any boyfriends. When I heard this story, it reminded me of the African-American woman in the film and her description of "false notions about beauty."

Some of my fondest memories are wrapped in the warmth of mealtimes. Special foods are part of special holidays. Watching generations of women cook and exchange recipes, taking in all the wonderful aromas and feeling their sense of pride and accomplishment as they fulfilled their understood role, was positive for me. Although their place of power was in the kitchen, I learned how that power worked. Being in the kitchen did not mean being passive or subservient. It meant doing your share of the business of parenting and partnering, since the kitchen is the center of family activity. It is a place of importance in the Latino household. Feeding those whom you care about is nurturing the entire unit, and eating all of your *arroz con pollo* means you are loved for your efforts in return.

There are many mixed messages to negotiate in a cross-cultural environment. Immigrants, like everyone else, want to belong. They find themselves trapped somewhere between the cultural values of their home and their host country. Although some can negotiate the conflict better than others, it nevertheless distorts views of the self. Reconciliation of different cultural repertoires is quite a challenge, especially for young Latinas who are trying to "fit in."   [1992]

 37

Homage to My Hips

LUCILLE CLIFTON

these hips are big hips
they need space to
move around in.
they don't fit into little
petty places. these hips
are free hips.
they don't like to be held back.
these hips have never been enslaved,
they go where they want to go

they do what they want to do.
these hips are mighty hips.
these hips are magic hips.
i have known them
to put a spell on a man and
spin him like a top!   [1987]

 38

Beauty: When the Other Dancer Is the Self

ALICE WALKER

It is a bright summer day in 1947. My father, a fat, funny man with beautiful eyes and a subversive wit, is trying to decide which of his eight children he will take with him to the county fair. My mother, of course, will not go. She is knocked out from getting most of us ready: I hold my neck stiff against the pressure of her knuckles as she hastily completes the braiding and then beribboning of my hair.

My father is the driver for the rich old white lady up the road. Her name is Miss Mey. She owns all the land for miles around, as well as the house in which we live. All I remember about her is that she once offered to pay my mother thirty-five cents for cleaning her house, raking up piles of her magnolia leaves, and washing her family's clothes, and that my mother—she of no money, eight children, and a chronic earache—refused it. But I do not think of this in 1947. I am two and a half years old. I want to go everywhere my daddy goes. I am excited at the prospect of riding in a car. Someone has told me fairs are fun. That there is room in the car for only three of us doesn't faze me at all. Whirling happily in my starchy frock, showing off my biscuit-polished patent-leather shoes and lavender socks, tossing my head in a way that makes my ribbons bounce, I stand, hands on hips, before my father. "Take me, Daddy," I say with assurance; "I'm the prettiest!"

Later, it does not surprise me to find myself in Miss Mey's shiny black car, sharing the back seat with the other lucky ones. Does not surprise me that I thoroughly enjoy the fair. At home that night I tell the unlucky ones all I can remember about the merry-go-round, the man who eats live chickens, and the teddy bears, until they say: that's enough, baby Alice. Shut up now, and go to sleep.

It is Easter Sunday, 1950. I am dressed in a green, flocked, scalloped-hem dress (handmade by my adoring sister, Ruth) that has its own smooth satin petticoat and tiny hot-pink roses tucked into each scallop. My shoes, new T-strap patent leather, again highly biscuit-polished. I am six years old and have learned one of the longest Easter speeches to be heard that day, totally unlike the speech I said when I was two: "Easter lilies/ pure and white/ blossom in/ the morning light." When I rise to give my speech I do so on a great wave of love and pride and expectation. People in the church stop rustling their new crinolines. They seem to hold their breath. I can tell they admire my dress, but it is my spirit, bordering on sassiness (womanishness), they secretly applaud.

"That girl's a little *mess*," they whisper to each other, pleased.

Naturally I say my speech without stammer or pause, unlike those who stutter, stammer, or, worst of all, forget. This is before the word "beautiful" exists in people's vocabulary, but "Oh, isn't she the *cutest* thing!" frequently floats my way. "And got so much sense!" they gratefully add . . . for which thoughtful addition I thank them to this day.

It was great fun being cute. But then, one day, it ended.

I am eight years old and a tomboy. I have a cowboy hat, cowboy boots, checkered shirt and pants, all red. My playmates are my brothers, two and four years older than I. Their colors are black and green, the only difference in the way we are dressed. On Saturday nights we all go to the picture show, even my mother; Westerns are her favorite kind of movie. Back home, "on the ranch," we pretend we are Tom Mix, Hopalong Cassidy, Lash LaRue (we've even named one of our dogs Lash LaRue); we chase each other for hours rustling cattle, being outlaws, delivering damsels from distress. Then my parents decide to buy my brothers guns. These are not "real" guns. They shoot "BBs," copper pellets my brothers say will kill birds. Because I am a girl, I do not get a gun. Instantly I am relegated to the position of Indian. Now there appears a great distance between us. They shoot and shoot at everything with their new guns. I try to keep up with my bow and arrows.

One day while I am standing on top of our makeshift "garage"—pieces of tin nailed across some poles—holding my bow and arrow and looking out toward the fields, I feel an incredible blow in my right eye. I look down just in time to see my brother lower his gun.

Both brothers rush to my side. My eye stings, and I cover it with my hand. "If you tell," they say, "we will get a whipping. You don't want that to happen, do you?" I do not. "Here is a piece of wire," says the older brother, picking it up from the roof; "say you stepped on one end of it and the other flew up and hit you." The pain is beginning to start. "Yes," I say. "Yes, I will say that is what happened." If I do not say this is what happened, I know my brothers will find ways to make me wish I had. But now I will say anything that gets me to my mother.

Confronted by our parents we stick to the lie agreed upon. They place me on a bench on the porch and I close my left eye while they examine the right. There is a tree growing from underneath the porch that climbs past the railing to the roof. It is the last thing my right eye sees. I watch as its trunk, its branches, and then its leaves are blotted out by the rising blood.

I am in shock. First there is intense fever, which my father tries to break using lily leaves bound around my head. Then there are chills: my mother tries to get me to eat soup. Eventually, I do not know how, my parents learn what has happened. A week after the "accident" they take me to see a doctor. "Why did you wait so long to come?" he asks, looking into my eye and shaking his head. "Eyes are sympathetic," he says. "If one is blind, the other will likely become blind too."

This comment of the doctor's terrifies me. But it is really how I look that bothers me most. Where the BB pellet struck there is a glob of whitish scar tissue, a hideous cataract, on my eye. Now when I stare at people—a favorite pastime, up to now—they will stare back. Not at the "cute" little girl, but at her

scar. For six years I do not stare at anyone, because I do not raise my head.

Years later, in the throes of a mid-life crisis, I ask my mother and sister whether I changed after the "accident." "No," they say, puzzled. "What do you mean?"

What do I mean?

I am eight, and, for the first time, doing poorly in school, where I have been something of a whiz since I was four. We have just moved to the place where the "accident" occurred. We do not know any of the people around us because this is a different county. The only time I see the friends I knew is when we go back to our old church. The new school is the former state penitentiary. It is a large stone building, cold and drafty, crammed to overflowing with boisterous, ill-disciplined children. On the third floor there is a huge circular imprint of some partition that has been torn out.

"What used to be here?" I ask a sullen girl next to me on our way past it to lunch.

"The electric chair," says she.

At night I have nightmares about the electric chair, and about all the people reputedly "fried" in it. I am afraid of the school, where all the students seem to be budding criminals.

"What's the matter with your eye?" they ask, critically.

When I don't answer (I cannot decide whether it was an "accident" or not), they shove me, insist on a fight.

My brother, the one who created the story about the wire, comes to my rescue. But then brags so much about "protecting" me, I become sick.

After months of torture at the school, my parents decide to send me back to our old community, to my old school. I live with my grandparents and the teacher they board. But there is no room for Phoebe, my cat. By the time my grandparents decide there *is* room, and I ask for my cat, she cannot be found. Miss Yarborough, the boarding teacher, takes me under her wing, and begins to teach me to play the piano. But soon she marries an African—a "prince," she says—and is whisked away to his continent.

At my old school there is at least one teacher who

loves me. She is the teacher who "knew me before I was born" and bought my first baby clothes. It is she who makes life bearable. It is her presence that finally helps me turn on the one child at the school who continually calls me "one-eyed bitch." One day I simply grab him by his coat and beat him until I am satisfied. It is my teacher who tells me my mother is ill.

My mother is lying in bed in the middle of the day, something I have never seen. She is in too much pain to speak. She has an abscess in her ear. I stand looking down on her, knowing that if she dies, I cannot live. She is being treated with warm oils and hot bricks held against her cheek. Finally a doctor comes. But I must go back to my grandparents' house. The weeks pass but I am hardly aware of it. All I know is that my mother might die, my father is not so jolly, my brothers still have their guns, and I am the one sent away from home.

"You did not change," they say.

Did I imagine the anguish of never looking up?

I am twelve. When relatives come to visit I hide in my room. My cousin Brenda, just my age, whose father works in the post office and whose mother is a nurse, comes to find me. "Hello," she says. And then she asks, looking at my recent school picture, which I did not want taken, and on which the "glob," as I think of it, is clearly visible, "You still can't see out of that eye?"

"No," I say, and flop back on the bed over my book.

That night, as I do almost every night, I abuse my eye. I rant and rave at it, in front of the mirror. I plead with it to clear up before morning. I tell it I hate and despise it. I do not pray for sight. I pray for beauty.

"You did not change," they say.

I am fourteen and baby-sitting for my brother Bill, who lives in Boston. He is my favorite brother and there is a strong bond between us. Understanding my feelings of shame and ugliness, he and his wife take me to a local hospital, where the "glob" is removed by a doctor named O. Henry. There is still a small bluish crater where the scar tissue was, but the ugly white stuff is gone. Almost immediately I became a different person from the girl who does not raise her head. Or so I think. Now that I've raised my head I win the boyfriend of my dreams. Now that I've raised my head I have plenty of friends. Now that I've raised my head classwork comes from my lips as faultlessly as Easter speeches did, and I leave high school as valedictorian, most popular student, and *queen,* hardly believing my luck. Ironically, the girl who was voted most beautiful in our class (and was) was later shot twice through the chest by a male companion, using a "real" gun, while she was pregnant. But that's another story in itself. Or is it?

"You did not change," they say.

It is now thirty years since the "accident." A beautiful journalist comes to visit and to interview me. She is going to write a cover story for her magazine that focuses on my latest book. "Decide how you want to look on the cover," she says. "Glamorous, or whatever."

Never mind "glamorous," it is the "whatever" that I hear. Suddenly all I can think of is whether I will get enough sleep the night before the photography session: if I don't, my eye will be tired and wander, as blind eyes will.

At night in bed with my lover I think up reasons why I should not appear on the cover of a magazine. "My meanest critics will say I've sold out," I say. "My family will now realize I write scandalous books."

"But what's the real reason you don't want to do this?" he asks.

"Because in all probability," I say in a rush, "my eye won't be straight."

"It will be straight enough," he says. Then, "Besides, I thought you'd made your peace with that."

And I suddenly remember that I have.

I remember:

I am talking to my brother Jimmy, asking if he remembers anything unusual about the day I was shot. He does not know I consider that day the last time my father, with his sweet home remedy of cool lily leaves, chose me, and that I suffered and raged inside because of this. "Well," he says, "all I remember is standing by the side of the highway with

Daddy, trying to flag down a car. A white man stopped, but when Daddy said he needed somebody to take his little girl to the doctor, he drove off."

I remember:

I am in the desert for the first time. I fall totally in love with it. I am so overwhelmed by its beauty, I confront for the first time, consciously, the meaning of the doctor's words years ago: "Eyes are sympathetic. If one is blind, the other will likely become blind too." I realize I have dashed about the world madly, looking at this, looking at that, storing up images against the fading of the light. *But I might have missed seeing the desert!* The shock of that possibility—and gratitude for over twenty-five years of sight—sends me literally to my knees. Poem after poem comes—which is perhaps how poets pray.

On Sight

I am so thankful I have seen
The Desert
And the creatures in the desert
And the desert itself.

The desert has its own moon
Which I have seen
With my own eye.
There is no flag on it.

Trees of the desert have arms
All of which are always up
That is because the moon is up
The sun is up
Also the sky
The stars
Clouds
None with flags.

If there *were* flags, I doubt
the trees would point.
Would you?

But mostly, I remember this:

I am twenty-seven, and my baby daughter is almost three. Since her birth I have worried about her discovery that her mother's eyes are different from other people's. Will she be embarrassed? I think. What will she say? Every day she watches a television program called "Big Blue Marble." It begins with a picture of the earth as it appears from the moon. It is bluish, a little battered-looking, but full of light, with whitish clouds swirling around it. Every time I see it I weep with love, as if it is a picture of Grandma's house. One day when I am putting Rebecca down for her nap, she suddenly focuses on my eye. Something inside me cringes, gets ready to try to protect myself. All children are cruel about physical differences, I know from experience, and that they don't always mean to be is another matter. I assume Rebecca will be the same.

But no-o-o-o. She studies my face intently as we stand, her inside and me outside her crib. She even holds my face maternally between her dimpled little hands. Then, looking every bit as serious and lawyerlike as her father, she says, as if it may just possibly have slipped my attention: "Mommy, there's a *world* in your eye." (As in, "Don't be alarmed, or do anything crazy.") And then, gently but with great interest: "Mommy, where did you *get* that world in your eye?"

For the most part, the pain left then. (So what, if my brothers grew up to buy even more powerful pellet guns for their sons and to carry real guns themselves. So what, if a young "Morehouse man" once nearly fell off the steps of Trevor Arnett Library because he thought my eyes were blue.) Crying and laughing I ran to the bathroom, while Rebecca mumbled and sang herself off to sleep. Yes indeed, I realized, looking into the mirror. There *was* a world in my eye. And I saw that it was possible to love it: that in fact, for all it had taught me of shame and anger and inner vision, I *did* love it. Even to see it drifting out of orbit in boredom, or rolling up out of fatigue, not to mention floating back at attention in excitement (bearing witness, a friend has called it), deeply suitable to my personality, and even characteristic of me.

That night I dream I am dancing to Stevie Wonder's song "Always" (the name of the song is really "As," but I hear it as "Always"). As I dance, whirling and joyous, happier than I've ever been in my life, another bright-faced dancer joins me. We dance and kiss each other and hold each other through the night. The other dancer has obviously come through all right, as I have done. She is beautiful, whole and free. And she is also me.   [1983]

Sexuality

Our sexual experiences, on both emotional and physical levels, are closely tied to what we learn about the meaning of sexuality and its relationship to other important dimensions of our lives. According to Virginia Reath, our fears, doubts, and expectations of sexuality reflect social and cultural messages of what it means to be female and sexual. As Sharon Thompson indicates, it is impossible to separate sexuality from other aspects of our relationships with one another. Lisa DeBoer considers the complexity of defining one's sexual identity and shares her experiences in this process.

The sexual experiences of lesbians are frequently ignored and/or dismissed in our society, which assumes that heterosexuality is the norm. Marilyn Frye examines the ways in which heterosexual definitions of sex are inappropriate for understanding lesbians' sexual relationships. She encourages lesbians to build a vocabulary that truly reflects the experiences of women loving women, to make meaningful discussions of sexuality possible.

Next, we explore emerging sexuality for heterosexual teen women. In "The Shame of Silence," a young woman recalls her early sexual experiences as a high school student in an affluent, Southern white community. Athena Devlin's account highlights the pervasive unchallenged power of boys, and the sometimes conflicting pressures on girls as they navigate the complex network of social expectations. Devlin speaks of the "bond of silence" that prevented young women in her school from challenging the sexism of teenage males. Recently, more and more young girls in junior high and high school have come forward with horrifying stories about sexual harassment and abuse, ranging from heckling to gang rape.

No discussion of contemporary sexuality would be complete without attention to the repercussions of AIDS on sexual attitudes and behaviors. In "Safe Sex Is Real Sex," Zoe Leonard explores some of the ways that AIDS has affected her sexual behavior. As she deals with the necessity of practicing safe sex, she presents strategies she has adopted that allow her to explore and enjoy her sexuality while also protecting her health.

What happens when women are able to move beyond the limited stereotypes of "acceptable" sexuality? The last two selections recount the experiences of women from different walks of life: one, a lesbian who is disabled; the other, an older African-American woman. The portrayal of these women as sexually active challenges the confining norms that our society proscribes for women's sexual behavior, and gives us a vision of the many possibilities that exist for the expression of women's sexuality.

39

Making the Sexual Revolution Work for Women

VIRGINIA REATH

Edited by Amy Kesselman

Sexuality encompasses far more than the genital activity of sex, with which it is often equated. It is a dynamic life force that is no more static than our physical growth patterns and is deeply connected to how we as human beings express ourselves; the way we express our sexuality changes throughout our lives. Although sex is thought to be "natural," our ideas and expectations about sex are socially constructed; we learn them through films, books, pornography, and in schoolyards. Like all socially constructed belief systems, ideas about sexuality have changed over time.

In the 1960s and 1970s, sexual ideas and practices underwent a radical change, a change that occurred on many levels. Abetted by the birth control pill, heterosexual couples flouted the taboos against premarital sex in unprecedented numbers. But while this "sexual revolution" made it acceptable to have heterosexual sex outside of marriage, it did not challenge the prevailing male-centered ideas about sexuality. In the 1970s, declaring that the "sexual revolution wasn't our war," activists and scholars from the feminist and lesbian and gay movements initiated the reevaluation of female sexuality. Their critique of the repressive nature of ideas about sexuality brought forth a revolution that continues to break apart myths and assumptions. They challenged the assumption that heterosexuality was the most natural form of sex, suggesting that it was not freely chosen in our society but coerced through injunctions against homosexuality; they declared that people had the right to choose their sexual partners among their own as well as the opposite sex. They championed women's right to sexual pleasure and denounced coercive sex. This movement was an attempt to redefine sex and sexuality; its clarion call was the right to

sexual pleasure: to pursue it, to write about it, to talk about it, and to experience it.

In particular, proponents of sexual liberty argued that the prevailing emphasis on penile-vaginal intercourse excluded a multitude of pleasurable experiences for women. In the early 1980s, Shere Hite's *The Hite Report* broke ground in revealing the unhealthy and unsatisfying sexual lives of many women. When women gave voice to their own experience in the pages of *The Hite Report* and in consciousness-raising groups around the country, the vaginal orgasm was dethroned and the clitoris was rediscovered. It seems odd that this organ, whose complex blood and nerve network make it the most responsive part of the female body, which serves no other function except to provide pleasure, had to be rediscovered. But it is not odd at all if we understand how threatening the female body can be to the society at large and how profoundly this knowledge challenges prevailing ideas about female sexuality. For two centuries a woman's sexuality had been defined in terms of her reproductive capacity. Denying the existence of the clitoris as a source of pleasure strengthened the link between sexuality and procreation for women and silenced women's dissatisfaction with sexual relationships.

The enormous amount of study and discussion of female sexuality that has taken place in the last thirty years, however, has not really made it out of the journals and conferences and into the bedrooms of most women. Our culture continues to bombard us with sexual images in which men are the subjects and women are the objects. These images affect all of us, but perhaps the people who are most vulnerable to them are adolescents. Although in theory adolescence is a time of self-discovery and growing autonomy, it is also a period in which young people are very vulnerable to the tyranny of cultural norms. Their fears of being rejected, disliked, teased, or disqualified are intensified. The question "Am I normal?" resounds in every teenager. This anxiety is often manifested in a cruel lack of tolerance for difference.

When we begin to relate sexually to others, we often feel as if we are playing a game with no rule book; the rules are there, but we have to discover them. We wonder what is normal and what isn't;

what is allowed and what isn't. In our need for certainty, we often adhere narrowly to sexual stereotypes in behavior and appearance without questioning their origins or reflecting on their implications for our lives. This contributes to the confusion and absence of pleasure that many young women experience during their first sexual encounter with a partner.

Even for women who are challenging the prevailing stereotypes of sexuality, pleasure can be an elusive goal because communication about sex is so difficult in our culture. The biological differences between men and women augment this problem by creating different expectations of sex. In general, the male response cycle is more rapid with orgasm coming sooner after arousal. Men often see penetration as the desired goal as soon as the penis becomes erect. However, the sexual response cycle of women is quite different. It usually takes women longer to experience orgasm but with continued attention to the clitoris, women can achieve multiple orgasms with brief intervals. When women are uncomfortable with the amount of time it takes to become aroused and achieve orgasm, they sometimes allow penetration before they are ready. This can result in vaginal pain and the absence of sexual pleasure. In the recent past, many women engaged in this kind of unsatisfying sex and experienced its repercussions: faked orgasm, sexual dysfunction, and being labeled frigid.

At this point in history, women are beginning to believe they have a right to pleasure and sexual fulfillment. But communicating about our sexual needs and desires remains difficult. One of the reasons for this difficulty is the inadequacy of our language. The available language for discussing sex is either clinical/medical or slang/pornographic. Clinical language seems unexciting and slang often has woman-hating connotations. These terms also limit sexual communication to genital organs and intercourse, and they can seem incapable of expressing intimacy and creating an atmosphere of trust and safety. Intimacy and trust develop out of self-respect and respect for the other. We need to develop a language that gives voice to a wide range of erotic activities, conveys respect as well as sexual energy, and is a meaningful vehicle for safe and trusting sexual play.

Can you list all the slang terms for male and female genitalia? What does this list convey?

But even if we have an adequate language, we need to figure out what we want to say. This is not as easy as it sounds, particularly for women, who have been taught to put aside our needs in order to care for others. To understand our sexual needs, we must discover and accept ourselves as sexual beings. This is a relatively new concept for women in Western culture. We are accustomed to seeing ourselves as dependent upon someone else for sexual satisfaction and abdicating responsibility in sexual matters. If we do not feel that we control our sexuality, it is inferred that it is not our own and can be taken, owned, used, and abused by others. This supposition has been harmful to all people but especially to women who for centuries were thought to be the property of men. Another dangerous myth is that women are responsible for male lust and its consequences. No man has ever died of "blue balls," but many women have suffered at the hands of men who could not take responsibility for their own sexual feelings. Both myths deny the basic truth that you *own your own body;* you are responsible for it; it has boundaries which *you* can define, and anyone who crosses them must have your consent.

These deep-seated ideas make it very difficult for women to claim their right to find out what they want sexually and ask for it. We can discover what we like through exploration of our bodies. Fortunately, today the taboo against female masturbation is less powerful than it was in the recent past. Masturbation requires no language, only the willingness to explore, and it can be a source of a great deal of information about what excites us. Communicating these discoveries to another person, however, collides with prevailing notions about the superiority of "natural" sex. Sex in our culture is supposed to be a matter of chemistry; we are all supposed to be like Adam and Eve and "just know"; we think the best sex is when we are "swept away." These seemingly romantic scripts have resulted in terrible consequences for women: pregnancy, disease, and emotional pain. They force us to rely on charades, telepathy, wishing and hoping, or silent waiting for our needs to be met.

For the sexual revolution to be meaningful for women, we need to talk to each other more about our sexual experiences and support each other's efforts to control our sexual lives. Essentially, the movement for sexual liberty is about people's right to create their sexual lives without fear of reprisal or discrimination. The freedom to express one's sexuality autonomously or in consensual relations with another person is important to fight for and to protect. We must guard this freedom vigilantly, questioning ideas and behaviors that serve to repress it and looking to our own experience for clues. Sexual ideas change with the tides of history; they are as susceptible to the influence of religion, culture, advertising, fashion, art, technology, politics, science, medicine, and education as we are, for they are part of us. By participating in the movement for sexual freedom in our daily lives, we become actors in this historical process.   [1992]

🌿 40

Reclaiming Our Bodies:
When the Personal
Is Political

SHARON R. THOMPSON

I am twenty-three, Black, feminist, single, celibate, heterosexual and thoroughly disgusted with men, patriarchy and sexism. How did I come to this place?

I remember at about eleven, cataloging all the ways my mother's and aunt's lives were more painful, literally and figuratively, than the men's lives—menstruation, pregnancy, childbirth, parenting, etc.—and wondering exactly why, in the face of all this, men were not far nicer to, if not in service of, women. It wasn't until I was in college that I realized there was a name for what I was feeling: feminism. There I threw away many of the restrictions and limitations the world had placed on me and began to discover and define myself as a Black woman.

I left college twenty-one, single and independent with a new understanding of what it meant to be Black and female in America. I was in control, confident and ready for the world.

Once in the world, I looked around and saw that in most heterosexual relationships, the woman is subjugated. Daily, I saw a million examples of violence against women ranging from blatant physical and verbal abuse to subtle manipulation. Even the rituals of heterosexual dating and courtship appear to serve men's needs and oppress women. I couldn't live with that. In addition, I began to know in a very real way that Black women are overlooked. Black women are nowhere in our culture's definitions of beauty, intelligence or success. Any billboard, movie or magazine beauty section proved that quite clearly. And just in case Black women somehow misunderstood those cues, Black men continually made the lesson clear when they chose white lovers, partners and wives.

In the "real world," I began to see the complex interconnections between the personal and political. Seemingly private decisions—who paid-for dinners; whether to keep, hyphenate or change the last name; what last name to give the children—were all connected to and reflective of greater societal issues. Similarly, larger issues like the absence of substantial, serious roles for women in film, or the universal use of the male pronoun in non-gender situations, which would appear to be unrelated to me, have a very real impact on my day-to-day living. Recognizing the very pervasiveness of oppression, I had to do something.

So I am twenty-three, thoroughly disgusted with men, patriarchy and sexism, celibate and feminist. Some days I long for the ability to deny the pain that I see in the faces and lives of other women. I ache for the skills that would allow me to ignore women's bodies being sold daily along with beer, cars and sports magazines; the tools that would help me to shut out the knowledge that none of the bodies, the sexiness, the beauty being sold included anything that I could ever achieve, even in unreality. Black women had been dismissed as "less than" from the start. I long to be able to go to school, to work, get married and raise a family without the constant awareness that sexism, racism, homophobia and capitalism are killing me and will kill my daughters.

But I do know and I can't go back. I can't *live* in that place, so what can I do here? What are the options for an educated Black, radical, feminist, heterosexual woman who wants to get married and have children? Where in the world does she live and love? Am I one of a kind or am I one of a generation of educated Black women who are realizing that our freedom and our very lives require education and political consciousness but our education and political consciousness keep us from participating fully in the life that exists?

In this place where I've found myself, my mind is freer to realize my own intelligence, beauty and worth and to appreciate that of other women. I *can* live here, but *how* do I live here? How do I live here without many of the things that define our society and culture? What of marriage and family? Are those lost to me now that I have arrived here? Perhaps the world will catch up. Perhaps there is a community where I can be and live.

I am beginning to think that mothers are more insightful than I realized. I have discovered what mothers may have been saying for generations. Perhaps "wait until your wedding night" might be restated as, "don't compromise, wait until you find the person, the relationship that allows *you* to *be*."

So, as most of us often find ourselves, I'm finally listening to my mother. I am waiting, waiting for that person, those people, that time when social interaction and cultural values are not so contaminated with oppression, where *I* can *be*. I have no idea what I am going to do here until then, besides hope that my daughters will find this story an interesting but remote artifact of my past.   [1992]

🌿 41

Living My Life: Thoughts on Sexual Identity

LISA DEBOER

"When we define ourselves, when I define myself, the place in which I am like you and the place in which I am not like you, I'm not excluding you from the joining—I'm broadening the joining."[1] In this quotation, Audre Lorde speaks about the existence of difference among people, and the meaning of self-definition. Although her statement seems obvious to me now, I couldn't fully understand it until I experienced the process of defining my own sexual identity. I've spent a lot of time thinking about sexual identity, and my thoughts have developed over the years as I've been exposed to various theories, ideas, and experiences.

All of my life I've had sexual feelings and attraction to women and to men. It never seemed strange, or felt like a problem. I joined my friends in heterosexual talk about boys, and read books about teenage girls and their boyfriends. I also read books about girls having deep friendships with other girls, and even crushes on them. I had crushes on female friends and teachers, the Beatles, and Adam Ant. As I grew older, my high school friends were people who accepted differences in sexual orientation. Within my group we were bisexual, straight, and gay: my first boyfriend told me he was bisexual, and later announced he was gay. In this supportive atmosphere, I began coming out publicly as bisexual. I felt that people's sex didn't matter to me; I was interested in them as people. I felt very comfortable with myself and my identity.

One day one of my friends told me she thought she was a lesbian. She was apprehensive and unsure, but willing to accept it. Because she had few lesbian or bisexual role models, she had difficulty interpreting her feelings towards women. She thought that if she had *any* interest in women, she must be a lesbian. In the ensuing months, she alternated between periods of being single and having boyfriends. When she was single, she called herself a lesbian. When she had boyfriends, she stopped talking about it. As she became more aware of her own feelings and desires, she accepted the fact that she was attracted to both men and women. She realized that her anxiety came from trying to make herself fit into a label that wasn't right for her. Through self-awareness, she succeeded in finding a way of expressing her sexual identity. She is presently a blissful bisexual activist.

Leaving my supportive environment behind, I ventured into the realm of college life. At my predominantly conservative midwestern state university, I lived a double life, with separate gay and straight worlds. For the first time in my life I met *lots* of lesbians and became involved with a thriving lesbian community. There were few other bisexuals around. During this time, I was often afraid to come out as bisexual. Rather than announce my identity, I allowed each community to assume I was just like them. Prejudices against bisexuals and fear of exclusion from both communities influenced my decision to remain silent. Eventually I did come out to people close to me, and though I was not ostracized, I found little open support for bisexuality.

As a bisexual, I came across most of the current stereotypes and misconceptions in both the straight and gay communities. While there is a multitude of ways these ideas are expressed, they fall into two main categories. The first consists of the denial of bisexual existence. People who spend part of their lives as bisexuals and then change to another orientation are often cited as proof that bisexuality is a transition phase or a denial of one's "true" identity. The second type of misconception is the belief that bisexuals do exist, but are dangerous, unhealthy, untrustworthy, perverse, desperate, and so on. Many people say they would never date a bisexual, because they assume all bisexuals have an inherent need to have someone of each sex all the time, and are therefore unfaithful.

While these stereotypes may be true for certain individuals, they hardly represent all bisexual people. Because bisexuality is not a polar opposite, like heterosexuality and homosexuality, it's harder to define. Bisexuals have fewer role models and less visibility than homosexuals and heterosexuals. In reality, there are many ways that people are bisexual, and for many people it is the healthiest, happiest, and most comfortable way for them to live.

As I encountered these prejudices, I discovered just how hard it is to maintain a bisexual identity in our society. The constant distortion, trivialization, and invalidation of bisexual existence can really wear a person down. One of the clearest societal messages is "Why don't you just choose? Why do you have to have both?" As I struggled against such restrictions, I wished everyone were bisexual—it would make everything so much easier! I fought for bisexual rights, advocated my bisexual identity, and promoted bisexual visibility.

Meanwhile, I studied feminist theory in my classes, and began to see sexual identity not as an innate trait that one discovers, but as socially constructed. Adrienne Rich's essay "Compulsory Heterosexuality and Lesbian Existence" had a particularly powerful effect on my thinking. Rich suggests that heterosexuality, rather than being an inevitable, natural form of sexual behavior, is taught and reinforced by a social structure in which bonding between women represents a threat to male power. I began to think about actively resisting the social pressure to be heterosexual. The idea of consciously shaping my own sexual identity fascinated me. If sexual identity is not biologically predetermined, it is fluid and changeable. We might change from heterosexual to lesbian to bisexual, or bisexual to lesbian, or any other possibility, as we move through our lives.

By my senior year, several major changes had occurred in my life. I had transferred college twice, and chosen a major in Women's Studies. I had relationships with both men and women that led me to look more closely at my sexual identity. The possibility of becoming a lesbian became all the more real. I realized that I felt a strong commitment to women, and felt myself to be women-identified. I began to shift from seeing myself as a person attracted to people regardless of gender, to someone who preferred women but was also attracted to men. I felt like I wanted to be a lesbian, and I felt like I *was* a lesbian—even though I was still sleeping with a man. The contradiction was almost too much for me, and I would stay up late ranting to my roommate about the disadvantages and limitations of these labels. Throughout this time I grappled with my sexual identity, and the thought of being both lesbian and heterosexual at the same time.

So why confine ourselves to terms like lesbian, straight, and bisexual? Why not be comfortable with broader definitions and concepts of sexuality? In an ideal world, each individual would choose lovers based on their own individual preference, and there would be no need for labels. But in this world, people are judged by their sexual orientation. Lesbians, gays, and bisexuals suffer from many forms of discrimination; they are denied jobs, housing, and child custody, are beaten and sometimes even killed.

We need to be able to organize politically and fight for our rights as lesbian, gay, and bisexual people. Labels can be personally and politically liberating, as a way for someone to publicly say, "This is who I am and who I love," despite society's hatred. As individuals openly speak about homosexuality and bisexuality, they challenge bigotry and homophobia by making others aware of our existence and our need for society to acknowledge and defend our civil and human rights. Labels also serve social and personal functions, by giving people a shorthand method of communicating preferences and potential availability. We can recognize each other and form communities more easily by using standard terms to describe our sexual orientation.

As I analyzed the functions of labels, I struggled to see what it could do for me in my own life. I still felt uneasy with the labels, despite my understanding of why they exist and why they are useful. I felt as if I didn't fit any of the labels, but I still wanted to find a way to describe my sexual identity to others. Then one night, while raving to my patient and understanding roommate, I experienced a revelation. The problem was in my perception of the relationship between identity and labels. In order to find a label that worked for me, I had to understand that labels serve many functions, but they do not define a person's entire identity. Identity is complex, and exists independently from terms used to describe it. Labels are the beginning of communication, not the end.

My bisexuality has changed into something quite different from my high school days, so now I call myself and identify as a lesbian. My primary interest is in women; men will always be my close friends, but it's extremely unlikely that any of them will be my lovers. However, I have not always been a lesbian, and the future is always uncertain. Bisexuality is an important part of my life that I don't want to forget, and I want others to know of it as well. So although I use the word lesbian to describe myself, I am aware that bisexuality remains an integral part of me.

Describing a self-defined sexual identity to other people can be difficult. While I have a clear understanding of who I am, it's not always easy to express it to others. It can be threatening enough to come out to someone else when you have a label to use and be understood; it's especially difficult when you have to come out and at the same time build a vocabulary with them in order to explain where you're coming from. It takes more energy and effort, and there's no guarantee that people will be able to understand. But it's worth it: through speaking the truth of our lives, we break the silences that keep us separated from each other.

While my story describes my experience and viewpoint, other people have different experiences of sexual orientation. Some people have the same sexual identity for their entire lives. For many people, claiming an identity as lesbian, gay, or bisexual is a positive experience that strengthens their sense of self. I hope to convey the idea that we each can come to our own understanding of our sexual identity, and that the discoveries we make based on our own experience are what matter most for our own happiness.

Living a self-defined life is challenging, as other people and society at large try to pigeonhole us all. But despite the problems, it's the most satisfying way for me to live. I've given up letting other people tell me who I am and what I'm allowed to do. I owe it to myself to be as fully me as I can, and not let other people's fears and insecurities limit me. I'm much happier now, and I feel in control of my life and more aware than ever of my possibilities. My horizons are broader, as I no longer feel limited by labels for my sexual identity. And my future options are all open; like my high school friends, my sexual orientation is something that can change and grow with me. I've realized I can continue to define my own life, and be true to the voice within me that strives to speak independently while living my life.

NOTES

1. From an interview in *The Feminist Renaissance. Sister Outsider, Essays and Speeches* by Audre Lorde. The Crossing Press, 1984.

Many thanks and hugs and kisses to Dawne Moon, Jerome O'Neill, Erin Clark, Kelly Scanlan and Joel Greenberg for their support and assistance in writing this paper.   [1993]

🌿 42

Lesbian "Sex"*

MARILYN FRYE

The reasons the word "sex" is in quotation marks in my title are two: one is that the term "sex" is an inappropriate term for what lesbians do, and the other is that whatever it is that lesbians do that (for a lack of a better word) might be called "sex" we apparently do damned little of it. For a great many lesbians, the gap between the high hopes we had some time ago for lesbian sex and the way things have worked out has turned the phrase "lesbian sex" into something of a bitter joke. I don't want to exaggerate this: things aren't so bad for all lesbians, or all of the time. But in our communities as a whole, there is much grumbling on the subject. It seems worthwhile to explore some of the meanings of the relative dearth of what (for lack of a better word) we call lesbian "sex."

Recent discussions of lesbian "sex" frequently cite the finding of a study on couples by Blumstein and Schwartz,[1] which is perceived by most of those who discuss it as having been done well, with a good sample of couples—lesbian, male homosexual, heterosexual non-married and heterosexual married couples. These people apparently found that lesbian couples "have sex" far less frequently than any other type of couple, that lesbian couples are less "sexual" as couples and as individuals than anyone else. In their sample, only about one-third of lesbians in relationships of two years or longer "had sex" once a week or more; 47% of lesbians in long-term relationships "had sex" once a month or less, while among heterosexual married couples only 15% had sex once a month or less. And they report that les-

bians seem to be more limited in the range of their "sexual" techniques than are other couples.

When this sort of information first came into my circle of lesbian friends, we tended to see it as conforming to what we know from our own experience. But on reflection, looking again at what has been going on with us in our long-term relationship, the nice fit between this report and our experience seemed not so perfect after all.

It was brought to our attention during our ruminations on this that what 85% of long-term heterosexual married couples do more than once a month takes on the average 8 minutes to do.[2]

Although in my experience lesbians discuss their "sex" lives with each other relatively little (a point to which I will return), I know from my own experience and from the reports of a few other lesbians in long-term relationships, that what we do that, on average, we do considerably less frequently, takes, on average, considerably more than 8 minutes to do. It takes about 30 minutes, at the least. Sometimes maybe an hour. And it is not uncommon that among these relatively uncommon occurrences, an entire afternoon or evening is given over to activities organized around doing it. The suspicion arises that what 85% of heterosexual married couples are doing more than once a month and what 47% of lesbian couples are doing less than once a month is not the same thing.

I remember that one of my first delicious tastes of old gay lesbian culture occurred in a bar where I was getting acquainted with some new friends. One was talking about being busted out of the Marines for being gay. She had been put under suspicion somehow, and was sent off to the base psychiatrist to be questioned, her perverted tendencies to be assessed. He wanted to convince her she had only been engaged in a little youthful experimentation and wasn't really gay. To this end, he questioned her about the extent of her experience. What he asked was, "How many times have you had sex with a woman?" At this, we all laughed and giggled: what an ignorant fool. What does he think he means, "times?" What will we count? What's to *count*?

Another of my friends, years later, discussing the same conundrum, said that she thought maybe every time you got up to go the bathroom, that marked a "time." The joke about "how many times" is still

---

*When I speak of "we" and "our communities," I actually don't know exactly who that is. I know only that I and my lover are not the only ones whose concerns I address, and that similar issues are being discussed in friendship circles and communities other than ours (as witness, e.g., discussion in the pages of the *Lesbian Connection*). If what I say here resonates for you, so be it. If not, at least you can know it resonates for some range of lesbians and some of them probably are your friends or acquaintances.

good for a chuckle from time to time in my life with my lover. I have no memory of any such topic providing any such merriment in my years of sexual encounters and relationships with men. It would have been very rare indeed that we would not have known how to answer the question "How many times did you do it?"

If what heterosexual married couples do that the individuals report under the rubric "sex" or "have sex" or "have sexual relations" is something that in most instances can easily be individuated into countable instances, this is more evidence that it is not what long-term lesbian couples do . . . or, for that matter, what short-term lesbian couples do.*

What violence did the lesbians do their experience by answering the same question the heterosexuals answered, as though it had the same meaning for them? How did the lesbians figure out how to answer the questions "How frequently?" or "How many times?" My guess is that different individuals figured it out differently. Some might have counted a two- or three-cycle evening as one "time" they "had sex"; some might have counted it as two or three "times." Some may have counted as "times" only the times both partners had orgasms; some may have counted as "times" occasions on which at least one had an orgasm; those who do not have orgasms or have them far more rarely than they "have sex" may not have figured orgasms into the calculations; perhaps some counted as a "time" every episode in which both touched the other's vulva more than fleetingly and not for something like a health examination. For some, to count every reciprocal touch of the vulva would have made them count as "having sex" more than most people with a job or a work would dream of having time for; how do we suppose those individuals counted "times"? Is there any good reason why they should *not* count all those as "times"? Does it depend on how fulfilling it was? Was anybody else counting by occasions of fulfillment?

We have no idea how the individual lesbians surveyed were counting their "sexual acts." But this also raises the questions of how heterosexuals counted *their* sexual acts. By orgasms? By *whose* orgasms? If the havings of sex by heterosexual married couples did take on the average 8 minutes, my guess is that in a very large number of those cases the women did not experience orgasms. My guess is that neither the women's pleasure nor the women's orgasms were pertinent in most of the individuals' counting and reporting the frequency with which they "had sex."

So, do lesbian couples really "have sex" any less frequently than heterosexual couples? I'd say that lesbian couples "have sex" a great deal less frequently than heterosexual couples: by the criteria that I'm betting most of the heterosexual people used to count "times," lesbians don't have sex at all. No male orgasms, no "times." (I'm willing to draw the conclusion that heterosexual women don't have sex either; that what they report is the frequency with which their partners had sex.)

It has been said before by feminists that the concept of "having sex" is a phallic concept; that it pertains to heterosexual intercourse, in fact, primarily to heterosex*ist* intercourse, i.e., male-dominant-female-subordinate-copulation-whose-completion-and-purpose-is-the-male's-ejaculation. I have thought this was true since the first time the idea was put to me, some 12 years ago.[3] But I have been finding lately that I have to go back over some of the ground I covered a decade ago because some of what I knew then I knew too superficially. For some of us, myself included, the move from heterosexual relating to lesbian relating was occasioned or speeded up or brought to closure by our knowledge that what we had done under the heading "having sex" was indeed male-dominant-female-subordination-copulation-whose-completion . . . etc. and it was not worthy of doing. Yet now, years later, we are willing to answer questionnaires that ask us how frequently we "have sex," and are dissatisfied with ourselves and with our relationships because we don't "have sex" enough. We are so dissatisfied that we keep a small army of therapists in business trying to help us "have sex" more.

We quit having sex years ago, and for excellent and compelling reasons. What exactly is our complaint now? . . .*

---

*This is the term used in the Blumstein and Schwartz questionnaire. In the text of their book, they use "have sex."

*Several pages that appeared in the original text have been omitted in this excerpt. The ideas discussed in the deleted passages are summarized in the following paragraph.

For some lesbians, using the words "sex" and "sexual" has led us to think and talk about ourselves in terms of a model that doesn't fit us—a model that best fits male experience. This may actually restrict our activities and our inventiveness, and it keeps us from developing a vocabulary that *does* fit us. And then, our lack of vocabulary interferes with our mutual communication and hence, our pleasure. . . .

My positive recommendation is this: Instead of starting with a point (a point in the life of a body unlike our own) and trying to make meanings along vectors from that point, we would do better to start with a wide field of our passions and bodily pleasures and make meanings that weave a web across it. To begin creating a vocabulary that elaborates and expands our meanings, we should adopt a very wide and general concept of "doing it." Let it be an open, generous, commodious concept encompassing all the acts and activities by which we generate with each other pleasures and thrills, tenderness and ecstasy, passages of passionate carnality of whatever duration or profundity. Everything from vanilla to licorice, from puce to chartreuse, from velvet to ice, from cuddles to cunts, from chortles to tears. Starting from there, we can let our experiences generate a finer-tuned descriptive vocabulary that maps and expresses the differences and distinctions among the things we do, the kinds of pleasures we get, the stages and styles of our acts and activities, the parts of our bodies centrally engaged in the different kinds of "doing it," and so on. I would not, at the outset, assume that all of "doing it" is good or wholesome, nor that everyone would like or even tolerate everything this concept includes; I would not assume that "doing it" either has or should have a particular connection with love, or that it hasn't or shouldn't have such a connection. As we explain and explore and define our pleasures and our preferences across this expansive and heterogeneous field, teaching each other what the possibilities are and how to navigate them, a vocabulary will arise among us and by our collective creativity.

The vocabulary will arise among us, of course, only if we talk with each other about what we're doing and why, and what it feels like. Language is social. So is "doing it."

I'm hoping it will be a lot easier to talk about what we do, and how and when and why, and in carnal sensual detail, once we've learned to laugh at foolish studies that show that lesbians don't have sex as often as, aren't as sexual as, and use fewer sexual techniques than other folks.

NOTES

This essay first appeared in *Sinister Wisdom,* vol. 35 (Summer/Fall 1988). In its first version, this essay was written for the meeting of the Society for Women in Philosophy, Midwestern Division, November, 1987, at Bloomington, Indiana. It was occasioned by Claudia Card's paper, "Intimacy and Responsibility: What Lesbians Do," (Published in the Institute for Legal Studies Working Papers, Series 2, University of Wisconsin-Madison, Law School, Madison, WI 53706). Carolyn Shafer has contributed a lot to my thinking here, and I am indebted also to conversations with Sue Emmert and Terry Grant.

1. Philip Blumstein and Pepper Schwartz, *American Couples* (NY: William Morrow and Company, 1983).
2. Dotty Calabrese gave this information in her workshop on long-term lesbian relationships at the Michigan Woman's Music Festival, 1987. (Thanks to Terry for this reference.)
3. By Carolyn Shafer. See pp. 156–7 of my book *The Politics of Reality* (The Crossing Press, 1983). [1989]

🌿 43

The Shame of Silence

ATHENA DEVLIN

As in every high school, there was in mine a set of especially powerful boys who were "popular." At my school in Texas, they were all football stars. When I was a freshman, and dying to make a good impression, I was invited by one of them to come over to his house to watch television. I don't think I will ever be able to forget (much to my embarrassment these days) how excited I was. By the time I left my house, my room looked like a clothes bomb had exploded in it. I was smiling from ear to ear, probably having visions of becoming a cheerleader. I forgot to ask myself *why* he had called me. I forgot to remember that I was *not* what you would call a popular girl. I rang his doorbell with a pounding heart and ridiculous aspirations. Bill let me in and led me into the living room. There, sitting on couches, were about eight boys. They were all watching a porno film on the VCR. They looked at me with open dislike and said "hi" pretty much in unison. I just stood there, frozen with disappointment while a blond woman acted out ecstasy on the television screen. No one spoke. After what seemed like a very long time, I turned away and walked into the kitchen just off the living room and sat at the table. I was embarrassed by my expectations. I felt like I had forgotten my "place." Now I remembered. I knew why I had been invited over. Bill let me stay in the kitchen by myself for about 20 minutes. When he finally walked in he just looked at me and said "You wanna go outside?" I said yes because it felt like the only way out. We went out to his back yard; to reclining deck chairs by a lit pool. We started making out. His hands were everywhere, his breath stank. I felt worthless and just let it happen. Then, when he leaned over to get to the hook of my bra, I looked up and there they all were, all eight of them standing on the second floor balcony watching us. I started yelling. Bill didn't say anything. He didn't tell them to go away, he didn't offer me an explanation. I suddenly got the feeling that it had all been planned this way. I was trying to stand and get my shirt back on when Bill took my hand and pulled me behind a fence at the back of the yard. When we got there, he turned and told me he wanted a hand job. I gave him one and left. I felt only one thing, and it wasn't anger; it was shame.

To be a "successful" girl in Highland Park was to be successful with boys. So, undeniably the girls that I grew up with viewed each other as less important than the boys they dated and more often than not, as would-be enemies. Nothing was ever as important as being accepted by men. And this, quite effectively, alienated us from one another. The key to success with boys in my high school was having the right kind of reputation, and reputation for a girl was for the most part focused narrowly on her looks and her sexual life. Importantly, it was the boys who decided what "type" a girl was sexually—which, in a social setting like this one, gave them a lot of power. What put them in this position was exactly that thing the girls lacked: each other. Maybe it was from all those hours of football practice where they had to depend on one another that did it, or maybe it was just because they felt important enough not to seek female approval as desperately as we sought theirs that made some sort of solidarity among them more

possible. But in any event, it was to their distinct advantage. For girls, trying to please the powers that be was very confusing because we were supposed to be attractive and sexually exciting in order to be accepted, while simultaneously prudish and innocent. We were supposed to be sweet and deferential towards them but we were also supposed to be able to stop them when they went too far. I suppose I never got that delicate balance down. I got one side of the equation but not the other.

Not surprisingly, then, the shame I felt by having been treated as worthless by boys was something I desperately wanted to *hide*. I had failed, it seemed in the most important way. I never told any of my girl friends about that night and, because of my shame, which covered everything, I wasn't even really aware of my anger, and it certainly did not occur to me to *show* any anger towards these boys. I had never heard a girl publicly denounce a boy for his behavior towards her, though I had seen many a girl be thoroughly disgraced in those hallways of Highland Park High. So, when the story of my night with the football stars got passed along by the boys, the girls who heard about it never tried to comfort me. They whispered about me instead, often to the very boys that had been involved. They were gaining points by disassociating themselves from me, because I was the one at fault. Boys will be boys after all. It's the girls who say yes that were held accountable at my high school—by both sexes.

About six months later when my reputation as a "slut" had been firmly established, I began hanging out with a girl named Cindy who had a similar public identity. Some of the boys from the group that participated in that horrible night often asked us out when their regular girl friends were away or safely tucked behind curfews. I usually said no, although I occasionally agreed because going out with them still felt like a form of acceptance. At least they thought I was pretty enough to make out with. But Cindy went out with them a lot. One Friday night something happened. To this day I do not know what actually went on (no surprise). I just knew she was upset and the following Monday, Will, one of the boys she went out with, started hassling her in the hall. She began to cry in the middle of passing period with everyone staring. Suddenly, and for the first time, I felt incredibly angry and before fear held me back, I began to yell at Will. I don't remember what I said exactly, but it was something to the effect of who did he think he was, and that I thought he was an asshole. I don't think he had ever been so surprised. He stared at me in complete amazement. And so did Cindy. Unfortunately, it didn't take him too long to recover and he told me in a voice loud enough for everyone in the building to hear, that I was a whore and everyone knew it, that I would sleep with anyone (I was still a virgin at the time), and that I was completely disgusting. The contempt in his voice was incredible. I started to feel ashamed again. One did not have scenes like this at Highland Park. But the surprise was Cindy hated me for it. In her opinion I had done an unforgivable thing in sticking up for her. And, what I learned was that girls didn't want each other's protection because it made them less attractive to boys. They feared focusing on each other too much.

For me, however, this incident was a turning point because afterwards these boys left me alone completely. I was released from the painful confusion of boys wanting me and disliking me at the same time—ignoring me or talking about me behind my back and then calling me up late on Friday night. I had yelled at a football star in front of everyone. That made me completely unacceptable as opposed to only marginally so. People began to make sure they didn't cross my path. I was left alone. Moreover, I was feared. It was then that I began to realize just how much the boys depended on the girls not do anything to defend themselves, that they depended heavily on our passivity. I saw that they lived in fear of us taking action. Any action. And I began to suspect that the isolation I noticed so many of the girls at my high school in Dallas feeling served a purpose useful enough to be a consequence of deliberateness. Still, I never made another scene.

But that was not really the greatest tragedy. Rather it was, and is, that girls grow up not knowing each other very well. And that while going through the same things, they are without both the benefit of each other's comfort and understanding, and more vulnerable to abuse. I am close to only one girl who went to high school with me, and that is probably only because we ended up at the same college. When I told her about writing this essay she told me, for the first time, some of her experiences at High-

land Park. They were as tortured and humiliating as mine, but I had never heard her stories before and she had never heard mine. High school obviously wasn't a great experience for either of us, and while we sat there tracing the damage through to our present lives, I desperately wished it had been different. And it could have been if we could have shaken off the terrible trap of shame and talked about our lives and found ways to support each other. It seems clear to me now that not only were the boys protecting each other, but we girls were protecting the boys through the silence that existed between us. [1992]

 44

Safe Sex Is Real Sex

ZOE LEONARD

I have a lover who is HIV positive.

I am HIV negative.

I want to talk about my experience with safe sex and loving someone who is HIV positive.

Safe sex is often spoken about as a major drag . . . necessary, but fundamentally unerotic. People never seem to say, "Yeah, I do this with my lover and it's really hot."

Well, I do it with my lover and it's really hot.

I knew he was HIV positive before I slept with him. I had felt surprised when I found out; he just looked so damned healthy. I didn't envision having a sexual relationship with him, mainly because I've been an out and happy lesbian for years. So, when we realized we had crushes on each other, it was a big shock and really scary. I was doing AIDS activism and supposedly I knew all about safe sex, but suddenly I couldn't remember what I knew. All the grey areas of "low-risk" and "safer" sex seemed unclear and menacing; was kissing really OK? Secret fears snuck in. What if everyone is wrong about safe sex, about saliva? I felt I couldn't ask about these scary thoughts, like I should know the answers and had no right to feel so threatened. I didn't want to reinforce the stigma that he fights: feeling infectious, reading about himself as an "AIDS carrier." It had been relatively easy to be supportive and accepting of my friends with AIDS, to be sex positive, to talk about safe sex, but now it was in my bedroom, and I'm wondering: can he put his finger inside me without a glove, can he go down on me, can I touch his penis? Safe sex is different when you know your partner is infected. I don't want to appear frightened. I don't want to make him feel bad by talking about it, but I really, really don't want to get infected. (I tested negative for HIV about two years ago, and swore that I would never again place myself at any risk whatsoever.) And, here I was, a dyke at that, kissing this man goodnight after our first date.

In the beginning I was overwhelmed, terrified after that first kiss. So, we didn't dive right into bed and "do the nasty." We took our time and messed around for months, figuring out what we were comfortable with. It was great, all that sex building up. I always came, but we never did anything outside the strictest confines of "no risk" sex without talking about it first. We talked a lot about limits and seeing each other's points of view: my understanding that he doesn't want to feel like a pariah, or like he represents disease, his understanding that I had a right to be frightened, cautious, curious. It is important that I never do anything out of pressure, out of a need to prove that I'm not prejudiced. I realize that, as much as he cares about my health, I have to decide for myself what is safe, and stick to it. I knew I would resent him if we did something I wasn't sure about, and I would fly into a panic the next day.

I also realize that he is at risk for any infection that I might be carrying, and that safe sex is to protect him, too. A mild infection that might be harmless to me could be devastating to him.

I'm afraid of making him sick. I had hepatitis this summer, and we were worried that I might give it to him. Hepatitis can be very dangerous to anyone with an impaired immune system. I felt frightened and guilty. Later on I got angry that my *being* sick was somewhat overlooked in the panic surrounding the possibility of his *getting* sick. I found myself anxious and worried about his health at a time when I needed comfort and care. Sometimes I don't feel legitimate in feeling sorry for myself or being concerned about my own health.

A great thing about safe sex is that we . . . don't have intercourse all the time. We get off a lot of different ways, so our sex is varied and we don't just fall into one pattern.

The main thing is not to form a hierarchy of what "real sex" is, or equate "real sex" with high-risk practices. We can't think that humping is fake and intercourse is real.

Condoms are great. They are really sexy to me now, like lingerie or the perfume of a lover. Maybe I'm just immature, or particularly responsive to Pavlovian training, but the mere sight of condoms, lube, or dental dams sends a sexy feeling through me. The tools of safe sex become as significant and fetishized as other toys for pleasure. I'm always hearing about how condoms and other latex barriers take away all the spontaneity, as if sex before AIDS was always spontaneous and perfect. There are many barriers to good sex, like being too anxious, too busy, or too tired, or the *phone ringing*, or not finding someone you want to have sex with in the first place.

You can use safe sex to tease each other, waiting until you want something really badly before you screw up the courage to ask for it (or beg for it). Then you stop, and hang in this state of anticipation, feeling like a teenager, waiting while he (for instance) gets the first condom out, squirts the lube in it, and gets it on. Then he gets the second condom out and on. It's tense and full of anticipation, and I rarely feel either of us cooling off. It can be exciting to admit what you want, to articulate it, and to know what your partner wants, and to use the confines of safe sex to create tension and escalate desire.

Also, it can be a gift, like the time we went away for the weekend and he showed up with a shopping bag full of every form of latex known to humankind. It's a way of showing that you care about someone's health, and that you want him or her to be considerate and romantic at the same time.

We've had to negotiate so many aspects of our relationship that otherwise might have remained mute, but this has given us the context to discuss other things: what feels good, what we want, what freaks us out. The need to figure all those things out has built trust between us; it's made us honest.

But divisions do occur between the sick and the well. My lover is asymptomatic, so HIV often seems like an abstract issue to me. When I'm talking about something in the future, he blurts out, "I don't know if I'll be alive in five years." Can I understand the depression? I feel guilty sometimes and cut off other times.

It's one thing to learn to [have safe sex] and quite another to feel committed to someone that you are afraid might get really sick or die. I think: can I do it? Will I have the patience, will I be adequate? What if he really does get sick, what then? . . . can I handle feeling this responsible? Do I want to take care of him? And what if he really does die? What about that?

I've had friends die of AIDS. I have visceral memories of Dan in the hospital just before he died, massaging his feet, feeling the thick lumps of KS lesions through his sweat socks. I remember him semiconscious, making noises, responding to the pressure of my hands, his lover saying yes, he likes that.

I was once very much in love with a woman who got cancer. For a year my whole world telescoped into just her room, her health. My life was filled with nightmares and worrying, cooking, obsessing. My days were spent in the hospital, knowing the staff, being a regular. I knew every detail of her treatment, read all the articles, took notes. Running into friends, everyone would ask, "How's Simone?" People stopped asking, "How are you?" There was a certain relief in turning myself over to this greater cause, where everything was always about her— humidifiers, macrobiotic food, appointments. Even now, we are friends, and still there is a subtext: will she get sick again, will she die?

I wonder, do I just thrive on drama? Do I have a martyr complex, or a death wish? Did I fall for him because of his status? Do I want to get infected; is this my most recent and subtle form of self-destruction? Friends and family are anxious, ask me about *it*. They tell me I'm crazy, and speak of illness and health in hushed tones.

And I have to admit, after all these months, sometimes I'm still scared. I see an article and I think, could I be the first case of saliva transmission? Why am I still scared? I forget for weeks, and then when I get sick, feverish, peaked, HIV is there like a threat. I worry secretly, and when I tell him, he's angry, defensive.

All around us, his friends, my friends, into the hospital, out of the hospital, dying. When will it start with him? He gets a cold, the flu. He's tired, glands swollen.

I hate this virus.

This started out to be about the joys of safe sex, but I guess it's complicated.

I am HIV negative, as of my last test. I've learned a lot and had some really hot sex and lots of flirty, sexy stuff, and there's been a lot of love and happiness in this relationship. There's a difference between rational fears and irrational ones. I try to act on the rational ones. I try to protect myself and my lover from real threats, and try to overcome the irrational fears.

You *can* make decisions about your life and love based on what you want, and not let illness, or fear of illness, make all the decisions for you.   [1990]

Demanding a Condom

KAT DOUD

Before I understood AIDS, who got it, and how it could be prevented, I was scared, really scared. I felt at risk but for the wrong reasons. I was afraid of casual contact with people instead of being afraid of having unsafe sex with a man I was seeing at the time. Max (not his real name) was putting a lot of pressure on me to get birth control pills for protection, [but] the only protection pills would offer would be for pregnancy—not AIDS. During this time, my fear of AIDS was growing. I was getting really paranoid, so I called the hotline. They talked a lot about condoms and safer sex. I went immediately to Max to tell him how I was feeling and that I wouldn't have sex with him without condoms. His reaction was horrible. He got very angry and full of contempt and accused me of having AIDS, and angry that I insinuated that he did. I began to try to explain, then realized he wasn't worth my time. Why would I want to sleep with this creature who didn't care about my life? I never saw him again after that night.   [1990]

🌿 45

Pleasures

DIANE HUGS

We both sat there, two disabled lesbians in our wheelchairs, each on opposite sides of the bed. Sudden feelings of fear and timidness came over us. But once we finished the transferring, lifting of legs, undressing and arranging of blankets, we finally touched. Softly and slowly we began to explore each other, our minds and bodies. Neither could make assumptions about the sensations or pleasures of the other. It was wonderful to sense that this woman felt that my body was worth the time it took to explore, that she was as interested in discovering my pleasure as I was in discovering hers.

From the first touch it was a stream of sensations; to listen to every breath, each sigh, and to feel every movement of our love intermingling. It was so intense, so mutual that I must say this beginning was one of the deepest and most fulfilling that I have ever experienced.

When I was an able-bodied lesbian, my approach to relating sexually had been to find out what moves turned someone on and go from there. Never before have I taken the time or had the opportunity to begin a relationship with such a beautiful feeling of pleasure, not only from the pot of gold at the end of the rainbow, but also from the exploration itself.

[1985]

🌿 46

My Man Bovanne

TONI CADE BAMBARA

Blind people got a hummin jones if you notice. Which is understandable completely once you been around one and notice what no eyes will force you

into to see people, and you get past the first time, which seems to come out of nowhere, and it's like you in church again with fat-chest ladies and old gents gruntin a hum low in the throat to whatever the preacher be saying. Shakey Bee bottom lip all swole up with Sweet Peach and me explainin how come the sweet-potato bread was a dollar-quarter this time stead of dollar regular and he say un hunh he understand, then he break into this *thizzin* kind of hum which is quiet, but fiercesome just the same, if you ain't ready for it. Which I wasn't. But I got used to it and the onliest time I had to say somethin bout it was when he was playin checkers on the stoop one time and he commenst to hummin quite churchy seem to me. So I says, "Look here Shakey Bee, I can't beat you and Jesus too." He stop.

So that's how come I asked My Man Bovanne to dance. He ain't my man mind you, just a nice ole gent from the block that we all know cause he fixes things and the kids like him. Or used to fore Black Power got hold their minds and mess em around till they can't be civil to ole folks. So we at this benefit for my niece's cousin who's runnin for somethin with this Black party somethin or other behind her. And I press up close to dance with Bovanne who blind and I'm hummin and he hummin, chest to chest like talkin. Not jammin my breasts into the man. Wasn't bout tits. Was bout vibrations. And he dug it and asked me what color dress I had on and how my hair was fixed and how I was doin without a man, not nosy but nice-like, and who was at this affair and was the canapés dainty-stingy or healthy enough to get hold of proper. Comfy and cheery is what I'm tryin to get across. Touch talkin like the heel of the hand on the tambourine or on a drum.

But right away Joe Lee come up on us and frown for dancin so close to the man. My own son who knows what kind of warm I am about; and don't grown men call me long distance and in the middle of the night for a little Mama comfort? But he frown. Which ain't right since Bovanne can't see and defend himself. Just a nice old man who fixes toasters and busted irons and bicycles and things and changes the lock on my door when my men friends get messy. Nice man. Which is not why they invited him. Grass roots you see. Me and Sister Taylor and the woman who does heads at Mamies and the man from the barber shop, we all there on account of we grass roots. And I ain't never been souther than

Brooklyn Battery and no more country than the window box on my fire escape. And just yesterday my kids tellin me to take them countrified rags off my head and be cool. And now can't get Black enough to suit em. So everybody passin sayin My Man Bovanne. Big deal, keep steppin and don't even stop a minute to get the man a drink or one of them cute sandwiches or tell him what's goin on. And him standin there with a smile ready case someone do speak he want to be ready. So that's how come I pull him on the dance floor and we dance squeezin past the tables and chairs and all them coats and people standin round up in each other face talkin bout this and that but got no use for this blind man who mostly fixed skates and skooters for all these folks when they was just kids. So I'm pressed up close and we touch talkin with the hum. And here come my daughter cuttin her eye at me like she do when she tell me about my "apolitical" self like I got hoof and mouf disease and there ain't no hope at all. And I don't pay her no mind and just look up in Bovanne shadow face and tell him his stomach like a drum and he laugh. Laugh real loud. And here come my youngest, Task, with a tap on my elbow like he the third grade monitor and I'm cuttin up on the line to assembly.

"I was just talkin on the drums," I explained when they hauled me into the kitchen. I figured drums was my best defense. They can get ready for drums what with all this heritage business. And Bovanne stomach just like that drum Task give me when he come back from Africa. You just touch it and it hum thizzm, thizzm. So I stuck to the drum story. "Just drummin that's all."

"Mama, what are you talkin about?"

"She had too much to drink," say Elo to Task cause she don't hardly say nuthin to me direct no more since that ugly argument about my wigs.

"Look here Mama," say Task, the gentle one. "We just tryin to pull your coat. You were makin a spectacle of yourself out there dancing like that."

"Dancin like what?"

Task run a hand over his left ear like his father for the world and his father before that.

"Like a bitch in heat," say Elo.

"Well uhh, I was goin to say like one of them sex-starved ladies gettin on in years and not too discriminating. Know what I mean?"

I don't answer cause I'll cry. Terrible thing when

your own children talk to you like that. Pullin me out the party and hustlin me into some stranger's kitchen in the back of a bar just like the damn police. And ain't like I'm old old. I can still wear me some sleeveless dresses without the meat hangin off my arm. And I keep up with some thangs through my kids. Who ain't kids no more. To hear them tell it. So I don't say nuthin.

"Dancin with that tom," say Elo to Joe Lee, who leanin on the folks' freezer. "His feet can smell a cracker a mile away and go into their shuffle number post haste. And them eyes. He could be a little considerate and put on some shades. Who wants to look into them blown-out fuses that—"

"Is this what they call the generation gap?" I say.

"Generation gap," spits Elo, like I suggested castor oil and fricassee possum in the milk-shakes or somethin. "That's a white concept for a white phenomenon. There's no generation gap among Black people. We are a col—"

"Yeh, well never mind," says Joe Lee. "The point is Mama . . . well, it's pride. You embarrass yourself and us too dancin like that."

"I wasn't shame." Then nobody say nuthin. Them standin there in they pretty clothes with drinks in they hands and gangin up on me, and me in the third-degree chair and nary a olive to my name. Felt just like the police got hold to me.

"First of all," Task say, holdin up his hand and tickin off the offenses, "the dress. Now that dress is too short, Mama, and too low-cut for a woman your age. And Tamu's going to make a speech tonight to kick off the campaign and will be introducin you and expecting you to organize the council of elders—"

"Me? Didn nobody ask me nuthin. You mean Nisi? She change her name?"

"Well, Norton was supposed to tell you about it. Nisi wants to introduce you and then encourage the older folks to form a Council of the Elders to act as an advisory—"

"And you going to be standing there with your boobs out and that wig on your head and that hem up to your ass. And people'll say, 'Ain't that the horny bitch that was grindin with the blind dude?'"

"Elo, be cool a minute," say Task, gettin to the next finger. "And then there's the drinkin. Mama, you know you can't drink cause next thing you know you be laughin loud and carryin on," and he grab another finger for the loudness. "And then there's the dancin. You been tattooed on the man for four records straight and slow draggin even on the fast numbers. How you think that look for a woman your age?"

"What's my age?"

"What?"

"I'm axin you all a simple question. You keep talkin bout what's proper for a woman my age. How old am I anyhow?" And Joe Lee slams his eyes shut and squinches up his face to figure. And Task run a hand over his ear and stare into his glass like the ice cubes goin calculate for him. And Elo just starin at the top of my head like she goin rip the wig off any minute now.

"Is your hair braided up under that thing? If so, why don't you take it off? You always did do a neat cornroll."

"Uh huh," cause I'm thinkin how she couldn't undo her hair fast enough talking bout cornroll so countrified. None of which was the subject. "How old, I say?"

"Sixtee-one or—"

"You a damn lie Joe Lee Peoples."

"And that's another thing," say Task on the fingers.

"You know what you all can kiss," I say, gettin up and brushin the wrinkles out my lap.

"Oh, Mama," Elo say, puttin a hand on my shoulder like she hasn't done since she left home and the hand landin light and not sure it supposed to be there. Which hurt me to my heart. Cause this was the child in our happiness fore Mr. Peoples die. And I carried that child strapped to my chest till she was nearly two. We was close is what I'm tryin to tell you. Cause it was more me in the child than the others. And even after Task it was the girlchild I covered in the night and wept over for no reason at all less it was she was a chub-chub like me and not very pretty, but a warm child. And how did things get to this, that she can't put a sure hand on me and say Mama we love you and care about you and you entitled to enjoy yourself cause you a good woman?

"And then there's Reverend Trent," say Task, glancin from left to right like they hatchin a plot and just now lettin me in on it. "You were suppose to be talking with him tonight, Mama, about giving us his basement for campaign headquarters and—"

"Didn nobody tell me nuthin. If grass roots mean you kept in the dark I can't use it. I really can't. And

Reven Trent a fool anyway the way he tore into the widow man up there on Edgecomb cause he wouldn't take in three of them foster children and the woman not even comfy in the ground yet and the man's mind messed up and—"

"Look here," say Task. "What we need is a family conference so we can get all this stuff cleared up and laid out on the table. In the meantime I think we better get back into the other room and tend to business. And in the meantime, Mama, see if you can't get to Reverend Trent and—"

"You want me to belly rub with the Reven, that it?"

"Oh damn," Elo say and go through the swingin door.

"We'll talk about all this at dinner. How's tomorrow night, Joe Lee?" While Joe Lee being self-important I'm wonderin who's doing the cookin and how come no body ax me if I'm free and do I get a corsage and things like that. Then Joe nod that it's O.K. and he go through the swingin door and just a little hubbub come through from the other room. Then Task smile his smile, lookin just like his daddy and he leave. And it just me in this stranger's kitchen, which was a mess I wouldn't never let my kitchen look like. Poison you just to look at the pots. Then the door swing the other way and it's My Man Bovanne standin there sayin Miss Hazel but lookin at the deep fry and then at the steam table, and most surprised when I come up on him from the other direction and take him on out of there. Pass the folks pushin up towards the stage where Nisi and some other people settin and ready to talk, and folks gettin to the last of the sandwiches and the booze fore they settle down in one spot and listen serious. And I'm thinkin bout tellin Bovanne what a lovely long dress Nisi got on and the earrings and her hair piled up in a cone and the people bout to hear how we all gettin screwed and gotta form our own party and everybody there listenin and lookin. But instead I just haul the man on out of there, and Joe Lee and his wife look at me like I'm terrible, but they ain't said boo to the man yet. Cause he blind and old and don't nobody there need him since they grown up and don't need they skates fixed no more.

"Where we goin, Miss Hazel?" Him knowin all the time.

"First we gonna buy you some dark sunglasses. Then you comin with me to the supermarket so I can pick up tomorrow's dinner, which is going to be a grand thing proper and you invited. Then we goin to my house."

"That be fine. I surely would like to rest my feet." Bein cute, but you got to let men play out they little show, blind or not. So he chat on bout how tired he is and how he appreciate me takin him in hand this way. And I'm thinkin I'll have him change the lock on my door first thing. Then I'll give the man a nice warm bath with jasmine leaves in the water and a little Epsom salt on the sponge to do his back. And then a good rubdown with rose water and olive oil. Then a cup of lemon tea with a taste in it. And a little talcum, some of that fancy stuff Nisi mother sent over last Christmas. And then a massage, a good face massage round the forehead which is the worryin part. Cause you gots to take care of the older folks. And let them know they still needed to run the mimeo machine and keep the spark plugs clean and fix the mailboxes for folks who might help us get the breakfast program goin, and the school for the little kids and the campaign and all. Cause old folks is the nation. That what Nisi was sayin and I mean to do my part.

"I imagine you are a very pretty woman, Miss Hazel."

"I surely am," I say just like the hussy my daughter always say I was.   [1972]

PART IV

Institutions That Shape Women's Lives

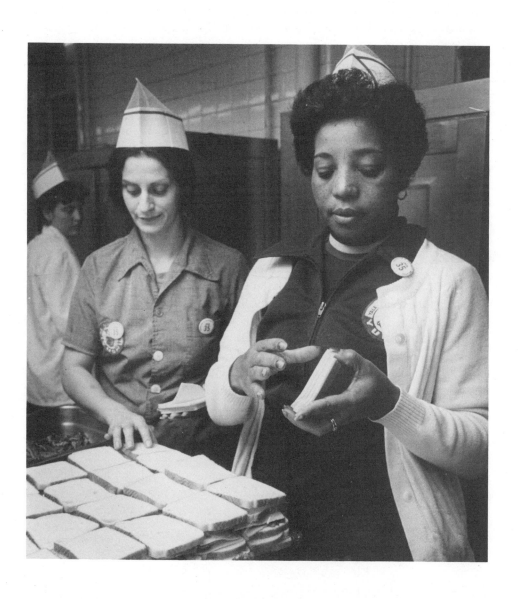

Parts I–III of *Women: Images and Realities* describe the ways that sexist attitudes about women's capabilities and social roles have stunted women's growth, distorted our sense of self, and undermined our self-confidence. Sexism, however, is more than a set of attitudes; it is firmly entrenched in the structure of society. Part IV examines the position of women in four of the major institutions that shape women's lives: the legal system, the workplace, the family, and the health care system. Together they have reinforced women's subordination in all areas of social life. Although we are accustomed to thinking of relationships such as family and motherhood as emotional and biological, they serve social and political purposes as well.

Feminist analysis has revealed that institutions tend to allocate power and resources in complex and subtle ways that systematically support patriarchy or male domination. While overt personal prejudice is apparent to most people, institutionalized sexism is so deeply embedded in our social life that it appears to be the natural order. Much of it remained unnoticed until the feminist movement called attention to it, revealing layer upon layer of discriminatory patterns. The deeper we look, the more patterns emerge. For example, women's analysis of the work force first revealed much outright discrimination. Employers paid women less and excluded them from jobs because they were women. But when the Equal Pay Act of 1963 and Title Seven of the Civil Rights Act of 1967 made such discrimination illegal, women remained in a disadvantaged position in the work force not only because of discrimination that eluded the law, but as a result of occupational segregation, the clustering of women into female-dominated occupations that pay less and offer fewer opportunities for advancement than male-dominated occupations.

Our society has been organized around the notion that the public arenas of work, politics, and education are the province of men and the private world of home and family is female terrain. While this division of activities and resources is powerful as an ideology, it has never been an accurate description of the lives of all women. As Patricia Hill Collins' essay demonstrates, for example, most black women have occupied both public and private worlds, bearing both economic and nurturing responsibility for families. Today a large proportion of women of all races and ethnic groups work outside the home. Despite these facts, the belief that women's natural role is in the family and men's is in the public world shapes the primary institutions of social life. The contradiction between the realities of many women's lives and the social institutions structured by the belief in this division of labor is one of the major sources of tension in contemporary American life.

One of the most powerful vehicles for enforcing the subordination of women has been the legal system. As recently as 1961, the Supreme Court upheld a law exempting women from jury service because "woman is still regarded as the center of home and family life"[1] and therefore not subject to the same public obligations as men are. Laws have changed in the last 30 years, and the courts now recognize women's right

---

[1] *Hoyt v. Florida,* 1961.

to equal protection, but the legal system remains male-dominated and biased against women in many ways.

Women have always played crucial economic roles both inside and outside the family. The work that women do in the home is absolutely essential to economic life. Because it is unpaid, however, it is invisible and difficult to measure. Women have also been working outside the home for centuries. Female slaves worked in the fields, and young female factory workers were the first employees of the American textile industry. Until the middle of the twentieth century, most white women left their jobs when they married, but African-American women continued to work outside the home while caring for home and children. In the past several decades, women of all racial and ethnic groups have entered the work force in increasing numbers. In 1989, women constituted 45% of the total work force. Nevertheless, the belief that women's primary role is in the home continues to shape our workplace experience, restricting opportunities, creating wage inequities and preserving women's responsibility for child care and housework even while we hold full-time jobs.

Although sex discrimination is now against the law, women continue to earn only 65% of what men earn and to encounter sexual harassment, sexual double standards, and what has been described as the glass ceiling, an invisible barrier of discrimination that has prevented women from advancing beyond a certain level. Recognizing that the clustering of women in low-paying, low-status jobs has been a major source of the wage inequities between women and men, some women have begun to enter occupations that have historically been male-dominated. Another approach to this problem is the demand for comparable worth or pay equity—the reevaluation of male- and female-dominated jobs on the basis of the required skill, effort, responsibility, and working conditions.

Women's responsibility for child care remains one of the biggest obstacles to economic equality for women. The United States lags behind other countries in providing child-care facilities, parental leave, and other features that make the workplace compatible with parenting. Without a fundamental restructuring of the workplace to accommodate workers with family responsibilities—both male and female—women will continue to be in a disadvantaged position. Because of the absence of affordable child care and the low pay of most women's jobs, many single women with children are dependent on welfare and condemned to poverty.

The position of women in the work force is thus inextricably connected with the position of women in the family. As Hisaye Yamamoto vividly demonstrates, the division of power and resources in the patriarchal family has often subordinated the needs of married women to those of their spouses. The sentimental rhetoric that often surrounds the family not only obscures unequal power relations but also conveys the impression that only the patriarchal family is legitimate. In fact, the family, a group of people who are committed to each other and share resources, can take a variety of forms. The African-American family, often sustained by mothers, aunts, and grandmothers, has proven remarkably durable in the face of almost insurmountable odds.

Feminist theorists have found it useful to view motherhood as an institution as well as a relationship between mother and child. As an institution, structured by the ideology of patriarchy, motherhood was long assumed to be women's primary function, one that made women unfit for full participation in other realms. The sentimentalization of motherhood obscures the realities of mothers' experience in a number of ways. While most mothers love and enjoy their children, motherhood can be lonely and sometimes painful in a society in which there are few social supports. When motherhood takes place outside the patriarchal family, the mantle of sentimentality disappears. Lesbian mothers have lost custody of their children, and single and teenage mothers face social censure. Sentimentalized motherhood also obscures the fact that not all women enjoy motherhood, and that mothers who have no other sources of identity and satisfaction can become disoriented when children grow up. The essays in this section tell the stories of real women whose lives belie the myths. They demonstrate the need to see motherhood as a more varied experience and to envision social supports that enable women to experience motherhood while participating fully in other aspects of human life.

One of the consequences of women's subordinate status in the workplace and family is male domination of the health care system. While women are the majority of health care consumers and do a great deal of the direct service work, most doctors, researchers, and managers of clinics and hospitals are men. As a result, women's health needs have not been adequately addressed. One particularly grievous example of this failure has been the slowness of the medical community to acknowledge the experience of women with AIDS. The women's health movement has been a vital part of the rebirth of feminism. Through such books as *The New Our Bodies, Ourselves* (Simon & Schuster, 1992), organizations like the National Black Women's Health project, and self-help groups, women have reclaimed their bodies, challenged the priorities of the medical establishment, and made our experiences and needs visible.

All these institutions are intimately connected to each other. Women's experience in one reinforces our position in another, indicating that change in the position of women in society needs to take place on many fronts. The selections in this part show that within our social institutions, gender, class, and race work together to shape female experience. While our culture teaches us to believe that hard work and talent will be rewarded, institutions place white men in advantageous social positions. Understanding these institutional barriers enables us to see that all people do not have equal opportunity in our society, and that to create it, we must make fundamental changes in our social institutions. Unless we recognize the historic advantages of white men, it is impossible to move toward a more equitable society. Affirmative action programs, which commit organizations to give preference to women and members of other historically disadvantaged groups, recognize that in many ways a "white male affirmative action program" has been in place for centuries.[2]

---

[2]Thanks to Karen Wynn for this phrase.

Finally, the selections in Part IV testify to the durability of patriarchy. While women have made significant advances in the past 30 years, sexism is proving to be a stubborn adversary. As women occupy new territory in our society, new problems emerge or come into view. We are just beginning to understand, for example, the extent to which sexual harassment of women has crippled us in the workplace, particularly in nontraditional occupations. When barriers to women's equality are toppled, they often reappear in different forms, requiring us to develop new strategies.

The Legal System

Laws shape women's experience of all institutions in our society. Although women have entered the legal profession in record numbers in the last decade, sexism continues to permeate the legal system.

In the first article, attorney Kristian Miccio paints both a historical and a contemporary picture of women's secondary status under the law. She describes the ways the legal system has constrained women and the ways feminists have used the law to fight for civil rights, in the areas of work, reproductive rights, and violence against women. Despite feminists' efforts, reforms have been slow to take effect because of the sexist attitudes that still shape police and attorney practices, judicial rulings, and jury verdicts. Miccio concludes that systemic change will "require the infusion of feminist politics at every level of the justice system from the police to the courts."

For example, during the 1980s, task forces were formed in many states to examine the place of women in the courts. Judges, lawyers, laypersons, academics, and others were interviewed to determine ways in which practices were unfair to women in the courts. Findings pointed to a wide range of sexist practices, from the way female attorneys were treated to patterns of assigning property rights and child support upon the dissolution of marriage. Recommendations for more equitable treatment for women in the courts were part of these reports. "The Courts' Enforcement of Women's Economic Rights" is a section from the report on the New York state court system.

 47

Women and the Law

KRISTIAN MICCIO

America prides itself on the notion that we are a society of laws. The legal system provides a framework upon which we as a society define ourselves. It is a statement of our collective values and traditions. Within the American context, law has an additional function. It is a compact between equals: A self-governance contract between the governed and the governors. Yet women have been conspicuously missing from the fabric of our legal traditions. In fact, women were at one time specifically excluded from the body politic.[1]

The framers of the Constitution believed that the public sphere and the exercise of citizenship were the domain of men. As Jefferson wrote, "Were the state a pure democracy there would still be excluded from our deliberation women, who, to prevent deprivation of morals and ambiguity of issues

---

[1]The Fourteenth Amendment to the Constitution, which enfranchised black men, specifically referred to males over the age of 21 as citizens with the right to vote. This excluded all women, regardless of race, class, or creed.

should not mix promiscuously in gatherings of men."[2] Clearly, Jefferson believed that the presence of women would pollute and corrupt not only the morals of men but the system itself. Jefferson's position echoed the prevailing view that women's social and political identity should be restricted and that her sexuality should be controlled.

The legal concept that women and men are equal before the law was not the original understanding of the Constitution's framers. Indeed, women's exclusion from the body politic was a direct consequence of our sex. Our body of law and our legal traditions restricted and confined women to that of the private sphere, and, in setting up this gilded cage, women's legal identity was shaped by and dependent on the men within the home.

In the eyes of the law, women were neither separate nor distinct legal beings. Simply put, because a woman derived her legal identity from men, she had no claim to rights commonly associated with citizenship. She could not vote, and her acquisition and control of private property was severely restricted.[3] Consequently, women's social status was defined by her ability to reproduce, and her legal status was shaped by her relationship to men within the family—as one's wife or as one's daughter. Women's legal identity, then, was subsumed into that of the husband or father. She had no separate legal character.

The British common-law tradition of "covered woman," which defined married women's legal status, was incorporated into American jurisprudence. William Blackstone, an eighteenth-century British legal theorist, summarized the doctrine of "femme couverte" in his Commentaries on the Law of England:

> By marriage, the husband and wife are one person in the law: that is, the very being or legal existence of the woman is suspended during the marriage, or at least is incorporated and consolidated into that of the husband; under whose wing, protection, and cover, she performs everything. . . . Upon this principle, of a union of person in husband and wife depend almost all the legal rights, duties and disabilities, that either of them acquire by the marriage. . . . a man can not grant anything to his wife, or enter into covenant with her: for the grant would be to suppose her separate existence; and to covenant with her would be only to covenant with himself and therefore it is also generally true that all compacts made between husband and wife, when single, are voided by the intermarriage. A woman indeed may be attorney for her husband, for that implies no separation from, but is rather a representation of her lord.[4]

This tradition guided our law until the mid-nineteenth century. With the passage of the Married Women's Property Act of 1848, many of the civil disabilities consistent with the acquisition of private property were lifted. Women as the sexual property of men and restrictions on their participation in public life remained intact until the late twentieth century.[5]

Upon marriage, a woman experienced a legal death. The first step in this process was the surrender of her name. This loss was more than a symbolic act; it was the initial step toward utter suspension of her legal existence.

Since married women were invisible in the eyes of the law, they could not take part in civil life. And the effects of such a civil death were profound. Women could not sue; they could not keep wages; they could not own property; they could not seek employment without spousal consent; they could not exercise any control over their children; and,

---

[2] Quoted in Kay, Herma Hill, *Sex Discrimination and the Law* (West Publications, 1988, p. 1).
[3] In *Minor v. Happersett,* 88 U.S. 162, 22 L.Ed. 627 (1874), Virginia Minor attempted to vote in the elections of 1872. The U.S. Supreme Court ruled that the right to vote was not among the "privileges and immunities" of United States or federal citizenship. Therefore, the States were not prohibited by the Constitution from inhibiting this right and restricting it, "[the] important trust to men alone." The Court did state, however, that women, like children, were "persons" and may be citizens within the meaning of the Fourteenth Amendment. Women received the right to vote with passage of the Nineteenth Amendment in 1920. This followed a century of struggle by the first wave of feminists (suffragists).

[4] *Blackstone's Commentaries* [1966 ed.], t. 430, as quoted in Kay, Herma Hill, *Sex Discrimination and the Law* (West Publications, 1988, p. 913).
[5] Marital rape exemptions fell in many states in the late 1980s; however, a limited number of jurisdictions still cling to this vestige of women as chattel.

finally, they had no control over their reproductive and sexual lives.

The doctrine of covered women transformed married women into the sexual property of their husbands. And because they were property, women could not exercise free will. Husbands, then, had complete control over their wives' bodies. Rape within marriage was not only a legal fiction, it was socially sanctioned and legally condoned. For women, the concept of a right to (bodily) privacy was alien.

A further consequence of "civil death" was economic dependency. Women could not work without the consent of their husbands. And if a woman was permitted to work outside the home, she was not entitled to keep her wages. This forced dependency kept women economically subservient and tied to hearth and home.

WOMEN AND WORK

In 1873, Myra Bradwell's application for a license to practice law was denied by the Illinois Supreme Court. This denial was due solely to her sex—she was born female. Bradwell's case was heard by the U.S. Supreme Court, and it upheld the lower state court's decision to deny her access to the legal profession. Justice Bradley, in a concurring opinion, written for himself and his brethren Justices Swayne sand Field, stated:

> The civil law, as well as nature herself, has always recognized a wide difference in the respective spheres and destinies of man and woman. Man is or should be woman's protector and defender. The natural and proper timidity and delicacy which belongs to the female sex evidently unfits it [*sic*] for many of the occupations of civil life. The constitution of the family organization, which is founded in divine ordinance, as well as in the nature of things, indicates the domestic sphere as that which properly belongs to the domain and function of womanhood. The harmony, not to say identity, of interests and views which belong, or should belong, to the family institution is repugnant to the idea of a woman adopting a distinct and independent career from that of her husband.[6]

Critical to Bradley's concurrence in *Bradwell* is his reliance on "divine ordinance" in upholding an arbitrary denial of admission to the Illinois bar. Once invoked, it is difficult to rebut the notion of the "divine ordinance," and in so doing, Justice Bradley couched a misogynist assumption in rather lofty and untouchable rhetoric.[7]

Such reliance on "divinity" formed the basis for Constitutional interpretations that denied women access to occupations and restricted the scope of their labor. By invoking "divine ordinance," the Court placed its imprimatur on a set of social values that defined women as reproductive instruments of the state.

In *Muller v. Oregon,* a decision that followed *Bradwell,* the Court clearly outlined its view of women in relationship to the state. Oregon had prohibited women from working in any mechanical establishment, factory, or laundry for more than 10 hours per day. Not less than three years before *Muller,* the Supreme Court in *Lochner* had declared restricting the hours of bakers as unconstitutional since such regulations violated the workers' liberty interest—the right to contract. The Court resolved this obvious conflict by focusing on the unique function of women's reproductive ability and its value to the state.

The *Muller* Court held that

> As healthy mothers are essential to vigorous offspring, the physical well-being of woman becomes an object of public interest in order to preserve the strength and vigor of the race. . . . The limitations which this statute places upon her contractual powers, upon her right to agree with her employer as to the time she shall labor are not imposed solely for her benefit, but also largely for the benefit of all. Many words cannot make this plainer. The two sexes differ in structure of body, in the functions to be performed by each, in the amount of physical

---

[6]83 U.S. (16 Wall) 130, 141–142, 21 L.Ed. 442 (1873).

[7]Notwithstanding reference to a "divine ordinance," the doctrine of separation of church and state was not violated. The Court's decision and Bradley's concurrence did not establish a state religion. Rather, it put into perspective the values and mores of society at the time the decision was written. It is important to note, however, that the Court has explicitly relied on Judeo-Christian doctrine to deny protections afforded by the Fourteenth Amendment to such groups as gay men and lesbians (*Hardwick v. Bowers*).

strength . . . the influence of vigorous health upon the future well-being of the race, the self-reliance which enables one to assert full rights, and in the capacity to maintain the struggle for subsistence. This difference justifies a difference in legislation and upholds that which is designed to compensate for some of the burdens which rest upon her.[8]

By viewing women's reproductive ability as a tool for the state, the Court was comfortable in restricting women's ability to contract freely. Yet in the nineteenth century, the right to contract was considered a fundamental right. Restrictions on this right were rare and only in those instances where the Court believed that the state had a strong or compelling interest. Limiting women's right to contract was premised solely on the state's interest in protecting the reproductive functions of women. Clearly, fundamental rights were premised on gender, and women did not hold this right in the same manner as men. And such "protection" carried with it a profound price—the eradication of a fundamental right.

Although much has changed concerning women's participation in the "public sphere," equality for women remains an ongoing struggle. It is important to recognize that the modern improvements women experience in the workplace were won through women's tireless campaign to ensure equality and to improve the quality of life for workers.

In 1963, women won a critical battle with the passage of the Equal Pay Act. Prior to its passage, employers were permitted to discriminate in pay, based on sex, notwithstanding similar work. With the EPA, employers were barred from paying women less as long as the work performed was of essentially the same nature as that performed by their male counterparts.

When issues of comparable worth are raised, EPA analysis is of little benefit. The EPA does not require that men and women be paid the same.

Rather, it requires that workers who perform the same job must be paid the same wage. Therefore, a woman firefighter could not be paid less than her male counterparts as long as she performed the same tasks. Sex alone was not sufficient to warrant a difference in pay. Where a wage differential is predicated on a "factor other than sex," e.g., market factors, this difference is permissible. Comparable worth cases have failed because litigants have been unable to demonstrate that pay differences are based on sex and the devaluation of women's work, rather than as a consequence of "market factors."

In the mid-1960s, the advent of the civil rights and women's movements brought substantial changes in employment opportunities for male members of the ethnic minority communities and for women. In 1964, the Civil Rights Acts were passed, and at the eleventh hour, at the behest of Rep. Martha Griffin, "sex" was added to Title VII of the Civil Rights Act. Title VII, in combination with various executive orders signed by President Johnson, paved the way for a sustained attack on gender asymmetry in the workplace.

Following passage of Title VII, it was unlawful to discriminate "against any individual with respect to . . . compensation, terms, conditions or privileges of employment because of that individual's race, color, religion, sex or national origin."[9] Additionally, with Johnson's executive orders in 1967, federal contractors were mandated to establish goals and timetables to eradicate past and/or continuing discrimination. The latter orders, commonly referred to as affirmative action programs, placed an affirmative burden on all recipients of federal moneys not only to hire qualified women and minorities but to construct a plan to compensate for past discrimination.

It was the affirmative action laws of the 1960s that opened up "nontraditional" job classifications for women and minorities. Women were finding both job training and employment in such industries as the building trades, uniform occupations (police, fire, and sanitation), and "white-collar" professions. These laws, in conjunction with Title IX of the Edu-

---

[8] It is important to note that the control of women's procreative ability served two functions: Women of "Yankee stock" should reproduce to propagate the (white) race, while immigrant and black women's reproductive ability was useful only in so much as their reproductive capabilities delivered future workers. *Muller v. Oregon;* 208 U.S. 412, 28 S. Ct. 324, 52 L.Ed 551 (1908).

---

[9] Title VII, Civil Rights Act, 1964.

cational Amendments which prohibited sexism in educational programs, did much to open doors previously closed to women.

With the election of Ronald Reagan in 1980 and his subsequent appointments to the Supreme Court and the federal bench, the gains made by women in employment were systematically eroded. Various Supreme Court decisions weakened the affirmative action laws of the 1960s, and the promise of the Civil Rights Act was broken. In the next century, women will have to recapture lost ground, while helping construct a legal theory that attacks the root cause of gender asymmetry in the workplace. This is a difficult task because it raises issues concerning biologic difference and challenges long-held notions concerning equal protection.

REPRODUCTIVE RIGHTS

Prior to 1965, women's control over their reproductive lives was tenuous at best. It was virtually impossible for any woman, irrespective of marital status, to receive information concerning birth control and abortion. In most states it was a criminal offense for doctors to give any information about birth control. Clearly, if the states could criminalize information, the actual procedures themselves should be legally proscribed.

Women, then, could not learn appropriate methods to stop unwanted pregnancies, nor could they terminate such pregnancies. Their reproductive lives fell outside their control, and implicit in the criminalization of birth control and abortion was the heavy hand of state regulation and control.

The state's position concerning birth control and abortion has been nothing short of schizophrenic. According to the common law, abortions in the U.S. were permitted before "quickening," the period at which the fetus became ensouled. Prior to this point, the fetus was viewed as part of the mother's body, and abortions were not proscribed. In the mid-nineteenth century, this common-law distinction was eradicated as state after state passed new laws criminalizing abortion. By the end of the nineteenth century, abortion was illegal at any stage of pregnancy throughout the U.S.

During the mid-1960s and early 1970s, challenges to the states' restrictive birth control and abortion laws were undertaken. Where legislative reform seemed hopeless, feminists turned to the courts to identify and protect women's right to reproductive freedom.[10]

Central to a feminist politic was the belief that women's control over their bodies was a fundamental right. To deny women the right to decide when and if to procreate was a denial of a basic civil liberty. Overturning restrictive abortion and birth control laws became a primary political goal of the feminist civil rights struggles of this era.

Birth Control

In 1965, the Supreme Court struck down a Connecticut law that criminalized counseling for and using contraceptives. The director of Planned Parenthood was convicted of providing a married couple with birth control information. He faced a possible fine and imprisonment of not less than 60 days and a maximum of one year. The case was appealed, and, after exhausting the state appellate process, the Supreme Court was petitioned to review the matter. In the now famous case of *Griswold v. Connecticut,* the Supreme Court ruled that the Connecticut statute was unconstitutional.

Writing for the majority, Justice William O. Douglas recognized that specific guarantees in the Bill of Rights "have penumbras, formed by emanations from those guarantees that help give them [the first ten amendments to the Constitution] life and substance . . . various guarantees create zones of privacy."[11] Douglas found that these zones of privacy included a marital right of privacy that was protected from intrusion by the state.

Central to the Court's analysis in *Griswold* was the belief that the decision to procreate is at the heart

---

[10]In 1970, New York state reformed its abortion laws. New York's new law was one of the most liberal abortion statutes, and it foreshadowed the *Roe* decision handed down by the U.S. Supreme Court in 1973.

[11]Since the Constitution does not specifically enumerate a right of privacy, the Court located this right in existing amendments and provisions. In doing this, the Court recognized that the Constitution is a living, breathing document, and that the already existing provisions, if understood historically and contextually, could accommodate a privacy right analysis. The Court did not create a "new right"; rather, it interpreted existing law as incorporating this right. See, by way of contrast, articles on original intent and strict constructionist theory.

of a cluster of constitutionally protected choices. No doubt the Court was repulsed by the idea that the state could intrude into a married couple's bedroom to regulate sexual practices and behavior,[12] but it was the nature of the decision (procreation) that the Court found worthy of privacy protection.

Following *Griswold,* the Court expanded the right of privacy to unmarried individuals. In *Eisenstadt v. Baird,* the Court struck down as unconstitutional a law that prohibited the distribution of contraceptives to unmarried persons. In *Eisenstadt,* the Court held that the liberty interest found in the Fourteenth Amendment involved a right of privacy, and "if the right of privacy [meant] anything, it [was] the right of the individual, married or single, to be free of unwarranted governmental intrusion into matters so fundamentally affecting a person as the decision whether to bear or beget a child."[13]

To the Court, marital status was irrelevant. What was critical and worthy of Constitutional protection was the decision to procreate. Such decisions, then, fell under the scope of Fourteenth Amendment protection.

Five years later, in *Carey v. Population Services,* the Supreme Court invalidated a New York law that regulated the availability of nonprescription contraceptives to minors.[14] Carey was a critical decision because it reaffirmed that women have a fundamental right not only to decide whether or not to procreate, but also to exercise that choice. Relying on *Roe v. Wade,* the abortion decision decided only four years earlier, the Court recognized that the right to decide or choose is meaningless without the right to access. In *Carey,* the Court strengthened the principle that women's reproductive freedom was more than a theoretical right. Rather, the exercise of this right was an inherent part of the "right to

choose." In the context of human existence, anything less would make it meaningless.

Abortion Decisions

In 1973, the Supreme Court expanded fundamental rights protection to the right to decide to terminate a pregnancy. In *Roe v. Wade,* the majority held that the Fourteenth Amendment liberty interest involved a right of privacy concerning a woman's decision to terminate a pregnancy. The state could only intrude on that decision if there existed a compelling state interest, and the means chosen (regulatory plan) was narrowly drawn and closely tailored to the governmental objective. The burden, then, was on the state to justify its position and its methodology if they restricted access to abortion.

In *Roe,* and its companion case *Doe v. Bolton,* the Court did not vest women with an absolute right to terminate a pregnancy. Rather, it recognized that the state has a compelling interest to regulate abortion in order to protect the right of the fetus and maternal health.[15] The Court, then, did not view the issue through the prism of a woman's right to exercise control over her body; rather, the Court recognized competing rights and interests of the state and that of the fetus. In doing so, it set the stage for the erosion of the original premise that the fundamental right to decide when and if to procreate was at the center of a "cluster" of constitutionally protected choices located in the Fourteenth Amendment.

Finally, by recognizing fetal rights at the point of viability, the Court not only compromised women's bodily integrity, it subordinated her right to that of the fetus and the state. Under the scheme articulated by the Court, the state could proscribe abortions at the point of fetal viability. At this time in the pregnancy, set at the third trimester, the state can prohibit all abortions unless this procedure is necessary

---

[12]This repulsion was dissipated when the Court was faced with the question of whether a right of privacy extends to homosexuality. In *Hardwick v. Bowers,* the Court upheld a Georgia statute that criminalized sodomy (a sex act anything other than intercourse) even if the acts were between consenting adults. The majority was quite clear that the right of privacy did not extend to the homosexual bedroom. Lurking behind the *Hardwick* decision was the majority's reliance on Judeo-Christian dogma. See *Hardwick v. Bowers,* specifically the Burger concurring opinion and Blackmun's dissent.

[13]*Eisenstadt v. Baird, supra,* 405 U.S. at 453.

[14]*Carey v. Population Services,* 431 U.S. 678 (1977).

---

[15]The Court set up an intricate system to accommodate what it viewed as conflicting rights and interests. During the first trimester, a woman's right to terminate a pregnancy was paramount; therefore, the state could not proscribe abortion. During the second trimester, the state's interest in protecting maternal health was compelling; therefore, the state could regulate the procedure as long as accessibility to abortion was not restricted. In the third trimester (viability), the combined interest of the state in protecting fetal life and the fetus's right to life were sufficiently compelling as to permit proscription of abortion unless maternal life was at issue.

to save the life of the mother. The woman's fundamental right to decide (which included accessibility), then, is now lessened in relation to that of the fetus's right to life and the state's interest in protecting fetal life. At the point of viability, the rights and interests of the woman, the fetus, and the state all converge, and it is the woman's right that is subordinated.

From 1976 to 1992, there was a series of abortion decisions that chipped away at the fundamental right articulated in *Roe*. These decisions were the consequence of two important factors. First, with the election of Ronald Reagan in 1980 and of George Bush in 1988, an anti-women's rights political attitude was reflected in the federal appointments made by both presidents. Five Supreme Court Justices were appointed during this 8-year period.[16] The Supreme Court was being filled with jurists who were hostile to women's reproductive freedom.

Second, following *Roe*, the Right-to-Life (RTL) Movement went on the political offensive. Through a combination of direct political action (such as the Operation Rescue blockade of abortion clinics), election politics, and community-based politics, the abortion issue was cast from the perspective of the anti-women's rights activists.

During this period, Medicaid funds for abortion were cut off (*McRae v. Harris*), minors' rights were subordinated to parents' rights (*Webster* and *Casey*), mandatory waiting periods were imposed (*Webster* and *Casey*), and the state's interest in promoting childbirth was recognized and elevated to a compelling interest.

The combined effects of these decisions resulted in weakening women's fundamental right. Access was no longer an inherent part of the right to decide. Unlike the birth control decisions, the right to decide was construed in its literal form—the mental process of reaching a decision in a social vacuum. The Court then permitted a cutoff of Medicaid funds to poor women who wished to exercise their right to terminate a pregnancy. The Court believed that the state's cutoff did not place an affirmative burden on the decision-making process since the state did not create poverty.

The Court decision in *Harris* was sinister for two reasons. First, it removed access from contemplation of what constitutes a right, thereby creating an abstract right. Second, it placed the state's interest in promoting childbirth on a par with a woman's right to reproductive freedom.[17] *Harris*, then, severely weakened *Roe* and women's right to choose.

In July of 1992, in *Planned Parenthood v. Casey*, the Court changed the compelling interest test to one of undue burden. This shifted the burden to women to prove that the state's actions were "unduly burdensome" before strict scrutiny could be triggered. This was a severe deviation from *Roe*, which had placed the onus on the state, thereby invoking strict scrutiny at the outset.

Although reaffirming *Roe*, *Casey* weakened the fundamental character of woman's right to terminate her pregnancy. Indeed, it is questionable at best if what remains of *Roe* is mere form over substance, since a woman's right to choose is no longer treated as a fundamental right.[18]

Conclusion

The Court's decisions in the abortion and birth control cases are dissimilar in one striking aspect. The

---

[16]Justices O'Connor, Kennedy, Scalia, Souter, and Thomas. Following the newest decision, *Casey*, it is clear that Thomas and Scalia are aligned with Chief Justice Rehnquist in his opposition to the right of privacy and the protections that this right affords women in deciding to terminate a pregnancy. O'Connor, Kennedy, and Souter are on the record in support of the right but would permit more extensive compromise of that right.

[17]At issue in *Harris* was the Hyde Amendment, which restricted Medicaid funds for pregnant poor women. Under Hyde, the federal government would reimburse states only for prenatal care and birthing. If a poor woman wanted to exercise her right to terminate her pregnancy, no federal funds could be used. In effect, due to the cost of hospitalization, poor women would have no other choice but to carry to term or revert to back-alley abortions. The framers of Hyde justified this total ban on poor women's right to abort in the state's right to promote and favor childbirth. The Court recognized this interest. Moreover, it held that since the state did not create poverty, it was under no affirmative duty to ensure that poor women could actualize their decision to abort. The dissent in *Harris* understood the effects of the majority decision. Characterizing the majority decision as callous, the dissenters recognized that *Harris* obliterated the access component of a right—but only for poor women.

[18]It is important to note that the Court is *one* vote away from overturning *Roe*. As Justice Blackmun, the architect of *Roe*, commented: "I am 83 years old. I shall not be on this Court much longer."

birth control cases did not exorcise access from fundamental rights analysis. The fundamental character of an *individual's* right to decide to use contraceptives remains undisturbed. In contrast, in the abortion cases, a woman's fundamental right of privacy has been severely compromised. This is due in large part to who holds the right (women) with the convergence of "rights" now vested in the fetus and the state. Abortion, unlike birth control, implicates the fundamental right only of the woman. In birth control, the Court protected the right of women and men to decide (and act). It is no coincidence, then, that the right to terminate a pregnancy has been circumscribed according to the sex of the person who is vested with it.

VIOLENCE AGAINST WOMEN

The problem of violence against women is at once simple and quite complex. It is simple because it is so obvious—indeed, such violence is everywhere. Women are beaten, abused, raped, and tortured on the streets, in the boardroom, and in the bedroom. Statistics tell us that violence against women is the leading cause of injury to women—more than car accidents, more than office-related accidents, and more than drug-related incidents.[19] Women are beaten, shot, and stabbed to death, not at the hands of strangers but by the men closest to them. In New York City in 1988, over 20,000 petitions for orders of protection were filed in New York County Family Court. Nationwide, 40% of all homicide victims are female; of that number, over 90% were killed by their husbands or boyfriends. Women are killed by intimates at a rate six times higher than men.[20]

The question is: Why are women killed and beaten at epidemic proportions?[21] Simply put, violence against women has been legally sanctioned and socially condoned. Wife-beating was legal, and marital rape is still sanctioned in some jurisdictions. This privilege extended to males was a direct outgrowth of the legal doctrine of "femme couverte," or "covered woman." Under this doctrine, women's legal existence was suspended or subsumed in that of the males. In the eyes of the law, women were invisible and, within the home, subject to the tyranny of the husband. Husbands could offer "subtle chastisement" or beat their wives as they beat their children.[22]

This cultural position vis-à-vis women's relationship to men in the family influenced American jurisprudence. The states codified this misogyny. Indeed, the decriminalization of assaults in the family and the marital rape exemption were a direct result of such misogyny in the law.

Prior to 1962 in New York state, assaults in the family that were low-level felonies if committed by strangers were routinely handled in family court. If a case managed to find its way into criminal court, it was automatically transferred because the criminal courts lacked "subject matter" jurisdiction.[23] Following hearings in the State Capitol, hearings that detailed the horrific violence experienced by women, New York modified its laws, and cases previously barred from prosecution were, theoretically, prosecutable under existing penal law statutes.

During the 1960s and 1970s, feminists were challenging the gender asymmetry of the laws involving "domestic violence." One such challenge called into question police-arrest avoidance in domestic violence cases. In *Bruno v. Codd,* the New York City Police Department (NYPD) was sued because line officers were refusing to arrest boyfriends and husbands accused of beating their girlfriends and wives. The plaintiffs in *Bruno* proved that the police were mediating cases even where the woman was beaten with a weapon. Clearly, the doctrine of "subtle chastisement" affected police performance.

A settlement agreement flowed from *Bruno,* and the NYPD assured battered women and their advocates that they would, at the very least, exercise discretion. Therefore, when responding to domestic violence incidents, the police would assess whether an arrest was warranted rather than engage in a *de facto* refusal to arrest in cases where the victim and assailant were known to each other.

In *Sorichetti v. NYPD,* all discretion was re-

---

[19]FBI Statistics, 1989.

[20]Department of Justice Statistics, 1990.

[21]Indeed, the U.S. Surgeon General has stated that domestic violence is the chief health risk faced by women.

[22]See *Blackstone's Commentaries, supra.*

[23]See NYS Family Court Act Section 813 and Besharov's Commentaries.

moved from police where violations of a court order of protection were at issue. In *Sorichetti,* the police refused to enforce an order of protection which mandated that the noncustodial father return the minor child at 5:00 p.m. following visitation and that he refrain from harassing and assaultive conduct.

The father in this case has been adjudicated an abuser in the New York Family Court, and he was known to the police as a "wife beater." When Ms. Sorichetti appealed to the police to look for her daughter and her ex-husband, she was rebuffed. Yet her fear was well grounded. After Ms. Sorichetti had dropped her daughter off for a visit with the father, he had made a death threat. In addition, he had failed to return the child at the time prescribed by the Court. The death threat and the failure to adhere to the time schedule constituted two separate violations of the order. Yet, notwithstanding a valid court order, two violations of the order, and a state law which said that the police should arrest where there has been a violation of an order of protection, the police refused to act.

Following repeated requests for assistance to enforce the order, the police searched for and found young Dina Sorichetti. Her father had carried through on his threat by attempting to dismember the child. In this case, the Court awarded Ms. Sorichetti and her daughter $2.3 million for the police's failure to enforce the order, which resulted in a failure to protect her and her daughter. As a result of this damage award, the NYPD changed its police procedures, mandating a must-arrest policy where there is probable cause to believe that an order of protection has been violated.

Such New York cases illustrate that the gender asymmetry in law has resulted in unequal protection for female citizens.[24]

Rape

Marital Rape Exemption   The marital rape exemption was a vestige of the common-law system that viewed women as inferior to men and as subjects of their husbands. At the core of this system

was the view that a woman is the property of either her husband or her father. The purpose of rape law generally was to preserve the "value" of the sexual object.[25] Under Mosaic law, the rapist of a virgin was penalized by forcing him to pay the bride price to the father to marry the woman.[26] Under ancient Babylonian law, criminal rape was the "theft of virginity, an embezzlement of the woman's fair price on the market."[27] These ancient laws found themselves in Western jurisprudence. According to common law, the female victim could save her attacker from death by marriage.[28]

Within the family and against a third party, the husband had a property interest in the body and a right to the "personal enjoyment of his wife."[29] Moreover, since the person of the married woman merged into that of the husband, it was a legal impossibility to hold the husband accountable for rape because it would be as if he were charged with raping himself.

Finally, based on the marital contract, because a woman was incapable of withholding consent, rape of one's wife was a legal nullity. As Lord Matthew Hale stated in the seventeenth century:

> But the husband cannot be guilty of rape committed by himself upon his lawful wife, for by their mutual matrimonial consent and contract, the wife hath given up *herself in this kind unto her husband which she cannot retract* [emphasis added].[30]

Jurisdictions accepted Hale's notion without any question and codified this exemption into their statutes.[31] States then willingly constructed a system of unequal justice based on marital status and gender. Indeed, the laws were allowed to stand in the face of the Fourteenth Amendment and various state constitutions, which incorporated equal protection standards from the federal constitution into their

---

[24]See also *Thurman v. Torrington.* Here, the police did nothing while Tracy Thurman's husband stomped on her face, threw her to the ground, and choked her. The police claimed that their refusal to arrest was premised on the fact that this was a domestic dispute.

[25]See S. Brownmiller, *Against Our Will: Men, Women, and Rape,* (New York: Simon & Schuster, 1975, p. 9).
[26]Deuteronomy 22:13–29.
[27]Brownmiller, p. 9.
[28]Rape and Battery Between Husband and Wife, 6 Stan. L.Rev. 719 724 & n. 2691954.
[29]*Oppenheim v. Krindel,* 140 N.E. 227, 228 (1923).
[30]I. Hale, *History of Pleas of the Crown;* pp. 6–9, as quoted in Kay, Herma Hill, *Sex Discrimination and the Law* (West Publications, 1992, p. 911).
[31]See *People v. Meli,* 19 NYS 365 (1922).

own. Woman as sexual property of the husband superseded the right of female citizens to be secure in their persons.

The marital rape exemptions of most jurisdictions did not fall until the 1980s. With the re-emergence of the battered women's and anti-rape movements, the states were confronted with legal challenges to these exemptions. Based on federal and state equal protection laws, the highest courts in the various states struck these provisions as constitutionally offensive.[32]

Rape: A Category of Crime Unto Itself   Cultural misogyny found its way into the rules of evidence as well as into the states' penal laws. Rape, therefore, was treated unlike any other crime. Up until recently, women's testimony was considered incredible as a matter of law. States, therefore, enacted strict corroboration requirements in sexual assault (rape) and sodomy cases.[33]

Under the independent corroboration rule, the testimony of the victim was insufficient to sustain an indictment for rape. The state needed evidence of a "different character" to make out every element of the crime. Therefore, to prove that the sex act had occurred, one would need either physical trauma to the vaginal or anal area, or evidence of semen. To prove the identity of the defendant, if unknown to the victim, one would need a witness. To meet the sufficiency burden concerning consent, evidence of bodily injury was critical. Rape is the only crime that required its victim to be victimized again—via assault (physical injury).

In addition, because most states required that force be viewed through the eyes of the defendant, where he interposed a reasonable belief that the victim consented, this operated as a complete defense. The level of fear, actual or perceived by the victim, was irrelevant in these jurisdictions.

Finally, women's character was under attack at trials involving rape charges. The prevailing defense theory was that if the complainant consented to sex once, this operated as a blanket consent and was relevant to the issue of "force" in current prosecution. It was not uncommon for a victim's past sexual history to be paraded before the Court.

Feminists systematically challenged the independent corroboration rules and the evidentiary "fishing expeditions" into the victim's prior sexual history. As a result, states passed rape shield laws and repealed the independent corroboration rule.

Nevertheless, because misogynist attitudes die hard, rape convictions are difficult to achieve where the victim has had a sexual life or has had a dating relationship with the defendant. The underlying premise is that a woman is not empowered to refuse sexual advances, especially when she has either socialized or had an intimate relationship with the defendant. Hence, marital rape, date rape, and acquaintance rape cases are still very difficult to prosecute. Juries are loathe to convict under these circumstances: They will do everything in their power to discredit the victim while crediting the defendant.

* * *

Although the law has been reformed to, theoretically, treat women as full human beings, these reforms are slow to take effect. This is because the justice system is still influenced by attitudes that view women as sexual property, reproductive instruments of the state, and unworthy of belief. Such attitudes shape police practices, prosecutorial discretion, judicial rulings, and jury verdicts.[34]

Creating systemic change will require the infusion of feminist politics at every level of the justice system, from the police to the courts. We will also need to evaluate the feminist theory and practice that has developed during the past decade to make

---

[32] See *People v. Liberta,* 64 NY 2d 152 [1984].

[33] Usually, such corroboration requirements exist when the victim (complainant) is either a minor or mentally incompetent. Under these circumstances, minors and mental incompetents could not normally testify under oath. Therefore, to sustain a conviction, the state needed independent corroboration to support the uncorroborated testimony of the victim. Such complainants were viewed, due to age and mental status, as legally incompetent.

[34] See New York State Task Force Report on Women in the Courts (1985), in which a judicial commission documented the misogyny in the justice system. It found that women litigants, rape victims, domestic violence victims, as well as female attorneys, were all treated with disrespect and in many cases with outright contempt. In New York, as in most states, women still await the full benefits of legal personage before the law.

sure that they adequately represent women's lives and defend women's rights. For example, the idea of the battered woman's syndrome was first developed by Lenore Walker to explain to juries why women who killed their assailants felt they had no choice even though there was a break in the violence. Further research and analysis has shown, however, that such situations often are, in fact, life-threatening to the woman. It does a disservice to the woman to refer to a psychological state rather than to see her as someone who has reasonably appraised her choices. Perhaps the real challenge of the twenty-first century will be to transform a legal system crafted to protect male power into one that brings women to the center of human discourse. *We* can then create a new legal tradition in which women's experience is no longer marginal.   [1992]

🌿 48

The Courts' Enforcement of Women's Economic Rights

NEW YORK STATE TASK FORCE
OF WOMEN IN THE COURTS

The "feminization of poverty"—the disproportionate representation of women among New York's poorest citizens—has impelled the legislative[151] and executive branches[152] of government to identify causes and seek solutions. For most women, unlike men, divorce causes extreme economic dislocation and thus has contributed significantly to the swelling ranks of female single-parent heads of households living in poverty.[153]

The courts directly influence the economic welfare of a substantial number of women in New York when they adjudicate women's rights to: (1) property and maintenance upon dissolution of a marriage; and (2) child support. To determine whether the courts have contributed to the well-documented trend of increased economic hardship for women, the Task Force examined the courts' decisions under the Equitable Distribution Law and child support laws.

1. THE EQUITABLE DISTRIBUTION LAW

New York's Equitable Distribution Law (EDL)[154]— the statute that governs the economic rights of husband and wife upon the dissolution of a marriage— was enacted in 1980. Immediately prior to the EDL's enactment, New York was one of few remaining states in which property—*i.e.*, real estate, securities, bank accounts, businesses and other assets—was distributed strictly to the title holder. Because wives rarely had assets in their own names, and because few assets other than the marital home were jointly held, property accumulated during the marriage usually went solely to the husband after divorce. A wife's years of contributions as primary caretaker for the children, homemaker and spouse had no impact on property distribution. Alimony was terminated on the husband's death and the former wife had no right to inheritance.

In 1985, the New York State Court of Appeals characterized the "conceptual base upon which the [EDL] rests" as an "economic partnership theory" of marriage.[155] The court expressly adopted a view of the EDL that one lower court "said so well":

---

[151] *See generally, The Status of Older Women: A Report on State-wide Public Hearings Conducted by the Assembly Task Force on Women's Issues and the Assembly Standing Committee on Aging* (New York State Assembly 1983); N.Y.C. Council, *The Feminization of Poverty, An Analysis of Poor Women in New York City* (1984).

[152] *See generally,* Minutes of Hearings, Department of State, Hearings on the Feminization of Poverty, Buffalo (June 5, 1984), Syracuse (June 6, 1984), White Plains (June 12, 1984), Hauppauge (June 13, 1984), New York City (June 14, 1984).

[153] *See* 1983 U. S. Department of Commerce, Bureau of the Census, *Child Support and Alimony;* Series P-23, No. 141,

July 1985; L. Weitzmann, *The Divorce Revolution: The Unexpected Social and Economic Consequences for Women and Children in America* (Free Press/MacMillan, 1985); Sterin and Davis, *Divorce Awards and Outcomes,* Federation for Community Planning/Cleveland Women's Council, 1981); J. Wallerstein and J. Kelley, *Surviving the Breakup* (Basic Books, Inc., 1980); D. Chambers, *Making Fathers Pay: The Enforcement of Child Support* (University of Chicago Press, 1979); Shaw, *Economic Consequences of Marital Disruption, National Longitudinal Study of Mature Women,* U. S. Department of Labor (June 1978); Hoffman and Holmes, *Husbands, Wives and Divorce in Five Thousand American Families— Patterns of Economic Progress,* Vol. IV, Institute for Social Research, University of Michigan (1975).

[154] L. 1980, ch. 281.

[155] *O'Brien v. O'Brien,* 66 N.Y.2d 576 (Case No. 629, slip op. at p. 12) (December 26, 1985). In *O'Brien,* the issue pre-

The function of equitable distribution is to recognize that when a marriage ends each of the spouses, based on the totality of contributions made to it, has a stake in and right to a share of the marital assets accumulated while it endured, not because that share is needed, but because those assets represent the capital product of what was essentially a partnership entity.[156]

Contributions to the formation and growth of marital assets are to be "recognized, considered, and rewarded" whether they are direct or indirect.[157] Indirect contributions not only include a spouse's services—such as child rearing and household management—that free the other spouse to pursue directly income-generating careers and the acquisition of assets, but also embrace the concept of opportunity cost. By undertaking homemaker's tasks, which require the development of skills not readily transferable to the paid labor market, the spouse makes an additional indirect contribution to the partnership enterprise by sacrificing her "own educational or career goals and opportunities."[158]

Over 20 witnesses appearing at the Task Force's public hearings presented their views on the EDL. Some submitted articles and written commentaries on the reported decisions. Professor Henry Foster and others stated that "New York's EDL is alive and well and is being fairly administered,"[159] and that women are in a substantially better position now than in pre-equitable distribution days.[160] Few witnesses concurred.

Current application of the EDL was overwhelmingly viewed as working "unfairness and undue hardship" on women.[161] New York City matrimonial attorneys, Harriet N. Cohen and Adria S. Hillman studied 70 reported EDL decisions and offered the following overview which was confirmed by a similar study submitted by Joel R. Brandes, Esq.:

> [D]ependent wives, whether they worked at home or in the paid market place were relegated to one or a combination of the following in an aggregate of 49 out of the 54 cases susceptible of this analysis; less than a fifty percent overall share of marital property; short term maintenance after long term marriages; *de minimis* shares of business and professional practices which, in addition, the courts undervalued; terminable and modifiable maintenance in lieu of indefeasible and equitable distribution or distributive awards; and inadequate or no counsel fee awards.[162]

---

sented was whether a license to practice medicine, "the parties' only asset of any consequence," is "marital property subject to equitable distribution," *Id.*, slip op. at p. 1. The Court of Appeals reversed a decision of the Appellate Division, Second Department, and overruled a decision of the Appellate Division, Fourth Department (*Lesman v. Lesman*, 88 A.D.2d 153 (4th Dept. 1982)). Judge Richard D. Simons wrote: "[t]he words [of the EDL] mean exactly what they say: that an interest in a profession or professional career potential is marital property which may be represented by direct or indirect contributions of the nontitle-holding spouse, including financial contributions and non-financial contributions made by caring for the home and family." *Id.* slip op. at pp. 7–8.

[156] *Id.*, slip op. at p. 12, quoting *Wood v. Wood*, 119 Misc. 2d 1076, 1079 (Sup. Ct. Suffolk Co. 1983).

[157] *Id.*, slip op. at p. 12.

[158] *Id.*, slip op. at p. 9.

[159] Foster, *A Second Opinion*, 17 Family Law Review 3 (1985), submitted to the Task Force on May 7, 1985 (hereinafter cited as Second Opinion). Even these individuals agreed that *pendente lite* awards for counsel and experts have been inadequate, *id.* at p. 8; that courts have applied the concept of rehabilitative maintenance inappropriately, *see* Testimony of Julia Perles, Family Law Section, Chairperson of the Committee on Equitable Distribution, New York State Bar Asso-

ciation, New York City I Tr. at p. 7 (hereinafter cited as Perles Testimony); and that substantial assets have been erroneously excluded from consideration as marital property. *See* Henry Foster, Esq., Letter to the Editor, N.Y.L.J., May 5, 1985, p. 2 col. 6. Perles Testimony at p. 9.

[160] Perles Testimony, *supra* note 159 at p. 2. Buffalo attorney Herbert Siegel stated "I don't mean to say for a moment that women are not doing much better today under equitable distribution than they were doing prior to 1980," but added, "it is my position in reference to day-to-day practice, that the economic partnership that I thought was established by way of the passage of the law is a long way off." Testimony of Herbert Siegel, Esq., Rochester Tr. at p. 172 (hereinafter cited as Siegel Testimony).

[161] Statement of Joel R. Brandes, Esq., at p. 2 (hereinafter referred to as Brandes Statement). *See also* Lester Wallman, a New York matrimonial lawyer and member of the committee that drafted EDL recently stated, "Judges are completely misconstruing it and women are being treated unjustly. . . . The answer is to make some very very substantive changes in the laws." *The New York Times*, Aug. 5, 1985 at A1. *See* Joint Public Hearings of the Senate and Assembly Standing Committees on the Judiciary Respecting Proposed Revisions to the Equitable Distribution Law, March 1985 and Joint Public Hearings of the Department of State and Division for Women Respecting the Feminization of Poverty, June 1984.

[162] Cohen and Hillman, "Analysis of Seventy Select Decisions After Trial Under New York State's Equitable Distribution Law, From January 1981 Through October 1984, Analyzed November 1, 1984" at p. 4 (hereinafter cited as Cohen-Hillman Study). *See also* Cohen and Hillman, "Report to the Task Force, Diagnosis is Confirmed: EDL is Ailing" (hereinafter cited as Diagnosis is Confirmed), at p. 4. The authors pointed out that only seventy EDL decisions were reported

The results of many lower court decisions involving property distribution and maintenance awards ignore the irretrievable economic losses women incur when they forego developing income-generating careers and vested retirement rights to become homemakers for the benefit of their families. Rather than recognizing the economic partnership theory of marriage, some judges appear predisposed to ensure that the EDL does not "make reluctant Santa Clauses out of ex-husbands."[163] Equitable sharing of this permanently lost earning capacity upon a marriage's dissolution does not, as some have written, confer a "free meal ticket" to the economically dependent spouse[164] but constitutes a recognition that each partner's contribution to the marital enterprise—whether through affirmative performance or through foregoing opportunity—will be equitably compensated out of assets accumulated during the marriage and the post-marriage earning capacity of each party.

(a) Distribution of Marital Property

The EDL directs the courts to consider two types of property upon the dissolution of a marriage: "marital" property and "separate" property. Separate property is defined as property acquired before the marriage or by descent or as a gift from a party other than the spouse or as compensation received for personal injuries. The appreciation in the value of separate property is not distributed and remains with the title-holding spouse "except to the extent that such appreciation is due in part to the contributions or efforts of the other spouse."[165]

Marital property is defined as "all property acquired by either or both spouses during the marriage and before the execution of a separation agreement or the commencement of a matrimonial action, regardless of the form in which title is held."[166] Assets deemed marital property must be divided "equitably" according to nine statutory factors and "any other factor which the court expressly finds to be just and proper."[167]

Judicial valuation and division of property determine many women's post-divorce economic well being.[168] Lower courts in New York have construed the provisions of the EDL relevant to property division in a manner that greatly disadvantages women and predetermines inequitable results. Economically dependent women's ability to litigate is hampered by inadequate awards of attorneys' and experts' fees. Property divisions place an inappro-

---

between July 1980 and October 15, 1984 and joined Mr. Brandes, who submitted an analysis of sixty-five cases, and other witnesses in urging that more decisions be published. They also noted that it is these seventy judicial decisions that set the parameters for the 90 percent of matrimonial cases that end in a negotiated settlement. Cohen-Hillman Testimony, New York City I Tr. at pp. 79, 87.

[163] *See* H. Foster & D. Freed, "Law and the Family" N.Y.L.J. 1/9/86, p. 1, col. 1 (chastising the "enemies of equitable distribution" as having "abandoned the principle of equal rights" and advocating " 'grandmother clauses' in order to make reluctant Santa Clauses out of ex-husbands they may have rejected.").

[164] *Id.*

[165] D.R.L. § 236B(1)(d)(3).

[166] D.R.L. § 236B(1)(c).

[167] Section 236B(5)(d) of the Domestic Relations Law provides that:

> In determining an equitable distribution of property, the court shall consider:
>
> (1) the income and property of each party at the time of marriage, and at the time of the commencement of the action;
>
> (2) the duration of the marriage and the age and health of both parties;
>
> (2) the need of a custodial parent to occupy or own the marital residence and to use or own its household effects;
>
> (4) the loss of inheritance and pension rights upon dissolution of the marriage as of the date of dissolution;
>
> (5) any award of maintenance under subdivision six of this part;
>
> (6) any equitable claim to, interest in, or direct or indirect contribution made to the acquisition of such marital property by the party not having title, including joint efforts or expenditures and contributions and services as a spouse, parent, wage earner and homemaker, and to the career or career potential of the other party;
>
> (7) the liquid or non-liquid character of all marital property;
>
> (8) the probable future financial circumstances of each party;
>
> (9) the impossibility or difficulty of evaluating any component asset or any interest in a business, corporation or profession, and the economic desirability of retaining such asset or interest intact and free from any claim or interference by the other party.

[168] Given the insufficiency of maintenance and child support awards and the extreme difficulty in enforcing them, many economically dependent wives rely heavily on marital property awards for economic security and survival.

priately low value on homemakers' services and permanently lost earning capacity.

(i) Women's Ability to Litigate The EDL empowers the courts to require either spouse to pay the other's attorney's fees so as "to enable that spouse to carry on or defend the action or proceeding."[169] Judges' refusals to award adequate or timely counsel and expert fees were repeatedly cited as critical barriers to women's receiving adequate representation in matrimonial cases.

> Most women do not have the necessary resources to retain an attorney who is very familiar with the law and its practice. No matter how well off the husband, by the time the parties are ready to retain lawyers the wife has been left with very little. Most attorneys require a retainer at the commencement of their representation and are forced to finance the case after the retainer has been used up. As a general rule, where an attorney has been paid a retainer, no matter how small the amount, the courts will not award *pendente lite* counsel fees. This creates financial pressure on the attorney to conclude the case and on the spouse who has to worry about the increasing cost of litigation.[170]

Respondents to the Attorneys' Survey said of counsel fees:

> The courts do not make reasonable allocations for legal services rendered to female litigants in matrimonial cases which has the effect of depriving female litigants of proper representation in situations where the husband controls the family purse strings and/or has the greater income—which is true in most cases. —*Seventy-year-old rural male*

> The greatest area of discrimination in Monroe County involves court awards of counsel fees to women. The courts are excessively stingy and inconsistent in cases where wife has no identifiable assets and husband is able to pay. As a result, members of the private bar will not accept this type of matrimonial case, and deserving women go unrepresented. —*Thirty-year-old rural male*

> I've curtailed my matrimonial practice because I can't afford to handle the cases. Most contested matters are guaranteed losers for the wife. Most of [those] I've handled, the husband has the resources to enter into protracted litigation while the wife does not. If I've invested $5,000–$10,000 worth of time into one of these divorces, the court might—on a good day—award me $2,500. The women who most need my services will never have the resources under the present system to be able to pay my fee. —*Thirty-six-year-old urban female*

The EDL provides that funds for retaining accountants and appraisers may be awarded to needy spouses "as justice requires."[171] Because the wife must prove the value of the husband's assets, business or professional practice, fees for experts are essential. This "prove it or lose it" aspect of EDL litigation often presents, in practice, acute problems for the economically dependent spouse.

Herbert M. Seigel, a Buffalo attorney, testified that "applications to the court . . . for accounting fees, for appraisal fees and evaluation fees are not being met kindly."[172] He described a case in which his firm advanced $5,000 for an appraisal of a husband's business and was awarded only $400 as reimbursement. Noting that few law offices are willing or able to make large disbursements for experts in matrimonial cases, Mr. Seigel concluded that "oftentimes women are not obtaining the necessary expert analysis that they should have prior to going to trial."[173]

(ii) Property Division The pattern of property division in reported decisions reveals that the view of marriage as an economic partnership has not taken hold. Lillian Kozak, C.P.A., Chair of the

[169] D.R.L. § 237.

[170] Brandes Statement, *supra* note 161 at p. 4. The Cohen-Hillman Study revealed that in the 47 reported decisions where counsel fees where at issue, 21 economically-dependent wives received no counsel fees at the conclusion of trial. Cohen-Hillman Study, *supra* note 162 at p. 7.

[171] *See* D.R.L. §§ 236(b)(5), 237; *Gueli v. Gueli*, 106 Misc. 2d 877, 878, 435 N.Y.S.2d 537, 538 (Sup. Ct. Nassau Co. 1981).

[172] Seigel Testimony, *supra* note 160 at p. 168. The Appellate Division, Second Department, has held that expert fees are not to be "granted routinely." *Ahern v. Ahern*, 94 A.D.2d 53, 58, 463 N.Y.S.2d 238, 241 (2d Dep't 1983).

[173] Seigel Testimony, *supra* note 160 at p. 168. The combined effect of a heavy burden of proof and the courts' denials and "often unrealistic," Second Opinion *supra* note 159 at p. 8, awards of *pendente lite* experts' fees significantly undercuts the EDL's purpose, making "possession . . . 9/10ths of the law." Brandes Statement, *supra* note 161 at p. 7.

NOW-New York State Domestic Relations Task Force testified:

> An examination of decisions reveals that the one family asset which is divided 50/50 most of the time, is the marital residence. Since the vast majority of houses are jointly owned and were therefore divided equally under the old law, the equal division of houses is hardly evidence of an egalitarian perspective. In the few cases where the wife has been awarded the whole marital residence, she has been deprived of far greater interest in income producing property, including businesses, and in pension plans or to obviously hidden wealth. Although cash savings are also being divided, where they have been substantial there has not been an equal division. In the realm of property division, the valuation of businesses . . . has been a hoax and the percentage of the hoax awarded the wife has been 25% or less. There seems to be no offset, in the main, for leaving the husband with this major income producing asset.[174]

The Cohen and Hillman Study analyzed fifteen reported cases in which a marital business property was at issue, of which thirteen involved marriages of long duration ranging from 7 years to 41 years. Eighteen percent of marital property was the median award to wives.[175] In only two were equal awards made. In six cases, the wife was completely denied a share of the business property.[176]

The courts appear to be ignoring wives' "contributions and services as a spouse, parent, wage earner and homemaker and to the career or career potential of the other party."[177] These criteria (which apply both to distribution of marital property and to awards of maintenance) require the courts to consider the contributions made to the "economic partnership," by the non-title-holding, non-wage-earning spouse.[178] Supreme Court Justice Betty Ellerin, Deputy Chief Administrative Judge for Courts within the City of New York, testified that "the value of a homemaker/wife's contribution to a marriage is again all too often valued in terms of societal attitudes that deprecate women's role or contribution."[179] Attendees at the Oswego County listening session reported that farmers' wives who have spent all their adult lives helping to keep a farm going do not have their contribution valued and end up with very little in equitable distribution.

One reason for the undervaluation of homemakers' contributions suggested by a survey respondent is that some judges "cannot conceive of a woman having a right to a share of 'the man's business' [which they] refer to as '*his* business' and '*his* house' and '*his* pension.' Under equitable distribution it should be thought of as 'their business' and 'their pension,' etc."

Among survey respondents, 72 percent of women and 32 percent of men reported that equitable distribution awards "sometimes," "often" or "always" reflect a judicial attitude that property belongs to the husband and a wife's share is based on how much he could give her without diminishing his current lifestyle.[180] Sixty-two percent (62%) of the male respondents and 20 percent of the female respondents reported that this occurs "rarely" or "never."

Seventy percent (70%) of women and 44 percent of men also reported that judges "sometimes," "of-

---

[174] Testimony of Lillian Kozak, Chair, NOW-NYS Domestic Relations Law Task Force, New York City I Tr. at p. 141 (hereinafter cited as Kozak Testimony).

[175] Cohen-Hillman Study, *supra*, note 162 at p. 90.

[176] There has been *dictum* in one appellate case to the effect that the wife's homemaker services should be rebuttably presumed to be equal in value to the husband's earnings. *Conner v. Conner*, 97 A.D.2d 88, 468 N.Y.S.2d 482 (2d Dep't 1983).

[177] D.R.L. § 236B(5)(d)(6) and (6)(a)(8).

[178] Professor Thomas Kershner of the Department of Economics at Union College, testified that "economists have made considerable economic advances in identifying and measuring the various jobs and tasks that homemakers, wives and mothers do." Testimony of Thomas Kershner, Albany Tr. at pp. 229–230. Judith Avner, Esq., Assistant Director of the New York State Women's Division, cautioned, however, that evaluation of the value of particular services as the sole measure of a homemaker's contribution, as opposed to the "joint enterprise" concept, can deteriorate into a debate at the level of whether the homemaker left a "ring-around-the-collar." Testimony of Judith Avner, Esq. Albany Tr. at p. 138. *See* Avner, *Valuing Homemakers Work: An Alternative to Quantification*, 4 Fairshare 11 (1984).

[179] Ellerin Testimony, *supra* note 78 at p. 284.

[180] Female and male survey respondents (F%/M%) reported that equitable distribution awards reflect a judicial attitude that property belongs to the husband and a wife's share is based on how much the husband could give her without diminishing his current lifestyle:

Always	Often	Sometimes	Rarely	Never	No Answer
12/2	35/10	25/20	13/31	7/31	9/6

ten" or "always" refuse to award 50 percent of property or more to wives even though financial circumstances are such that even with such an award husbands will not have to substantially reduce their standard of living but wives will.[181] Forty-nine percent (49%) of the men and 18 percent of the women reported that this occurs "rarely" or "never."

Other witnesses and respondents stressed the fact that the judiciary is overwhelmingly male and may have little understanding of what homemaking involves. Some judges appear unaware of the economic opportunity cost to the one who has devoted long years to unpaid labor for her family. Rockland County Legislator Harriet Cornell observed:

> [M]ale perspective on family life has skewed decisions in equitable distribution cases. The perception of most men—and the judiciary is mostly male—is that care of the house and children can be done with one hand tied behind the back. Send the kids out to school, put them to bed, and the rest of the time free to play tennis and bridge. They think any woman—no matter her age or lack of training—can find a nice little job and a nice little apartment and conduct her later years as she might have done at age 25.[182]

Lillian Kozak's reference to the valuation of businesses as "a hoax" was also noted in the Cohen-Hillman study, which cited several cases in which courts credited the husband's experts' valuation even while acknowledging the husband's financial chicanery. These cases can be read as encouraging a husband to undervalue or hide assets because such behavior is ultimately rewarded in the division of marital property.[183]

(b) Maintenance

The EDL provides for the ordering of "temporary maintenance or maintenance to meet the reasonable needs of a party to the matrimonial action in such an amount as justice requires" as determined by ten factors.[184] In his legislative memorandum in support of the EDL, Gordon Burrows of the Assembly Judiciary Committee, stated:

> The objective of the maintenance provision is to award the recipient spouse an opportunity to achieve independence. However, in marriages of long duration, or where the former spouse is out of the labor market and lacks sufficient resources, or has sacrificed her business or professional career to serve as a parent and homemaker, "maintenance" on a permanent basis may be necessary.[185]

Maintenance awards are critical to the economic security of the vast majority of economically dependent wives. Lillian Kozak testified: "The greatest asset in most families is the earning power of the supporting spouse to which the homemaker has

---

[181] Female and male survey respondents (F%/M%) reported that judges refuse to award 50% of property or more to wives even though the probable future financial circumstances indicate that even with such an award husbands will not have to substantially reduce their standard of living but wives will:

Always	Often	Sometimes	Rarely	Never	No Answer
10/2	41/16	19/26	12/31	6/18	11/8

[182] Testimony of Hon. Harriet Cornell, Albany Tr. at pp. 51–52 (hereinafter cited as Cornell Testimony),

[183] Cohen-Hillman Study, *supra,* note 162 at p. 7.

[184] Section 236B(6)(a) of the Domestic Relations Law provides, in relevant part that:

> [I]n any matrimonial action the court may order temporary maintenance or maintenance to meet the reasonable needs of a party to the matrimonial action in such amount as justice requires. . . . In determining the amount and duration of maintenance the court shall consider:
>
> (1) the income and property of the respective parties including marital property distributed pursuant to subdivision five of this part;
> (2) the duration of the marriage and the age and health of both parties;
> (3) the present and future capacity of the person having need to be self-supporting;
> (4) the period and training necessary to enable the person having need to become self-supporting;
> (5) the presence of children of the marriage in the respective homes of the parties;
> (6) the standard of living established during the marriage where practical and relevant;
> (7) the tax consequences to each party;
> (8) contributions and services of the party seeking maintenance as a spouse, parent, wage earner and homemaker, and to the career or career potential of the other party;
> (9) the wasteful dissipation of family assets by either spouse; and
> (10) any other factor which the court shall expressly find to be just and proper.

[185] Memorandum of Assemblyman Gordon W. Burrows, 1980 New York State Legislative Annual at p. 130. The fact that the term "permanent maintenance" is not used in the statute may mislead some judges. At a New York City regional meeting an attorney described an argument before a Nassau County judge who insisted that the EDL bars permanent maintenance.

contributed. The only possible distribution of this asset is via alimony/maintenance."[186]

(i) Duration of Award   The Legislature intended maintenance awards to be short-term when the non-wage-earning or economically dependent spouse is young or has a strong potential to become self-supporting after a period of support for education or training. The Task Force found that this concept of "rehabilitative" maintenance is being widely abused. Judges are too frequently awarding minimal, short-term maintenance or no maintenance at all to older, long-term, full or part-time homemakers with little or no chance of becoming self-supporting at a standard of living commensurate with that enjoyed during the marriage.[187] Among survey respondents, 62 percent of women and 38 percent of men reported that older, long-term homemakers with little chance of obtaining employment above minimum wage are "sometimes," "rarely," or "never" awarded permanent alimony. Survey comments on maintenance included:

> While I generally support rehabilitative maintenance, I do not believe that a 50-year-old woman who has always been a housewife can be rehabilitated. However, permanent awards for such women are almost non-existent.
> — *Thirty-six-year-old urban female*

> I am *very disturbed* by the court's reluctance and often refusal to award adequate and/or long-term maintenance orders to wives especially those from lengthy marriages (15–30+ years). I am also disturbed by the meager temporary (*pendente lite*) awards of support which are usually "barely getting by" awards, especially when the cases involve husbands and fathers with significant income ($50,000 and more). [emphasis in original]
> — *Fifty-four-year-old rural male*

A woman who is minimally self-supporting often receives no maintenance or minimal ($25-$50/

week) for a limited period of time, when the man may be earning $30,000–$50,000/year.[188]
> — *Twenty-eight-year-old urban female*

Cohen and Hillman analyzed fifty reported decisions involving requests for maintenance. In forty-four of these cases, the marriages ranged from 7½ years to 57 years in duration. In ten cases economically dependent wives married between 10 and 57 years (with 18 years of marriage being the median) were totally denied a maintenance award. In fifteen cases, economically dependent women who had been married for between 8 and 36 years (20 years of marriage being the median) were awarded only rehabilitative maintenance for periods ranging from 1½ years to 5 years. In the remaining nineteen cases economically dependent women were awarded long-term or permanent maintenance.[189]

(ii) Amount of Award   Some judges appear to be ignoring "the standard of living established during the marriage" and are relying on parsimonious interpretation of the wife's "reasonable needs." As a result, even women who can obtain employment enjoy a far less generous post-divorce standard of living than do their husbands. The question of post-divorce parity was raised by Herbert Seigel, Esq., who asked:

> When it comes to equitable distribution and the talk of economic partnership, why should there not be

---

[186] Kozak Testimony, *supra* note 174 at p. 143.

[187] Female and male survey respondents (F%/M%) reported that older displaced homemakers, with little chance of obtaining employment above minimum wage, are awarded permanent maintenance after long-term marriages:

Always	Often	Sometimes	Rarely	Never	No Answer
4/15	24/43	36/24	21/10	5/2	10/6

[188] Seeking to explain the reasons behind courts' failure to award appropriate maintenance, another survey respondent wrote:

> The attitude seems to be one of "You've gotten your fair share of the marital assets and you're capable of working (whether the wife is 25 or 55 years old; having been married 5 years or 35 years), therefore if you are careful and invest what you have received you will be able to get along." This attitude prevails irrespective of the standard of living of the couple prior to divorce, the presence of children in the wife's home (pre-school or otherwise), past employment or lack thereof by the wife, her level of education or job training, and the disparity of post-divorce income of the couple. (Almost no effort is given to fashioning parity, even for a short duration.) . . . The inequities are apparent, yet the courts (including the appellate courts) have for the most part chosen to ignore them. . . . The insensitivity of the courts in this regard is egregious.
> — *Forty-nine-year-old urban male*

[189] Cohen-Hillman Study, *supra* note 162 at p. 93. The range of duration of marriage of this group was 7½ to 41 years with the median at 17 years.

an economic partnership not only in property, but in the ability to support themselves or live in a way to maintain a certain standard of living? . . . I think there should be some parity when it comes to the dissolution of marriages and the question of maintenance itself.[190]

Julia Perles, Esq., Chairperson on the Equitable Distribution Committee of the Family Law Section of the New York State Bar Association, testified that inadequate maintenance awards are "unfair," but they are "not the fault of the EDL. I think it's the fault and the prejudice of particular judges who hear the cases."[191]

Justice William Rigler, Presiding Judge of Special Term, Part 5 (the matrimonial part) in Kings County Supreme Court suggested that the problem is that this kind of gender bias is injected by the parties themselves. He cited a case in which a physician husband admitted to a net annual income of about $50,000 and the wife, who had worked to put the husband through medical school and had no college degree, requested support for herself and her children and funds to complete her education. The husband rejected this request and submitted his own estimates of what his wife's expenses should be. "His list included only the bare necessities for his wife, while his own list of expenses was quite expansive and generous, taking into account the social and professional position as a physician."[192]

(c) Provisional Remedies and Enforcement

Despite statutory provisions for full financial disclosure, the preservation of assets, enforcement of awards and interest on arrears, enforcement is seriously deficient.

Practitioners assert that there are no useful sanctions in the EDL to compel disclosure. As a result, "stonewalling" is commonplace.[193] If effective temporary restraining orders are granted to maintain the status quo for equitable distribution,[194] judges rarely impose meaningful sanctions when they are violated.[195]

In an enforcement action, the EDL requires a judge to enter a judgment for arrears unless "good cause" is shown for failure to seek relief from the amount of maintenance awarded.[196] Ex-husbands often respond to enforcement actions with meritless motions for downward modification or claims that they are financially unable to comply. Myrna Felder, Esq., Chair of the Matrimonial Committee of the Women's Bar Association of the State of New York testified that a motion for downward modification "automatically stops enforcement proceedings in their tracks,"[197] leading to nine to twelve months of delay before the Special Referee's hearing and confirmation of the Referee's report by the Supreme Court Judge who made the reference.

> If a year later, after hearings and the entry of contempt, it turns out that he was able to comply all along, is there a penalty for the man? No. Are there damages? No. Is there an extraordinary counsel fee? No. The fellow has learned a lesson that our courts are teaching the men around the state: It's better not to be so quick to pay.[198]

Survey respondents reported that Courts do not uniformly grant maintenance retroactive to the initial motion date as required by the Domestic Rela-

---

[190] Seigel Testimony, *supra* note 160, at pp. 170–171.
Female and male survey respondents (F/M) reported the duration of rehabilitative maintenance awards based on length of marriage as:

Duration of Marriage	Average of Years Maintenance
Less than 10	3/3
10–20	4/5
20–30	6/8
More than 30	8/9

[191] Perles Testimony, *supra* note 159, at p. 29.
[192] Testimony of Hon. William Rigler, New York City II Tr. at pp. 100–101 (hereinafter cited as Rigler Testimony).

[193] Brandes Testimony, *supra* note 161 at 181.
[194] Female and male survey respondents (F%/M%) reported that effective temporary restraining orders are granted to maintain the status quo for equitable distribution:

Always	Often	Sometimes	Rarely	Never	No Answer
2/4	15/30	35/37	33/15	4/5	11/8

[195] Female and male survey respondents (F%/M%) reported that judges impose meaningful sanctions, including civil commitment, when injunctions are violated:

Always	Often	Sometimes	Rarely	Never	No Answer
*/2	5/9	12/20	46/45	26/14	10/10

[196] Domestic Relations Law § 244.
[197] Testimony of Myrna Felder, Esq., New York City I Tr. at 247 (hereinafter cited as Felder testimony).
[198] *Id.* at 248.

tions Law and Family Court Act,[199] or effectively enforce the maintenance awarded.[200] Sixty percent (60%) of women and 56 percent of men survey respondents reported that interest is "rarely" or "never" awarded on arrears.[201] The inability of women to afford counsel and the refusal of the courts to award realistic counsel fees were also cited as a factor in enforcement problems.[202]

SUMMARY OF FINDINGS

1. The manner in which judges distribute a family's assets and income upon divorce profoundly affects many women's economic welfare. Women who forego careers to become homemakers usually have limited opportunities to develop their full potential in the paid labor force.

2. The New York Court of Appeals has recognized that the Equitable Distribution Law embraces the view of marriage as an economic partnership in which the totality of the non-wage-earning spouse's contributions—including lost employment opportunity and pension rights—is to be considered when dividing property and awarding maintenance.

3. Many lower court judges have demonstrated a predisposition not to recognize or to minimize the homemaker spouse's contributions to the marital economic partnership by:

    a. awarding minimal, short-term maintenance or no maintenance at all to older, long-term, full or part-time homemakers with little or no chance of becoming self-supporting at a standard of living commensurate with that enjoyed during the marriage.

    b. awarding homemaker-wives inequitably small shares of income-generating or business property.

4. Economically dependent wives are put at an additional disadvantage because many judges fail to award attorneys' fees adequate to enable effective representation or experts' fees adequate to value the marital assets.

5. Many judges fail to order provisional remedies that ensure assets are not diverted or dissipated.

6. After awards have been made, many judges fail to enforce them.   [1985]

---

[199] Domestic Relations Law § 236(b)(6)(a); Family Court Act § 440(1). Female and male survey respondents (F%/M%) reported that maintenance is granted retroactive to the initial motion date:

Always	Often	Sometimes	Rarely	Never	No Answer
10/16	19/29	26/23	31/20	5/6	9/6

[200] Female and male survey respondents (F%/M%) reported that the courts effectively enforce maintenance awards:

Always	Often	Sometimes	Rarely	Never	No Answer
1/4	12/27	27/38	45/22	10/3	4/5

[201] Female and male survey respondents (F%/M%) reported that interest on arrears is awarded as provided by statute:

Always	Often	Sometimes	Rarely	Never	No Answer
2/4	10/5	19/17	40/39	20/17	10/7

[202] The importance of fees sufficient to vigorously litigate was expressed by a survey respondent who wrote:

> The courts' failure to enforce child support and maintenance awards, whether *pendente lite* or after trial, is a disgrace. I am ashamed to tell my female clients that an award of maintenance and/or child support and/or arrears for same is generally not worth the paper it is written on unless (a) there is an endless supply of money to litigate enforcement or (b) the defendant-husband voluntarily complies with the orders directing the award.
> —*Fifty-five-year-old NYC female*

Work

The selections in this section consider the ways that sexism shapes women's work both inside and outside the home and suggest approaches to change.

Although the media give the impression that women have unlimited opportunities and have made unprecedented career advances, the reality of the workplace is much more discouraging. While women have made significant progress in a few areas, the majority face a sex-segregated labor market that devalues the work that most women do. Cynthia Marano is director of Wider Opportunities for Women, a Washington, D.C.-based national organization that works to achieve economic independence and equality of opportunity for women. In her article, she points out how various forms of sex discrimination limit opportunities for female workers.

The work that women do in the home—housework, child care, and nurturing—is extremely demanding in time, energy, and skill. Women still do most of the work in the home despite their increasing participation in the labor force. "The Politics of Housework" is a classic piece from the early days of the women's liberation movement that points to the struggle involved in getting men to take responsibility for housework. Because it is associated with women, housework is seen as demeaning and lacking in value. Like many of the writings from this period, it demonstrates that an activity that has been treated as private is indeed political; that is, it involves the allocation of power and resources.

Women experience discrimination in the workplace in many forms. While sexual harassment has shaped women's work experience for centuries, it has only recently been named and challenged. Sexual harassment has a damaging impact on women's economic security and advancement at work, as well as on their mental and physical health. Susan Brownmiller and Dolores Alexander's piece describes the ways women have struggled to expose the sexual harassment that large numbers of women face.

The lack of institutional support for parents is a serious disadvantage to women in the workplace. The U.S. is far behind other developed countries in providing government programs to support wage-earning women and their families, as June Jordan discusses in a later section. Michelle Harrison's recollections testify to the difficulties women face when they try to combine parenting with professional work in institutions resistant to anything less than a full-time commitment.

The dual role female workers are expected to play combined with inequities in the workplace trap many women in poverty. When women have children and can't find work that pays enough to support their families and pay for child care, they often must rely on the welfare system to survive. Women on welfare are frequently blamed for their situation and criticized for being "lazy." Welfare mothers, Diane Dujon, Judy Gradford, and Dottie Stevens describe the reality of their lives.

As Norma Burgess demonstrates, the experience of African-American women in the world of paid work has been significantly different from that of white women.

While black women have spent more time in the paid work force and contributed more of their family income than white women, racial discrimination has excluded them from many of the jobs occupied by white women. Burgess documents recent improvements as a result of civil rights and equal employment legislation and the improved education of black women, but concludes that much more needs to be done to improve the work lives of African-American women.

Women have struggled over time to have their work taken seriously and to be paid fairly. In their discussion of comparable worth as a strategy for raising women's wages, Teresa Amott and Julie Matthaei demonstrate that efforts to reevaluate jobs that have historically been performed by women can both augment women's earning power and raise fundamental questions about the free market, and the value of various forms of labor. Through this approach and others, feminists continue to challenge discriminatory patterns and press for equity for women's work.

49

Running Harder to Catch Up: Women, Work and the Future

CYNTHIA MARANO

Over the past several years, government and corporate leaders have expressed optimism at the prospects women workers [will] face over the next decade. The current rhetoric proclaims: "more jobs for women . . . more opportunities for women . . . greater employer interest in women workers . . . women breaking the glass ceiling."

Because of anticipated worker shortages and the predominance of new female job entrants expected over the next decade, it is assumed by many that women's problems in the job market are going to disappear or diminish greatly before our entry into the 21st century. I would counter this view of the future as incomplete and dangerously naive.

Instead, we must focus on the difficult problems women workers will face over the next decade. My view of the situation confronting women workers is considerably less promising than the rhetoric of Workforce 2000 commentators. Moreover, the problems women workers will face are old prob-

lems, exacerbated by new economic realities. The picture confronting women workers is bleak precisely *because* we have not found program and policy solutions to the labor market inequities identified in American society since the mid-'60s and early '70s. Additional social and economic problems have intensified the occupational inequities: the failure of our schools to fully develop the needed skills for employment; an employment system which is not structured to utilize workers' higher order skills; and the fiscal crisis in public systems coupled with a conservative political climate. With the confluence of these problems, women workers in the United States face a world in which occupational segregation will be more pronounced; a larger proportion of the female workforce will hold jobs but live in poverty; the glass ceiling of corporate management will remain unbroken; more women will fall into the ranks of the long-term unemployed; many women-owned businesses will fail; and more employers will find that a significant segment of the female workforce is ill-prepared to help keep American business competitive.

In addition, many women will continue to head households alone and in poverty, extending the cycle of poverty into several additional generations. Many of the family-related services provided by America's traditional homemakers will be left undone or will be provided by service businesses, employing women at low wages, but charging prices which will make the services inaccessible to middle- and low-income families. Women will be economically pressed to work outside the home and to provide the home and family services in the evenings. Many women will need to hold two jobs or mix full-time work with school or retraining to hold their own in the competition for a living wage. <u>The image of a working mother running harder to catch up with her previous standard of living is the image I see as typical</u> for the working women of the next decade. It is hardly a secure or comfortable image as contrasted with the businesswoman of the future who "has it all"—the popular image celebrated throughout the media.

Why is there such a gap between the <u>media image</u> (an image fostered by government leaders as well) and the realities that will be faced by the majority of women in the workforce of the future? What do labor force and other data indicate about the status of working women in the future? Let's review the statistics and highlight some of the factors affecting the status of women, work, and the U.S. economic future as we enter the 21st century.

WOMEN'S WORKFORCE PARTICIPATION: WHO WILL BE LEFT OUT?

Between 1990 and the year 2000, two-thirds of new workforce entrants will be female. Between 30 and 35 percent of new entrants will be male. Among new women workers, <u>women of color will make up the greatest proportion of new workforce entrants:</u>[1]

- There will be an 85 percent increase in the number of Latinas entering the labor force.
- There will be a 33 percent increase of African-American women in the labor force.
- One in ten new workforce entrants will be Asian, Native American, or Alaskan native women.

This picture might lead us to infer that the decade will be one in which all women will be employed, that there will be a great expansion of labor market opportunity for women workers. In fact, however, two-thirds of the workers who will be filling jobs over the next decade are already in the labor force. White men will continue to be the dominant workforce group, especially in the managerial and technical jobs at the top of the wage scale. Women in general—and African-American, Latina, Asian

and Native American women, in particular—will continue to face substantial disadvantages in the labor market.

Women will also continue to make up a significant percentage of <u>the unemployed</u>. In fact, it is clear that those at the greatest risk of unemployment in the year 2000 will include: individuals who lack a high school diploma, those with little paid work experience, individuals who lack a basic knowledge of technology, individuals who have a history of persistent poverty, and those whose employment skills have become obsolete. Among these target groups are alarming numbers of women.

It is estimated that only 14 percent of jobs by the year 2000 will be available to workers who hold a high school diploma or less. Currently, 58 percent of women workers have a high school diploma or less. Among unemployed women ages 25–64, 69 percent have attained a high school diploma or less. At particular risk of unemployment over the next decade are single mothers and displaced homemakers, more than half of whom lack a high school diploma. One-third of Latina workers and one-fifth of African-American women workers have also completed less than four years of high school education. These populations of women will face critical barriers to employment without significant intervention in education and training.

For African-American women, while workforce participation rates have been slightly higher than for white women, unemployment and <u>occupational segregation at the bottom of the wage scale</u> is a critical issue. Access to higher wage occupations and increased access to college education—especially in technical professional and science fields—are key agenda items for the decade. For Latinas, whose labor force participation will skyrocket between now and the year 2000, an increase in earnings and access to year round, full-time work are critical. The earnings of Latinas are the lowest of all U.S. women, and—even with gains over the past decade—remain significantly lower than the earning of African-American and white women. Investment in greater skills training—especially for Puerto Rican and Mexican American women—is critical. Among Asian and Pacific Islander women, a focus on the needs of those with highest rates of poverty is important—Vietnamese, Chinese, and Korean women, especially those who are recent immigrants. For Native American women, job creation and economic development—sensitive to the cultures of native peoples—will be needed because of extraordinary rates of unemployment.[2]

Yet, other groups of women stand at great risks in the Workforce 2000 as well. A significant proportion of women will continue to work at home as unpaid homemakers and caregivers. The National Displaced Homemakers Network cautions that women who make this choice over the next decade will face even greater labor force disadvantages. They note that, "In 1988, over 16 million women aged 25–59 were *not* in the paid labor force. Of these women, 13.9 million had no plans to look for work in the next year. Of those who were planning to enter the labor market, 881,000 had not worked in the last five years, if ever."[3]

Similarly, high unemployment will continue in specific geographic areas across the United States into the next century. Women in rural areas will suffer especially from the decline in manufacturing jobs projected over the next decade. Rural women's wage-earning jobs, such as apparel manufacturing, are especially vulnerable to exportation overseas. What development initiatives targeted to rural areas are planned to take the place of dying industries that have provided rural women and their families with needed income and often their only link to health and other benefits?

OCCUPATIONAL SEGREGATION: A WORSENING PICTURE

Only nine percent of women workers in the United States are now employed in nontraditional jobs—those in which 25 percent or less of the workforce is female. Seventy-seven percent of women workers are employed in the 20 occupations in which women make up more than 80 percent of the workforce. Will the increase in female job entrants affect this picture?

Evidence indicates that this historic occupational segregation may worsen as we enter the 21st century. First, the majority of jobs being created are in traditionally female categories. Among the ten occupations projected to have the greatest growth between now and the year 2000, six are traditionally female occupations. Second, the pipeline of education and employment training programs for women serves, in most cases, to reinforce this segregation. For example, more than 30 percent of women trained in Job Training Partnership Act (JTPA) programs have been trained for clerical occupations. Less than 15 percent of female JTPA trainees have been trained or placed in nontraditional or technical occupations.[4] This picture of sex segregation does not change significantly when we look at vocational education programs or welfare employment programs.

Advances in reducing occupational segregation over the past decade have occurred mainly in the professions, such as law, medicine, and accounting. Among the other, non-professional occupations, little desegregation has occurred. Rather, in some job categories, the establishment of new female job ghettoes has occurred. This is most visible in the area of electronic assembly, a nontraditional occupation for women in the early '70s. Today, electronic assembly has a 70 percent female workforce, and wages have declined as the occupation has become more predominantly female.

In fact, advances in technology which were once thought to offer promise in breaking down occupational segregation have not fulfilled this promise. Today certain categories of technical employment are predominantly female—those at the bottom of the wage spectrum. At the top of the wage spectrum in technical occupations, women are usually less than 10 percent of the workforce. Even then, however, the wage gap never disappears.

WOMEN'S POVERTY: SHIFTS AHEAD

One of the most disturbing realities about the Workforce 2000 is the estimated number of American women workers who will be working, but living in poverty. This is in spite of the fact that, according to the Rand Corporation, the wage gap between men and women will have been reduced by nearly 10 percent. However, one of the reasons that the wage gap will decrease is that wages of both men and women will have declined, with greater numbers of men joining the ranks of workers at the bottom of the wage scale, a trend that has been escalating since the mid-'70s. From 1978 to 1985, the number of Americans working full-time but living below the poverty line increased by 50 percent.[5]

Moreover, among the new jobs being created, the majority fall into low-wage categories. Between 1973 and 1979, one in five newly created jobs was a low-wage job. But in the next six years, the percentage more than doubled. By 1985, 44 percent of all newly created jobs paid the equivalent of $7,400 or less a year for full-time work. During the same period, high-wage jobs, paying the equivalent of $29,600 or above, decreased from 50 percent of new jobs to 10 percent of new jobs.[6] The result of this trend is that many Americans are struggling with declining wages and standards of living. In 1988, 4.5 million American women held jobs but lived in poverty.

Sociologist Dr. Diana Pearce of the Women and Poverty Project has explored the implications of this data for the next decade. Studying the gender breakdown of those who entered low-wage jobs between 1975 and 1984, she has documented that while 10 percent more women entered the labor force, 60 percent of these women entered as low-wage workers. When looking ahead to the year 2000, Pearce projects an increase in the "feminization of poverty"—the number of women heading households alone and in poverty—as well as an increase in the number of women who will be working but poor.[7] The minimum wage could be a solution to the inadequate incomes currently generated by women working in low-wage jobs. Yet the changes voted into law by the 101 Congress in 1989 were not large enough to move such workers, of whom more than 60 percent are female, to wages above the poverty level.

WOMEN'S UNPAID WORK: MAINTAINING FAMILIES

With the increase in the number of women working outside the home and the increase in women working at low-wage jobs, a further set of disturbing questions must be addressed. Families and society have traditionally relied upon the unpaid work of women at home to provide vital services to the family. These services, which include child care; housekeeping; care of sick, aged, and disabled family; and community volunteerism, are far more difficult to balance with full-time or even part-time work. Yet women's wages are the base of support among the many households headed by women and

are increasingly necessary to keep family income above the poverty level in dual-career families. In fact, the incomes of 50 percent of dual-earner families would fall below the poverty level if the wife did not work.

One solution, of course, is the development of businesses that provide these services to families who need them. This is a trend that was highly visible in the 1970s and 1980s with the dramatic growth in the caregiving industry. Unfortunately, while these services are increasingly needed, they are now being provided at a cost which a declining number of families can afford to pay. They also rely on predominantly female workers who are paid low wages to perform the services. Families earning low wages cannot afford to purchase these services or are able to purchase only marginal services so that female family members can participate in the labor force. The quality of family life and caretaking can therefore be expected to decline. Many women are caught in an unending cycle of low-wage work, caregiving at home, and the recognition that family needs are being poorly met. This will be an even more common tragedy as the decade comes to a close.

CONCLUSION

As politicians and business leaders discuss the Workforce 2000, little attention has been paid to these issues—or to the sex, race, age, and other forms of discrimination that have kept women disadvantaged in the labor force during the 20th century. Little discussion has been generated about the problems facing women in rural areas, where unemployment is rising dramatically; among Native American women, whose communities and cultures are threatened; or among American women workers whose jobs are being eliminated either through the direct impact of technology or through the exportation of jobs out of the country to lower-wage economies.

To assess women's workforce status for the future, it is necessary to explore both the macro-picture and the micro-picture: to take a look at the broad spectrum of women workers and at groups of women who will face disproportionately difficult times ahead. It is my premise that the United States and all its sectors must face up to the problems facing women workers if we are to design and implement strategies that will lead us to a healthy economy, competitiveness in the world market, safe and secure families, and a democratic and equitable society. To face these problems will take persistence, resources, and willingness to change. First, however, it takes information and the will to look at ourselves squarely. We must recognize and understand the risks to be willing to tackle the challenge.

NOTES

1. Bureau of Labor Statistics, *Monthly Labor Review* (September 1987).
2. Wider Opportunities for Women, *Risks and Challenges: Women, Work and the Future* (Washington, DC: 1990).
3. Jill Miller and Jean Cilik, "Homemakers, Displaced Homemakers, and the Workplace of the Future," in *Risks and Challenges: Women, Work and the Future* (Washington, DC: Wider Opportunities for Women, 1990), p. 38.
4. U.S. General Accounting Office, *Job Training Partnership Act: Information on Training, Placements and Wages of Male and Female Participants* (GAO/HRD-89-152FS (Washington, DC: GAO, 1989).
5. Sar Levitan and Isaac Shapiro, *Working But Poor, America's Contradiction* (Baltimore: Johns Hopkins University Press, 1987).
6. Barry Bluestone and Bennett Harrison, *The Great American Job Machine: The Proliferation of Low-Wage Employment in the U.S. Economy,* a study prepared for the Joint Economic Committee (U.S. Congress, 1986).
7. Diane Pearce, "Women's Poverty: Moving to the Workplace," in *Risks and Challenges: Women, Work and the Future* (Washington DC: Wider Opportunities for Women, 1990).

 50

The Politics of Housework

PAT MAINARDI OF REDSTOCKINGS

Though women do not complain of the power of husbands, each complains of her own husband, or of the husbands of her friends. It is the same in all other cases of servitude; at least in the commencement of the emancipatory movement. The serfs did not at first complain of the power of the lords, but only of their tyranny.

—John Stuart Mill
On the Subjection of Women

Liberated women—very different from Women's Liberation! The first signals all kinds of goodies, to warm the hearts (not to mention other parts) of the most radical men. The other signals—HOUSE-

WORK. The first brings sex without marriage, sex before marriage, cozy housekeeping arrangements ("I'm living with this chick") and the self-content of knowing that you're not the kind of man who wants a doormat instead of a woman. That will come later. After all, who wants that old commodity anymore, the Standard American Housewife, all husband, home and kids? The New Commodity, the Liberated Woman, has sex a lot and has a Career, preferably something that can be fitted in with the household chores—like dancing, pottery, or painting.

On the other hand is Women's Liberation—and housework. What? You say this is all trivial? Wonderful! That's what I thought. It seemed perfectly reasonable. We both had careers, both had to work a couple of days a week to earn enough to live on, so why shouldn't we share the housework? So I suggested it to my mate and he agreed—most men are too hip to turn you down flat. You're right, he said. It's only fair.

Then an interesting thing happened. I can only explain it by stating that we women have been brainwashed more than even we can imagine. Probably too many years of seeing television women in ecstasy over their shiny waxed floors or breaking down over their dirty shirt collars. Men have no such conditioning. They recognize the essential fact of housework right from the very beginning. Which is that it stinks.

Here's my list of dirty chores: buying groceries, carting them home and putting them away; cooking meals and washing dishes and pots; doing the laundry, digging out the place when things get out of control; washing floors. The list could go on but the sheer necessities are bad enough. All of us have to do these things, or get someone else to do them for us. The longer my husband contemplated these chores, the more repulsed he became, and so proceeded the change from the normally sweet, considerate Dr. Jekyll into the crafty Mr. Hyde who would stop at nothing to avoid the horrors of—housework. As he felt himself backed into a corner laden with dirty dishes, brooms, mops and reeking garbage, his front teeth grew longer and pointier, his fingernails haggled and his eyes grew wild. Housework trivial? Not on your life! Just try to share the burden.

So ensued a dialogue that's been going on for several years. Here are some of the high points:

- "I don't mind sharing the housework, but I don't do it very well. We should each do the things we're best at." MEANING: Unfortunately I'm no good at things like washing dishes or cooking. What I do best is a little light carpentry, changing light bulbs, moving furniture (how often do *you* move furniture?). ALSO MEANING: Historically the lower classes (black men and us) have had hundreds of years experience doing menial jobs. It would be a waste of manpower to train someone else to do them now. ALSO MEANING: I don't like the dull, stupid, boring jobs, so you should do them.

- "I don't mind sharing the work, but you'll have to show me how to do it." MEANING: I ask a lot of questions and you'll have to show me everything every time I do it because I don't remember so good. Also don't try to sit down and read while I'M doing my jobs because I'm going to annoy hell out of you until it's easier to do them yourself.

- "We used to be so happy!" (Said whenever it was his turn to do something.) MEANING: I used to be so happy. MEANING: Life without housework is bliss. No quarrel here. Perfect Agreement.

- "We have different standards, and why should I have to work to your standards? That's unfair." MEANING: If I begin to get bugged by the dirt and crap I will say, "This place sure is a sty" or "How can anyone live like this?" and wait for your reaction. I know that all women have a sore called "Guilt over a messy house" or "Household work is ultimately my responsibility." I know that men have caused that sore—if anyone visits and the place *is* a sty, they're not going to leave and say, "He sure is a lousy housekeeper." You'll take the rap in any case. I can outwait you. ALSO MEANING: I can provoke innumerable scenes over the housework issue. Eventually doing all the housework yourself will be less painful to you than trying to get me to do half. Or I'll suggest we get a maid. She will do my share of the work. You will do yours. It's women's work.

- "I've got nothing against sharing the housework, but you can't make me do it on your schedule." MEANING: Passive resistance. I'll do it when I damned well please, if at all. If my job is doing dishes, it's easier to do them once a week. If taking out laundry, once a month. If washing the floors, once a year. If you don't like it, do it yourself oftener, and then I won't do it at all.

- "I hate it more than you. You don't mind it so much." MEANING: Housework is garbage work. It's the worst crap I've ever done. It's degrading and humiliating for someone of *my* intelligence to do it. But for someone of *your* intelligence. . . .

- "Housework is too trivial to even talk about." MEANING: It's even more trivial to do. Housework is beneath my status. My purpose in life is to deal with matters of significance. Yours is to deal with matters of insignificance. You should do the housework.

- "This problem of housework is not a man-woman problem. In any relationship between two people one is going to have a stronger personality and dominate." MEANING: That stronger personality had better be *me*.

- "In animal societies, wolves, for example, the top animal is usually a male even where he is not chosen for brute strength but on the basis of cunning and intelligence. Isn't that interesting? MEANING: I have historical, psychological, anthropological and biological justification for keeping you down. How can you ask the top wolf to be equal?

- "Women's liberation isn't really a political movement." MEANING: The revolution is coming too close to home. ALSO MEANING: I am only interested in how I am oppressed, not how I oppress others. Therefore the war, the draft and the university are political. Women's liberation is not.

- "Man's accomplishments have always depended on getting help from other people, mostly women. What great man would have accomplished what he did if he had to do his own housework?" MEANING: Oppression is built into the system and I, as the white American male, receive the benefits of this system. I don't want to give them up.

Participatory democracy begins at home. If you are planning to implement your politics, there are certain things to remember.

1. He *is* feeling it more than you. He's losing some leisure and you're gaining it. The measure of your oppression is his resistance.

2. A great many American men are not accustomed to doing monotonous, repetitive work which never issues in any lasting, let alone important, achievement. This is why they would rather repair a cabinet than wash dishes. If human endeavors are

like a pyramid with man's highest achievements at the top, then keeping oneself alive is at the bottom. Men have always had servants (us) to take care of this bottom stratum of life while they have confined their efforts to the rarefied upper regions. It is thus ironic when they ask of women—Where are your great painters, statesmen, etc.? Mme Matisse ran a military shop so he could paint. Mrs. Martin Luther King kept his house and raised his babies.

3. It is a traumatizing experience for someone who has always thought of himself as being against any oppression or exploitation of one human being by another to realize that in his daily life he has been accepting and implementing (and benefiting from) this exploitation; that his rationalization is little different from that of the racist who says, "Black people don't feel pain" (women don't mind doing the shitwork); and that the oldest form of oppression in history has been the oppression of 50 percent of the population by the other 50 percent.

4. Arm yourself with some knowledge of the psychology of oppressed peoples everywhere, and a few facts about the animal kingdom. I admit playing top wolf or who runs the gorillas is silly but as a last resort men bring it up all the time. Talk about bees. If you feel really hostile bring up the sex life of spiders. They have sex. She bites off his head.

The psychology of oppressed peoples is not silly. Jews, immigrants, black men and all women have employed the same psychological mechanisms to survive: admiring the oppressor, glorifying the oppressor, wanting to be like the oppressor, wanting the oppressor to like them, mostly because the oppressor held all the power.

5. In a sense, all men everywhere are slightly schizoid—divorced from the reality of maintaining life. This makes it easier for them to play games with it. It is almost a cliché that women feel greater grief at sending a son off to a war or losing him to that war because they bore him, suckled him, and raised him. The men who foment those wars did none of those things and have a more superficial estimate of the worth of human life. One hour a day is a low estimate of the amount of time one has to spend "keeping" oneself. By foisting this off on others, man has seven hours a week—one working day more to play with his mind and not his human needs. Over the course of generations it is easy to

see whence evolved the horrifying abstractions of modern life.

6. With the death of each form of oppression, life changes and new forms evolve. English aristocrats at the turn of the century were horrified at the idea of enfranchising working men—were sure that it signaled the death of civilization and a return to barbarism. Some working men were even deceived by this line. Similarly with the minimum wage, abolition of slavery, and female suffrage. Life changes but it goes on. Don't fall for any line about the death of everything if men take a turn at the dishes. They will imply that you are holding back the revolution (their revolution). But you are advancing it (your revolution).

7. Keep checking up. Periodically consider who's actually *doing* the jobs. These things have a way of backsliding so that a year later once again the woman is doing everything. After a year make a list of jobs the man has rarely if ever done. You will find cleaning pots, toilets, refrigerators and ovens high on the list. Use time sheets if necessary. He will accuse you of being petty. He is above that sort of thing (housework). Bear in mind what the worst jobs are, namely the ones that have to be done every day or several times a day. Also the ones that are dirty—it's more pleasant to pick up books, newspapers, etc., than to wash dishes. Alternate the bad jobs. It's the daily grind that gets you down. Also make sure that you don't have the responsibility for the housework with occasional help from him. "I'll cook dinner for you tonight" implies it's really your job and isn't he a nice guy to do some of it for you.

8. Most men had a rich and rewarding bachelor life during which they did not starve or become encrusted with crud or buried under the litter. There is a taboo that says women mustn't strain themselves in the presence of men—we haul around 50 pounds of groceries if we have to but aren't allowed to open a jar if there is someone around to do it for us. The reverse side of the coin is that men aren't supposed to be able to take care of themselves without a woman. Both are excuses for making women do the housework.

9. Beware of the double whammy. He won't do the little things he always did because you're now a "Liberated Woman," right? Of course he won't do anything else either. . . .

I was just finishing this when my husband came in and asked what I was doing. Writing a paper on housework. Housework? he said. *Housework? Oh my god how trivial can you get?* A paper on housework. [1970]

🌿 51

From Carmita Wood to Anita Hill

SUSAN BROWNMILLER and
DOLORES ALEXANDER

Professor Anita Hill's testimony last October at the Senate Judiciary Committee hearing may have been some people's first exposure to the legal concept of sexual harassment on the job, but the issue had been named and developed in the mid-1970s.

The women's movement was full blown by the time Lin Farley, a 29-year-old activist, was teaching an experimental course on women and work at Cornell University in 1974. During a consciousness-raising session with her class, students talked about disturbing behavior they had been subjected to on summer jobs; in all the cases, the women had been forced off the job by these unwanted advances.

Coincidentally, Carmita Wood, a 44-year-old administrative assistant, walked out the office of a Cornell physicist after becoming physically ill from the stress of fending off his advances. When Ms. Wood filed for unemployment compensation in Ithaca, New York, claiming it wasn't her fault she had quit her job, the nascent movement acquired its first heroine, as well as a clear delineation of a problem as endemic as the abuse itself. The credibility of an office worker, a mother of four, was pitted against the reputation of an eminent scientist whose status was—and remains—so lofty that to this day his name has not appeared in accounts of her case.

Farley and two Cornell colleagues, Susan Meyer and Karen Sauvigné, found a lawyer for Wood and brainstormed to invent a name for their newly identified issue: "sexual harassment." The young feminists and their complainant proceeded to hold a movement-style speakout (a technique that had been used effectively to articulate the issues of abortion and rape) in a community center in Ithaca in May 1975. A questionnaire collected after the meeting showed that an astonishing number of women had firsthand experience to contribute.

Eleanor Holmes Norton, then chair of the New York City Commission on Human Rights, was conducting hearings on women and work that year. Farley came to testify, half expecting to be laughed out of the hearing room. "The titillation value of sexual harassment was always obvious," Farley recalls. "But Norton treated the issue with dignity and great seriousness." Norton, who had won her activist spurs in the civil rights movement, was to put her understanding of sexual harassment to good use during her later tenure in Washington, D.C., as head of the Equal Employment Opportunity Commission (EEOC). But we are moving ahead of our history.

Reporter Enid Nemy covered the Human Rights Commission hearings for the *New York Times*. Her story, "Women Begin to Speak Out Against Sexual Harassment at Work," appeared in the *Times* on August 19, 1975, and was syndicated nationally, to a tidal wave of response from women across the country.

Sauvigné and Meyer set up the Working Women's Institute in New York City as a clearinghouse for inquiries, and to develop a data bank with an eye toward public policy. Wood lost her case; the unemployment insurance appeals board ruled her reasons for quitting were personal. Lin Farley's breakthrough book, *Sexual Shakedown: The Sexual Harassment of Women on the Job*, was published by McGraw-Hill in 1978—after 27 rejections. "I thought my book would change the workplace," Farley says. "It is now out of print."

Things had begun to percolate on the legal front. Working with a large map and color-coded push-pins, Sauvigné and Meyer matched up complainants with volunteer lawyers and crisis counselors. Initially, aggrieved women sought redress by filing claims for unemployment insurance after they'd quit their jobs under duress, or by bringing their complaints to local human rights commissions. Ultimately, the most important means of redress became the EEOC, the federal agency charged with

Going Public

ELLEN BRAVO

Every April, in honor of Secretaries Week, 9 to 5 sponsors a national contest called "Nominate Your Boss: The Good, the Bad and the Downright Unbelievable." We use Public Service Announcements to attract entries to the contest. Subsequent publicity about the "winners" helps draw attention to sexual harassment, keeps the spotlight on offenders, calls attention to positive steps taken by employers, and honors the courageous women who are turning their private pain into public action. The winners:

THE GOOD

In Canada, the United Steelworkers Union begins every conference and convention, whatever its topic, with a presentation defining what sexual harassment is and stating that it will not be tolerated at that meeting. Anyone violating this rule, it is announced, will be sent home with a letter to the local Executive Board detailing the offense.

THE BAD

Louette Colombano was one of the first female police officers in her San Francisco district. While listening to the watch commander, she and the other officers stood at attention with their hands behind their backs. The officer behind her unzipped his fly and rubbed his penis against her hands.

THE DOWNRIGHT UNBELIEVABLE

Katherine Young, who worked for a hotel chain, claimed her boss had fired her for refusing his advances, Alabama Judge E. B. Haltom ruled against her. The boss couldn't possibly have been interested in harassing Young, the judge noted, because unlike the boss's wife, Young "wore little or no makeup, and her hair was not colored in any way."

[1992]

---

investigating and mediating discrimination cases under Title VII of the 1964 Civil Rights Act. (The inclusion of sex discrimination in the 1964 act had been introduced at the last minute in an attempt to defeat the bill.)

By 1977, three cases argued at the appellate level (*Barnes* v. *Costle; Miller* v. *Bank of America; Tomkins* v. *Public Service Electric & Gas*) had established a harassed woman's right, under Title VII, to sue the corporate entity that employed her. "A few individual women stuck their necks out," says Nadine Taub, the court-appointed attorney for Adrienne Tomkins against the New Jersey utilities company.

The Tomkins case, in particular, made it clear that the courts would no longer view harassment as a personal frolic, but as sex discrimination for which the employer might be held responsible. A young woman named Catharine MacKinnon had followed these cases with avid interest while a law student at Yale; later she published an impassioned, if somewhat obfuscating, treatise, *Sexual Harassment of Working Women,* in 1979.

Job-threatening though it was, sexual harassment remained on a back burner of the public conscience, as life-threatening issues—rape, battery, child abuse, and the ongoing pro-choice battle—continued to dominate feminist activity and media attention.

"We felt so alone out there," remembers Freada Klein, whose Boston area advocacy group was called the Alliance Against Sexual Coercion. "There was a *Redbook* survey in 1976 and a *Ms.* speakout and cover story in 1977. That was all." Peggy Crull, director of research for the New York City Commission on Human Rights, recalls that by the close of the decade, however, "every women's magazine had run a piece."

Slowly and quietly, case law broadened the definition of unlawful harassment. As women entered the work force in greater numbers, committing themselves not only to jobs but to careers, new cases went beyond those situations in which a boss suggested sex to a subordinate as a quid pro quo for keeping her job or getting a promotion. A court decision in Minnesota established that coworker harassment was as inimical to working conditions as harassment by a boss. A New York decision held that a receptionist could not be required to wear revealing clothes that brought her unwanted attention.

Meanwhile, a clerk-typist named Karen Nussbaum was pursuing her own mission to organize women office workers through a national network she called 9 to 5. An old friend from the antiwar movement, Jane Fonda, visited her headquarters in Cleveland with the idea of making a movie about underpaid and unappreciated secretaries in a large U.S. corporation.

9 to 5, produced by Fonda's IPC Films, and starring Fonda, Lily Tomlin, and Dolly Parton, was released in 1980, with Parton playing the plucky secretary who fends off her lecherous boss. The loopy movie, a commercial success, used broad comedic strokes to highlight the women's perspective.

In the waning days of the Carter administration, when Eleanor Holmes Norton was chair of the EEOC, she seized the initiative by issuing a set of federal guidelines on sexual harassment. The guidelines, a single-page memorandum issued on November 10, 1980, as Norton's tenure was running out, stated with admirable brevity that sexual activity as a condition of employment or promotion was a violation of Title VII. The creation of an intimidating, hostile, or offensive working environment was also a violation. Verbal abuse alone was deemed sufficient to create a hostile workplace. The guidelines encouraged corporations to write their own memoranda and inform employees of appropriate means of redress.

Guidelines are interpretations of existing statutes and do not have the full authority of law. But in 1981 (while Anita Hill was working for Clarence Thomas at the Department of Education), the EEOC was required to defend itself in *Bundy* v. *Jackson,* said the former EEOC general counsel Leroy D. Clark. The

Factory Harassment

APRIL GERTLER

Sexual harassment is not confined to an office setting. North Carolina poultry workers consistently are told to dress up in mini skirts and keep the health and safety inspectors "busy." According to Sarah Fields-Davis, Executive Director of the Center for Women's Economic Alternatives in Ashokie, poultry plant owners—the biggest employers in the region—maintain an economic stronghold over employees' lives. Owners guarantee loans for their workers to purchase home mortgages and cars. Employers in North Carolina are not bound by law to have "reasonable cause" to fire their employees. As a result, women poultry workers are too vulnerable to speak out individually or collectively in the persistent atmosphere of sexual harassment.

Fields-Davis said that "though there are times of knock-down drag-out screaming sessions where employees voice their grievances outside of work, women generally rely on their faith to get them through." Sexual harassment is about power. In this situation of economic dependency, women turn to the highest power they know.　　　　[1992]

District of Columbia circuit court ruled in favor of Sandra Bundy, a corrections department employee, and accepted the EEOC's guidelines as law, holding that Title VII could be violated even if a woman remained on the job.

Employers who were caught off guard were in for another surprise. During that same first year of the Reagan administration, the Merit Systems Protection Board, a regulatory agency that seldom makes news, released the results of a random survey of 20,100 federal employees. The findings revealed that a staggering 42 percent of the government's female workers had experienced an incident of sexual harassment on the job in the previous two years. "It was the first decent methodological study," says Freada Klein, who served as an adviser. "They did it again in 1988 and came up with the same figures."

It took the U.S. Supreme Court until 1986 to affirm unanimously, in *Meritor Savings Bank* v. *Vinson,* that sexual harassment even without economic harm was unlawful discrimination, although the court drew back in some measure from employer liability in hostile-environment cases.

Five years later, Anita Hill's testimony to 14 white male senators, and the merciless attacks on her credibility, echoed the agonies of her predecessors from Carmita Wood to Mechelle Vinson, who came forward at the risk of ridicule to tell about an abuse of power by a favored, institutionally protected, high-status male.

Detractors of the feminist role in social change have sought to create the impression that sexual harassment is yet another nefarious plot cooked up by an elite white movement to serve middle-class professionals. As it happens, veterans of the battle have been struck time and again by the fact that the plaintiffs in most of the landmark cases, brave women every one, have been working-class and African American: Paulette Barners, payroll clerk; Margaret Miller, proofing machine operator; Diane Williams, Justice Department employee; Rebekah Barnett, shop clerk; Mechelle Vinson, bank teller trainee.

We collected many speculations as to why black women have led this fight, but the last word goes to Eleanor Holmes Norton, who said, succinctly, "With black women's historic understanding of slavery and rape, it's not surprising to me."   [1992]

 52

A Woman in Residence

MICHELLE HARRISON

When I started to investigate potential programs, I found that few hospitals offered part-time residency positions, and none I could find actually had a part-time resident in obstetrics and gynecology (OB-GYN). To a letter of inquiry I wrote to a hospital which must have been mistakenly listed in the part-time registry, this reply came back: "We do not offer part-time residencies ever. Please note that full time is twenty-four hours a day."

An interview at another hospital—where I didn't go—went as follows:

Chairman of Dept. of OB-GYN: Why don't you send your child away to live?
Me: I can't do that.
He: If you aren't willing to give up your child, you don't deserve to be an obstetrician-gynecologist. Dr. Harrison, your problem is that you lack motivation.

Doctors Hospital, in Everytown, was well known in the Midwest for its intent to provide humanitarian care to patients.

At an interview at Doctors Hospital:

Dr. Walter Pierce: I'd be willing to offer you a position right now, pending receipt of your credentials.
Me: There's a hooker.
He: What's that?
Me: I have a child.
He: That's no hooker.
Me: And I want to do it part-time.
He: That's a hooker.

Dr. Pierce, an accomplished GYN endocrinologist and head of the Dept. of OB-GYN at Doctors Hospital, was known for his liberal attitude toward women in training. This resulted in a higher than usual percentage of women residents in his department, but even so, he was uncertain he wanted to take anyone part-time. A full-time program at his hospital ranged from ninety to one hundred and forty hours a week. It was a schedule I didn't think I could manage as a single parent. We negotiated for a long time and Dr. Pierce finally offered me a po-

Office Double Standards

A businessman is aggressive, a businesswoman is pushy.
He's careful about details, she's picky.
He follows through, she doesn't know when to quit.
He's firm, she's stubborn.
He makes judgments, she reveals her prejudices.
He's a man of the world, she's "been around."
He exercises authority, she's bossy.
He's discreet, she's secretive.
He says what he thinks, she's opinionated.

(original sources, unfortunately, unknown)

---

sition that was two-thirds time for half salary. I would have to work out the specific hours with the chief residents, who would be directly responsible for my daily activities.

Although I had met with Dr. Pierce to talk about the possibility of starting training the following year, eleven months hence, Pierce now said I could have the job if I could be in Everytown to start work in four weeks. He had just fired a resident that week, so he needed someone at once. With no certainty that the offer would be good the following year, I felt I had to take advantage of this opportunity.

I left Pierce's office astounded because I had the offer I had wanted, in a city where I had friends, in a program with a chairperson who was supportive of women, in a residency program with other women. And because I was going to one of the finest and most humanitarian of hospitals, the difficulties would at least be fewer than elsewhere. All I needed to do was gather letters and credentials from all the places I'd been, negotiate with the chief residents about the schedule, and move halfway across the country. Each piece seemed manageable.

There would be three chief residents—all women—each for a period of four months during the year. They had started together three years before, and now, in their final year of residency, they would take turns being chief residents. Carol, a woman I knew from work in the women's health movement, was currently the chief. She had almost four months to go.

Carol was the person who had urged me to call

Dr. Pierce to talk about a position, telling me, "He likes strong women."

"He offered me the job!" I reported to her ecstatically later in the day.

"I know. I've already talked with him. We have to talk about the hours."

When she found that the other residents were opposed to my coming into the program part-time, Carol had had to do her own negotiating about me. I knew I would need the support of at least the chief residents if I were to succeed at all. Jackie, who would be chief in the spring, wanted to talk with me before any final agreements were made since, as she told me that evening, "I have to live with the decisions that are made now. I'll be your chief in the spring."

Jackie and I talked on the phone. She was worried and doubtful the arrangement would work. "You know, politically I'm in favor of what you are trying to do, but I don't want to be left to do your work." However, she was surprised that the schedule tentatively worked out by Carol and me called for me to work many more hours than she had expected. "My husband once knew a part-time resident in opthalmology who was never there and never did her work," she said.

Jackie went on, thinking out loud as she tried to create a schedule that would best help the hospital but would not be full-time. Interspersed with her listing possible duties, shifts, days of greater surgery, were her doubts about my plans. "I don't think you can really do this if you have kids," she said. "I decided a long time ago that I'd have an abortion if I got pregnant while in training.

"A lot of others will resent you," she added.

"I know that."

"They can make it tough for you."

"I know that, too; that's why I wanted to be sure that at least you and Carol felt all right about my coming here. I don't expect it to be easy."

"Everyone here is overworked, so there will always be excess demands on your time. You're going to have to be able to protect yourself. No one will ever be satisfied with what you do because there is always more work to be done."

Jackie finally presented a plan. I would come in five mornings at six o'clock and see patients until eight. On Monday and Tuesday I would then be free to leave for the day. If I was to be on call for the night, I would return to the hospital at five and stay either until morning or through the next day. On Wednesday, Thursday and Friday I would work from six in the morning until six o'clock at night. I would take night and weekend call every sixth night, as Carol and I had already agreed.

"But can you take orders?" Jackie asked as though needing to satisfy one more doubt of hers; Dr. Pierce had already asked me the same question.

"Jackie, I know the rules of the game. I think I can take it. I've told myself I'll take whatever I have to in order to make it through. I'm giving up a lot to be here."

We were both worn out by the end of the phone call. Jackie had to be at work at six, and soon I would be there too. The following morning I was on the phone sending telegrams to schools, training programs and jobs where I had been, authorizing them to send letters to Dr. Pierce.   [1982]

 53

Reports from the Front: Welfare Mothers Up in Arms

DIANE DUJON, JUDY GRADFORD, and DOTTIE STEVENS

Women on welfare know they are in constant battle to provide for themselves and their children. Their "enemies" are

multiple, often including husbands, the welfare bureaucracy, and the attitudes of the general public. In this essay representatives from a group of welfare recipients in the Boston area who have organized into a welfare-rights group called ARMS (Advocacy for Resources for Modern Survival) describe some of the skirmishes they face every day.*

OUR LIVES NO LONGER BELONG TO US

One of my sons was diagnosed as having a high lead level in his blood. The Welfare Department placed my son under protective services and told me that I would have to find another place to live or they would put my son into a foster home. With six children on a welfare budget, it's not easy to find an apartment. And I had to find one within thirty days! To keep the state from taking my son, I was forced to move into the first available housing I could find.

Since I was an emergency case and eligible for a housing subsidy, my name was placed at the top of the list. I had to take the first available unit offered by the Housing Authority. The offer: a brand new town-house-type apartment *fifty miles* away in a white, middle-class suburb!

I knew this move would devastate my family because we would be so far away from our relatives and friends. When you're poor, you have to depend on your family and friends to help you through when you don't have the money to help yourself. At least two or three times every month I take my children to my mother's house to eat. How would we ever be able to get to her house from fifty miles away?

I also knew that my neighbors would not welcome me and my children: a black single woman with six children. I imagined the sneers of the merchants as I paid for my groceries with food stamps and the grunts of the doctors as I pulled out my Medicaid card.

I thought about the problems of transportation that were sure to crop up. How would I get my children to school? What if they got sick; how far was the nearest hospital? I envisioned the seven of us walking for miles with grocery bags. In short, I felt no relief at having found a nice clean apartment within the allotted time, but my back was against the wall. I could not refuse or my son would be put into foster care.

---

*In addition to the three authors, several other members of the ARMS collective should be mentioned for their contributions to the larger unpublished paper from which this essay is taken, "Welfare Mothers Up in Arms." They are Angela Hannon, Marion Graham, Jeannie MacKenzie, Carolyn Turner, and Hope Habtemarian. The quotations in this essay are taken from interviews with various ARMS members.

We now live in a totally hostile environment severed from our family and friends. And although we live in a physically beautiful development, life for us is hard. A poor family with no transportation is lost in the suburbs. We are as isolated as if we lived on a remote island in the Pacific.

Situations like the one described by this woman show how our lives no longer belong to us. We have, in effect, married the state. To comply with the conditions of our recipient status, we cannot make any personal decisions ourselves. We must consult the Welfare Department first, and the final decision is theirs. The state is a domineering, chauvinistic spouse.

Politicians often boast or complain about the many services and benefits welfare recipients receive. For us, these services and benefits are the bait that the predatory department uses to entrap us and our families. Like the wiley fox, we are driven by hunger to the trap. We must carefully trip the trap, retrieve the bait, and escape, hopefully unscathed. Also similar to the fox, our incompetence can lead to starvation, disease, and death for ourselves and our families.

This may seem an unlikely analogy to some; but the Welfare Department, in its *eagerness* to help us constantly adopts policies that put us in catch-22 situations. We are continuously in a dilemma over whether we should seek the help we desperately need or not. The purportedly "free" social services that are available to us extort a usurer's fee in mental and physical anguish. So, although there are several services available, we are often unable or reluctant to receive them. Below we describe some of the catch-22's that constitute mental cruelty for us.

CATCH-22: A LOW BUDGET

The first catch-22 we encounter is living under the conditions set up by the state for recipients. Under penalty of law we are required adequately to house, clothe, feed, and otherwise care for our children on a budget that is two thirds of the amount considered to be at the poverty line. If we fail to fulfill our obligation in the opinion of friends, strangers, neighbors, relatives, enemies, or representatives of the Welfare Department, the state can and *will* take our children from our homes. Anyone can call the department anonymously and report that we are neglecting or abusing our children. With no further

questions, the state initiates an investigation, which further jeopardizes our family stability. While it is necessary for the state to protect children from abuse and neglect, a large portion of the investigations are based on unfounded allegations for which no one can be held accountable. It is no easy task to fulfill the basic obligation of surviving on welfare, because we often pay as much as 85 to 95 percent of our income for rent and utilities.

On the other hand, there is no reward for a job well done. If we manage to clothe, feed, and house our children, the risk is the same: at the least, biting remarks from people in public, and at the most, an investigation of fraud.

We are constantly under public scrutiny. We are made to feel uncomfortable if we wear jewelry, or buy a nice blouse, or own a warm coat. It's as if we're not supposed to have families or friends who love us and might give us a birthday or Christmas present. Absolutely no thought is given to the fact that we may have had a life before welfare! Heaven forbid that anyone should honor the great job we must do as shoppers!

There are a few legal ways in which welfare mothers can supplement their monthly grant. Some of these supports are available upon eligibility for Aid to Families with Dependent Children (AFDC); others, termed "social services," have additional individual eligibility requirements. Each has its quota of catch-22's.

CATCH-22: EMERGENCY ASSISTANCE

I was $300 in arrears with my electric bill. The electric company sent me several reminders, but I didn't have the money to pay my bill. It made me very nervous. It was winter, and although I had oil, if my electricity were turned off, my pilot light would go out and my children would be cold.

I took my bill and the warning notices to my social worker at the Welfare Department. She told me that I could receive up to $500 of Emergency Assistance per year, but that only one such grant could be made in any twelve-month period. However, I could not receive any Emergency Assistance until I received a "shut-off" notice. She further explained that I should wait because if I received the $300 EA grant, I could not get the additional $200 to which I was entitled that year. I would have to wait twelve months before I could be eligible for another grant. I really wasn't interested in getting all I could, I just wanted to be able to sleep at night; but since I didn't have a shut-off notice, I had no choice but to wait.

I received a shut-off notice when my bill was about $400. I applied for, and received, the EA grant.

The very next year, I was in a similar situation. I again attempted to wait for the shut-off notice. One day I received a notice from the electric company stating that I was scheduled for a "field collection." My social worker reminded me that EA can only be awarded upon my receipt of a shut-off notice. Even though the notice stated that my service would be "interrupted" if I failed to honor the collector, it did not have the specific words *shut off* and, therefore, I was ineligible for EA. I couldn't believe what she was telling me! To become eligible, I had to go to the electric company to ask them to stamp "shut off" on my bill. I was angry that I was being forced to humiliate myself by revealing my personal business to the electric company representative.

CATCH-22: MEDICAID

Medicaid is the most treasured benefit to families who must depend on AFDC, but it, too, falls short of the expectations of beneficiaries. Doctors, hospitals, druggists, and other health providers often refuse to accept Medicaid patients. The amount of paper work that is required for each and every patient is tedious and time-consuming. Medicaid also sets limits on the type and amount of treatments it will cover.

Every trip to the doctor is a grueling, costly, and time-consuming event. First, we must search for a doctor or medical facility that will accept Medicaid. If we are lucky enough to have a neighborhood health center nearby, we will often go the clinic. In either situation, we usually have to wait for hours to receive the medical attention we need. Doctors often remark about the amount of paperwork that is required by the state and the fact that they often have to wait six to eight months to obtain their fees from the state. It is exceedingly distressing to be sick and to have to hear about the doctor's problems.

I had periodontal disease once. The dentist explained that an infection had settled under my gums and he would have to cut my gums and scrape the infection away. Since I was on Medicaid, I was required to wait until Medicaid approved the dental procedure.

After several weeks, the approval arrived. My dentist informed me that although Medicaid approved the procedure, the amount approved was too low to allow him to use gas as was customary. I had a choice: either I could pay him the difference, and *enjoy* a painless procedure; or I could have the procedure done for the cost Medicaid allotted and he could use novocaine, which would be at least moderately painful.

I didn't have the money to pay the difference, but I knew that if I delayed the operation I stood a good chance of losing my teeth. I decided to brave the novocaine.

The dentist had to cut deep into my gums and the novocaine did nothing for the pain below the surface. I tried hard to be still and keep my mouth open wide, but I was in agony with the pain. The procedure took four hours and required sixty-four stitches and forty-seven injections of novocaine!

CATCH-22: FOOD STAMPS

Food Stamps are a symbol of the government's benevolence. Rather than increase the amount of the welfare budget so that we can afford to buy more food, the government *supplements* our budgets with food stamps. As the name suggests, food is all that can be purchased with them. And not much food at that. Households receiving the maximum amount of food stamps receive an average of forty cents per meal per person. All other commodities, such as soap, detergent, toilet paper, diapers, etc., must be separated at the time of purchase. Food, by anyone's definition, is a necessity for sustaining life. Why, then, do we feel as if food is a luxury?

Contrary to public opinion, we pay for these food stamps at a cost significantly higher than a cup of coffee per meal. We pay with the anguish of wondering how we are going to maintain healthy children on $1.20 per day. Food stamps last an average of ten days, depending on the supply of staples (flour, sugar, cereal, salt, spaghetti, etc.) we have on hand; the rest of the month we struggle to keep up with the milk, eggs, juice, fruits, vegetables, and bread so vital to good health. The last two weeks we are challenged to use our imaginations to ensure that our children receive the best nutrition possible. For those of us who are lucky enough to be able to commit "fraud" through friends and relatives, it's a little easier; but for many of us it's often an impossible task!

The way the food stamp budget is calculated, it's as if our diet is supposed to shrink in the summer. Our fuel costs are counted as an expense in the winter, so we receive more food stamps in the winter and less in the summer. This budget policy is ludicrous because most of our fuel costs in the winter are paid with Fuel Assistance.

I had trouble one time receiving my food stamps. Every month I would have to commute to the next town where my welfare office was located to report that I had not received my food stamps. Each time I was interrogated by the food stamps worker about whether I had cashed my food stamps and was trying to get some more under false pretenses. I had to sign a sworn statement to the effect that I had not received my food stamps before they could issue replacement stamps.

I finally decided that rather than go through the hassle and expense of picking up my food stamps from the welfare office each month, I would purchase a post office box. When I went to inform my worker of my box number, I was told that food stamps could not be sent to a post office box. This policy was supposed to deter fraud. I was forced to continue to pick up my stamps from the welfare office each month.

Food stamp redemption centers are generally located in areas that are virtually inaccessible to those of us without cars. Much of the money we are supposed to be saving with food stamps is spent on transportation to the centers.

My food stamps usually come on the due date, but my welfare check is often late. This creates a problem for me because I always need the food, but with no cash money it is almost impossible to do the shopping I need to do the first time. I have to make at least two trips to the supermarket; the first trip for food only with the food stamps and the second, when my check comes, to buy soap, cleaning products, etc. Two trips to the store doubles the amount of transportation expenses, too.

CATCH-22: WELFARE FRAUD

Fraud within the welfare system might also be called "devising a way to survive." The federal and state laws call it fraud if a welfare recipient uses up her allotment for any reason and seeks assistance from a friend, relative, or acquaintance (be it ten cents or $10). If she does not report this money to the welfare office, she is technically considered to be defrauding the Welfare Department. Such unrealistic definitions leave all of us vulnerable to fraud and make it difficult to separate honest need from intentional deception.

According to the narrow, unrealistic guidelines of the state and federal government, most or all welfare recipients could be accused of having committed fraud at some time during their ordeal with the welfare system, even though they would not have meant to defraud anyone. We are stuck in a system that inadequately provides for us and that even the social workers know, depends upon our having a "little help from our friends." However, if we are caught doing what we all have to do to survive, we may even be made into an "example" and used to discredit the difficulties faced by women on welfare.

We are poor because we do not receive enough money from the Welfare Department to live decently. If we lack family or friends, we may feel forced to find ways to get a little extra money for our families. Many who have been discovered working to buy Christmas presents, for example, have been brought to court by the Welfare Department and either fined, jailed, or made to pay back all monies received while working.

Although there seems to be large-scale vendor fraud among those who supply Medicaid services, it is seldom investigated or taken to court. While we are hounded for minor infractions, little is done to the unscrupulous doctors, dentists, druggists, nursing-home operators, and others in the health field who blatantly commit welfare fraud as a regular practice. Because of their "respectability" in the community, these providers are in a position to bill Medicaid for services never rendered, and they do so with some regularity. When these abuses are publicized, pubic outcry is minimal and fleeting at best. It is so much easier to blame "those people."

Even in the event of discovery by a Medicaid "fraud squad," the welfare recipient, rather than the health professional suspected of illegally using the system, often becomes the target of their investigation.

I was ordered by our Medicaid fraud squad to appear at my local welfare office within the week. A dentist who had done surgery on my mouth for a periodontal disease was under suspicion of committing fraud.

I arrived at the office not knowing what to expect. Two men who resembled G-Men arrived and hustled me into a cubicle and began interrogating me. Not being satisfied with my answers, they proceeded to look into my mouth at every tooth in my head to prove I had fillings where they were not supposed to be, according to the computer printout they were studying. They also wanted me to account for every filling, extraction, check-up, and cleaning of my three children, which had been done by the same dentist. This took me another week.

I was treated as if I was guilty of something. When you are on welfare, no one cares about your feelings—they don't count.

The welfare system, in reality, has been set up to promote fraud as a means of survival. They *know* we can't live on budgets "below the poverty line." With a more reasonable system of providing financial assistance, there would be less "fraud" because people on welfare would be less desperate. But as it is, women are punished for being on welfare and pushed into impossible binds.

ENOUGH ALREADY

Families who must rely on the welfare system to survive are constantly torn to pieces by the bureaucratic policies that supply the services they need. Each benefit comes with its own rules and regulations, which must be followed if recipients are to remain eligible. The policies are designed separately, with little regard to policies of other agencies, so we are continuously in compromising positions.

Welfare policies are written in "still life." Like the prepackaged vegetables in the supermarkets, they look fine on the surface: but turn them over and look beneath the surface and you may see rotten spots. Living, breathing people need policies that allow for individuality and flexibility. No two families are alike or have the same needs. We should not be lumped together and threatened with extinction if we complain. Women who are already in crises do not need the added stress of conflicting policies among the services that are ours by right. We are strong, capable, and often wise beyond our years. We demand that we be allowed to have some control over our own lives. No governor, president, general, or legislator should be able to dictate to us where we live,

what we eat, or where, or even, whether we should work outside the home when we are already taking care of our children.   [1986]

🦎 54

*African-American Women and Work: The Discriminating Difference**

NORMA J. BURGESS

Women of African descent in the United States face a dual dilemma. On the one hand, both racism and sexism are present in the job market, since most employers can choose not to hire, support, mentor or promote African-American† women. On the other hand, the double status of being female and an American of African descent distorts what few gains have been made, leaving only stereotypes and misconceptions about what can and cannot be changed. Scholarly research, unlike popular literature, does not support the notion that being African American and female is an advantage. Economically, contemporary African-American women continue to be concentrated in low-status occupations. Positions in middle-status occupations such as clerical work, and high-status occupations other than teaching, excluded African-American women almost completely until the mid-twentieth century. Despite the fact that African-American women have been in the labor market for longer periods of time overall, they tend to earn less than comparably trained African-American and white men and most white women.

*Grateful acknowledgement to the National Science Foundation for its support and the Center for Research on Women, Memphis State University. Neither the Foundation nor the Center bears responsibility for the contents herein.
†The term "African American," as opposed to the anthropological term "black," is used to acknowledge African ancestry for the women under consideration in this essay.

African-American women also continue to perform traditional household tasks and assume responsibility for child rearing. African-American mothers are more likely than white mothers to work for wages. As a result, there is an ongoing tension between career aspirations and familial duties. African-American women perform a delicate balancing act, walking both race and gender tightropes. Whether the African-American female achiever is single or married, her race and gender interface in perplexing ways, contributing to confusion, contradictions, and dilemmas. Because she occupies a marginal position in society, chances for isolation are also increased.

Many studies of women's work patterns are based on the experience of white women and erroneously applied to African-American women. It is important to understand that the employment experiences of women vary with race and social class. Understanding African-American women's unique work patterns requires a historical perspective. It is virtually impossible to understand African-American women today without placing them in the context of their African background and the experience of slavery. African-American women did not come to this country willingly, and they came primarily as workers. Familial and spousal roles for these women were redefined to accommodate the slave owners. While enslaved Africans were forced to outwardly embrace alien norms, values, and roles, African cultural values and belief systems survived and helped shape African-American patterns of work and family.

AFRICAN-AMERICAN WOMEN AND WORK: 1940–1980

During the World War II labor shortage, white women in large numbers entered the labor force for the first time. In addition, the great migration from the south to the north among African-Americans occurred. This 40-year period in employment history reflects significant changes for men and women in the labor force and therefore is used as a benchmark for changes in occupational patterns. Prior to 1940, African-American women were concentrated in low-status occupations and were almost completely absent from professions such as clerical work

and the professions other than teaching. In 1940, African-American women were confined to domestic service and farm labor. Approximately 60% of African-American women were domestic servants. African-American men and women were not allowed access to many blue-collar and service-sector jobs (except in private households) and were excluded from virtually all clerical sales and professional jobs (except teaching).

While African-American women moved from domestic service to factory work, fewer than 10% of African-American women workers held positions in middle- or high-status occupations. By contrast, white women worked in a variety of occupations, with more than one-half employed in clerical or sales-related occupations. After the war, rapid job growth and antidiscrimination legislation allowed large numbers of African-American women to enter white-collar jobs. Between 1950 and 1970, female clerical employment grew significantly, and the percentage of African-American women workers in these jobs increased from 5% to 21%. Professional employment almost doubled but still represented only 11% of African-American women's jobs in 1970 (U.S. Commission on Civil Rights, 1990). The lowering of racial barriers in the public sector under affirmative action accounted for a large number of these new jobs, and by 1979, almost one-third of employed African-American women worked for the federal, state, or local government, compared to less than one-fifth of white women (Amott and Matthaei, 1991).

Despite improvements in occupations and wages, African-American women continue to be underrepresented in managerial and professional occupations and overrepresented in low-status occupations. Restricted job opportunities played a significant role in limiting the progress among women. African-American women found jobs in emerging southern industries but always in the lowest paid and most dangerous jobs (Amott and Matthaei, 1991). Southern industries could not absorb all the individuals who were displaced by agriculture. Regionally, southern African-American women fared worse than their counterparts in other regions because of institutionalized discrimination, receiving lower wages and attaining lower occupational stature than white women (U.S. Commission on Civil Rights, 1990). Outside the south, African-American women who were not domestic servants found employment as operatives and service workers. By 1980, African-American women had left their jobs as farm laborers and domestic servants and made substantial progress into occupations once dominated by males and whites. In addition, African-American women worked in clerical positions but continued to be overrepresented in low-status office jobs and underrepresented in middle- and high-status occupations. Clerical workers represented about 25% of white women but employed less than 2% of African-American women.

The legacy of past racial discrimination has limited African-American women's economic status. Labor market discrimination by employers, co-workers, and customers have taken the form of lowering African-American women's wages, excluding them from certain occupations and denying them occupational mobility. It is not by happenstance that occupations dominated by African Americans and women generally rank lower in prestige and salary levels. The U.S. Commission on Civil Rights (1990) found that discrimination in hiring, referrals, and promotions appears to be a major problem for African-American women. Discrimination in the labor market appears to have been a significant factor in African-American women's acquiring less human capital (training and education) than white women (Feagin, 1991). Discrimination in education limits access to quality schooling, which directly limits African-American women's access to on-the-job training and skill augmentation. Although racial differences in educational attainment, regional distribution, urban-rural residence, and age can partially account for African-American women's lower occupational status from 1940 to 1980, it is likely that occupational discrimination against African-American women played a far greater role in limiting African-American women's access to occupations commonly held by white women.

INCOME AND EARNINGS

Family income and wealth among African-American women tend to be lower; they also experience higher unemployment, welfare, and poverty rates than white women. The earnings of African-American women make up a much larger fraction of their family income than do those of white women, especially among married women. Work status, then, is crucial to elevating the status of women. The lower labor force participation rates among unmarried African-American women could be the indirect result of labor market discrimination.

Family structures of African-American women also play a significant role in their economic status. Roughly two-thirds of African-American women are not married. They are also more likely to have children present in their homes. This fact suggests that the African-American woman is likely to be the only adult wage earner in her family, as well as having the responsibility for children.

The economic well-being of African-American women and their families depends on whether or not they work. Employed African-American women have higher family incomes than those who are not working. Among married women, African-Americans are much more likely to work full-time than whites, but as we have seen, African-American male and female workers are clustered in the low-wage sector of the economy.

SUMMARY

African-American women made progress between 1970 and 1980 in entering higher-paying jobs. Relative concentrations increased in top-level engineering, sales, administrative, and managerial positions. A function of the successes gained by African-American women over time is a direct result of human capital investment, specifically education and job training. Recent adjustments in affirmative action mandates and civil rights legislation may threaten continued progress in these areas. Many of African-American women's professions, such as teaching and social service work, are largely in the public sector. Inside and outside the public sector, most female professionals are found in jobs that serve African-American, mostly poor and working class, clients. Hence, the progress made is both partial and tenuous: partial because their employment opportunities are still limited, and tenuous because their jobs are dependent upon the size of the government sector in an era of budget austerity and lessening commitment to affirmative action (Amott and Matthaei, 1991).

REFERENCES

Amott, Teresa, and Matthaei, Julie. 1991. Race, Gender and Work. Boston: South End Press.

Burgess, Norma J. (forthcoming). "Gender Roles Revisited: The Development of the Woman's Place among African American Women in the United States." Journal of Black Studies.

Feagin, Joe. 1991. "The continuing significance of race: The Black middle class experience." Paper presented at the annual meeting of the American Sociological Association, Cincinnati, Ohio.

Rodgers-Rose, LaFrances. 1980. The Black Woman. Beverly Hills: Sage.

U.S. Commission on Civil Rights. 1990. The Economic Status of Black Women: An Exploratory Investigation. Washington, D.C.   [1993]

🦎 55

The Promise of Comparable Worth: A Socialist-Feminist Perspective

TERESA AMOTT and JULIE MATTHAEI

THE HISTORY OF THE COMPARABLE WORTH STRATEGY

Although the concept of comparable worth first emerged from discussions within the War Labor Board in 1943, the first comparable worth suit was brought against General Electric and Westinghouse by the United Electrical Workers of America (UE) in 1945. In the suit, UE attacked the companies' job descriptions as thinly veiled attempts to pay different, and divisive, wages to men and women.[1]

Comparable worth did not emerge as a broadly-based strategy for the women's movement until the mid-1970s, at which time the "second wave" of feminism took up the demand and argued it as an issue for women rather than solely an aspect of labor movement solidarity. The second wave of pay equity campaigns arose as women's advocates discovered that the 1973 Equal Pay Act, which prohibited unequal pay only in the case of equal (i.e., identical) work, was of limited applicability to women. Partly because the Act was so weak, the average income for women working full-time remained roughly 60 per-

cent of men's income throughout the 1960s and 1970s.

The constancy of the wage gap in the face of civil rights legislation drew attention to the fact that women and men are rarely found in the same jobs, since women have historically been concentrated in a few occupations and excluded from many others. To this day, most women work in occupations with low pay and few opportunities for advancement. These jobs often center around nurturing and serving others—for example, nursing, secretarial and clerical work, teaching, and food service. Throughout the 1970s, for example, over 40 percent of all women workers were crowded into 10 occupations, most of which were over 70 percent female.* Men, especially white men, have more job options and generally earn higher pay. For instance stock clerks, who are predominantly male, earn more than bank tellers, who are predominantly female. Similarly, registered nurses earn less than mail carriers.

The concept of comparable worth was devised to raise wages in female-dominated occupations up to the level paid in male occupations "of comparable worth." Pay equity advocates argue that this is the best strategy for raising women's pay since the majority of women work in sex-typed jobs with no chance, or in some cases no desire, to enter male occupations. The concept requires that jobs deemed to be of "equal value to the employer" pay the same, regardless of their sex-typing.

In no cases are comparable worth adjustments made by lowering the wages of higher-paid jobs. Generally speaking, equity is achieved by larger percentage increases for lower-paid job categories over a period of time until the inequity is eliminated.

All pay equity campaigns in the U.S. have been limited to achieving equity in the wage structure of an individual employer, and there is presently no mechanism or campaign which would permit com-

---

* These statistics actually underestimate the extent of firm- or plant-level segregation. For example, while 4 percent of the registered nurses in the U.S. are male, many hospitals have no male nurses at all. An excellent discussion of the firm-level segregation can be found in Francine Blau, "Sex Segregation of Workers by Enterprise in Clerical Occupations," in Richard C. Edwards, Michael Reich, and David M. Gordon, eds., *Labor Market Segmentation* (Lexington, MA: D. C. Heath & Co., 1975).

parisons of jobs across industries.* Most pay equity campaigns in the U.S. have also applied only to full-time workers, although there is no technical reason why the wages of part-timers couldn't also be raised using comparable worth techniques. However, since many part-time workers are excluded from union membership, they have not participated in pay equity campaigns. Comparable worth can also be applied to race-typing in occupations, but to date, most comparable worth efforts have focused on wage differences originating from sex-based segregation.

Pay equity campaigns can take three forms: litigation, collective bargaining, and legislation. Often a combination of these strategies is employed.

Litigation

Prior to *County of Washington v. Gunther,* a 1981 Supreme Court decision which ordered a narrowing of pay differentials between male prison guards and female jail matrons, the courts were unfriendly to comparable worth cases. The importance of this landmark case lay in establishing the applicability of Title VII of the 1964 Civil Rights Act to pay differences arising across similar, but not identical, jobs.

Since 1981, pay equity litigation has expanded substantially. The largest pay equity suit to date was won by the American Federation of State, County, and Municipal Employees (AFSCME) against the state of Washington in 1983. A district court awarded $800 million in back pay and damages to 15,000 state workers in female-dominated jobs.†

Collective Bargaining

Many unions, including AFSCME, the Communications Workers of America (CWA), the International Union of Electrical, Radio and Machine Workers (IUE), the Service Employees International (SEIU), the United Auto Workers (UAW), the UE and others, have adopted pay equity as a goal in bargaining, membership education and lobbying. Most of these efforts have focused on public employees, partly because state agencies may be more vulnerable to public pressure brought through community-labor alliances. In addition, state workers perform a wide array of jobs with varying degrees of sex and race segregation, making the public sector an ideal place for pay equity comparisons across jobs.

The 1984 strike of Yale clerical workers and an earlier strike of city employees of San Jose, California, attracted the most media attention, but there have been many other instances in which comparable worth principles have been introduced in collective bargaining. In Massachusetts, for instance, women's jobs in all grades of state employment have been reclassified upwards in negotiations with all participating unions. In addition, an IUE local won raises for women General Electric workers and Boston University clericals have organized for pay equity. Pay equity has even made inroads in states where the political environment is considerably more anti-union, such as Texas, where CWA completed a pay equity study in December 1984.[2]

Legislation

Under political pressure, many states have adopted legislation calling for pay equity studies, and others, including California, Minnesota, Washington, and Wisconsin, have passed statutes which require public sector wages to be set on the basis of comparable worth. Public sector clerical workers in Idaho won a 16 percent pay increase through pay equity legislation, and in New Mexico, funds were appropriated

---

*Canada and Australia have national legislation requiring equal pay for work of comparable worth. In Australia, women's wages as a percentage of men's jumped from 60 percent to 77 percent in just 6 years as a result of the law. See *Dollars and Sense,* September 1985, p. 18.

†The ruling was overturned by the 9th Circuit Court of Appeals in September of last year, but the ruling had little effect; one month earlier AFSCME and the state had announced that they would begin talks to settle the issue out of court and the state legislature had appropriated $42 million for pay equity raises in female-dominated jobs. The state and AFSCME have since settled and the first paychecks have gone out to women workers. By 1993, when the pay equity adjustments will be completed, the cumulative cost of the settlement will be $482 million. The appeals court verdict was one of several rulings in recent years which are consistent with Reagan ad-

---

ministration doctrine that plaintiffs in discrimination cases must prove an *intent* to discriminate, in contrast to previous decisions which rested on statistical proof of de facto discrimination. Other recent court rulings have been mixed.

to raise pay for the lowest-paid state employees, many of them Native Americans and Chicanos. . . .[3]

UNDERMINING PATRIARCHY

It is commonly believed that women are paid less than men because they are less productive, less skilled, or less able. The notion of comparable worth attacks an essential element of this patriarchal ideology. It does so by identifying and highlighting cases in which women are paid less than men although they are equally productive. By showing the extent to which women are discriminated against in pay, comparable worth supports feminist demands for change.

Comparable worth will also increase women's earnings (up to 25 percent, even if job evaluation studies reward job characteristics as the market presently does), and hence give women more economic power relative to men. If groups commissioning such studies also challenge the masculine bias operating in the established point factor systems, greater pay increases can be achieved. For instance, if skills needed for women's jobs, such as nurturing, guidance, and communication, are recognized and rewarded, the points awarded to traditionally female jobs will be considerably higher.

We can also expect that comparable worth will help reduce occupational segregation by sex. As long as "women's" work is considered socially inferior, and is paid as such, men will continue to shun traditionally female occupations. Higher wages in female-dominated jobs would lessen this stigmatization and attract men into these jobs. This would have the double result both of breaking down their sex-typing, and of bringing greater value to activities which are traditionally feminine. It may also have the indirect result of making male-dominated jobs more accessible to women.

In addition, by raising women's wages, comparable worth would weaken a crucial link in the vicious circle of women's oppression. If women were paid equitably, they would be able to support themselves and their children, and would not depend upon men for their economic survival. Women would face less economic coercion to marry or to remain in exploitative relationships with men, and would be freer to pursue nontraditional relationships and living arrangements, such as staying single, relating to men without living together, or being a lesbian. Men would have to offer women more than just their paychecks to attract them to, and keep them in, subservient roles.

Furthermore, there would be much less pressure on heterosexual couples to reproduce the traditional division of household labor. Once comparable worth brings women's earnings up to par with those of their male partners, women could more feasibly choose to give less priority to unpaid housework and childcare, and more priority to market work. In the same vein, greater wage equality would make it more logical to share the burdens and pleasures of both home and market work, perhaps with some specialization according to preferences and talents. . . .

COMPARABLE WORTH'S CHALLENGE TO CAPITALISM

In their struggle to alter the existing wage structure, comparable worth advocates have challenged the free market mythology which is used so successfully to defend the status quo. Comparable worth attacks the traditional supposition that the market pays workers "what they're worth." Are market apologists really willing to claim that parking lot attendants are more productive than registered nurses? Assembly-line workers more productive than secretaries? Accepting the premise that a fair wage structure rewards workers according to their relative contributions to their employers, comparable worth advocates use job evaluation studies to show that the wage structure is far from fair. Once it is shown that there is not a direct link between wages and productivity, the other traditional defense of wage inequality—that the market uses wages to motivate increased effort and productivity—is shattered as well.

In addition to undermining two major free market premises, comparable worth raises broader questions about the way in which wages are determined. If wages are not set fairly and efficiently by the forces of supply and demand, as orthodox free market theorists claim, *what is going on?* Why are some workers and some industries paid more than others? A comparable worth strategy exposes the true nature of the market: it is not an impersonal, fair mediator between individuals, but rather a crucible in which those with power exploit those without it. . . .

COMPARABLE WORTH AND RACISM

Those who are concerned that the women's movement is too narrowly based in the self-interests of middle-class white women have criticized comparable worth as being "a white women's issue." While we share that concern, we believe that comparable worth efforts can also bring about wage increases for women and men of color.

The numerical dominance of whites in the labor force virtually ensures that whites will constitute the majority of workers in any job category. Nonetheless, most women of color are found in female-dominated jobs. This means that wage increases secured through sex-based pay equity campaigns will be of substantial benefit to women of color. In other words, there is no *economic* reason why pay equity should not be a demand with major relevance for women of color.

The post World War II era brought about major changes in the occupational distribution of women of color, particularly black women. During this period, there was a sharp expansion of employment for women of color in jobs traditionally performed by white women, such as clerical, some professional and technical work, and sales. In addition, service occupations grew rapidly as traditional household work like childcare and food preparation was commodified. As employment expanded, black, Latina, Asian and Native American women could enter new occupations without displacing white women, and thus without arousing as much political opposition as would have occurred if they were replacing white workers. These new jobs for women of color constituted a marked change from the private household and farm labor jobs of their mothers and grandmothers.[4]

Pay equity cases usually single out for scrutiny job categories that are over 70 percent female—clerical work, nursing, elementary schoolteaching, food service, childcare, and health technicians, to name a few. Contrary to popular myths, substantial numbers of women of color are now employed in these job categories, as shown in Figure 1.* According to 1980 census data, over half of white women are employed in jobs which are over 70 percent female, but the same percentage of black, and just under half of all Native American, and Asian women are also found in those job categories.

It is true that detailed occupational breakdowns often reveal further race segregation *within* women's jobs. For instance, senior typists might all be white while junior typists might be predominantly women of color. Yet sex-based pay equity studies would still single out a job dominated by black women for pay equity upgrading by comparing it to a comparable male-dominated job (which might be held by a man of any race). Therefore, pay equity has the potential to raise wages for the women of color.

Whether it does so or not depends partly on the character of the comparable worth campaign. Much media attention to the comparable worth issue has been directed at professional women—librarians and registered nurses in particular—but pay equity comparisons between men and women can be made *at all levels of the skills hierarchy.* For example, a pay equity campaign might raise the wages of women who clean an office building at night to the same level as the wages of male janitors who clean a factory for the same employer. Job evaluation studies which encompass all the jobs in a firm or government agency will have a greater effect on women of color than those which are aimed only at professional workers. Most state and local government job evaluation initiatives are across-the-board studies of all sex-stereotyped job categories at all skill levels.

Collective bargaining efforts can also be made more relevant to women of color by litigating on behalf of job categories in which large numbers of women of color are found. For example, black women workers in Illinois and Cook County welfare departments won a $15 million back pay award in a 1984 pay equity suit based on the sex-segregated nature of their work.[5] Progressive activists must

---

*Since most comparable worth initiatives are based in a single employer or worksite, this figure to some degree understates the segregation of women of color. For instance, in the city of Chicago, virtually all welfare service aides are black and Latina—but they are also women. As a result, they were able to win a pay equity case based on sex.

Occupation (Percent female)

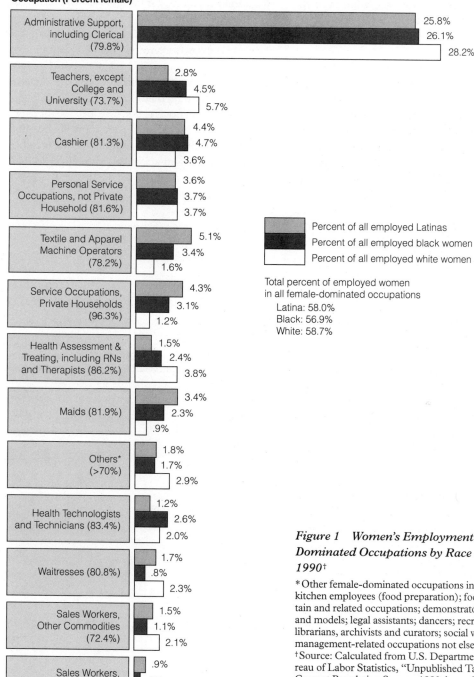

Administrative Support, including Clerical (79.8%)	25.8% / 26.1% / 28.2%
Teachers, except College and University (73.7%)	2.8% / 4.5% / 5.7%
Cashier (81.3%)	4.4% / 4.7% / 3.6%
Personal Service Occupations, not Private Household (81.6%)	3.6% / 3.7% / 3.7%
Textile and Apparel Machine Operators (78.2%)	5.1% / 3.4% / 1.6%
Service Occupations, Private Households (96.3%)	4.3% / 3.1% / 1.2%
Health Assessment & Treating, including RNs and Therapists (86.2%)	1.5% / 2.4% / 3.8%
Maids (81.9%)	3.4% / 2.3% / .9%
Others* (>70%)	1.8% / 1.7% / 2.9%
Health Technologists and Technicians (83.4%)	1.2% / 2.6% / 2.0%
Waitresses (80.8%)	1.7% / .8% / 2.3%
Sales Workers, Other Commodities (72.4%)	1.5% / 1.1% / 2.1%
Sales Workers, Apparel (82%)	.9% / .5% / .7%

Percent of all employed Latinas
Percent of all employed black women
Percent of all employed white women

Total percent of employed women in all female-dominated occupations
Latina: 58.0%
Black: 56.9%
White: 58.7%

Figure 1   Women's Employment in Female-Dominated Occupations by Race and Ethnicity, 1990†

*Other female-dominated occupations include dressmakers; kitchen employees (food preparation); food counter, fountain and related occupations; demonstrators, promoters and models; legal assistants; dancers; recreation workers; librarians, archivists and curators; social work teachers; management-related occupations not elsewhere classified.
†Source: Calculated from U.S. Department of Labor, Bureau of Labor Statistics, "Unpublished Tabulations from the Current Population Survey: 1990 Annual Averages," with research assistance from Sumi Kailasapathy. Chart by Virginia Blaisdell.

pressure unions to take into consideration the employment patterns and wage levels of women of color. . . .

THE POLITICS OF COMPARABLE WORTH

As with any reform, comparable worth may be economically problematic and politically divisive if it is not pursued as part of a larger program. Conservative economists have warned that comparable worth, by raising the wages for women's work, would create uncontrollable inflation. In fact, the inflationary impact would depend upon the magnitude of the pay equity adjustment in a particular time period, as well as the ability of firms and government to pass on the costs to consumers and taxpayers. To address this concern, workers could propose to utilize wage-price controls if inflationary problems develop.

Others worry that firms and state agencies may respond to the increase in the price of women's labor by initiating labor-saving technical change, eliminating state programs, and moving factories to countries in which women still provide a super-exploitable labor force. In the absence of comparable worth, office automation is already threatening the jobs of clerical workers, and the movement of jobs to the Third World has created massive structural unemployment in the US. In order for comparable worth not to exacerbate these problems, it must be pursued in conjunction with demands for job security, retraining, and plant-closing legislation.

Comparable worth is unlikely to help the millions of people, many of them women heading households, who live in poverty because they are forced to accept seasonal or part-time work, or cannot find work at all. Only a broader agenda which includes the right to a job and adequate income will address the needs of these people. . . .

NOTES

1. See Ruth Milkman, "The Reproduction of Job Segregation by Sex: A Study of the Sexual Division in the Auto and Electrical Manufacturing Industries in the 1960s," Ph.D. Dissertation, University of California at Berkeley, 1981.
2. See Alice Cook, *Comparable Worth: A Case Book of Experiences in States and Localities* (University of Hawaii, 1985).
3. For nontechnical discussion of job evaluation techniques, see Joy Ann Grune, ed., *Manual on Pay Equity*.
4. We thank Kim Christiansen for this observation, a central premise of her unpublished Ph.D. dissertation in the Economics Department, University of Massachusetts at Amherst.
5. Conversation with Jean Fairfax, Director, Division of Legal Information and Community Service, NAACP Legal Defense and Educational Fund, Inc.   [1988]

The Family

The family and motherhood are often thought of as "natural" entities rather than institutions that, in traditional forms, reinforce sexism and maintain women's subordinated status. The selections in this section first explore women's situation in the family and then some of our varied experiences with motherhood. The fictional pieces serve to highlight the emotional realities of some women's lives in the family, realities that are often obscured by rosy cultural images of family life.

While families can be a source of support for some women, sexism in families can hurt us in various ways. Women no longer lose their legal identity and right to contract as they did in earlier centuries, yet, as Susan Lehrer points out, "the nuclear family is a different place for women and men." The family offers women the hope of love, but also the potential of entrapment, as Rosie learns in Hisaye Yamamoto's short story.

At the same time that women are limited by the institution of the family, we are sometimes blamed for its problems. June Jordan points to the way that black single mothers in particular are blamed for the cause of black poverty. Rather than eliminating the racism and sexism in our society that undermines black families and praising black women for their success in keeping families together, the media "experts" and government officials "talk about our mamas." Jordan points to the institutional and social changes necessary to support all women and families.

As discussed in the introduction to Part IV, feminists distinguish the experience of mothering from the institution of motherhood. "A Long Story" depicts the pain experienced by mothers when the state's prerogatives, rather than women's emotional ties to their children, define motherhood.

In our struggle to survive, or in response to sexism and racism, women have both individually and collectively challenged the constraints of our situations and reshaped the experience of motherhood. Patricia Hill Collins contrasts motherhood in African-American communities with the "cult of true womanhood," a set of ideas dominant in the white middle class of the nineteenth century that equated "true womanhood" with domesticity, purity, piety, and submission. She points to the involvement of "othermothers" and the importance of work outside the home as significant aspects of motherhood for black women.

56

Family and Women's Lives

SUSAN LEHRER

We tend to think about the family as a natural, biological unit. After all, everyone knows it takes two to make a baby. What is meant by family is more than biological relations, of course. In current debates, one specific form of family is referred to as "traditional": the nuclear family—mother, father, and their children, living together, with the father the main breadwinner and the mother responsible for the home. It is maintained and reinforced by law and the state, and forms the basis for social policy toward women and children. Yet only about 25% of American households are married couples and their children; the "traditional" version, in which the father is the sole family breadwinner, accounts for only 8.2% of American households and certainly does not reflect the realities of most of us (U.S. Bureau of the Census, 1991, p. 145).

Overwhelmingly, women's family life includes responsibility for children and the home (called "women's work"), But women also work outside the home in the paid labor force—including over half of women with children under one year of age. Using the outdated, inaccurate picture of "family," however, prevents the needs of women and real-life families from being recognized. This essay explores some of the broad historical changes that have changed the family, and the way in which family structure defines the opportunities, economic situation, and social position of women.

HISTORICAL OVERVIEW

Before industrialization, the family was a working, productive unit, with women producing goods for family consumption, as well as maintaining the family's health and material well-being. For example, in *Little House on the Prairie,* Laura Ingalls Wilder describes her childhood frontier family in which Ma's contribution was clear and valued, and Pa's work took place within the family setting as well. This continued into the late nineteenth and early twentieth centuries in rural areas.

With the beginnings of industrialization, a major shift occurred, as "work" became something done outside the home, for pay, by men. "Women's work" within the home (called housework) was not paid labor and hence not seen as "real work." Thus, the roles of breadwinner and homemaker that are often taken for granted as "natural" are the result of specific historical changes like industrialization, and are, as Jesse Bernard (1981) put it, specific to a very short period in human history. The household itself changed from a unit of production to one primarily of consumption.

Although men were the main workers (for pay), right from the beginning of industrialization, women also worked outside their homes. For example, in making cloth (which was one of the first industries affected by the Industrial Revolution), young women were the main source for factory workers, because men's labor was needed in agricultural production and therefore scarce. Women received wages that were one-quarter to one-half those of men. From the beginning of wage labor and capitalist production for profit, the wage structure itself has been different (and lower) for female workers than for male workers. Although male workers were not well paid, their wages were expected to support a family; women were not expected to be self-supporting, let alone able to support anyone else. This meant women were dependent upon men for support, even when they did work outside the home.

The "power of the purse" reinforced the husband's control over his family. Under English common law, which our legal system is based on, when a woman married, she lost her own legal identity and her legal right to contract. For instance, her husband had control over all money and property of the family, including her wages. Marriage represented a legal contract in which women's status was subordinate to her husband's. Women's current subordination in marriage is rooted in legal tradition as well as in economic arrangements.

As commercial and industrial development expanded and a national economy emerged in the later 1800s, women's world was still supposed to be centered within the household—she was the "angel of the hearth," available to provide material and emotional comfort for the man, who braved the world of commercial competition. This idealized version of family was never quite accurate even in the nineteenth century. For middle-class women, it meant complete economic dependence on the goodwill of their husbands and fathers. Less well-off women worked in factories and sweatshops as young women or whenever they were not supported by a man's income. Women also added to the household income by taking in boarders or doing washing—usually ignored by official counts of family income and employment (Bose, 1987:113).

Enslaved African-American women were expected to perform similar tasks as men, and in the United States, unlike other countries, even slave marriage was not recognized by white law. African-American women worked in the fields as well as in the slave master's household. Nonetheless, studies indicate that many enslaved families sought to maintain strong ties (which amounted to an act of subversion under slavery), and after emancipation, large-scale relocations of African Americans were often an attempt to reunite families broken apart by slavery (Gutman, 1983). After slavery, whites still expected African-American wives to work for them; they were considered lazy if they presumed to stay home and act like ladies (Jones, 1985:59). Thus we see that the "traditional" family was only expected to apply to certain groups and not others—white, middle-class families primarily.

From this brief historical background, it is clear that the family is not a natural, unchanging entity, but it changes along with social and economic shifts in the larger social world. We are again in a time when these larger social forces are visibly changing the way families function. Although the number of women working outside the home has been slowly increasing since the early 1900s, the increase in the past two decades has been astounding. The vast majority of women now combine outside work and family life, and in addition, the proportion of women who are heads of households, never married, and working has also increased dramatically.

THE NUCLEAR FAMILY: IT'S A DIFFERENT PLACE FOR WOMEN THAN MEN

The idealized image of family relationships is that they are warm, loving, and occasionally quarrel-

some but, in the long run, supportive. As the saying goes, family is where, when you go there, they have to take you in. The image of the nuclear family—with the father the main money-maker and responsible for making the important decisions in the family—continues to be a very strong influence on family lifestyles. Choices made within the family setting that appear to be simply logical or natural are, in fact, the consequence of the nuclear family structure. For instance, since the man's job is considered the mainstay of the family, his occupational shifts take first place over other family concerns. Because his earnings are likely to be greater than his wife's if she works, her job is considered the logically expendable one. If they have children, the wife is the one who is going to quit work and "stay home with the baby." If his career plans favor relocating to a different city, hers are likely to suffer. This, in turn, reinforces the disparity in their earnings, making it seem natural that his job is the one that is really important, while hers is secondary. Many women's reluctance to plan a career (as distinguished from a job to earn money) reflects the reality that they are expected to fit it in around everything else in the family. Many men agree that their wife's education, job, and career plans are worthwhile, as long as dinner is still on the table, the house in order, and the kids taken care of when he walks in the door. Some men still talk about taking responsibility for their own child as "baby-sitting."

The reality is that different family members experience the "same" family very differently. Where money is short, it is women who "bridge the gap between what a household's resources really are and what a family's position is supposed to be" (Rapp, 1982:175). They stretch the available food, clothing, and resources to make ends meet. Where a family consistently comes up short at the end of the paycheck, it is the woman who eats less and does without, in order that the kids and husband can have enough. To talk about a family's standard of living as if all family members shared the same level of well-being or poverty is misleading. Yet social scientists typically use the husband's occupation in defining social class and just assume that the rest of the family is included. And defining a family's class by the husband's occupation does not provide a basis for understanding the very different life chances that men and women face within the "same" family, given the realities of divorce and single parenthood.

FAMILIES: A MULTITUDE OF POSSIBILITIES

Probably the most talked-about change in American families in recent years has been the increase in family households headed by women. Women heading families face a series of obstacles that reflect the unwillingness of policy makers to recognize and address their condition. In order to work and support their families, women must have child care; then they must earn enough to provide for their families. Women's earnings are still less than 70% of men's. The good news is that this is a greater proportion than it has been in the recent past; the bad news is that this is because of the relative *decline* in men's earnings rather than an increase in women's overall income. This means that women heading households are more likely to be poor, not only because there is only one earner in the family but because that earner is a woman. It also means that the lack of affordable child care hits women who are heads of family especially hard. Yet American social policy has not recognized that child care is just as much a social necessity as educating children. The United States is far behind most European countries, which train child-care specialists and provide care for children from the youngest ages.

For many women, the descent to poverty occurs as a result of divorce. This is more likely to happen for white women than for black women, partly because of the overall lower earnings of black men relative to white men. Despite all the jokes about men paying their life fortune in alimony to ex-wives, the reality is that men's standard of living goes *up* following divorce, while women's drops precipitously. One study found that a year after divorce, men's standard of living improved 42%, while women's *dropped* by 73% (Weitzman, 1985).

The transition from Mrs. to ex-Mrs. is especially difficult for older, long-married women, who often do not have marketable skills to support themselves. The tragic irony is that it is precisely those women who acceded to cultural expectations to stay at home and be good wives and mothers who suffer the most, both economically and emotionally. Women whose whole sense of identity centers around being a wife and mother must cope with profound loss of meaning as well as the economic shock of divorce. These older women are the ones more likely to get alimony (as distinguished from child support). Younger women from shorter-term marriages are unlikely to be awarded alimony and often are unable to even collect child support. In 1990, there were 10 million women living with children whose fathers were not in the home; only half were awarded child support at all, and only half of those received the full amount (U.S. Bureau of the Census, Feb. 1992, p. 2). Responsibility for children following divorce still rests overwhelmingly with the mother, despite all the movies depicting the hilarious, heart-warming adventures of men raising children.

The reasons for the increase in families headed by women are complex and cannot be reduced to a simple explanation. Young women are more likely to have worked. Shotgun weddings are less common now than in the past (judging by the fact that many fewer pregnant women marry before their first child is born (U.S. Bureau of the Census, 1992, p. 2). The options of abortion, and refusing to marry someone you don't like, are more acceptable now. Other explanations look at economic factors affecting couples' financial prospects as they consider marriage. There is extensive urban unemployment and poverty among young people, for whom education is less likely to lead to jobs that pay enough to support a family. The reality is, almost 25% of families with children were headed by women in 1990, compared with less than 12% in 1970. Single-parent families are 28% of families with children under 18; less than 14% of them are headed by the father. Many African-American families are headed by women—56%, compared with 19% for white families and 29% for Hispanic-American families. And remember, not all families involve children—they also include elders or other relatives in the household (U.S. Bureau of the Census, 1992, p. 7).

Married couples with children still depend upon the wife to do the "second shift"—the housework. Even when both husband and wife work full-time, throughout the 1980s, two-thirds of working wives reported that they did most or all of the housework. The time women spent on housework remained about the same whether they worked or not.

This may be beginning to change—partly because women have simply stopped doing so much of it, but also because couples believe in sharing household work (Schor, 1991:103).

Despite the variety of social arrangements in which people live their lives, social policy and law penalize those who do not live in nuclear family settings. One of the ways this happens is by excluding non-legally married family members from health insurance plans—without which Americans cannot afford to be sick. The high cost of medical coverage has now reached crisis proportions nationally. The United States is the only major industrial nation (besides South Africa) that does not have national health coverage for everybody. Hospitals frequently restrict visits for very ill people to "immediate family," meaning legal spouses, and also deny information and decision making to non-legally married couples of any sort. This exclusion especially affects gay couples (Thompson and Andrzejewski, 1988). The increasing numbers of people affected by these exclusions are being encouraged to declare so-called "living wills" and powers of attorney so that the person they designate will be accorded the rights and responsibilities that a legal spouse would be without question.

MOM AND APPLE PIE?

The conservatives who attack the women's movement for being anti-family have a specific form of the family in mind—one that certainly does not correspond to what real families are like. These fundamentalist doctrines of the political far right rigidly interpret the Bible to justify the patriarchal family, attack women's rights, and use the power of the laws to support their views. It is interesting that in times of social change—like the mid-1800s in the throes of industrialization, and our own time—ideologies advocating a return to an earlier, past "golden age" surface.

Now, even the basic, biological fact that it takes two to make a baby seems to be blurring at the edges with the advances of reproductive technologies. A woman may be pregnant and give birth to a child to whom she is not genetically related, from an ovum that was fertilized in vitro (outside the woman's body). The child then may potentially have two completely different sets of parents. What is the le-

gal status of the woman who was pregnant with the child? What "rights," if any, has she to be considered the "mother"? Is a "contract" to give up the child after birth enforceable if she changes her mind? These are unresolved questions. Typically, the couple wishing to become parents is wealthy enough to pay large medical and legal fees, while the woman having the child has much lower income and less to spend on lawyers. Our thinking about women, pregnancy, parenting, and family will need to take these issues into account.

Another possibility is that a woman who wants to become pregnant but is having difficulties can opt for series of fertility treatments or implanting of fertilized eggs—procedures that are experimental and extremely expensive, uncomfortable, and uncertain. Others want to be parents but not within a male-female household, either gay/lesbian couples or single persons. All of these can also become families with parents who raise children, wipe sniffly noses, and clap at school plays. The challenge is to creatively respond to changed conditions, and to help shape that change in ways that will enhance rather than stifle peoples' lives.

REFERENCES

Bernard, Jessie. "The Good Provider Role: Its Rise and Fall," *American Psychologist* vol. 36, No. 1, Jan. 1981, pp. 1–12.

Bose, Christine, "Devaluing Women's Work: The Undercount of Women's Employment in 1900 and 1980," in Christine Bose, Roslyn Feldberg, and Natalie Sokoloff, eds. *Hidden Aspects of Women's Work.* New York: Praeger, 1987, pp. 95–115.

Gutman, Herbert, "Persistent Myths About the Afro-American Family," in Michael Gordon, ed. *The American Family in Social-Historical Perspective,* 3rd ed. New York: St. Martins Press, 1983, pp. 459–481.

Jones, Jacqueline. *Labor of Love, Labor of Sorrow: Black Women, Work and the Family from Slavery to the Present.* New York: Vintage, 1985.

Rapp, Rayna. "Family and Class in Contemporary America: Notes Toward an Understanding of Ideology," in Barrie Thorne and Marilyn Yalom, eds. *Rethinking the Family: Some Feminist Questions.* New York: Longman, 1982.

Schor, Juliet. *The Overworked American: The Unexpected Decline of Leisure.* New York: Basic Books, 1991.

Thompson, Karen, and Andrzejewski, Julie. *Why Can't Sharon Kowalski Come Home?* San Francisco: Spinster/Aunt Lute Book Company, 1988.

U.S. Bureau of the Census, U. S. Department of Commerce, "Household and Family Characteristics: March 1990 and 1989," *Current Population Reports,* Population Characteristics, Series P-20, No. 447, 1991.

U.S. Bureau of the Census, U.S. Department of Commerce, "How We're Changing, Demographic State of the Nation:

1991," *Current Population Reports,* Special Studies Series P–23, No. 177, February 1992.

Weitzman, Lenore. *The Divorce Revolution: The Unexpected Consequences for Women and Children in America.* New York: Free Press, 1985.   [1992]

🦎 57

Seventeen Syllables

HISAYE YAMAMOTO

The first Rosie knew that her mother had taken to writing poems was one evening when she finished one and read it aloud for her daughter's approval. It was about cats, and Rosie pretended to understand it thoroughly and appreciate it no end, partly because she hesitated to disillusion her mother about the quantity and quality of Japanese she had learned in all the years now that she had been going to Japanese school every Saturday (and Wednesday, too, in the summer). Even so, her mother must have been skeptical about the depth of Rosie's understanding, because she explained afterwards about the kind of poem she was trying to write.

See, Rosie, she said, it was a *haiku,* a poem in which she must pack all her meaning into seventeen syllables only, which were divided into three lines of five, seven, and five syllables. In the one she had just read, she had tried to capture the charm of a kitten, as well as comment on the superstition that owning a cat of three colors meant good luck.

"Yes, yes, I understand. How utterly lovely," Rosie said, and her mother, either satisfied or seeing through the deception and resigned, went back to composing.

The truth was that Rosie was lazy; English lay ready on the tongue but Japanese had to be searched for and examined, and even then put forth tentatively (probably to meet with laughter). It was so much easier to say yes, yes, even when one meant no, no. Besides, this was what was in her mind to say: I was looking through one of your magazines from Japan last night, Mother, and towards the back I found some *haiku* in English that delighted me. There was one that made me giggle off and on until

I fell asleep—

It is morning, and lo!
I lie awake, *comme il faut,*
sighing for some dough.

Now, how to reach her mother, how to communicate the melancholy song? Rosie knew formal Japanese by fits and starts, her mother had even less English, no French. It was much more possible to say yes, yes.

It developed that her mother was writing the *haiku* for a daily newspaper, the *Mainichi Shimbun,* that was published in San Francisco. Los Angeles, to be sure, was closer to the farming community in which the Hayashi family lived and several Japanese vernaculars were printed there, but Rosie's parents said they preferred the tone of the northern paper. Once a week, the *Mainichi* would have a section devoted to *haiku,* and her mother became an extravagant contributor, taking for herself the blossoming pen name, Ume Hanazono.

So Rosie and her father lived for awhile with two women, her mother and Ume Hanazono. Her mother (Tome Hayashi by name) kept house, cooked, washed, and, along with her husband and the Carrascos, the Mexican family hired for the harvest, did her ample share of picking tomatoes out in the sweltering fields and boxing them in tidy strata in the cool packing shed. Ume Hanazono, who came to life after the dinner dishes were done, was an earnest, muttering stranger who often neglected speaking when spoken to and stayed busy at the parlor table as late as midnight scribbling with pencil on scratch paper or carefully copying characters on good paper with her fat, pale green Parker.

The new interest had some repercussions on the household routine. Before, Rosie had been accustomed to her parents and herself taking their hot baths early and going to bed almost immediately afterwards, unless her parents challenged each other to a game of flower cards or unless company dropped in. Now if her father wanted to play cards, he had to resort to solitaire (at which he always cheated fearlessly), and if a group of friends came over, it was bound to contain someone who was also writing *haiku,* and the small assemblage would be split in two, her father entertaining the non-literary members and her mother comparing ecstatic notes with the visiting poet.

If they went out, it was more of the same thing. But Ume Hanazono's life span, even for a poet's, was very brief—perhaps three months at most.

One night they went over to see the Hayano family in the neighboring town to the west, an adventure both painful and attractive to Rosie. It was attractive because there were four Hayano girls, all lovely and each one named after a season of the year (Haru, Natsu, Aki, Fuyu), painful because something had been wrong with Mrs. Hayano ever since the birth of her first child. Rosie would sometimes watch Mrs. Hayano, reputed to have been the belle of her native village, making her way about a room, stooped, slowly shuffling, violently trembling (*always* trembling), and she would be reminded that this woman, in this same condition, had carried and given issue to three babies. She would look wonderingly at Mr. Hayano, handsome, tall, and strong, and she would look at her four pretty friends. But it was not a matter she could come to any decision about.

On this visit, however, Mrs. Hayano sat all evening in the rocker, as motionless and unobtrusive as it was possible for her to be, and Rosie found the greater part of the evening practically anaesthetic. Too, Rosie spent most of it in the girls' room, because Haru, the garrulous one, said almost as soon as the bows and other greetings were over, "Oh, you must see my new coat!"

It was a pale plaid of grey, sand, and blue, with an enormous collar, and Rosie, seeing nothing special in it, said, "Gee, how nice."

"Nice?" said Haru, indignantly. "Is that all you can say about it? It's gorgeous! And so cheap, too. Only seventeen-ninety-eight, because it was a sale. The saleslady said it was twenty-five dollars regular."

"Gee," said Rosie. Natsu, who never said much and when she said anything said it shyly, fingered the coat covetously and Haru pulled it away.

"Mine," she said, putting it on. She minced in the aisle between the two large beds and smiled happily. "Let's see how your mother likes it."

She broke into the front room and the adult conversation and went to stand in front of Rosie's mother, while the rest watched from the door. Rosie's mother was properly envious. "May I inherit it when you're through with it?"

Haru, pleased, giggled and said yes, she could, but Natsu reminded gravely from the door, "You promised me, Haru."

Everyone laughed but Natsu, who shamefacedly retreated into the bedroom. Haru came in laughing, taking off the coat. "We were only kidding, Natsu," she said. "Here, you try it on now."

After Natsu buttoned herself into the coat, inspected herself solemnly in the bureau mirror, and reluctantly shed it, Rosie, Aki, and Fuyu got their turns, and Fuyu, who was eight, drowned in it while her sisters and Rosie doubled up in amusement. They all went into the front room later, because Haru's mother quaveringly called to her to fix the tea and rice cakes and open a can of sliced peaches for everybody. Rosie noticed that her mother and Mr. Hayano were talking together at the little table—they were discussing a *haiku* that Mr. Hayano was planning to send to the *Mainichi*, while her father was sitting at one end of the sofa looking through a copy of *Life*, the new picture magazine. Occasionally, her father would comment on a photograph, holding it toward Mrs. Hayano and speaking to her as he always did—loudly, as though he thought someone such as she must surely be at least a trifle deaf also.

The five girls had their refreshments at the kitchen table, and it was while Rosie was showing the sisters her trick of swallowing peach slices without chewing (she chased each slippery crescent down with a swig of tea) that her father brought his empty teacup and untouched saucer to the sink and said, "Come on, Rosie, we're going home now."

"Already?" asked Rosie.

"Work tomorrow," he said.

He sounded irritated, and Rosie, puzzled, gulped one last yellow slice and stood up to go, while the sisters began protesting, as was their wont.

"We have to get up at five-thirty," he told them, going into the front room quickly, so that they did not have their usual chance to hang onto his hands and plead for an extension of time.

Rosie, following, saw that her mother and Mr. Hayano were sipping tea and still talking together, while Mrs. Hayano concentrated, quivering, on raising the handleless Japanese cup to her lips with both her hands and lowering it back to her lap. Her father, saying nothing, went out the door, onto the bright porch, and down the steps. Her mother looked up and asked, "Where is he going?"

"Where is he going?" Rosie said, "He said we were going home now."

"Going home?" Her mother looked with embarrassment at Mr. Hayano and his absorbed wife and then forced a smile. "He must be tired," she said.

Haru was not giving up yet. "May Rosie stay overnight?" she asked, and Natsu, Aki, and Fuyu came to reinforce their sister's plea by helping her make a circle around Rosie's mother. Rosie, for once having no desire to stay, was relieved when her mother, apologizing to the perturbed Mr. and Mrs. Hayano for her father's abruptness at the same time, managed to shake her head no at the quartet, kindly but adamant, so that they broke their circle and let her go.

Rosie's father looked ahead into the windshield as the two joined him. "I'm sorry," her mother said. "You must be tired." Her father, stepping on the starter, said nothing. "You know how I get when it's *haiku*," she continued, "I forget what time it is." He only grunted.

As they rode homeward silently, Rosie, sitting between, felt a rush of hate for both—for her mother for begging, for her father for denying her mother. I wish this old Ford would crash, right now, she thought, then immediately, no, no, I wish my father would laugh, but it was too late: already the vision had passed through her mind of the green pick-up crumpled in the dark against one of the mighty eucalyptus trees they were just riding past, of the three contorted, bleeding bodies, one of them hers.

Rosie ran between two patches of tomatoes, her heart working more rambunctiously than she had ever known it to. How lucky it was that Aunt Taka and Uncle Gimpachi had come tonight, though, how very lucky. Otherwise she might not have really kept her half-promise to meet Jesus Carrasco. Jesus was going to be a senior in September at the same school she went to, and his parents were the ones

helping with the tomatoes this year. She and Jesus, who hardly remembered seeing each other at Cleveland High where there were so many other people and two whole grades between them, had become great friends this summer—he always had a joke for her when he periodically drove the loaded pick-up up from the fields to the shed where she was usually sorting while her mother and father did the packing, and they laughed a great deal together over infinitesimal repartee during the afternoon break for chilled watermelon or ice cream in the shade of the shed.

What she enjoyed most was racing him to see which could finish picking a double row first. He, who could work faster, would tease her by slowing down until she thought she would surely pass him this time, then speeding up furiously to leave her several sprawling vines behind. Once he had made her screech hideously by crossing over, while her back was turned, to place atop the tomatoes in her green-stained bucket a truly monstrous, pale green worm (it had looked more like an infant snake). And it was when they had finished a contest this morning, after she had pantingly pointed a green finger at the immature tomatoes evident in the lugs at the end of his row and he had returned the accusation (with justice), that he had startlingly brought up the matter of their possibly meeting outside the range of both their parents' dubious eyes.

"What for?" she had asked.

"I've got a secret I want to tell you," he said.

"Tell me now," she demanded.

"It won't be ready till tonight," he said.

She laughed. "Tell me tomorrow then."

"It'll be gone tomorrow," he threatened.

"Well, for seven hakes, what is it?" she asked, more than twice, and when he had suggested that the packing shed would be an appropriate place to find out, she had cautiously answered maybe. She had not been certain she was going to keep the appointment until the arrival of her mother's sister and her husband. Their coming seemed a sort of signal of permission, of grace, and she had definitely made up her mind to lie and leave as she was bowing them welcome.

So as soon as everyone appeared settled back for the evening, she announced loudly that she was going to the privy outside, "I'm going to the *benjo!*" and slipped out the door. And now that she was actually on her way, her heart pumped in such an undisciplined way that she could hear it with her ears. It's because I'm running, she told herself, slowing to a walk. The shed was up ahead, one more patch away, in the middle of the fields. Its bulk, looming in the dimness, took on a sinisterness that was funny when Rosie reminded herself that it was only a wooden frame with a canvas roof and three canvas walls that made a slapping noise on breezy days.

Jesus was sitting on the narrow plank that was the sorting platform and she went around to the other side and jumped backwards to seat herself on the rim of a packing stand. "Well, tell me," she said without greeting, thinking her voice sounded reassuringly familiar.

"I saw you coming out the door," Jesus said. "I heard you running part of the way, too."

"Uh-huh," Rosie said. "Now tell me the secret."

"I was afraid you wouldn't come," he said.

Rosie delved around on the chicken-wire bottom of the stall for number two tomatoes, ripe, which she was sitting beside, and came up with a left-over that felt edible. She bit into it and began sucking out the pulp and seeds. "I'm here," she pointed out.

"Rosie, are you sorry you came?"

"Sorry? What for?" she said. "You said you were going to tell me something."

"I will, I will," Jesus said, but his voice contained disappointment, and Rosie fleetingly felt the older of the two, realizing a brand-new power which vanished without category under her recognition.

"I have to go back in a minute," she said. "My aunt and uncle are here from Wintersburg. I told them I was going to the privy."

Jesus laughed. "You funny thing," he said. "You slay me!"

"Just because you have a bathroom *inside,*" Rosie said, "Come on, tell me."

Chuckling, Jesus came around to lean on the stand facing her. They still could not see each other very clearly, but Rosie noticed that Jesus became very sober again as he took the hollow tomato from her hand and dropped it back into the stall. When he took hold of her empty hand, she could find no words to protest; her vocabulary had become dis-

tressingly constricted and she thought desperately that all that remained intact now was yes and no and oh, and even these few sounds would not easily come out. Thus, kissed by Jesus, Rosie fell for the first time entirely victim to a helplessness delectable beyond speech. But the terrible, beautiful sensation lasted no more than a second, and the reality of Jesus' lips and tongue and teeth and hands made her pull away with such strength that she nearly tumbled.

Rosie stopped running as she approached the lights from the windows of home. How long since she had left? She could not guess, but gasping yet, she went to the privy in back and locked herself in. Her own breathing deafened her in the dark, close space, and she sat and waited until she could hear at last the nightly calling of the frogs and crickets. Even then, all she could think to say was oh, my, and the pressure of Jesus' face against her face would not leave.

No one had missed her in the parlor, however, and Rosie walked in and through quickly, announcing that she was next going to take a bath. "Your father's in the bathhouse," her mother said, and Rosie, in her room, recalled that she had not seen him when she entered. There had been only Aunt Taka and Uncle Gimpachi with her mother at the table, drinking tea. She got her robe and straw sandals and crossed the parlor again to go outside. Her mother was telling them about the *haiku* competition in the *Mainichi* and the poem she had entered.

Rosie met her father coming out of the bathhouse. "Are you through, Father?" she asked. "I was going to ask you to scrub my back."

"Scrub your own back," he said shortly, going toward the main house.

"What have I done now?" she yelled after him. She suddenly felt like doing a lot of yelling. But he did not answer, and she went into the bathhouse. Turning on the dangling light, she removed her denims and T-shirt and threw them in the big carton for dirty clothes standing next to the washing machine. Her other things she took with her into the bath compartment to wash after her bath. After she had scooped a basin of hot water from the square wooden tub, she sat on the grey cement of the floor and soaped herself at exaggerated leisure, singing

"Red Sails in the Sunset" at the top of her voice and using da-da-da where she suspected her words. Then, standing up, still singing, for she was possessed by the notion that any attempt now to analyze would result in spoilage and she believed that the larger her volume the less she would be able to hear herself think, she obtained more hot water and poured it on until she was free of lather. Only then did she allow herself to step into the steaming vat, one leg first, then the remainder of her body inch by inch until the water no longer stung and she could move around at will.

She took a long time soaking, afterwards remembering to go around outside to stoke the embers of the tin-lined fireplace beneath the tub and to throw on a few more sticks so that the water might keep its heat for her mother, and when she finally returned to the parlor, she found her mother still talking *haiku* with her aunt and uncle, the three of them on another round of tea. Her father was nowhere in sight.

At Japanese school the next day (Wednesday, it was), Rosie was grave and giddy by turns. Preoccupied at her desk in the row for students on Book Eight, she made up for it at recess by performing wild mimicry for the benefit of her friend Chizuko. She held her nose and whined a witticism or two in what she considered was the manner of Fred Allen; she assumed intoxication and a British accent to go over the climax of the Rudy Vallee recording of the pub conversation about William Ewart Gladstone; she was the child Shirley Temple piping, "On the Good Ship Lollipop"; she was the gentleman soprano of the Four Inkspots trilling, "If I Didn't Care." And she felt reasonably satisfied when Chizuko wept and gasped, "Oh, Rosie, you ought to be in the movies!"

Her father came after her at noon, bringing her sandwiches of minced ham and two nectarines to eat while she rode, so that she could pitch right into the sorting when they got home. The lugs were piling up, he said, and the ripe tomatoes in them would probably have to be taken to the cannery tomorrow if they were not ready for the produce haulers tonight. "This heat's not doing them any good. And we've got no time for a break today."

It *was* hot, probably the hottest day of the year, and Rosie's blouse stuck damply to her back even

under the protection of the canvas. But she worked as efficiently as a flawless machine and kept the stalls heaped, with one part of her mind listening in to the parental murmuring about the heat and the tomatoes and with another part planning the exact words she would say to Jesus when he drove up with the first load of the afternoon. But when at last she saw that the pick-up was coming, her hands went berserk and the tomatoes started falling in the wrong stalls, and her father said, "Hey, hey! Rosie, watch what you're doing!"

"Well, I have to go to the *benjo*," she said, hiding panic.

"Go in the weeds over there," he said, only half-joking.

"Oh, Father!" she protested.

"Oh, go on home," her mother said. "We'll make out for awhile."

In the privy Rosie peered through a knothole toward the fields, watching as much as she could of Jesus. Happily she thought she saw him look in the direction of the house from time to time before he finished unloading and went back toward the patch where his mother and father worked. As she was heading for the shed, a very presentable black car purred up the dirt driveway to the house and its driver motioned to her. Was this the Hayashi home, he wanted to know. She nodded. Was she a Hayashi? Yes, she said, thinking that he was a good-looking man. He got out of the car with a huge, flat package and she saw that he warmly wore a business suit. "I have something here for your mother then," he said, in a more elegant Japanese than she was used to.

She told him where her mother was and he came along with her, patting his face with an immaculate white handkerchief and saying something about the coolness of San Francisco. To her surprised mother and father, he bowed and introduced himself as, among other things, the *haiku* editor of the *Mainichi Shimbun*, saying that since he had been coming as far as Los Angeles anyway, he had decided to bring her the first prize she had won in the recent contest.

"First prize?" her mother echoed, believing and not believing, pleased and overwhelmed. Handed the package with a bow, she bobbed her head up and down numerous times to express her utter gratitude.

"It is nothing much," he added, "but I hope it

will serve as a token of our great appreciation for your contributions and our great admiration of your considerable talent."

"I am not worthy," she said, falling easily into his style. "It is I who should make some sign of my humble thanks for being permitted to contribute."

"No, no, to the contrary," he said, bowing again.

But Rosie's mother insisted, and then saying that she knew she was being unorthodox, she asked if she might open the package because her curiosity was so great. Certainly she might. In fact, he would like her reaction to it, for personally, it was one of his favorite Hiroshiges.

Rosie thought it was a pleasant picture, which looked to have been sketched with delicate quickness. There were pink clouds, containing some graceful calligraphy, and a sea that was a pale blue except at the edges, containing four sampans with indications of people in them. Pines edged the water and on the far-off beach there was a cluster of thatched huts towered over by pine-dotted mountains of grey and blue. The frame was scalloped and gilt.

After Rosie's mother pronounced it without peer and somewhat prodded her father into nodding agreement, she said Mr. Kuroda must at least have a cup of tea after coming all this way, and although Mr. Kuroda did not want to impose, he soon agreed that a cup of tea would be refreshing and went along with her to the house, carrying the picture for her.

"Ha, your mother's crazy!" Rosie's father said, and Rosie laughed uneasily as she resumed judgment on the tomatoes. She had emptied six lugs when he broke into an imaginary conversation with Jesus to tell her to go and remind her mother of the tomatoes, and she went slowly.

Mr. Kuroda was in his shirtsleeves expounding some *haiku* theory as he munched a rice cake, and her mother was rapt. Abashed in the great man's presence, Rosie stood next to her mother's chair until her mother looked up inquiringly, and then she started to whisper the message, but her mother pushed her gently away and reproached, "You are not being very polite to our guest."

"Father says the tomatoes. . . ." Rosie said aloud, smiling foolishly.

"Tell him I shall only be a minute," her mother said, speaking the language of Mr. Kuroda.

When Rosie carried the reply to her father, he did not seem to hear and she said again, "Mother says she'll be back in a minute."

"All right, all right," he nodded, and they worked again in silence. But suddenly, her father uttered an incredible noise, exactly like the cork of a bottle popping, and the next Rosie knew, he was stalking angrily toward the house, almost running in fact, and she chased after him crying, "Father! Father! What are you going to do?"

He stopped long enough to order her back to the shed. "Never mind!" he shouted. "Get on with the sorting!"

And from the place in the fields where she stood, frightened and vacillating, Rosie saw her father enter the house. Soon Mr. Kuroda came out alone, putting on his coat. Mr. Kuroda got into his car and backed out down the driveway onto the highway. Next her father emerged, also alone, something in his arms (it was the picture, she realized), and, going over to the bathhouse woodpile, he threw the picture on the ground and picked up the axe. Smashing the picture, glass and all (she heard the explosion faintly), he reached over for the kerosene that was used to encourage the bath fire and poured it over the wreckage. I am dreaming, Rosie said to herself, I am dreaming, but her father, having made sure that his act of cremation was irrevocable, was even then returning to the fields.

Rosie ran past him and toward the house. What had become of her mother? She burst into the parlor and found her mother at the back window watching the dying fire. They watched together until there remained only a feeble smoke under the blazing sun. Her mother was very calm.

"Do you know why I married your father?" she said without turning.

"No," said Rosie. It was the most frightening question she had ever been called upon to answer. Don't tell me now, she wanted to say, tell me tomorrow, tell me next week, don't tell me today. But she knew she would be told now, that the telling would combine with the other violence of the hot afternoon to level her life, her world to the very ground.

It was like a story out of the magazines illustrated in sepia, which she had consumed so greedily for a period until the information had somehow reached her that those wretchedly unhappy autobiographies, offered to her as the testimonials of living men and women, were largely inventions: Her mother, at nineteen, had come to America and married her father as an alternative to suicide.

At eighteen she had been in love with the first son of one of the well-to-do families in her village. The two had met whenever and wherever they could, secretly, because it would not have done for his family to see him favor her—her father had no money; he was a drunkard and a gambler besides. She had learned she was with child; an excellent match had already been arranged for her lover. Despised by her family, she had given premature birth to a stillborn son, who would be seventeen now. Her family did not turn her out, but she could no longer project herself in any direction without refreshing in them the memory of her indiscretion. She wrote to Aunt Taka, her favorite sister in America, threatening to kill herself if Aunt Taka would not send for her. Aunt Taka hastily arranged a marriage with a young man of whom she knew, but lately arrived from Japan, a young man of simple mind, it was said, but of kindly heart. The young man was never told why his unseen betrothed was so eager to hasten the day of meeting.

The story was told perfectly, with neither groping for words nor untoward passion. It was as though her mother had memorized it by heart, reciting it to herself so many times over that its nagging vileness had long since gone.

"I had a brother then?" Rosie asked, for this was what seemed to matter now; she would think about the other later, she assured herself, pushing back the illumination which threatened all that darkness that had hitherto been merely mysterious or even glamorous. "A half-brother?"

"Yes."

"I would have liked a brother," she said.

Suddenly, her mother knelt on the floor and took her by the wrists. "Rosie," she said urgently, "Promise me you will never marry!" Shocked more by the request than the revelation, Rosie stared at her mother's face. Jesus, Jesus, she called silently, not certain whether she was invoking the help of the son of the Carrascos or of God, until there returned sweetly the memory of Jesus' hand, how it had touched her and where. Still her mother waited for an answer, holding her wrists so tightly that her

hands were going numb. She tried to pull free. Promise, her mother whispered fiercely, promise. Yes, yes, I promise, Rosie said. But for an instant she turned away, and her mother, hearing the familiar glib agreement, released her. Oh, you, you, you, her eyes and twisted mouth said, you fool. Rosie, covering her face, began at last to cry, and the embrace and consoling hand came much later than she expected.   [1988]

 58

"Don't You Talk About My Mama!"

JUNE JORDAN

I got up that morning, with malice toward no one. Drank my coffee and scanned the front page of *The New York Times*. And there it was. I remember, even now, the effrontery of that headline four years ago: "Breakup of Black Family Imperils Gains of Decades." I could hardly believe it. Here were these clowns dumping on us yet again. That was 1983, three years into the shameless Real Deal of Ronald Reagan. He'd taken or he'd shaken everything we Black folks needed just to hang in here, breathing in and out. And yet the headline absolutely failed to give credit where it was due. Instead, "politicians and scholars—black and white" dared to identify the *victims*—the Black single mothers raising 55 percent of all of our Black children *with no help from anybody anywhere*—as the cause of Black poverty! These expense-account professionals presumed to identify "the family crisis" of Black folks as "a threat to the future of Black people without equal." And this was not somebody's weird idea about how to say "thank you." (I could relate to that: somebody finally saying thank you to Black women!) No: This was just another dumb, bold insult to my mother.

Now when I was growing up, the one sure trigger to a down-and-out fight was to say something—anything—about somebody's mother. As a matter of fact, we refined things eventually to the point where you didn't have to get specific. All you had to do was push into the face of another girl or boy, close as you could, almost nose to nose, and just spit out the two words: "Your mother!" This item of our code of honor was not negotiable, and clearly we took it pretty seriously: Even daring to refer to someone's mother put you off-limits. From the time you learned how to talk, everybody's mama remained the holiest of holies. And we did not ever forget it, this fact, that the first, the last and the most, that the number-one persevering, resourceful, resilient and devoted person in our lives was, and would always be, your mother and my mother.

But sometimes, as you know, we grow up without growing wise. Sometimes we become so sophisticated we have to read *The New York Times* in order to figure out whether it's a hot or a rainy day. We read the fine print in order to find out the names of our so-called leaders. But what truly surprises me is Black folks listening to a whole lot of white blasphemy against Black feats of survival, Black folks paying attention to people who never even notice us except to describe us as "female-headed" or something equally weird. (I would like to know, for a fact, has anybody ever seen a female-headed anything at all? What did it look like? What did it do?)

Now I am not opposed to sophistication per se, but when you lose touch with your mama, when you take the word of an absolute, hostile stranger over and above the unarguable truth of your own miraculous, hard-won history, and when you don't remember to ask, again and again, "Compared to what?" I think you don't need to worry about enemies anymore. You'd better just worry about yourself.

Back in 1965, Daniel P. Moynihan (now a U.S. senator from New York) issued a broadside insult to the national Black community. With the full support of a Democratic administration that was tired of Negroes carrying on about citizenship rights and integration and white racist violence, Moynihan came through with the theory that we, Black folks, and we, Black women in particular, constituted "the problem." And now there are Black voices joining the choruses of the absurd. There are national Black organizations and purported Black theoreticians who have become indistinguishable from the verified enemies of Black folks in this country. These sophisticated Black voices jump to the forefront of delighted mass-media exposure because they are willing to lament and to defame the incredible triumph of Black women, the victory of Black mothers that is the victory of our continuation as a people in America.

Archly delivering jargon phrases about "the collapse of Black family structure" and "the destructive culture of poverty in the ghetto" and, of course, "the crisis of female-headedness," with an additional screaming reference to "the shame of teenage pregnancy," these Black voices come to us as the disembodied blatherings of peculiar offspring: Black men and women who wish to deny the Black mother of their origins and who wish to adopt white Daniel P. Moynihan as their father. I happen to lack the imagination necessary to forgive, or understand, this phenomenon. But the possible consequences of this oddball public outcry demand our calm examination.

According to these new Black voices fathered by Mr. Moynihan, it would seem that the Black family subsists in a terrible, deteriorating state. That's the problem. The source of the problem is The Black Family (that is, it is not white; it suffers from "female-headedness"). The solution to The Black Family Problem is—you guessed it—The Black Family. It must become more white—more patriarchal, less "female-headed," more employed more steadily at better and better-paying jobs.

Now I would agree that the Black family is not white. I do not agree that the problem is "female-headedness." I would rather suggest that the problem is that women in general and that Black women in particular cannot raise our children and secure adequately paying jobs because this is a society that hates women and that believes we are replaceable, that we are dispensable, ridiculous, irksome facts of life. American social and economic hatred of women means that any work primarily identified as women's work will be poorly paid, if at all. Any work open to women will be poorly paid, at best, in comparison to work open to men. Any work done by women will receive a maximum of 64 cents on the dollar compared with wages for the same work done by men. Prenatal, well-baby care, day care for children, children's allowances, housing allowances for parents, paid maternity leave—all of the elemental provisions for the equally entitled citizenship of women and children are ordinary attributes of industrialized nations, except for one: the United States.

The problem, clearly, does not originate with women in general or Black women specifically, who, whether it's hard or whether it's virtually impossible, nevertheless keep things together. Our hardships follow from the uncivilized political and economic status enjoined upon women and children in our country, which has the highest infant mortality rate among its industrial peers. And, evidently, feels fine, thank you, about that. (Not incidentally, Black infant-mortality rates hold at levels twice that for whites.)

The Black Family persists *despite* the terrible deteriorating state of affairs prevailing in the United States. This is a nation unwilling and progressively unable to provide for the well-being of most of its citizens: Our economic system increasingly concentrates our national wealth in the hands of fewer and fewer interest groups. Our economic system increasingly augments the wealth of the richest sector of the citizenry, while it diminishes the real wages and the available livelihood of the poor. Our economic system refuses responsibility for the equitable sharing of national services and monies among its various peoples. Our economic system remains insensitive to the political demands of a democracy, and therefore it does not yield to the requirements of equal entitlement of all women and all children and Black, Hispanic and Native American men, the elderly and the disabled. If you total the American people you have an obvious majority of Americans squeezed outside the putative benefits of "free enterprise."

Our economic system continues its trillion-dollar commitment *not* to the betterment of the lives of its citizens but, rather, to the development and lunatic replication of a military-industrial complex. In this context, then, the Black family persists, yes, in a terrible deteriorating state. But we did not create this state. Nor do we control it. And we are not suffering "collapse." Change does not signify collapse. The nuclear, patriarchal family structure of white America was never our own; it was not *African*. And when we arrived to slavery here, why or how should we have emulated the overseer and the master? We who were counted in the Constitution as three-fifths of a human being? We who could by law neither marry nor retain our children against the preda-

tions of the slave economy? Nonetheless, from under the whip through underpaid underemployment and worse, Black folks have formulated our own family, our own home base for nurture and for pride. We have done this through extended kinship methods. And even Black teenage parents are trying, in their own way, to perpetuate the Black family.

The bizarre analysis of the Black family that blames the Black family for being not white and not patriarchal, not endowed with steadily employed Black husbands and fathers who enjoy access to middle-income occupations is just that: a bizarre analysis, a heartless joke. If Black men and Black women *wanted* Black men to become patriarchs of their families, if Black men wanted to function as head of the house—shouldn't they probably have some kind of a job? Can anyone truly dare to suggest that the catastrophic 46-percent unemployment rate now crippling working-age Black men is something that either Black men or Black women view as positive or desirable? Forty-six percent! What is the meaning of a man in the house if he cannot hold out his hand to help his family make it through the month, and if he cannot hold up his head with the pride and authority that regular, satisfying work for good pay provides? How or whom shall he marry and on what basis? Is it honestly puzzling to anyone that the 46-percent, Depression-era rate of unemployment that imprisons Black men almost exactly mirrors the 50 percent of Black households now maintained by Black women? Our Black families persist despite a racist arrangement of rewards such as the fact that the median Black family has only about 56 cents to spend for every dollar that white families have to spend. And a Black college graduate still cannot realistically expect to earn more than a white high-school graduate.

We, children and parents of Black families, neither created nor do we control the terrible, deteriorating state of our unjust and meanly discriminating national affairs. In its structure, the traditional Black family has always reflected our particular jeopardy within these unwelcome circumstances. We have never been "standard" or predictable or stabilized in any normative sense, even as our Black lives have never been standard or predictable or stabilized in a benign national environment. We have been flexible, ingenious and innovative or we have perished. And we have not perished. We remain and we remain different, and we have become necessarily deft at distinguishing between the negative differences—those imposed upon us—and the positive differences—those that joyously attest to our distinctive, survivalist attributes as a people.

Today we must distinguish between responsibility and consequence. We are not responsible for the systematic underemployment and unemployment of Black men or women. We are not responsible for racist hatred of us, and we are not responsible for the American contempt for women per se. We are not responsible for a dominant value system that quibbles over welfare benefits for children and squanders deficit billions of dollars on American pie in the sky. But we must outlive the consequences of this inhumane, disposable-life ideology. We have no choice. And because this ideology underpins our economic system and the political system that supports our economy, we no longer constitute a minority inside America. We are joined in our precarious quandary here by all women and by children, Hispanic Americans and Native Americans and the quickly expanding population of the aged, as well as the temporarily or permanently disabled.

At issue now is the "universal entitlement" of American citizens (as author Ruth Sidel terms it in her important book *Women and Children Last: The Plight of Poor Women in Affluent America* [Viking Press, 1986]): What should American citizenship confer? What are the duties of the state in relation to the citizens it presumes to tax and to govern?

It is not the Black family in crisis but American democracy in crisis when the majority of our people oppose U.S. intervention in Central America and, nevertheless, the President proceeds to intervene. It is not the Black family in crisis but American democracy at stake when the majority of our people abhor South African apartheid and, nonetheless, the President proceeds to collaborate with the leadership of that evil. It is not the Black family in crisis but American democracy at risk when a majority of American citizens may no longer assume that social programs beneficial to them will be preserved and/or developed.

But if we, Black children and parents, have been joined by so many others in our precarious quandary here, may we not also now actively join with these other jeopardized Americans to redefine and

to finally secure universal entitlement of citizenship that will at last conclude the shameful American history of our oppression? And what should these universal entitlements—our new American Bill of Rights—include?

1. Guaranteed jobs and/or guaranteed income to ensure each and every American in each and every one of the 50 states an existence *above* the poverty line.

2. Higher domestic minimum wages and, for the sake of both our narrowest and broadest self-interests, a coordinated, international minimum wage so that exhausted economic exploitation in Detroit can no longer be replaced by economic exploitation in Taiwan or Soweto or Manila.

3. Government guarantees of an adequate minimum allowance for every child regardless of the marital status of the parents.

4. Equal pay for equal work.

5. Affirmative action to ensure broadly democratic access to higher-paying occupations.

6. Compensation for "women's work" equal to compensation for "men's work."

7. Housing allowances and/or state commitments to build and/or to subsidize acceptable, safe and affordable housing for every citizen.

8. Comprehensive, national health insurance from prenatal through geriatric care.

9. Availability of state education and perpetual reeducation through graduate levels of study on the basis of student interest and aptitude rather than financial capacity.

10. A national budget that will invariably commit the main portion of our collective monies to our collective domestic needs for a good life.

11. Comprehensive provision for the well-being of all our children commensurate with the kind of future we are hoping to help construct. These provisions must include paid maternity and paternity leave and universal, state-controlled, public child-care programs for working parents.

12. Nationalization of vital industries to protect citizen consumers and citizen workers alike from the greed-driven vagaries of a "free market."

13. Aggressive nuclear-disarmament policies and, concurrently, aggressive state protection of what's left of the life-supportive elements of our global environment.

I do not believe that a just, a civilized nation can properly regard any one of these 13 entitlements as optional. And yet not one of them is legally in place in the United States. And why not? I think that, as a people, we have yet to learn how to say thank you in real ways to those who have loved us enough to keep us alive despite inhumane and unforgivable opposition to our well-being. For myself, I do not need any super-sophisticated charts and magical graphs to tell me my own mama done better than she could, and my mama's mama, *she* done better than I could. And *everybody's mama* done better than anybody had any right to expect she would. And that's the truth!

And I hope you've been able to follow my meaning. And a word to the wise, they say, should be sufficient. So, I'm telling you real nice: Don't you talk about my mama!   [1987]

🌿 59

A Long Story

BETH BRANT

Dedicated to my Great-Grandmothers
Eliza Powless and Catherine Brant

"About 40 Indian children took the train at this depot for the Philadelphia Indian School last Friday. They were accompanied by the government agent, and seemed a bright looking lot."

                     —*The Northern Observer*
          (Massena, New York, July 20, 1892)

"I am only beginning to understand what it means for a mother to lose a child."

          —Anna Demeter, *Legal Kidnapping*
               (Beacon Press, Boston, 1977)

1890

It has been two days since they came and took the children away. My body is greatly chilled. All our blankets have been used to bring me warmth. The women keep the fire blazing. The men sit. They talk among themselves. We are frightened by this sudden child-stealing. We signed papers, the agent said. This gave them rights to take our babies. It is good for them, the agent said. It will make them civilized, the agent said. I do not know *civilized*.

I hold myself tight in fear of flying apart in the air. The others try to feed me. Can they feed a dead woman? I have stopped talking. When my mouth opens, only air escapes. I have used up my sound screaming their names—She Sees Deer! He Catches The Leaves! My eyes stare at the room, the walls of scrubbed wood, the floor of dirt. I know there are people here, but I cannot see them. I see a darkness, like the lake at New Moon. Black, unmoving. In the center, a picture of my son and daughter being lifted onto the train. My daughter wearing the dark blue, heavy dress. All of the girls dressed alike. Never have I seen such eyes! They burn into my head even now. My son. His hair cut. Dressed as the white men, his arms and legs covered by cloth that made him sweat. His face, streaked with tears. So many children crying, screaming. The sun on our bodies, our heads. The train screeching like a crow, sounding like laughter. Smoke and dirt pumping out the insides of the train. So many people. So many children. The women, standing as if in prayer, our hands lifted, reaching. The dust sifting down on our palms. Our palms making motions at the sky. Our fingers closing like the claws of the bear.

I see this now. The hair of my son held in my hands. I rub the strands, the heavy braids coming alive as the fire flares and casts a bright light on the black hair. They slip from my fingers and lie coiled on the ground. I see this. My husband picks up the braids, wraps them in cloth; he takes the pieces of our son away. He walks outside, the eyes of the people on him. I see this. He will find a bottle and drink with the men. Some of the women will join him. They will end the night by singing or crying. It is all the same. I see this. No sounds of children playing games and laughing. Even the dogs have ceased their noise. They lay outside each doorway, waiting. I hear this. The voices of children. They cry. They pray. They call me. *Nisten ha.* I hear this. *Nisten ha.**

1978

I am wakened by the dream. In the dream my daughter is dead. Her father is returning her body to me in pieces. He keeps her heart. I thought I screamed . . . *Patricia!* I sit up in bed, swallowing air as if for nourishment. The dream remains in the air. I rise to go to her room. Ellen tries to lead me back

---

*Mother.

to bed, but I have to see once again. I open her door. She is gone. The room empty, lonely. They said it was in her best interests. How can that be? She is only six, a baby who needs her mothers. She loves us. This has not happened. I will not believe this. Oh god, I think I have died.

Night after night, Ellen holds me as I shake. Our sobs stifling the air in our room. We lie in our bed and try to give comfort. My mind can't think beyond last week when she left. I would have killed him if I'd had the chance! He took her hand and pulled her to the car. The look in his eyes of triumph. It was a contest to him, Patricia the prize. He will teach her to hate us. He will! I see her dear face. That face looking out the back window of his car. Her mouth forming the words *Mommy, Mama*. Her dark braids tied with red yarn. Her front teeth missing. Her overalls with the yellow flower on the pocket, embroidered by Ellen's hands. So lovingly she sewed the yellow wool. Patricia waiting quietly until she was finished. Ellen promising to teach her designs— chain stitch, french knot, split stitch. How Patricia told everyone that Ellen made the flower just for her. So proud of her overalls.

I open the closet door. Almost everything is gone. A few things hang there limp, abandoned. I pull a blue dress from the hanger and take it back to my room. Ellen tries to take it from me, but I hold on, the soft blue cotton smelling of my daughter. How is it possible to feel such pain and live? "Ellen?!" She croons my name. "Mary, Mary, I love you." She sings me to sleep.

1890

The agent was here to deliver a letter. I screamed at him and sent curses his way. I threw dirt in his face as he mounted his horse. He thinks I'm a crazy woman and warns me, "You better settle down Annie." What can they do to me? I am a crazy woman. This letter hurts my hand. It is written in their hateful language. It is evil, but there is a message for me.

I start the walk up the road to my brother. He works for the whites and understands their meanings. I think about my brother as I pull the shawl closer to my body. It is cold now. Soon there will be snow. The corn has been dried and hangs from our cabin, waiting to be used. The corn never changes. My brother is changed. He says that *I* have changed

and bring shame to our clan. He says I should accept the fate. But I do not believe in the fate of child-stealing. There is evil here. There is much wrong in our village. My brother says I am a crazy woman because I howl at the sky every evening. He is a fool. I am calling the children. He says the people are becoming afraid of me because I talk to the air and laugh like the raven overhead. But I am talking to the children. They need to hear the sound of me. I laugh to cheer them. They cry for us.

This letter burns my hands. I hurry to my brother. He has taken the sign of the wolf from over the doorway. He pretends to be like those who hate us. He gets more and more like the child-stealers. His eyes move away from mine. He takes the letter from me and begins the reading of it. I am confused. This letter is from two strangers with the names Martha and Daniel. They say they are learning civilized ways. Daniel works in the fields, growing food for the school. Martha cooks and is being taught to sew aprons. She will be going to live with the school-master's wife. She will be a live-in girl. What is a *live-in girl?* I shake my head. The words sound the same to me. I am afraid of Martha and Daniel, these strangers who know my name. My hands and arms are becoming numb.

I tear the letter from my brother's fingers. He stares at me, his eyes traitors in his face. He calls after me, "Annie! Annie!" That is not my name! I run to the road. That is not my name! There is no Martha! There is no Daniel! This is witch work. The paper burns and burns. At my cabin, I quickly dig a hole in the field. The earth is hard and cold, but I dig with my nails. I dig, my hands feeling weaker. I tear the paper and bury the scraps. As the earth drifts and settles, the names Martha and Daniel are covered. I look to the sky and find nothing but endless blue. My eyes are blinded by the color. I begin the howling.

1978

When I get home from work, there is a letter from Patricia. I make coffee and wait for Ellen, pacing the rooms of our apartment. My back is sore from the line, bending over and over, screwing the handles on the doors of the flashy cars moving by. My work protects me from questions, the guys making jokes at my expense. But some of them touch my shoulder lightly and briefly as a sign of understanding.

The few women, eyes averted or smiling in sympathy. No one talks. There is no time to talk. No room to talk, the noise taking up all space and breath.

I carry the letter with me as I move from room to room. Finally I sit at the kitchen table, turning the paper around in my hands. Patricia's printing is large and uneven. The stamp has been glued on halfheartedly and is coming loose. Each time a letter arrives, I dread it, even as I long to hear from my child. I hear Ellen's key in the door. She walks into the kitchen, bringing the smell of the hospital with her. She comes toward me, her face set in new lines, her uniform crumpled and stained, her brown hair pulled back in an imitation of a french twist. She knows there is a letter. I kiss her and bring mugs of coffee to the table. We look at each other. She reaches for my hand, bringing it to her lips. Her hazel eyes are steady in her round face.

I open the letter. *Dear Mommy. I am fine. Daddy got me a new bike. My big teeth are coming in. We are going to see Grandma for my birthday. Daddy got me new shoes. Love, Patricia.* She doesn't ask about Ellen. I imagine her father standing over her, coaxing her, coaching her. The letter becomes ugly. I tear it in bits and scatter them out the window. The wind scoops the pieces into a tight fist before strewing them in the street. A car drives over the paper, shredding it to garbage and mud.

Ellen makes a garbled sound. "I'll leave. If it will make it better, I'll leave." I quickly hold her as the dusk moves into the room and covers us. "Don't leave. Don't leave." I feel her sturdy back shiver against my hands. She kisses my throat, and her arms tighten as we move closer. "Ah Mary, I love you so much." As the tears threaten our eyes, the taste of salt is on our lips and tongues. We stare into ourselves, touching the place of pain, reaching past the fear, the guilt, the anger, the loneliness.

We go to our room. It is beautiful again. I am seeing it new. The sun is barely there. The colors of cream, brown, green mixing with the wood floor. The rug with its design of wild birds. The black ash basket glowing on the dresser, holding a bouquet of dried flowers bought at a vendor's stand. I remember the old woman, laughing and speaking rapidly in Polish as she wrapped the blossoms in newspaper. Ellen undresses me as I cry. My desire for her breaking through the heartbreak we share. She pulls

the covers back, smoothing the white sheets, her hands repeating the gestures done at work. She guides me onto the cool material. I watch her remove the uniform of work. An aide to nurses. A healer of spirit.

She comes to me in full flesh. My hands are taken with the curves and soft roundness of her. She covers me with the beating of her heart. The rhythm steadies me. Her heat is centering me. I am grounded by the peace between us. I smile at her face above me, round like a moon, her long hair loose and touching my breasts. I take her breast in my hand, bring it to my mouth, suck her as a woman—in desire, in faith. Our bodies join. Our hair braids together on the pillow. Brown, black, silver, catching the last light of the sun. We kiss, touch, move to our place of power. Her mouth, moving over my body, stopping at curves and swells of skin, kissing, removing pain. Closer, close, together, woven, my legs are heat, the center of my soul is speaking to her, I am sliding into her, her mouth is medicine, her heart is the earth, we are dancing with flying arms, I shout, I sing, I weep salty liquid, sweet and warm it coats her throat. This is my life. I love you Ellen, I love you Mary, I love, we love.

1891

The moon is full. The air is cold. This cold strikes at my flesh as I remove my clothes and set them on fire in the withered corn field. I cut my hair, the knife sawing through the heavy mass. I bring the sharp blade to my arms, legs, and breasts. The blood trickles like small red rivers down my body. I feel nothing. I throw the tangled webs of my hair into the flames. The smell, like a burning animal, fills my nostrils. As the fire stretches to touch the stars, the people come out to watch me—the crazy woman. The ice in the air touches me.

They caught me as I tried to board the train and search for my babies. The white men tell my husband to watch me. I am dangerous. I laugh and laugh. My husband is good only for tipping bottles and swallowing anger. He looks at me, opening his mouth and making no sound. His eyes are dead. He wanders from the cabin and looks out on the corn. He whispers our names. He calls after the children. He is a dead man.

Where have they taken the children? I ask the

question of each one who travels the road past our door. The women come and we talk. We ask and ask. They say there is nothing we can do. The white man is like a ghost. He slips in and out where we cannot see. Even in our dreams he comes to take away our questions. He works magic that resists our medicine. This magic has made us weak. What is the secret about them? Why do they want our children? They sent the Blackrobes many years ago to teach us new magic. It was evil! They lied and tricked us. They spoke of gods who would forgive us if we believed as they do. They brought the rum with the cross. This god is ugly! He killed our masks. He killed our men. He sends the women screaming at the moon in terror. They want our power. They take our children to remove the inside of them. Our power. They steal our food, our sacred rattle, the stories, our names. What is left?

I am a crazy woman. I look to the fire that consumes my hair and see their faces. My daughter. My son. They still cry for me, though the sound grows fainter. The wind picks up their keening and brings it to me. The sound has bored into my brain. I begin howling. At night I dare not sleep. I fear the dreams. It is too terrible, the things that happen there. In my dream there is wind and blood moving as a stream. Red, dark blood in my dream. Rushing for our village. The blood moves faster. There are screams of wounded people. Animals are dead, thrown in the blood stream. There is nothing left. Only the air echoing nothing. Only the earth soaking up blood, spreading it in the four directions, becoming a thing there is no name for. I stand in the field watching the fire, The People watching me. We are waiting, but the answer is not clear yet. A crazy woman. That is what they call me.

1979

After taking a morning off work to see my lawyer, I come home, not caring if I call in. Not caring, for once, at the loss in pay. Not caring. My lawyer says there is nothing more we can do. I must wait. As if there has been something other than waiting. He has custody and calls the shots. We must wait and see how long it takes for him to get tired of being a mommy and a daddy. So, I wait.

I open the door to Patricia's room. Ellen and I keep it dusted and cleaned in case my baby will be allowed to visit us. The yellow and blue walls feel like a mockery. I walk to the windows, begin to systematically tear down the curtains. I slowly start to ripe the cloth apart. I enjoy hearing the sounds of destruction. Faster, I tear the material into strips. What won't come apart with my hands, I pull at with my teeth. Looking for more to destroy, I gather the sheets and bedspread in my arms and wildly shred them to pieces. Grunting and sweating, I am pushed by rage and the searing wound in my soul. Like a wolf, caught in a trap, gnawing at her own leg to set herself free, I begin to beat my breasts to deaden the pain inside. A noise gathers in my throat and finds the way out. I begin a scream that turns to howling, then becomes hoarse choking. I want to take my fists, my strong fists, my brown fists, and smash the world until it bleeds. Bleeds! And all the judges in their flapping robes, and the fathers who look for revenge, are ground, ground into dust and disappear with the wind.

The word *lesbian*. Lesbian. The word that makes them panic, makes them afraid, makes them destroy children. The word that dares them. Lesbian. *I am one.* Even for Patricia, even for her, *I will not cease to be!* As I kneel amidst the colorful scraps, Raggedy Anns smiling up at me, my chest gives a sigh. My heart slows to its normal speech. I feel the blood pumping outward to my veins, carrying nourishment and life. I strip the room naked. I close the door.   [1985]

 60

The Meaning of Motherhood in Black Culture

PATRICIA HILL COLLINS

BLOODMOTHERS, OTHERMOTHERS, AND WOMEN-CENTERED NETWORKS

In African-American communities, the boundaries distinguishing biological mothers of children from other women who care for children are often fluid and changing. Biological mothers or bloodmothers are expected to care for their children. But African and African-American communities have also recognized that vesting one person with full responsibility for mothering a child may not be wise or possible. As a result, "othermothers," women who assist bloodmothers by sharing mothering responsibilities, traditionally have been central to the institution of Black motherhood.[1]

The centrality of women in African-American extended families is well known.[2] Organized, resilient, women-centered networks of bloodmothers and othermothers are key in understanding this centrality: Grandmothers, sisters, aunts, or cousins acted as othermothers by taking on childcare responsibilities for each other's children. When needed, temporary childcare arrangements turned into long-term care or informal adoption.[3]

In African-American communities, these women-centered networks of community-based childcare often extend beyond the boundaries of biologically related extended families to support "fictive kin."[4] Civil rights activist Ella Baker describes how informal adoption by othermothers functioned in the Southern, rural community of her childhood:

> My aunt who had thirteen children of her own raised three more. She had become a midwife, and a child was born who was covered with sores. Nobody was particularly wanting the child, so she took the child and raised him . . . and another mother decided she didn't want to be bothered with two children. So my aunt took one and raised him . . . they were part of the family.[5]

Even when relationships were not between kin or fictive kin, African-American community norms were such that neighbors cared for each other's children. In the following passage, Sara Brooks, a Southern domestic worker, describes the importance of the community-based childcare that a neighbor offered her daughter. In doing so, she also shows how the African-American cultural value placed on cooperative childcare found institutional support in the adverse conditions under which so many Black women mothered.

> She kept Vivian and she didn't charge me nothin either. You see, people used to look after each other,
> but now it's not that way. I reckon it's because we all was poor, and I guess they put theirself in the place of the person that they was helpin.[6]

Othermothers were key not only in supporting children but also in supporting bloodmothers who, for whatever reason, were ill-prepared or had little desire to care for their children. Given the pressures from the larger political economy, the emphasis placed on community-based childcare and the respect given to othermothers who assume the responsibilities of childcare have served a critical function in African-American communities. Children orphaned by sale or death of their parents under slavery, children conceived through rape, children of young mothers, children born into extreme poverty; or children, who for other reasons have been rejected by their bloodmothers, have all been supported by othermothers who, like Ella Baker's aunt, took in additional children, even when they had enough of their own.

PROVIDING AS PART OF MOTHERING

The work done by African-American women in providing the economic resources essential to Black family well-being affects motherhood in a contradictory fashion. On the one hand, African-American women have long integrated their activities as economic providers into their mothering relationships. In contrast to the cult of true womanhood where work is defined as being in opposition to and incompatible with motherhood, work for Black women has been an important and valued dimension of Afrocentric definitions of Black motherhood. On the other hand, African-American women's experiences as mothers under oppression were such that the type and purpose of work Black women were forced to do greatly impacted on the type of mothering relationships bloodmothers and othermothers had with Black children.

While slavery both disrupted West African family patterns and exposed enslaved Africans to the gender ideologies and practices of slaveowners, it simultaneously made it impossible, had they wanted to do so, for enslaved Africans to implement slaveowner's ideologies. Thus, the separate spheres of providing as a male domain and affective nurturing as a female domain did not develop within African-

American families.[7] Providing for Black children's physical survival and attending to their affective, emotional needs continued as interdependent dimensions of an Afrocentric ideology of motherhood. However, by changing the conditions under which Black women worked and the purpose of the work itself, slavery introduced the problem of how best to continue traditional Afrocentric values under oppressive conditions. Institutions of community-based childcare, informal adoption, greater reliance on othermothers, all emerge as adaptations to the exigencies of combining exploitative work with nurturing children.

In spite of the change in political status brought on by emancipation, the majority of African-American women remained exploited agricultural workers. However, their placement in Southern political economies allowed them to combine childcare with field labor. Sara Brooks describes how strong the links between providing and caring for others were for her:

> When I was about nine I was nursin my sister Sally—I'm about seven or eight years older than Sally. And when I would put her to sleep, instead of me goin somewhere and sit down and play, I'd get my little old hoe and get out there and work right in the field around the house.[8]

Black women's shift from Southern agriculture to domestic work in Southern and Northern towns and cities represented a change in the type of work done, but not in the meaning of work to women and their families. Whether they wanted to or not, the majority of African-American women had to work and could not afford the luxury of motherhood as a non-economically productive, female "occupation."

COMMUNITY OTHERMOTHERS AND SOCIAL ACTIVISM

Black women's experiences as othermothers have provided a foundation for Black women's social activism. Black women's feelings of responsibility for nurturing the children in their own extended family network have stimulated a more generalized ethic of care where Black women feel accountable to all the Black community's children.

This notion of Black women as community othermothers for all Black children traditionally allowed Black women to treat biologically unrelated children as if they were members of their own families. For example, sociologist Karen Fields describes how her grandmother, Mamie Garvin Fields, draws on her power as a community othermother when dealing with unfamiliar children.

> She will say to a child on the street who looks up to no good, picking out a name at random, "Aren't you Miz Pinckney's boy?" in that same reproving tone. If the reply is, "No, *ma'am*, my mother is Miz Gadsden," whatever threat there was dissipates.[9]

The use of family language in referring to members of the Black community also illustrates this dimension of Black motherhood. For example, Mamie Garvin Fields describes how she became active in surveying the poor housing conditions of Black people in Charleston.

> I was one of the volunteers they got to make a survey of the places where we were paying extortious rents for indescribable property. I said "we," although it wasn't Bob and me. We had our own home, and so did many of the Federated Women. Yet we still felt like it really was "we" living in those terrible places, and it was up to us to do something about them.[10]

To take another example, while describing her increasingly successful efforts to teach a boy who had given other teachers problems, my daughter's kindergarten teacher stated, "You know how it can be—the majority of the children in the learning disabled classes are *our children*. I know he didn't belong there, so I volunteered to take him." In these statements, both women invoke the language of family to describe the ties that bind them as Black women to their responsibilities to other members of the Black community as family.

Sociologist Cheryl Gilkes suggests that community othermother relationships are sometimes behind Black women's decisions to become community activists.[11] Gilkes notes that many of the Black women community activists in her study became involved in community organizing in response to the needs of their own children and of those in their communities. The following comment is typical of how many of the Black women in Gilkes' study relate to Black children: "There were a lot of summer programs springing up for kids, but they were exclusive . . . and I found that most of *our kids* (emphasis mine) were excluded."[12] For many women, what began as the daily expression of their obligations as community othermothers, as was the case for the kindergarten teacher, developed into full-fledged roles as community leaders.

NOTES

1. The terms used in this section appear in Rosalie Riegle Troester, "Turbulence and Tenderness: Mothers, Daughters, and Othermothers" in Paule Marshall's *Brown Girl, Brownstones,*" *SAGE: A Scholarly Journal on Black Women* 1 (Fall 1984), pp. 13–16.

2. See Tanner's discussion of matrifocality, 1974; see also Carrie Allen McCray, "The Black Woman and Family Roles," in *The Black Woman,* ed. LaFrances Rogers-Rose (Beverly Hills, CA: Sage, 1980), pp. 67–78; Elmer Martin and Joanne Mitchell Martin, *The Black Extended Family* (Chicago: University of Chicago, 1978); Joyce Aschenbrenner, *Lifelines, Black Families in Chicago* (Prospect Heights, IL: Waveland, 1975); and Carol B. Stack, *All Our Kin* (New York: Harper & Row, 1974).

3. Martin and Martin, 1978; Stack, 1974; and Virginia Young, "Family and Childhood in a Southern Negro Community," *American Anthropologist* 72 (1970), pp. 269–288.

4. Stack, 1974.

5. Ellen Cantarow, *Moving the Mountain: Women Working for Social Change* (Old Westbury, NY: Feminist Press, 1980), p. 59.

6. Thordis Simonsen, ed., *You May Plow Here, The Narrative of Sara Brooks* (New York: Touchstone, 1986), p. 181.

7. Deborah White, *Arn't I a Woman? Female Slaves in the Plantation South* (N.Y.: WW Norton, 1984); Dill, 1986; Leith Mullings, "Uneven Development: Class, Race and Gender in the United States Before 1900," in *Women's Work, Development and the Division of Labor by Gender,* eds. Eleanor Leacock and Helen Safa (South Hadley, MA: Bergin & Garvey, 1986), pp. 41–57.

8. Simonsen, 1986, p. 86.

9. Mamie Garvin Fields and Karen Fields, *Lemon Swamp and Other Places: A Carolina Memoir* (New York: Free Press, 1983), p. xvii.

10. Ibid, p. 195.

11. Cheryl Gilkes, "'Holding Back the Ocean with a Broom,' Black Women and Community Work," in Rogers-Rose, 1980, pp. 217–231; "Going Up for the Oppressed: The Career Mobility of Black Women Community Workers," *Journal of Social Issues* 39 (1983), pp. 115–139.

12. Gilkes, 1980, p. 219.   [1992]

Health Care

Historically, women have been healers; we have supported each other with skill and understanding when experiencing physical pain. The legacy of midwives in this country is one example. Yet beginning in the late eighteenth century, male physicians in the U.S. led a successful campaign to eliminate midwives. In the mid-nineteenth century, they also mounted an assault against the many female medical practitioners who were trained outside the male-dominated medical establishment. In the words of Lila Wallis and Perri Klass, "Women have not been treated kindly by the established medical profession, neither as health care consumers nor as health care providers nor as subjects of medical research."

Although health care is an important topic for feminism, this section is relatively short because many of you will also be reading *The New Our Bodies, Ourselves*, an excellent source of information about women's health care (Simon & Schuster, 1992). *Our Bodies, Ourselves* was written by the Boston Women's Health Book Collective, a group of women who, impelled by the lack of available information about women's bodies, began meeting in 1969 to share information and experiences and publish what became the first of many editions of *Our Bodies, Ourselves*. Women of varied racial and class backgrounds from different parts of the country organized similarly to spawn the now extensive women's health movement.

Despite the strength of this movement, sexism in the medical system is wide-ranging. Members of the Boston Women's Health Book Collective report patterns of the following types of abuse of women by personnel in medical settings who have: not listened to them or believed what they said; withheld knowledge or lied; treated them without their consent; not warned of risks; experimented on them; discriminated against them because of race, sexual preference, age, or disability; offered tranquilizers or moral advice instead of medical care or useful help from community resources; administered treatments that were unnecessarily mutilating; performed unnecessary operations; or sexually abused them.

The selections in this section provide further evidence of sexism in the medical system. Physicians Lila Wallis and Perri Klass present an overview of the ways women have been treated as both health care consumers and providers. The essay "Women and AIDS: HIV, the National Scandal" points to ways women continue to be discriminated against in their efforts to obtain quality health care.

🦎 61

Toward Improving Women's Health Care*

LILA A. WALLIS and PERRI KLASS

Historically, women have not been treated kindly by the established medical profession, neither as health care consumers nor as health care providers nor as subjects of medical research. Margaret Eichler, PhD, identified four ways that gender bias may present itself,[1] and, along with Elaine Borins, MD, and Anna Reisman, MD, of Toronto, adapted that concept to medical research.[2] (1) *Androcentricity* is when the world is depicted from a man's perspective; in research it can take various forms, including female invisibility or using an all-male frame of reference. (2) *Overgeneralization* occurs when a study deals with one sex but presents itself as if it were applicable to both sexes. (3) *Gender insensitivity* consists of ignoring sex as a socially or medically important variable. Lack of knowledge of sex similarities and differences impedes appropriate progress in subsequent research, making it impossible to devise gender sensitive treatments for men and women. (4) *Double standards* involve evaluation, treatment, or measurement of identical behaviors, traits, or situations by different means.

Dominated by men, the medical profession was until very recently not eager to welcome female recruits. There was less prestige attached to specializing in diseases and disorders unique to women, and many female complaints were never properly studied. Not infrequently, these complaints were inadequately treated or even brushed aside as "hysterical," a word derived from the Greek *hystera* meaning womb. We will all recall being told in physiology classes that the average weight of a human being is 70 kg—a vivid and common example of androcentricity. When it came to diseases that affected both men and women, studies were often done on all-male groups and the results generalized to women, as if men were truly the generic humans.

Many studies of such conditions as atherosclerotic heart disease, strokes, and cancer were done on all-male groups, even though the titles of the papers suggested an "all people" inclusive population. For instance, a study from the *New England Journal of Medicine* was entitled "Work Activity and Coronary Mortality,"[3] but actually considered an all-male group. Overgeneralization is dangerous, as it may lead to incorrect treatment of women when only men are the subjects of research.

The famous concept of the Type A personality, the ambitious, aggressive workaholic, was developed from a study of 4,000 California businessmen.[4] This study demonstrated that "Type A behaviors" were associated with an increased incidence of coronary artery disease. Pundits promptly began to warn that women,[5] as they penetrated the higher echelons of the working world, would sacrifice serenity, develop the Type A personalities that their new jobs demanded, and pay the price in heart attacks. Since the male investigators *assumed* that women would follow the male pattern, their study reflected both overgeneralization and gender insensitivity.

Indeed, in a 1980 study,[6] Suzanne Haynes looked at women who were participating in the Framingham Heart Study and found that, *overall,* working women as a group did not have significantly higher rates of coronary artery disease than housewives. Women who held clerical jobs, however, had *twice* the rate of coronary disease as women who stayed home. Moreover, they pinpointed specific stresses as particularly likely to be associated with heart disease in women. These included feelings of suppressed hostility, having a nonsupportive boss, decreased job mobility, and being married to a blue-collar worker. Single working women had the lowest incidence of coronary artery disease. Hence, these observations tended to refute the idea that the stress of holding down a job *per se* is responsible for the shorter male life expectancy and higher rate of heart disease in men.

It is of interest that married men tend to live longer than single men. Is marriage protective of men's health? Does employment protect the coronary arteries of single women? The stresses of life, work, and family seem to have different impacts on male bodies and female bodies, and specific studies are needed before anyone can make predictions or give advice. The stresses of socioeconomic status

---

*Portions of this paper appeared in the October 1989 edition of *Lear's* magazine.

need to be studied, as well as the stresses of different kinds of jobs, not just the effects of "working" or "not working." If clerical jobs, for example, hold particular risks, that should be of special interest to women. Haynes commented that female clerical workers experience "a lack of autonomy and control over the work environment, underutilization of skills, and lack of recognition of accomplishment."[6] Do these stresses increase the risk of heart disease? How do they compare, for women and for men, with the different stresses of holding a powerful, decision-wielding position? Will it turn out that instead of paying the Type A personality price, women thrive on a balanced mixture of high-powered work and family? Would they be even healthier than if they married and stayed home?

Women have repeatedly complained that their doctors don't take them seriously, that their symptoms are cast aside as imaginary or "psychosomatic." In 1979, a research team[7] investigated the way that doctors responded to five medical complaints common in both men and women: chest pain, back pain, headache, dizziness, and fatigue. The investigators examined the extent of the workup doctors ordered on patients with these complaints. Of course, the extent of the workup is determined by the physician's assessment of the patient's complaint—how alarming the symptoms are and how real the risk of serious disease appears to be. For instance, depending on the physician's approach, assessment, and intuition, the extent of the workup for headache may range from a brief history and physical examination with a prescription for a tranquilizer, to much more extensive testing that includes an electroencephalogram, CT scan, and MRI.

In the 1979 study, the investigators found that, across the board, "Men received a more extensive workup than women for all complaints studied."[7] They could not explain the difference on medical facts alone and suggested that, perhaps, in fact, doctors did not take complaints as seriously when they came from women. Clearly, this is an example of a double standard influencing diagnostic workup.

Until recent times, when women *were* studied, the research was conducted almost exclusively on conditions associated with the female reproductive tract. And, as there has been a tendency to look at women's health "from the waist down," women pa-

tients seem to have absorbed some of this attitude. Most women go to gynecologists for their primary health care, as if this one body system determined absolutely their state of health, and as if it were the only system worth checking out on a regular basis. And when women are studied largely in terms of this one physiological system, when students are taught about women's health only in terms of disorders of the breast, uterus, cervix, and vagina, then—for some doctors—the very state of being female almost comes to imply pathology, while the norm is so eminently male.

Yet despite the relative emphasis on the clinical care of women's reproductive systems, many related women's health problems have received insufficient research attention. Areas in which intensive research needs to be conducted include: *primary* prevention of breast cancers, development of a painless mammography technique, development of serological markers for ovarian cancer—an insidious, nearly always fatal disease that evades early detection. Additionally, much work is needed to improve our treatment of depression as well as of alcohol, drug, and other substance abuse, conditions that are either more common in women or have distinct characteristics when they occur in women.

As they move into positions of power and influence in various fields, successful women will probably be of interest as subjects of study both to grant givers and to those who do the research. With more families relying on two incomes, and with an increase in the numbers of single-parent families, the effects of multiple role stresses on all aspects of women's health should be studied systematically. Women in this country occupy an ever enlarging piece of the workforce and still are largely responsible for the upbringing of the next generation. It makes sense for the federal government to invest funds in research on the greatest resource this country will ever have, namely, the health of its women.

Although women are going into medicine in larger numbers, they still occupy only a tiny fraction of leadership positions. And the health care of women will not become a priority by itself; affirmative action for women's issues must be taken to close the gaps in research and funding. Though there are now more detailed studies of women than there used to be, there is a lot of catching up to do, and there is no evidence that fundamental attitudes have changed. It would be comforting to think that as women claim a more significant voice in medicine, we will also claim a larger territory, our lives will be studied more carefully, our ailments treated more appropriately. As we cease to be the exception within the profession itself, we might also cease to be seen as the exception in our patterns of health and sickness. But it hasn't happened yet, and it won't happen without a deliberate effort on our part.

How can we help? Who are the potential players in this effort? Women constitute 52% of the population and account for about 70% of all health provider/consumer interactions, yet they represent only a small fraction of the *decision-making* groups in medical education, training, practice, and policy. Even now in the early 1990s, only 5% of all physician full professors in medical faculty are women, only 5% of our legislators are women, and only 2% of all medical school deans are women. Our answer is to elect more women legislators and to empower women in medical academia to seek and assume crucial decision-making positions.

Women's health does not exist yet as a recognized specialty with its own board, but it is practiced daily by many hundreds, perhaps thousands, of women doctors. There are, moreover, groups of women doctors who are working on a curriculum for postgraduate training in women's health. Indeed, several physicians convened at the 75th Annual Meeting of AMWA in Philadelphia recently to discuss proposed curricula. The recognition of the need for special training of doctors who will be taking care of 52% of the American public will not be universal because there are powerful opposing forces, including the American Academy of Family Physicians, American College of Obstetricians and Gynecologists, and even the American College of Physicians. Perhaps, in order not to provoke "turf" battles that are divisive and futile, we should not be speaking about a specialty and a board of women's health, but of the *training* needed to take care of women effectively. Those who wish to take care of women patients should consider intensive training in internal medicine, office gynecology, and psychiatry, along with immersion in nutrition, orthopedics, urology, and preventive medicine.

What else can we do to promote better health care for women? *All* women can play an important role: women doctors and medical students, women health workers, women taxpayers, women voters, and women patients. Various women's health organizations must work together and support each other in order to bring about changes in medical education, training, and practice. Such organizations as the American Medical Women's Association, the National Council on Women in Medicine, the National Association of Women's Health Professionals, and the American Nurses Association should, at the very least, exchange newsletters and co-sponsor conferences on common issues. At best, we should form coalitions and perhaps consortiums.

As taxpayers, women can demand that the National Institutes of Health reexamine their agendas and show us how much of our tax money is being spent to study the various segments of the population. We can inform our legislators that women care about how research dollars are spent and encourage those most directly involved with funding and health care to look closely at their priorities. Clearly, legislators need to know that women's health should assume greater importance in NIH grant giving. Indeed, the Congressional Caucus on Women's Issues, under the leadership of Patricia Schroeder and Olympia Snowe, have charged the General Accounting Office with ascertaining how compliant the NIH grant givers are with the gender equality regulation requiring NIH grantees to include an equal number of women in their studies. A multidisciplinary women's health division in the existing Institutes or perhaps, in the future, a separate National Institute on Women's Health could be envisioned.

As health care providers, we can teach individual women patients to exert their muscle as consumers of medical care. They must make certain that their doctors care for them appropriately as women, their reproductive systems neither ignored nor emphasized to the exclusion of other body parts. When a woman chooses a primary health care provider, she should seek a physician who incorporates different aspects of her health care, not just her reproductive health. She should insist that her prospective primary doctor include pelvic and breast examinations in the general physical exam. Such services should be an integral part of the woman patient's general health care; she should not have to make an additional appointment to see yet another specialist.

More medical research on women will bring us

better health care only if it has an impact on medical education, training, and practice. Greater emphasis on women's health in medical education will allow the additional information to percolate to the level of clinical practice. Creation of women's health as a medical specialty separate from obstetrics-gynecology will be a great step forward.

We need to push at all five levels—as voters, as taxpayers, as supporters of women in medical academia, as supporters of our organizations, and as individual health practitioners educating and empowering women health consumers—for changes that will reshape the concept of the male norm, opening our profession to a truer, more diverse, and infinitely more interesting view of the woman patient. The result would certainly be better health care for women—and probably better health care for everyone.

REFERENCES

1. Eichler M: *Nonsexist Research Methods—A Practical Guide.* Boston, Allen and Unwin, 1988.
2. Eichler M, Reisman A, Borins E: Gender bias in medical research. Paper read before Conference on Gender, Science and Medicine, November 5, 1988, Toronto, Ontario, Canada.
3. Paffenberger RS, Hole WE: Work activity and coronary heart mortality. *N Engl J Med* 1975;292:545–550.
4. Rosenman RH, Brand RJ, Jenkins CD, et al: Coronary heart disease in the Western Collaborative Group Study; Final follow-up experience of 8½ years. *JAMA* 1976;233:872–877.
5. Garbus SB, Garbus SB: Will improvement in the socioeconomic status of women increase their cardiovascular morbidity and mortality? *JAMWA* 1980;35:257–261.
6. Haynes SG, Feinleib M: Women, work and coronary heart disease: Prospective findings from the Framingham heart study. *Am J Public Health* 1980;70:133–141.
7. Armitage KJ, Schneiderman LJ, Bass RA: Response of physicians to medical complaints in men and women. *JAMA* 1979;241:2186–2187.   [1990]

62

"You're a Doctor?"

MONTANA KATZ

The following excerpt is from an oral history of a young black doctor in her late twenties. She had been a practicing obstetrician/gynecologist for two years at the time of the interview.

I can remember one time, I'll never forget this. I was sitting at the nurses' station. It was like the front desk. There's a clerk there, and usually the interns and other doctors will hang around that station checking labs on the computer or writing notes or something. So one of my preceptors was a black woman who was an attending. I was sitting next to her, and the two of us had a patient's chart open in front of us and were discussing the patient's chart and our plan of management. I had a stethoscope around my neck and I was wearing a white coat. She was wearing street clothes. So we were sitting there talking and this intern or some guy, he was either an intern or a resident, came around. He was mulling around looking for a piece of paper in the clerk's filing desk. He was mulling around looking for an X-ray form or something like that. So he interrupts us. We're in the middle of talking. He doesn't say excuse me. He just says, "Can I have an X-ray form, please?" So I said, "Well, I don't know where they are, I'm sorry," so we went back to our discussion. So then he comes around behind us and leans over, looking for this form and says, "Look, I can't find these forms." So I said, "Well, I suggest that you ask the clerk," which was kind of obnoxious at that point.

So then a few minutes later, he doesn't quit, you know. He's looking for the form and he speaks up. He says, "Look, I'm looking for this form. I need to get this form for my patient and I don't see why you two can't stop what you're doing and help me." So my preceptor who was an attending said, "Listen, I'm Dr. X and I'm having a discussion with Dr. Y about this patient, and why are you disturbing us?" And he said, "Oh, I didn't know you're a doctor. I'm sorry." And then she says, "You know, just because we are black females sitting at the nurses' station doesn't mean we're nurses and it doesn't mean we're clerks. And even if we were nurses or clerks, you should at least have the courtesy of saying excuse me if you're interrupting our conversation." And the guy bolts out of there.

This is a perfect example of the way it is. He never thought for two seconds that we could be doctors because we're black women. And therefore he could talk to us however he likes. That's something that we have to face all the time. Even to this day, I hear it all the time. When I go to the hospital and say I'm Dr. Y. And they say, "You're a doctor?" Most of the time they'll say, "Oh, you look too young to be a doctor," or something like that. But you know if I were a man they probably wouldn't say that. There's just a subtle sense that you get that people are always questioning your ability and who you are.   [1993]

63

Women and AIDS: HIV, the National Scandal

PEG BYRON

Harlem Hospital's HIV outpatient clinic was emptying into the gray afternoon and Wilda Correa was still waiting to see the doctor. Nervous, but trying to be cooperative, she had already waited three months for the appointment since taking the blood test for HIV, the human immunodeficiency virus responsible for AIDS. Inside the crowded clinic, Correa, a 43-year-old mother of three, knew it would take a lot to keep the once-silent virus from totally destroying her immune system.

In many ways, Correa epitomizes the people who are at great risk yet are most ignored in the U.S. AIDS epidemic: poor women of color and IV drug users, who, because of sex, race, and class, are viewed as the "throwaways" of society. But Harlem is not the only place in the U.S. where women must wait too long to get HIV care. And delays mean deterioration as the infection destroys the immune system and spirals into devastating diseases, and, often, death.

AIDS might be described most accurately as a late stage of HIV disease. There are some long-term AIDS survivors, but the outlook for most women is bleak. One small New Jersey survey found that women diagnosed with AIDS live an average of barely four *months,* while white gay men with AIDS live 1.3 to 1.7 *years;* studies conducted in New York and San Francisco corroborate the differential. African American women in 1988 died at nine times the rate of European American women. Does this reflect the difference in the quality of health care available to these groups? Is HIV affecting women in different ways? Are different epidemics striking different communities? Experts say they don't know.

They don't know because these questions remain unexplored. But the lack of interest and the high death rate for women are two sides of the same crime: women are being ignored in the AIDS epidemic.

Women continue to get the attention of most AIDS researchers only as possible infectors of children and men. It is as if HIV-infected women are viewed solely as carriers of disease. Seen as pregnancy risks and troublesome with their child care and transportation problems, women also are widely excluded from experimental drug trials— making up only 7 percent of the enrollment in AIDS treatment research. Yet such drug trials are usually the only sources of potentially crucial medicine for this as yet incurable condition.

More often than men, women with HIV/AIDS suffer from lack of money or insurance for basic care. Yet without the data to define how they get sick with HIV differently from men, many women are denied desperately needed disability benefits.

Still, no major research has addressed the question of whether women may experience any symptoms different from men's. Dr. Daniel Hoth, AIDS division director for the National Institute of Allergy and Infectious Diseases (NIAID), a man who controls millions of research dollars, reluctantly concedes he has sponsored no studies about women's health. And the situation is the same at the National Cancer Institute; together, the two institutes get the bulk of U.S. AIDS research dollars, but neither has gotten around to asking what AIDS looks like in women.

According to Dr. Kathryn Anastos, director of HIV primary care services at Bronx-Lebanon Hospital Center in New York, one third to one half of all HIV-infected women have gynecological complications before the appearance of any other symptoms, except possibly fatigue; 32 percent to 86 percent of HIV-infected women have abnormal Pap smears and are at risk for cervical cancer; there is some evidence that pelvic inflammatory disease (PID) is more aggressive and caused by a wider array of organisms; irregular periods and infertility have been reported, suggesting unknown hormonal effects.

For at least three years, reports in medical journals have warned about severe, hard-to-treat gynecological infections linked to HIV (see *Ms.,* July

1988). But not a single female genital complication is included in the federal guidelines set by the Centers for Disease Control (CDC) for AIDS diagnoses or even as signs of HIV infection.

"It's a major problem," said Dr. Mardge Cohen, who is the director of the Women and Children with AIDS Project at Cook County Hospital in Chicago. "It would make more sense to consider gynecological manifestations as representative of the clinical spectrum of AIDS. If it's not AIDS by the official definition, we see women who are desperate for those benefits."

The very definition of AIDS, as set forth by the federal government, excludes women. The CDC has characterized AIDS based on what government scientists knew when clusters of gay men were stricken in the early 1980s. Originally called GRID, for Gay-Related Immune Deficiency, AIDS was gradually defined. If many women or intravenous drug users were dying in similar ways then, they were not noticed and their particular symptoms were not included in the AIDS definition. The human cost of that exclusion continues today each time a woman confronts her HIV problems.

"Look at my hands," Correa says, still waiting for her clinic appointment. They are covered with strange, reddish-brown spots, a few of which faintly scatter her cheek. "It feels like something crawling up my face. They itch." The spots appeared during the summer when Correa first got sick and lost 30 pounds with a severe bout of diarrhea.

She saw a doctor about fatigue and shortness of breath just two years earlier. He did not suggest an HIV test, though intravenous drug use accounts for over 50 percent of all U.S. women who have been diagnosed with AIDS and he knew she had a ten-year-long heroin habit. He diagnosed an enlarged heart and warned her to clean up her lifestyle. Since then, she's been off both heroin and methadone.

Dr. Wafaa El-Sadr calls Correa into one of the clinic's examining rooms and decides to hospitalize her to get her heart and blood pressure under control before starting HIV treatment. Chief of the hospital's infectious disease department, El-Sadr says Correa does not have what is officially AIDS. She will try an antibacterial ointment on Correa's rash, which she says is not Kaposi's sarcoma lesions (common among gay men with AIDS but almost never seen on others diagnosed with AIDS).

Did Correa have any unusual gynecological symptoms? The doctor says she doesn't know. While the city-run clinic supplies at no cost an expensive regimen of drugs, it does not have the equipment to do pelvic exams. The examining tables don't even have stirrups.

The doctor describes the clinic's almost 600 patients as "desperately poor," many of them homeless. Women make up 30 percent of her AIDS caseload—triple the national AIDS rate for women. The Egyptian-born El-Sadr says the high percentage of women she treats are the leading edge of the epidemic. "We're seeing the evolution of the epidemic."

Women throughout the country are the fastest growing part of the AIDS epidemic. Several years ago, they made up 7 percent of all those who were diagnosed. Now, women with AIDS number about 15,000; of these, 72 percent are African American or Latina. "If AIDS has done anything for us, it has magnified the other social and health problems that exist for women of color," said Dàzon Dixon, executive director of SISTERLOVE, an affiliate of the National Black Women's Health Project.

By 1993, women will make up 15 percent of the people with AIDS in the U.S., according to the CDC; several AIDS researchers argue that the CDC's figures on women are at least 40 percent too low, in part because of its failure to count many of women's HIV-induced illnesses as AIDS.

Even when examining tables have stirrups, most researchers aren't interested in the woman, but in the fetus she is bearing. For a new national AZT study called protocol 076, 700 pregnant women are being sought to determine if the drug reduces the chance of an infected woman transmitting the virus to the baby. The protocol, still under review, as recently as last March included no evaluation of the women's health or the drug's impact on the mothers. A letter from NIAID's Hoth explained that protocol 076 "was not designed to be a study of pregnant women, although this topic is most important. . . . " NIAID has since revised the study to include a maternal health component, but it is not for purposes of the woman's health.

Hoth said in an interview, "As we move on in our thinking, we realize we have two patients to account for in pregnancy studies." This startling revelation is a chilling reminder of the history of interference with women's reproductive choices, from forced sterilizations and denial of abortions to the current concern for fetal rights.

For a woman with HIV, pregnancy poses a dilemma: if she wants to deliver (the odds of having a healthy baby are estimated to be 70 percent), she may be pressured to end the pregnancy. But if she chooses to abort, many clinics refuse to assist anyone who has HIV, and 37 states do not allow Medicaid or other public funds to be used for abortion.

In the limited studies that do involve pelvic exams, abnormal cervical Pap smears have been detected at rates five to eight times greater than in non-HIV women in the same communities. Other studies suggest a dangerous synergy between HIV and a common virus that causes genital warts, called the human papillomavirus, or HPV. Women with both HIV and HPV infections are 29 times more likely than non-HIV women to have cervical cancer, one study found.

"HPV is a ubiquitous virus. It is found in the inner cities, the upper classes. Some studies suggest that it is found in a third of all adolescents in the inner cities and a quarter of all women," said Dr. Sten Vermund, chief of epidemiology for NIAID. He warns that once HIV-infected women start reaching the same life expectancy as HIV-infected men, an epidemic in cervical cancer may emerge due to the HIV-HPV combination. Doctors who treat many women with HIV infections (in clinics with properly equipped examining tables) say they already see higher rates of abnormal cervical conditions rapidly progressing to invasive cancers.

Advanced HPV with HIV, argues Vermund, should be considered one of the opportunistic infections that define AIDS—making many more women count in both the AIDS toll and benefit programs. "I'm having trouble getting people's attention on this matter. I have had a paper about it in review at the *American Journal of Obstetrics and Gynecology* for a god-awful long time," said Vermund.

Dr. Mathilde Krim of the American Foundation for AIDS Research (AmFAR) says how women are counted "matters a lot when it comes to entitlement to disability payments or Medicare. The rest of the government relies on this definition. And where women are left out of the system, the lack of treatment can shorten their lives."

There are conflicts over the hierarchy of AIDS illnesses, which not only affects who qualifies for limited disability benefits but how the shape and scope of the epidemic [are] defined. And that affects how both public and private agencies must respond.

The battles pit the sick against the dying in a fight over money. Scientists and doctors, for example, are in a fierce competition for limited research funding: the scientists are focused on long-range goals to stop HIV with the development of antiviral drugs and a vaccine, while doctors are desperate for ways to treat people already infected. But President Bush and the Congress—which will spend a projected $800 billion on the S&L crisis and $2.2 billion a month in the Persian Gulf—have capped NIAID's AIDS research funding at $432.6 million and NCI's at $161 million for fiscal year 1991.

AIDS activist Maxine Wolfe, who demonstrated and sat in at CDC and NIAID offices as part of the Women's Caucus of AIDS Coalition to Unleash Power (ACT UP), says: "The whole size of the epidemic is being squashed. Can you imagine if they added TB with HIV, or vaginal thrush with HIV, or PID or syphilis with HIV? The number of cases out there would be enormous. By not having that number, they [the feds] justify so little government money for research and treatment."

Following pressure from activists as well as the Congressional Caucus for Women's Issues, NIAID sponsored a special conference on women and HIV in December to help prioritize women's needs. At another meeting at NIAID last year, Wolfe, a professor at the City University of New York Graduate Center, and other ACT UP activists confronted NIAID chief Dr. Anthony Fauci, Hoth, and other officials to demand that "women be treated as women and not as fetus-bearers." Even Fauci had to concede that there had been few women included in AIDS drug trials.

Not surprisingly, the blind sexism of the NIH establishment is also reflected in the institute's attitudes toward women researchers. According to Dr. Deborah Cotton, an assistant professor of medicine at Harvard Medical School who chaired the session on women in clinical trials at NIAID's December conference, condescension was the typical response to criticisms from her and other women of the Food and Drug Administration committee reviewing protocol 076.

"As a woman, part of the problem in talking about clinical trials in women is that people don't listen," said Cotton. "They consider it a political statement . . . as if we are overstating what the scientific issues are." Pressure from women's advocates has helped, she said. "I think it did take that kind of advocacy to put women at the top of the agenda."

Legal pressure may also help. A class-action lawsuit has been filed against Health and Human Services Secretary Louis Sullivan, who oversees the Social Security Administration as well as CDC, NIH, and NCI. The suit seeks to grant disability benefits for a broader range of HIV diseases, including HIV-induced gynecological diseases. Legal services attorney Theresa McGovern filed the case from her cramped New York City office after hearing from dozens of people like S.P., a 23-year-old with two children in foster care.

S.P. said she can't have her name published because she must keep her HIV condition a secret from her father, with whom she shares a tiny, dilapidated apartment. She can't afford her own apartment unless she receives Social Security Disability insurance and Supplemental Security Income benefits. Without adequate housing, she has been unable to convince the family court to return her children.

"I get headaches, throw up a lot. I've got a lot of pain in my side," S.P. said. She has outbreaks of painful pelvic inflammatory disease for which she has been hospitalized. Her immune system is nearly depleted.

The benefits would mean a monthly grant of $472 instead of the $113 she gets from local assistance programs. Despite her own doctor's testimony at a hearing last fall that she is unable to work, an administrative law judge deemed the rail-thin woman's testimony "not credible" and denied her claim. The class-action suit, in U.S. District Court in Manhattan, could affect thousands of women as well as male IV drug users.

"This should have been a national class action but we just didn't have the money to do it," McGovern says. Other nonprofit legal service groups joined in the suit, including the gay-rights oriented Lambda Legal Defense and Education Fund. But McGovern said that support from major AIDS groups has been slower in coming.

McGovern's lawsuit—like the Women's AIDS Network in San Francisco and the handful of other such efforts for women—has been run on a shoestring. These groups get little of the money that flows, for example, to New York's Gay Men's Health Crisis (GMHC), the country's biggest AIDS service group. GMHC, for its part, did not join the lawsuit, though it made a small donation.

Even when better funded AIDS groups sponsor programs needed by women with HIV, they may set entrance criteria women can't meet. Even large groups like GMHC have restricted their client services to serve only those diagnosed with AIDS or AIDS-related conditions, as set by the male-oriented CDC definition; GMHC has long refused services to anyone still using drugs. Given the barriers women face getting diagnosed correctly, plus the high percentage who get AIDS from IV drug use, women are falling through the cracks even in community HIV service groups.

Some doctors are uneasy about women bringing new demands to the fray. They are critical of demands to include women's genital tract infections among AIDS-defining illnesses. "Some of these infections are very common," said Dr. Paula Shuman, infectious disease specialist at Wayne State University School of Medicine in Detroit. "It would terrify a lot of women into thinking it means they have HIV." No one wants to promote unnecessary anxiety, but viewing women as hysterics who would place extra demands on doctors is a common reason given to deny better research and medical care to women.

Women's organizations themselves are also guilty of ignoring the threat of HIV to women. Center for Women Policy Studies Executive Director Leslie Wolfe says her group will be pushing women's organizations to start giving AIDS priority, after years of groups insisting HIV is not a women's issue.

"If women don't fit some stereotype, HIV won't be considered," said Cohen of Chicago's Cook County Hospital. For women of color, the poor, and IV drug users who are the majority of women with AIDS, HIV adds a grim dimension to the neglect they always have experienced; for middle-class European American women, HIV is often missed because AIDS is what happens to other people.

Older women also suffer from doctor biases. According to Dr. Mary A. Young, who sees scores of infected women at her office in the Georgetown University Medical Center in Washington, D.C., one 62-year-old was given cancer tests for a year before anyone thought to take her sexual history and recommend an HIV test. It was positive. "No one had considered this widow might be sexually active," Young said.

But women with HIV have been organizing among themselves to try to answer the questions that the AIDS establishment has ignored. Michelle Wilson, 39, a legal services aide from Washington, D.C., started a newsletter and an organization called "The Positive Woman" for women like herself who live with the virus. Sex is one of the toughest topics.

"Initially, it made me feel unclean," she said about trying to have sex after learning of her infection last year. "I felt like my husband couldn't touch me without infecting himself." For a while, he didn't wear a condom because he thought it would make her feel bad. "It was hard to relax and feel good. I couldn't keep feeling sexually aroused because I knew what the condom meant. But at some point, a coping mechanism kicks in and you feel, 'Now what a guy—our lovemaking remains unchanged because he really loves me.' And that keeps us a loving and sexual couple."

Wilson gets calls from around the country about the newsletter. Many women describe frustrations when they look for support from male-oriented service groups. "You're reluctant if you're in a room filled with men to raise your hand and say, 'I have lesions on my vagina,'" Wilson said.

Lesbians with HIV find their existence even more widely denied. Drug use, alternative methods of fertilization, blood transfusions, and sex with infected men are known routes of HIV into the lesbian population. As for lesbian sexual HIV transmission, several possible cases have been reported in letters to medical journals, but the risk remains unclear. CDC epidemiologist Susan Chu, the lead author of a recent report that looked for AIDS in lesbians, said she found no cases of female-to-female transmission.

But Chu states flatly that her study did not rule out HIV risks in lesbian sex. Notably, the study used the CDC's narrow definition of AIDS, not a cross section of HIV-infected women. And the authors defined "lesbian" more strictly than would many lesbian women: they omitted any women mentioned in CDC AIDS reports through 1989 who had had sex with men since 1977, leaving 79 lesbians, or 0.8 percent of all reported adult women with AIDS in the country. Almost all were intravenous drug users and 5 percent were described as infected through transfusions. This gives no help for lesbians who, for whatever reason, are infected. The CDC has not found the question of lesbian risk significant enough to warrant safer sex guidelines.

As far as menstrual blood is concerned, Chu said she doesn't know if it is as HIV-laden as circulating blood in infected women. She could not say if sex during menses was riskier for one's sex partner, although the menstruating woman might be at more risk of infection herself, because her cervix is more open.

In trying to assess their own risk, women probably should consider the geographic prevalence of the virus where they or their sexual partners have had sex, shared hypodermic needles, had blood transfusions, maybe even had tattoos and electrolysis performed since the late 1970s. Perhaps most tangled is the daisy chain of sex tied to everyone's history that is both invisible and sometimes distorted by guilt.

The answer to uncertain risk—"just wear a condom"—ignores the fact that women don't wear condoms. Men do and most don't like it; some admit it gives them performance anxiety and others say it is "unnatural." For some, says Dooley Worth, Ph.D., an anthropologist and adviser to New York's Health and Hospitals Corporation, condoms are unwelcome symbols of extra-relationship activity. Worth also warns that no relationship is static and commitment to condom use can diminish over time. And condom campaigns ignore the real pressures in women's relationships that sometimes make unsafe sex seem the less risky alternative.

"Women may be getting battered, or fear the possibility of battery or of losing the relationship," said Sally Jue, the mental health program manager for AIDS Project Los Angeles. "For many Asian and Hispanic women, being assertive and getting their men to wear condoms is a ludicrous idea."

In one study of women in prostitution, only 4 percent of nearly 600 women reported they regularly had customers use condoms. In a more encouraging study, the Alan Guttmacher Institute recently reported that levels of condom use among Latino teenagers had tripled during the 1980s.

But if condoms are not known as perfect birth control, why are they so great when it comes to a question of life and death? After all, condom failure in pregnancy prevention ranges between 3 percent for older, white married women and 36 percent for younger, nonmarried women of color. With HIV protection, less is known. One study concluded that condom use reduces HIV infection risk for women by a factor of 10.

There are mixed recommendations about antiviral spermicides, containing nonoxynol 9, sodium oxychlorosene, or benzalkonium chloride. Although these are in the woman's control, they are less effective than condoms. Also, spermicides can irritate both mucous membranes lining the vagina and anus, making them more vulnerable to infection.

As a long-term public health strategy, condoms are not the answer for women wanting control over their health. But federal officials were dumbfounded when Representative Constance Morella (R.-Md.) and other congresswomen asked what was being done to give women control of HIV protection. "They have not been doing anything," said Morella, whose district includes the NIH's sprawling research campus.

The concept that women's health counts as much as men's is long overdue. Last summer, the Congressional Caucus for Women's Issues forced the formation of an Office of Research on Women's Health at NIH. The caucus also introduced the Women's Health Equity Act, which includes AIDS initiatives written by the Center for Women Policy Studies in Washington.

"The activists are right," said AmFAR's Krim. "But unless politicians also feel pressure from the mainstream, from groups like NOW and the League of Women Voters, they won't do it for women." Certainly, scientists and doctors, when asked to spend time and money on women's health, must stop reacting like men who have been asked to wear condoms.

Women cannot afford to let the Health Equity Act follow the path of the ERA. Unless true health equity is addressed, thousands and thousands of women, especially in the inner cities and gradually across the country, as sentenced to death as HIV in the U.S. begins to take on the global pattern on AIDS.

Suzanne Wilson
Dallas, Texas
Age 29

I met Cragg in a restaurant/bar four and a half years ago. It was love at first sight. I walked right up to him and said, "You are the sexiest man I've ever seen in my life." We got married three months later.

Even with my knowledge that Cragg had been an IV drug user, I still did not think it was going to happen to me. He had been clean for almost four years when I met him. You just don't think it's going to touch your life. If I knew then what I know now, I would not be infected. I still would have married Cragg, but I would have used a rubber.

I quit my job at Neiman-Marcus after almost six years to work on renovating this house Cragg and I got three years ago. That's what we were doing when he got sick last January. We're both asymptomatic now. We're both on AZT.

When people ask me what's different between our lifestyle and somebody else's, I tell them our biggest difference is that on our kitchen table, instead of just salt and pepper, we have a bottle of AZT. Ninety percent of the time, Cragg and I lead a very normal life. There's that 10 percent where we sit down and cry.

But I don't look at what's been taken away from me now. I look at things that God gives me every day. That's real hard to do when you've got one set of dreams that have been smashed. You say, O.K., they're smashed, what do we do? Well, you set new ones, except on a day-to-day basis. I don't project two years from now.

My mother calls me an innocent victim. I got this because I fell in love with someone. I can look at it like that, and I can cry about it and feel real sorry for myself, but I can't dwell on it. I think that everybody who contracts AIDS is an innocent victim.

"Alice"
San Francisco, California
Age 45

Being a third-generation Japanese American had a lot to do with my accepting that I have this disease and also communicating that to the family, because of the need not to bring shame on your family or yourself. My parents, brother, and sister-in-law know finally. They were tremendously supportive. My anonymity is because my extended family doesn't know and in the community there's still that negative stigma.

About a year ago I went to one of the local street fairs in Japantown, and parked a few feet away from a table for the Asian AIDS Project. I watched people of my own community whiz past the table like they didn't even see it. If this is happening in my community, how can I expect to get any help? But this year there were a lot more Asian faces staffing the table and more active involvement by the people walking by. It made me feel good that there were changes—slow—but little victories count.

My partner was bisexual, I'm heterosexual. I'm not promiscuous, and I thought I was pretty selective.

The idea that women are promiscuous is a biggie with the media. I want to tell women that they shouldn't stop having sex. It's one of the most beautiful things in the world for two people to share. But we need to arm ourselves—with education, and with a sense of our own responsibility and our partners'.

I found out I had HIV in 1987 and worked as an accountant until the winter of 1988. Social Security—I swear to God—almost made me commit suicide. I applied in March

and didn't get a determination until June. This involved numerous bus trips downtown, and here I am in pain. I said, "I am a person with AIDS and I was told you could expedite things." And they said, "Well, ma'am, we're sorry, we can't be expediting applications for everybody with AIDS." In my frustration and anger I said, "You're just going to drag your feet and hope we die in the meantime."

I have what is called peripheral neuropathy, which is numbness in my lower extremities. When I have food cravings, I jump on them because I've lost about ten pounds. Every day I want a hamburger, even if it gets monotonous, and a real, homemade-style milkshake. It's just a little game you play with your body. You've got to keep your sense of humor, or you'll go stir-crazy. Friends ask me how I get around, and I say, "Very slowly"—but I get there eventually.   [1990]

PART V

The Differences Among Us:
Divisions and Connections

Sisterhood is powerful," proclaimed Robin Morgan in 1970. The strength that some women felt in the early days of the second wave of feminism has carried beyond the initial excitement to form bonds that support our continuing efforts to make social change. But these ties have not been strong enough to overcome many of the social divisions and barriers, often rooted in competition, that have separated women.

Although sexism influences the lives of all women, it is inextricably intertwined with other forms of oppression that have separated women from each other and sometimes pitted them against one another. Part V focuses on the effects of race, class, and sexual orientation on the relationships among women. The selections examine the ways institutional discrimination as well as pervasive prejudice can prevent us from understanding the experiences we have in common and appreciating the differences among us as a rich resource. Some of the articles make these divisions visible by focusing on the often painful dynamics in our daily lives that reinforce them. Because the barriers between women are strengthened by ignorance, there are many first-person and fictional accounts that present women's experiences through their own eyes. In these stories and essays, the divisions among women emerge in different forms and play a variety of roles in women's lives. As you read these accounts, notice how institutional and cultural racism, class bias, and discrimination against lesbians affect the relationships among individual women.

Several pieces are about childhood. As we grow up, we first try to make sense of ourselves in relation to others, an experience that can often be painful for people who feel marginal. Carrie Castro's poem, for example, describes the anguish of a young woman "longing to be someone else instead of 'me'." Angela Davis describes the process of learning the skills of surviving as a young African-American woman in a racist society. In Minnie Bruce Pratt's essay, which appears at the end of this part, a white woman discovers that what "has been presented to me as an accurate view of the world is frequently a lie." She then makes an effort to make sense of her racial and class privileges.

Distrust and prejudice stunt the relationships among adult women and limit our participation in the world. Poems such as "Salad" and "I Am Not Your Princess" show that even seemingly benign stereotypes, such as viewing Asian people as neat, erase a person's humanity. Similarly, stereotypes have defined lesbians by their sexual orientation and made them seem dangerously different from other women.

While individual prejudice serves to perpetuate divisions between people, discriminatory structures are deeply embedded in the workplace, schools, health care institutions, and the political and legal systems. Just as sexism, which grants men power and privilege, is embedded in the social institutions that shape our lives, racism, which grants white people power and privilege, is similarly entrenched in our social, economic, and political systems and our cultural norms. Racism pervades our society, excluding people of color from resources and power, subjecting them to acts of violence and hatred, and rendering them marginal in academia, the media, the law, and the business world.

Racism affects all of us, influencing the way we relate to each other and the way we see the world. Because our society marginalizes people of color, white people often think their experience is universal and don't recognize or value other people's activities, needs, or contributions. In an essay entitled "Disloyal to Civilization," Adrienne Rich describes what she calls white "solipsism." This, she argues, is "not the consciously held *belief* that one race is inherently superior to all others, but a tunnel-vision which simply does not see non-white experience or existence as precious or significant, unless in spasmodic, impotent guilt reflexes. . . ." She argues that to get beyond this perception, white women must listen closely to what the "politics of skin color" has meant to women of color.[1] This may include outright discrimination. For example, the leaders of white women's suffrage organizations in the early twentieth century restricted the participation of African-American women in their movement because they feared alienating white southern politicians. The politics of skin color, however, may take subtler forms, which white women can understand better by hearing from women of color about their experience.

The class system has functioned in similar ways. Economic inequality is reinforced by social institutions and cultural values. Some women have greater access to education, health care, employment opportunities, and other resources, and they have sometimes worked for their own advancement, excluding and ignoring poor women. For example, middle-class and upper-class women in Puerto Rico in the 1920s worked for a law that allowed only literate women over 21 to vote, excluding thousands of illiterate women even though many of them had been working for decades to win suffrage. Today, defending the legal right to abortion without also demanding *access* to abortion for women who depend on welfare and public health clinics would sacrifice the reproductive rights of thousands of women. Some of the selections illustrate the ways class divisions separate women.

Prejudice and discrimination against lesbians in our culture are a reflection of what Adrienne Rich calls "compulsory heterosexuality," a complex web of laws, practices, and attitudes that enforce heterosexuality as a norm and render love relationships between people of the same sex "deviant."[2] As a result of institutional discrimination against lesbians and gay men, sometimes called heterosexism, lesbian mothers have been denied custody of their children, lesbian partners cannot get health coverage for each other, and lesbians have been fired from jobs because of their sexual orientation. Because of these and other sanctions, many lesbians have hidden their sexual orientation from employers, family, and friends. Prejudice against lesbians thrives in an atmosphere in which lesbian lives and history are hidden. As a result, myths and misconceptions about lesbians are numerous in our culture. For example, prejudice against lesbians on the part of the adults in Julie Carter's story "Cat" isolated Cat and destroyed her relationship with Julie.

As Suzanne Pharr demonstrates in "Homophobia and Sexism," taboos against love between women have constrained the lives of all women. The fear of being la-

---

[1] Adrienne Rich, "Disloyal to Civilization," in Adrienne Rich, *Lies, Secrets and Silence* (New York: Norton, 1979), pp. 306–307.
[2] Adrienne Rich, "Compulsory Heterosexuality and Lesbian Existence," *Signs: Journal of Culture and Society* 5 (4) (Summer 1980), 631–660.

beled a lesbian often deters women from acting and speaking freely. For example, women have sometimes been afraid to develop close friendships for fear of being perceived as lesbians, and have sometimes been reluctant to participate in activities that violate the norms of "femininity." As long as the accusation, "What are you—some kind of dyke?" still has the power to scare women, no woman can be free. Freedom to love whomever we choose is a central ingredient of feminism.

Becoming aware of the institutional inequities in our society encourages us to challenge what Peggy McIntosh describes as "the myth of meritocracy." This is the belief, which permeates our culture, that one's success is purely the result of one's own abilities and efforts. McIntosh, reflecting on her white woman's perceptions of the world, points out that since whole groups of people in our society are subjected to discrimination, one's success is not entirely determined by one's individual merits. Systems of power and privilege affect both the advantaged and the disadvantaged, and some groups of people have considerably more access to resources than others.

The stories, essays, and poems in Part V address the many dimensions of prejudice and institutional discrimination as they affect women. They also reveal some of the attitudes that have prevented women from honestly addressing the differences among us, such as the assumptions that some people's experience is universal while others is marginal and deviant, the fear of conflict, the desire to feel safe. By seeing differences from various women's points of view, we can begin to move beyond the distrust of difference that permeates our culture and use our varied experiences to enrich our analysis of society and understanding of human life.

Take a Closer Look: Racism in Women's Lives

Racism in our society operates on many levels and implicates all of us—whether we are conscious of it or not. Despite the advances of the civil rights movement, people of color continue to encounter racism both in institutions and among individuals. Because our society remains highly segregated by race and ethnicity, most of us grow up ignorant of the experiences and feelings of other groups of people.

All the selections in this section tell of the scars of racism through the eyes of its victims. They enable us to see both the enormously destructive power of racism and the will of the human spirit to resist it. They also reveal the various forms racism can take. The authors of the first two poems demonstrate the ways that racial stereotypes obliterate their individuality. "Take a Closer Look" and the excerpt from Angela Davis's *Autobiography* describe the agony of children trying to develop a sense of themselves in a racist world. While struggling to survive the daily hostility and contempt of white people in the South in the 1940s and 1950s, Davis developed methods of maintaining her dignity and self-respect. This section concludes by focusing on institutional racism through "Lullaby," a story about the devastation perpetrated on a Navaho family by the practices of the Bureau of Indian Affairs.

64

Salad

JANICE MIRIKITANI

The woman
did not mean to
offend me,

her blue eyes
blinking
at the glint
of my blade,

as I cut
precisely
like magic
the cucumber in
exact, even,
quick slices.

Do you orientals
do everything
so neatly?   [1982]

65

I Am Not Your Princess

CHRYSTOS

especially for Dee Johnson

Sandpaper between two cultures which tear one
        another apart I'm not
a means by which you can reach spiritual
        understanding or even
learn to do beadwork
I'm only willing to tell you how to make fry bread
1 cup flour, spoon of salt, spoon of baking powder

Stir   Add milk or water or beer until it holds
   together
Slap each piece into rounds   Let rest
Fry in hot grease until golden
This is Indian food only if you know that Indian is
   a government word
which has nothing to do with our names for
   ourselves
I won't chant for you
I admit no spirituality to you
I will not sweat with you or ease your guilt with fine
   turtle tales
I will not wear dancing clothes to read poetry or
   explain hardly anything at all
I don't think your attempts to understand us are
   going to work so I'd rather
you left us in whatever peace we can still scramble
   up
after all you continue to do
If you send me one more damn flyer about how to
   heal myself for $300
with special feminist counseling I'll probably set
   fire to something
If you tell me one more time that I'm wise I'll throw
   up on you
Look at me
See my confusion   loneliness   fear   worrying
   about all our struggles to keep
what little is left for us
Look at my heart   not your fantasies
Please don't ever again tell me about your
   Cherokee great-great grandmother
Don't assume I know every other Native Activist in
   the world personally ·
That I even know the names of all the tribes
or can pronounce names I've never heard
or that I'm expert at the peyote stitch
If you ever
again tell me
how strong I am
I'll lay down on the ground & moan so you'll see
at last   my human weakness   like your own
I'm not strong   I'm scraped
I'm blessed with life while so many I've known are
   dead
I have work to do   dishes to wash   a house to
   clean   There is no magic

See my simple cracked hands which have washed
   the same things you wash
See my eyes dark with fear in a house by myself
   late at night
See that to pity me or to adore me are the same
1 cup flour, spoon of salt, spoon of baking powder
   & liquid to hold
remember this is only my recipe   There are many
   others
Let me rest
here
at least   [1987]

 66

Take a Closer Look

CARRIE CASTRO

Can you see as you
take a closer look
beyond how I appear
to be so self assured
of who I am.
My name alone
   morena
does not reveal
the inner thoughts
of uneasiness
I sometimes feel.

Let me take you
back
to a time
when I was young
and didn't understand
the significance
of colored skins
when I didn't realize
they made a difference.

Back
to a time
when I became
aware of the division
some say existed

between those born
here and those who
come from "over there,"
we made the difference.

Back
to a time
when I grew older
and longed to be
someone else
instead of "me"
because I didn't feel
that was good enough,
I made the difference.

Take a closer look
because inside
my insecurities
you will find
that the reasons
arise from the
cobwebbed minds
of those who cannot see
any beauty in faces
darker than their own.   [1980]

 67

An Autobiography (excerpt)

ANGELA DAVIS

The big white house on top of the hill was not far from our old neighborhood, but the distance could not be measured in blocks. The government housing project on Eighth Avenue where we lived before was a crowded street of little red brick structures—no one of which was different from the other. Only rarely did the cement surrounding these brick huts break open and show patches of green. Without space or earth, nothing could be planted to bear fruit or blossoms. But friends were there—and friendliness.

In 1948 we moved out of the projects in Birmingham, Alabama, to the large wooden house on Center Street. My parents still live there. Because of its steeples and gables and peeling paint, the house was said to be haunted. There were wild woods in back with fig trees, blackberry patches and great wild cherry trees. On one side of the house was a huge Cigar tree. There was space here and no cement. The street itself was a strip of orange-red Alabama clay. It was the most conspicuous house in the neighborhood—not only because of its curious architecture but because, for blocks around, it was the only house not teeming inside with white hostility. We were the first Black family to move into that area, and the white people believed that we were in the vanguard of a mass invasion.

At the age of four I was aware that the people across the street were different—without yet being able to trace their alien nature to the color of their skin. What made them different from our neighbors in the projects was the frown on their faces, the way they stood a hundred feet away and glared at us, their refusal to speak when we said "Good afternoon." An elderly couple across the street, the Montees, sat on their porch all the time, their eyes heavy with belligerence.

Almost immediately after we moved there the white people got together and decided on a border line between them and us. Center Street became the line of demarcation. Provided that we stayed on "our" side of the line (the east side) they let it be known we would be left in peace. If we ever crossed over to their side, war would be declared. Guns were hidden in our house and vigilance was constant.

Fifty or so yards from this hatred, we went about our daily lives. My mother, on leave from her teaching job, took care of my younger brother Benny, while waiting to give birth to another child, my sister Fania. My father drove his old orange van to the service station each morning after dropping me off at nursery school. It was next door to the Children's Home Hospital—an old wooden building where I was born and where, at two, I had my tonsils removed. I was fascinated by the people dressed in white and tried to spend more time at the hospital than at the nursery. I had made up my mind that I was going to be a doctor—a children's doctor.

Shortly after we moved to the hill, white people began moving out of the neighborhood and Black families were moving in, buying old houses and building new ones. A Black minister and his wife, the Deyaberts, crossed into white territory, buying the house right next to the Montees, the people with the hateful eyes.

It was evening in the spring of 1949. I was in the bathroom washing my white shoelaces for Sunday School the next morning when an explosion a hundred times louder than the loudest, most frightening thunderclap I had ever heard shook our house. Medicine bottles fell off the shelves, shattering all around me. The floor seemed to slip away from my feet as I raced into the kitchen and my frightened mother's arms.

Crowds of angry Black people came up the hill and stood on "our" side, staring at the bombed-out ruins of the Deyaberts' house. Far into the night they spoke of death, of white hatred, death, white people, and more death. But of their own fear they said nothing. Apparently it did not exist, for Black families continued to move in. The bombings were such a constant response that soon our neighborhood became known as Dynamite Hill.

The more steeped in violence our environment became, the more determined my father and mother were that I, the first-born, learn that the battle of white against Black was not written into the nature of things. On the contrary, my mother always said, love had been ordained by God. White people's hatred of us was neither natural nor eternal. She knew that whenever I answered the telephone and called to her, "Mommy, a white lady wants to talk to you," I was doing more than describing the curious drawl. Every time I said "white lady" or "white man" anger clung to my words. My mother tried to erase the anger with reasonableness. Her experiences had included contacts with white people seriously committed to improving race relations. Though she had grown up in rural Alabama, she had become involved, as a college student, in anti-racist movements. She had worked to free the Scottsboro Boys and there had been whites—some of them Communists—in that struggle. Through her own political work, she had learned that it was possible for white people to walk out of their skin and respond with the integrity of human beings. She tried hard to make her little girl—so full of hatred and confusion—see white people not so much as what they were as in terms of their potential. She did not want

me to think of the guns hidden in drawers or the weeping black woman who had come screaming to our door for help, but of a future world of harmony and equality. I didn't know what she was talking about.

When Black families had moved up on the hill in sufficient numbers for me to have a group of friends, we developed our own means of defending our egos. Our weapon was the word. We would gather on my front lawn, wait for a car of white people to pass by and shout the worst epithets for white people we knew: Cracker. Redneck. Then we would laugh hysterically at the startled expressions on their faces. I hid this pastime from my parents. They could not know how important it was for me, and for all of us who had just discovered racism, to find ways of maintaining our dignity.   [1974]

 68

Lullaby

LESLIE MARMON SILKO

The sun had gone down but the snow in the wind gave off its own light. It came in thick tufts like new wool—washed before the weaver spins it. Ayah reached out for it like her own babies had, and she smiled when she remembered how she had laughed at them. She was an old woman now, and her life had become memories. She sat down with her back against the wide cottonwood tree, feeling the rough bark on her back bones; she faced east and listened to the wind and snow sing a high-pitched Yeibechei song. Out of the wind she felt warmer, and she could watch the wide fluffy snow fill in her tracks, steadily, until the direction she had come from was gone. By the light of the snow she could see the dark outline of the big arroyo a few feet away. She was sitting on the edge of Cebolleta Creek, where in the springtime the thin cows would graze on grass already chewed flat to the ground. In the wide deep creek bed where only a trickle of water flowed in the summer, the skinny cows would wander, looking for new grass along winding paths splashed with manure.

Ayah pulled the old Army blanket over her head

like a shawl. Jimmie's blanket—the one he had sent to her. That was a long time ago and the green wool was faded, and it was unraveling on the edges. She did not want to think about Jimmie. So she thought about the weaving and the way her mother had done it. On the tall wooden loom set into the sand under a tamarack tree for shade. She could see it clearly. She had been only a little girl when her grandma gave her the wooden combs to pull the twigs and burrs from the raw, freshly washed wool. And while she combed the wool, her grandma sat beside her, spinning a silvery strand of yarn around the smooth cedar spindle. Her mother worked at the loom with yarns dyed bright yellow and red and gold. She watched them dye the yarn in boiling black pots full of beeweed petals, juniper berries, and sage. The blankets her mother made were soft and woven so tight that rain rolled off them like birds' feathers. Ayah remembered sleeping warm on cold windy nights, wrapped in her mother's blankets on the hogan's sandy floor.

The snow drifted now, with the northwest wind hurling it in gusts. It drifted up around her black overshoes—old ones with little metal buckles. She smiled at the snow which was trying to cover her little by little. She could remember when they had no black rubber overshoes; only the high buckskin leggings that they wrapped over their elkhide moccasins. If the snow was dry or frozen, a person could walk all day and not get wet; and in the evenings the beams of the ceiling would hang with lengths of pale buckskin leggings, drying out slowly.

She felt peaceful, remembering. She didn't feel cold any more. Jimmie's blanket seemed warmer than it had ever been. And she could remember the morning he was born. She could remember whispering to her mother, who was sleeping on the other side of the hogan, to tell her it was time now. She did not want to wake the others. The second time she called to her, her mother stood up and pulled on her shoes; she knew. They walked to the old stone hogan together, Ayah walking a step behind her mother. She waited alone, learning the rhythms of the pains while her mother went to call the old woman to help them. The morning was already warm even before dawn and Ayah smelled the bee flowers blooming and the young willow growing at the springs. She could remember that so clearly, but his birth merged into the births of the other children and to her it became all the same birth. They named him for the summer morning and in English they called him Jimmie.

It wasn't like Jimmie died. He just never came back, and one day a dark blue sedan with white writing on its doors pulled up in front of the boxcar shack where the rancher let the Indians live. A man in a khaki uniform trimmed in gold gave them a yellow piece of paper and told them that Jimmie was dead. He said the Army would try to get the body back and then it would be shipped to them; but it wasn't likely because the helicopter had burned after it crashed. All of this was told to Chato because he could understand English. She stood inside the doorway holding the baby while Chato listened. Chato spoke English like a white man and he spoke Spanish too. He was taller than the white man and he stood straighter too. Chato didn't explain why; he just told the military man they could keep the body if they found it. The white man looked bewildered; he nodded his head and he left. Then Chato looked at her and shook his head, and then he told her, "Jimmie isn't coming home anymore," and when he spoke, he used the words to speak of the dead. She didn't cry then, but she hurt inside with anger. And she mourned him as the years passed, when a horse fell with Chato and broke his leg, and the white rancher told them he wouldn't pay Chato until he could work again. She mourned Jimmie because he would have worked for his father then; he would have saddled the big bay horse and ridden the fence lines each day, with wire cutters and heavy gloves, fixing the breaks in the barbed wire and putting the stray cattle back inside again.

She mourned him after the white doctors came to take Danny and Ella away. She was at the shack alone that day they came. It was back in the days before they hired Navajo women to go with them as interpreters. She recognized one of the doctors. She had seen him at the children's clinic at Cañoncito about a month ago. They were wearing khaki uniforms and they waved papers at her and a black ballpoint pen, trying to make her understand their English words. She was frightened by the way they looked at the children, like the lizard watches the fly. Danny was swinging on the tire swing on the elm tree behind the rancher's house, and Ella was toddling around the front door, dragging the broomstick horse Chato made for her. Ayah could see they wanted her to sign the papers, and Chato had taught her to sign her name. It was something she was proud of. She only wanted them to go, and to take their eyes away from her children.

She took the pen from the man without looking at his face and she signed the papers in three different places he pointed to. She stared at the ground by their feet and waited for them to leave. But they stood there and began to point and gesture at the children. Danny stopped swinging. Ayah could see his fear. She moved suddenly and grabbed Ella into her arms; the child squirmed, trying to get back to her toys. Ayah ran with the baby toward Danny; she screamed for him to run and then she grabbed him around his chest and carried him too. She ran south into the foothills of juniper trees and black lava rock. Behind her she heard the doctors running, but they had been taken by surprise, and as the hills became steeper and the cholla cactus were thicker, they stopped. When she reached the top of the hill, she stopped to listen in case they were circling around her. But in a few minutes she heard a car engine start and they drove away. The children had been too surprised to cry while she ran with them. Danny was shaking and Ella's little fingers were gripping Ayah's blouse.

She stayed up in the hills for the rest of the day, sitting on a black lava boulder in the sunshine where she could see for miles all around her. The sky was light blue and cloudless, and it was warm for late April. The sun warmth relaxed her and took the fear and anger away. She lay back on the rock and watched the sky. It seemed to her that she could walk into the sky, stepping through clouds endlessly. Danny played with little pebbles and stones, pretending they were birds eggs and then little rabbits. Ella sat at her feet and dropped fistfuls of dirt into the breeze, watching the dust and particles of sand intently. Ayah watched a hawk soar high above them, dark wings gliding; hunting or only watching, she did not know. The hawk was patient and he circled all afternoon before he disappeared around the high volcanic peak the Mexicans called Guadalupe.

Late in the afternoon, Ayah looked down at the gray boxcar shack with the paint all peeled from the wood; the stove pipe on the roof was rusted and crooked. The fire she had built that morning in the oil drum stove had burned out. Ella was asleep in her lap now and Danny sat close to her, complaining that he was hungry; he asked when they would go to the house. "We will stay up here until your father comes," she told him, "because those white men were chasing us." The boy remembered then and he nodded at her silently.

If Jimmie had been there he could have read those papers and explained to her what they said. Ayah would have known then, never to sign them. The doctors came back the next day and they brought a BIA policeman with them. They told Chato they had her signature and that was all they needed. Except for the kids. She listened to Chato sullenly; she hated him when he told her it was the old woman who died in the winter, spitting blood; it was her old grandma who had given the children this disease. "They don't spit blood," she said coldly. "The whites lie." She held Ella and Danny close to her, ready to run to the hills again. "I want a medicine man first," she said to Chato, not looking at him. He shook his head. "It's too late now. The policeman is with them. You signed the paper." His voice was gentle.

It was worse than if they had died: to lose the children and to know that somewhere, in a place called Colorado, in a place full of sick and dying strangers, her children were without her. There had been babies that died soon after they were born, and one that died before he could walk. She had carried them herself, up to the boulders and great pieces of the cliff that long ago crashed down from Long Mesa; she laid them in the crevices of sandstone and buried them in fine brown sand with round quartz pebbles that washed down the hills in the rain. She had endured it because they had been with her. But she could not bear this pain. She did not sleep for a long time after they took her children. She stayed on the hill where they had fled the first time, and she slept rolled up in the blanket Jimmie had sent her. She carried the pain in her belly and it was fed by everything she saw: the blue sky of their last day together and the dust and pebbles they played with; the swing in the elm tree and broomstick horse choked life from her. The pain filled her stomach and there was no room for food or for her lungs to fill with air. The air and the food would have been theirs.

She hated Chato, not because he let the policeman and doctors put the screaming children in the government car, but because he had taught her to sign her name. Because it was like the old ones always told her about learning their language or any of their ways: it endangered you. She slept alone on the hill until the middle of November when the first snows came. Then she made a bed for herself where the children had slept. She did not lie down beside Chato again until many years later, when he was sick and shivering and only her body could keep him warm. The illness came after the white rancher told Chato he was too old to work for him anymore, and Chato and his old woman should be out of the shack by the next afternoon because the rancher had hired new people to work there. That had satisfied her. To see how the white man repaid Chato's years of loyalty and work. All of Chato's fine-sounding English talk didn't change things.

It snowed steadily and the luminous light from the snow gradually diminished into the darkness. Somewhere in Cebolleta a dog barked and other village dogs joined with it. Ayah looked in the direction she had come, from the bar where Chato was buying the wine. Sometimes he told her to go on ahead and wait; and then he never came. And when she finally went back looking for him, she would find him passed out at the bottom of the wooden steps to Azzie's Bar. All the wine would be gone and most of the money too, from the pale blue check that came to them once a month in a government envelope. It was then that she would look at his face and his hands, scarred by ropes and the barbed wire of all those years, and she would think, this man is a stranger; for forty years she had smiled at him and cooked his food, but he remained a stranger. She stood up again, with the snow almost to her knees, and she walked back to find Chato.

It was hard to walk in the deep snow and she felt the air burn in her lungs. She stopped a short distance from the bar to rest and readjust the blanket. But this time he wasn't waiting for her on the bottom step with his old Stetson hat pulled down and his shoulders hunched up in his long wool overcoat.

She was careful not to slip on the wooden steps. When she pushed the door open, warm air and cigarette smoke hit her face. She looked around slowly

and deliberately, in every corner, in every dark place that the old man might find to sleep. The bar owner didn't like Indians in there, especially Navajos, but he let Chato come in because he could talk Spanish like he was one of them. The men at the bar stared at her, and the bartender saw that she left the door open wide. Snowflakes were flying inside like moths and melting into a puddle on the oiled wood floor. He motioned to her to close the door, but she did not see him. She held herself straight and walked across the room slowly, searching the room with every step. The snow in her hair melted and she could feel it on her forehead. At the far corner of the room, she saw red flames at the mica window of the old stove door; she looked behind the stove just to make sure. The bar got quiet except for the Spanish polka music playing on the jukebox. She stood by the stove and shook the snow from her blanket and held it near the stove to dry. The wet wool smell reminded her of new-born goats in early March, brought inside to warm near the fire. She felt calm.

In past years they would have told her to get out. But her hair was white now and her face was wrinkled. They looked at her like she was a spider crawling slowly across the room. They were afraid; she could feel the fear. She looked at their faces steadily. They reminded her of the first time the white people brought her children back to her that winter. Danny had been shy and hid behind the thin white woman who brought them. And the baby had not known her until Ayah took her into her arms, and then Ella had nuzzled close to her as she had when she was nursing. The blonde woman was nervous and kept looking at a dainty gold watch on her wrist. She sat on the bench near the small window and watched the dark snow clouds gather around the mountains; she was worrying about the unpaved road. She was frightened by what she saw inside too: the strips of venison drying on a rope across the ceiling and the children jabbering excitedly in a language she did not know. So they stayed for only a few hours. Ayah watched the government car disappear down the road and she knew they were already being weaned from these lava hills and from this sky. The last time they came was in early June, and Ella stared at her the way the men in the bar were now staring. Ayah did not try to pick her up; she smiled at her instead and spoke cheerfully to

Danny. When he tried to answer her, he could not seem to remember and he spoke English words with the Navajo. But he gave her a scrap of paper that he had found somewhere and carried in his pocket; it was folded in half, and he shyly looked up at her and said it was a bird. She asked Chato if they were home for good this time. He spoke to the white woman and she shook her head. "How much longer?" he asked, and she said she didn't know; but Chato saw how she stared at the boxcar shack. Ayah turned away then. She did not say good-bye.

She felt satisfied that the men in the bar feared her. Maybe it was her face and the way she held her mouth with teeth clenched tight, like there was nothing anyone could do to her now. She walked north down the road, searching for the old man. She did this because she had the blanket, and there would be no place for him except with her and the blanket in the old adobe barn near the arroyo. They always slept there when they came to Cebolleta. If the money and the wine were gone, she would be relieved because then they could go home again; back to the old hogan with a dirt roof and rock walls where she herself had been born. And the next day the old man could go back to the few sheep they still had, to follow along behind them, guiding them, into dry sandy arroyos where sparse grass grew. She knew he did not like walking behind old ewes when for so many years he rode big quarter horses and worked with cattle. But she wasn't sorry for him; he should have known all along what would happen.

There had not been enough rain for their garden in five years; and that was when Chato finally hitched a ride into the town and brought back brown boxes of rice and sugar and big tin cans of welfare peaches. After that, at the first of the month they went to Cebolleta to ask the postmaster for the check; and then Chato would go to the bar and cash it. They did this as they planted the garden every May, not because anything would survive the summer dust, but because it was time to do this. The journey passed the days that smelled silent and dry like the caves above the canyon with yellow painted buffaloes on their walls.

He was walking along the pavement when she found him. He did not stop or turn around when he heard her behind him. She walked beside him and she noticed how slowly he moved now. He smelled strong of woodsmoke and urine. Lately he had been forgetting. Sometimes he called her by his sister's name and she had been gone for a long time. Once she had found him wandering on the road to the white man's ranch, and she asked him why he was going that way; he laughed at her and said, "You know they can't run that ranch without me," and he walked on determined, limping on the leg that had been crushed many years before. Now he looked at her curiously, as if for the first time, but he kept shuffling along, moving slowly along the side of the highway. His gray hair had grown long and spread out on the shoulders of the long overcoat. He wore the old felt hat pulled down over his ears. His boots were worn out at the toes and he had stuffed pieces of an old red shirt in the holes. The rags made his feet look like little animals up to their ears in snow. She laughed at his feet; the snow muffled the sound of her laugh. He stopped and looked at her again. The wind had quit blowing and the snow was falling straight down; the southeast sky was beginning to clear and Ayah could see a star.

"Let's rest awhile," she said to him. They walked away from the road and up the slope to the giant boulders that had tumbled down from the red sandrock mesa throughout the centuries of rainstorms and earth tremors. In a place where the boulders shut out the wind, they sat down with their backs against the rock. She offered half of the blanket to him and they sat wrapped together.

The storm passed swiftly. The clouds moved east. They were massive and full, crowding together across the sky. She watched them with the feeling of horses—steely blue-gray horses startled across the sky. The powerful haunches pushed into the distances and the tail hairs streamed white mist behind them. The sky cleared. Ayah saw that there was nothing between her and the stars. The light was crystalline. There was no shimmer, no distortion through earth haze. She breathed the clarity of the night sky; she smelled the purity of the half moon and the stars. He was lying on his side with his knees pulled up near his belly for warmth. His eyes were closed now, and in the light from the stars and the moon, he looked young again.

She could see it descend out of the night sky: an

icy stillness from the edge of thin moon. She recognized the freezing. It came gradually, sinking snow-flake by snowflake until the crust was heavy and deep. It had the strength of the stars in Orion, and its journey was endless. Ayah knew that with the wine he would sleep. He would not feel it. She tucked the blanket around him, remembering how it was when Ella had been with her; and she felt the rush so big inside her heart for the babies. And she sang the only song she knew to sing for babies. She could not remember if she had ever sung it to her children, but she knew that her grandmother had sung it and her mother had sung it:

The earth is your mother,
   she holds you.

The sky is your father,
   he protects you.
Sleep,
sleep.
Rainbow is your sister,
   she loves you.
The winds are your brothers,
   they sing to you.
Sleep,
sleep.
We are together always
We are together always
There never was a time
when this
was not so.   [1981]

The Legacy of Class

In the United States, people don't talk about class very much. Nevertheless, most people are aware of class differences by the way people look, talk, and move through the world. This awareness affects the way we relate to each other. Our class backgrounds have a powerful effect on our values, the way we see ourselves, and the choices we have in our lives. For example, work outside the home has seemed, to women who grew up in middle-class homes, as a form of liberation, while women in poor and working class families have always worked and often at alienating, dead-end jobs.

This section includes several stories and an essay that explore the meaning of class in women's lives. The first selection is an excerpt from an autobiographical novel, *Daughter of Earth,* by Agnes Smedley, a socialist activist during the early twentieth century. It describes a poor child's anguish and confusion when treated with contempt and condescension by wealthier people. For Bernice Mennis, being Jewish and working class are closely intertwined, in her recollections of making sense of a world where she often felt different.

 The feminist ideal of sisterhood among women is often challenged by class divisions. In "Sisters," both women are African American, united by the racism and sexism in their lives but divided by class. Jealousy, competition, and the belief that one can make it on one's own if one is "tough enough" keeps them from offering each other the support each desperately needs. In "The Pocketbook Game," the inequalities between the narrator and the woman she works for breed suspicion and distrust. But rather than passively accepting her employer's treatment, the narrator found a creative way to call attention to her exploitative and condescending behavior.

🌿 69

The Birthday Party

AGNES SMEDLEY

Then it was that the little white girl invited me to her birthday party. My mother objected to buying bananas as a present, but after I had cried and said everyone else was taking things, she grudgingly bought three.

"They are rich people," she protested bitterly, looking at the precious bananas, "an' there's no use givin' 'em any more."

When I arrived at the little girl's home I saw that other children had brought presents of books, silver pieces, handkerchiefs and lovely things such as I had never seen in my life. Fairy tales mentioned them but I never thought they really existed. They were all laid out on a table covered with a cloth shot through with gold. I had to walk up before them all and place my three bananas there, covertly touching the cloth shot through with gold. Then I made my way to a chair against the wall and sat down, trying to hide my feet and wishing that I had never come.

The other little girls and boys were quite at ease—they had been at parties before. They were not afraid to talk or laugh and their throats didn't become whispery and hoarse when anyone asked them a question. I became more and more miserable with each passing moment. In my own world I could reply and even lead, and down beyond the tracks no boy dared touch me or my brother George. If he did he faced me with a jimpson weed as a weapon. But this was a new kind of hurt. In school I had not felt like this before the little white girl: there I had learned an invaluable lesson—that she was clean and orderly, but that I could *do* and learn things that she couldn't. Because of that and because of my teacher's protecting attitude toward me, she had been ashamed not to invite me to her party.

"Of course, if you're too busy to come, you must not feel that you ought, just because I've invited you," she had said. She was not much over ten, yet she had been well trained. I felt vaguely that something was wrong, yet I looked gratefully at her and replied:

"I'll come. I ain't got nothin' to do!"

Now here I was in a gorgeous party where I wasn't wanted. I had brought three bananas at a great sacrifice only to find that no other child would have dreamed of such a cheap present. My dress, that seemed so elegant when I left home, was shamefully shabby here. I was disturbed in my isolation by a number of mothers who called us into another room and seated us at a long table covered with a white tablecloth, marvelous cakes and fruit such as made my heart sink when I compared them with my three bananas. Only my desire to tell my mother all about it, and my desire to know everything in the world even if it hurt, kept me from slipping out of the door when no one was looking, and rushing home. I was seated next to a little boy at the table.

"What street do you live on?" he asked, trying to start a polite conversation.

"Beyond th' tracks."

He looked at me in surprise. "Beyond the tracks! Only tough kids live there!"

I stared back trying to think of something to say, but failed. He sought other avenues of conversation.

"My papa's a lawyer—what's yours?"

"Hauls bricks."

He again stared at me. That made me long to get him over beyond the tracks—he with his eye-glasses and store-made clothes! We used our sling-shots on such sissies. He was stuck-up, that was what he was! But what about I couldn't see.

"*My* papa don't haul bricks!" he informed me, as if to rub it in. Wherein the insult lay I couldn't see, yet I knew one was meant. So I insulted back.

"My papa can lick your papa I bet!" I informed him, just as a pleasant elegant mother bent over us with huge plates of yellow ice cream in her hands.

"Well, Clarence, and what are you talking about?" she asked affectionately.

"Her father hauls bricks and she lives beyond the tracks and she says her father can lick my father!" Clarence piped.

"That doesn't matter, dear, that doesn't matter! Now, now, just eat your ice cream." But I saw her eyes rest disapprovingly on me and I knew it did matter.

Clarence plunged his spoon into his ice cream and henceforth ignored me. I picked up my spoon, but it clattered against the plate. A dainty little girl in blue, with flaring white silk ribbons on her braid of hair, glanced at me primly. I did not touch the spoon again, but sat with my hands under me watching the others eating in perfect self-possession and without noise. I knew I could never eat like that and if I tried to swallow, the whole table would hear. The mother returned and urged me to eat, but I said I didn't like ice cream or cake! She offered me fruit and I took it, thinking I could eat it at home. But when the children left the table I saw that they carried no fruit. So I left mine beside the precious ice cream and cake.

In the next room little boys and girls were choosing partners for a game, and the little white girl was actually sitting at the piano ready to play. My eyes were glued on her—to think of being able to play the piano! Everyone was chosen for the game but me. No little boy bowed to me and asked:

"Will you be my partner, please?" I saw them avoid me deliberately . . . some of them the same little boys who were so stupid in school!

The mother of my little hostess tried to be kind:

"Are you sick, Marie?" she asked. "Would you like to go home?"

"Yes, mam." My voice was hoarse and whispery.

She took me to the door and smiled kindly, saying she hoped I had had a nice time.

"Yes, mam," my hoarse voice replied.

The door closed behind me. The game had started inside and voices of the children were shouting in laughter. In case anyone should be looking out of the window and think I cared, I turned my head and gazed sternly at a house across the street as I walked rapidly away.

And in case anyone I knew saw me with tears in my eyes I would say . . .   [1973]

✤ 70

Jewish and Working Class

BERNICE MENNIS

When I was called to speak at this conference about working-class experience, my immediate reaction was: "No, get someone else." One voice said: "I have nothing worthwhile to say." A second voice said: "I was not born poor. I always ate well. I never felt deprived. I have not suffered enough to be on this panel." Both voices silenced me. The first came from my class background—a diminished sense of competence, ability, control, power. ("Who are you anyway? You have nothing to say. No one cares or will listen.") The second, the guilt voice, comes from a strange combination of my Jewishness, my fear of anti-Semitism, my own psychological reaction to my own deprivations: a denial of my own pain if someone else seems to suffer more.

Economic class has been a matter of both shame and pride for me, depending on the value judgments of the community with which I identified. The economic class reality has always remained the same: My father had a very small outdoor tomato and banana stand and a small cellar for ripening the fruit. Until he was 68, he worked twelve hours a day, six days a week, with one week vacation. Although he worked hard and supported our family well, my father did not feel proud of his work, did not affirm his strength. Instead, he was ashamed to have me

visit his fruit stand; he saw his work as dirty, himself as an "ignorant greenhorn." The legacy of class.

And I accepted and echoed back his shame. In elementary school, when we had to go around and say what work our parents did, I repeated my father's euphemistic words: "My father sells wholesale and retail fruits and vegetables." It's interesting that later, when I was involved in political actions, my shame turned to pride of that same class background. The poorer one was born, the better, the more credit.

Both reactions—shame and pride—are based on a false assumption that one has control and responsibility for what one is born into. (Society—those in power, institutions—is responsible for people being born into conditions of economic limitation and suffering, for racism and classism. But as individuals we do not choose our birth.) That blame/credit often prevents us from seeing clearly the actual effects of growing up in a certain class: what it allows, what it inhibits, blocks, destroys. Also, if we take credit for what is out of our control, we sometimes do not take sufficient credit and responsibility for what is in our control: our consciousness, our actions, how we shape our lives.

What becomes difficult immediately in trying to understand class background is how it becomes hopelessly entangled with other issues: the fact that my father was an immigrant who spoke with a strong accent, never felt competent to write in English, always felt a great sense of self-shame that he projected onto his children; that my father had witnessed pogroms and daily anti-Semitism in his tiny *shtetl* in Russia, that we were Jewish, that the Holocaust occurred; that neither of my parents went to school beyond junior high school; that I was the younger daughter, the "good" child who accepted almost everything without complaining or acknowledging pain; that my sister and I experienced our worlds very differently and responded in almost opposite ways. It's difficult to sort out class, to see clearly. . . .

Feelings of poverty or wealth are based on one's experiences and where one falls on the economic spectrum. The economic class and the conditions we grow up under are very real, objective, but how we label and see those circumstances is relative, shaped by what we see outside ourselves. Growing up in the Pelham Parkway–Lydig Avenue area of the Bronx, I heard my circumstances echoed everywhere: Everyone's parents spoke Yiddish and had accents; they all spoke loudly and with their hands; few were educated beyond junior high school; no one dressed stylishly or went to restaurants (except for special occasions) or had fancy cars or dishwashers or clothes washers. (Our apartment building had, and still has, only one washing machine for 48 apartments. The lineup of baskets began early in the morning. My mother and I hung the clothes on the roof.) We ate good kosher food and fresh fruits and vegetables (from my uncle's stand). My mother sewed our clothes or we would shop in Alexander's and look for bargains (clothes with the manufacturers' tags removed). Clothes were passed between sisters, cousins, neighbors. I never felt poor or deprived. I had no other perspective, no other reality from which to judge our life.

When I went to the World's Fair and watched the G.E. exhibit of "Our Changing World," I remember being surprised that what I believed was a modern-day kitchen—an exact duplicate of our kitchen at home—was the kitchen of the '40s. When I received a fellowship for graduate school, I was surprised to discover I was eligible for the maximum grant because my parents' income fell in the lowest income category. I was surprised when I met friends whose parents talked about books and psychology and art, when I met people who noticed labels and brand names and talked about clothes and cars (but never mentioned costs and money).

What I also didn't see or appreciate was all the work and struggle of my parents to maintain and nourish us, work done silently and without any credit for many years. A few years ago I wrote a poem called "The Miracle" about my mother and her skilled unacknowledged work.

Clearly our assumptions, expectations, and hopes are unconsciously shaped by our class backgrounds. At a very young age I learned to want only what my parents could afford. It was a good survival mechanism that allowed me never to feel deprived or denied. At a later age, when I would read in natural history books about the "immortal species," the lesson was reaffirmed: The key to survival was always to become smaller, to minimize needs. Those species that had become dependent on more luxuriant conditions perished during hard times. Those used to less survived.

There is something powerful about surviving by adapting to little. The power comes from an independence of need, an instinct that allows us to get by. But it is a defense, and, like any defense, its main fault was that it never allowed me to feel the edge of my own desires, pains, deprivations. I defined my needs by what was available. Even now I tend to minimize my needs, to never feel deprived—a legacy of my class background.

Class background reveals itself in little ways. Around food, for example. My family would sip their soup loudly, putting mouth close to bowl. We would put containers directly on the table and never use a butter dish. We would suck bone marrow with gusto, pick up chicken bones with our hands, crunch them with our teeth, and leave little slivers on our otherwise empty plates. We would talk loudly and argue politics over supper. Only later did I become conscious of the judgment of others about certain behavior, ways of eating, talking, walking, dressing, being. Polite etiquette struck me as a bit absurd, as if hunger were uncivilized: the delicate portions, the morsels left on the plate, the proper use of knife and fork, the spoon seeming to go in the opposite direction of the mouth. The more remote one was from basic needs, the higher one's class status. I usually was unconscious of the "proper behavior": I did not notice. But if I ever felt the eye of judgment, my first tendency would be to exaggerate my "grossness" in order to show the absurdity of others' snobbish judgments. I would deny that that judgment had any effect other than anger. But I now realize that all judgment has effect. Some of my negative self-image as *klutz, nebbish,* ugly, unsophisticated is a direct result of the reflection I saw in the judging, sophisticated eye of the upper class.

Lack of education and lack of money made for an insecurity and fear of doing almost anything, a fear tremendously compounded by anti-Semitism and World War II. My parents were afraid to take any risks—from both a conviction of their own incompetence and a fear that doing anything big, having any visibility, would place them in danger. From them I inherited a fear that if I touched something, did anything, I would make matters worse. There was an incredible nervousness in my home around fixing anything, buying anything big, filling out any forms. My mother still calls me to complete forms for her. When my father was sick, my parents needed me to translate everything the doctor said, not because they did not understand him, but because their fear stopped them from listening when anyone very educated or in authority spoke.

I did not inherit the fear of those in authority. In fact, my observation of people's condescension, use of authority, and misuse of power helped shape my politics at a young age. I identified with the underdog, was angry at the bully, fought against the misuse of power. But I did inherit their fear of taking risks, of doing anything big, of trying anything new. I have trouble with paper forms; I've never been able to write a grant proposal; I have no credit cards. I sometimes seek invisibility as a form of safety.

For poorer people, for people who experience prejudice, there is a strong feeling that one has no power, no ability to affect or control one's environment. For nine years my family and I lived in a very small three-room apartment; my sister and I had no bedroom of our own. When we moved from the fifth floor to the sixth, we got a tiny room just big enough for two beds and a cabinet. I never thought to put up a picture, to choose a room color or a bedspread. I had no notion of control over private space, of shaping my environment.

That feeling of lack of control over one's environment, of no right to one's own space, was psychologically intensified by my parents' experiences of anti-Semitism and by the Holocaust. These fostered a deep sense of powerlessness and vulnerability and, on an even more basic level, a doubt whether we really had a right to exist on this earth.

In college I took a modern dance class. A group of us began "dancing" by caving in on ourselves, slinking around the side walls of the gym. I remember the teacher saying that to dance one needed to be able to open one's arms and declare the beauty of one's being, to take up one's space on the dance floor: to say "I am here." For many women who experience poverty and prejudice this kind of self-assertion feels foreign, impossible, dangerous. One of the unconscious effects of being born wealthy is a natural sense of one's right to be here on this earth, an essential grace that comes from the feeling of be-

longing. (The danger, of course, is that wealthier people often take up too much space. They do not see the others crushed under their wide flinging steps.) Where the poorer person's danger is the self-consciousness that shrinks us into invisibility, the wealthier one's is the unconscious arrogance that inflates.

But what happens when one feels self-conscious and small and is seen as large, wealthy, powerful, controlling? At a young age, I knew the anti-Semitic portrait of the wealthy, exploitative Jew. I also knew that I did not feel powerful or controlling. My parents and I felt powerless, fearful, vulnerable. We owned nothing. All my parents saved, after working fifty years, would not equal the cost of one year of college today. What does it mean to have others' definition of one's reality so vastly different from one's experience of it? The effects are confusion, anger, entrapment. I lost touch with what was real, what my own experiences really were.

As a political person I felt particularly vulnerable to the hated image of "the Jew." I knew it was a stereotype and not my experience or the experience of the Jews I grew up with—but it still made me feel guilt, not pride, for any success I did have, for any rise in status. If the stereotype said "Jews have everything," the only way I could avoid that stereotype would be to have nothing. If you are poor, you are not a Jew. If you are successful, you are a bad Jew. The trap.

The economic and professional success of many second-generation Jews became tinged for me, as if we had done something wrong. To feel bad about achievement, to hold back one's power, is very destructive. My aunts and uncles, my parents, my friends' parents all had little education and little money. Yet we—my cousins, my sister, my friends—not only went to college, but even to graduate school and law school. I was speaking the other day with my aunt, who was saying what a miracle it was that her four children were all professionals and she was poor and uneducated. But the miracle was not really a miracle at all. It was the result of parents who saw education as very, very important—as a way out of the entrapment of class and prejudice. It was the result of parents who worked desperately hard so that their children could have that way out. It was a City College system in New York City that provided completely free education while we worked and lived at home.

In one generation we created an incredible economic, class, professional, and educational distance between ourselves and our parents. The danger of this success is that we forget the material soil that nourished us, the hard work that propped us up; that we lose our consciousness of the harm and evil of condescension, exploitation, oppression, the pain of being made to feel inferior and invisible. Anzia Yezierska, a Jewish immigrant writer, says "Education without a heart is a curse." But to keep that consciousness and that heart and to be able to step onto the dance floor of life and say "I am here," reflecting back to our parents the beauty and strength we inherited from them, that would be a very real "miracle" indeed.   [1987]

71

Sisters

BARBARA NEELY

. . . and are we not one
daughter of the same dark mother's child
breathing one breath from a multitude of mouths . . .
    —from the Sisterhood Song of the Yenga Nation

The offices of Carstairs and Carstairs Management Consultants had that hushed, forbidden air of after five o'clock. No light shone from beneath any of the office doors bordering the central typing pool which was also deserted, except for the new cleaning woman working her way among the desks. Lorisa was the last of the office staff to leave. She'd pushed the button for the elevator before she remembered the notes on Wider Housewares she wanted to look over before tomorrow morning's meeting. She turned and took a shortcut through the typing pool to her office.

"Good evening," she said to the grey uniform-clad back of the cleaning woman as the woman reached down to pick up a wastebasket. Lorisa automatically put on her polite, remote smile, the one

that matched the distance in her tone, while she waited for the woman to move out of her way.

Jackie turned with the wastebasket still in her hand and let her eyes roam so slowly over the woman who'd spoken to her that she might have been looking for something in particular. Then she nodded, briefly, curtly, before turning, lifting the basket and dashing its contents into the rolling bin she pushed along ahead of her. Only then did she step aside.

Lorisa hurried into her office, careful not to slam the door and show her irritation. Where did they find the cleaning staff, the asylum for the criminally insane? The woman had given her a look cold enough to cut stone and barely acknowledged her greeting—as though she were not worth the time it took to be pleasant. She, who was always careful to speak to the gum-chewing black girls who worked in the mail room, the old man who shined shoes in the lobby, the newspaper man and any other of her people she met in the building who did menial work. None of them had ever been anything but equally polite to her. She had noticed the shoeshine man always had something pleasant to say to the mailroom girls and only a "Good day" to her. But considering the difference in their positions, his reticence with her seemed only natural and nothing like the attitude of the cleaning woman.

Although she'd only returned for her notes, she found herself moving papers from one side of her desk to the other, making a list of small tasks for tomorrow, staving off the moment when she would have to confront the cleaning woman once again. But Lorisa realized it wasn't the woman's curt nod or the slowness with which she'd moved aside that made her reluctant to leave her office. It was those eyes. Big, black, dense eyes with something knowing in them—something that had made her feel as though her loneliness and her fear of it, her growing uneasiness about her job, the disturbing hollowness where pleasure in her comfortable life should be, and all her other fears and flaws were as visible to the cleaning woman as so many wrinkles and smudges on her dress. When their eyes had met, the sense of secret knowledge already shared had filled her with an almost overwhelming desire to say something, to explain something about a part of herself she couldn't name. The woman's look of cold disdain had only corroborated her feeling of having been revealed and found wanting. "Your shit ain't so hot, honey, and you know it," the woman's eyes seemed to say. It didn't occur to Lorisa that the way she'd spoken to the cleaning woman could have anything to do with the woman's response. She was tired, with too much work and too little rest. And she was always over-imaginative when her period was about to start. She forced herself to open the door to her office and was nearly lightheaded with relief to find the cleaning woman nowhere in sight.

In the descending elevator, she realized that the term "cleaning woman" rang false against the face and figure she'd just encountered. Cleaning women were fat and full of quiet kindness and mother wit. They were not women who looked to be in their late twenties—her own age—with faces strong and proud as her own. They didn't have lean, hard-muscled arms and eyes like onyx marbles. She remembered her grandmother, her father's squat, black, broad-nosed mother who had cooked and cleaned for white people all of her life. On those rare occasions when Lorisa's mother had consented to a visit from her mother-in-law, or, rarer still, when the family paid the older woman a visit in North Carolina, Grandmother would wait on everyone. She would slip into your room while you were in the bathroom in the morning and make your bed, hang up your clothes, and spirit away anything that looked the least bit in need of mending, washing, or pressing. But her dedication didn't earn her much praise.

"Young black girls learn enough about being mammies without your mother to set an example," Lorisa had once heard her mother say to her father. Her mother was explaining why it was impossible for Lorisa to spend part of her summer with her grandmother, despite Lorisa's and her grandmother's wishes. She'd been sent to camp instead, a camp at which, she remembered now, the white kids had called her and the three other black girls "niggers" and put spiders in their beds. As she crossed the lobby, it occurred to her that her grandmother had once been young, just like the woman cleaning the typing pool. Had there been fire in her grandmother's eyes, too, when she was young? Had she spit in

the white folks soup, the way the slaves used to do? How long did it take to make a *real* cleaning woman?

* * *

Jackie banged another wastebasket against her bin with such vigor she left a dent in the basket. What had made her act like that? She slammed the basket down beside the desk and moved on to the next one. The woman was only trying to be polite. But a mean, evil rage had risen up at the very sight of her—walking around like she owned the place, having her own office. And those shoes! She must have paid a hundred dollars for them shoes! Who'd she think she was? Jackie dumped the last basket and began dry mopping the floor with an over-sized dustmop. A college education didn't give her the right to give nobody that uptight little greeting, like an icicle down somebody's back, she thought. She'd run into three or four other black women with really good jobs in other buildings where she cleaned. A couple of them had had that air of doing you a favor when they spoke to you, too. But they'd been light-skinned and looked like models, which somehow made their hinciness less personal. This woman's smooth dark face and big round eyes reminded Jackie of a girl she'd hung out with in school; and she had a cousin with the same big legs and small waist. She didn't need for no plain ole everyday-looking black woman to speak to her because she thought she ought to. She got more than enough of being practically patted on her head, if not her behind, from the phony whites she worked for. She wasn't taking that stuff from one of her own, too!

She let her mind slip into a replay of her latest run-in with her snooty white supervisor in which she'd once again had to point out that she only gave respect when she got it. She was hoping to draw a parallel between the two situations and thereby relieve herself of the knowledge that in the moment when she'd first seen the woman standing there— as crisp and unused as a new dollar bill, as far removed from emptying other people's wastebaskets as a black woman was likely to get—she had been struck dumb by jealousy. She swung the mop in wide arcs, putting more energy into the chore than was called for.

She was just finishing up the Men's Room when

she heard the elevator bell. When she left the bathroom no light showed from beneath the woman's door. Although she'd already cleaned the private offices, Jackie crossed the typing pool and tiptoed into the woman's office. She stood in the middle of the room. Light from the street below made turning on the overhead light unnecessary. A hint of some peppery perfume lingered in the air, like a shadow of the woman who worked there. It was a good-sized office, with a beige leather sofa under an abstract painting in shades of blues and brown; a glass and chrome coffee table with dried flowers in a bowl. A big, shiny, wooden desk.

Jackie ran her fingers along the edge of the desk as she walked slowly round it. She stood in front of the leather desk chair and placed the fingertips of both hands lightly on the desk. She leaned forward and looked toward the sofa as though addressing an invisible client or underling. Then she sat—not as she usually sat, with a sigh of relief at getting off her feet as she plopped solidly down. She sat slowly, her head held high, her back straight. In her imagination, she wore Lorisa's raw silk shirtwaist and turquoise beads. Gold glistened at her ears and on her small, manicured hands. Her hair was long and pulled back into a sleek chignon. The desk hid her suddenly corn-free feet, sporting one hundred dollar shoes. And she knew things—math, the meaning of big words, what to tell other people to do . . . things that meant you were closer to being the boss than to being bossed.

Once, so long ago it seemed like the beginning of time, she'd thought she might be something— nothing grand enough for an office like this. Being a secretary is what she'd dreamed about: dressing real neat, walking with her legs close together, in that switchy way secretaries always had on TV, typing and filing and so forth. She must have been about ten years old when she'd hoped for that, not old enough to know that chubby-butt, black-skinned, unwed mothers with GED diplomas and short, nappy hair didn't get jobs as downtown secretaries or very much else, besides floor-moppers or whores, unless they had a college education. She'd had to drop out of school to take care of her son. She'd never considered marrying Carl's father and he had never asked if she wanted to get married. They were

both fifteen and had only had sex twice. Since then, it seemed she only met two kinds of men—those she didn't like who liked her and those she liked who weren't interested in her. Her marriage dream was no more real than any of her other dreams. She lifted a slim, black pen from its desk holder, shined it on the edge of the apron she wore over her uniform, and quickly replaced it.

But hadn't she at least suspected, even back when she was ten and still dreaming about secretarial school and happy-ever-after, that this was what her life was going to be—just what her mother's life had been and that of all her girlfriends who were not in jail or on dope or working themselves to death for some pimp or factory owner? Hadn't she known that questions like: "And what do you want to be when you grow up, little girl?" were only grownups' way of not talking to her, since they already knew the limits of her life?

A longing beyond words welled up from her core and threatened to escape into a moan so deep and so wrenching its gathering made her suddenly short of breath. She rose quickly from the chair and headed for the door.

What happened to the part of yourself that dreams and hopes, she wondered. Was it just a phase of growing up, to believe you might amount to something, might do something with your life besides have babies and be poor? And how come some people got to have their dreams come true and others didn't?

*   *   *

Lorisa lay with her head thrown back against the edge of the high steel tub, droplets from the swirling water gently splashing her face, tightening the skin across her forehead. She stopped by the spa for a whirlpool bath and fifteen minutes in the steam room every day after work. As a reward, she told herself, without thinking about what there was about her work that warranted rewarding. She shifted her weight, careful to keep her feet from the sucking pipe that pulled the water in and forced it out to knead and pummel her muscles, dissolving the tension across her shoulders. But not quite.

Jim Daily's face rose behind her eyelids—a pale, oval moon altering the landscape of her leisure with its sickly light. She pressed her eyelids down as hard as possible, but Daily's face remained.

"You notice how much she looks like the maid in that cleanser commercial? You know the one I mean," he'd gone on to whoever was in earshot, to whoever would listen, as he'd circled her, trapped her with his penetrating voice. "Go ahead," he told her, "Put your hand on your hip and say, 'Look, chile!'" He'd transformed his voice into a throaty falsetto. His pale blue gaze had pinned her to the spot where she stood, like a spotlight, as he'd waited for her to perform, to act like some nigger clown in some minstrel show. All in fun, of course; just joking, of course; no offense intended, of course. A hot flush of shame had warmed her cheeks. Is that how she looked to him, to them? she'd wondered, searching her mind for real similarities between herself and the commercial caricature of whom Daily spoke, even though she knew in her heart that he never saw her, that all black women's faces were most likely one to him.

Lorisa tried to let go of the memory, to give herself over to the soothing water, but her back was stiff now, her tongue pressed too firmly to the roof of her mouth behind tightly clenched teeth. All the rage she couldn't let herself release at the time came rolling to the surface in a flood of scenes in which she said all the things she might have said to him, if she'd had the luxury of saying and acting as she pleased—like the cleaning woman in her office. She saw herself putting her hand on her hip and telling daily what an ignorant, racist dog he was. A stiletto-thin smile curved her lips at the thought of how he would have looked, standing there with his face gone purple and his whiny nasal voice finally silenced.

Of course, from Daily's point of view, from the firm's point of view, she would only have proved conclusively that all blacks were belligerent and had no sense of proportion, none of the civilizing ability to laugh at themselves. And, of course, she would have lost her job. Daily was slightly senior to her. He was also a white male in a white male firm where she, and the two white women consultants, did everything they could to distract attention from the fact that they were not biologically certified for the old boys' club. And Lorisa knew she was on even shakier ground than the white women on staff.

She was the one who got the smallest and most mundane clients with whom to work. It was her ideas that were always somehow attributed to someone else. She was invariably the last to know about changes in the firm's policies or procedures and office gossip was stone cold by the time she heard it. For a while, she'd been fairly successful at convincing herself all this was due to her being a very junior member of the staff, that race had nothing to do with it. Of course, she realized, with the seventh sense of a colored person in a white society, which members of the firm hated her silently and politely because of her color. Daily was not alone in his racism and he was probably less dangerous, with his overt ignorance, than the quiet haters. But they were individuals. The firm was different. The firm was only interested in making all the money it could. It didn't really care who did the work. Wasn't that what she'd been taught in her college economics courses? But more and more, as men with less seniority and skills than she were given serious responsibilities, she was increasingly unable to plaster over the cracks in the theory that the firm was somehow different from the individuals of which it is composed. More and more she was forced to accept the very good possibility that she'd been hired as a token and would be kept as a company pet, as long as she behaved herself . . . or until some other type of token/pet became more fashionable.

It seemed ironic that in college she'd been one of the black students most involved in trying to better race relations. She'd helped organize integrated retreats and participated in race workshops. She'd done her personal share by rooming with a white girl who became her best friend, costing her what few black girlfriends she'd had on campus. She could almost count the number of dates she'd had on one hand. There were only a few black boys on campus to begin with and a third of them were more interested in her white roommate or light-skinned colored girls than they'd been in the likes of her. Those who had dated her had done so only once and spread the word that she was "lame," and "cold." She quickly evaded the thought that her love life hadn't improved appreciably since college. Back then, there were times when she had felt more comfortable with some of the white kids than she had with some of the black ones, although she'd denied this vehemently when a black girl accused her of it.

And she'd originally liked being the only black at Carstairs and Carstairs. She'd thought she'd have more of a chance to get ahead on her own, without other blacks and their problems and claims to her allegiance.

"We're so proud of our Lorisa," her mother's prim school teacher's voice repeated inside Lorisa's head. The occasion had been a family dinner honoring Lorisa's completion of graduate school and the job offer from Carstairs. "Yes, indeed," her mother had gone on, "Lorisa is a fine example of what a young colored woman can do, if she just puts all this race and sex mess behind her and steps boldly, acts forcefully on her own behalf."

Lorisa wondered what her mother would say if she knew how often her daughter longed for just one pair of dark eyes in one brown face in which to see herself mirrored and know herself whole in moments when she was erased by her co-workers' assumptions about her ability or brains based on her color, not to mention her sex. It was only now that she, herself, realized how much she needed for that brown face to belong to a woman. How long had it been since she'd had one of those I-can-tell-you-cause-you're-just-like-me talks that she remembered from her late childhood and early teens? But that was before she and her girlfriends had been made to understand the ways in which they were destined to compete and to apprehend the generally accepted fact that women could not be trusted.

Still, she'd been smart to keep her mouth shut with Daily. The economy wasn't all that good and lots of companies were no longer interested in trying to incorporate blacks. She could have opened her mouth and ended up with nothing more than her pride. No job. No money. No future. She picked at the possibility like a worrisome scab, imagining herself unable to pay the rent on her newly furnished and decorated apartment or meet the payments on her new car, living a life of frozen fish sticks and cheap pantyhose in a roach-ridden apartment. She saw herself clerking in a supermarket or department store, waiting on people who had once waited on her. Or worse. The face of the cleaning woman from her office replaced Daily's in her mind's eye—the woman's scowl, her hands in cheap rubber gloves, her eyes showing something hot and unsettling, like the first glow of an eruption-bound volcano.

They said it wasn't like the old days. Nowadays, blacks could do anything whites could do. Hadn't a black man gone into space? Hadn't a black woman been named Miss America? Then why was it, she wondered, that the minute she began to contemplate being out of work and what would be available to her, it was only work near the bottom that she expected to find? It was as though her degrees, her experience and skills would amount to nothing, once she descended into the ranks of the black unemployed.

But she was not going to be unemployed. She was not going to be on the outside. She was from a family of achievers. Her father was the first black to get an engineering degree from his alma mater. Her mother had been named best teacher by the local parent-teacher's association for three years in a row. How could she ever explain getting fired to them? Or to members of the black business women's association she'd recently joined? No. She intended to stay right where she was and prove to Carstairs and Carstairs that she was just as dedicated to profit margins and sales, just as adept at sniffing out a rival's weakness and moving in for the kill, just as practiced in the fine art of kissing her superior's ass, as any white boy they could find. She rose quickly from the tub and snatched her towel off the rack, irritated that relaxation had once again eluded her.

* * *

The room was starting to have that acrid, funky odor of people in danger of losing their last dime. Jackie looked around the card table. Light bounced off Big Red's freckled forehead; his belly was a half-submerged beach ball bobbing above the table. Mabel's lips were pressed near to disappearance. It was a look she'd wear as long as there were cards on the table. Her gambling mask, she called it. Bernice was half drunk. Jackie hated playing cards with drunks. They either knocked over a drink and soaked the cards, or started some shit with one of the other players. Bernice had already signified to Alma about the whereabouts and doings of Alma's old man, Rickie, a good-looking Puerto Rican with a Jones for blue-black thighs. Ramrod Slim sat just like his name. His color and the millions of tiny wrinkles on his face reminded Jackie of raisins and prunes.

Jackie riveted her eyes and attention on Slim's

hands as he passed out the cards. The hand he dealt her was as indifferent as all the other hands she'd been dealt tonight. Sweat formed a film separating her fingers from the cards. Oh Jesus! If she could just win a couple of hands, win just enough to pay on Carl's dental bill so the dentist would adjust the child's braces. She gritted her teeth at the memory of the note Carl had brought home when he went for his last visit, a note saying he shouldn't return without at least a fifty-dollar payment. Bastard! Honky bastard! All they ever cared about was money. But, of course, it was more than the dentist's money she needed now.

When she'd decided to get in the game, she'd told herself she had twelve dollars' card-playing money. If she lost it, she would leave the game and not have lost anything other than the little bit of extra money she had left over from her bills and other necessities. If she won, there'd be money for the dentist and the shoes she needed so badly. She'd found a quarter on the way to work—a sure sign of luck.

But not only had she lost her twelve dollars, she'd also lost her light bill money, all of her carfare for next week and was now in danger of losing part of her grocery money. She gripped her cards and plucked. Damn! Shit on top of shit. She wasn't hardly in the way of winning this hand. She longed for a drink to take away the taste of defeat, to drown the knowledge of once again having made the wrong decision, taken the wrong risk. She would have to get some money from somewhere. She let her mind run over her list of friends in order of the likelihood of their being able to lend her something and was further disheartened. Almost everybody she knew was either laid off or about to be. Those who were working steady were in debt and had kids to feed, too. She didn't have a man at the moment. The last one had borrowed twenty-five dollars from her and disappeared. But she would have to find the money somewhere, somehow. She wondered what it would be like to be able to lose this little bit of cash—not much more than a pair of those alligator pumps that woman had worn in the building where she'd cleaned yesterday. She tried to make space in her anxious mind in which to imagine having enough money not to constantly be concerned about it.

"Girl! Is you gonna play cards or daydream?" Big Red grumbled.

Jackie made a desultory play, waited for her inevitable loss, indifferent to whom the winner might be.

* * *

The Carstairs were consummate party givers. They liked entertaining. They liked the accolades providing lavish amounts of expensive food and drink brought them. It was what they did instead of donating to charity. Mr. Carstairs invariably invited all the professional members of the firm and made no secret of how much pleasure it gave him when they were all in attendance. As usual, on party nights, the front door of the Carstairs' twenty-room country place was wide open. A jumble of voices underscored the music that danced out to meet Lorisa as she walked slowly up the front steps.

She hoped it would be different this time. Perhaps, just this once, they would not all turn toward her when she first entered the room and leave her feeling blotted out by their blank, collective stare. She could have made it easier on herself by bringing a date, but she didn't know a man she disliked and trusted enough to subject to one of the Carstairs' parties, or a man who liked her well enough to make the sacrifice. Nevertheless, she attended all the Carstairs' parties, always leaving just as someone started banging out "Dixie" on the piano or telling the latest Jewish, Polish, or gay joke. She knew who would be the butt of the next go-round.

But tonight, she would do more than put in a respectful appearance. Tonight she would prove she was prepared to make whatever sacrifice necessary to play on the team. For she'd decided that it was her non-team player behavior—her inability to laugh at a good joke, no matter who was the butt of it; her momentary appearances at office social functions; her inability to make other staff accept that she was no different from them in any way that counted—that kept her from total acceptance into the firm. Tonight, she would break through the opaque bubble that seemed to keep her from being seen or heard, making her as murky to the whites on staff as they were to her.

After the usual genuflection before the Carstairs and the obligatory exchange of comments about how very glad they were she could come and how pleased she was to be there, Lorisa ordered a stiff drink from the barman and began to circulate with determination. She stopped at one small grouping after another, asking about wives and children, looking interested in golf scores, remaining noncommittal on the issues of busing and affirmative action until her tongue felt swollen, her lips parched and stretched beyond recovery. And still she pressed on: dancing with Bill Steele; laughing at Daily's tasteless joke about a crippled child; listening to Mrs. Carstairs reminisce about Annie Lee, the dear, dead, colored woman who had raised her, while her mama languished on a chaise lounge with a twenty-year-old migraine. And still she pressed on.

And she thought she made her point. She was sure she saw some of them, the ones who counted—the ones who watched the junior staff for signs of weakness or leadership—smile in her direction, nodding their heads as though dispensing a blessing when she caught their eye. Her success was clear in the gentle hug from Mrs. Carstairs, a sign of approval that all the women in the office had come to covet. It was this sense of having proved herself worthy that made her decide to speak to Jill Franklin.

She'd had no intention of trying to enlist anyone in the firm in her struggles with Daily. While she felt one or two of them—including Jill—might be sympathetic, none of them had ever attempted to intervene on her behalf or had even shown overt empathy for her. But the flush of acceptance made her feel as though she had a right to make requests of staff, just like any other member of the firm. She'd been talking to Jill and Ken Horton, whose offices bordered her own, about baseball, until Ken's wife dragged him away. For a few moments, both of the women were quiet. Lorisa gathered strength from the silence, then spoke.

"Listen, Jill, I need to ask you something. You've been working with Jim Daily for a while, now. And you seem to know him well, get along with him. Tell me, is there anything I can do to make him stop?"

"Stop what?" Jill's voice was full of innocent curiosity, her face bland as milk.

For the first time, since she'd arrived at the party, Lorisa looked someone directly in the eye. Jill's eyes had that same blue distance she saw in Daily's eyes.

"Stop . . ." she began, searching desperately for something safe to say to cover her error.

"Hey, you two! This is a party, come out of that corner!" Somebody Lorisa didn't recognize grabbed Jill's hand and pulled her out to the patio where some people were dancing. Lorisa went in search of the Carstairs and made her good-nights.

*   *   *

Jackie spotted Mr. Gus as soon as she pushed open the door. He was where she'd expected him to be this time of evening: on his favorite stool near the far end of the bar, away from the juke box in the front of the long room, but not too close to the bathrooms at the back.

"Hey, Miz Pretty." Harold rubbed his grungy bar cloth in a circle and gave her a wink. Cissy and her old man, Juice (so called for his love of it), sat in a booth opposite the bar and stared past each other. Miz Hazel, who ran the newspaper stand, nursed a mug of beer and half a shot of something while she and Harold watched a baseball game on the portable TV at their end of the bar. Jackie was glad for the game. Talking to Mr. Gus would be easier than if the juke box was going. And she did have to talk to Mr. Gus. She'd tried all her girlfriends, her mother and even her hairdresser. Everyone was broke as she was. Mr. Gus was her last hope. She stopped thinking about all the years she'd promised herself that no matter how broke she got, she wouldn't turn to this sly, old brown coot.

She slid onto a stool three up from Mr. Gus and told Harold to bring her a vodka and orange juice. She glanced at Mr. Gus in the long mirror hanging behind the rows of bottles in front of her. He was looking at the newspaper lying on the bar beside his glass. He didn't lean over the paper, the way most people would. He sat with his back straight, his head slightly inclined, his folded hands resting on the edge of the bar in front of his drink. The white of his shirt glistened in the blue bar light. She had never seen him without shirt and tie, despite the fact that he wore a uniform at work, just like her.

"How you doin', Mr. Gus?"

He looked up as though surprised to find her there, as though he hadn't seen her from the moment she stepped in the door, as though he hadn't been waiting for her since she was a little girl. Mr. Gus was a neighborhood institution. Being a man who understood the economic realities of most black women's lives, he'd cultivated two generations of little girls and was working on a third generation. He took them for rides in his car, gave them candy—all on the up and up, of course. He would never touch a child. He got a portion of his pleasure from waiting, anticipating. Many of Jackie's little play-mates had come to learn they could depend on their old friend, nice Mr. Gus, for treats in their adult lives, too. Only now the candy was cash and the price was higher than a "Thank you, Mr. Gus." But despite the fact that she made next-to-no salary and had a child to raise, Jackie had never come around. Until now. Mr. Gus smiled.

"Anything in the paper about that boy who got shot on Franklin Street, last night?" Jackie craned her neck in his direction, her eyes seeming to search the front page of the paper, her chest thrust forward, in her low-cut sweater. She skipped her behind over the barstools between them, still pretending to be in-tent upon the headlines. But she was mindful of the cat-with-cream smile on his face. It was a smile that made her sure he knew why she was there; that he had sensed, in that special way some men have, that she was vulnerable, could be run to ground like a wounded doe.

She hadn't meant to drink so much, but Mr. Gus was generous. And he was an excellent listener. There was something about his attitude, his stillness and sympathetic expression that allowed women to tell him things they wouldn't reveal to their best friends. They told their men's secrets, what they had dreamed about the night before and anything else that was on their minds, as though injected with a truth-inducing drug. To many women, what was a little sex for badly needed cash, after this kind of intimacy? It was a line of thinking Mr. Gus encouraged.

And so, Jackie had rattled on about her lousy job and what her supervisor had said to her and how hard it was trying to raise a boy alone. Mr. Gus nod-ded and tsked, asked a question or two to prime the pump when she hesitated, ordered more drinks and waited for the beg, the plea. And, of course, the payback.

But in the end, Jackie couldn't do it. She told him how badly Carl needed his braces adjusted and what a fool she'd been to lose her carfare and light bill money in a card game. But when it came to asking him could he see his way clear to let her have seventy-five or even fifty dollars, the same hard glint in his eye that had put her off as a child made her hold her tongue. She did try to get him to say his lines—to ask why she sighed so forlornly, or what she meant when she said, in that frightened voice, that she didn't know what she was going to do. But Mr. Gus refused to play. He wanted the beg. He'd been waiting for it for a long, long time.

They left the bar together. Jackie now a little rocky on her feet, Mr. Gus unwilling to lose when he was so very close. He took her up to his place for one last drink. The smell of old men's undershirts sobered her a bit.

"I sure hate to see you in such a bad way," he said as she sat at his kitchen table trying to adjust her breathing to the bad air.

"Course, you coulda had all I got." He poured another dollop of Seagrams in her jelly glass. Jackie quickly drank it down.

"I don't know why you always been so mean to me, Miz Jackie." He rose and walked to stand be-hind her chair, kneading her left shoulder with pudgy fingers that radiated damp heat, like a moist heat pad. She willed herself not to pull her shoulder away. He breathed like a cat purring.

"Why you so mean, Miz Jackie?" He spoke in a wheedling, whiny tone, as though he, not she, were on the beg.

"You know Mr. Gus ain't gon let you and little Carl go wanting. Don't you know that, now?" He crept closer to the back of her chair, still moving his fingers in damp slow circles.

"I got me a little piece of money, right here in the bedroom; and I want you to have it."

* * *

At first, Lorisa had considered it a sign of her grow-ing esteem among her superiors that she was chosen to take Stanley Wider, of Wider Housewares, to din-ner for a preliminary discussion about his signing a contract with the firm. She was so grateful for any indication of growing favor that it hadn't occurred to her to wonder why she, a junior member of the firm, with no real experience with prestigious clients, should be given this plum. The Wider account had the potential for being very big, very important to the career of whoever pulled him in. Now that dinner with Wider was nearly over, Lorisa understood why she'd been chosen.

Mr. Wider was what the women in the office called "a lunch man"—a client who turned into a sex fiend after dark and could, therefore, only be talked to over lunch. Looking at him, anyone would think he was a kindly, trustworthy genteel man—like Walter Cronkite. Only his eyes and his words told the truth about him. She smiled up from her Peach Melba into his lean, clean-shaven face to find his eyes once again caressing her breasts. He smiled sheepishly, boyishly, when he realized he'd been caught. But his eyes remained cold and hard.

Ralph Wider was a serious pursuer of young corporate women on the rise. In the sixties, when women began pressuring for more room at the top, he'd been bitterly against the idea. But a chance encounter with an extremely ambitious female sales representative had shown him the benefits of affirmative active. In his analysis, women in business fell into two categories: those who were confident and competent enough to know they didn't need to take their panties down to do business; and those who could be convinced that in at least his case, a little sex would get them more business than a lot of facts. He didn't meet many black ones and the ones he met were always smart. He figured they had to be to get high enough to deal with him. But he had a fairly good record of convincing category-one women to slip down a notch. The challenge added spice to his business dealings.

"We're very excited about the possibility of working with your people," Lorisa began, trying once again to introduce the reason for their having dinner together. "We think we can . . ."

"You know, I've always admired black women. You all are so . . . so uninhibited." He stretched the last word out into an obscenity. "I bet you can be a very friendly young lady, when you want to be."

This man is important, not just to the firm, but to my career, Lorisa reminded herself before she spoke.

"I'm afraid I've never been particularly famous for my friendliness, Mr. Wider, but I am a first rate efficiency specialist and I've got some ideas about how to increase . . ."

He lifted his glass in a toast as she spoke. "To freedom" he said with a sly grin.

Twice more she tried to raise the subject of business. Each time he countered with another invitation to spend a weekend on his boat or take a ride in his plane, or have dinner with him in his hotel room the following night.

She knew what she should say to him. She'd practiced gently and firmly explaining that she did not appreciate passes as a part of her work. But she'd never had occasion to use that speech, before. And this man had the power to greatly improve her position in the firm, simply by what he said about their evening together.

"Excuse me," she said between dessert and cognac. She could feel his eyes poking at her behind as she headed for the Ladies Room.

She wrapped wet paper towels around her neck, careful not to dampen her blouse and held her wrists under the cold water tap to calm herself. Tears quickened in her eyes at the sudden desire to tell some woman her woes; to explain about *him* being out there waiting for her and what ought she to do. Somebody deep inside urged her to go out there, pour a glass of ice water in his lap and run like hell—the same someone who'd urged her to talk to Daily as though he had a tail; the same someone who'd urged her to major in archeology instead of business and to stop smiling at white people, at least on weekends. But she was no fool. She wanted the Wider account and the prestige of getting it. She wanted her salary, her vacations, her car. She wanted to prove she was just as good as anybody else in the firm. At the moment, she just didn't know why she needed to prove it.

Lorisa dried her hands, checked her make-up and straightened her shoulders. She couldn't come apart now. She couldn't let them think she was incapable of handling any task the firm gave her. For all she knew, she was being tested. She brushed at her hair and willed that frightened look out of her eyes. I have a contract to get, she told herself as she opened the door.

She stared at his slim, distinguished figure as she crossed the room. So deceiving, she thought, like a bright shiny apple turned to maggotty mush on the inside. But if she could just get him to agree to look at the prospectus. He rose as she returned to her seat.

"I mean it, little lady," he said as he sat down, "I think you're really something special. I'm sure I can do business with you!" he added with a smile as his leg brushed hers beneath the table.

* * *

If there'd been any way for Lorisa to avoid getting on the elevator with Jackie, she'd have done so. If there'd been other people she'd have had no hesitation about getting on. Other people would have kept her from speaking, as she now feared she might. She didn't look at the woman as she entered the elevator, but she didn't need to. She remembered those eyes. The elevator doors hissed shut before her. The lobby button was already lit so she had only to stand there. She kept her eyes straight ahead and wondered if the elevator always moved this slowly or if the damned thing was going to stall, leaving them alone together for the rest of the night.

Jackie studied Lorisa's back and tried to get up the courage to say something. This was the first time she'd seen the woman since their encounter a couple of evenings ago. She still felt bad about how she'd responded. She wanted to apologize, maybe even change her luck by doing so.

"I'm real sorry for the way I acted the other day. Let me buy you a drink to make up for it," she practiced in her head, even though she didn't have enough money to buy herself a drink. She saw the two of them walking down the street to Libby's Place where she knew she could buy a round or two on credit. They would sit in a booth near the back. The juke box would be off, so the place would be quiet enough for talk. The woman would buy her a drink in return and they would talk about what they needed to talk about. Wasn't no black woman's life without something that needed talking about. But none of that was really going to happen. She could tell from the way the woman stood that she didn't want to be bothered.

As the elevator reached the lower floors, Lorisa reached in her pocket, pulled out her leather driving gloves and smoothed them on over long, slim fingers. She tried to keep her attention focused on what she was doing and away from her urge to somehow make herself acceptable to the woman standing behind her.

"Girl, you sure are evil!" she heard herself saying in a way that smacked of respect for the woman's willingness to give her economic betters hell. She saw them walking out of the building together. She would tell the woman her name and offer her a lift. Their talk in the car would be slow but easy. They might discover they liked one another.

But, of course, that whole scene was irrational. Why should she take a chance on being insulted again? Why should it make any difference to her whether this woman considered her somebody worth being pleasant to? She pressed her lips firmly together as the elevator finally slid to a stop. She stepped quickly forward and brisk-stepped her way to the other door, trying to put as much distance between herself and the cleaning woman as possible, before she did something she would regret.

After all, it wasn't as though they had anything in common.   [1985]

72

The Pocketbook Game

ALICE CHILDRESS

Marge . . . day's work is an education! Well, I mean workin' in different homes you learn much more than if you was steady in one place. . . . I tell you, it really keeps your mind sharp tryin' to watch for what folks will put over on you.

What? . . . No, Marge. I do not want to help shell no beans, but I'd be more than glad to stay and have supper with you, and I'll wash the dishes after. Is that all right? . . .

Who put anything over on who? . . . Oh yes! It's like this. . . . I been working for Mrs. E. one day a week for several months and I notice that she has some peculiar ways. Well, there was only one thing that really bothered me and that was her pocketbook habit . . . No, not those little novels . . . I mean her purse—her handbag.

Marge, she's got a big old pocketbook with two long straps on it . . . and whenever I'd go there, she'd be propped up in a chair with her handbag double wrapped tight around her wrist, and from room to room she'd roam with that purse hugged to her bosom. . . . Yes, girl! This happens every time! No, there's *nobody* there but me and her. . . . Marge, I couldn't say nothin' to her! It's her purse, ain't it? She can hold onto it if she wants to!

I held my peace for months, tryin' to figure out how I'd make my point. . . . Well, bless Bess! *Today was the day!* . . . Please, Marge, keep shellin' the beans so we can eat! I know you're listenin', but you listen with your ears, not your hands. . . . Well, anyway, I was almost ready to go home when she steps in the room hangin' onto her bag as usual and says, "Mildred, will you ask the super to come up and fix the kitchen faucet?" "Yes, Mrs. E.," I says, "as soon as I leave." "Oh, no," she says, "he may be gone by

then. Please go now." "All right," I says, and out the door I went, still wearin' my Hoover apron.

I just went down the hall and stood there a few minutes . . . and then I rushed back to the door and knocked on it as hard and frantic as I could. She flung open the door sayin', "What's the matter? Did you see the super?" . . . "No," I says, gaspin' hard for breath. "I was almost downstairs when I remembered . . . *I left my pocketbook!*"

With that I dashed in, grabbed my purse and then went down to get the super! Later, when I was leavin' she says real timid-like, "Mildred, I hope that you don't think I distrust you because . . ." I cut her off real quick. . . . "That's all right, Mrs. E., I understand. 'Cause if I paid anybody as little as you pay me, I'd hold my pocketbook too!"

Marge, you fool . . . lookout! . . . You gonna drop the beans on the floor! [1986]

Breaking Chains and Encouraging Life

ALICE WALKER

In Shockley's essay on the absence of black lesbians in American literature, she quotes Muhammed Ali's response to a female reporter for the *Amsterdam News* who asked him to comment on the ERA and the equalizing of economic opportunities. Ali replied: ". . . some professions shouldn't be open to women because they can't handle certain jobs, like construction work. Lesbians, maybe, but not women."

A black woman, perhaps (let us say) our daughter, needs to work. Has to work. Wants to work. Wants to work at construction. She reads Ali's words and knows all her community will respect and believe what he says. Our daughter's spirit is torn. If she takes the job her head is bent, her shoulders hunched against the assaults of ignorance. If she does not take the job, she starves, goes on welfare, or is easily defeated by a world that prefers broken black spirits anyway.

In this one comment Ali undermines our daughter's belief in the wholeness of her maternal ancestors (were not our slave great-grandmothers, to whom modern-day construction work would doubtless seem easy, women?), threatens her present existence, and narrows her future. As surely as if he clamped a chain on her body, he has clamped a chain on her spirit. And by our silence, our fear of being labeled lesbian, we help hold it there. *And this is inexcusable.* Because we know, whatever else we don't know and are afraid to guess, black lesbians *are* black women. It is in our power to say that the days of intimidating black women with impunity are over. [1983]

"Are You Some Kind of Dyke?"
The Perils of Heterosexism

Attitudes toward lesbians vary across cultures and have changed over time. In the U.S., loving, sensual relationships between women were not seen as deviant in the seventeenth through nineteenth centuries; it was women who passed as men who were punished. In the late nineteenth century, medical experts began to define lesbianism as an illness, and close connections among women became suspect. After World War II, the taboos against lesbianism became extremely powerful, resulting in the erasure of lesbian experience from history; discrimination against lesbians in social, political, and economic institutions; and the proliferation of prejudices, misconceptions, and myths about lesbian life.

The essays and short story in this section examine the consequences of heterosexism for all women, exploring the ways that heterosexuality is enforced through prejudice, fear, and the denial of resources to lesbian couples. Suzanne Pharr demonstrates that homophobia, the fear of homosexuality, and heterosexism, the assumption that heterosexuality is a superior way of life, are used to prevent all women from challenging sexism. In "Cat," love between two young girls feels natural to them until the prejudice of adults destroys it. Lindsy Van Gelder argues that by participating in the institution of marriage, heterosexual couples reinforce the disadvantaged position of lesbians. Carla Trujillo describes the ways that Chicana lesbians are threatening to the established power relations in the Chicano community and urges Chicanas to recognize the commonalities among lesbian and heterosexual women.

73

Homophobia and Sexism

SUZANNE PHARR

Homophobia works effectively as a weapon of sexism because it is joined with a powerful arm, heterosexism. Heterosexism creates the climate for homophobia with its assumption that the world is and must be heterosexual and its display of power and privilege as the norm. Heterosexism is the systemic display of homophobia in the institutions of society. Heterosexism and homophobia work together to enforce compulsory heterosexuality and that bastion of patriarchal power, the nuclear family. The central focus of the rightwing attack against women's liberation is that women's equality, women's self-determination, women's control of our own bodies and lives will damage what they see as the crucial societal institution, the nuclear family. The attack has been led by fundamentalist ministers across the country. The two areas they have focused on most consistently are abortion and homosexuality, and their passion has led them to bomb women's clinics and to recommend deprogramming for homosexuals and establishing camps to quarantine people with AIDS. To resist marriage and/or heterosexuality is to risk severe punishment and loss.

It is not by chance that when children approach puberty and increased sexual awareness they begin to taunt each other by calling these names: "queer," "faggot," "pervert." It is at puberty that the full force of society's pressure to conform to hetero-sexuality and prepare for marriage is brought to bear. Children know what we have taught them, and we have given clear messages that those who deviate from standard expectations are to be made to get back in line. The best controlling tactic at puberty is to be treated as an outsider, to be ostracized at a time when it feels most vital to be accepted. Those who are different must be made to suffer loss. It is also at puberty that misogyny begins to be more apparent, and girls are pressured to conform to societal norms that do not permit them to realize their full potential. It is at this time that their academic achievements begin to decrease as they are coerced into compul-sory heterosexuality and trained for dependency upon a man, that is, for economic survival.

There was a time when the two most condemn-ing accusations against a woman meant to ostracize and disempower her were "whore" and "lesbian." The sexual revolution and changing attitudes about heterosexual behavior may have led to some lessen-ing of the power of the word *whore*, though it still has strength as a threat to sexual property and pros-titutes are stigmatized and abused. However, the word *lesbian* is still fully charged and carries with it the full threat of loss of power and privilege, the threat of being cut asunder, abandoned, and left outside society's protection.

To be a lesbian is to be *perceived* as someone who has stepped out of line, who has moved out of sex-ual/economic dependence on a male, who is woman-identified. A lesbian is perceived as someone who can live without a man, and who is therefore (how-ever illogically) against men. A lesbian is perceived as being outside the acceptable, routinized order of things. She is seen as someone who has no societal institutions to protect her and who is not privileged to the protection of individual males. Many hetero-sexual women see her as someone who stands in contradiction to the sacrifices they have made to conform to compulsory heterosexuality. A lesbian is perceived as a threat to the nuclear family, to male dominance and control, to the very heart of sexism. Gay men are perceived also as a threat to male dominance and control, and the homophobia ex-pressed against them has the same roots in sexism

as does homophobia against lesbians. Visible gay men are the objects of extreme hatred and fear by heterosexual men because their breaking ranks with male heterosexual solidarity is seen as a damaging rent in the very fabric of sexism. They are seen as betrayers, as traitors who must be punished and eliminated. In the beating and killing of gay men we see clear evidence of this hatred. When we see the fierce homophobia expressed toward gay men, we can begin to understand the ways sexism also affects males through imposing rigid, dehumanizing gen-der roles on them. The two circumstances in which it is legitimate for men to openly physically affec-tionate with one another are in competitive sports and in the crisis of war. For many men, these two experiences are the highlights of their lives, and they think of them again and again with nostalgia. War and sports offer a cover of all-male safety and domi-nance to keep away the notion of affectionate open-ness being identified with homosexuality. When gay men break ranks with male roles through bonding and affection outside the arenas of war and sports, they are perceived as not being "real men," that is, as being identified with women, the weaker sex that must be dominated and that over the centuries has been the object of male hatred and abuse. Misogyny gets transferred to gay men with a vengeance and is increased by the fear that their sexual identity and behavior will bring down the entire system of male dominance and compulsory heterosexuality.

If lesbians are established as threats to the status quo, as outcasts who must be punished, homo-phobia can wield its power over all women through lesbian baiting. Lesbian baiting is an attempt to control women by labeling us as lesbians because our behavior is not acceptable, that is, when we are being independent, going our own way, living whole lives, fighting for our rights, demanding equal pay, saying no to violence, being self-assertive, bonding with and loving the company of women, assuming the right to our bodies, insisting upon our own authority, making changes that include us in soci-ety's decision-making; lesbian baiting occurs when women are called lesbians because we resist male dominance and control. And it has little or nothing to do with one's sexual identity.

To be named as lesbian threatens all women, not just lesbians, with great loss. And any woman who steps out of role risks being called a lesbian. To understand how this is a threat to all women, one must understand that any woman can be called a lesbian and there is no real way she can defend herself: there is no way to credential one's sexuality. ("The Children's Hour," a Lillian Hellman play, makes this point when a student asserts two teachers are lesbians and they have no way to disprove it.) She may be married or divorced, have children, dress in the most feminine manner, have sex with men, be celibate—but there are lesbians who do all those things. *Lesbians look like all women and all women look like lesbians.* There is no guaranteed method of identification, and as we all know, sexual identity can be kept hidden. (The same is true for men. There is no way to prove their sexual identity, though many go to extremes to prove heterosexuality.) Also, women are not necessarily born lesbian. Some seem to be, but others become lesbians later in life after having lived heterosexual lives. Lesbian baiting of heterosexual women would not work if there were a definitive way to identify lesbians (or heterosexuals).

We have yet to understand clearly how sexual identity develops. And this is disturbing to some people, especially those who are determined to discover how lesbian and gay identity is formed so that they will know where to start in eliminating it. (Isn't it odd that there is so little concern about discovering the causes of heterosexuality?) There are many theories: genetic makeup, hormones, socialization, environment, etc. But there is no conclusive evidence that indicates that heterosexuality comes from one process and homosexuality from another.

We do know, however, that sexual identity can be in flux, and we know that sexual identity means more than just the gender of people one is attracted to and has sex with. To be a lesbian has as many ramifications as for a woman to be heterosexual. It is more than sex, more than just the bedroom issue many would like to make it: it is a woman-centered life with all the social interconnections that entails. Some lesbians are in long-term relationships, some in short-term ones, some date, some are celibate, some are married to men, some remain as separate as possible from men, some have children by men, some by alternative insemination, some seem "feminine" by societal standards, some "masculine," some are doctors, lawyers and ministers, some laborers, housewives and writers: what all share in common is a

sexual/affectional identity that focuses on women in its attractions and social relationships.

If lesbians are simply women with a particular sexual identity who look and act like all women, then the major difference in living out a lesbian sexual identity as opposed to a heterosexual identity is that as lesbians we live in a homophobic world that threatens and imposes damaging loss on us for being *who we are,* for choosing to live whole lives. Homophobic people often assert that homosexuals have the choice of not being homosexual; that is, we don't have to act out our sexual identity. In that case, I want to hear heterosexuals talk about their willingness not to act out their sexual identity, including not just sexual activity but heterosexual social interconnections and heterosexual privilege. It is a question of wholeness. It is very difficult for one to be denied the life of a sexual being, whether expressed in sex or in physical affection, and to feel complete, whole. For our loving relationships with humans feed the life of the spirit and enable us to overcome our basic isolation and to be interconnected with humankind.

If, then, any woman can be named a lesbian and be threatened with terrible losses, what is it she fears? Are these fears real? Being vulnerable to a homophobic world can lead to these losses:

- *Employment.* The loss of job leads us right back to the economic connection to sexism. This fear of job loss exists for almost every lesbian except perhaps those who are self-employed or in a business that does not require societal approval. Consider how many businesses or organizations you know that will hire and protect people who are openly gay or lesbian.
- *Family.* Their approval, acceptance, love.
- *Children.* Many lesbians and gay men have children, but very, very few gain custody in court challenges, even if the other parent is a known abuser. Other children may be kept away from us as though gays and lesbians are abusers. There are written and unwritten laws prohibiting lesbians and gays from being foster parents or from adopting children. There is an irrational fear that children in contact with lesbians and gays will become homosexual through influence or that they will be sexually abused. Despite our knowing that 95 percent of those who sexually abuse children are heterosexual men, there are no policies keeping heterosexual men

from teaching or working with children, yet in almost every school system in America, visible gay men and lesbians are not hired through either written or unwritten laws.

• *Heterosexual privilege and protection.* No institutions, other than those created by lesbians and gays—such as the Metropolitan Community Church, some counseling centers, political organizations such as the National Gay and Lesbian Task Force, the National Coalition of Black Lesbians and Gays, the Lambda Legal Defense and Education Fund, etc.,—affirm homosexuality and offer protection. Affirmation and protection cannot be gained from the criminal justice system, mainstream churches, educational institutions, the government.

• *Safety.* There is nowhere to turn for safety from physical and verbal attacks because the norm presently in this country is that it is acceptable to be overtly homophobic. Gay men are beaten on the streets; lesbians are kidnapped and "deprogrammed." The National Gay and Lesbian Task Force, in an extended study, has documented violence against lesbians and gay men and noted the inadequate response of the criminal justice system. One of the major differences between homophobia/heterosexism and racism and sexism is that because of the Civil Rights Movement and the women's movement racism and sexism are expressed more covertly (though with great harm); because there has not been a major, visible lesbian and gay movement, it is permissible to be overtly homophobic in any institution or public forum. Churches spew forth homophobia in the same way they did racism prior to the Civil Rights Movement. Few laws are in place to protect lesbians and gay men, and the criminal justice system is wracked with homophobia.

• *Mental health.* An overtly homophobic world in which there is full permission to treat lesbians and gay men with cruelty makes it difficult for lesbians and gay men to maintain a strong sense of well-being and self-esteem. Many lesbians and gay men are beaten, raped, killed, subjected to aversion therapy, or put in mental institutions. The impact of such hatred and negativity can lead one to depression and, in some cases, to suicide. The toll on the gay and lesbian community is devastating.

• *Community.* There is rejection by those who live in homophobic fear, those who are afraid of association with lesbians and gay men. For many in the gay and lesbian community, there is a loss of public acceptance, a loss of allies, a loss of place and belonging.

• *Credibility.* This fear is large for many people: the fear that they will no longer be respected, listened to, honored, believed. They fear they will be social outcasts.

The list goes on and on. But any one of these essential components of a full life is large enough to make one deeply fear its loss. A black woman once said to me in a workshop, "When I fought for Civil Rights, I always had my family and community to fall back on even when they didn't fully understand or accept what I was doing. I don't know if I could have borne losing them. And you people don't have either with you. It takes my breath away."

What does a woman have to do to get called a lesbian? Almost anything, sometimes nothing at all, but certainly anything that threatens the status quo, anything that steps out of role, anything that asserts the rights of women, anything that doesn't indicate submission and subordination. Assertiveness, standing up for oneself, asking for more pay, better working conditions, training for and accepting a nontraditional (you mean a man's?) job, enjoying the company of women, being financially independent, being in control of one's life, depending first and foremost upon oneself, thinking that one can do whatever needs to be done, but above all, working for the rights and equality of women.

In the backlash to the gains of the women's liberation movement, there has been an increased effort to keep definitions man-centered. Therefore, to work on behalf of women must mean to work against men. To love women must mean that one hates men. A very effective attack has been made against the word *feminist* to make it a derogatory word. In current backlash usage, *feminist* equals *man-hater* which equals *lesbian.* This formula is created in the hope that women will be frightened away from their work on behalf of women. Consequently, we now have women who believe in the rights of women and work for those rights while from fear deny that they are feminists, or refuse to use the word because it is so "abrasive."

So what does one do in an effort to keep from being called a lesbian? She steps back into line, into the role that is demanded of her, tries to behave in such a way that doesn't threaten the status of men, and if she works for women's rights, she begins modifying that work. When women's organizations begin doing significant social change work, they inevitably are lesbian-baited; that is, funders or institutions or community members tell us that they can't work with us because of our "man-hating attitudes" or the presence of lesbians. We are called too strident, told we are making enemies, not doing good.

The battered women's movement has seen this kind of attack: the pressure has been to provide services only, without analysis of the causes of violence against women and strategies for ending it. To provide only services without political analysis or direct action is to be in an approved "helping" role; to analyze the causes of violence against women is to begin the work toward changing an entire system of power and control. It is when we do the latter that we are threatened with the label of man-hater or lesbian. For my politics, if a women's social change organization has not been labeled lesbian or communist, it is probably not doing significant work; it is only "making nice."

Women in many of these organizations, out of fear of all the losses we are threatened with, begin to modify our work to make it more acceptable and less threatening to the male-dominated society which we originally set out to change. The work can no longer be radical (going to the root cause of the problem) but instead must be reforming, working only on the symptoms and not the cause. Real change for women becomes thwarted and stopped. The word *lesbian* is instilled with the power to halt our work and control our lives. And we give it its power with our fear.   [1988]

 74

Cat

JULIE CARTER

It is three days after my twelfth birthday and my mother is sitting beside me on the edge of my bed.

She is holding a box of sanitary napkins and a little booklet that reads "What Every Young Girl Should Know" and telling me for the third straight year that I am to read the book and keep the pads hidden from the sight of Daddy and Leroy. I am hardly listening. I am sneaking furtive glances out the window and patiently waiting for her to finish so I can meet the boys out on the lot for our softball game.

My mother is saying, "Look, you've thrown your pretty dress on the floor." She is bending down to pick it up. It is a white flared dress with large yellow flowers. Daddy bought it for my birthday. I am remembering the party, the coconut cake with the twelve ballerinas holding twelve pink candles. Momma had straightened my hair but refused to wave it tight to my head so it would look like a process, the way I usually wear it. Instead she has fluffed up the curls like she does my sister Dee Dee's hair. Momma is serving punch in a white apron or just standing around with her hands in the pockets. When she catches my eye she motions with her head for me to go over and talk with the other girls who are standing in a cluster around the record player. I smile nervously back at her, but remain where I am. My friends are all acting strange. Leroy, my brother and very best friend, has been stuck up under Diedra Young all evening and Raymond and Zip-Zip are out on the back steps giggling with Peggy and Sharon. Jeffrey teases me about my knobby black knees under my new dress until I threaten to punch him in the mouth. I wander out to the kitchen to play with Fluffy, our cat, until Momma misses me and comes to drag me back to the party.

Now, sitting on my bed with Momma, she is saying she will have to get me a training bra. I self-consciously reach up and touch my breasts then jerk my hands down again. I hate them. I'm always hurting them when I bump into things and now when I fight I not only have to protect my face and head I have to worry about getting hit in the breast too.

"Momma, can I go now? I gotta pitch today," I say. Momma puts her arm around my shoulder and pulls me closer to her. "Sugar, you've got to stop playing with those boys all the time; why don't you go play with Sheila, that nice young girl who's staying with the Jenkins?"

"But I don't know her."

"Well, you can get to know her. She's a nice girl

and she doesn't know anybody. You can introduce her to the rest of the girls."

"But Dee Dee know them better than I do."

"Yeah, sugar, but Sheila doesn't have any girlfriends and you don't either, so you could be friends with each other."

I pull away from her. "I got friends," I say. I'm getting annoyed with the conversation, I want to go out and play. I get up and walk over to the window and stand there with my back to her.

"O.K.," Momma says finally, "but I've invited the Jenkins over for lunch Sunday and if you want to be friends with Sheila fine, if not . . ." She shrugs her shoulders.

"You gonna make Dee Dee be there too?"

"Yup."

"Can we invite Zip-Zip and Jeffrey?"

She hesitates a moment. ". . . Maybe next time."

"O.K., can I go now?" I am inching towards the door.

"All right, scoot." She pats me on the butt as I pass her. I am running down the steps, jumping over the last two. Dee Dee, who has been listening at the door, says, "Can I go with you, Cat?"

"No."

"Why not?"

"'Cause you can't."

I reach the vacant lot where we play ball. There is no game today. The boys are busy gathering ammunition—dirt clods, rocks, bottles—for the fight with the white boys from across the tracks.

Dee Dee whines to Leroy: "Leroy, I wanna go."

"You can't," Leroy says.

"How come?"

"'Cause you're too young."

"I'm just as old as Jeffrey!"

"You can't go," Leroy says, ". . . besides you're a girl."

"Cat's a girl," she says indignantly.

We all ignore her. We are gathering sticks and rocks and throwing them into an empty milk crate.

"How come I can't go? Huh? How come?" Nobody answers her. We are all walking across the lot. Raymond and Leroy are carrying the ammunition; Dee Dee is standing where we left her, yelling, "I'm gonna tell Momma what you're up to! I'm gonna tell you going cross the tracks to fight with those white boys." Then, after a moment or two: ". . . And Cat's

got Kotex in her dresser drawer!" My neck burns but I keep walking.

I am sixteen years old and sitting in Sheila's dining room. We are playing checkers and I am losing and not minding at all. Her cousin Bob comes in. He is stationed in Georgia and on leave from the army. He says hi to Sheila, ignores me completely and walks through to the back with his green duffel bag in his left hand. His voice drifts in from the kitchen, "Where'd the little bulldagger come from?" Sheila springs back from the table so fast her chair overturns. She yells in the kitchen doorway, "You shut your nasty mouth, Bob Jenkins!" The next day we are supposed to make cookies for her aunt's birthday but she calls to suggest we do it over my house instead. I do not go back over Sheila's again unless Dee Dee is with me, or there is no one home.

We are in Fairmount Park within some semienclosed shrubbery. Sheila and I are lying on our backs on an old army blanket. We look like Siamese twins joined together at the head. The sky is blue above us and I am chewing on the straw that came with my coke.

"Cat, tell me again how you used to almost be late for school all the time 'cause you used to be waiting for me to come out of my house so we could walk to school together," Sheila says.

"I've told you three thousand times already."

"Well, tell me again, I like to hear it."

"If you hadn't been peeping from behind the curtains yourself and waiting for *me* to come out we'd both have gotten to school on time."

She laughs softly then turns over on her stomach.

"I want a kiss," she says.

I lean up on my elbow, check around to make sure nobody's peeping through the bushes then turn and press my lips to hers. After a few seconds she pulls away. "Man, Cat, I never felt this way about anybody before."

"Me neither." I reach over and touch her hand. We kiss again, briefly, our lips just touching. Then we turn and lie as we were before but continue holding hands.

"Cat?"

"Yeah?"

"I think I'm in love."

"Me too."

She squeezes my hand. I squeeze hers back.

"What would you do if Bob came by and saw us now?" Sheila asks.

"What would you do?"

"I don't know. I'd just say hi, I guess."

"Then I would too," I say.

The sun has moved and is now shining directly over us. I cover my eyes with my arm.

"Bob would say we're both bulldaggers," Sheila says after a while.

"Yeah, I guess he would," I say.

"We aren't bulldaggers, are we, Cat?"

"No, bulldaggers want to be men and we don't want to be men, right?"

"Right, we just love each other and there's nothing wrong with loving someone."

"Yeah and nobody can choose who you fall in love with."

"Right."

Sheila and I are in her bedroom; her uncle is standing over the bed shouting, "What the hell's going on here?" He is home from work early. Sheila and I scramble for the sheet and clutch it across our bodies. I am waiting for her uncle to leave so I can get up and dressed, but he just stands there staring, thunder in his face. Finally I release my end of the sheet and scramble to the foot of the bed. Sheila's stockings are entwined in my blouse. I cram panties into my pocket and pull blue jeans over naked, ashen legs. I am trembling. Her uncle's eyes follow me around the room like harsh spotlights.

Later at my house, Momma, Daddy and I are in the dining room. Leroy and Dee Dee are in their rooms, the doors are shut tight; they've been ordered not to open them. My mother sits on the couch wringing her hands. I sit stiffly forward on the edge of a straight backed chair. My head down. My teeth clenched. My father stomps back and forth across the floor, his hands first behind him, holding each other at the butt, then gesturing out in front of him. He is asking, "What's this I hear about you being in bed with the Jenkins girl?" I sit still on the edge of my chair, looking straight ahead.

"I'm talking to you, Catherine!" His voice is booming to the rafters, I'm sure the neighbors hear.

It is dark outside and a slight breeze puffs out the window curtains. I am holding a spool of thread that had been on the table. I am squeezing it in my hands, the round edges intrude into my palms. I continue to squeeze.

"You hear me talking to you, girl?" He is standing directly over me now, his voice reverberates in my ear. I squeeze the spool of thread and stare at a spider-shaped crack in the wall above the light switch. There is an itch on my left leg, below my knee. I do not scratch. Dogs bark in the backyards and one of the Williams kids is getting a spanking. I hear the strap fall, a child wailing, and an angry female voice.

My father is saying, "Look, you'd better say something, you brazen heifer!" He jerks my head around to face him. I yank it back to stare at the crack in the wall.

"You're lucky Tom Jenkins didn't have you arrested—forcing yourself on that girl like that. . . ."

"What? What? What force? Sheila didn't say I forced her to do anything!"

"If you didn't force her, then what happened?"

"Sheila didn't say that! She didn't say it! Mr. Jenkins must have said it!" I am on my feet and trembling, and screaming at the top of my lungs.

"Then what did happen?" my father screams back at me. I sit back down in the chair and again stare at the crack in the wall over the light switch. Trying to concentrate on it, blot out my father's voice. I cannot. I get up and run to the chair where my mother sits. I am pulling on her arm. "Momma, Sheila didn't say that, did she? She didn't say I forced her?"

Momma sits there biting on her bottom lip and wringing her hands. She does not look at me. She lays her hand on my head and does not speak. My father grabs my arm and yanks me away. I am enveloped in his sour breath as he shouts, "Look, I'm a man of God and don't you dare doubt my word!" I yank my arm from his grip and run towards the steps, toward the safety of my bedroom.

"I haven't dismissed you!" I hear my father's footsteps behind me. He grabs me by my tee shirt and swings me around. I lose my footing and fall at the bottom of the steps.

"Arthur, Arthur!" My mother is running behind

us. My father's knee is in my chest; he is yelling in a hoarse angry voice, "Catherine Johnson, I have one more thing to say to you, then we needn't discuss it anymore, but you listen carefully because I mean every word I say: There will be no bulldaggers in my house, do you understand me? THERE WILL BE NO BULLDAGGERS IN MY HOUSE!"

I am sitting beside Sheila on a bench in Fairmount Park; we are within walking distance of the spot where we used to meet with our lunch on Daddy's old army blanket. The grass is completely green except for one long crooked brown streak where the boys trampled a short cut to the basketball court. The leaves are green too, save for one or two brown and yellow ones beneath the bench at our feet. Sheila's head is bent.

"I'm sorry," she is saying. She is picking minute pieces of lint from a black skirt. "I'm really sorry but you don't know how my uncle is when he gets mad." I am silent. I am watching three boys play basketball on the court about twenty yards away. A tall white kid leaps up and dunks the ball.

"I just didn't know what else to do," Sheila continues. "I was scared and Uncle Jim kept saying, 'She made you do it, didn't she? She made you do it, didn't she?' And before I knew it, I'd said 'yes'." A short black kid knocks the ball out of bounds and a fat boy in a green shirt darts out to retrieve it.

"Cathy?" Her hand is on my forearm and I turn to look her full in the face. "I'm sorry, Cat, I just didn't know what else to do." I turn again towards the basketball court. The tall white boy is holding the ball under his arm and shaking the hand of a short kid. The fat boy in the green sweat shirt is pulling a navy blue poncho on over his head.

"Cathy, please?" Sheila is saying. I turn to look her full in the face. "It's all right, Sheila, it's all right." It is getting windy. The basketball court empties and Sheila asks if I'll meet her at our spot next Saturday. I lie and say yes. She checks to make sure no one's looking, pecks me on the cheek, then gets up to leave. I sit watching the empty basketball court for a long time, then I get up and take the long way home. [1983]

 75

Marriage as a Restricted Club

LINDSY VAN GELDER

Several years ago, I stopped going to weddings. In fact, I no longer celebrate the wedding anniversaries or engagements of friends, relatives, or anyone else, although I might wish them lifelong joy in their relationships. My explanation is that the next wedding I attend will be my own—to the woman I've loved and lived with for nearly six years.

Although I've been legally married to a man myself (and come close to marrying two others), I've come, in these last six years with Pamela, to see heterosexual marriage as very much a restricted club. (Nor is this likely to change in the near future, if one can judge by the recent clobbering of what was actually a rather tame proposal to recognize "domestic partnerships" in San Francisco.) Regardless of the *reason* people marry—whether to save on real estate taxes or qualify for married students housing or simply to express love—lesbians and gay men can't obtain the same results should they desire to do so. It seems apparent to me that few friends of Pamela's and mine would even join a club that excluded blacks, Jews, or women, much less assume that they could expect their black, Jewish, or female friends to toast their new status with champagne. But probably no other stand of principle we've ever made in our lives has been so misunderstood, or caused so much bad feeling on both sides.

Several people have reacted with surprise to our views, it never having occurred to them that gay people *can't* legally marry. (Why on earth did they think that none of us had bothered?) The most common reaction, however, is acute embarrassment, followed by a denial of our main point—that the about-to-be-wed person is embarking on a privileged status. (One friend of Pamela's insisted that lesbians are "lucky" not to have to agonize over whether or not to get married.) So wrapped in gauze is the institution of marriage, so ingrained the expectation that brides and grooms can enjoy the world's delighted approval, that it's hard for me not to feel put on the defensive for being so mean-spirited, eccentric, and/or politically rigid as to boycott such a happy event.

Another question we've fielded more than once (usually from our most radical friends, both gay and straight) is why we'd want to get married in the first place. In fact, I have mixed feelings about registering my personal life with the state, but—and this seems to me to be the essence of radical politics—I'd prefer to be the one making the choice. And while feminists in recent years have rightly focused on puncturing the Schlaflyite myth of the legally protected homemaker, it's also true that marriage does confer some very real dollars-and-cents benefits. One example of inequity is our inability to file joint tax returns, although many couples, both gay and straight, go through periods when one partner in the relationship is unemployed or makes considerably less money than the other. At one time in our relationship, Pamela—who is a musician—was between bands and earning next to nothing. I was making a little over $37,000 a year as a newspaper reporter, a salary that put me in the 42 percent tax bracket—about $300 a week taken out of my paycheck. If we had been married, we could have filed a joint tax return and each paid taxes on half my salary, in the 25 or 30 percent bracket. The difference would have been nearly $100-a-week in our pockets.

Around the same time, Pamela suffered a months'-long illness which would have been covered by my health insurance if she were my spouse. We were luckier than many; we could afford it. But on top of the worry and expense involved (and despite the fact that intellectually we believe in the ideal of free medical care for everyone), we found it almost impossible to avoid internalizing a sense of personal failure—the knowledge that *because of who we are, we can't take care of each other.* I've heard of other gay people whose lovers were deported because they couldn't marry them and enable them to become citizens; still others who were barred from intensive-care units where their lovers lay stricken because they weren't "immediate family."

I would never begrudge a straight friend who got married to save a lover from deportation or staggering medical bills, but the truth is that I no longer sympathize with most of the less tangible justifications. This includes the oft-heard "for the sake of the children" argument, since (like many gay people, especially women) I *have* children, and I resent the implication that some families are more "legitimate" than others. (It's important to safeguard one's children's rights to their father's property, but a legal contract will do the same thing as marriage.)

But the single most painful and infuriating rationale for marriage, as far as I'm concerned, is the one that goes: "We wanted to stand up and show the world that we've made a *genuine* commitment." When one is gay, such sentiments are labeled "flaunting." My lover and I almost never find ourselves in the public settings outside the gay ghetto where we are (a) perceived to be a couple at all (people constantly ask us if we're sisters, although we look nothing like each other), and (b) valued as such. Usually we're forced to choose between being invisible and being despised. "Making a genuine commitment" in this milieu is like walking a high-wire without a net—with most of the audience not even watching and a fair segment rooting for you to fall. A disproportionate number of gay couples do.

I think it's difficult for even my closest, most feminist straight women friends to empathize with the intensity of my desire to be recognized as Pamela's partner. (In fact, it may be harder for feminists to understand than for others; I know that when I was straight, I often resented being viewed as one half of a couple. My struggle was for an independent identity, not the cojoined one I now crave.) But we are simply not considered *authentic,* and the reminders are constant. Recently at a party, a man I'd known for years spied me across the room and came over to me, arms outstretched, big happy-to-see-you grin on his face. Pamela had a gig that night and wasn't at the party; my friend's wife was there but in another room, and I hadn't seen her yet. "How's M—?" I asked the man, "Oh, she's fine," he replied, continuing to smile pleasantly. "Are you and Pam still together?"

Our sex life itself is against the law in many states, of course, and like all lesbians and gay men, we are without many other rights, both large and small. (In Virginia, for instance, it's technically against the law for us to buy liquor.) But as a gay couple, we are also most likely to be labeled and discriminated against in those very settings that, for most heterosexual Americans, constitute the most relaxed and personal parts of life. Virtually every tiny public act of togetherness—from holding hands on the street to renting a hotel room to dancing—requires us constantly to risk humiliation (I think, for example, of the two California women who were recently thrown out of a restaurant that had special romantic tables for couples), sexual harassment (it's astonishing how many men can't resist coming on to a lesbian couple), and even physical assault. A great deal of energy goes into just expecting possible trouble. It's a process which, after six years, has become second nature for me—but occasionally, when I'm in Provincetown or someplace else with a large lesbian population, I experience the *absence* of it as a feeling of virtual weightlessness.

What does all this have to do with my friends' weddings? Obviously, I can't expect my friends to live my life. But I do think that lines are being drawn in this "pro-family" Reagan era, and I have no choice about what side I'm placed on. My straight friends do, and at the very least, I expect them to acknowledge that. I certainly expect them to understand why I don't want to be among the rice-throwers and well-wishers at their weddings; beyond that, I would hope that they would commit themselves to fighting for my rights—preferably in personally visible ways, like marching in gay pride parades. But I also wish they wouldn't get married, period. And if that sounds hard-nosed, I hope I'm only proving my point—that not being able to marry isn't a minor issue.

Not that my life would likely be changed as the result of any individual straight person's symbolic refusal to marry. (Nor, for that matter, do all gay couples want to be wed.) But it's a political reality that heterosexual live-together couples are among our best tactical allies. The movement to repeal state sodomy laws has profited from the desire of straight people to keep the government out of *their* bedrooms. Similarly, it was a heterosexual New York woman who went to court several years ago to fight her landlord's demand that she either marry her live-in boyfriend or face eviction for violating a lease

clause prohibiting "unrelated" tenants—and whose struggle led to the recent passage of a state rent law that had ramifications for thousands of gay couples, including Pamela and me.

The right wing has seized on "homosexual marriage" as its bottomline scare phrase in much the same way that "Would you want your sister to marry one?" was brandished 25 years ago. *They* see marriage as their turf. And so when I see feminists crossing into that territory of respectability and "sinlessness," I feel my buffer zone slipping away. I feel as though my friends are taking off their armbands, leaving me exposed.   [1984]

76

Chicana Lesbians: Fear and Loathing in the Chicano Community

CARLA TRUJILLO

The vast majority of Chicano heterosexuals perceive Chicana lesbians as a threat to the community. Homophobia, that is, irrational fear of gay or lesbian people and/or behaviors, accounts, in part, for the heterosexist response to the lesbian community. However, I argue that Chicana lesbians are perceived as a greater threat to the Chicano community because their existence disrupts the established order of male dominance, and raises the consciousness of many Chicanas regarding their own independence and control. Some writers have addressed these topics,[1] however, an analysis of the complexities of lesbian existence alongside this perceived threat has not been undertaken. While this essay is by no means complete, it attempts to elucidate the underlying basis of these fears which, in the very act of the lesbian existence, disrupt the established norm of patriarchal oppression.

SEXUALITY

As lesbians, our sexuality becomes the focal issue of dissent. The majority of Chicanas, both lesbian and heterosexual, are taught that our sexuality must conform to certain modes of behavior. Our culture voices shame upon us if we go beyond the criteria of passivity and repression, or doubts in our virtue if we refuse.[2] We, as women, are taught to suppress our sexual desires and needs by conceding all pleasure to the male. As Chicanas, we are commonly led to believe that even talking about our participation and satisfaction in sex is taboo. Moreover, we (as well as most women in the United States) learn to hate our bodies, and usually possess little knowledge of them. Lourdes Arguelles did a survey on the sexuality of 373 immigrant Latinas and found that over half of the women possessed little knowledge of their reproductive systems or their own physiology. Most remarked they "just didn't look down there."[3]

Not loving our bodies affects how we perceive ourselves as sexual beings. As lesbians, however, we have no choice but to confront our sexuality before we can confront our lesbianism. Thus the commonly held viewpoint among heterosexuals that we are "defined by our sexuality" is, in a way, partially true. If we did not bring our sexuality into consciousness, we would not be able to confront ourselves and come out.

After confronting and then acknowledging our attraction, we must, in turn, learn to reclaim that what we're told is bad, wrong, dirty, and taboo—namely our bodies, and our freedom to express ourselves in them. Too often we internalize the homophobia and sexism of the larger society, as well as that of our own culture, which attempts to keep us from loving ourselves. As Norma Alarcón states, "[Chicana lesbians] must act to negate the negation."[4] A Chicana lesbian must learn to love herself, both as a woman and a sexual being, before she can love another. Loving another woman not only validates one's own sexuality, but also that of the other woman, by the very act of loving. Understanding this, a student in a workshop Cherríe Moraga and I conducted on lesbian sexuality stated, "Now I get it. Not only do you have to learn to love your own vagina, but someone else's too."[5] It is only then that the subsequent experiences of love and commitment, passion and remorse can also become our dilemmas, much like those of everyone else. The effort to consciously reclaim our sexual selves forces Chicanas to either confront their own sexuality or,

in refusing, castigate lesbians as *vendidas** to the race, blasphemers to the church, atrocities against nature, or some combination.

IDENTIFICATION

For many Chicanas, our identification as women, that is, as complete women, comes from the belief that we need to be connected to a man.[6] Ridding ourselves of this parasitic identification is not always easy, for we grow up, as my Chicana students have pointed out, defined in a male context: daddy's girl, some guy's girlfriend, wife, or mother. Vying for a man's attention compromises our own personal and intellectual development. We exist in a patriarchal society that undervalues women.[7] We are socialized to undervalue ourselves, as well as anything associated with the concept of self. Our voice is considered less significant, our needs and desires secondary. As the Chicanas in the MALCS workshop indicated,[8] our toleration of unjust behavior from men, the church, the established order, is considered an attribute. How much pain can we bear in the here-and-now so that we may be better served in the afterlife? Martyrdom, the cloth of denial, transposes itself into a gown of cultural beauty.

Yet, an alliance with a man grants a woman heterosexual privileges, many of which are reified by the law, the church, our families and, of course, "la causa." Women who partake in the privileges of male sexual alliance may often do so at the cost of their own sense of self, since they must often subvert their needs, voice, intellect, and personal development in these alliances. These are the conditional contradictions commonly prescribed for women by the patriarchy in our culture and in the larger society. Historically, women have been viewed as property.[9] Though some laws have changed, ideologically little else has. Upon marriage, a father feels he can relinquish "ownership" and "responsibility" of his daughter to her husband. The Chicana feminist who confronts this subversion, and critiques the sexism of the Chicano community, will be called *vendida* if she finds the "male defined and often anti-feminist" values of the community difficult to accept.[10]

---

*traitors.

The behaviors necessary in the "act of pursuing a man" often generate competition among women, leading to betrayal of one another.[11] When a woman's sense of identity is tied to that of a man, she is dependent on this relationship for her own self-worth. Thus, she must compete with other women for his attention. When the attention is then acknowledged and returned, she must work to ensure that it is maintained. Ensuring the protection of this precious commodity generates suspicion among women, particularly single, unattached women. Since we're all taught to vie for a man's attention, we become, in a sense, sexual suspects to one another. The responsibility is placed entirely upon the woman with little thought given to the suspected infidelity of the man.

We should ask what role the man places himself in regarding his support of these behaviors. After all, the woman is commonly viewed as his possession. Hence, in the typical heterosexual relationship both parties are abetting the other, each in a quest that does not improve the status of the woman (nor, in my view, that of the man), nor the consciousness of either of them.

How does the Chicana lesbian fit into this picture? Realistically, she doesn't. As a lesbian she does many things simultaneously: she rejects "compulsory heterosexuality";[12] she refuses to partake in the "game" of competition for men; she confronts her own sexuality; and she challenges the norms placed upon her by culture and society, whose desire is to subvert her into proper roles and places. This is done, whether consciously or unconsciously, by the very aspect of her existence. In the course of conducting many workshops on lesbian sexuality, Chicana heterosexuals have often indicated to me that they do not associate with lesbians, since it could be assumed that either (1) they, too, must be lesbians, or (2) if they're not, they must be selling out to Anglo culture, since it is implied that Chicana lesbians do and thus any association with lesbians implicates them as well. This equivocation of sexual practice and cultural alliance is a retrograde ideology, quite possibly originating from the point of view that the only way to uplift the species is to propagate it. Thus, homosexuality is seen as "counter-revolutionary."

Heterosexual Chicanas need not be passive victims of the cultural onslaught of social control. If anything, Chicanas are usually the backbone of every *familia,* for it is their strength and self-sacrifice which often keeps the family going. While heterosexual Chicanas have a choice about how they want to live their lives (read: how they choose to form their identities[13]), Chicana lesbians have very little choice, because their quest for self-identification comes with the territory. This is why "coming out" can be a major source of pain for Chicana lesbians, since the basic fear of rejection by family and community is paramount.[14] For our own survival, Chicana lesbians must continually embark on the creation or modification of our own *familia,* since this institution, as traditionally constructed, may be nonsupportive of the Chicana lesbian existence.[15]

MOTHERHOOD

The point of view that we are not complete human beings unless we are attached to a male is further promoted by the attitude that we are incomplete as women unless we become mothers. Many Chicanas are socialized to believe that our chief purpose in life is raising children.[16] Not denying the fact that motherhood can be a beautiful experience, it becomes, rather, one of the few experiences not only supported [by] but expected in a traditional Chicano community. Historically, in dual-headed households, Chicanas (as well as other women) were relegated to the tasks of home care and child rearing, while the men took on the task of earning the family's income.[17] Economic need, rather than feminist consciousness, has been the primary reason for the change to two-income households. Nevertheless, for many Chicanas, motherhood is still seen by our culture as the final act in establishing our "womanhood."

Motherhood among Chicana lesbians does exist. Many lesbians are mothers as by-products of divorce, earlier liaisons with men, or through artificial insemination. Anecdotal evidence I have obtained from many Chicana lesbians in the community indicates that lesbians who choose to become mothers in our culture are seen as aberrations of the traditional concept of motherhood, which stresses male-female partnership. Choosing to become a mother via alternative methods of insemination, or even adopting children, radically departs from society's view that lesbians and gay men cannot "success-fully" raise children. Therefore, this poses another threat to the Chicano community, since Chicana lesbians are perceived as failing to partake in one of their chief obligations in life.

RELIGION

Religion, based on the tradition of patriarchal control and sexual, emotional, and psychological repression, has historically been a dual means of hope for a better afterlife and social control in the present one. Personified by the Virgen de Guadalupe, the concept of motherhood and martyrdom go hand in hand in the Catholic religion. Nevertheless, as we are all aware, religion powerfully affects our belief systems concerning life and living. Since the Pope does not advocate a homosexual lifestyle,[18] lesbians and gay men are not given sanction by the largely Catholic Chicano community—hence, fulfilling our final threat to the established order. Chicana lesbians who confront their homosexuality must, in turn, confront (for those raised in religious households) religion, bringing to resolution some compromise of religious doctrine and personal lifestyle. Many choose to alter, modify, or abandon religion, since it is difficult to advocate something which condemns our existence. This exacerbates a sense of alienation for Chicana lesbians who feel they cannot wholly participate in a traditional religion.

In sum, Chicana lesbians pose a threat to the Chicano community for a variety of reasons, primarily because they threaten the established social hierarchy of patriarchal control. In order to "come-out," Chicana lesbians must confront their sexuality, therefore bringing a taboo subject to consciousness. By necessity, they must learn to love their bodies, for it is also another woman's body which becomes the object of love. Their identities as people alter and become independent of men, hence there is no need to submit to, or perform the necessary behaviors that cater to wooing, the male ego. Lesbians (and other feminist women) would expect to treat and be treated by men as equals. Men who have traditionally interacted with women on the basis of their gender (read: femininity) first, and their brains second, are commonly left confused when the lesbian (or feminist) fails to respond to the established pecking order.

Motherhood, seen as exemplifying the final act of our existence as women, is practiced by lesbians, but usually without societal or cultural permission. Not only is it believed that lesbians cannot become mothers (hence, not fulfilling our established purpose as women), but if we do, we morally threaten the concept of motherhood as a sanctified entity, since lesbianism doesn't fit into its religious or cultural confines. Lastly, religion, which does not support the homosexual lifestyle, seeks to repudiate us as sinners if we are "practicing," and only tolerable if not. For her personal and psychological survival, the Chicana lesbian must confront and bring to resolution these established cultural and societal conflicts. These "confrontations" go against many of the values of the Chicano community, since they pose a threat to the established order of male control. Our very existence challenges this order, and in some cases challenges the oftentimes ideologically oppressive attitudes toward women.

It is widely assumed that lesbians and heterosexual women are in two completely different enclaves in regard to the type and manner of the oppression they must contend with. As illustrated earlier in this essay, this indeed, may be true. There do exist, however, different levels of patriarchal oppression which affect all of us as women, and when combined inhibit our collective liberation. If we, as lesbian and heterosexual Chicanas, can open our eyes and look at all that we share as women, we might find commonalities even among our differences. First and foremost among them is the status of woman. Uttered under any breath, it implies subservience; cast to a lower position not only in society, but in our own culture as well.

Secondly, the universal of the body. We are all female and subject to the same violations as any woman in society. We must contend with the daily threat of rape, molestation, and harassment—violations which affect all of us as women, lesbian or not.

As indicated earlier, our sexuality is suppressed by our culture—relegated to secrecy or embarrassment, implicating us as wrongful women if we profess to fulfill ourselves sexually. Most of us still grow up inculcated with the dichotomy of the "good girl-bad girl" syndrome. With virtue considered as the most admirable quality, it's easy to understand which we choose to partake. This generates a cloud of secrecy around any sexual activity, and leads, I am convinced, to our extremely high teenage pregnancy rate, simply because our families refuse to acknowledge the possibility that young women may be sexually active before marriage.

We are taught to undervalue our needs and voices. Our opinions, viewpoints, and expertise are considered secondary to those of males—even if we are more highly trained. Time and again, I have seen otherwise sensible men insult the character of a woman when they are unable to belittle her intellectual capacities.[19] Character assassinations are commonly disguised in the familiar "*vendida* to the race" format. Common it seems, because it functions as the ultimate insult to any conscientious *política*. Because many of us are taught that our opinions matter little, we have difficulty at times, raising them. We don't trust what we think, or believe in our merits. Unless we are encouraged to do so, we have difficulty thinking independently of male opinion. Chicanas must be constantly encouraged to speak up, to voice their opinions, particularly in areas where no encouragement has ever been provided.

As Chicanas (and Chicanos), most of us are subject to the effects of growing up in a culture besieged by poverty and all the consequences of it: lack of education, insufficient political power and health care, disease and drugs. We are all subject to the effects of a society that is racist, classist and homophobic, as well as sexist, and patriarchally dominant. Colonization has imposed itself and affected the disbursement of status and the collective rights of us as individuals. Chicanas are placed in this order at a lower position, ensconced within a tight boundary which limits our voices, our bodies, and our brains. In classic dissonant fashion, many of us become complicit in this (since our survival often depends on it) and end up rationalizing our very own limitations.

The collective liberation of people begins with the collective liberation of half its constituency—namely women. The view that our hierarchical society places Chicanos at a lower point, and they in turn must place Chicanas lower still, is outmoded and politically destructive. Women can no longer be relegated to supporting roles. Assuaging delicate male egos as a means of establishing our identities is retrograde and subversive to our own identities as women. Chicanas, both lesbian and heterosexual, have a dual purpose ahead of us. We must fight for our own voices as women, since this will ultimately serve to uplift us as a people.

NOTES

1. Cherríe Moraga, *Loving in the War Years: Lo que nunca pasó por sus labios* (Boston: South End Press, 1983), 103, 105, 111, 112, 117.
2. See Ana Castillo's essay on sexuality: "La Macha: Toward a Beautiful Whole Self" in *Chicana Lesbians: The Girls Our Mothers Warned Us About,* ed. Carla Trujillo (Berkeley: Third Woman Press, 1991). Also see *The Sexuality of Latinas, Third Woman* 4 (1989).
3. Lourdes Arguelles, "A Survey of Latina Immigrant Sexuality," presented at the National Association for Chicano Studies Conference, Albuquerque, New Mexico, March 29–April 1, 1990.
4. Norma Alarcón, personal communication, MALCS (Mujeres Activas en Letras y Cambio Social) Summer Research Institute, University of California, Los Angeles, August 3–6, 1990.
5. Chicana Leadership Conference, Workshop on Chicana lesbians, University of California, Berkeley, Feb. 8–10, 1990.
6. This was spoken of in great detail in a workshop on Chicana Empowerment and Oppression by Yvette Flores Ortiz at the MALCS, 1990.
7. There are multitudes of feminist books and periodicals which attest to the subordinate position of women in society. Listing them is beyond the scope of this essay.
8. Yvette Flores Ortiz, MALCS, 1990.
9. Peggy R. Sanday, "Female Status in the Public Domain," in *Women, Culture & Society,* eds. Michelle Rosaldo and Louise Lamphere (Stanford: Stanford University Press, 1974), 189–206.
10. *Loving in the War Years,* 113.
11. See Ana Castillo's "La Macha: Toward a Beautiful Whole Self." See also *Loving in the War Years,* 136.
12. Adrienne Rich, "Compulsory Heterosexuality and Lesbian Existence," in *Women: Sex and Sexuality,* eds. Catharine R. Stimpson and Ethel Spector Person (Chicago: University of Chicago Press, 1980), 62–91.
13. As Moraga states, "only the woman intent on the approval can be affected by the disapproval," *Loving in the War Years,* 103.
14. Rejection by family and community is also an issue for gay men; however, their situation is muddied by the concomitant loss of power.
15. Cherríe Moraga attests to the necessity of Chicanas needing to "make *familia* from scratch" in *Giving Up the Ghost* (Los Angeles: West End Press, 1986), 58.
16. *Loving in the War Years,* 113.
17. Karen Sacks, "Engels Revisited: Women, the Organization of Production and Private Property" in *Women, Culture & Society,* 207–222.
18. Joseph Cardinal Ratzinger, Prefect, and Alberto Bouone, Titular Archbishop of Caesarea in Numedia, Secretary, "Letter to the Bishops of the Catholic Church in the Pastoral Care of Homosexual Persons," October 1, 1986. Approved by Pope John Paul II, adopted in an or-

dinary session of the Congregation for the Doctrine of Faith and ordered published. Reprinted in *The Vatican and Homosexuality,* eds. Jeannine Gramick and Pat Furey (New York: Crossroad Publishing Co., 1988), 1–10.

19. This occurred often to the women MeChA (Movimiento Estudiantil Chicano de Aztlán) leaders who were on the Berkeley campus between 1985 and 1989. It also occurred to a Chicana panel member during a 1990 National Association for Chicano Studies presentation, when a Chicano discussant disagreed with the recommendations based on her research.   [1991]

Understanding and Valuing Difference

The first step to bridging the differences between us is to broaden our view of female experience, to understand the complex ways in which various forms of discrimination and prejudice affect the lives of different women. We hope the previous sections have been useful in this regard. In an effort to deepen our understanding of divisions among women, we have also found it useful to reexamine our experience with a view to understanding the privileges granted by various systems of domination. Minnie Bruce Pratt, a white southern woman, reaches back to her childhood to remember the exclusiveness and narrowness of the world she inherited. As a woman, however, her relationship to the privilege and power of the white men of her class was always ambivalent. Peggy McIntosh, recognizing that being white has given her unearned advantages in a racist society, struggles to look at these advantages from the point of view of people who do not share them.

We conclude this section with an influential essay by Audre Lorde, a black writer who died of cancer in 1993. Lorde warns us of the dangers of ignoring difference, and urges us to work harder with ourselves and each other to ensure that our differences, rather than dividing us, will enrich our struggle and our vision.

77

"Who Am I If I'm Not My Father's Daughter?"

MINNIE BRUCE PRATT

As a white woman, raised small-town middle-class, Christian, in the Deep South, I was taught to be a *judge,* of moral responsibility and punishment only in relation to *my ethical system;* was taught to be a *preacher,* to point out wrongs and tell others what to do; was taught to be a *martyr,* to take all the responsibility for change and the glory, to expect others to do nothing; was taught to be a *peacemaker,* to mediate, negotiate between opposing sides because *I* knew the right way. When I speak, or speak up, about anti-Semitism and racism, I struggle not to speak with intonations, the gestures, the assumption of these roles, and not to speak out of any role of

ought-to; I ask that you try not to place me in that role. I am trying to speak today to women like myself, out of need: as a woman who loves other women passionately and wants us to be able to be together as friends in this unjust world.

But where does the need come from, if by skin color, ethnicity, birth culture, we are women who are in a position of material advantage, where we gain at the expense of others, of other women? A place where *we* can have a degree of safety, comfort, familiarity, just by staying put. Where is our *need* to change what we were born into? What do we have to gain?

When I try to think of this, I think of my father, of how, when I was about eight years old, he took me up the front marble steps of the courthouse in my town. He took me inside, up the worn wooden steps, stooped under the feet of the folks who had gone up and down to be judged, or to gawk at others being judged, up past the courtroom where my grandfather had leaned back his chair and judged for more than 40 years, up to the attic, to some narrow steps that went to the roof, to the clock tower with a walled ledge.

What I would have seen at the top: on the streets around the courthouse square: the Methodist church, the limestone building with the county health department, board of education, welfare department (my mother worked there), the yellow brick Baptist church, the Gulf station, the pool hall (no women allowed), Cleveland's grocery, Ward's shoe store; then all in a line, connected: the bank, the post office, Dr. Nicholson's office, one door for whites, one for blacks, then separate: the Presbyterian church, the newspaper office, the yellow brick jail, same brick as the Baptist church, and as the courthouse.

What I could not have seen from the top: the sawmill, or Four Points where the white mill folks lived, or the houses of blacks in Veneer Mill quarters.

This is what I would and would not have seen, or so I think, for I never got to the top. When he told me to go up the steps in front of him, I tried to, crawling on hands and knees, but I was terribly afraid. I couldn't—or wouldn't—do it. He let me crawl down: he was disgusted with me, I thought. I think now that he wanted to show me a place he had climbed to as a boy, a view that had been his father's, and his, and would be mine. But I was *not* him. I had not learned to take that height, that being set apart as my own: a white girl, not a boy.

And yet I know I have been shaped by my relation to those buildings, and to the people in the buildings, by ideas of who should be working in the board of education, of who should be in the bank handling money, of who should have the guns and the keys to the jail, of who should be *in* the jail; I have been shaped by what I didn't see, or didn't notice, on those streets.

Each of us carries around with us those growing-up places, the institutions, a sort of backdrop, a stage-set. So often we act out the present against a backdrop of the past, within a frame of perception that is so familiar, so safe that it is terrifying to risk changing it even when we know our perceptions are distorted, limited, constricted by that old view.

So this is one gain for me as I change: I learn a way of looking at the world that is more accurate, complex, multilayered, multidimensioned, more truthful: to see the world of overlapping circles, like movement on the millpond after a fish has jumped, instead of the courthouse square with me in the middle. I feel the *need* to look differently because I've learned that what is presented to me as an accurate view of the world is frequently a lie: so that to look through an anthology of women's studies that has little or no work by women of color is to be up on that ledge above the town and be thinking that I see the town, without realizing how many lives have been pushed out of sight, beside unpaved roads. I'm learning that what I think that I *know* is an accurate view of the world is frequently a lie: as when I was in a discussion about the Women's Pentagon Action with several women, four of us Christian-raised, one Jewish. In describing the march through Arlington Cemetery, one of the four mentioned the rows of crosses. I had marched for a long time through that cemetery; I nodded to myself, visualized rows of crosses. No, said the Jewish woman, they were headstones, with crosses or Stars of David engraved above the names. We four objected; we had all seen crosses. The Jewish woman had some photographs of the march through the cemetery, laid them on the table. We saw rows and rows of rectangular gravestones, and in the foreground, clearly visible, one inscribed with a name and a Star of David.

So I gain truth when I expand my constricted eye, an eye that has only let in what I have been taught to see. But there have been other constrictions: the fear around my heart when I must deal with the *fact* of folk who exist, with their own lives, in other places besides the narrow circle I was raised in. I have learned that my fear of these folks is kin to a terror that has been in my birth culture for years, for centuries, the terror of people who have set themselves apart and *above*, who have wronged others and feel they are about to be found out and punished. It is the terror that in my culture has been expressed in lies about dirty Jews who kill for blood, sly Arab hordes who murder, brutal Indians who massacre, animal blacks who rise in rebellion in the middle of the night and slaughter. It is the terror that has *caused* the slaughter of all these peoples. It is the terror that was my father with his stack of John Birch newspapers, his belief in a Communist-Jewish-Black conspiracy. It is the desperate terror, the knowledge that something is *wrong,* and tries to end fear by attack.

I get afraid when I am trying to understand myself in relation to folks different from me, when there are discussions, conflicts about anti-Semitism and racism among women, criticisms, criticisms of *me;* when, for instance, in a group discussion about race and class, I say I feel we have talked too much about race, not enough about class, and a woman of color asks me in anger and pain if I don't think her skin has something to do with class; when, for instance, I say carelessly to a Jewish friend that there were no Jews where I grew up, she begins to ask me: How do I know? Do I hear what I'm saying? and I get afraid; when I feel my racing heart, breath, the tightening of my skin around me, literally defenses to protect my narrow circle, I try to say to myself: yes, that fear is there, but I will try to be at the edge between my fear and the outside, on the edge at my skin, listening, asking what new thing will I hear, will I see, will I let myself feel, beyond the fear. I try to say to myself: that to acknowledge the complexity of another's existence is not to deny my own. I try to say: when I acknowledge what my people, what those who are like me, have done to people with less power and less safety in the world, I can make a place for things to be different, a place where I can feel grief, sorrow, not to be sorry *for* the others, but to mourn, to expand my circle of self, follow my need to loosen the constrictions of fear, be a break in the cycle of fear and attack.

To be caught within the narrow circle of the self is not just a fearful thing, it is a *lonely* thing. When I could not climb the steps that day with my father, maybe I knew on some level that my place was with women, not with men, that I did not want his view of the world. Certainly, I have felt this more and more strongly since my coming out as a lesbian. Yet so much has separated me from other women, ways in which my culture set me apart by race, by ethnicity, by class. I understood abruptly one day how lonely this made me when a friend, a black woman, spoke to me casually in our shared office: and I heard how she said my name: the lingering accent, so much like how my name is said at home. Yet I knew enough of her history and mine to know how much separated us: the chasm of murders, rapes, lynchings, the years of daily humiliations done by

my people to hers. I went and stood in the hallway and cried, thinking of how she said my name like home, and how divided our lives were.

It is a pain I come to over and over again when, for instance, I realize how *habitually* I think of my culture, my ethics, my morality, as the culmination of history, as the logical extension of what has gone before; the kind of thinking represented by my use, in the past, of the word *Judeo-Christian,* as if Jewish history and lives have existed only to culminate in Christian culture, the kind of thinking that the U.S. government is using now to promote Armageddon in the Middle East; the kind of thinking that I did until recently about Indian lives and culture in my region, as if Indian peoples have existed only in museums since white folks came in the 1500s; the kind of thinking that separates me from women in cultures different from mine, makes their experience less central, less important than mine. It is painful to keep understanding this separation, within myself and in the world. Yet I have felt that the need to be with other women can be the breaking through the shell around me, painful, but a coming through into a new place, where with understanding and change, the loneliness won't be necessary.

If we have these things to gain, and more, by struggling against racism and anti-Semitism in ourselves, what keeps us from doing so, at any one moment, what keeps us from action? In part, I know I hesitate because I have struggled painfully, for years, to make this new place for myself with other women, and I hesitate to disrupt it.

In part I hesitate because the process of uncovering my complicity is so painful: it is the stripping down, layer after layer, of my identity: skin, blood, heart: to find out how much of what I am has been shaped by my skin and family, to find out which of my thoughts and actions I need to change, which I need to keep as my own. Sometimes I fear that stripping away the layers will bring me to nothing, that the only values that I and my culture have are based on negativity, exclusion, fear.

Often I have thought: *what* of who I am is worth saving? worth taking into the future? But I have learned that as the process of shaping identity was long, so the process of change is long. I know that change speeds up the more able I am to put into material shape what I have learned from struggling with anti-Semitism and racism, to begin to act for change can widen perception, loosen fear, ease loneliness. I know that we can choose to act in ways that get us closer to the longed-for but unrealized world, a world where we each are able to live, but not by trying to make someone less than us, not by someone else's blood or pain.   [1984]

 78

White Privilege: Unpacking the Invisible Backpack

PEGGY MCINTOSH

Through work to bring materials from Women's Studies into the rest of the curriculum, I have often noticed men's unwillingness to grant that they are over-privileged, even though they may grant that women are disadvantaged. They may say they will work to improve women's status, in the society, the university, or the curriculum, but they can't or won't support the idea of lessening men's. Denials which amount to taboos surround the subject of advantages which men gain from women's disadvantages. These denials protect male privilege from being fully acknowledged, lessened or ended.

Thinking through unacknowledged male privilege as a phenomenon, I realized that since hierarchies in our society are interlocking, there was most likely a phenomenon of white privilege which was similarly denied and protected. As a white person, I realized I had been taught about racism as something which puts others at a disadvantage, but had been taught not to see one of its corollary aspects, white privilege, which puts me at an advantage.

I think whites are carefully taught not to recognize white privilege, as males are taught not to recognize male privilege. So I have begun in an untutored way to ask what it is like to have white privilege. I have come to see white privilege as an invisible package of unearned assets which I can count on cashing in each day, but about which I was 'meant' to remain oblivious. White privilege is like an invisible weightless backpack of special provisions, maps, passports, codebooks, visas, clothes, tools and blank checks.

Describing white privilege makes one newly accountable. As we in Women's Studies work to reveal male privilege and ask men to give up some of their power, so one who writes about having white privilege must ask, "Having described it, what will I do to lessen or end it?"

After I realized the extent to which men work from a base of unacknowledged privilege, I understood that much of their oppressiveness was unconscious. Then I remembered the frequent charges from women of color that white women whom they encounter are oppressive. I began to understand why we are justly seen as oppressive, even when we don't see ourselves that way. I began to count the ways in which I enjoy unearned skin privilege and have been conditioned into oblivion about its existence.

My schooling gave me no training in seeing myself as an oppressor, as an unfairly advantaged person, or as a participant in a damaged culture. I was taught to see myself as an individual whose moral state depended on her individual moral will. My schooling followed the pattern my colleague Elizabeth Minnich has pointed out: whites are taught to think of their lives as morally neutral, normative, and average, and also ideal, so that when we work to benefit others, this is seen as work which will allow "them" to be more like "us."

I decided to try to work on myself at least by identifying some of the daily effects of white privilege in my life. I have chosen those conditions which I think in my case *attach somewhat more to skin-color privilege* than to class, religion, ethnic status, or geographical location, though of course all these other factors are intricately intertwined. As far as I can see, my African American co-workers, friends and acquaintances with whom I come into daily or frequent contact in this particular time, place, and line of work cannot count on most of these conditions.

1. I can if I wish arrange to be in the company of people of my race most of the time.

2. If I should need to move, I can be pretty sure of renting or purchasing housing in an area which I can afford and in which I would want to live.

3. I can be pretty sure that my neighbors in such a location will be neutral or pleasant to me.

4. I can go shopping alone most of the time, pretty well assured that I will not be followed or harassed.

5. I can turn on the television or open to the front page of the paper and see people of my race widely represented.

6. When I am told about our national heritage or about "civilization," I am shown that people of my color made it what it is.

7. I can be sure that my children will be given curricular materials that testify to the existence of their race.

8. If I want to, I can be pretty sure of finding a publisher for this piece on white privilege.

9. I can go into a music shop and count on finding the music of my race represented, into a supermarket and find the staple foods which fit with my cultural traditions, into a hairdresser's shop and find someone who can cut my hair.

10. Whether I use checks, credit cards, or cash, I can count on my skin color not to work against the appearance of financial reliability.

11. I can arrange to protect my children most of the time from people who might not like them.

12. I can swear, or dress in second hand clothes, or not answer letters, without having people attribute these choices to the bad morals, the poverty, or the illiteracy of my race.

13. I can speak in public to a powerful male group without putting my race on trial.

14. I can do well in a challenging situation without being called a credit to my race.

15. I am never asked to speak for all the people of my racial group.

16. I can remain oblivious of the language and customs of persons of color who constitute the world's majority without feeling in my culture any penalty for such oblivion.

17. I can criticize our government and talk about how much I fear its policies and behavior without being seen as a cultural outsider.

18. I can be pretty sure that if I ask to talk to "the person in charge," I will be facing a person of my race.

19. If a traffic cop pulls me over or if the IRS audits my tax return, I can be sure I haven't been singled out because of my race.

20. I can easily buy posters, postcards, picture books, greeting cards, dolls, toys, and children's magazines featuring people of my race.

21. I can go home from most meetings of organizations I belong to feeling somewhat tied in, rather than isolated, out-of-place, outnumbered, unheard, held at a distance, or feared.

22. I can take a job with an affirmative action employer without having co-workers on the job suspect that I got it because of race.

23. I can choose public accommodation without fearing that people of my race cannot get in or will be mistreated in the places I have chosen.

24. I can be sure that if I need legal or medical help, my race will not work against me.

25. If my day, week, or year is going badly, I need not ask of each negative episode or situation whether it has racial overtones.

26. I can choose blemish cover or bandages in "flesh" color and have them more or less match my skin.

I repeatedly forgot each of the realizations on this list until I wrote it down. For me white privilege has turned out to be an elusive and fugitive subject. The pressure to avoid it is great, for in facing it I must give up the myth of meritocracy. If these things are true, this is not such a free country; one's life is not what one makes it; many doors open for certain people through no virtues of their own.

In unpacking this invisible backpack of white privilege, I have listed conditions of daily experience which I once took for granted. Nor did I think of any of these perquisites as bad for the holder. I now think that we need a more finely differentiated taxonomy of privilege, for some of these varieties are only what one would want for everyone in a just society, and others give licence to be ignorant, oblivious, arrogant and destructive.

I see a pattern running through the matrix of white privilege, a pattern of assumptions which were passed on to me as a white person. There was one main piece of cultural turf; it was my own turf, and I was among those who could control the turf. *My skin color was an asset for any move I was educated to want to make.* I could think of myself as belonging in major ways, and of making social systems work for me. I could freely disparage, fear, neglect, or be oblivious to anything outside of the dominant cultural forms. Being of the main culture, I could also criticize it fairly freely.

In proportion as my racial group was being made confident, comfortable, and oblivious, other groups were likely being made inconfident, uncomfortable, and alienated. Whiteness protected me from many kinds of hostility, distress, and violence, which I was being subtly trained to visit in turn upon people of color.

For this reason, the word "privilege" now seems to me misleading. We usually think of privilege as being a favored state, whether earned or conferred by birth or luck. Yet some of the conditions I have described here work to systematically overempower certain groups. Such privilege simply *confers dominance* because of one's race or sex.

I want, then, to distinguish between earned strength and unearned power conferred systematically. Power from unearned privilege can look like strength when it is in fact permission to escape or to dominate. But not all of the privileges on my list are inevitably damaging. Some, like the expectation that neighbors will be decent to you, or that your race will not count against you in court, should be the norm in a just society. Others, like the privilege to ignore less powerful people, distort the humanity of the holders as well as the ignored groups.

We might at least start by distinguishing between positive advantages which we can work to spread, and negative types of advantages which unless rejected will always reinforce our present hierarchies. For example, the feeling that one belongs within the human circle, as Native Americans say, should not be seen as privilege for a few. Ideally it is an *unearned entitlement.* At present, since only a few have it, it is an *unearned advantage* for them. This paper results from a process of coming to see that some of the power which I originally saw as attendant on being a human being in the U.S. consisted in *unearned advantage* and *conferred dominance.*

I have met very few men who are truly distressed about systemic, unearned male advantage and con-

ferred dominance. And so one question for me and others like me is whether we will be like them, or whether we will get truly distressed, even outraged, about unearned race advantage and conferred dominance and if so, what we will do to lessen them. In any case, we need to do more work in identifying how they actually affect our daily lives. Many, perhaps most, of our white students in the U.S. think that racism doesn't affect them because they are not people of color; they do not see "whiteness" as a racial identity. In addition, since race and sex are not the only advantaging systems at work, we need similarly to examine the daily experience of having age advantage, or ethnic advantage, or physical ability, or advantage related to nationality, religion, or sexual orientation.

Difficulties and dangers surrounding the task of finding parallels are many. Since racism, sexism, and heterosexism are not the same, the advantaging associated with them should not be seen as the same. In addition, it is hard to disentangle aspects of unearned advantage which rest more on social class, economic class, race, religion, sex and ethnic identity than on other factors. Still, all of the oppressions are interlocking, as the Combahee River Collective Statement of 1977 continues to remind us eloquently.

One factor seems clear about all of the interlocking oppressions. They take both active forms which we can see and embedded forms which as a member of the dominant group one is taught not to see. In my class and place, I did not see myself as a racist because I was taught to recognize racism only in individual acts of meanness by members of my group, never in invisible systems conferring unsought racial dominance on my group from birth.

Disapproving of the systems won't be enough to change them. I was taught to think that racism could end if white individuals changed their attitudes. [But] a "white" skin in the United States opens many doors for whites whether or not we approve of the way dominance has been conferred on us. Individual acts can palliate, but cannot end, these problems.

To redesign social systems we need first to acknowledge their colossal unseen dimensions. The silences and denials surrounding privilege are the key political tool here. They keep the thinking about equality or equity incomplete, protecting unearned advantage and conferred dominance by making these taboo subjects. Most talk by whites about equal opportunity seems to me now to be about equal opportunity to try to get into a position of dominance while denying that *systems* of dominance exist.

It seems to me that obliviousness about white advantage, like obliviousness about male advantage, is kept strongly inculturated in the United States so as to maintain the myth of meritocracy, the myth that democratic choice is equally available to all. Keeping most people unaware that freedom of confident action is there for just a small number of people props up those in power, and serves to keep power in the hands of the same groups that have most of it already.

Though systematic change takes many decades, there are pressing questions for me and I imagine for some others like me if we raise our daily consciousness on the perquisites of being light-skinned. What will we do with such knowledge? As we know from watching men, it is an open question whether we will choose to use unearned advantage to weaken hidden systems of advantage, and whether we will use any of our arbitrarily-awarded power to try to reconstruct power systems on a broader base.

[1989]

🌿 79

Age, Race, Class, and Sex: Women Redefining Difference*

AUDRE LORDE

Much of Western European history conditions us to see human differences in simplistic opposition to each other: dominant/subordinate, good/bad, up/

*Paper delivered at the Copeland Colloquium, Amherst College, April 1980.

down, superior/inferior. In a society where the good is defined in terms of profit rather than in terms of human need, there must always be some group of people who, through systematized oppression, can be made to feel surplus, to occupy the place of dehumanized inferior. Within this society, that group is made up of Black and Third World people, working-class people, older people, and women.

As a forty-nine-year-old Black lesbian feminist socialist mother of two, including one boy, and a member of an interracial couple, I usually find myself a part of some group defined as other, deviant, inferior, or just plain wrong. Traditionally, in american society, it is the members of oppressed, objectified groups who are expected to stretch out and bridge the gap between the actualities of our lives and the consciousness of our oppressor. For in order to survive, those of us for whom oppression is as american as apple pie have always had to be watchers, to become familiar with the language and manners of the oppressor, even sometimes adopting them for some illusion of protection. Whenever the need for some pretense of communication arises, those who profit from our oppression call upon us to share our knowledge with them. In other words, it is the responsibility of the oppressed to teach the oppressors their mistakes. I am responsible for educating teachers who dismiss my children's culture in school. Black and Third World people are expected to educate white people as to our humanity. Women are expected to educate men. Lesbians and gay men are expected to educate the heterosexual world. The oppressors maintain their position and evade responsibility for their own actions. There is a constant drain of energy which might be better used in redefining ourselves and devising realistic scenarios for altering the present and constructing the future.

Institutionalized rejection of difference is an absolute necessity in a profit economy which needs outsiders as surplus people. As members of such an economy, we have *all* been programmed to respond to the human differences between us with fear and loathing and to handle that difference in one of three ways: ignore it, and if that is not possible, copy it if we think it is dominant, or destroy it if we think it is subordinate. But we have no patterns for relating across our human differences as equals. As a result, those differences have been misnamed and misused in the service of separation and confusion.

Certainly there are very real differences between us of race, age, and sex. But it is not those differences between us that are separating us. It is rather our refusal to recognize those differences, and to examine the distortions which result from our misnaming them and their effects upon human behavior and expectation.

Racism, the belief in the inherent superiority of one race over all others and thereby the right to dominance. Sexism, the belief in the inherent superiority of one sex over the other and thereby the right to dominance. Ageism. Heterosexism. Elitism. Classism.

It is a lifetime pursuit for each one of us to extract these distortions from our living at the same time as we recognize, reclaim, and define those differences upon which they are imposed. For we have all been raised in a society where those distortions were endemic within our living. Too often, we pour the energy needed for recognizing and exploring difference into pretending those differences are insurmountable barriers, or that they do not exist at all. This results in a voluntary isolation, or false and treacherous connections. Either way, we do not develop tools for using human difference as a springboard for creative change within our lives. We speak not of human difference, but of human deviance.

Somewhere, on the edge of consciousness, there is what I call a *mythical norm,* which each one of us within our hearts knows "that is not me." In america, this norm is usually defined as white, thin, male, young, heterosexual, christian, and financially secure. It is with this mythical norm that the trappings of power reside within this society. Those of us who stand outside that power often identify one way in which we are different, and we assume that to be the primary cause of all oppression, forgetting other distortions around difference, some of which we ourselves may be practicing. By and large within the women's movement today, white women focus upon their oppression as women and ignore differences of race, sexual preference, class, and age. There is a pretense to a homogeneity of experience covered by the word *sisterhood* that does not in fact exist.

Unacknowledged class differences rob women of each others' energy and creative insight. Recently a women's magazine collective made the decision for one issue to print only prose, saying poetry was a less "rigorous" or "serious" art form. Yet even the form our creativity takes is often a class issue. Of all the art forms, poetry is the most economical. It is the one which is the most secret, which requires the least physical labor, the least material, and the one which can be done between shifts, in the hospital pantry, on the subway, and on scraps of surplus paper. Over the last few years, writing a novel on tight finances, I came to appreciate the enormous differences in the material demands between poetry and prose. As we reclaim our literature, poetry has been the major voice of poor, working class, and Colored women. A room of one's own may be a necessity for writing prose, but so are reams of paper, a typewriter, and plenty of time. The actual requirements to produce the visual arts also help determine, along class lines, whose art is whose. In this day of inflated prices for material, who are our sculptors, our painters, our photographers? When we speak of a broadly based women's culture, we need to be aware of the effect of class and economic differences on the supplies available for producing art.

As we move toward creating a society within which we can each flourish, ageism is another distortion of relationship which interferes without vision. By ignoring the past, we are encouraged to repeat its mistakes. The "generation gap" is an important social tool for any repressive society. If the younger members of a community view the older members as contemptible or suspect or excess, they will never be able to join hands and examine the living memories of the community, nor ask the all important question, "Why?" This gives rise to a historical amnesia that keeps us working to invent the wheel every time we have to go to the store for bread.

We find ourselves having to repeat and relearn the same old lessons over and over that our mothers did because we do not pass on what we have learned, or because we are unable to listen. For instance, how many times has this all been said before? For another, who would have believed that once again our daughters are allowing their bodies to be hampered and purgatoried by girdles and high heels and hobble skirts?

Ignoring the differences of race between women and the implications of those differences presents the most serious threat to the mobilization of women's joint power.

As white women ignore their built-in privilege of whiteness and define *woman* in terms of their own experience alone, then women of Color become "other," the outsider whose experience and tradition is too "alien" to comprehend. An example of this is the signal absence of the experience of women of Color as a resource for women's studies courses. The literature of women of Color is seldom included in women's literature courses and almost never in other literature courses, nor in women's studies as a whole. All too often, the excuse given is that the literatures of women of Color can only be taught by Colored women, or that they are too difficult to understand, or that classes cannot "get into" them because they come out of experiences that are "too different." I have heard this argument presented by white women of otherwise quite clear intelligence, women who seem to have no trouble at all teaching and reviewing work that comes out of the vastly different experiences of Shakespeare, Molière, Dostoyefsky, and Aristophanes. Surely there must be some other explanation.

This is a very complex question, but I believe one of the reasons white women have such difficulty reading Black women's work is because of their reluctance to see Black women as women and different from themselves. To examine Black women's literature effectively requires that we be seen as whole people in our actual complexities—as individuals, as women, as human—rather than as one of those problematic but familiar stereotypes provided in this society in place of genuine images of Black women. And I believe this holds true for the literatures of other women of Color who are not Black.

The literatures of all women of Color recreate the textures of our lives, and many white women are heavily invested in ignoring the real differences. For as long as any difference between us means one of us must be inferior, then the recognition of any difference must be fraught with guilt. To allow women of Color to step out of stereotypes is too guilt provoking, for it threatens the complacency of those women who view oppression only in terms of sex.

Refusing to recognize difference makes it impossible to see the different problems and pitfalls facing us as women.

Thus, in a patriarchal power system where white-skin privilege is a major prop, the entrapments used to neutralize Black women and white women are not the same. For example, it is easy for Black women to be used by the power structure against Black men, not because they are men, but because they are Black. Therefore, for Black women, it is necessary at all times to separate the needs of the oppressor from our own legitimate conflicts within our communities. This same problem does not exist for white women. Black women and men have shared racist oppression and still share it, although in different ways. Out of that shared oppression we have developed joint defenses and joint vulnerabilities to each other that are not duplicated in the white community, with the exception of the relationship between Jewish women and Jewish men.

On the other hand, white women face the pitfall of being seduced into joining the oppressor under the pretense of sharing power. This possibility does not exist in the same way for women of Color. The tokenism that is sometimes extended to us is not an invitation to join power; our racial "otherness" is a visible reality that makes that quite clear. For white women there is a wider range of pretended choices and rewards for identifying with patriarchal power and its tools.

Today, with the defeat of ERA, the tightening economy, and increased conservatism, it is easier once again for white women to believe the dangerous fantasy that if you are good enough, pretty enough, sweet enough, quiet enough, teach the children to behave, hate the right people, and marry the right men, then you will be allowed to co-exist with patriarchy in relative peace, at least until a man needs your job or the neighborhood rapist happens along. And true, unless one lives and loves in the trenches it is difficult to remember that the war against dehumanization is ceaseless.

But Black women and our children know the fabric of our lives is stitched with violence and with hatred, that there is no rest. We do not deal with it only on the picket lines, or in dark midnight alleys, or in the places where we dare to verbalize our resistance. For us, increasingly, violence weaves through the daily tissues of our living—in the supermarket, in the classroom, in the elevator, in the clinic and the schoolyard, from the plumber, the baker, the saleswoman, the bus driver, the bank teller, the waitress who does not serve us.

Some problems we share as women, some we do not. You fear your children will grow up to join the patriarchy and testify against you, we fear our children will be dragged from a car and shot down in the street, and you will turn your backs upon the reasons they are dying.

The threat of difference has been no less blinding to people of Color. Those of us who are Black must see that the reality of our lives and our struggle does not make us immune to the errors of ignoring and misnaming difference. Within Black communities where racism is a living reality, differences among us often seem dangerous and suspect. The need for unity is often misnamed as a need for homogeneity, and a Black feminist vision mistaken for betrayal of our common interests as a people. Because of the continuous battle against racial erasure that Black women and Black men share, some Black women still refuse to recognize that we are also oppressed as women, and that sexual hostility against Black women is practiced not only by the white racist society, but implemented within our Black communities as well. It is a disease striking the heart of Black nationhood, and silence will not make it disappear. Exacerbated by racism and the pressures of powerlessness, violence against Black women and children often becomes a standard within our communities, one by which manliness can be measured. But these women-hating acts are rarely discussed as crimes against Black women.

As a group, women of Color are the lowest paid wage earners in america. We are the primary targets of abortion and sterilization abuse, here and abroad. In certain parts of Africa, small girls are still being sewed shut between their legs to keep them docile and for men's pleasure. This is known as female circumcision, and it is not a cultural affair as the late Jomo Kenyatta insisted, it is a crime against Black women.

Black women's literature is full of the pain of frequent assault, not only by a racist patriarchy, but also by Black men. Yet the necessity for and history of shared battle have made us, Black women, particularly vulnerable to the false accusation that anti-sexist is anti-Black. Meanwhile, womanhating as a recourse of the powerless is sapping strength from Black communities, and our very lives. Rape is on the increase, reported and unreported, and rape is not aggressive sexuality, it is sexualized aggression. As Kalamu ya Salaam, a Black male writer points out, "As long as male domination exists, rape will exist. Only women revolting and men made conscious of their responsibility to fight sexism can collectively stop rape."*

Differences between ourselves as Black women are also being misnamed and used to separate us from one another. As a Black lesbian feminist comfortable with the many different ingredients of my identity, and a woman committed to racial and sexual freedom from oppression, I find I am constantly being encouraged to pluck out some one aspect of myself and present this as the meaningful whole, eclipsing or denying the other parts of self. But this is a destructive and fragmenting way to live. My fullest concentration of energy is available to me only when I integrate all the parts of who I am, openly, allowing power from particular sources of my living to flow back and forth freely through all my different selves, without the restrictions of externally imposed definition. Only then can I bring myself and my energies as a whole to the service of those struggles which I embrace as part of my living.

A fear of lesbians, or of being accused of being a lesbian, has led many Black women into testifying against themselves. It has led some of us into destructive alliances, and others into despair and isolation. In the white women's communities, heterosexism is sometimes a result of identifying with the white patriarchy, a rejection of that interdependence between women-identified women which allows the self to be, rather than to be used in the service of men. Sometimes it reflects a die-hard belief in the protective coloration of heterosexual relationships, sometimes a self-hate which all women have to fight against, taught us from birth.

Although elements of these attitudes exist for all women, there are particular resonances of heterosexism and homophobia among Black women. Despite the fact that woman-bonding has a long and honorable history in the African and African-

---

*From "Rape: A Radical Analysis, An African-American Perspective" by Kalamu ya Salaam in *Black Books Bulletin,* vol. 6, no. 4 (1980).

american communities, and despite the knowledge and accomplishments of many strong and creative women-identified Black women in the political, social and cultural fields, heterosexual Black women often tend to ignore or discount the existence and work of Black lesbians. Part of this attitude has come from an understandable terror of Black male attack within the close confines of Black society, where the punishment for any female self-assertion is still to be accused of being a lesbian and therefore unworthy of the attention or support of the scarce Black male. But part of this need to misname and ignore Black lesbians comes from a very real fear that openly women-identified Black women who are no longer dependent upon men for their self-definition may well reorder our whole concept of social relationships.

Black women who once insisted that lesbianism was a white woman's problem now insist that Black lesbians are a threat to Black nationhood, are consorting with the enemy, are basically un-Black. These accusations, coming from the very women to whom we look for deep and real understanding, have served to keep many Black lesbians in hiding, caught between the racism of white women and the homophobia of their sisters. Often, their work has been ignored, trivialized, or misnamed, as with the work of Angelina Grimke, Alice Dunbar-Nelson, Lorraine Hansberry. Yet women-bonded women have always been some part of the power of Black communities, from our unmarried aunts to the amazons of Dahomey.

And it is certainly not Black lesbians who are assaulting women and raping children and grandmothers on the streets of our communities.

Across this country, as in Boston during the spring of 1979 following the unsolved murders of twelve Black women, Black lesbians are spearheading movements against violence against Black women.

What are the particular details within each of our lives that can be scrutinized and altered to help bring about change? How do we redefine difference for all women? It is not our differences which separate women, but our reluctance to recognize those differences and to deal effectively with the distortions which have resulted from the ignoring and misnaming of those differences.

As a tool of social control, women have been encouraged to recognize only one area of human difference as legitimate, those differences which exist between women and men. And we have learned to deal across those differences with the urgency of all oppressed subordinates. All of us have had to learn to live or work or coexist with men, from our fathers on. We have recognized and negotiated these differences, even when this recognition only continued the old dominant/subordinate mode of human relationship, where the oppressed must recognize the masters' difference in order to survive.

But our future survival is predicated upon our ability to relate within equality. As women, we must root out internalized patterns of oppression within ourselves if we are to move beyond the most superficial aspects of social change. Now we must recognize differences among women who are our equals, neither inferior nor superior, and devise ways to use each other's difference to enrich our visions and our joint struggles.

The future of our earth may depend upon the ability of all women to identify and develop new definitions of power and new patterns of relating across difference. The old definitions have not served us, nor the earth that supports us. The old patterns, no matter how cleverly rearranged to imitate progress, still condemn us to cosmetically altered repetitions of the same old exchanges, the same old guilt, hatred, recrimination, lamentation, and suspicion.

For we have, built into all of us, old blueprints of expectations and response, old structures of oppression, and these must be altered at the same time as we alter the living conditions which are a result of those structures. For the master's tools will never dismantle the master's house. As Paulo Freire shows so well in *The Pedagogy of the Oppressed*,* the true focus of revolutionary change is never merely the oppressive situations which we seek to escape, but that piece of the oppressor which is planted deep within each of us, and which knows only the oppressors' tactics, the oppressors' relationships.

Change means growth, and growth can be pain-

---

* Seabury Press, New York, 1970.

ful. But we sharpen self-definition by exposing the self in work and struggle together with those whom we define as different from ourselves, although sharing the same goals. For Black and white, old and young, lesbian and heterosexual women alike, this can mean new paths to our survival.

We have chosen each other
and the edge of each others battles
the war is the same

if we lose
someday women's blood will congeal
upon a dead planet
if we win
there is no telling
we seek beyond history
for a new and more possible meeting.*   [1980]

———————————

*From "Outlines," unpublished poem.

PART VI

The Consequences of Sexism:
Current Issues

As women speak about the realities of our lives, shattering the myths that have surrounded female experience, issues emerge that have previously been hidden or ignored. Some of the issues facing contemporary women have been discussed earlier in this book. In Part VI, we focus on three areas that have not been fully explored: aging, reproductive health, and violence against women. The implications of the attitudes, policies, and practices we have considered earlier become clear as we look at the meaning of aging for women today, the violence we face in our homes and in the streets, and our diminishing ability to control our reproductive lives.

For example, the disadvantaged position of women in the work force and the lack of financial compensation for women's work in the home results in far more women over 65 living in poverty than their male contemporaries. As the article by the Older Women's League points out, women living alone are disproportionately represented among the elderly poor, and their poverty often results in inadequate health care. Old women who live alone are often the victims of criminals and indifferent and paternalistic social service and health care agencies. Improving the position of all women in the work force will address some of these problems. But changes in social policy will be required to provide adequate health care and pensions for people who have spent much of their lives outside the work force, and to ensure that affordable housing is available for the thousands of old women living alone.

The emphasis on physical beauty as a measure of female worth, and the popular equation of female beauty with youthfulness, contribute to the marginalization of old women. While aging men are often considered "distinguished," women are offered a panoply of cosmetics, surgery, and hair products to camouflage their age. As Cynthia Rich points out, even language trivializes old women's actions. While usually not meant maliciously, phrases such as "little old lady" demean and belittle old women. Despite the disdain they often encounter, however, old women, like Basha and her friends at the Senior Center studied by Barbara Meyerhoff, treat aging as a challenge for which they develop ingenious coping strategies. Meyerhoff's study suggests that women's experience in providing for their daily needs and those of their families enables them to adapt more easily to aging.

As Margaret Sanger said in 1914, "enforced motherhood is the most complete denial of a woman's right to life and liberty."[1] Women have tried to control their reproductive lives throughout history, sharing contraceptive and abortion information among themselves. In the early twentieth century, Sanger led the crusade to legalize birth control and improve the contraceptive technology available to women. Undeterred by arrests and harassment, she and other crusaders succeeded in establishing birth control clinics throughout the country and legalizing the distribution of birth control information and devices.

While birth control was widely used by the 1960s, some states still restricted its use until the Supreme Court declared such restrictions unconstitutional in 1965 (*Griswold v. Connecticut*). As we showed in the discussion of women and the law (Part IV), in *Roe v. Wade,* the Supreme Court in 1973 drew on the "right to privacy"

---

[1] Margaret Sanger, *The Woman Rebel,* 1914, p. 25.

ideas articulated in the *Griswold* decision to declare unconstitutional state laws that criminalized abortion. Since 1973, women's reproductive rights have been under fierce attack, and the Supreme Court has retreated from its support of all women's right to choose.

The activities of the anti-abortion movement have brought reproductive rights to the center of the political stage in the last decade. Opponents of abortion have harassed abortion clinics and doctors who perform abortion, pressured legislatures to limit abortions, and succeeded in getting the Republican Party to adopt an anti-abortion platform. The advocates of women's reproductive rights call themselves the "pro-choice" movement, emphasizing a woman's right to choose when she has a child. The anti-abortion forces have called themselves the "right to life" movement, contending that human life exists from the moment of conception. Beneath this argument lie conflicting views of sexuality, women's role in society, and individual liberty. As Kristin Luker has shown in *Abortion and the Politics of Motherhood,* most activists in the "right to life" movement adhere to traditional views about women's role, believe that sexuality should be confined to the family, and that women's most important role is motherhood.[2] Advocates of women's right to choose believe that these decisions should be made by individual women, and that all women have a right to choose how we live, with whom we have sex, and when and if we have children. The debate about abortion is inextricably entangled with the broader debate about women's position in society.

Although the majority of Americans favor legal abortion, the "right to life" movement has succeeded in severely curtailing women's access to abortion. Several states have restricted women's right to abortion in various ways, including parental consent requirements for minors. Abortion services are becoming more difficult to obtain because harassment of clinics and doctors has reduced the number of doctors who will perform abortion. Without access to abortion services, the legal right is meaningless. For this reason Byllye Avery, founder of the National Black Woman's Health Project, has urged feminists to speak of reproductive *health,* which includes both the right to make decisions about one's reproductive life and access to the services required to make that right a reality.

As the selections in Part VI make clear, returning to the days of illegal abortion would not eliminate abortion; women would continue to try to control their reproductive lives and would find illegal and sometimes unsafe ways to accomplish their goal. Because they would have even less access to safe abortions than they do today, it is poor women who would suffer. Since many women of color are poor, a majority of the women who died of illegal abortions before *Roe v. Wade* were women of color. Women of color have also been denied control of their reproductive lives through involuntary sterilization. Believing that poor women of color were having too many babies, doctors in poor communities, often supported by federal funds, have sterilized thousands of women (as they were delivering babies) without their informed consent. Latina, African-American, and Native American women pressured govern-

---

[2] Kristin Luker, *Abortion and the Politics of Motherhood* (Berkeley: University of California Press, 1984).

ment agencies to establish guidelines to protect women from being deprived of their rights through sterilization abuse.

The anti-choice forces in the United States, in asserting the right of the state to control the behavior of pregnant women, are not only elevating the fetus to the status of human life, but relegating the woman to the status of carrier, or, as the writer Katha Pollitt puts it, "potting soil."[3] As Ruth Hubbard points out in her article, however, the concern for fetal life that allegedly motivates the regulation of pregnant women's behavior appears hypocritical when little is being done to improve the social and economic conditions of poverty that endanger so many babies.

Violence against women, while it has existed for centuries, has been hidden behind the cloak of privacy that has surrounded the family. The feminist insistence on the political nature of private life has enabled women to talk about the experience of violence, revealing how widespread it is. As the selections make clear, women of all backgrounds have experienced violence, often at the hands of men they love.

The roots of violence against women lie in the soil of the patriarchal family. The belief that a wife is the possession of a male head of household who should control the behavior of all other family members is deeply embedded in the traditions of our society. Women's disadvantaged position in the work force and their continued responsibility for raising children reinforces their economic dependence on their husbands, making it difficult for women to leave abusive relationships. For years, domestic violence eluded the criminal justice system because police were reluctant to interfere in family life. Women who have been trained all their lives to believe that they should adjust to men's needs and fix any problems that arise in their relationships are often trapped in violent relationships by their own feelings of guilt and shame.

In the past two decades, women have organized to make the criminal justice system more effective in dealing with domestic violence by educating police and changing laws to ensure that women get the protection they need from law enforcement agencies. Women have also organized a network of shelters for women who are fleeing abusive relationships, but these shelters can only house a fraction of those who need them. Today, violence against women is more openly discussed than it was in the recent past, and victims are more likely to know where to turn for help. Despite these advances, however, violence remains a part of the lives of thousands of women.

Sexual violence affects the lives of all women. The fear of rape shapes women's behavior from childhood, restricting our movements and limiting our freedom. But despite the precautions women learn to take, thousands of women and girls are raped and molested each year. In 1992 alone, 109,062 rapes were reported to the FBI. Rape is, however, a grossly underreported crime, and estimates of the actual number of rapes in the U.S. range from 200,000 to 900,000 annually. Researchers estimate that somewhere between 15% and 40% of women are victims of rape or attempted rape during their lifetime.[4]

---

[3] Katha Pollitt, "The New Assault on Feminism," *The Nation,* March 26, 1990, p. 418.
[4] Committee on Children, Youth, and Families of the House of Representatives, *Fact Sheet on Rape* (Washington, DC: 1988).

Despite its pervasiveness, women's experience of sexual violence was, until recently, rarely discussed in public. In 1979, Susan Griffin's article, "Rape: The All American Crime," which begins the final section, broke the silence about rape and called attention to the ways that images of sexual violence pervade Western culture. Susan Brownmiller's comprehensive study *Against Our Will*, continued this investigation, tracing the history of rape in Western culture and demonstrating that far from being a problem of individual psychopaths, sexual violence against women has been reinforced by our legal and criminal justice systems and prevailing ideas about gender and sexuality.[5] The belief that women are the sexual property of men is still alive today, embodied in the statutes of the thirty-six states in which it is legal for a man to rape his wife. The notion that women are responsible for male sexual behavior is reflected in the humiliating questions rape victims are often asked about their sexual histories and contributes to the low rate of conviction in rape trials.

Racism has shaped the experience of rape in our culture, from the systematic rape of African-American women in slavery to the false charges of rape that were used as a pretext for lynching African-American men in the South in the early twentieth century. African-American rape victims are less frequently believed by white juries and African-American men are more frequently convicted. The popular myth of the black rapist clouds the reality that most rapes are committed by men who are of the same race as their victims.

Among the myriad misconceptions that surround the subject of rape is the notion that most rapes are committed by strangers. In fact, researchers estimate that 60–80% of all rapes are acquaintance rapes and, as Robin Warshaw shows, many of them are in dating situations. The traditions of sexual conquest, in which women are seen as sexual objects and male sexuality is assumed to be uncontrollable, make it particularly difficult for the victims of date rape to speak out and be taken seriously. Male culture on college campuses, particularly in fraternities, has encouraged the treatment of women as sexual prey and celebrated male lust. Wherever it occurs, rape is an expression of women's subordinate status. To combat it, we must assert our right to say no to unwanted sex and to be seen as sexual actors, not objects.

The sexual abuse of young girls by a trusted adult is another form of sexual violence that has surfaced in horrifying proportions in recent years. Researchers estimate that one in four girls are victims of sexual abuse. Girls are often painfully confused when molested by an adult from whom they crave affection and approval. Feelings of betrayal often follow women into adulthood. Like the other forms of sexual violence, the molestation of young girls is a violation of female bodily integrity and a cruel exercise of power.

Because they confront us with some of most horrifying consequences of sexism, the selections that follow are upsetting. However, acknowledging the contempt with which women have often been treated enables us to take action against it, as the women described in the next two parts of this book have done.

---

[5] Susan Brownmiller, *Against Our Will: Men, Women, and Rape* (New York: Simon & Schuster, 1975).

Aging

Aging is a painful process for many midlife and older women whose lives are marked by vulnerability to poverty, crime, poor health, and inadequate housing. The selections in this section address these realities, focusing on the general living conditions of many older women, as well as the personal experiences of older women who are struggling on their own.

We begin with an overview of the economic, social, and health concerns of older women. These data, collected by the Older Women's League, document the realities of many older women's lives. A national membership organization in Washington, DC, the Older Women's League is dedicated to achieving economic, political, and social equity for midlife and older women through education, research, and public advocacy. The Older Women's League advocates for a national, universal health care system, reform of the Social Security system, and government policies to end discrimination at work and to provide affordable housing for older women.

Another aspect of older women's vulnerability is depicted in "The Women in the Tower," which recounts the struggles of older black women to obtain adequate security in their apartment building. As these women make their needs and rights known to the housing authority, the media present them in stereotypically negative terms, casting them as insignificant and diminishing their efforts.

Old women are often caught between their desire for independence and their physical fragility. In the last two selections, we hear the experiences of Basha, a Jewish woman who attends a senior citizens' program at the Aliyah Center, and Nani, who lives alone in Los Angeles. Both women strive to maintain their autonomy despite the changes in their lives, such as poor health and a fixed income.

 80

The Realities of Older Women's Lives

OLDER WOMEN'S LEAGUE

INTRODUCTION

For many women, the discrimination which they face as young women becomes magnified as they age. Despite attempts by the media and others to pit the young against the old and to portray the elderly as financially secure and greedy, the Older Women's League (OWL) knows differently. These are myths which are as ugly and crippling as they are false. They mask the realities of women's lives and enable policymakers and society to ignore the needs posed by this vulnerable group of citizens. To the extent that national leaders accept this image of old age as a life of leisure and affluence, America is enacting laws based on fairy tales.

Older women are much less likely to reap the economic benefits from a lifetime of work than men. They are more likely to live in poverty and isolation. Rather than being cared for, they are likely to continue to sacrifice their health and their livelihood to care for others.

The disturbing truth is that four out of every ten older women are poor or near poor. The median income for women age 65 and older in 1990 was $8,044. The mere fact that one is a woman increases the chances of being poor by 60%. Of the elderly who are poor, nearly three quarters (72%) are women. If one is Black or Hispanic, the chances of falling below the government's poverty threshold escalate. Approximately one in three Black women are poor, half over age 75 are poor. In 1990 the median annual income for a Black woman over 65 was $5,617 and for a Hispanic woman $5,373.

As a recent U.S. Census Bureau report indicates, women have different prospects as they age than men. Men tend to die earlier than women but if they survive, men are more likely to be healthy, self-sufficient and living with their families rather than alone. Most older men are married while most older women live alone. Of the 9 million elderly living alone, 81% are women. The differences are more stark in the over 85 age group, the fastest growing segment of the population, where women currently outnumber men 5 to 2. Women over age 85 are three times as likely to be poor and twice as likely to be living alone. The Commonwealth Foundation warns that by the year 2020, poverty among elderly Americans will be confined to women living alone. The two-elderly generation-ratio has risen steadily in the past four decades and is projected to continue increasing to 2010. This means that the young-old, primarily women, will increasingly be caring for the old-old, also primarily women.

A woman's income is adversely affected by her continuing responsibilities in the home, whether she is child-rearing or caregiving to a spouse, parents or friends. OWL's 1989 Mother's Day Report, *Failing America's Caregivers,* revealed that a woman can expect to spend 17 years of her life caring for her children and 18 years caring for older family members. Seventy-two percent of the providers of unpaid care to the frail elderly are women and their average age is 57 years old. One-third of these caregivers are over age 65.

Non-entry or late entry into the job market, job interruptions and temporary or part-time employment characterize a woman's employment history when she is the primary caregiver in the family. Such an employment record has a devastating impact on her employment, health, and retirement benefits, as well as her income.

Undervalued in the home and underpaid in the workforce, old age for most women is nothing short of an economic nightmare. And the numbers who will experience that nightmare are increasing.

THE OLDER WOMEN'S LEAGUE: ISSUES AND AGENDA

Health Care

OWL's 1992 Mother's Day Report, *Critical Condition,* made clear that America's health care system is inaccessible to many midlife and older women, because of its connection to employment benefits and the type of health coverage available. Lack of financial resources, changes in marital status, and the inability to obtain decent-paying, full-time work make midlife women especially vulnerable to a loss of health insurance coverage. As a result, 5 million women between the ages of 40 and 45 have no health insurance. Approximately 1.5 million women or 11.5% of women between the ages of 55 and 64 have no health insurance.

Federal law (COBRA) permits some individuals who lose their health insurance to continue group insurance, at their own expense, but that is only for 18 to 36 months. Many with pre-existing conditions are unable to find alternative coverage when this period expires.

Women live longer than men, but they are not necessarily healthier. Older women can expect increased and longer periods of chronic health problems with devastating economic consequences. While men experience acute illness, the chronic nature of older women's health problems places long-term limitations on their everyday activities.

If not already poor, an older woman's health care costs can push her over the brink into poverty. On average, women over 65 spend one-third of their annual income on health care, despite the existence of Medicare. Women are the primary users of long-term care, yet Medicare provides minimal assistance for home care and requires a family to spend

Gender differences

down to near poverty to be reimbursed for institutionalized care. Spouses of institutionalized patients may still experience financial hardship, if not impoverishment. Forty percent of those who need long-term care are under the age of 65, millions of whom are children and disabled adults.

Discrimination in the Workplace and the Image of Midlife and Older Women

Midlife and older women are subject to dual discrimination—sex and age. Midlife and older women comprise a disproportionate share of "discouraged workers" (those who no longer even seek employment, thus do not show up in the unemployment statistics), part-time and seasonal low-paid workers, and those stuck in dead-end jobs. When a midlife or older woman loses her job, she is unemployed longer than a man of the same age.

Although midlife and older women comprise an increasing portion of the workforce, gains in workforce participation will not necessarily mean a decent living or equal opportunity in the workplace of the future.

Today 14 million midlife and older women earn significantly less than men. In 1990, the median earnings of midlife and older women who worked full time were less than two-thirds those of men. Older women tend to be segregated in low-paying jobs in the sales, clerical and service sectors of the economy. Even within female dominated occupations, men earn more than women and move up the career ladder while women stay clustered at the bottom. By the year 2000, 22 million women age 45 and over will hold paying jobs, and likely still earn less than men.

The results of this discrimination are carried into retirement when a woman's Social Security (and pension, if any) are low because of her low pay and lack of fringes while working. This directly results in the fact that almost twice as many women over the age of 65 fall near or below the poverty line than men (23.4% vs. 12.8%).

Pension Coverage

When today's 25-year-old woman retires, after having been employed for as long as 35 years, she can expect to receive the same retirement benefits that her mother received—which are inadequate for both generations.

Today only 27% of older women receive a pension, either public or private, based on their own work record or that of their spouse, compared to 49% of men. Businesses aren't required to have pension plans, and female workers are clustered in those businesses least likely to offer pensions. In addition, women are over-represented among seasonal and part-time workers, jobs that seldom qualify for pension coverage.

Women are also more mobile in the job market, thus decreasing their chances of vesting. The result is that a minority of women receive pension income upon retirement, and of those that do, their pensions average less than half of a man's ($269 vs. $591 a month in 1990).

Women need strong pension income even more than men, because they: (1) have to pay for one-third more retirement years than men; (2) start retirement with a lower financial base; and (3) are six times more likely than men to end their lives single.

Social Security System and SSI

Retirement income is a key concern of older women. Although retirement income security is theoretically sustained by Social Security, pensions, and savings, older women depend primarily on Social Security and, as a last resort, Supplemental Security Income (SSI). Although Social Security is a lifeline for older women, it does not always treat them fairly or adequately, essentially because women's work is undervalued at the workplace and in the home. Older women have less Social Security income than men, approximately $458 a month, compared with $627 for men. Women age 65 or older are more likely to rely on Social Security for their sole source of support than are men of the same age.

Social Security best serves so-called "traditional" families that consist of a lifelong breadwinner, a lifelong homemaker, and two children. Fewer than 10% of American families fit that definition; even fewer will fit it in the future. Social Security discriminates against women by penalizing dual earner families, caregivers, divorced spouses, and people who retire early and live long. Wives who are entitled to both benefits on their own work record and benefits from their husband may collect only one. With women's wages remaining low, most collect from their husband's contribution. Since 1960, the percentage of women receiving a dependent's benefit has remained more than 60 percent, despite more women in the work force.

The current benefit standard for the Supplemental Security Income (SSI) program is $5,064. This represents less than 75% of the poverty level. Only a few states provide enough of a supplement to raise the incomes of SSI recipients over the poverty level. Today's SSI asset limits of less than $2,000 for a single person and $3,000 for a married couple are only $500 more for a single person and $750 more for couples than when the program was established 18 years ago.

Housing

The national housing crisis is very much a midlife and older women's issue. Although 62% of older women living alone own their own homes, homeownership presents hardships: taxes, utilities, and upkeep may leave them impoverished. Midlife and older women have a real need for affordable, accessible, secure housing.

Zoning laws restrict ECHO housing, accessory apartments, collective housing and other innovative forms of housing for the older population. Builders resist spending a few dollars on making minor structural modifications to increase the accessibility of the home to older and disabled residents.

Laws favoring landlords continue to expose older residents to unsafe and uninhabitable rental units. Older women face a growing shortage of affordable rental housing, due in part to government policies of the last 12 years against building affordable housing and rent increases over the rate of inflation. Twenty-two percent of all renters who live alone are older women while only 6% are older men.

CONCLUSION

It would take an unusual woman, indeed, to avoid the lifelong consequences of pay discrimination, inadequate retirement income, and a decline in health. However, a national agenda which includes the positions supported by OWL can mean a healthier and more secure future for 40 million midlife and older women.   [1992]

 81

The Women in the Tower

CYNTHIA RICH

In April, 1982 a group of Black women demand a meeting with the Boston Housing Authority. They are women between the ages of sixty-six and eighty-one. Their lives, in the "housing tower for the elderly" where they live, are in continual danger. "You're afraid to get on the elevator and you're afraid to get off," says Mamie Buggs, sixty-six. Odella Keenan, sixty-nine, is wakened in the nights by men pounding on her apartment door. Katherine Jefferson, eighty-one, put three locks on her door, but "I've come back to my apartment and found a group of men there eating my food."

The menace, the violence, is nothing new, they say. They have reported it before, but lately it has become intolerable. There are pictures in the *Boston Globe* of three of the women, and their eyes flash with anger. "We pay our rent, and we're entitled to some security," says Mamie Buggs. Two weeks ago, a man attacked and beat up Ida Burres, seventy-five, in the recreation room. Her head wound required forty stitches.

"I understand your desire for permanent security," says Lewis Spence, the BHA representative. "But I can't figure out any way that the BHA is going to be offering 24-hour security in an elderly development." He is a white man, probably in his thirties. His picture is much larger than the pictures of the women.

The headline in the *Boston Globe* reads, "Elderly in Roxbury building plead with BHA for 24-hour security." Ida Burres is described in the story as "a feisty, sparrow-like woman with well-cared for gray hair, cafe au lait skin and a lilting voice." The byline reads "Viola Osgood."

I feel that in my lifetime I will not get to the bottom of this story, of these pictures, of these words.

Feisty, sparrow-like, well-cared for gray hair, cafe au lait skin, lilting voice.

Feisty. Touchy, excitable, quarrelsome, like a mongrel dog. "Feisty" is the standard word in newspaperspeak for an old person who says what she thinks. As you grow older, the younger person sees your strongly felt convictions or your protest against an intolerable life situation as an amusing over-reaction, a defect of personality common to mongrels and old people. To insist that you are a person deepens the stigma of your Otherness. Your protest is not a specific, legitimate response to an outside threat. It is a generic and arbitrary quirkiness, coming from the queer stuff within yourself—sometimes annoying, sometimes quaint or even endearing, never, never to be responded to seriously.

Sparrow-like. Imagine for a moment that you have confronted those who have power over you, demanding that they do something to end the terror of your days and nights. You and other women have organized a meeting of protest. You have called the press. Imagine then opening the newspaper and seeing yourself described as "sparrow-like." That is no simple indignity, no mere humiliation. The fact that you can be described as "sparrow-like" is in part why you live in the tower, why nobody attends. Because you do not look like a natural person—that is, a young or middle-aged person—you look like a sparrow. The real sparrow is, after all, a sparrow and is seen merely as homely, but a woman who is sparrow-like is unnatural and ugly.

A white widow tells of smiling at a group of small children on the street and one of them saying, "You're ugly, ugly, ugly." It is what society has imprinted on that child's mind: to be old, and to look old, is to be ugly, so ugly that you do not deserve to live. Crow's feet. Liver spots. The media: "I'm going to wash that gray right out of my hair and wash in my 'natural' color." "Get rid of those unsightly spots." And if you were raised to believe that old is ugly, you play strange tricks in your own head. An upper middle class white woman, a woman with courage and zest for life, writes in 1982: "When we love we do not see our mates as the young view us—wrinkled, misshapen, unattractive." But then she continues: "We still retain, somewhere, the *memory* of one another as beautiful and lustful, and we see each other at our *once-best.*"

Old is ugly and unnatural in a society where power is male-defined, powerlessness disgraceful. A society where natural death is dreaded and concealed, while unnatural death is courted and glori-fied. But old is ugliest for women. A white woman newscaster in her forties remarks to a sportscaster who is celebrating his sixtieth birthday: "What women really resent about men is that *you* get more attractive as you get older." A man is as old as he feels, a woman as old as she looks. You're ugly, ugly, ugly.

Aging has a special stigma for women. When our wombs are no longer ready for procreation, when our vaginas are no longer tight, when we no longer serve men, we are unnatural and ugly. In medical school terminology, we are a "crock"; in the language of the street, we are an "old bag." The Sanskrit word for widow is "empty." But there is more than that.

Sparrow-like. The association of the old woman with a bird runs deep in the male unconscious. Apparently, it flows back to a time when men acknowledged their awe of what they were outsiders to—the interconnected, inseparable mysteries of life and death, self and other, darkness and light. Life begins in genital darkness, comes into light, and returns to darkness as death. The child in the woman's body is both self and other. The power to offer the breast is the power to withhold it. The Yes and the No are inextricable. In the beginning was the Great Mother, mysteriously, powerfully connected to the wholeness of Nature and her indivisible Yeses and Nos. But for those outside the process, the oneness was baffling and intolerable, and the Great Mother was split. Men attempted to divide what they could not control—nature and women's relationship to it. The Great Mother was polarized into separate goddesses or into diametrically opposed aspects of a single goddess. The Good Mother and the Terrible Mother. The Good Mother created life, spread her bounty outward, fertilized the crops, nourished and protected, created healing potions. The Terrible Mother, the original old Witch, dealt in danger and destruction, devoured children as food for herself, concocted poisons. Wombs ≠ tomb, light ≠ darkness, other ≠ self. A world of connectedness was split down the middle.

The Terrible Mother was identified with the winged creatures that feed on mammals: vultures, ravens, owls, crows, bats. Her images in the earliest known culture of India show her as old, birdlike, hideous: "Hooded with a coif or shawl, they have high, smooth foreheads above their staring circular eye holes, their owl-beak nose and grim slit mouth. The result is terrifying . . . the face is a grinning skull."

Unable to partake of the mystery of wholeness represented by the Great Mother, men first divided her, then wrested more and more control of her divided powers. The powerful Good Mother—bounteous life-giver, creator and nurturer of others—became the custodian of children who "belong" to the man or the male state. She can no longer even bear "his" child without the guiding forceps or scalpel of a man. She is the quotidian cook (men are the great chefs) who eats only after she has served others. She is the passive dispenser—as nurse, mother, wife—of the "miracles" of modern medicine created by the brilliance of man.

The Terrible Mother—the "old Woman of the West," guardian of the dead—represented men's fear of the powerful aspect of woman as intimate not only with the mysteries of birth but also of death. Today men are the specialists of death—despite a recent study that suggests that men face natural death with much more anxiety than women do. Today male doctors oversee dying, male priests and rabbis perform the rituals of death, and even the active role of laying out the dead no longer belongs to woman (now the work of male undertakers). Woman is only the passive mourner, the helpless griever. And it is men who vie with each other to invent technologies that can bring about total death and destruction.

The Terrible Mother—the vulture or owl feeding on others—represented the fear of death, but also the fear of woman as existing not only to create and nurture others but to create and nurture her Self. Indeed, the aging woman's body is a clear reminder that women have a self that exists not only for others; it descends into her pelvis as if to claim the womb-space for its own. Woman's Self—her meeting of her own needs, seen by men as destructive and threatening—has been punished and repressed, branded "unnatural" and "unwomanly."

In this century, in rural China, they had a practice called "sunning the jinx." If a child died, or there was some similar misfortune, it was seen as the work of a jinx. The jinx was always an old, poor woman, and she was exposed to the searing heat of the summer sun until she confessed. Like the witches burned throughout Europe in the fifteenth to seventeenth centuries, she was tortured by double-think. If she died without confessing, they had eliminated the jinx. If she confessed her evil powers, she was left in the sun for three more days to "cure her." In Bali today, the Terrible Mother lingers on in magic plays, as Ranga, the witch who eats children, "a huge old woman with drooping breasts and a mat of white hair that comes down to her feet." It is a man who plays her part, and he must be old since only an old man can avoid the evil spirit of the Terrible Mother.

In present-day white culture, men's fear of the Terrible Mother is managed by denial: by insisting on the powerlessness of the old woman, her harmless absurdity and irrelevance. The dread of her power lingers, reduced to farce—as in the Hansel and Gretel story of the old witch about to devour the children until the boy destroys her, or in the comic juxtaposition of Arsenic and Old Lace. The image of her winged power persists, totally trivialized, in the silly witch flying on her broomstick, and in "old bat," "old biddy," "old hen," "old crow," "crow's feet," "old harpy." Until, in April of 1982, an old woman's self-affirmation, her rage at her disempowerment, her determination to die naturally and not at the hands of men, can be diminished to feistiness, and she can be perceived as sparrow-like.

Sparrow-like. Writing for white men, did Viola Osgood unconsciously wish to say, "Ida Burres is not a selfish vulture—even though she is doing what old women are not meant to do, speak for their own interests (not their children's or grandchildren's but their own). She is an innocent sparrow, frail and helpless"? Or had she herself so incorporated that demeaning image—sparrow-like—that she saw Ida Burres through those eyes? Or both?

Well-cared for gray hair. Is that about race? About class? An attempt to dispel the notion that a poor Black woman is unkempt? Would Viola Osgood describe a Black welfare mother in terms of her "well-groomed afro"? Or does she mean to dispel the notion that this *old* woman is unkempt? Only the young can afford to be careless about their hair, their dress. The care that the old woman takes with her appearance is not merely to reduce the stigma of ugly; often it is her most essential tactic for survival: it signals to the person who sees her, I am old, but I am not senile. My hair is gray but it is well-cared for. Because to be old is to be guilty of craziness and incapacity unless proven otherwise.

Cafe au lait skin. Race? Class? Age? Not dark black like Katherine Jefferson, but blackness mitigated. White male reader, who has the power to save these women's lives, you can't dismiss her as Black, poor, old. She is almost all right, she is almost white. She is Black and old, but she has something in common with the young mulatto woman whose skin you have sometimes found exotic and sensual. And she is not the power of darkness that you fear in the Terrible Mother.

A lilting voice. I try to read these words in a lilting voice: "I almost got my eyes knocked out. A crazy guy just came in here and knocked me down and hit me in the face. We need security." These words do not lilt to me. A woman is making a demand, speaking truth to power, affirming her right to live— Black, Old, Poor, Woman. Is the "lilting" to say, "Although her words are strong, although she is bonding with other women, she is not tough and dykey"? Is the "lilting" to say, "Although she is sparrow-like, although she is gray-haired, something of the mannerisms you find pleasing in young women remain, so do not ignore her as you routinely do old women"?

I write this not knowing whether Viola Osgood is Black or white. I know that she is a woman. And I know that it matters whether she is Black or white, that this is not a case of one size fits all. But I know that Black or white, any woman who writes news articles for the *Globe,* or for any mainstream newspaper, is mandated to write to white men, in white men's language. That any messages to women, Black or white, which challenge white men's thinking can at best only be conveyed covertly, subversively. That any messages of appeal to those white men must be phrased in ways that do not seriously threaten their assumptions, and that such language itself perpetuates the power men have assumed for themselves. And I know that Black or white, ageism blows in the wind around us and certainly through

the offices of the *Globe.* I write this guessing that Viola Osgood is Black, because she has known that the story is important, cared enough to make sure the photographer was there. I write this guessing that the story might never have found its way into the *Globe* unless through a Black reporter. Later, I find out that she is Black, thirty-five.

And I think that Viola Osgood has her own story to tell. I think that I, white Jewish woman of fifty, still sorting through to find the realities beneath the lies, denials and ignorance of my lifetime of segregations, cannot write this essay. I think that even when we try to cross the lines meant to separate us as women—old and young, Black and white, Jew and non-Jew—the seeds of division cling to our clothes. And I think this must be true of what I write now. But we cannot stop crossing, we cannot stop writing.

Elderly in Roxbury building plead with BHA for 24-hour security. Doubtless, Viola Osgood did not write the headline. Ten words and it contains two lies—lies that routinely obscure the struggles of old woman. *Elderly.* This is not a story of elderly people, it is the story of old women, Black old women. Three-fifths of the "elderly" are women; almost all of the residents of this tower are women. An old woman has half the income of an old man. One out of three widows—women without the immediate presence of a man—lives below the official poverty line, and most women live one third of their lives as widows. In the United States, as throughout the world, old women are the poorest of the poor. Seven percent of old white men live in poverty, forty-seven percent of old Black women. "The Elderly," "Old People," "Senior Citizens," are inclusive words that blot out these differences. Old women are twice unseen—unseen because they are old, unseen because they are women. Black old women are thrice unseen. "Elderly" conveniently clouds the realities of power and economics. It clouds the convergence of racial hatred and fear, hatred and fear of the aged, hatred and fear of women. It also clouds the power of female bonding, of these women in the tower who are acting together as women for women.

Plead. Nothing that these women say, nothing in their photographs, suggests pleading. These women are angry, and if one can demand where there is no leverage—and one can—they are demanding. They are demanding their lives, to which they know full well they have a right. Their anger is clear, direct, unwavering. "Pleading" erases the force of their confrontation. It allows us to continue to think of old women, if we think of them at all, as meek, cowed, to be pitied, occasionally as amusingly "feisty," but not as outraged, outrageous women. Old women's anger is denied, tamed, drugged, infantilized, trivialized. And yet anger in an old woman is a remarkable act of bravery, so dangerous is her world, and her status in that world so marginal, precarious. Her anger is an act of insubordination—the refusal to accept her subordinate status even when everyone, children, men, younger women, and often other older women, assumes it. "We pay our rent, and we're entitled to some security." When will a headline tell the truth: Old, Black, poor women confront the BHA demanding 24-hour security?

The housing tower for the elderly. A tall building filled with women, courageous women who bond together, but who with every year are less able to defend themselves against male attack. A tower of women under siege. A ghetto within a ghetto. The white male solution to the "problem of the elderly" is to isolate the Terrible Mother.

That tower, however, is not simply architectural. Nor is the male violence an "inner city problem." Ten days later, in nearby Stoughton, a man will have beaten to death an eighty-seven-year-old white woman, leaving her body with "multiple blunt injuries around her face, head, and shoulders." This woman was not living in a housing tower for the elderly. She lived in the house where she was born. "She was very, very spry. She worked in her garden a lot and she drove her own car," reports a neighbor. She had the advantages of race, class, a small home of her own, a car of her own. Nor did she turn away from a world that rejects and demeans old women ("spry," like "feisty," is a segregating and demeaning word). At the time of her murder, she was involved in planning the anniversary celebration at her parish.

Yet she was dead for a week before anyone found her body. Why? The reporter finds it perfectly natural. "She outlived her contemporaries and her circle of immediate relatives." Of course. How natural. Unless we remember de Beauvoir: "One of the ruses of oppression is to camouflage itself behind a natu-

ral situation since, after all, one cannot revolt against nature."* How natural that young people, or even the middle aged, should have nothing in common with an old woman. Unthinkable that she should have formed friendships with anyone who was not in her or his seventies or eighties or nineties. It is natural that without family, who must tolerate the stigma, or other old people who share the stigma, she would have no close ties. And it is natural that no woman, old or young, anywhere in the world, should be safe from male violence.

But it is not natural. It is not natural, and it is dangerous, for younger women to be divided as by a taboo from old women—to live in our own shaky towers of youth. It is intended, but it is not natural that we be ashamed of, dissociated from, our future selves, sharing men's loathing for the women we are daily becoming. It is intended, but it is not natural that we be kept ignorant of our deep bonds with old women. And it is not natural that today, as we reconnect with each other, old women are still an absence for younger women.

As a child—a golden-haired Jew in the segregated South while the barbed wire was going up around the Warsaw ghetto—I was given fairy tales to read. Among them, the story of Rapunzel, the golden-haired young woman confined to a tower by an old witch until she was rescued by a young prince. My hair darkened and now it is light again with gray. I know that I have been made to live unnaturally in a tower for most of my fifty years. My knowledge of my history—as a woman, as a lesbian, as a light-skinned woman in a world of dark-skinned women, as the Other in a Jew-hating world—shut out. My knowledge of my future—as an old woman—shut out.

Today I reject those mythic opposites: young/old, light/darkness, life/death, other/self, Rapunzel/Witch, Good Mother/Terrible Mother. As I listen to the voices of the old women of Warren Tower, and of my aging self, I know that I have always been aging, always been dying. Those voices speak of wholeness: To nurture Self = to defy those who endanger that Self. To declare the I of my unique existence = to assert the We of my connections with

---

*Simone de Beauvoir, *The Ethics of Ambiguity* (New York: Citadel, 1948), p. 83.

other women. To accept the absolute rightness of my natural death = to defend the absolute value of my life. To affirm the mystery of my daily dying and the mystery of my daily living = to challenge men's violent cheapening of both.

But I cannot hear these voices clearly if I am still afraid of the old witch, the Terrible Mother in myself, or if I am estranged from the real old women of this world. For it is not the wicked witch who keeps Rapunzel in her tower. It is the prince and our divided selves.

Note: There was no follow-up article on the women of the tower, but Ida Burres, Mamie Buggs, Mary Gordon, Katherine Jefferson, Odella Keenan, and the other women of Warren Tower, did win what they consider to be adequate security—"of course, it is never all that you could wish," said Vallie Burton, President of the Warren Tower Association. They won because of their own bonding, their demands, and also, no doubt, because of Viola Osgood.   [1983]

 82

The Women of the Aliyah Center

BARBARA MEYERHOFF

Every morning I wake up in pain. I wiggle my toes. Good. They still obey. I open my eyes. Good. I can see. Everything hurts but I get dressed. I walk down to the ocean. Good. It's still there. Now my day can start. About tomorrow I never know. After all, I'm eighty-nine. I can't live forever.

Death and the ocean are protagonists in Basha's life. They provide points of orientation, comforting in their certitude. One visible, the other invisible, neither hostile nor friendly, they accompany her as she walks down the boardwalk to the Aliyah Senior Citizens' Center.

Basha wants to remain independent above all. Her life at the beach depends on her ability to perform a minimum number of basic tasks. She must shop and cook, dress herself, care for her body and her one-room apartment, walk, take the bus to the market and the doctor, be able to make a telephone call in case of emergency. Her arthritic hands have a difficult time with the buttons on her dress. Some days her fingers ache and swell so that she cannot fit them into the holes of the telephone dial. Her hands shake as she puts in her eyedrops for glaucoma. Fortunately, she no longer has to give herself injections for her diabetes. Now it is controlled by pills, if she is careful about what she eats. In the neighborhood there are no large markets within walking distance. She must take the bus to shop. The bus steps are very high and sometimes the driver objects when she tries to bring her little wheeled cart aboard. A small boy whom she has befriended and occasionally pays often waits for her at the bus stop to help her up. When she cannot bring her cart onto the bus or isn't helped up the steps, she must walk to the market. Then shopping takes the better part of the day and exhausts her. Her feet, thank God, give her less trouble since she figured out how to cut and sew a pair of cloth shoes so as to leave room for her callouses and bunions.

Basha's daughter calls her once a week and worries about her mother living alone and in a deteriorated neighborhood. "Don't worry about me, darling. This morning I put the garbage in the oven and the bagels in the trash. But I'm feeling fine." Basha enjoys teasing her daughter whose distant concern she finds somewhat embarrassing. "She says to me, 'Mamaleh, you're sweet but you're so *stupid*.' What else could a greenhorn mother expect from a daughter who is a lawyer?" The statement conveys Basha's simultaneous pride and grief in having produced an educated, successful child whose very accomplishments drastically separate her from her mother. The daughter has often invited Basha to come and live with her, but she refuses.

What would I do with myself there in her big house, alone all day, when the children are at work? No one to talk to. No place to walk. Nobody talks Yiddish. My daughter's husband doesn't like my cooking, so I can't even help with meals. Who needs an old lady around, somebody else for my daughter to take care of? They don't keep the house warm like I like it. When I go to the bathroom at night, I'm afraid to flush, I shouldn't wake anybody up. Here I have lived for thirty-one years. I have my friends. I have the fresh air. Always there are people to talk to on the benches. I can go to the Center whenever I like and always there's something doing there. As long as I can manage for myself, I'll stay here.

Managing means three things: taking care of herself, stretching her monthly pension of three hundred and twenty dollars to cover expenses, and filling her time in ways that have meaning for her. The first two are increasingly hard and she knows that they are battles she will eventually lose. But her free time does not weigh on her. She is never bored and rarely depressed. In many ways, life is not different from before. She has never been well-off, and she never expected things to be easy. When asked if she is happy, she shrugs and laughs. "Happiness by me is a hot cup of tea on a cold day. When you don't get a broken leg, you could call yourself happy." . . .

Basha dresses simply but with care. The purchase of each item of clothing is a major decision. It must last, should be modest and appropriate to her age, but gay and up-to-date. And, of course, it can't be too costly. Basha is not quite five feet tall. She is a sturdy boat of a woman—wide, strong of frame, and heavily corseted. She navigates her great monobosom before her, supported by broad hips and thin, severely bowed legs, their shape the heritage of her malnourished childhood. Like most of the people who belong to the Aliyah Center, her early life in Eastern Europe was characterized by relentless poverty.

Basha dresses for the cold, even though she is now living in Southern California, wearing a babushka under a red sun hat, a sweater under her heavy coat. She moves down the boardwalk steadily, paying attention to the placement of her feet. A fall is common and dangerous for the elderly. A fractured hip can mean permanent disability, loss of autonomy, and removal from the community to a convalescent or old age home. Basha seats herself on a bench in front of the Center and waits for friends. Her feet are spread apart, well-planted, as if growing up from the cement. Even sitting quite still, there is an air of determination about her. She will withstand

attacks by anti-Semites, Cossacks, Nazis, historical enemies whom she conquers by outliving. She defies time and weather (though it is not cold here). So she might have sat a century ago, before a small pyramid of potatoes or herring in the marketplace of the Polish town where she was born. Patient, resolute, she is a survivor.

Not all the Center women are steady boats like Basha. Some, like Faegl, are leaves, so delicate, dry, and vulnerable that it seems at any moment they might be whisked away by a strong gust. And one day, a sudden wind did knock Faegl to the ground. Others, like Gita, are birds, small and sharp-tongued. Quick, witty, vain, flirtatious, they are very fond of singing and dancing. They once were and will always be pretty girls. This is one of their survival strategies. Boats, leaves, or birds, at first their faces look alike. Individual features are blurred by dentures, heavy bifocals, and webs of wrinkles. The men are not so easy to categorize. As a group, they are quieter, more uniform, less immediately outstanding except for the few who are distinctive individuals, clearly distinguishable as leaders.

As the morning wears on, the benches fill. Benches are attached back to back, one side facing the ocean, one side the boardwalk. The people on the ocean side swivel around to face their friends, the boardwalk, and the Center.

Bench behavior is highly stylized. The half-dozen or so benches immediately to the north and south of the Center are the territory of the members, segregated by sex and conversation topic. The men's benches are devoted to abstract, ideological concerns—philosophical debate, politics, religion, and economics. The women's benches are given more to talk about immediate, personal matters—children, food, health, neighbors, love affairs, scandals, and "managing." Men and women talk about Israel and its welfare, about being a Jew and about Center politics. On the benches, reputations are made and broken, controversies explored, leaders selected, factions formed and dissolved. Here is the outdoor dimension of Center life, like a village plaza, a focus of protracted, intense sociability.

Basha had decided that she could no longer live on her own. A series of blows had demoralized her: an obscene phone call, her purse had been snatched, her new dentures could not be made to fit properly causing her endless digestive problems, then she lost her Social Security check and took this as a final sign that she was no longer able to take care of herself. If she waited much longer, it might be too late—she might become really dependent and she dreaded her friends' pity more than leaving them and the community. Sonya scolded her. "Look here, Basha. I don't like this attitude of yours. I've known you for thirty-eight years and you were always a brave woman. You're giving up and there's no excuse for it." But Basha was resolute. She was going to an old age home twenty miles away and would probably never see the Center again. From time to time a few friends would find ways to visit her there, and phone or send notes, but she knew this was all she could hope for in salvaging ties that had endured for three decades. She had had her hair washed and set in a beauty parlor for the first time in her life just before she left.

A few days before her departure, Basha invited Olga, Sonya, Hannah, and me to her room for tea. She had packed nearly everything. The room was oppressively clean. Basha was not ordinarily a neat housekeeper. Her room had been crammed with the material remains of her own and her parents' lives. Photographs of everyone but her father—who had been unwilling to "become an idol" by having his picture taken—hung on the walls, alongside a night school certificate, an award for completion of a course from the Singer Sewing Machine Company, and her Graduation-Siyum diploma. Books, newspapers, greeting cards, buttons, and scraps of material had mingled unselfconsciously on every surface.

Basha's room was really one big kitchen. She had arranged this when she first moved in by removing a partition that separated the cooking facilities from the sleeping-sitting room. The space was dominated by a table and chairs and in the center of the table, a fine brass samovar that Basha's mother had managed to hold on to through a lifetime of movement and adversity. Basha had kept it out to use for this afternoon. In one corner of the room was a narrow couch-bed and in the other Basha's old iron sewing machine with its splendid worked iron treadle. "This machine goes with me wherever I go," she had told me when I first visited her. "In the middle of a room, it makes of it a home. With this machine you could change everything, making from a

shmatte a Purim gown.* You sew on a ribbon here, a feather there, pretty soon you're done up like a queen."

Someone from the thrift shop that supported a Jewish hospital was coming out to take the machine away later on in the day.

We had all dressed up for the occasion. Olga swept in in a flowing black cape. "For what else would I use it if not here?" she asked. "Lately no one has asked me to the Grand Ball." Sonya wore a bright red jumper that accentuated the straight delicate lines of her back and neck. She brought a plate of organic squash latkes, which were received with pleasure. Basha politely rejected my box of fancy cookies. "Too much refined sugar for us, dolly, maybe you could give them to some of the ones at the Center who could not afford luxuries." I should have known better. They did not approve of spending money on delicacies and Basha was not about to accept anything from me just because this might be my last chance to give her something.

Everyone made much over Basha's new hairdo. Pleased and proud, she refused our compliments. "A dressed-up potato is still a potato," she quoted in Yiddish. "You shouldn't be taken in by an old lady."

I sat in Basha's kitchen thinking about how ingenious and resourceful these old women were, and they thought so, too, it was clear. "Basha, darling," Olga said, "you will be all right wherever you are. Above all, when you get to the new home you should adapt yourself. The worst part will be having a roommate. If you're lucky you won't end up with someone who snores all night. Try to be cheerful. And you could do like I do in the Guest House. Whenever I want a snack, I go into the kitchen and make jokes with the girl there. If you get people to laugh, they help you and they won't pity you neither. Last week I went to the doctor. They put on me one of those foolish paper robes. I had everybody in stitches. I told them if they would give me a broom I would fly away to the Witches' Sabbath. If people see you're a person and not a ghost, they do nice little things for you. You've seen how I am on the boardwalk. Everybody knows me and calls me 'Grandma.' I can walk anywhere I want without getting hurt. Now I have no husband, and a woman

---

* *Shmatte* is a rag; *Purim* is a Jewish holiday.

needs a male escort, so I tell everyone I'm out for a stroll with my boyfriend. My cane is my boyfriend, best one I ever had. He is faithful, strong, and never talks back to me. Between him and my smile, I feel safe wherever I go."

"That's right. Adapt and have a sense of humor about you," said Hannah. "When I was to go to the hospital I spent two days cooking. My neighbor comes in and says, 'Hannah, what are you doing?' Are you planning on having a party or going for an operation?' 'I'll tell you, dear,' I says, 'I'm going to cook all this food and freeze it. If I come back, I'll have that to eat, nourishing food to recover on. If I don't, my friends should have all the best food to eat for my wake, just the way I would cook it myself.' She got a kick out of that."

The women were describing some of the strategies they had cultivated for coping with their circumstances—growing old, living alone and with little money. Each in a different way, with a different specialization had improvised techniques for growing old with originality and dedication. For these women, aging was a career, . . . a serious commitment to surviving, complete with standards of excellence, clear, public, long-term goals whose attainment yielded community recognition and inner satisfaction.

When middle-aged or young people look at the situation of the elderly, inevitably they compare it with their own. Then aging seems only a pathetic series of losses—money, freedom, relationships, roles, strength, beauty, potence, and possibilities. Aging is usually discussed from this point of view; whether compassionately or patronizingly, this stance is *external*, describing aging as it appears to one who is not old. We are rarely presented with the views of old people about themselves and given an opportunity to hear how aging is experienced by them, "from inside the native's head," so to speak. This approach, basic to anthropology, yields the "aging as a career" concept, to replace the usual "series of losses" notion that results when younger people regard the elderly from their own perspective. Another advantage accrues to the study of aging from an anthropological point of view: attention to the correspondences—or lack of them—between action and ideas, or real and idealized conduct. For example, many of the Center people's verbal state-

ments about aging were as grim as anything said or written about them by younger people, but their behavior often belied their words. Even those who stated flatly that old age was a curse, with no redeeming features, could be seen living engaged lives, passionate and original. Nearly every person in the Center community—men and women—had devised some career, some activity or purpose to which he/she was committed. They had provided themselves with new possibilities to replace those that had been lost, regularly set new standards for themselves in terms of which to measure growth and achievement, sought and found meaning in their lives, in the short run and the long.

The elders were not deluded and knew quite well the difference between careers in aging and those in the outside "real world of work." Thus, Sadie, whose career was composing and singing her songs, said, "Myself, when I sing I am in glory. My only regret is I never had the chance for a real career. I had talent but I had to sacrifice. I had to choose between myself and my children. But now when I sing I try to get better all the time, and then I really lose myself." There were many other careers: Basha's ceaseless efforts on behalf of Israeli causes; Gita's passion for dancing; the involvement of many of the women with the philanthropic work; Hannah's devotion to the pigeons she fed every day, gathering huge bags of crumbs from neighbors, stores, and restaurants. Olga told and retold a cycle of highly polished, nearly invariant stories about herself that showed how she handled hostility and indifference with courage and dignity; these tales become her special lifework.

With considerable pride she recounted a story we had all heard many times:

"One Saturday afternoon near Christmas, it was very dark, and as usual, I was out walking. All of a sudden about ten big boys about fifteen, sixteen years old, surrounded me. 'Hi, Grandma,' they said. 'How do you do? It's not a very nice day,' I answered them real polite. 'Spread out, guys,' one of them told the others and they surrounded me. 'Are you Jewish?' he asks me, looking real mean. 'Yes,' I say. 'Do you believe in Jesus?' 'It all depends,' I answer. 'Do you believe he is here walking with us?' he asks. 'No, I don't,' I say. 'How do you know he isn't here with us?' he asks me real menacing. 'Because if he would be here, he would come up to me and say, "Hello,

Olga, how are you?" After all, he was my cousin before yours.' After that they laughed and separated to let me go on my way. That's how I handle people."

It was one of her favorite stories, sanctified and validated by use and intent, and everyone nodded appreciatively.

Sonya was just as proud of the neat, well-spelled minutes that she kept so faithfully for Center meetings. And she made truly elegant dresses out of scraps and castoffs that she bought in rummage sales, her self-satisfaction doubled because the money she laid out for materials went to Israel.

And for all of them, getting up each morning, being independent, living up to their goals, despite incredible odds, managing for themselves, whether it was only dressing, cooking, shopping, demanding and getting satisfaction from a hardhearted or indifferent doctor or welfare official—these, too, should be counted as successful examples of the lifework of aging.

[1987]

 83

The Day Nani Fell and I Wasn't There to Catch Her

ANNA MARIE QUEVEDO

Nana
lives alone in Echo Park
    Allison Street
one block above the Sunset

Sundays
before glaucoma clouded eyes
ruined her independence
she went to mass

sometimes at La Placita
once in awhile Saint Vibiana's
occasionally Saint Anthony's
every single Sunday
every novena Friday

my nana
at the bus stop
waiting patiently for the #10 going downtown
arriving amid clouds of stinking gasoline fumes

        (she'd complain to me
            "Los Angeles is an ugly city"
                she wished she'd never left Silver.)

after church
shopping at the Grand Central
another walk to the bus stop
#28 going home

suddenly she stumbled!
hand stretched out to break the fall
too late
collarbone snapped, shoulder blade broken
downtown L.A. strangers hardly noticed

Nana
went to a medi-cal hungry doctor
told her it was only a sprain and didn't set it
now her shoulder is slumped
her arm permanently crippled

in Silver City someone would have softened the fall
[1982]

Rights and Choices: Reproductive Health

The *Roe v. Wade* decision of 1973 legalized abortion in the United States, guaranteeing for the first time a woman's right to choose between pregnancy and abortion. Since this landmark decision, however, women's right to safe and legal abortions has been steadily eroded. The controversy about abortion reflects an often simplistic attempt to pit the rights of women against the rights of the fetus. Ellen Willis argues that the "right to life" position is flawed because it is based on the assumption that fetal rights are separate from women's rights. Commenting on college students' positions on this issue, Laura Wells observes that many students have been influenced by anti-choice positions, even when they support general feminist ideals. These two pieces convey the complex nature of the abortion rights controversy.

The heated debate over women's right to choose can distance one from the human side of the abortion rights question. Judy Simmons offers a personal account of her decision to terminate an unwanted pregnancy during a time when legal abortions were not available. Her words show us the dilemma she faced, and confirm that women choosing abortion struggle seriously with issues that are difficult and painful.

Anti-abortion legislation, particularly parental consent and notification laws that require teenage women to obtain a parent's approval for abortion, have diminished women's right to legal abortions. The devastating effects of such legislation on young women are explored in "Abortion Denied." William Bell provides a personal narrative of the tragic consequences of Indiana's parental consent laws. His daughter, Becky, was 18 years old when she died from an infection resulting from an illegal abortion. Rather than risk her parents' disappointment by telling them about her pregnancy, Becky had chosen to obtain an abortion on her own. As "Abortion: Cost, Funding and Access" shows, poor women have been hurt most by such restrictions on abortions.

The concept of reproductive rights extends beyond the right to safe, legal abortions, and includes women's choices and rights regarding all aspects of reproductive health. Ruth Hubbard shows that pregnant women's rights are often subordinated to those of the fetus, and argues for meeting the economic, social, and educational needs of women and their children.

84

Abortion: Is a Woman a Person?

ELLEN WILLIS

If propaganda is as central to politics as I think, the opponents of legal abortion have been winning a psychological victory as important as their tangible gains. Two years ago, abortion was almost always discussed in feminist terms—as a political issue affecting the condition of women. Since then, the grounds of the debate have shifted drastically; more and more, the right-to-life movement has succeeded in getting the public and the media to see abortion as an abstract moral issue having solely to do with the rights of fetuses. Though every poll shows that most Americans favor legal abortion, it is evident that many are confused and disarmed, if not convinced, by the antiabortionists' absolutist fervor. No one likes to be accused of advocating murder. Yet the "pro-life" position is based on a crucial fallacy—that the question of fetal rights can be isolated from the question of women's rights.

Recently, Garry Wills wrote a piece suggesting that liberals who defended the snail-darter's right to life and opposed the killing in Vietnam should condemn abortion as murder. I found this notion breathtaking in its illogic. Environmentalists were protesting not the "murder" of individual snail-darters but the practice of wiping out entire species of organisms to gain a short-term economic benefit; most people who opposed our involvement in Vietnam did so because they believed the United States was waging an aggressive, unjust and/or futile war. There was no inconsistency in holding such positions and defending abortion on the grounds that women's welfare should take precedence over fetal life. To claim that three very different issues, each with its own complicated social and political context, all came down to a simple matter of preserving life was to say that all killing was alike and equally indefensible regardless of circumstance. (Why, I wondered, had Wills left out the destruction of hapless bacteria by penicillin?) But aside from the general mushiness of the argument, I was struck by one

peculiar fact: Wills had written an entire article about abortion without mentioning women, feminism, sex, or pregnancy.

Since the feminist argument for abortion rights still carries a good deal of moral and political weight, part of the antiabortionists' strategy has been to make an end run around it. Although the mainstream of the right-to-life movement is openly opposed to women's liberation, it has chosen to make its stand on the abstract "pro-life" argument. That emphasis has been reinforced by the movement's tiny left wing, which opposes abortion on pacifist grounds and includes women who call themselves "feminists for life." A minority among pacifists as well as right-to-lifers, this group nevertheless serves the crucial function of making opposition to abortion respectable among liberals, leftists, and moderates disinclined to sympathize with a right-wing crusade. Unlike most right-to-lifers, who are vulnerable to charges that their reverence for life does not apply to convicted criminals or Vietnamese peasants, antiabortion leftists are in a position to appeal to social conscience—to make analogies, however facile, between abortion and napalm. They disclaim any opposition to women's rights, insisting rather that the end cannot justify the means—murder is murder.

Well, isn't there a genuine moral issue here? If abortion *is* murder, how can a woman have the right to it? Feminists are often accused of evading this question, but in fact an evasion is built into the question itself. Most people understand "Is abortion murder?" to mean "Is the fetus a person?" But fetal personhood is ultimately as inarguable as the existence of God; either you believe in it or you don't. Putting the debate on this plane inevitably leads to the nonconclusion that it is a matter of one person's conscience against another's. From there, the discussion generally moves on to broader issues: whether laws defining the fetus as a person violate the separation of church and state; or conversely, whether people who believe an act is murder have not only the right but the obligation to prevent it. Unfortunately, amid all this lofty philosophizing, the concrete, human reality of the pregnant woman's dilemma gets lost, and with it an essential ingredient of the moral question.

Murder, as commonly defined, is killing that is unjustified, willful, and malicious. Most people would agree, for example, that killing in defense of one's life or safety is not murder. And most would accept a concept of self-defense that includes the right to fight a defensive war or revolution in behalf of one's independence or freedom from oppression. Even pacifists make moral distinctions between defensive violence, however deplorable, and murder; no thoughtful pacifist would equate Hitler's murder of the Jews with the Warsaw Ghetto rebels' killing of Nazi troops. The point is that it's impossible to judge whether an act is murder simply by looking at the act, without considering its context. Which is to say that it makes no sense to discuss whether abortion is murder without considering why women have abortions and what it means to force women to bear children they don't want.

We live in a society that defines child rearing as the mother's job; a society in which most women are denied access to work that pays enough to support a family, child-care facilities they can afford, or any relief from the constant, daily burdens of motherhood; a society that forces mothers into dependence on marriage or welfare and often into permanent poverty; a society that is actively hostile to women's ambitions for a better life. Under these conditions the unwillingly pregnant woman faces a terrifying loss of control over her fate. Even if she chooses to give up the baby, unwanted pregnancy is in itself a serious trauma. There is no way a pregnant woman can passively let the fetus live; she must create and nurture it with her own body, in a symbiosis that is often difficult, sometimes dangerous, always uniquely intimate. However gratifying pregnancy may be to a woman who desires it, for the unwilling it is literally an invasion—the closest analogy is to the difference between lovemaking and rape. Nor is there such a thing as foolproof contraception. Clearly, abortion is by normal standards an act of self-defense.

Whenever I make this case to a right-to-lifer, the exchange that follows is always substantially the same:

RTL: If a woman chooses to have sex, she should be willing to take the consequences. We must all be responsible for our actions.

EW: Men have sex, without having to "take the consequences."

RTL: You can't help that—it's biology.

EW: You don't think a woman has as much right as a man to enjoy sex? Without living in fear that one slip will transform her life?

RTL: She has no right to selfish pleasure at the expense of the unborn.

It would seem, then, that the nitty-gritty issue in the abortion debate is not life but sex. If the fetus is sacrosanct, it follows that women must be continually vulnerable to the invasion of their bodies and loss of their freedom and independence—unless they are willing to resort to the only perfectly reliable contraceptive, abstinence. This is precisely the "solution" right-to-lifers suggest, usually with a touch of glee; as Representative Elwood Rudd once put it, "If a woman has a right to control her own body, let her exercise control before she gets pregnant." A common ploy is to compare fucking to overeating or overdrinking, the idea being that pregnancy is a just punishment, like obesity or cirrhosis.

In 1979 it is depressing to have to insist that sex is not an unnecessary, morally dubious self-indulgence but a basic human need, no less for women than for men. Of course, for heterosexual women giving up sex also means doing without the love and companionship of a mate. (Presumably, married women who have had all the children they want are supposed to divorce their husbands or convince them that celibacy is the only moral alternative.) "Freedom" bought at such a cost is hardly freedom at all and certainly not equality—no one tells men that if they aspire to some measure of control over their lives, they are welcome to neuter themselves and become social isolates. The don't-have-sex argument is really another version of the familiar antifeminist dictum that autonomy and femaleness—that is, female sexuality—are incompatible; if you choose the first, you lose the second. But to pose this choice is not only inhumane; it is as deeply disingenuous as "Let them eat cake." No one, least of all the antiabortion movement, expects or wants significant numbers of women to give up sex and marriage. Nor are most right-to-lifers willing to allow abortion for rape victims. When all the cant about "responsibility" is stripped away, what the right-to-life position comes down to is, if the effect of prohibiting abortion is to keep women slaves to their biology, so be it.

In their zeal to preserve fetal life at all costs,

antiabortionists are ready to grant fetuses more legal protection than people. If a man attacks me and I kill him, I can plead self-defense without having to prove that I was in danger of being killed rather than injured, raped, or kidnapped. But in the annual congressional battle over what if any exceptions to make to the Medicaid abortion ban, the House of Representatives has bitterly opposed the funding of abortions for any reason but to save the pregnant woman's life. Some right-to-lifers argue that even the danger of death does not justify abortion; others have suggested "safeguards" like requiring two or more doctors to certify that the woman's life is at least 50 percent threatened. Antiabortionists are forever worrying that any exception to a total ban on abortion will be used as a "loophole": better that any number of women should ruin their health or even die than that one woman should get away with not having a child "merely" because she doesn't want one. Clearly this mentality does not reflect equal concern for all life. Rather, antiabortionists value the lives of fetuses above the lives and welfare of women, because at bottom they do not concede women the right to an active human existence that transcends their reproductive function. Years ago, in an interview with Paul Krassner in *The Realist,* Ken Kesey declared himself against abortion. When Krassner asked if his objection applied to victims of rape, Kesey replied—I may not be remembering the exact words, but I will never forget the substance—"Just because another man planted the seed, that's no reason to destroy the crop."* To this day I have not heard a more eloquent or chilling metaphor for the essential premise of the right-to-life movement: that a woman's excuse for being is her womb. It is an outrageous irony that antiabortionists are managing to pass off this profoundly immoral idea as a noble moral cause.

The conservatives who dominate the right-to-life movement have no real problem with the antifeminism inherent in their stand; their evasion of the issue is a matter of public relations. But the politics of antiabortion leftists are a study in self-contradiction: in attacking what they see as the violence of abortion, they condone and encourage violence against women. Forced childbearing does violence to a woman's body and spirit, and it contributes to other kinds of violence: deaths from illegal abortion; the systematic oppression of mothers and women in general; the poverty, neglect, and battering of unwanted children; sterilization abuse.

Radicals supposedly believe in attacking a problem at its roots. Yet surely it is obvious that restrictive laws do not keep women from seeking abortions; they just create an illicit, dangerous industry. The only way to drastically reduce the number of abortions is to invent safer, more reliable contraceptives, ensure universal access to all birth control methods, eliminate sexual ignorance and guilt, and change the social and economic conditions that make motherhood a trap. Anyone who is truly committed to fostering life should be fighting for women's liberation instead of harassing and disrupting abortion clinics (hardly a nonviolent tactic, since it threatens the safety of patients). The "feminists for life" do talk a lot about ending the oppression that drives so many women to abortion; in practice, however, they are devoting all their energy to increasing it.

Despite its numerical insignificance, the antiabortion left epitomizes the hypocrisy of the right-to-life crusade. Its need to wrap misogyny in the rhetoric of social conscience and even feminism is actually a perverse tribute to the women's movement; it is no longer acceptable to declare openly that women deserve to suffer for the sin of Eve. I suppose that's progress—not that it does the victims of the Hyde Amendment much good.   [1981]

---

*A reader later sent me a copy of the Kesey interview. The correct quotation is "You don't plow under the corn because the seed was planted with a neighbor's shovel."

🌿 85

In Response to a "Moderate" View of Abortion

LAURA WELLS

As a teacher of an introductory women's studies course at a public, four-year college for nearly five years, I have been impressed by students' overall enthusiasm and receptivity to feminist principles. Many students embrace feminist perspectives on work and family, health, law, and the media. In discussions of abortion, however, I can detect the success of the anti-abortion movement in blurring the issues and putting advocates for choice on the defensive. This is evident when meaningful abortion discussion is derailed by a statement that is offered as if it is a reasonable compromise between two extremist positions: "I think abortion should be legal, but I'm against it when women use it for birth control."

One glaring problem with the statement is, of course, that abortion *is* a means of birth control. For what other purpose might women "use" abortion? Recreation? Political gain? Social status? Personal enrichment? Obviously not. Because our reproductive capabilities cannot be separated from other aspects of our lives, women sometimes terminate unwanted pregnancies. Studies show that this has been true throughout history, and worldwide. We are fortunate when we have contraceptive options as well. However, there are virtually *no* circumstances under which women have absolute control over contraception/conception. The "compromise" argument suggests that any woman who wants to avoid pregnancy can do so if only her will is great enough. To see the fallacy in this view, one has only to consider the many familiar problems with contraceptive methods.

To be effective, all contraceptive methods require that users understand human reproduction and the functions of the various contraceptive methods. Further, women need to know which methods are appropriate and how to use them. Our class discussions reveal that this information is by no means universally accessible to women, either in schools or in their communities. When they do gain access to contraception, cost often affects whether it is used reliably.

There are few methods over which women have absolute control. Most require some degree of cooperation by sexual partners. Inequality and abuses of power, in forms ranging from rape to ridicule, threats to promises, readily affect contraceptive use. And sometimes contraceptives simply fail, even under the best of circumstances. In *Taking Chances:*

Abortion and the Decision Not to Contracept, Kristin Luker demonstrates that in our culture, where motherhood is idealized and sex romanticized, women don't always think clearly about long-term effects and take risks they may later regret.[1] For all of these reasons, unwanted pregnancies do occur in women's lives, sometimes more than once.

Students who maintain that abortion should be legal, but oppose abortion when it's "used for birth control," reveal their ignorance of the various conditions that contribute to unwanted pregnancies. Fortunately, education can replace existing myths and misconceptions with an understanding of these issues.

However, these students' view also reflects a terrible assumption: that someone can determine whether women are *deserving* of abortion alternatives based on their (presumed) actions/conditions at the time of impregnation. Does this mean that a woman could be excused from a "the-condom-broke" kind of unwanted pregnancy, although another is punished for pregnancy that results from "he'd leave me if I made him use one"? Is a first abortion tolerable on the basis that "we all make mistakes," while subsequent abortions are judged to be evidence of a woman's utter negligence? Are we really willing to return to the old notion that pregnancy is a suitable punishment for "bad girls"?

Contempt for woman who "use abortion as birth control" is not only deeply woman-blaming, but also falsely self-righteous. Isn't it really a thinly veiled justification for rejecting another woman's need for an abortion, while preserving the right for oneself?

For all of these reasons, the students' statement is not a compromise position. It is neither reasonable nor logical, but disguises age-old misogyny as moderation, and deceives the speaker into thinking that her statement is pro-choice when, in fact, it is profoundly threatening to the reproductive rights of all women.   [1992]

---

[1] Kristin Luker, *Taking Chances: Abortion and the Decision Not to Contracept* (Berkeley: University of California Press, 1975).

🦎 86

Abortion:
A Matter of Choice

JUDY D. SIMMONS

Abortion is a great equalizer of women. Whatever their age, class or race, women tend to walk the same way after ending a pregnancy. They sort of hunch their shoulders, fold their arms rather protectively across their upper bodies, and take small steps. Of course, they're pretty woozy when they come out; most stay in the recovery room only long enough to get conscious and unsteadily upright. Nobody wants to spend a lot of time sipping tea and eating cookies in the clinic, any more than she hangs around the dentist's office after oral surgery or looks forward to a chummy tête-à-tête following an audit by the Internal Revenue Service.

Aborting a pregnancy isn't the high point of a woman's day. Nor, however, is it the melodramatic tragedy, social cancer, mortal sin, legislative crisis or genocidal master plan that various segments of the American public represent it to be. Women have been preventing and aborting pregnancies as long as they've been women. African queen and pharaoh Hatshepsut, who reigned in Egypt between 1500 and 1479 B.C., invented a method of birth control. Numerous African women enslaved in the United States aborted pregnancies rather than bear children into slavery or give birth to the products of slave masters' rapes, notes Paula Giddings in her book, *When and Where I Enter*. A sixty-seven-year-old woman I know who has lived in a number of places in this country told me that every town she was ever in had its abortionist, and everyone knew where to find him or her. Abortion has been either legal or not a matter of public-policy intervention in many nations for ages. Like so many things one deals with in life, abortion is an uncomfortable but not uncommon experience. In the case of a girl we'll call Renee—a fifteen-year-old with a troubled home life, some emotional deficits and little practical awareness—abortion is a necessity, a mercy and a chance to build a better life.

These were my thoughts a few years back as I sat in a Westchester County, New York, women's clinic waiting for Renee to emerge from the inner sanctum where the abortions are done. These thoughts are a good deal more reasonable and coherent than the ones I had when I ended my first pregnancy in 1963. At that time, abortions were illegal in the United States. I traveled to Tijuana, Mexico, from Sacramento, California, where I lived and went to college. I can remember having one clear idea: If the place looked and felt like a butcher shop, I'd come home and let the pregnancy come to term. I had heard about the coat-hanger and knitting-needle abortions that were the standard methods for poor and non-white women before the 1973 *Roe v. Wade* Supreme Court decision that legalized abortion; and I had read about women being rendered sterile or dying as the aftermath of "back-alley" abortions. My thoughts at that time were sheer, simple fear and an awful sadness. A phase of my life was ending—an innocence, if you'll allow me that. Deciding to *have an abortion* went against every dream I'd had since I was seven or eight and found out how interestingly babies are made.

I was always a dreamy girl. As a preschooler I dreamed that I flew around heaven with a blue-eyed, blond-haired Jesus. I dreamed—until I actually did it at seventeen—that I'd be reunited with my father, who had divorced me and my mother when I was five. From the time I went from Rhode Island to segregated Alabama when I was seven, I dreamed I'd escape the red-clay dust, the gnats, the slop pails and the prejudiced white folks and get back up North to be Somebody.

Naturally, the deepest dream was that I would marry an intelligent, handsome, God-fearing man, be his divine helpmeet, have six children (to compensate for my only-child loneliness, I guess) and live happily ever after. To me, love, sex, marriage, children, goodness and happiness were all wrapped up in one romantic religious package that automatically came in the mail when you were old enough. Finding out that this wasn't so, in a scant three months of 1963, emotionally devastated me.

As I waited for Renee I pondered the similarities and differences in our abortion situations. In the twenty-odd years gone by between the two experiences, abortion has been legalized in the United States—that is an obvious difference. What's not so obvious, perhaps, is the psychological difference that makes. Renee didn't have to contact what amounted to an underground network and have a password (a previous patient's code name) to make her appointment. She didn't have to fly far away from home, family and friends and cross a national border feeling as if she had a flashing neon sign on her forehead saying ABORTION. She didn't have to fear being arrested when she went for a post-abortion checkup if the doctor decided to help some lout of a prosecutor polish his reputation by meddling in a personal matter that should never be part of the legal system.

Renee wasn't totally ignorant about the procedure and what to expect following it. I thought I'd have terrible cramps and bleed to the point of hemorrhage. Imagine my surprise when I returned to the hotel, fell asleep and woke up feeling wonderful, with only the discomfort of being famished from not having eaten all day. I then proceeded to eat the most delicious fried chicken ever sold by a restaurant. Relief is a great flavor-enhancer. If there's one cause I might take up the gun for, it's that girls and women should always be able to get safe, legal, caring, "sunshine" abortions. No one should be subjected to the terror of clandestine activity in addition to the other stresses that usually surround a decision to abort.

The similarities between Renee's experience and mine are an old story. Renee was impregnated by a man ten years her senior who said he was going to marry her. My "fiancé" was thirteen years older than I. Renee's seducer was in an authority position—a security guard at her junior high school. Mine was my thirty-one-year-old languages professor (white and, it later turned out, gay). Renee was hungry for love and protection to make her feel wanted and worthwhile. So was I. Like most young girls—indeed, like many people in the United States—Renee imposed fantasy on reality, acting on the assumption that what she felt and wanted to happen was really what was happening. So did I. But it ain't easy, especially when you're a teenager whose awakening glands can make you think mud looks like fudge and smells like perfume.

The similarity between Renee and me that makes me angry is that adult women never talked to us *realistically* about being a woman, lover and mother.

When I spoke with Renee the day before she went for the abortion, she showed no awareness of why her mother might stay married to Renee's tyrant of a stepfather, who was making advances toward Renee and terrorizing the family with physical violence, meanness about money and refusal to allow them visitors and telephone calls. . . .

I know a woman who had her first child out of wedlock at thirteen, another at seventeen, then got married and had two more kids before her husband left her. The woman was very nearly crazy with bills and parental responsibilities. When she suspected that her sixteen-year-old daughter might be messing around, she responded to my query about a heart-to-heart mother-daughter discussion of responsible sex and birth control with a haughty "I'm not going to talk to her about those things. She'll think I'm condoning sex." Condoning sex! Did this woman's mother "condone" her having sex and a baby at thirteen? "My mother? Hell, no." Did that stop her from doing both? "I don't care. If my daughter's going to mess around, she'll just have to take the consequences." I ran screaming into the night.

Why, why, generation after generation, do we send young girls out ignorant? Sure, I remember comments from women such as "You better take care of yourself" and "You lie down with dogs, you get up with fleas," or "Girl, it's hard to be a woman." These are vague warnings indeed when the lust tide of puberty rises; when the guys are so sleek, sweet, masterful and full of smiles; when the experimental necking and petting sets the heated sap to running; when the first real manly hand touches your breast, and you feel a strange, silky saliva slide down your throat and discover a new reason for panties to get wet. Don't grown women remember what it's like to be fresh meat and jailbait? You have to beat dudes off with a stick. Sometime, somewhere, somebody's gonna get ya.

In theory, it's fine to say that men have an equal responsibility to protect against pregnancy and disease. In fact, God bless the child who's got her own, and God helps her who helps herself. Giving young girls a chance to develop their intellectual and spiritual possibilities, protecting them with supervision, information and devices as necessary, schooling them in the realities of sex, mating and motherhood counter the pervasive fantasies and compelling hungers of body and soul—all this is women's work, women's responsibility, women's mission. 'Cause we're the ones who get jammed up. . . .

Obviously, I'm not as concerned about an embryo's right to life as I am about a child's quality of life, and the things that destroy it. What about war—nuclear and otherwise—social injustice and the irrevocable death penalty? What about the bombing of children in Libya, the slaughter in the Middle East and South Africa, or the United States government's devoting a hundred million dollars to sustain and heighten violence in Nicaragua? What about classism and racism, which condemn children to falling down elevator shafts and out of windows in slum houses, or poor nutrition, lousy medical care, police brutality and unemployed, crazed or simply juvenile parents? What about the feminization of poverty that results from too many girls and women having children before developing intellectual coping skills and economic positioning, whether or not there are husbands present?

Perhaps we can moderate the notion that becoming a mother means one has done something intrinsically special and sacred. Every species of animal and plant I've heard of reproduces itself. It doesn't take a creative genius or intellectual giant to have sex and reproduce other human animals, although it may take both to rear the human animal into a decent human being in this complex perilous time. It's the rearing that separates the women from the girls, not the birthing.

Had I been clear about these things when I aborted my pregnancy, I wouldn't have substituted the role of "tragic abortee" for the rejected role of "mother," nor punished myself for going against the prevailing notion that becoming a mother should be the crowning fulfillment of every woman's life. Biologically speaking, what I aborted at eight weeks wasn't a cute, cuddly baby. Between eight weeks and nine months anything could happen: spontaneous abortion, a car accident, the world blowing up, a thalidomide distortion—you name it. There's no guarantee that pregnancy means getting a perfect reflection of oneself in a lovely little package. Of course, chances are that I would have had a healthy baby, but my point is that it was foolish and unnecessary to torture myself with guilt over an *assumption,* a hope, a fantasy, that the embryonic cells

might have become another Dr. Martin Luther King, Jr. They might also have become Charles Manson, or have never become a fully developed human being at all.

My decision to abort was quite practical as well. At the time, I was living with three roommates in Sacramento, financed by student loans and part-time jobs. The jobs I'd had—waitress, telephone magazine sales, nannying and civil-service clerkships—were dead-end enough to convince me I'd never make it into financial comfort and an advantaged lifestyle if I didn't get a degree, and certainly not if I were supporting and rearing a child. Plus, it had been understood from the day I was born that I would get a bachelor's degree at least, if not a master's. It would disgrace the whole family if I came home with a big belly, no degree and no husband. Out-of-wedlock wasn't fashionable or respectable in 1963. Having a child and releasing her or him for adoption was out as far as I was concerned. No kid of mine was going to wander the planet without my knowing its circumstances. . . .

I think it's very important for girls and women to give themselves the chance to develop more than their biological and emotional abilities. This doesn't mean not being mothers and wives, but rather being other things as well. The world is profoundly in need of the "feminine" characteristics—empathy, cooperation and conciliation, nurturing and sharing.

Women cannot affect human affairs beyond the personal and familial by being only mothers and marginal survival workers. The hand that rocks the cradle does not, in fact, rule the world—it just rocks the cradle. Harriet Tubman, Sojourner Truth and Mary McLeod Bethune didn't educate and free enslaved Africans by just rocking cradles. Women didn't get the vote, found Planned Parenthood or get abortion legalized in this country by only rocking cradles. Dorothy Height (National Council of Negro Women), Jewell Jackson McCabe (National Coalition of 100 Black Women), Faye Wattleton (Planned Parenthood), Marian Wright Edelman (Children's Defense Fund) and Barbara C. Jordan (professor and former Texas congresswoman) have not contributed to the improvement of hundreds of thousands of lives by rocking cradles. They rock the boat.

To be all that we can be—even if we join the

Army—we must control the timing and circumstances of motherhood. Since telling people to abstain from something as necessary, basic and pleasurable as sex doesn't seem to work, that means using contraception in the first place and abortion as a last resort. I'm not saying that every young mother lives a blighted life. I just want to maximize the odds in favor of girls, women and children. That's the name of this tune.   [1990]

 87

Abortion Denied

FEMINIST MAJORITY FOUNDATION

In 1973, safe, legal abortion became every American woman's right. Thousands of senseless deaths from unsafe, illegal abortions stopped. Since then the Supreme Court, in a series of decisions upholding repressive state laws, has chipped away abortion rights—first for low-income women, then for seriously ill women and *now, for young women.*

In June 1990, the Supreme Court upheld two more harsh anti-abortion laws dramatically restricting a young woman's right to legal abortion.

While laws requiring a teenage woman to notify or get permission from her parents for abortion may seem reasonable, *the overwhelming evidence shows that parental consent and notification laws are devastating to young women.*

LETHAL IMPACT OF LAWS

In 1988, Becky Bell, 17 years old, was a victim of Indiana law PL-106 which demands parental consent for an abortion for women under 18. Becky was intimidated by Indiana's law that blocks access to legal abortion.

Panicked by the legal requirement that she tell her parents—because she did not want to disappoint them—and believing she could not obtain a judge's waiver through a court hearing, she instead obtained an illegal abortion.

Becky was killed by a massive deadly infection—the result of that back-alley abortion.

A GROWING NATIONAL THREAT

Parental consent and notification laws have passed in 34 states. Though many have been blocked by the courts, 14 states now enforce these laws. The recent Supreme Court decisions upholding the Ohio and Minnesota laws invite many more states to follow suit. Both types of laws have exactly the same dangerous impact—*they risk young women's lives.*

Young women often cannot tell their parent(s) for a host of compelling reasons: *fear of abuse, physical violence, being thrown out of the house, or tarnishing their image with their parents.*

In restrictive states, young unmarried women under 18 years old who want an abortion must:

1. seek parental notification or consent;
2. travel long distances to an unrestricted state;
3. petition for a court bypass; *or*
4. obtain an illegal abortion.

And although 50% of young women *do* voluntarily go to one or both parents, those who feel they cannot will risk almost anything, including their lives, to avoid exposure.

FAILURE OF COURT BYPASS

The court bypass procedure, which forces young women to convince judges that they can't involve their parent(s), is discriminatory and frequently does not work. Young women seeking a bypass tend to be white, suburban, middle-class, college bound, and self-confident.

Young women must reveal their personal lives to the scrutiny of stranger(s), chiefly older white, male attorneys and judges. The legal maze they must maneuver is intimidating and is especially discriminatory against women of color and those with low incomes.

Teenage women are denied their right to privacy and often have to face up to 23 people in the process. Many have reported harassment from anti-abortion judges.

The court bypass delays essential medical care and causes many young women to enter the second trimester of a pregnancy.

After the Minnesota law passed, the percentage of teenage women needing riskier, more costly second trimester abortions *increased* by 26.5%. Even so, the U.S. Supreme Court said this was not an undue burden.

Court bypass hearings are not easy to come by. In Massachusetts, many judges refuse to hear abortion cases. In Minnesota, court hearings and abortions are available in only two locations. In Ohio, the bypass process could take 22 days, but the U.S. Supreme Court still approved the law.

An analysis of court bypass procedures indicates that a young woman's right to abortion is dependent on where she lives.

For instance, an extensive clinic survey in Indiana reveals that permission has been *granted only about a dozen times per year* in the 4 years the law has been in effect.

In comparison, in Minnesota and Massachusetts, thousands of court waivers were granted in that same time period.

MEDICAL OPPOSITION TO FORCED PARENTAL CONSENT

Medical and health professionals do not support parental consent and notification of abortion. Organizations filing court briefs against the Minnesota and Ohio laws included:

- Amer. College of Ob/Gyn (ACOG)
- Amer. Acad. of Child and Adolescent Psychiatry
- Amer. Acad. of Pediatrics
- Amer. Medical Women's Assn.
- Amer. Nurses Assn.
- Amer. Psychiatric Assn.
- Nurses' Assn. of Amer. College of Ob/Gyn
- Society for Adolescent Medicine

In most states, teenagers do not need parental consent or notification to receive treatment for drug or alcohol abuse, venereal diseases, or to carry a pregnancy to term.

Adolescents are 200% more likely to die in childbirth than women in their 20s—and adolescents under the age of 15 face the highest risk. Their risk of death in childbirth is 1000% greater than the risk to women in their 20s. In fact, for a young teen to have a baby, it is 24 times more dangerous than to have an early abortion.

HIGH SOCIAL COST FOR TEENAGE PREGNANCY

Over one million U.S. teenagers become pregnant each year. One in four teenage mothers drops out of high school and only 1 in 50 finishes college. Children of teens are *twice* as likely to die in infancy than those born to women in their 20s or 40s. The total cost to American taxpayers for families started by teenage women is $20 billion annually in AFDC, food stamps and medicaid benefits.

THE ADOPTION MYTH

Some people believe the answer to these social costs is adoption. In fact, the most likely woman to place a child for adoption is a white teen under 18.

Yet, there are some 35,000 children waiting to be adopted with no homes in sight. Adoptive parents usually seek white, healthy infants, often paying large fees to baby brokers or agencies, while infants of color and disabled children wait, often indefinitely, for homes.

In fact, brokers can charge up to $100,000 for a healthy white infant, and fees of $30,000 are standard. Most adoption agencies are more moderate, but fees vary from agency to agency and frequently by type of infant. Agency fees can go to a high of 12% of the adoptive parents' gross annual income. In some agencies, fees for white, healthy infants are higher than for minority or special needs children. It is worth noting that some anti-abortion groups operate adoption agencies.

Also, America's foster care system is breaking

Pregnancy Rates in Industrialized Nations for Women 15–17

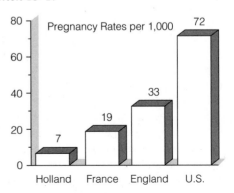

down. There are now 450,000 children who have been temporarily removed from their families and, by the year 2000, there will be one million.

A WORLDWIDE KILLER

The U.S. teen pregnancy rate is the highest among developed nations. It is more than double that of England, triple that of France, and 10 times greater than Holland. The teenage sexual activity rates are equal, but other countries have better sex education, access to contraception and birth control information.

The U.S. ranks tenth among 15 industrialized countries in the availability of birth control to minors, behind countries such as Canada, Italy, and Czechoslovakia.

Worldwide, 1 woman dies every 3 minutes from illegal abortion and young women rank high among the casualties. Throughout the world, denial of sex education, birth control, and abortion shatters the lives of young women and girls.   [1990]

 88

Testimony of William Bell (on Raised Bill #5447)

CONNECTICUT STATE LEGISLATURE

My name is Bill Bell and I reside in Indianapolis, Indiana with my wife Karen and my 20 year old son Bill.

I submit this testimony with mixed emotions: dreading to relive the death of my daughter but also realizing a responsibility to others, that the punitive and restrictive laws that are being heard before this committee are understood by all. In writing and in theory these laws appear reasonable and safe. But in practice they are punishing.

My daughter Becky made a mistake and became pregnant. Parental consent laws, very similar to those you are considering today, dictated that in order to terminate her pregnancy she must obtain approval of her parents, petition the courts, or travel to another state that would allow her a safe clinical

abortion, *or* seek back-alley assistance. She died [from] an illegal abortion.

In confiding with her best friend she said, "I don't want to disappoint my mother and dad, I love them so much."

Knowing my daughter, I believe that the judicial option would have been too intimidating, given her desperate emotional state. She would also have been faced with the prospect of appearing before a pro-life judge. Hardly a reasonable option considering the fact that she had decided to terminate her pregnancy. She chose the last option available to her, an illegal abortion.

Unfortunately, we have been unable to piece together all the circumstances and today we struggle with the question, why did our daughter have to endure such mental torture in making what turned out to be her final decision?

She was intelligent enough to pursue her options, yet we live with the pain of knowing our daughter was desperate and alone, and because of these punishing and restrictive laws, she further compounded her initial mistake with another, and paid for it with her life.

My daughter was a quality child. She was raised in a functional family environment and was encouraged to develop her own thinking and reasoning skills. Yet, in her time of crisis, others had dictated how she must react, thus denying her a legitimate option that all women should enjoy, the right of self-determination.

Had our daughter come to us, her mother and I would have counseled her, made her aware of all her options, the circumstances and the consequences, to the best of our ability. But I can state emphatically that the final decision would have been hers.

As it stands today, legislators, judges, self-appointed moralists, and parents are making the decisions for these young women, allowing little or no input from them. Decisions that are clearly along the lines of their own political, moral or religious beliefs. How can we legislate or dictate that families communicate? How can we dictate to people how they must act or react in a time of crisis?

I realize a great number of young women are going to their parents for counsel and for this I am grateful. Since the death of our daughter, my wife and I have counseled several young women and have been fortunate to get the parents involved. But what about the young woman who doesn't want to disappoint her family?

If I understand correctly, the legislation before you offers no accommodation for a real life situation like that of a Becky Bell. Nor does it consider the young lady from a dysfunctional home who may fear her physical well-being. These laws speak to theories and hypotheticals, they do not address the real life issues taking place today. I submit to you, these punitive and restrictive laws being considered, if enacted, will serve to further isolate the young women of this state. They will serve as a punishment to those who have made a mistake. In the interest of political gain and in the name of God, my daughter was punished.

Others took it upon themselves to decide my daughter's fate, thus denying her a safe option, the best care. Their theories and political stance were placed ahead of and valued more than the life of my daughter.

These laws clearly denied her a safe and reasonable option. And because she had decided to terminate her pregnancy, forced her into making a fatal mistake. My beautiful Becky Bell died on September 16th, 1988.

My daughter's death *will* count for something. She was somebody, somebody beautiful. I will not sit idly by and not speak out to others that could face the same torment that the Bell family now lives with. Not as long as there are those who will go to any length to take away basic human rights.

I am not promoting abortion, far from it. But I am speaking out against those who want to punish, who suggest that we can reduce teenage pregnancy through legislation. I am speaking out against those who will simply not address the needs of birth control and sex education.

Sex among teenagers will not be regulated by legislation, nor will it be eliminated.

I am a man with a broken heart, and it is my desire that speaking out will in some way prevent others from living this same nightmare.

I urge you to consider real life situations and not punish the young women of this state and uphold the rights of all the people of Connecticut, not just the parents.

Rebecca Suzanne Bell was not a theory, she was a beautiful human being. She was my daughter, taken away because others *thought* they had all of the answers. The bill before you doesn't have all of the answers either and I urge you to defeat this legislation.   [1990]

 89

Abortion: Cost, Funding and Access

NOW LEGAL DEFENSE AND
EDUCATION FUND

THE PROBLEM

America's health care system deprives poor women, particularly women of color and rural women, of not only the right to basic health care, but also the access to reproductive choice. This is because access to health care, including reproductive health care, is generally dependent on one's ability to pay for it. In contrast to citizens of other developed countries, a significant number of Americans must rely solely on their own resources to pay for health care. Nearly 18% of all Americans have no health insurance and millions of others have coverage so limited that they may as well be uninsured. The figures are even worse for Americans of color. Safety net coverage for those without insurance is inadequate. Medicaid covers less than half of those below the poverty level. Almost 88% of the uninsured are working poor and their families, those who make too much to qualify for Medicaid yet not enough to live above the poverty level.

Increasingly, poverty and the consequent lack of adequate health care are suffered primarily by women and children. Poverty is disproportionately prevalent among women and children of color and among rural women and children. Two out of three adults living below the poverty level are women and more than half of poor families are headed by women. Of all women aged 18–24, 30% have no insurance coverage. Of women aged 15–44 living below the poverty level, 36% are uninsured. Among women in the same age group living at 100–149% of the poverty level, 30% are uninsured. A woman's lack of insurance affects her children's health as well. Babies born to women without insurance are 30% more likely to die or be seriously ill at birth.

FUNDING LIMITATIONS

Poor women must thus deal with inadequate health care funding for all their health problems. In the area of reproductive health, additional hardships have been imposed. Obstetricians and gynecologists do not participate in Medicaid to as great an extent as other types of physicians. The greatest impediment to poor women receiving proper reproductive care is that even where they have access to an "ob-gyn" who does accept Medicaid payment, the federal government still bars Medicaid funding of abortions except in cases where the woman's life is in danger. (In October 1989, President Bush vetoed a bill passed by Congress that would have permitted Medicaid funding of abortions in cases of promptly reported rape or incest.) Although the states are free to pay for abortions that do not meet the federal standards, 30 states provide funding only when the woman's life is endangered, 8 states provide funding in certain additional circumstances (rape, incest or grave fetal abnormalities), and only 12 states fund all abortions necessary to preserve or protect a woman's health. Ironically, 44 states and the District of Columbia extend Medicaid coverage to all pregnant women and infants living in families with incomes below the poverty level; the only non-covered health care is pregnancy termination, except in limited circumstances.

In 1987, $64 million in public funds went to abortions, but the federal government contributed less than 1% of that. Nearly all of the state-funded abortions were performed in states that fund all medically necessary abortions, and *none* of the states that provide funding only when a woman's life is endangered used state revenues for abortion services. Such restrictions on funding are a major cause for Medicaid-eligible women either to delay their abortions while they save for the fee or to bear unwanted children.

The lack of federal abortion funding is especially disquieting when compared to federal funding of sterilization. In 1987, $65 million in government money went to fund sterilization procedures. The federal government provided 97% of these funds (compared to less than 1% for abortions, see above), 91% through Medicaid. The government's willingness to fund sterilization must be viewed against the shocking sterilization abuses which were uncovered in the 1970's—abuses aimed at women of color and poor women. Some of the horrifying events that occurred involved public assistance officials tricking illiterate Black welfare recipients into consenting to sterilization of their teenage daughters; doctors agreeing to deliver babies of Black Medicaid recipients or perform abortions on condition that the women be sterilized; and doctors performing radical hysterectomies on Native American women under age 21 without informed consent. Non-English speaking women were even less likely to have given informed consent because of communication difficulties. As of 1983, 25% of women of color had been sterilized, compared to 16% of white women. Many women who are being sterilized today still are not being informed that sterilization is not reversible. One 1988 study of low-income clinic patients planning to be sterilized revealed that only between 64 and 70 percent knew that sterilization makes it impossible to have children in the future.

Raising the money for an abortion can be difficult for poor women. The cost of an abortion ranges from $125 to over $2,000. Even if a woman is covered by Medicaid she often must pay cash up front, something very difficult for poor women to do. Early abortions cost less and are safer than abortions performed later in the pregnancy. Thus, delays caused by lack of funds increase the final cost of the abortion and subject women to unnecessary risk. Financial problems may also increase the risks of later abortions. Among the methods for second trimester abortions, dilation and evacuation (D&E) is the fastest and safest. D&E's, however, are not widely available and may be too expensive for poor women. If anti-choice forces are able to pass laws like those recently upheld in *Webster v. Reproductive Health Services,* the cost of an abortion will increase even more, placing a greater burden on poor women. It is estimated that the viability tests required by the Missouri statute challenged in *Webster* could add $125–$200 to the cost of an abortion.

Government-funded reproductive health services further limit poor women's choices. Under the regulations now on the books, Title X programs, which are funded by the federal government to provide contraceptive counseling and services, cannot perform abortions, counsel women about abortion, or provide referrals for abortions. Also, programs must keep their Title X programs completely separate from any abortion-related activity. Although these regulations are being challenged in court and some of them are currently enjoined, they provide one more threat to poor women seeking abortions. If the regulations are ultimately upheld by the courts, Title X programs will not even be able to tell a pregnant woman that abortion is an option or where she can obtain more information about abortion. Furthermore, the rules regarding keeping programs separate could force some programs to shut down entirely, further limiting reproductive choice.

ACCESS LIMITATIONS

Poor women rely heavily on public hospitals for all their health care. These facilities are not, however, meeting women's needs for reproductive health care. In 1985, only 17% of public hospitals reported performing abortions. This dismal situation will only worsen if states follow Missouri's lead and pass restrictive laws such as those upheld in *Webster*. Under the Missouri law no "public facility" may assist or perform abortions unless the woman's life is in danger. "Public" is defined very broadly. As the dissent in *Webster* noted, the law bans abortions at the Truman Medical Center in Kansas City—where, in 1985, 97% of all Missouri hospital abortions at 16 weeks gestation or later were performed—even though the Center is a private hospital, staffed primarily by private doctors and administered by a private corporation. The Center is defined as "public" only because it is located on land leased from the city government.

The repercussions of *Webster*-like laws go beyond limitations on access. Such bans on abortions at "public" facilities would mean that few physicians and nurses will be trained in abortion techniques, because most training is done in hospitals, not clinics. If the broadly-defined "public" hospitals thus prohibited from providing abortions were to be added to the Catholic hospitals that already choose not to perform abortions, doctors seeking abortion training would have few places to turn. The ultimate losers, however, would be women seeking affordable, quality reproductive health care.

Limitations on access to hospital abortions compromise women's health. Some women seeking abortion may not require an abortion to save their lives, but may have a high-risk medical condition which mandates that an abortion be carried out in a hospital setting. Although most abortions can be safely performed on an out-patient basis, hospital facilities must remain available for women in special circumstances and for late-term abortions.

Anti-choice groups seek to limit abortions performed in clinics and doctors' offices as well. In the 1989–90 term, the Supreme Court agreed to review an Illinois case challenging extensive abortion regulations. Among its many requirements, Illinois's complex licensing scheme required that abortions be performed in hospitals, or out-patient clinics licensed as Ambulatory Surgical Treatment Centers (ASTCs); that ASTCs meet exacting physical standards and be equipped with certain medical equipment; and that anyone seeking to open an ASTC get a certificate of need from the Department of Public Health after a public hearing and a 120-day review period. These regulations required ASTCs to be the "functional equivalent of small hospitals." The requirements would add 10% or more to the cost of an abortion, force some clinics to close down, and prevent others from ever opening. Before the Supreme Court could issue a ruling, the State of Illinois agreed in a settlement to withdraw the challenged regulatory scheme. It is possible that other states might attempt to impose similar restrictions. Obviously, the ramifications for cost and access would be devastating.

PARTICULAR PROBLEMS

Even without these added restrictions, certain segments of the population face intensified difficulties in obtaining access to abortion. For rural women, locating a facility that will perform abortions is a major problem. In 82% of the counties in the United States (home to 30% of all women of reproductive age) there are no abortion providers. Hardest hit are rural women—79% of them live in counties with no abortion providers. This is a particularly severe aspect of an overall rural health care problem. A car, necessary to reach most health care facilities, especially reproductive health care facilities, is beyond the means of many of the rural poor. Even a routine health care visit requires a substantial investment of time and resources.

Native American women also face both funding and access problems. No Indian Health Service clinic or hospital may perform abortions, even when the woman is able to pay for it herself. For Native American women who live on reservations, Indian Health Service facilities are usually the only health care provider within hundreds of miles. Thus, a Native American woman seeking an abortion must have enough money to cover both the cost of an abortion *and* the cost of traveling a great distance to an abortion provider.

Although women in the most disadvantaged segments of our society face the most severe obstacles, access and funding problems have broader impact. Women *above* the poverty level also have difficulty paying for abortions. Many women who work part-time or in small companies, service industries, or temporary jobs do not have health insurance. Even women who have insurance may not have adequate coverage when it comes to reproductive health care. Some states have passed laws prohibiting state employees' health insurance from covering abortions except in cases where the woman's life is in danger. Other states have passed laws which mandate that private insurance policies may cover abortion only if an added premium is paid. In the absence of state laws, many insurance companies decide on their own not to offer coverage for abortions.   [1989]

✿ 90

Using Pregnancy to Control Women

RUTH HUBBARD

Strange things have been happening to this culture's ideas about pregnancy. More and more, physicians,

judges, legislators, and the media are presenting pregnancy as a contest in which pregnant women and the embryos and fetuses we nourish in our bodies are represented as lined up on opposing sides. But construing the "interests" of embryos and fetuses as opposed to those of the women whose bodies sustain them makes no sense biologically or socially. A pregnant woman's body is an organic unit, of which the fetus is a part. She shares with her fetus one blood supply as well as other essential functions. Any foods or digestive products, hormones or drugs, or anything else that involves either can have an impact on the other.

This does not mean that pregnant women should scan all their feelings, thoughts, and actions for possible ill effects on the fetus within them. It is probably true that stresses they experience will be transmitted to the fetus, but that includes the stresses and anxieties that would arise from trying to live a life free of stress and anxiety. What it does mean, however, is that it is counterproductive to heap needless stress on pregnant women by worrying them about possible sources of harm to their fetus and by subjecting them to often still-experimental tests and procedures to detect fetal disabilities for which they or the fetus are not specifically predicted to be at risk. Some of today's stresses of pregnancy are evoked by exaggerated concerns and watchfulness intended to avert relatively unlikely risks.

Precisely because anything that is done to a pregnant woman or to her fetus has an impact on both, pregnant women must be the ones to decide whether to carry their pregnancy to term. Only they can know whether they are prepared to sustain the pregnancy as well as the future relationship to their child.

As part of this trend of looking upon embryos and fetuses as though their "interests" could be separated from those of the women whose bodies sustain them, we have been witnessing: (1) prosecutions of pregnant women or of women who have recently given birth for so-called fetal abuse; (2) court-mandated Caesarean sections; and (3) so-called fetal protection practices in which employers bar women of child-bearing age (defined in one instance as 16 to 54 years) from certain kinds of jobs that are said to put a potential fetus at risk, in case these women become pregnant.

I want to look at these three situations and then speculate about why this is happening now and why only in the United States.

"DISTRIBUTING DRUGS TO A MINOR"

Across the nation in the last few years women have been charged with the crime of "distributing drugs to a minor via the umbilical cord" or similarly Orwellian accusations. Since the legal status of the fetus is uncertain, most of these have not stood up in court. Presumably for this reason, in Florida, Jennifer Johnson, a woman who had just birthed her baby, so that it was now legally a born child, was charged with delivering an illicit drug to a minor via the umbilical cord while it was still attached to the cord. Despite the absurdity of this construct, she was convicted. .

It seems reasonable to assume that drug use during pregnancy can harm the fetus, though it is not at all clear how dangerous it is. The designation "crack baby" usually is not the result of health-care workers noting behavioral abnormalities in a newborn. It came on the scene because a test was devised that can detect metabolic products resulting from women's drug use close to the time of birth. As a result, babies of mothers who fall into certain "suspect" categories—young, unmarried, poor, of color—are tested more or less routinely and especially in public hospitals. (In one recent instance where the test result was challenged by the young woman and her mother—though not until after the young woman and her baby had been forcibly separated—it turned out that the drugs the test detected were medically administered to the woman during labor.)

A recent article in the medical journal *The Lancet* explains that there are no accurate assessments of the dangers to the fetus of drug use by pregnant women. Its authors show that Canada's Society of Pediatric Research between 1980 and 1989 much more frequently accepted papers for presentation at its annual meeting that documented adverse effects of drug use during pregnancy than papers of the same, or superior, scientific quality that failed to detect any harm. As the authors point out, this kind of bias in publication of research reports makes it impossible to know how great the risk actually is. But even if we go with the common wisdom that drugs

taken by pregnant women are likely to harm the fetus, the problem is that very few drug-treatment programs accept women, fewer yet pregnant women, and even fewer, women on Medicaid. In fact, Jennifer Johnson's sentence in Florida included as a condition of her fifteen-year probation that she enter a drug-treatment program, something she had tried, but been unable, to do while pregnant. Another was that she be gainfully employed, something she had also tried, but been unable, to achieve. In other words, she was first victimized by an unresponsive system and then blamed for not availing herself of the remedies she had tried, but been unable, to obtain. She ended up convicted for the government's negligence and neglect.

It is important to realize that just about all the women who have been prosecuted for prenatal injuries to their babies have been poor and of color. Most of them have had little or no prenatal care and have given birth in public or teaching hospitals. None has been a white, suburban drug user, in the care of a private obstetrician. The so-called war on drugs requires public hospitals to report instances of suspected drug use, while private physicians can avoid doing so. Obviously, this policy is counterproductive, since it will make women who could benefit from medical and social services avoid them for fear of being declared unfit to care for their children.

COURT-MANDATED CAESAREANS

In most cases, a woman submits to a Caesarean section when a physician warns that giving birth vaginally would endanger her baby. This is true in this country, as elsewhere, despite the fact that the incidence of Caesarean sections in the United States is higher (about one in four) than in any other industrialized country (it is one in ten in the Netherlands, which has one of the lowest infant mortality rates in the world). But occasionally, a woman refuses on religious grounds, out of fear of surgery, or for other reasons. Whereas physicians and attorneys argued in print as late as 1979 that physicians have it in their power to cajole or threaten, but that cutting someone open against her will constitutes battery, since 1980 obstetricians have been granted court orders for performing Caesarean sections against the explicit will of the pregnant woman. In a number of instances pregnant women have escaped the operation by going underground or by giving birth vaginally before the court order could be implemented. In all of them the babies have been born unharmed, despite the obstetrician's direst predictions. In one case, the physician had testified that without a Caesarean there was a 99 percent risk that the baby would die and a 50 percent risk of death to the woman if she gave birth vaginally. She did, and both she and the baby were fine, which just shows that birth outcomes are notoriously unpredictable, except to say that most births end well. These situations, too, have involved mostly poor women—many of them of color, and whose primary language is not English—presumably because of the range of power imbalances between obstetricians and pregnant women. The prevalent differences in class, race, sex, and education that interfere with communication even in the best of circumstances are exacerbated when the women have unusual religious convictions or are young or unmarried or don't speak the same language as the doctor.

There is hope that a recent decision handed down by the District of Columbia Court of Appeals may make courts more reluctant to order Caesareans against the wishes of pregnant women. On April 26, 1990, this court ruled on the case of Angela Carder, a woman who was pregnant and dying of cancer. After 26 weeks of gestation, when it became clear that she would not survive until the end of her pregnancy, Georgetown Hospital in Washington, D.C., got a court order to perform a Caesarean section against her wishes as well as those of her parents, her husband, and her attending physicians. Both she and the baby died within 24 hours of surgery. The American Public Health Association, the American Medical Association, the American College of Obstetricians and Gynecologists, and other health and civil liberties organizations joined, as friends of the court, in a suit brought against the hospital. The majority of the D.C. Court of Appeals held that "in virtually all cases, the question of what is to be done is to be decided by the patient—the pregnant woman—on behalf of herself and the fetus." Though this decision governs only in the District of Columbia, we can hope that it will lend weight to refusals of surgery by pregnant women in other jurisdictions.

FETAL ENDANGERMENT IN THE WORKPLACE

Reproductive hazards in the workplace were cited in 1977 as grounds for requiring five women at the American Cyanamid plant in Willow Island, West Virginia, to be sterilized, if they wanted to retain jobs paying $225 per week plus substantial overtime instead of being transferred to janitorial jobs at $175 per week with no extras. None of these women was pregnant or planning a pregnancy, yet without the operation, they were considered "potentially pregnant." A number of such situations have arisen since, and currently the U.S. Supreme Court has agreed to hear an appeal against a lower court decision supporting Johnson Controls' "fetal protection" policy. . . .*

The grounds for barring the women have been that the work involves exposure to lead or other chemicals or radiation that could endanger a fetus, despite the fact that these agents also put men's reproductive processes, and specifically sperm, at risk. And these situations have only occurred relative to higher-paying jobs, traditionally occupied by men, to which women have been newcomers. Comparable concerns have not been raised about women employed in traditionally female jobs in which they are routinely exposed to hazardous chemicals or radiation, such as surgical operating room or x-ray technician, nurse, beautician, or indeed, clerical or domestic worker. Whether the women are planning to have children appears to be irrelevant. Rather, fertile women, as a class, are always considered "potentially pregnant." This is just one more way to keep women out of higher-paying jobs by dressing up sex discrimination as fetal protection. Of course, it also enhances the status of the fetus as a person, while relegating all women, pregnant or not, to the status of fetal carriers.

These kinds of "protections" make no sense from the viewpoint of health, because any substance that endangers a fetus is also dangerous for workers—female *and* male. But it is cheaper for compa-

---

*Editor's note: In March, 1991 in *UAW v. Johnson Controls, Inc.*, the Supreme Court unanimously declared unconstitutional Johnson Controls' policy of excluding women of childbearing capacity from jobs in which they would be exposed to lead.

nies to fire "potentially pregnant" workers (which means any woman who cannot prove she is infertile) than to clean up the workplace so that it becomes safe for everyone. Employers claim they are barring women because they are afraid of lawsuits, should a worker whose baby is born with a disability, claim that disability was brought on by workplace exposure. But, in fact, no such suit has ever been filed and, considering the problems Vietnam veterans have experienced in suits claiming reproductive damages from exposure to Agent Orange and farm workers from exposure to toxic pesticides, such a suit is not likely to present a major risk to employers.

WHY?

So, why are these various fetal protection activities happening and why only in the United States? Indeed, why do many cities and states post warnings in bars and subways, now also appearing on liquor bottles, that read: "Warning! Drinking alcoholic beverages during pregnancy can cause birth defects"? (Note: any alcoholic beverage, no specification of how much or of alcohol content, and no mention of possible detrimental effects on sperm.)

No doubt, the antiabortion movement has helped raise "the fetus" to mythic proportions. Perhaps also prenatal technologies, especially ultrasound imaging, have made fetuses seem more real than before. Not so long ago, physicians could find out about a fetus' health only by touching or listening to a pregnant woman's distended belly. Now, in the minds of many people, fetuses have an identity separate from that of the woman whose body harbors them, since it is not unusual for their future parents to know their sex and expected health status.

But that doesn't explain why these activities are peculiar to the United States. Europeans often assume that anything that is accepted in the United States today will be accepted in Europe tomorrow—or, if not tomorrow, the next day. But pregnancy is not like Coca Cola. It is embedded in culture and framed by a network of economic and social policies. We cannot understand the profound differences between the ways pregnant women are regarded here and in other Western countries unless we face the fact that this country alone among industrialized nations has no coherent programs of health insurance, social and economic supports for

pregnant women, maternal and child care, and protection of workers' rights. This has been true since the beginning of this century, but the situation has been aggravated since the dismemberment of the, however meager, social policies that existed before the Reagan era. Recent pronouncements by "drug czar" William Bennett and Secretary of Health and Human Services Louis Sullivan, urging that drug use during pregnancy be taken as prima facie evidence of child abuse, are among the ways the administration is shifting blame for the disastrous economic and social policies that have resulted in huge increases in poverty, homelessness, and unprecedented levels of drug use onto the victims of these policies.

While the economic circumstances of women and children, and especially those of color, are deteriorating and disparities in access to services and in infant mortality rates are increasing, what a fine trick it is to individualize these conditions and blame women for selfishly putting their fetuses at risk. Yet taking women to court for fetal endangerment creates more low-income women and more babies that will be warehoused in hospitals or shuttled among an insufficient number of adequate foster homes by overloaded social-service systems. These are not solutions. They are merely ways of diverting attention from the enormous systemic problems that have been aggravated by the Reagan-Bush years and of shifting blame for the consequences onto the most vulnerable people.

The editorial in the June [1990] issue of the *American Journal of Public Health* (Vol. 80, No. 6) calls attention to the longstanding correlation of birthweight with parental income and living environment, regardless of maternal age, education, or marital status. The author points out that although U.S. infant mortality has declined since the 1940s, the overall decline slowed during the conservative Eisenhower and Reagan-Bush years. He also shows that, though infant mortality has gone down overall since 1947, Black/white infant mortality *ratios* have risen from 1.61 in 1947 to 2.08 in 1987 (where race, as usual, is to be interpreted as an indicator of the range of disadvantages that result from racism and not as a biological signifier).

Again and again, studies have documented the deleterious effects of adverse economic and social conditions on maternal and infant health. But it continues to be far easier to get money for yet another study than for the policies and programs that could ameliorate or, indeed, eliminate the dismal conditions that jeopardize the health and welfare of women and children.

WHAT TO DO?

We have to take whatever political actions we can to support the efforts of various community organizations and to pressure government agencies at all levels to provide the economic, social, and educational supports that will let women and children live *above* the poverty level, not below it. We need what other industrialized nations have: adequate education, job security, proper nutrition, subsidized housing, universal health care, accessible drug-treatment programs, and so on. The lack of these is responsible for the disproportionate U.S. infant mortality and disability rates, not women's neglectful behavior during pregnancy.

A friend recently suggested that, rather than being sued, pregnant women should sue in the name of "the fetus" for access to the economic, social, and health measures that are necessary for successful pregnancy outcomes. Of course, this concept suffers from the fact that it, too, makes the fetus a person. Furthermore, such suits probably would not hold up in court, since, while the U.S. Constitution guarantees certain freedoms and rights, it does not guarantee the economic and social conditions necessary for every one to be able to exercise them. Despite this, a well-orchestrated campaign of this sort could educate and politicize people about the shallowness and hypocrisy of the government's supposed efforts at fetal protection, and so could be used to rally support for the kinds of measures that can improve the needlessly dismal economic and social circumstances in which large sectors of the U.S. population live. [1990]

Violence Against Women in Intimate Relationships

Physical violence directed against women by their partners has made the home a frightening and dangerous place for the millions of women who are abused each year. For many of these women, fear of social judgment often prevents them from speaking out about their lives, thereby gaining support and possibly changing their relationships. This section begins with the voices of two women who have found the courage to expose their abuse. The risks these women take in breaking their silence reveal that all too often, society tacitly condones violence against women in intimate relationships.

Myths and misconceptions prevent many people from understanding the experiences of battered women and the reasons why they stay in abusive relationships. Margaret Anderson provides an overview of violence against women in the home, and examines the realities of battered women's lives. Myrna Zambrano confronts the myths about battered women and asserts that abused women are not responsible for men's violence against them.

91

A Letter from a Battered Wife

DEL MARTIN

A friend of mine received the following letter after discussing wife-beating at a public meeting.

I am in my thirties and so is my husband. I have a high school diploma and am presently attending a local college, trying to obtain the additional education I need. My husband is a college graduate and a professional in his field. We are both attractive and, for the most part, respected and well-liked. We have four children and live in a middle-class home with all the comforts we could possibly want.

I have everything, except life without fear.

For most of my married life I have been periodically beaten by my husband. What do I mean by "beaten"? I mean that parts of my body have been hit violently and repeatedly, and that painful bruises, swelling, bleeding wounds, unconsciousness, and combinations of these things have resulted.

Beating should be distinguished from all other kinds of physical abuse—including being hit and shoved around. When I say my husband threatens me with abuse I do not mean he warns me that he may lose control. I mean that he shakes a fist against my face or nose, makes punching-bag jabs at my shoulder, or makes similar gestures which may quickly turn into a full-fledged beating.

I have had glasses thrown at me. I have been kicked in the abdomen when I was visibly pregnant. I have been kicked off the bed and hit while lying on the floor—again, while I was pregnant. I have been whipped, kicked and thrown, picked up again and thrown down again. I have been punched and kicked in the head, chest, face, and abdomen more times than I can count.

I have been slapped for saying something about politics, for having a different view about religion, for swearing, for crying, for wanting to have intercourse.

I have been threatened when I wouldn't do something he told me to do. I have been threatened when he's had a bad day and when he's had a good day.

I have been threatened, slapped, and beaten after stating bitterly that I didn't like what he was doing with another woman.

After each beating my husband has left the house and remained away for a few days.

Few people have ever seen my black and blue face or swollen lips because I have always stayed indoors afterwards, feeling ashamed. I was never able to drive following one of these beatings, so I could not get myself to a hospital for care. I could never have left my young children alone, even if I could have driven a car.

Hysteria inevitably sets in after a beating. This hysteria—the shaking and crying and mumbling—is not accepted by anyone, so there has never been anyone to call.

My husband on a few occasions did phone a day or so later so we could agree on an excuse I would use for returning to work, the grocery store, the dentist appointment, and so on. I used the excuses—a car accident, oral surgery, things like that.

Now, the first response to this story, which I myself think of, will be "Why didn't you seek help?"

I did. Early on in our marriage I went to a clergyman who, after a few visits, told me that my husband meant no real harm, that he was just confused and felt insecure. I was encouraged to be more tolerant and understanding. Most important, I was told to forgive him the beatings just as Christ had forgiven me from the cross. I did that, too.

Things continued. Next time I turned to the doctor. I was given little pills to relax me and told to take things a little easier. I was just too nervous.

I turned to a friend, and when her husband found out, he accused me of either making things up or exaggerating the situation. She didn't, but she could no longer really help me. Just by believing me she was made to feel disloyal.

I turned to a professional family guidance agency. I was told there that my husband needed help and that I should find a way to control the incidents. I couldn't control the beatings—that was the whole point of my seeking help. At the agency I found I had to defend myself against the suspicion that I wanted to be hit, that I invited the beatings.

Good God! Did the Jews invite themselves to be slaughtered in Germany?

I did go to two more doctors. One asked me what I had done to provoke my husband. The other asked if we had made up yet.

I called the police one time. They not only did not respond to the call, they called several hours later to ask if things had "settled down." I could have been dead by then!

I have nowhere to go if it happens again. No one wants to take in a woman with four children. Even if there were someone kind enough to care, no one wants to become involved in what is commonly referred to as a "domestic situation."

Everyone I have gone to for help has somehow wanted to blame me and vindicate my husband. I can see it lying there between their words and at the end of their sentences. The clergyman, the doctor, the counselor, my friend's husband, the police—all of them have found a way to vindicate my husband.

No one has to "provoke" a wife-beater. He will strike out when he's ready and for whatever reason he has at the moment.

I may be his excuse, but I have never been the reason.

I know that I do not want to be hit. I know, too, that I will be beaten again unless I can find a way out for myself and my children. I am terrified for them also.

As a married woman I have no recourse but to remain in the situation which is causing me to be painfully abused. I have suffered physical and emotional battering and spiritual rape because the social structure of my world says I cannot do anything about a man who wants to beat me. . . . But staying with my husband means that my children must be subjected to the emotional battering caused when they see their mother's beaten face or hear her screams in the middle of the night.

I know that I have to get out. But when you have nowhere to go, you know that you must go on your own and expect no support. I have to be ready for that. I have to be ready to support myself and the children completely, and still provide a decent environment for them. I pray that I can do that before I am murdered in my own home.

I have learned that no one believes me and that I cannot depend upon any outside help. All I have left is the hope that I can get away before it is too late.

I have learned also that the doctors, the police, the clergy, and my friends will excuse my husband for distorting my face, but won't forgive me for looking bruised and broken. The greatest tragedy is that I am still praying, and there is not a human person to listen.

Being beaten is a terrible thing; it is most terrible of all if you are not equipped to fight back. I recall an occasion when I tried to defend myself and actually tore my husband's shirt. Later, he showed it to a relative as proof that I had done something terribly wrong. The fact that at that moment I had several raised spots on my head hidden by my hair, a swollen lip that was bleeding, and a severely damaged cheek with a blood clot that caused a permanent dimple didn't matter to him. What mattered was that I tore his shirt! That I tore it in self-defense didn't mean anything to him.

My situation is so untenable I would guess that anyone who has not experienced one like it would find it incomprehensible. I find it difficult to believe myself.

It must be pointed out that while a husband can beat, slap, or threaten his wife, there are "good days." These days tend to wear away the effects of the beating. They tend to cause the wife to put aside the traumas and look to the good—first, because there is nothing else to do; second, because there is nowhere and no one to turn to; and third, because the defeat is the beating and the hope is that it will not happen again. A loving woman like myself always hopes that it will not happen again. When it does, she simply hopes again, until it becomes obvious after a third beating that there is no hope. That is when she turns outward for help to find an answer. When that help is denied, she either resigns herself to the situation she is in or pulls herself together and starts making plans for a future life that includes only herself and her children.

For many the third beating may be too late. Several of the times I have been abused I have been amazed that I have remained alive. Imagine that I have been thrown to a very hard slate floor several times, kicked in the abdomen, the head, and the chest, and still remained alive!

What determines who is lucky and who isn't? I could have been dead a long time ago had I been hit the wrong way. My baby could have been killed or deformed had I been kicked the wrong way. What saved me?

I don't know. I only know that it has happened and that each night I dread the final blow that will kill me and leave my children motherless. I hope I can hang on until I complete my education, get a good job, and become self-sufficient enough to care for my children on my own.   [1983]

92

The Club

MITSUYE YAMADA

He beat me with the hem of a kimono
worn by a Japanese woman
this prized
painted
wooden statue
carved to perfection
in Japan or maybe Hong Kong.

She was usually on display
in our living room atop his bookshelf
among his other overseas treasures
I was never to touch.
She posed there most of the day
her head tilted
her chin resting lightly
on the white pointed fingertips
of her right hand
her black hair
piled high on her head
her long slim neck bared
to her shoulders.
An invisible hand
under the full sleeve
clasped her kimono
close to her body
its hem flared
gracefully around her feet.

That hem
made fluted red marks
on these freckled arms
my shoulders

my back.
That head
inside his fist
made camel
bumps
on his knuckles.
I prayed for her
that her pencil thin neck
would not snap
or his rage would be unendurable.
She held fast for me
didn't even chip or crack.

One day, we were talking
as we often did the morning after.
Well, my sloe-eyed beauty, I said
have you served him enough?
I dared to pick her up with one hand
I held her gently by the flowing robe
around her slender legs.
She felt lighter than I had imagined.
I stroked her cold thighs
with the tips of my fingers
and felt a slight tremor.

I carried her into the kitchen and wrapped her
in two sheets of paper towels
We're leaving
I whispered
you and I
together.

I placed her
between my clothes in my packed suitcase.
That is how we left him
forever.   [1989]

 93

Violence in the Family

MARGARET L. ANDERSON

This discussion of the family shows that isolation is both an ideological and a structural characteristic of the modern family. We have already seen the contradictions and dilemmas that isolation poses for mothers. But the effects of isolation and the ethic of family privacy are no more vividly seen than in the high incidence of violence against women in the family. Wife battering, child abuse, and incest have only recently been brought to the public's attention, but all of them make the tensions of family life clear. Violence in families also reveals the continuing presence of patriarchal relations within families.

Only in recent years has the sanctity of the private household been breached so that these issues have come to our attention. What were once hidden problems now seem disturbingly common. Although accurate measures of the extent of family violence are difficult to establish, researchers estimate that the problem is widespread across families in all classes and races (Dobash and Dobash 1979; Strauss, Gelles, and Steinmetz 1980). With regard to wife battering and child abuse, indirect evidence of their extent also comes from police records of domestic disturbances (Martin 1976), hospital emergency room files, family court records, homicide rates of women killed by husbands and lovers (Wolfgang 1958), and the great number of divorces that cite violence as the primary reason for ending the marriage (Chester and Streather 1972; Levinger 1966). Information on incest is even harder to obtain because social taboos against it make it one of the most hidden of social problems. But as victims of incest have spoken out, we have begun to see its high incidence across class and race. While we have tended to think of violence as most prevalent in lower classes and among minority groups, it is important to point out that it occurs in all groups, although the middle and upper classes have more ability to keep it secret.

BATTERED WOMEN

Studies indicate that the overwhelming amount of domestic violence is directed against women (Dobash and Dobash 1979). Coupled with the idea that violence is purposeful behavior, this fact leads to the conclusion that violence against wives is a form of social control—one that emerges directly from the patriarchal structure and ideology of the family (Barry 1979). Historically, wife beating has been a legitimate way to express male authority. Scholars contend that the transformation from the feudal patriarchal household to the nuclear family had the effect of strengthening the husband's power over his wife by placing systems of authority directly in the hands of individual men, not in the indirect rule of the state. Thus, throughout the seventeenth, eighteenth, and nineteenth centuries, men could, within the law, beat their wives, and there was little community objection to their doing so as long as the method and extent of violence remained within certain tacit, and sometimes formally documented, limits. For example, eighteenth-century French law restricted violence against wives to "blows, thumps, kicks, or punches on the back if they leave no traces" and did not allow the use of "sharp edged or crushing instruments" (Castan, cited in Dobash and Dobash 1979:56–57). One ancient code, from which we get the phrase *rule of thumb*, allowed a man to beat his wife with a stick no thicker than his thumb (Dobash and Dobash 1977).

The historical context of wife beating provides a perspective with which to view the contemporary problem. Now, although wife beating is socially abhorred, it is at the same time widely legitimated through its humorous portrayal and through attitudes protecting privacy in marriage. Additionally, the attitude that victims bring violence on themselves (by not leaving) seems to discourage social intervention in violent relationships. As a result, the phenomenon of violence is widely misunderstood. Dobash and Dobash's (1979) study of Scottish wives gives us some understanding of how violence emerges in marriage and how it is tied to the social isolation of women in the family.

Dobash and Dobash traced the course of 109 relationships that resulted in battering, beginning with the initial courtship phase. During the period when couples first met, both maintained separate lives, including an independent social life with friends and individual commitments to their family, jobs, and education. As the couples' commitment to each other increased, the partners modified their social lives, although women did so more than men. One-quarter of the women studied went out with their own friends once a week or more, compared with nearly half of the men. The more serious the relationship became, the less time women spent with their own friends.

Prior to marriage, the women reported that sexual jealousy was the major conflict in the relationship, although arguments over jealousy seem to have had the purpose of confirming the couple's commit-

ment to each other. The women became increasingly isolated from their friends prior to the marriage, and they reported believing that love would take care of any problems that existed in the relationship.

Both partners entered marriage with ideals about how the marriage would work, although after a time it was clear that the husband's ideals would rule. Marriage, for the wife, involved an extreme constriction of her social world, and the husband began to believe that he could monopolize his wife, although she could not put similar demands upon him. He, as the representative to the outside world, was supposed to have authority, independence, and freedom; she could not question his movements.

In this study, 41 percent of the wives experienced their first attack within six months of the wedding; another 18 percent experienced an attack within the first year of marriage. The wives' response was one of surprise, shock, shame, and guilt, although both partners treated the incident as an exception and assumed, without discussion, that the issue had been resolved. Yet, as the marriage continued, conflicts repeatedly surfaced. Nearly two-thirds of the couples reported sexual jealousy and expectations about domestic work as the source of conflict leading to violent episodes. The women reported that their social world moved more apart from their husband's as the marriage went on. The wives were mostly involved in the everyday matters of household management and child care, whereas the husbands were involved in their own work. However, the husbands still expected their wives to meet their immediate needs.

What is striking about these case studies is how common the patterns in these relationships are. Clearly, wife battering emerges from institutional arrangements that isolate women in the home and give men authority over them. Moreover, once a pattern of violence is established, wives believe they have no options. Most will, at some point, leave—even if temporarily—(Dobash and Dobash 1979)—but their feeling that they have no place to go is usually a realistic assessment of their economic situation and their powerlessness to effect changes within the relationship (Martin 1976). When wives do stay in abusive relationships, they tend to rationalize the violence to themselves. Research on women who did not leave after battering finds that they use several types of rationalizations, including believing that the man can be "saved" and denying the battering by seeing it as the result of external forces.

In the courts, battered wives are faced with the problem of having to prosecute a man who is both their husband and, possibly, the father of their children. Moreover, even if the wife brings charges, when the husband is released he returns to the home—perhaps more angry than when the violence began (Martin 1976). The movement to establish refuges for battered women has assisted many victims in responding to battering, and such centers have proliferated in communities throughout the country. But difficulties in funding such centers have caused many to close, and current cutbacks in social services funding seem likely to pose additional setbacks. Finally, the attitude that family problems are a private matter, to be resolved between two equal partners and within the confines of the home, creates resistance to social changes that could assist battered wives.

MARITAL RAPE

Marital rape is defined as "forced sexual activity demanded of a wife by her husband" (Frieze 1983). Legal definitions of marital rape vary from state to state, and in many states forced sex is not considered a crime in marriage. Nonetheless, studies of marital rape show it to be a serious problem, affecting probably 10 percent of all married women (Finkelhor and Yllo, 1985; Frieze 1983; Russell 1982).

Marital rape is most commonly associated with other physical violence in the relationship. Victims of marital rape, like other rape victims, experience rape trauma syndrome, including physical injury, anger, depression, fear, and loss of interest in sex (Burgess and Holmstrom 1978).

Studies of marital rape find that wives who have several children, who have never been employed before marriage, and who have less formal education are more likely to be raped in marriage, compared with battered wives who are not raped. Husbands who rape their wives are more dominant in the marriage relationship and are also more likely to have drinking problems. Marital rape is more likely to occur also where husbands associate sex with violence, have extramarital affairs, and are unreasonably jealous (Frieze 1983). One of the most disturbing findings in the research on marital rape is that one of its causes is a husband's anger that his wife has been raped by someone else.

Wives in these marriages have few resources of their own to draw on, exacerbating their powerlessness in this situation. Moreover, the belief that sexual access is a right in marriage makes it appear that they have not been raped. Nonetheless, the evidence on marital rape shows the extent to which the definition of women as the property of men continues to affect marital relationships.

INCEST AND SEXUAL ABUSE

Accurate estimates of the extent of incest and sexual abuse are very difficult to establish. Man–girl incest is said to involve at least 1 percent of all girls, although one in five girls and one in eleven boys say they have had sexual experience as a child with a much older person (Finkelhor 1979).

Feminist clinicians who have studied incest have challenged traditional Freudian assumptions about incest that children lie or fantasize about incestuous sexual encounters. Incest victims do try to stop the incest by seeking help or striking back, though often they are not believed. Research from feminist clinicians has shown that families where incest occurs tend to share several characteristics, the most significant of which is the estrangement of mother and daughter.

Mothers may be aware of incestuous abuse, but they are typically powerless to stop it. A mother may become a silent bystander because her emotional and/or economic dependence on her husband prevents her from confronting the situation (Armstrong and Begus 1982). Particularly in families where mothers are unusually powerless because of battering, disability, mental illness, or repeated childbearing, there is an especially high risk of sexual abuse, especially among daughters who have taken on the household responsibilities; in such families, the daughter is often led to believe that she must comply with the father's demands if she is to hold the family together (Herman and Hirschman 1977). Moreover, molested daughters in this situation are still dependent upon their fathers for care and, since this may be the only affection they receive, victims often report warm feelings for their fathers, who make them feel special (Herman 1981).

This research finds that the father/assailant feels

no contrition about his behavior. When mothers were incapacitated, fathers did not take on the nurturing functions, nor did they express nurturing feelings for the victim or understand the destructiveness of the incest. Fathers typically blamed their wife or their daughter for the incest and, distressingly, Herman finds that daughters often reinforce this view, blaming the mother and herself, while exonerating the father (Herman 1981).

This portrait of incestuous behavior underscores that the intersection of power and gender relations in families is a contributing fact in incestuous behavior. Researchers also are only now beginning to see the multiple consequences of sexual abuse. A study of female prostitutes and drug users finds that as many as 44 percent were sexually abused as children (MacFarlane 1978). Sexually abused female runaways are also more likely than nonabused female runaways to engage in delinquent and criminal activities (McCormack, Janus, and Burgess 1986). These findings also suggest that sexual abuse is important for practitioners to consider when developing treatment programs.

Feminists have pointed to violence as the logical result of both women's powerlessness in the family and a male culture that emphasized aggression, domination, and violence. The modern form of the family leads women to be dependent on men economically and emotionally, and, as a result, the traditional family is a source of social conflict and a haven only for men (Hartmann 1981). The phenomenon of violence in the family shows clearly the problems that traditional family structures create for women. Feminist criticism of the family rests, in part, on the psychological, physical, and economic threats families pose for women. And it is for these reasons that feminists argue for a change in traditional family structures. These changes, intended to empower women, would not necessarily abolish the family, but they would create new values regarding women's work in the family and new rewards for women in the family, regardless of whether they are also working in the public labor force.   [1988]

REFERENCES

Armstrong, P., and Begus, S. "Daddy's Right: Incestuous Assault." In Irene Diamond (ed.), *The Family, Politics and the State.* New York: Longman's Press, 1982.

Barry, K. *Female Sexual Slavery.* Englewood Cliffs, NJ.: Prentice Hall, 1979.

Burgess, L. L., and Holmstrom, A. W. *The Victim of Rape: Institutional Reactions.* New York: Wiley, 1978.

Chester, R., and Streather, J., "Cruelty in English Divorce: Some Empirical Findings." *Journal of Marriage and the Family,* 34(1972): 706–710.

Dobash, R. E., and Dobash, R. "Love, Honor, and Obey: Institutional Ideologies and the Struggle for Battered Women." *Contemporary Crises,* 1(1977): 403–415.

———. *Violence Against Wives.* New York: Free Press, 1979.

Finkelhor, D. *Sexually Victimized Children.* New York: Free Press, 1979.

——— (ed.). *The Dark Side of Families: Current Family Violence Research.* Beverly Hills, CA: Sage Publications, 1983.

Finkelhor, D., and Yllo, K. *License to Rape: Sexual Abuse of Wives.* New York: Free Press, 1979.

Frieze, I. H. "Investigating the Causes and Consequences of Marital Rape." *Signs,* 8(Spring 1983): 532–553.

Hartmann, H. "The Family as the Locus of Gender, Class, and Political Struggle: The Example of Housework." *Signs,* 6(Spring 1981): 366–394.

Herman, J. *Father-Daughter Incest.* Cambridge, MA: Harvard University Press, 1981.

Herman, J., and Hirschman, L. "Father-Daughter Incest." *Signs,* 2(Summer 1977): 735–756.

Levinger, G. "Sources of Marital Dissatisfaction Among Applicants for Divorce." *American Journal of Orthopsychiatry,* 36(1966): 803–807.

MacFarlane, K. "Sexual Abuse of Children." In J. R. Chapman and M. Gates (eds.), *The Victimization of Women.* Beverly Hills, CA: Sage Publications, 1978, pp. 81–109.

Martin, D. *Battered Wives.* San Francisco: Gilde, 1976.

McCormack, A., Janus, M. D., and Burgess, A. W. "Runaway Youths and Sexual Victimization: Gender Differences in an Adolescent Runaway Population." *Child Abuse and Neglect,* 10(1986): 387–395.

Pagelow, M. D. "Double Victimization of Battered Women." Paper presented at the Annual Meeting of the American Society of Criminology, San Francisco, November 1980.

Russell, D. E. H. *Rape in Marriage.* New York: Macmillan, 1982.

Strauss, M. A., Gelles, R., and Steinmetz, S. *Behind Closed Doors.* Garden City, NY: Doubleday-Anchor, 1980.

Wolfgang, M. *Patterns in Criminal Homicide.* New York: Wiley, 1958.

 94

Social and Cultural Reasons for Abuse

MYRNA ZAMBRANO

IS IT TRUE WHAT THEY SAY ABOUT BATTERED WOMEN?

People say many things about why women are beaten by their husbands or boyfriends. You may have heard that it's because the family is poor, or the woman has a job and isn't home, or because she is not very smart. But women of *all* cultures and races, of all income levels, and of all personalities can be and are physically and emotionally abused by the men they are involved with. Most of what is said about battered women is meant to excuse behavior that is violent, irrational, and illegal. Most of what is said is cleverly designed to get around the basic fact that one person beating another is wrong and cannot be excused. Most of it also blames the person being beaten instead of the person doing the beating. But why should the men be protected and the women blamed? When people, or the men themselves, try to make excuses for the violence or blame women as the cause, they are denying and ignoring a very serious, complex problem. Perhaps worse, they perpetuate "myths" about domestic violence—false ideas and false reasons why men abuse women (and why women should accept it as natural) that circulate throughout society in movies, magazines, bars and beauty salons until they are so widespread that no one questions them and everyone believes they are true. The most terrible and untruthful thing is that these myths make abused women believe that it is all their fault and that they can control the violence if they really want to.

Don't believe these myths—they are false. They don't change or help the situation, they allow it to get worse. They let men get away with cruelty and brutality, and make women fearful and submissive. Instead of believing what people say, you can learn some of the facts about domestic violence that can help to change your anger and frustration into action and fulfillment.

MYTHS AND REALITIES

Myth #1 Battered women like it or else they would leave.

FALSE No one likes being threatened, slapped, shoved, thrown around, choked, hit or kicked. But it is difficult to leave a man who is your only support, or who has sworn to kill you if you leave. It is difficult to leave if you don't know where to go and have children to think about and provide for. A woman doesn't stay in a violent relationship because she likes it, she stays because many times pressure from her family, church and community leaves her feeling she has few, if any, alternatives.

Myth #2 If the battered woman sticks it out long enough, the relationship will change for the better.

FALSE If the woman doesn't leave, get legal help or counseling, the beatings and mental torture are likely to get worse, not better. Many women stay hoping the abuse will eventually stop. Some finally leave when the violence is so bad they want to kill the abuser or know that the next time he will kill them. It's dangerous to wait until this point of desperation; almost half of all women killed in the United States are killed by their boyfriends or husbands.*

Myth #3 If he didn't drink he wouldn't beat his wife or partner.

FALSE Although in many relationships alcohol appears to provoke or encourage violent behavior, women are physically abused by men who are sober and by men who don't drink. Alcohol is just a part of the reason he hits. At times the alcohol gives men a false sense of power. It cannot be said that it is the only cause, or that if he stops drinking the beating will stop.

Myth #4 Women deserve to be beaten because of the way they behave.

FALSE No one deserves to be beaten no matter what she does. Women who are beaten know only too well that it happens most of the time for no reason at all. If the dinner is served late she gets beaten, if she serves dinner on time she gets beaten. He is never pleased or satisfied with anything she does. His anger and his desire to have total control are the causes of his outbursts, not her actions.

Myth #5 If he works, is a good provider, and good with the children, a woman shouldn't ask for more. She should tolerate some of his character defects.

FALSE A husband who is good with the kids and brings home a paycheck shouldn't be excused from violent behavior. *Violence in the home shouldn't be tolerated under any circumstances.* The wife deserves to be well-treated, just like any member of the family. No one would approve of staying with a man because he only beat the children!

---

*R. E. Dobash, R. Dobash, *Violence Against Wives: A Case Against the Patriarchy,* The Free Press, 1979, p. 17.

Myth #6   Battering doesn't affect the children. They are just kids and don't notice these things.

FALSE   Battering most definitely affects children. In fact, a high percentage of men who are batterers saw their own mothers beaten.* Battering can be learned. It is very possible that if your children witness beatings, they too will grow up to be batterers or the victims of abuse. Also, living in the midst of an explosive situation frequently contributes to learning and personality problems in children. Although kids may not talk about the violence, they know it exists, and it has a deep impression on them.

Myth #7   This is God's will and no one should interfere.

FALSE   God may plan for much of what happens in our lives, but he would never plan for a woman to be regularly beaten by her partner. We may not be able to avoid something like a fatal disease or the death of a child, but what control we do have over our lives can be used to help stop the violence. It is far more likely that it is God's will that we live in peace and harmony than in the middle of violence.

Myth #8   Yes, women shouldn't be beaten, but what goes on in a home is no one else's business.

FALSE   Domestic violence is everyone's problem. Women are maimed and killed every day. Physical assault is wrong and it is illegal. We are all responsible for its end. Your husband has no more right to

---

*M. Straus, R. Gellis, S. Steinmetz, *Beyond Closed Doors: Violence in the American Family,* Anchor Press, 1980, p. 100.

harm you than a stranger, who would be convicted and sent to jail if he beat you or tried to rape you in your home.

Myth #9   If women would fight back, men wouldn't keep on beating them.

FALSE   Even if women do fight back they are beaten, sometimes even more severely. Most women are physically smaller than most men and no match when it comes to a fist fight.

Myth #10   Battering is a problem of the poor and uneducated.

FALSE   Battering is a crime against women that affects *all* communities. Abused women can be rich or poor; they can be white, Black, or Latina; they can have a high school education or a college degree. Although you may know only of poor women who are beaten, wealthy women are also victims of domestic violence. These women usually have more resources to keep their bruises from public view. They can see private doctors instead of emergency rooms, they can consult lawyers instead of legal aid, they may live in less crowded areas where people don't hear what's going on. They are less likely to ask for help from public agencies and are better able to keep their problems private. Admitting you are being battered does not show you are poor or uneducated. It says that you are being taken advantage of physically and mentally and that your partner needs immediate help. The violence in your home should not be a shameful secret that keeps you from getting help.   [1985]

Rape and Sexual Abuse

Sexual violence against women and girls is a specific form of abuse that, like battering, is surrounded by images and myths that mask the realities of assaulted women's lives. Whether we fear the possibility of assault or are actually raped or abused, all women feel the effects of these crimes every day.

Susan Griffin broke the silence about rape in 1971 in the first selection in this section. Her article drew rape out of the realm of inexplicable atrocities and placed it squarely in the context of patriarchy. It generated a good deal of analysis about the connection between rape and prevailing ideas about women, men, and sexuality. This analysis has led more recently to a movement against marital and acquaintance rape.

Rape is an abuse of power that is expressed through sexual violence. Many misconceptions about rape suggest that assaulted women somehow "provoked" their attackers into raping them. However, as Ntosake Shange's poem shows, the irrational violence of rape occurs "with no immediate cause."

While stranger rape and acquaintance rape are similar, they differ in significant ways. Perhaps the most notable characteristic of acquaintance rape is the betrayal of trust experienced by a woman when someone she knows, and may care about, rapes her. Robin Warshaw confronts the myths about acquaintance rape that prevent many women from naming their experience as rape.

Sexual abuse of a girl by a relative or close family friend has been shrouded in secrecy, even though it occurs to approximately one out of four girl children. In the short story "Hey, Hey Annamae," Annamae exposes her secret when she tells her girlfriends about her abuse. What happens to Annamae, and her friends' reactions to her story, provide examples of the continuing anguish and "conspiracy of silence" that scar the lives of many incest survivors.

🌿 95

Rape: The All-American Crime

SUSAN GRIFFEN

I

I have never been free of the fear of rape. From a very early age I, like most women, have thought of rape as part of my natural environment—something to be feared and prayed against like fire or lightning. I never asked why men raped; I simply thought it one of the many mysteries of human nature.

I was, however, curious enough about the violent side of humanity to read every crime magazine I was able to ferret away from my grandfather. Each issue featured at least one "sex crime," with pictures of a victim, usually in a pearl necklace, and of the ditch or the orchard where her body was found. I was never certain why the victims were always women, nor what the motives of the murderer were, but I did guess that the world was not a safe place for women.

I observed that my grandmother was meticulous about locks, and quick to draw the shades before anyone removed so much as a shoe. I sensed that danger lurked outside.

At the age of eight, my suspicions were confirmed. My grandmother took me to the back of the house where the men wouldn't hear, and told me that strange men wanted to do harm to little girls. I learned not to walk on dark streets, not to talk to strangers, or get into strange cars, to lock doors, and to be modest. She never explained why a man would want to harm a little girl, and I never asked.

If I thought for a while that my grandmother's fears were imaginary, the illusion was brief. That year, on the way home from school, a schoolmate a few years older than I tried to rape me. Later, in an obscure aisle of the local library (while I was reading *Freddy the Pig*) I turned to discover a man exposing himself. Then, the friendly man around the corner was arrested for child molesting.

My initiation to sexuality was typical. Every woman has similar stories to tell—the first man who attacked her may have been a neighbor, a family friend, an uncle, her doctor, or perhaps her own father. And women who grow up in New York City always have tales about the subway. . . .

When I was very young, my image of the "sexual offender" was a nightmarish amalgamation of the bogey man and Captain Hook: he wore a black cape, and he cackled. As I matured, so did my image of the rapist. Born into the psychoanalytic age, I tried to "understand" the rapist. Rape, I came to believe, was only one of many unfortunate evils produced by sexual repression. Reasoning by tautology, I concluded that any man who would rape a woman must be out of his mind.

Yet, though the theory that rapists are insane is a popular one, this belief has no basis in fact. According to Professor Menachem Amir's study of 646 rape cases in Philadelphia, *Patterns in Forcible Rape*, men who rape are not abnormal. Amir writes, "Studies indicate that sex offenders do not constitute a unique or psychopathological type; nor are they as a group invariably more disturbed than the control groups to which they are compared." Alan Taylor, a parole officer who has worked with rapists

in the prison facilities at San Luis Obispo, California, stated the question in plainer language, "Those men were the most normal men there. They had a lot of hang-ups, but they were the same hang-ups as men walking out on the street."

Another canon in the apologetics of rape is that, if it were not for learned social controls, all men would rape. Rape is held to be natural behavior, and not to rape must be learned. But in truth rape is not universal to the human species. Moreover, studies of rape in our culture reveal that far from being impulsive behavior, most rape is planned. Professor Amir's study reveals that in cases of group rape (the "gangbang" of masculine slang), 90 percent of the rapes were planned; in pair rapes, 83 percent of the rapes were planned; and in single rapes, 58 percent were planned. These figures should significantly discredit the image of the rapist as a man who is suddenly overcome by sexual needs society does not allow him to fulfill.

Far from the social control of rape being learned, comparisons with other cultures lead one to suspect that, in our society, it is rape itself that is learned. (The fact that rape is against the law should not be considered proof that rape is not in fact encouraged as part of our culture.)

This culture's concept of rape as an illegal, but still understandable, form of behavior is not a universal one. In her study *Sex and Temperament*, Margaret Mead describes a society that does not share our views. The Arapesh do not ". . . have any conception of the male nature that might make rape understandable to them." Indeed our interpretation of rape is a product of our conception of the nature of male sexuality. A common retort to the question, why don't women rape men, is the myth that men have greater sexual needs, that their sexuality is more urgent than women's. And it is the nature of human beings to want to live up to what is expected of them.

And this same culture which expects aggression from the male expects passivity from the female. Conveniently, the companion myth about the nature of female sexuality is that all women secretly want to be raped. Lurking beneath her modest female exterior is a subconscious desire to be ravished. The following description of a stag movie, written by Brenda Starr in Los Angeles' underground paper, *Everywoman,* typifies this male fantasy. The movie "showed a woman in her underclothes reading on her bed. She is interrupted by a rapist with a knife. He immediately wins her over with his charm and they get busy sucking and fucking." An advertisement in the *Berkeley Barb* reads, "Now as all women know from their daydreams, rape has a lot of advantages. Best of all it's so simple. No preparation necessary, no planning ahead of time, no wondering if you should or shouldn't; just whang! bang!" Thanks to Masters and Johnson even the scientific canon recognizes that for the female, "whang! bang!" can scarcely be described as pleasurable.

Still, the male psyche persists in believing that, protestations and struggles to the contrary, deep inside her mysterious feminine soul, the female victim has wished for her own fate. A young woman who was raped by the husband of a friend said that days after the incident the man returned to her home, pounded on the door and screamed to her, "Jane, Jane. You loved it. You know you loved it."

The theory that women like being raped extends itself by deduction into the proposition that most or much of rape is provoked by the victim. But this too is only myth. Though provocation, considered a mitigating factor in a court of law, may consist of only "a gesture," according to the Federal Commission on Crimes of Violence, only 4 percent of reported rapes involved any precipitative behavior by the woman.

The notion that rape is enjoyed by the victim is also convenient for the man who, though he would not commit forcible rape, enjoys the idea of its existence, as if rape confirms that enormous sexual potency which he secretly knows to be his own. It is for the pleasure of the armchair rapist that detailed accounts of violent rapes exist in the media. Indeed, many men appear to take sexual pleasure from nearly all forms of violence. Whatever the motivation, male sexuality and violence in our culture seem to be inseparable. James Bond alternately whips out his revolver and his cock, and though there is no known connection between the skills of gun-fighting and love-making, pacifism seems suspiciously effeminate. . . .

In the spectrum of male behavior, rape, the perfect combination of sex and violence, is the penultimate act. Erotic pleasure cannot be separated from culture, and in our culture male eroticism is wedded to power. Not only should a man be taller and stronger than a female in the perfect love-match, but he must also demonstrate his superior strength in gestures of dominance which are perceived as amorous. Though the law attempts to make a clear division between rape and sexual intercourse, in fact the courts find it difficult to distinguish between a case where the decision to copulate was mutual and one where a man forced himself upon his partner.

The scenario is even further complicated by the expectation that, not only does a woman mean "yes" when she says "no," but that a really decent woman ought to begin by saying "no," and then be led down the primrose path to acquiescence. Ovid, the author of Western Civilization's most celebrated sex-manual, makes this expectation perfectly clear:

> . . . and when I beg you to say "yes," say "no." Then let me lie outside your bolted door. . . . So Love grows strong. . . .

That the basic elements of rape are involved in all heterosexual relationships may explain why men often identify with the offender in this crime. But to regard the rapist as the victim, a man driven by his inherent sexual needs to take what will not be given him, reveals a basic ignorance of sexual politics. For in our culture heterosexual love finds an erotic expression through male dominance and female submission. A man who derives pleasure from raping a woman clearly must enjoy force and dominance as much or more than the simple pleasures of the flesh. Coitus cannot be experienced in isolation. The weather, the state of the nation, the level of sugar in the blood—all will affect a man's ability to achieve orgasm. If a man can achieve sexual pleasure after terrorizing and humiliating the object of his passion, and in fact while inflicting pain upon her, one must assume he derives pleasure directly from terrorizing, humiliating and harming a woman. According to Amir's study of forcible rape, on a statistical average the man who has been convicted of rape was found to have a normal sexual personality, tending to be different from the normal, well-adjusted male only in having a greater tendency to express violence and rage.

And if the professional rapist is to be separated from the average dominant heterosexual, it may be mainly a quantitative difference. For the existence of rape as an index to masculinity is not entirely metaphorical. Though this measure of masculinity seems to be more publicly exhibited among "bad boys" or aging bikers who practice sexual initiation through group rape, in fact, "good boys" engage in the same rites to prove their manhood. In Stockton, a small town in California which epitomizes silent-majority America, a bachelor party was given last summer for a young man about to be married. A woman was hired to dance "topless" for the amusement of the guests. At the high point of the evening the bridegroom-to-be dragged the woman into a bedroom. No move was made by any of his companions to stop what was clearly going to be an attempted rape. Far from it. As the woman described, "I tried to keep him away—told him of my *herpes genitalis*, et cetera, but he couldn't face the guys if he didn't screw me." After the bridegroom had finished raping the woman and returned with her to the party, far from chastising him, his friends heckled the woman and covered her with wine.

It was fortunate for the dancer that the bridegroom's friends did not follow him into the bedroom for, though one might suppose that in group rape, since the victim is outnumbered, less force would be inflicted on her, in fact, Amir's studies indicate, "the most excessive degrees of violence occurred in group rape." Far from discouraging violence, the presence of other men may in fact encourage sadism, and even cause the behavior. In an unpublished study of group rape by Gilbert Geis and Duncan Chappell, the authors refer to a study by W. H. Blanchard which relates, "The leader of the male group . . . apparently precipitated and maintained the activity, despite misgivings, because of a need to fulfill the role that the other two men had assigned to him. 'I was scared when it began to happen,' he says. 'I wanted to leave but I didn't want to say it to the other guys—you know—that I was scared.'"

Thus it becomes clear that not only does our culture teach men the rudiments of rape, but society, or more specifically other men, encourage the practice of it.

II

Every man I meet wants to protect me. Can't figure out what from.
                                                        —*Mae West*

. . . According to the male mythology which defines and perpetuates rape, it is an animal instinct inherent in the male. The story goes that sometime in our pre-historical past, the male, more hirsute and burly than today's counterparts, roamed about an uncivilized landscape until he found a desirable female. (Oddly enough, this female is *not* pictured as more muscular than the modern woman.) Her mate does not bother with courtship. He simply grabs her by the hair and drags her to the closest cave. Presumably, one of the major advantages of modern civilization for the female has been the civilizing of the male. We call it chivalry.

But women do not get chivalry for free. According to the logic of sexual politics, we too have to civilize our behavior. (Enter chastity. Enter virginity. Enter monogamy.) For the female, civilized behavior means chastity before marriage and faithfulness within it. Chivalrous behavior in the male is supposed to protect that chastity from involuntary defilement. The fly in the ointment of this otherwise peaceful system is the fallen woman. She does not behave. And therefore she does not deserve protection. Or, to use another argument, a major tenet of the same value system: what has once been defiled cannot again be violated. One begins to suspect that it is the behavior of the fallen woman, and not that of the male, that civilization aims to control.

The assumption that a woman who does not respect the double standard deserves whatever she gets (or at the very least "asks for it") operates in the courts today. While in some states a man's previous rape convictions are not considered admissible evidence, the sexual reputation of the rape victim is considered a crucial element of the facts upon which the court must decide innocence or guilt. . . .

According to the double standard, a woman who has had sexual intercourse out of wedlock cannot be raped. Rape is not only a crime of aggression against the body; it is a transgression against chastity as defined by men. When a woman is forced into a sexual relationship, she has, according to the male ethos, been violated. But she is also defiled if she does not behave according to the double standard, by maintaining her chastity, or confining her sexual activities to a monogamous relationship.

One should not assume, however, that a woman can avoid the possibility of rape simply by behaving. Though myth would have it that mainly "bad girls" are raped, this theory has no basis in fact. Available statistics would lead one to believe that a safer course is promiscuity. In a study of rape done in the District of Columbia, it was found that 82 percent of the rape victims had a "good reputation." Even the Police Inspector's advice to stay off the streets is rather useless, for almost half of reported rapes occur in the home of the victim and are committed by a man she has never before seen. Like indiscriminate terrorism, rape can happen to any woman, and few women are ever without this knowledge.

But the courts and the police, both dominated by white males, continue to suspect the rape victim, *sui generis,* of provoking or asking for her own assault. According to Amir's study, the police tend to believe that a woman without a good reputation cannot be raped. The rape victim is usually submitted to countless questions about her own sexual mores and behavior by the police investigator. This preoccupation is partially justified by the legal requirements for prosecution in a rape case. The rape victim must have been penetrated, and she must have made it clear to her assailant that she did not want penetration (unless of course she is unconscious). A refusal to accompany a man to some isolated place to allow him to touch her does not in the eyes of the court, constitute rape. She must have said "no" at the crucial genital moment. And the rape victim, to qualify as such, must also have put up a physical struggle—unless she can prove that to do so would have been to endanger her life.

But the zealous interest the police frequently exhibit in the physical details of a rape case is only partially explained by the requirements of the court. A woman who was raped in Berkeley was asked to tell the story of her rape four different times "right out in the street," while her assailant was escaping. She was then required to submit to a pelvic examination to prove that penetration had taken place. Later, she was taken to the police station where she was asked the same questions again: "Were you forced?" "Did he penetrate?" "Are you sure your life was in danger and you had no other choice?" This woman had

been pulled off the street by a man who held a 10-inch knife at her throat and forcibly raped her. She was raped at midnight and was not able to return to her home until five in the morning. Police contacted her twice again in the next week, once by telephone at two in the morning and once at four in the morning. In her words, "The rape was probably the least traumatic incident of the whole evening. If I'm ever raped again, . . . I wouldn't report it to the police because of all the degradation. . . ."

If white women are subjected to unnecessary and often hostile questioning after having been raped, third world women* are often not believed at all. According to the white male ethos (which is not only sexist but racist), third world women are defined from birth as "impure." Thus the white male is provided with a pool of women who are fair game for sexual imperialism. Third world women frequently do not report rape and for good reason. When blues singer Billie Holliday was 10 years old, she was taken off to a local house by a neighbor and raped. Her mother brought the police to rescue her, and she was taken to the local station crying and bleeding:

> When we got there, instead of treating me and Mom like somebody who called the cops for help, they treated me like I'd killed somebody. . . . I guess they had me figured for having enticed this old goat into the whorehouse. . . . All I know for sure is they threw me into a cell . . . a fat white matron . . . saw I was still bleeding, she felt sorry for me and gave me a couple glasses of milk. But nobody else did anything for me except give me filthy looks and snicker to themselves.
>
> After a couple of days in a cell they dragged me into a court. Mr. Dick got sentenced to five years. They sentenced me to a Catholic institution.

Clearly the white man's chivalry is aimed only to protect the chastity of "his" women.

As a final irony, that same system of sexual values from which chivalry is derived has also provided womankind with an unwritten code of behavior, called femininity, which makes a feminine woman the perfect victim of sexual aggression. If being chaste does not ward off the possibility of assault,

---

*Editor's note: "Third World" was used to describe women of color in the U.S. at the time this article was written.

being feminine certainly increases the chances that it will succeed. To be submissive is to defer to masculine strength; is to lack muscular development or any interest in defending oneself; is to let doors be opened, to have one's arm held when crossing the street. To be feminine is to wear shoes which make it difficult to run; skirts which inhibit one's stride; underclothes which inhibit the circulation. Is it not an intriguing observation that those very clothes which are thought to be flattering to the female and attractive to the male are those which make it impossible for a woman to defend herself against aggression?

Each girl as she grows into womanhood is taught fear. Fear is the form in which the female internalizes both chivalry and the double standard. Since, biologically speaking, women in fact have the same if not greater potential for sexual expression as do men, the woman who is taught that she must behave differently from a man must also learn to distrust her own carnality. She must deny her own feelings and learn not to act from them. She fears herself. This is the essence of passivity, and of course, a woman's passivity is not simply sexual but functions to cripple her from self-expression in every area of her life.

Passivity itself prevents a woman from ever considering her own potential for self-defense and forces her to look to men for protection. The woman is taught fear, but this time fear of the other; and yet her only relief from this fear is to seek out the other. Moreover, the passive woman is taught to regard herself as impotent, unable to act, unable even to perceive, in no way self-sufficient, and, finally, as the object and not the subject of human behavior. It is in this sense that a woman is deprived of the status of a human being. She is not free to be. . . .

III

If the basic social unit is the family, in which the woman is a possession of her husband, the superstructure of society is a male hierarchy, in which men dominate other men (or patriarchal families dominate other patriarchal families). And it is no small irony that, while the very social fabric of our male-dominated culture denies women equal access to political, economic and legal power, the literature,

myth and humor of our culture depicts women not only as the power behind the throne, but the real source of the oppression of men. The religious version of this fairy tale blames Eve for both carnality and eating of the tree of knowledge, at the same time making her gullible to the obvious devices of a serpent. Adam, of course, is merely the trusting victim of love. Certainly this is a biased story. But no more biased than the one television audiences receive today from the latest slick comedians. Through a media which is owned by men, censored by a State dominated by men, all the evils of this social system which make a man's life unpleasant are blamed upon "the wife." The theory is: were it not for the female who waits and plots to "trap" the male into marriage, modern man would be able to achieve Olympian freedom. She is made the scapegoat for a system which is in fact run by men.

Nowhere is this more clear than in the white racist use of the concept of white womanhood. The white male's open rape of black women, coupled with his overweening concern for the chastity and protection of his wife and daughters, represents an extreme of sexist and racist hypocrisy. While on the one hand she was held up as the standard for purity and virtue, on the other the Southern white woman was never asked if she wanted to be on a pedestal, and in fact any deviance from the male-defined standards for white womanhood was treated severely. (It is a powerful commentary on American racism that the historical role of Blacks as slaves, and thus possessions without power, has robbed black women of legal and economic protection through marriage. Thus black women in Southern society and in the ghettoes of the North have long been easy game for white rapists.) The fear that black men would rape white women was, and is, classic paranoia. Quoting from Ann Breen's unpublished study of racism and sexism in the South "*The New South: White Man's Country,*" Frederick Douglass legitimately points out that, had the black man wished to rape white women, he had ample opportunity to do so during the civil war when white women, the wives, sisters, daughters and mothers of the rebels, were left in the care of Blacks. But yet not a single act of rape was committed during this time. The Ku Klux Klan, who tarred and feathered black men and lynched them in the honor of the purity of white womanhood, also applied tar and feathers to a Southern white woman accused of bigamy, which leads one to suspect that Southern white men were not so much outraged at the violation of the woman as a person, in the few instances where rape was actually committed by black men, but at the violation of his property rights." In the situation where a black man was found to be having sexual relations with a white woman, the white woman could exercise skin-privilege, and claim that she had been raped, in which case the black man was lynched. But if she did not claim rape, she herself was subject to lynching.

In constructing the myth of white womanhood so as to justify the lynching and oppression of black men and women, the white male has created a convenient symbol of his own power which has resulted in black hostility toward the white "bitch," accompanied by an unreasonable fear on the part of many white women of the black rapist. Moreover, it is not surprising that after being told for two centuries that he wants to rape white women, occasionally a black man does actually commit that act. But it is crucial to note that the frequency of this practice is outrageously exaggerated in the white mythos. Ninety percent of reported rape is intra- not inter-racial. . . .

Indeed, the existence of rape in any form is beneficial to the ruling class of white males. For rape is a kind of terrorism which severely limits the freedom of women and makes women dependent on men. Moreover, in the act of rape, the rage that one man may harbor toward another higher in the male hierarchy can be deflected toward a female scapegoat. For every man there is always someone lower on the social scale on whom he can take out his aggressions. And that is any woman alive.

This oppressive attitude towards women finds its institutionalization in the traditional family. For it is assumed that a man "wears the pants" in his family—he exercises the option of rule whenever he so chooses. Not that he makes all the decisions— clearly women make most of the important day-to-day decisions in a family. But when a conflict of interest arises, it is the man's interest which will prevail. His word, in itself, is more powerful. He lords it over his wife in the same way his boss lords it over him, so that the very process of exercising his power becomes as important an act as obtaining whatever it is his power can get for him. This notion of power is key to the male ego in this culture, for the two acceptable measures of masculinity are a man's power over women and his power over other men. A man may boast to his friends that "I have 20 men working for me." It is also aggrandizement of his ego if he has the financial power to clothe his wife in furs and jewels. And, if a man lacks the wherewithal to acquire such power, he can always express his rage through equally masculine activities—rape and theft. Since male society defines the female as a possession, it is not surprising that the felony most often committed together with rape is theft. . . .

* * *

Rape is an act of aggression in which the victim is denied her self-determination. It is an act of violence which, if not actually followed by beatings or murder, nevertheless always carries with it the threat of death. And finally, rape is a form of mass terrorism, for the victims of rape are chosen indiscriminately, but the propagandists for male supremacy broadcast that it is women who cause rape by being unchaste or in the wrong place at the wrong time—in essence, by behaving as though they were free.

The threat of rape is used to deny women employment. (In California, the Berkeley Public Library, until pushed by the Federal Employment Practices Commission, refused to hire female shelvers because of perverted men in the stacks.) The fear of rape keeps women off the streets at night. Keeps women at home. Keeps women passive and modest for fear that they be thought provocative.

It is part of human dignity to be able to defend oneself, and women are learning. Some women have learned karate; some to shoot guns. And yet we will not be free until the threat of rape and the atmosphere of violence is ended, and to end that the nature of male behavior must change.

But rape is not an isolated act that can be rooted out from patriarchy without ending patriarchy itself. The same men and power structure who victimize women are engaged in the act of raping Vietnam, raping Black people and the very earth we live upon. Rape is a classic act of domination where, in the words of Kate Millett, "the emotions of hatred, con-

tempt, and the desire to break or violate personality," take place. This breaking of the personality
characterizes modern life itself. No simple reforms
can eliminate rape. As the symbolic expression of
the white male hierarchy, rape is the quintessential
act of our civilization, one which, Valerie Solanis
warns, is in danger of "humping itself to death."

[1971]

96

With No Immediate Cause

NTOSAKE SHANGE

every 3 minutes a woman is beaten
every five minutes a
woman is raped/every ten minutes
a lil girl is molested
yet i rode the subway today
i sat next to an old man who
may have beaten his old wife
3 minutes ago or 3 days/30 years ago
he might have sodomized his
daughter but i sat there
cuz the young men on the train
might beat some young women
later in the day or tomorrow
i might not shut my door fast
enuf/push hard enuf
every 3 minutes it happens
some woman's innocence
rushes to her cheeks/pours from her mouth
like the betsy wetsy dolls have been torn
apart/their mouths
mensis red & split/every
three minutes a shoulder
is jammed through plaster & the oven door/
chairs push thru the rib cage/hot water or
boiling sperm decorate her body
i rode the subway today
& bought a paper from a
man who might
have held his old lady onto
a hot pressing iron/i dont know

maybe he catches lil girls in the
park & rips open their behinds
with steel rods/i cdnt decide
what he might have done i only
know every 3 minutes
every 5 minutes every 10 minutes/so
i bought the paper
looking for the announcement
there has to be an announcement
of the women's bodies found
yesterday/the missing little girl
i sat in a restaurant with my
paper looking for the announcement
a yng man served me coffee
i wondered did he pour the boiling
coffee/on the woman cuz she waz stupid/
did he put the infant girl/in
the coffee pot/with the boiling coffee/cuz she cried
    too much
what exactly did he do with hot coffee
i looked for the announcement
the discovery/of the dismembered
woman's body/the
victims have not all been
identified/today they are
naked & dead/refuse to
testify/one girl out of 10's not
coherent/i took the coffee
& spit it up/i found an
announcement/not the woman's
bloated body in the river/floating
not the child bleeding in the
59th street corridor/not the baby
broken on the floor/
    "there is some concern
    that alleged battered women
    might start to murder their
    husbands & lovers with no
    immediate cause"
i spit up   i vomit   i am screaming
we all have immediate cause
every 3 minutes
every 5 minutes
every 10 minutes
every day
women's bodies are found
in alleys & bedrooms/at the top of the stairs

before i ride the subway/buy a paper/drink
coffee/i must know/
have you hurt a woman today
did you beat a woman today
throw a child cross a room
   are the lil girl's panties
   in yr pocket
did you hurt a woman today

i have to ask these obscene questions
the authorities require me to
establish
immediate cause

every three minutes
every five minutes
every ten minutes
every day   [1970]

🌿 97

The Reality of Acquaintance Rape

ROBIN WARSHAW

Women raped by men they know—acquaintance rape—is not an aberrant quirk of male-female relations. If you are a woman, your risk of being raped by someone you know is *four times greater* than your risk of being raped by a stranger.

A recent scientific study of acquaintance rape on 32 college campuses conducted by *Ms.* magazine and psychologist Mary P. Koss showed that significant numbers of women are raped on dates or by acquaintances, although most victims never report their attacks.

Ms. SURVEY STATS
- 1 in 4 women surveyed were victims of rape or attempted rape.
- 84 percent of those raped knew their attacker.
- 57 percent of the rapes happened on dates.

Those figures make acquaintance rape and date rape more common than left-handedness or heart attacks or alcoholism. These rapes are no recent campus fad or the fantasy of a few jilted females. They are real. And they are happening all around us.

Most states define rape as sexual assault in which a man uses his penis to commit vaginal penetration of a victim against her will, by force or threats of force or when she is physically or mentally unable to give her consent. Many states now also include unwanted anal and oral intercourse in that definition and some have removed gender-specific language to broaden the applicability of rape laws.

In acquaintance rape, the rapist and victim may know each other casually—having met through a common activity, mutual friend, at a party, as neighbors, as students in the same class, at work, on a blind date, or while traveling. Or they may have a closer relationship—as steady dates or former sexual partners. Although largely a hidden phenomenon because it's the least reported type of rape (and rape, in general, is the most underreported crime against a person), many organizations, counselors, and social researchers agree that acquaintance rape is the most prevalent rape crime today.

Only 90,434 rapes were reported to U.S. law enforcement agencies in 1986, a number that is conservatively believed to represent a minority of the actual rapes of all types taking place. Government estimates find that anywhere from three to ten rapes are committed for every one rape reported. And while rapes by strangers are still underreported, rapes by acquaintances are virtually nonreported. Yet, based on intake observations made by staff at various rape-counseling centers (where victims come for treatment, but do not have to file police reports), 70 to 80 percent of all rape crimes are acquaintance rapes.

Those rapes are happening in a social environment in which sexual aggression occurs regularly. Indeed, less than half the college women questioned in the *Ms.* survey reported that they had experienced *no* sexual victimization in their lives thus far (the average age of respondents was 21). Many had experienced more than one episode of unwanted sexual touching, coercion, attempted rape, or rape.

Using the data collected in the study, . . . [a] profile can be drawn of what happens in just one year of "social life" on America's college campuses.

Over the years, other researchers have documented the phenomenon of acquaintance rape. In 1957, a study conducted by Eugene J. Kanin of Purdue University in West Lafayette, Indiana, showed that 30 percent of women surveyed had suffered attempted or completed forced sexual intercourse while on a high school date. Ten years later, in 1967, while young people donned flowers and beads and talked of love and peace, Kanin found that more than 25 percent of the male college students surveyed had attempted to force sexual intercourse on a woman to the point that she cried or fought back. In 1977, after the blossoming of the women's movement and countless pop-culture attempts to extol the virtues of becoming a "sensitive man," Kanin found that 26 percent of the men he surveyed had tried to force intercourse on a woman and that 25 percent of the women questioned had suffered attempted or completed rape. In other words, two decades had passed since Kanin's first study, yet women were being raped by men they knew as frequently as before.

In 1982, a doctoral student at Auburn University in Auburn, Alabama, found that 25 percent of the undergraduate women surveyed had at least one experience of forced intercourse and that 93 percent of those episodes involved acquaintances. That same year, Auburn psychology professor and acquaintance-rape expert Barry R. Burkhart conducted a study in which 61 percent of the men said they had sexually touched a woman against her will.

Further north, at St. Cloud State University in St. Cloud, Minnesota, research in 1982 showed 29 percent of women surveyed reported being physically or psychologically forced to have sexual intercourse.

In 1984, 20 percent of the female students questioned in a study at the University of South Dakota in Vermillion, South Dakota, said they had been physically forced to have intercourse while on a date. At Brown University in Providence, Rhode Island, 16 percent of the women surveyed reported they were raped by an acquaintance and 11 percent of the men said they had forced sexual intercourse on a woman. And another study coauthored by Auburn's Burkhart showed 15 percent of the male respondents reporting having raped a date.

That same year, the study of acquaintance rape moved beyond the serenity of leafy college quadrangles into the hard reality of the "dangerous" outside world. A random sample survey of 930 women living in San Francisco, conducted by researcher Diana Russell, showed that 44 percent of the women questioned had been victims of rape or attempted rape—and that 88 percent of the rape victims knew their attackers. A Massachusetts Department of Public Health study, released in 1986, showed that two-thirds of the rapes reported at crisis centers were committed by acquaintances.

These numbers stand in stark contrast to what most people think of as rape: that is, a stranger (usually a black, Hispanic, or other minority) jumping out of the bushes at an unsuspecting female, brandishing a weapon, and assaulting her. The truth about rape—that it usually happens between people who know each other and is often committed by "regular" guys—is difficult to accept.

Most people never learn the truth until rape affects them or someone they care about. And many women are so confused by the dichotomy between their acquaintance-rape experience and what they thought rape really was that they are left with an awful new reality: Where once they feared strange men as they were taught to, they now fear strange men *and* all the men they know.

LORI'S STORY

How can a date be a rape?

The pairing of the word "date," which conjures up an image of fun shared by two companions, with the word "rape," which evokes the total loss of control by one person to the will of another, results in the creation of a new phrase that is nearly impossible for most people to comprehend. To understand how date rape happens, let's look at a classic case.

The Setup

It was natural. Normal. Lori's friend Amy wanted to go out with Paul, but felt awkward and shy about going out with him alone. So when Paul's roommate, Eric, suggested that he and Lori join Amy and Paul for a double date, it made sense. "I didn't feel anything for Eric except as a friend," Lori says of her reaction to the plan. "I said, 'Okay, maybe it will make Amy feel better.'"

Agreeing to go out with Eric was no great act of charity on Lori's part. He *was* attractive—tall, good-looking, in his mid-20s and from a wealthy family. Lori, who was 19 at the time, knew Eric and Paul as frequent customers at the popular Tampa Bay restaurant where she worked as a waitress when she was between college semesters.

On the day of the date, Eric called several times to change their plans. Finally, he phoned to say that they would be having a barbecue with several of his friends at the house he and Paul shared. Lori agreed.

We went to his house and I mentioned something about Paul and Amy and he kind of threw it off, like, "Yeah, yeah." I didn't think anything of it. There we are, fixing steaks, and he was saying, "Well, this is obviously something to help Amy."

He kept making drinks all night long. He kept saying, "Here, have a drink," "Here, drink this." I didn't because I didn't want it. He was just downing them right and left.

The Attack

Unknown to Lori, Amy had canceled her plans to see Paul the day before. Paul told Eric, but Eric never told Lori. As the barbecue party progressed and her friend failed to show up, Lori questioned Eric again. He then lied, telling her that Paul had just called to say he and Amy weren't coming.

I was thinking to myself, "Well, okay." Not in my wildest dreams would I have thought he was plotting something. Then all of his friends started leaving. I began to think, "Something is wrong, something is going on," but I've been known to overreact to things, so I ignored it.

After his friends left, we're sitting on the couch and he leans over and he kisses me and I'm thinking, "It's a date, it's no big deal." So then we started kissing a little bit more and I'm thinking, "I'm starting to enjoy this, maybe this isn't so bad." Then the phone rang and when he came back I was standing up. He grabbed me from behind and picked me up. He had his hands over my eyes and we were walking through his house. It was really dark and I didn't know where on earth he was taking me. I had never actually walked through his house.

He laid me down [on a bed] and kissed me. . . . He starts taking off my clothes and I said,

"Wait—time out! This is not what I want, you know," and he said to me something like this is what I owed him because he made me dinner.

I said, "This is wrong, don't do this. I didn't go out with you with this intent."

He said, "What do you call that on the couch?"

I said, "I call it a kiss, period."

And he said, "Well, I don't."

The two struggled until Eric rolled off her momentarily. Lori jumped up and went into the bathroom. Her plan was to come out in a few minutes and tell him it was time to take her home.

The whole time I'm thinking, "I don't believe this is happening to me." I didn't even have time to walk fully out of the bathroom door when he grabbed me and threw me on the bed and started taking my clothes off. I'm yelling and hitting and pushing on him and he just liked that. He says, "I know you must like this because a lot of women like this kind of thing." Then he says, "This is the adult world. Maybe you ought to grow up some."

I finally got to the point where there was nothing I could do.

Eric pushed his penis into her and, after a few minutes, ejaculated. Lori had had only one other experience with sexual intercourse, about a year before with a longtime boyfriend.

Then Eric just rolled over and I started to get my clothes together. He said, "Don't tell me you didn't like that." I looked at him and said, "No," and by this time I'm crying because I don't know what else to do. I never heard of anybody having that happen to them.

The Aftermath

Finally, Eric took her home.

In the car he said, "Can I call you tomorrow? Can I see you next weekend?" I just looked at him and he just looked at me and started laughing.

My mom had gone out and I just laid on my bed with the covers up. Everything I could possibly put on I think I put on that night—leg warmers, thermal underwear—everything imaginable in the middle of summer I put on my body. That night I dreamed it was all happening again. I dreamed I was standing there watching him do it.

For two weeks I couldn't talk. People would talk to me and I felt nothing. I felt like a zombie. I couldn't cry, I couldn't smile, I couldn't eat. My mom said, "What's wrong with you? Is something going on?" I said, "Nothing's wrong."

I thought it was my fault. What did I do to make him think he could do something like that? Was I wrong in kissing him? Was I wrong to go out with him, to go over to his house?

After two weeks, she told her mother what happened and they talked about what to do. Lori decided not to report it to the police for fear Eric would blame her. Eric continued to frequent the restaurant where she worked. Several weeks after their date, he cornered her in a hallway near the kitchen.

He touched me and I said, "Get your hands off me." At first, he thought it was funny. He said, "What's wrong?" then he started pulling me, trying to hug me. I pushed him and said, "Leave me alone," and I was starting to get a little loud. As I was walking away, he said, "Oh, I guess you didn't get enough."

I walked in the kitchen and picked up this tray full of food. I don't know how it happened, I just dropped the whole tray and it went everywhere. My friend, another waitress, went to the manager and said, "She's not going to be much good to you tonight," so they sent me home.

Lori decided to move to a town about 150 miles away to avoid continued encounters with Eric. There she found work as an office assistant and cashier and enrolled for a few classes at a new college. . . .

THE MYTHS ABOUT ACQUAINTANCE RAPE

Like most women with date-rape or acquaintance-rape experiences, Lori did not report the incident to police and did not, at first, even understand it to be rape. Instead, she felt almost totally isolated and blamed herself for what happened. She changed her life in order to feel physically safe from her attacker. She is now filled with doubts about her own judgment, fears socializing with men, and despairs about her ability to have a "normal" relationship.

But ask a group of college students what they think of a story like Lori's and they might tell you:

- "She deserved it."
- "What did she expect? After all, she went to his house."
- "That's not rape. Rape is when a guy you don't know grabs you and holds a gun to your head."
- "She wasn't a virgin, so no harm was done."
- "He bought her dinner. She owed him."
- "She liked kissing him. What's the big deal if he went farther?"
- "She just 'cried rape' later because she felt guilty about having sex."

Those are the kinds of comments heard recently on all kinds of campuses—Ivy League, state universities, small schools—when date rape was discussed by both male and female undergraduates. But let's not blame college students alone for their views: Their parents, indeed most of our society, would agree with one or more of those statements.

These are the myths that have formed what we believe to be the truth about women who are raped by men they know. But the actual truth is different indeed. Here are several of the most common myths about acquaintance rape juxtaposed with the reality:

Myth	Reality
Rape is committed by crazed strangers.	Most women are raped by "normal" acquaintances.
A woman who gets raped deserves it, especially if she agreed to go to the man's house or ride in his car.	No one, male or female, deserves to be raped. Being in a man's house or car does not mean a woman has agreed to have sex with him.
Women who don't fight back haven't been raped.	You have been raped when you are forced to have sex against your will, whether you fight back or not.
If there's no gun or knife, you haven't been raped.	It's rape whether the rapist uses a weapon or his fists, verbal threats, drugs or alcohol, physical isolation, your own diminished physical or mental state, or simply the weight of his body to overcome you.

It's not really rape if the victim isn't a virgin.

If a woman lets a man buy her dinner or pay for a movie or drinks, she owes him sex.
Agreeing to kiss or neck or pet with a man means that a woman has agreed to have intercourse with him.

When men are sexually aroused, they need to have sex or they will get "blue balls." Also, once they get turned on, men can't help themselves from forcing sex on a woman.

Women lie about being raped, especially when they accuse men they date or other acquaintances.

Rape is rape, even if the woman isn't a virgin, even if she willingly had sex with the man before.
No one owes sex as a payment to anyone else, no matter how expensive the date.
Everyone has the right to say "no" to sexual activity, regardless of what has preceded it, and to have that "no" respected.
Men don't physically need to have sex after becoming aroused any more than women do. Moreover, men are still able to control themselves even after becoming sexually excited.
Rape really happens—to people you know, by people you know.

Like most of our beliefs, we absorb these myths as we grow up: from the people around us, from the books we read, from the movies and television programs we watch, even from the way products are sold to us in advertisements.

Because of the myths, the reality of acquaintance rape is largely ignored. On college campuses, when a woman is raped in a dormitory or fraternity house by another student, university officials announce new plans for better lighting in the parking lots and expanded hours for escort services—positive safety precautions that have nothing to do with stopping acquaintance rape. The few women who report their date rapes (and whose cases are accepted for prosecution) are usually met with skepticism and disbelief from jurors and judges when they testify about being raped by a man they knew or chose to be with in a social setting.

No wonder that while many rape-prevention activists would like to see more prosecutions for acquaintance-rape cases, many admit privately that they counsel women not to press charges because of the difficulty of convincing jurors—whose views are shaped by the myths—that a rape has really taken place.

RAPE IS RAPE

Rape that occurs on dates or between people who know each other should not be seen as some sort of misguided sexual adventure: Rape is violence, not seduction. In stranger rape *and* acquaintance rape, the aggressor makes a decision to force his victim to submit to what he wants. The rapist believes he is entitled to force sexual intercourse from a woman and he sees interpersonal violence (be it simply holding the woman down with his body or brandishing a gun) as an acceptable way to achieve his goal.

"All rape is an exercise in power," writes Susan Brownmiller in her landmark book *Against Our Will: Men, Women and Rape.* Specifically, Brownmiller and others argue, rape is an exercise in the imbalance of power that exists between most men and women, a relationship that has forged the social order from ancient times on.

Today, that relationship continues. Many men are socialized to be sexually aggressive—to score, as it were, regardless of how. Many women are socialized to submit to men's wills, especially those men deemed desirable by society at large. Maintaining such roles helps set the stage for acquaintance rape.

But despite their socialization, most men are not rapists. That is the good news.

The bad news, of course, is that so many are.

Ms. SURVEY STAT
• 1 in 12 of the male students surveyed had committed acts that met the legal definitions of rape or attempted rape.

BLAMING THE ACQUAINTANCE-RAPE VICTIM

Without question, many date rapes and acquaintance rapes could have been prevented by the woman—if she hadn't trusted a seemingly nice guy, if she hadn't gotten drunk, if she had acted earlier on the "bad feeling" that many victims later report they felt but ignored because they didn't want to seem rude, unfriendly, or immature. But acknowledging that in some cases the woman might have prevented the rape by making a different decision does not make her responsible for the crime. Says a counselor for an Oregon rape-crisis agency: "We have a saying here: 'Bad judgment is not a rapeable offense.'"

As a society, we don't blame the victims of most crimes as we do acquaintance-rape survivors. A mugging victim is not believed to "deserve it" for wearing a watch or carrying a pocketbook on the street. Likewise, a company is not "asking for it" when its profits are embezzled; a store owner is not to blame for handing over the cash drawer when threatened. These crimes occur because the perpetrator decides to commit them.

Acquaintance rape is no different. There are ways to reduce the odds, but, like all crimes, there is no way to be certain that it will not happen to you.

Yet acquaintance-rape victims are seen as responsible for the attacks, often more responsible than their assailants. "Date rape threatens the assumption that if you're good, good things happen to you. Most of us believe that bad things don't happen out of the blue," says psychologist Koss, chief investigator of the *Ms.* study, now affiliated with the department of psychiatry at the University of Arizona Medical School in Tucson, Arizona. Society, in general, is so disturbed by the idea that a "regular guy" could do such a thing—and, to be sure, many "regular guys" are made uncomfortable by a concept that views their actions as a crime—that they would rather believe that something is wrong with the woman making such an outlandish claim: She is lying, she has emotional problems, she hates men, she is covering up her own promiscuous behavior. In fact, the research in the *Ms.* survey shows that women who have been raped by men they know are not appreciably different in any personal traits or behaviors than women who are not raped.

Should we ask women not to trust men who seem perfectly nice? Should we tell them not to go to parties or on dates? Should we tell them not to drink? Should we tell them not to feel sexual? Certainly not. *It is not the victim who causes the rape. . . .*

DATE RAPE AND ACQUAINTANCE RAPE ON COLLEGE CAMPUSES

Despite philosophical and political changes brought about by the women's movement, dating relationships between men and women are still often marked by passivity on the woman's part and aggression on the man's. Nowhere are these two seen in stronger contrast than among teenagers and young adults who often, out of their own fears, insecurity, and ignorance, adopt the worst sex-role stereotypes. Such an environment fosters a continuum of sexual victimization—from unwanted sexual touching to psychologically coerced sex to rape—that is tolerated as normal. "Because sexually coercive behavior is so common in our male-female interactions, rape by an acquaintance may not be perceived as rape," says Py Bateman, director of Alternatives to Fear, a Seattle rape-education organization.

Indeed, we speak of "the battle of the sexes" and, for many, it is just that. In their teens, many boys are counseled by their friends and older males to practice the "4Fs" when dealing with women: "Find 'em; feel 'em; fuck 'em; forget 'em." On the other hand, many girls, who have been admonished to "save it" for Mr. Right, want sexual intercourse to take place in the context of a relationship with some continuity attached to it. Kurt Weis and Sandra S. Borges, researchers at the University of California at Berkeley, pointed out in a 1973 paper that dating places individuals with these highly socialized but differing expectations into an ambiguous situation in which there is maximum privacy.

That is, dating can easily lead to rape.

Not surprising, then, that the risk of rape is four times higher for women aged 16 to 24, the prime dating age, than for any other population group. Approximately half of all men arrested for rape are also 24 years old or younger. Since 26 percent of all 18- to 24-year-olds in the United States attend college, those institutions have become focal points for studying date rape and acquaintance rape, such as the *Ms.* research.

Ms. SURVEY STAT

• For both men and women, the average age when a rape incident occurred (either as perpetrator or victim) was 18½ years old.

Going to college often means going away from home, out from under parental control and protection and into a world of seemingly unlimited freedoms. The imperative to party and date, although strong in high school, burgeons in this environment.

Alcohol is readily available and often used in stultifying amounts, encouraged by a college world that practically demands heavy drinking as proof of having fun. Marijuana, cocaine, LSD, methamphetamines, and other drugs are also often easy to obtain.

Up until the 1970s, colleges adopted a "substitute parent" attitude toward their students, complete with curfews (often more strict for females than males), liquor bans, and stringent disciplinary punishments. In that era, students were punished for violating the three-feet-on-the-floor rules during coed visiting hours in dormitories or for being caught with alcohol on college property. Although those regulations did not prevent acquaintance rape, they undoubtedly kept down the number of incidents by making women's dorms havens of no-men-allowed safety.

Such regulations were swept out of most schools during the Vietnam War era. Today, many campuses have coed dorms, with men and women often housed in alternating rooms on the same floor, with socializing unchecked by curfews or meaningful controls on alcohol and drugs. Yet, say campus crisis counselors, many parents still believe that they have properly prepared their children for college by helping them open local bank accounts and making sure they have enough underwear to last until the first trip home. By ignoring the realities of social pressures at college on male and female students—and the often catastrophic effects of those pressures—parents help perpetuate the awareness vacuum in which date rape and acquaintance rape continue to happen with regularity.

"What's changed for females is the illusion that they have control and they don't," says Claire P. Walsh, program director of the Sexual Assault Recovery Service at the University of Florida in Gainesville. "They know that they can go into chemical engineering or medical school and they've got their whole life planned, they're on a roll. They transfer that feeling of control into social situations and that's the illusion."

When looking at the statistical results of the *Ms.* survey, it's important to remember that many of these young people still have years of socializing and dating ahead of them, years in which they may encounter still more acquaintance rape. Students, parents of college students, and college administrators should be concerned. But many are not, lulled

by the same myths that pervade our society at large: Rape is not committed by people you know, against "good" girls, in "safe" places like university campuses.   [1988]

 98

Hey, Hey, Annamae

CHRISTINA GLENDENNING

When I was growing up back East all the neighborhood women and children would sit on their green or brown painted porch steps and gossip from dinner till dusk. The custom was called stoop-setting. You got to know everyone on the block and you knew about everyone on the block. You knew who beat on his wife, who had done time and whose car had been repossessed. We kids kept our ears open. It was an uneasy neighborhood and gossip was our most important source of survival.

It was the 1950's in Pittsburgh. Most of the neighborhood didn't have televisions or televisions that worked. Our entertainment was each other. And it was hot, steelmills polluting the air with oppressive grey-brown smoke. Come early evening the porches were cool, offering easy relief from the heat of cooking and washing up. We'd sit on the stoops and shout back and forth across the street, waiting for a breeze.

Mrs. Lloyd lived in the house directly across from us. Ernie, her youngest son and mean as sin, bullied the rest of us. About seven o'clock or so she'd bring her kitchen stool onto the sidewalk and sit down. Balancing her coffee cup on her knee she'd complain about her son to all the other mothers within earshot. "You mark my words, Blanche, not even the army's gonna take that one," she'd lament over a cigarette. My Aunt Millie liked to gossip with Flo Lloyd and Mrs. Bracco. If Betty Bracco wasn't sitting on her porch it was because her husband had beaten her and she was too embarrassed to socialize. My aunt would shake her head with a commiserative nod.

"That Betty is a saint putting up with that man. That's what you get with a drinker, nothing but grief." Then she'd remember Arlene's father was an alcoholic. "Sometimes, kids, sometimes it's like that with drinking men."

My best friend Arlene and I would sit on our old green glider and play records. Songs that made promises of love and escape. We had been friends since we met in fifth grade. Ar was the eldest of five daughters and as her mother worked the night shift she spent most of her time at our house. We watched our neighbors and exchanged knowledgeable looks. "If my husband blackened my eye, I'd break his neck."

"Sure thing, Ar, you're sooo strong. Shit. I'd put Drano in his dinner and watch his stomach burn out. That Betty Bracco is one lazy bitch and he works two jobs. Don't ever see her cleaning house. You know the youngest kid paints his fingernails! Yeah . . . pink. She's nuts that one."

By our logic, anyone who let her old man beat on her deserved it. We would never be that stupid. It was taken for granted that we kids got beat and that our mothers either would not or could not come to our aid. And somewhere, so very close to the surface, we hated them for their weakness. We were tough in those days, our barriers carefully erected. I dyed my hair black and I smoked, butt dangling from my lip when I talked. We watched the neighborhood with bemused detachment. Street-wise and soul-weary, at sixteen we knew our lives would be different. Annamae changed all that.

Annamae Schoewalter was the fattest girl in the whole school. Her roundness was emphasized because she was so short. Buddy Weiss called her a human basketball and she would laugh, her grey pixie-pleated skirt shaking rhythmically on her hips. She shuffled when she dragged her body about, dingy anklets half in, half out of her shoes. When we were younger all the kids would chant, "Hey, hey Annamae, take your toys and go away." But she would simply join in the laughter and tag along, seemingly unaware that we were laughing at her. There was no sport in teasing a person who was too stupid to cry. She was obviously delighted to be the center of attention. As we got older, we tolerated her. Her playmates were the children younger than she and with them she seemed more comfortable. Annamae was "slow" and while we considered her retarded and we teased her we also felt some sense

of protection towards her. Her family was odd and gave you an uneasy feeling when you went to the house. In our own homes if company came the fighting stopped, the beer bottles were tidied up and soon coffee was brewing on the stove. But in Annamae's house nobody even tried to cover-up and there was this feeling of walking into something that threatened to overpower you. We avoided her house and because she was perfunctorily passed from one grade to the next, she remained on the periphery of our lives.

Lunchtime always meant a cigarette break. I'd wait for Ar by her locker. "Come on, already, lunch will be over 'till you get a move on," I'd prod her. On this particular day I could tell from her sour mood that something was wrong. The past week she had asked her dad for clothes money and they fought. He had pushed her down the basement stairs and locked the door. But that was last week, past history. Of course I would never ask her what the matter was; we were best friends and didn't mess with the necessary balance we presented to the world. She would have simply shrugged in reply and returned to whatever she was doing. Being cool was important; people didn't mess with you if you kept face. I told her dirty jokes to cajole her. Soon we were laughing and ready for a cigarette in the girl's room. Phyllis and Jody were already combing their hair by the back stall when we arrived.

"Phil has a date with Ernie Lloyd," teased Jody. But she had allowed a bit of concern to tighten the corners of her mouth.

"You nuts, girl?" Ar blurted out as she touched up her mascara. "He's nasty. A good dancer but he's got a mouth on him. You know he punched out Linda when she broke up with him? Even his own mother can't stand him."

I smiled at the look on Phil's face; nearly as green as the walls and twice as faded. I lit another cigarette. Faded, dirty green walls that probably were painted when my mother was a junior. More than likely she stared at that same chipped plaster. I reminded myself to ask her when I got home. It would give us something to talk about. I broke into the silence, "Hey, you heard Joyce Weiss is preggers? My aunt says . . ."

The finger-smudged door slowly opened. The familiar shuffling came closer.

"Hey, hey, it's Annamae!" giggled Phyllis. "You want a cig, Annie?"

She shook her head and walked past us into the first stall. We ignored her as we usually did and returned to the gossip about Joyce. That was hot news. The toilet flushed and Annamae cut through our circle to get to the sink. I removed my Luckys from behind the faucet and watched her in the mirror. The amorphous features were hidden by fat.

"Come on, Annie, have a smoke. You know how? Here, watch me." Jody inhaled deeply and blew the smoke out in perfect rings. "You try," she said as she passed the butt to Annamae.

The chubby hand reached hesitantly for the cigarette. Encouraged by the friendly gesture, she tried to inhale. When she had coughed out all the smoke we laughed and took turns showing her the proper way to exhale. Jody took her eyebrow pencil and scratched an obscenity on the wall. "It matches the decor, don't you think?" she quipped at Annie.

We got back to Phil about Ernie Lloyd. What is now termed peer pressure was our way of protecting each other. Once a girl got a reputation, that was it. Not even her friends could help her and our families would force us to drop her as a friend.

"Enough, already!" protested Phil. "I'll tell him something came up. I'll pester you guys instead." We laughed. The sunlight filtered in through the dirty windowpanes making the walls appear less grey.

"Annie, you got a hickey on your neck. Look at that." Jody squealed and winked at Ar.

Annamae smiled and rubbed her stubby fingers over the mark. Her face lit up with a strange sort of recognition as she looked at herself in the mirror. Shyly, she asked, "Can I tell you guys a secret and you won't tell no one?"

"Okay, woman of the world, who's the guy?" I laughed as Ar rolled her eyes and elbowed Jody in the ribs.

Annamae beamed with pleasure. She was one of the girls at last. Her tone was conspiratorial and we formed a tighter circle. "I was sleeping last night and I woke up and guess who was in bed with me?" She began a nervous giggle in response to our stares. "My uncle."

Through the window I could see the sun dart under a cloud, the bathroom walls darkened once more. A grey-green shadow spread over Annie's face and hid her eyes from me. Jody and Phil passed a secret gaze between them. "Holy Jesus," muttered Ar.

I took the cigarette from my lip and held it under the dripping faucet. The grey ash streaked the sink. "What did you do, Annie, when . . . you saw him?" I asked nonchalantly. Cool, got to remain cool. Take it easy . . .

"Nothing, he's my uncle silly. He likes me and buys me stuff. . . ."

Ar cut her off. "Look, Annie, what we mean is . . . uh . . ." She couldn't finish.

Annie's eyes clouded over and the humor left her voice. "But he says I'm pretty . . . Jody . . . Phil?" She searched our faces for affirmation. I did not want to look at her. I did not want to hear her secrets. I had too many secrets of my own.

"You are pretty, sure thing, Annie . . . only . . . maybe you shouldn't tell anyone but us. A girl has to protect her reputation, huh?" My words disguised the sick feeling spreading in my stomach as my fingers traced a pattern in the wet cigarette ashes.

Annamae brightened. "Oh, I know what you mean," she laughed. "I won't tell the rest. Well, I gotta go to gym. Bye." Annie waved and smiled like she had just stopped by to tell us a really funny joke. The door closed and we heard the shuffling fade into the hallway.

Ar leaned over the sink and swore under her breath. Jody and Phil tried to giggle but could not. "Her uncle?" Ar looked directly into my eyes, looked into eyes where my father dwelt amid lies and silences. "I know she's an M.R. but . . ." Our bravado almost failed us. "Come on, Ar, that whole family is crazy, remember?" She nodded her head, losing herself in her own private thoughts while we walked to class.

Annamae was always on my mind after the incident in the girl's room. I'd sit on the porch after dinner just as before, but it was different. The cool indifference was gone and the grey-brown smoke that hung in the air depressed me. The neighborhood houses looked older and dingier than before. I no longer smirked at the neighborhood women and their misfortunes. Pittsburgh closed in on me and escape seemed suddenly improbable. I pictured myself sitting on a different porch fifteen years later sporting a black eye every other week. The image frightened me. But it was too soon for me to realize that Betty Bracco wasn't beat because she was slovenly but that she was slovenly because she had been hit so often. Yet, the shadow of that knowledge fell across my mind and shaded my perceptions.

Annamae got pregnant over summer vacation and had to leave school. Buddy Weiss laughed for days. He said he couldn't imagine anybody making it with a human basketball. And he would dribble an imaginary ball across the floor and roll his eyes. We all told him to shove it.

I would walk out of my way to pass Annie's house trying to catch a glimpse of her, but she never seemed to be around. Someone said she had been packed off to some relative in Cleveland. Months later the family moved over to Rankin and all traces of Annamae were gone. I had asked her, manipulated, really, her soft mind into keeping silence. Her silence, my silence. But I had cunning to protect myself and intelligence to cushion my fall. She had neither and I could not help her. But I could not let her expose the nightmare of our lives because Ar and I and the rest of our friends would have gone under in its wake.

I watched the neighbors, their voices echoing up and down the street. The children playing on the sidewalk, always keeping one ear open, learning how to become victims. And I knew I had to leave, had to follow that shadow, that hint of an idea that things were really not as they seemed. I took the guilt over Annamae with me. She never took her toys and she never went away.　　　　　　　　　　　　[1982]

PART VII

Changing Our Lives

The feminist belief in women's right to shape our own lives has had both personal and political implications. It has inspired individual women to transform their lives and challenge sexist notions of what is appropriate for women. It has also meant organizing to change political, economic, and social institutions that undermine women's right to self-determination. Parts VII and VIII of *Women: Images and Realities* are about personal and social change. Because feminists believe that the roots of many of women's "personal" problems are to be found in social, political, and economic structures, these last two parts are closely connected.

In Part VII, we meet women who are making decisions about their lives, asserting their right to live and love in accordance with their own needs, and redefining their relationships with each other, with men, and with families. In a world where women are often defined by their relationships with others—as mothers, daughters, grandmothers, or wives—we have often had to struggle to claim our personal identities. For some women, like Anne Waters, a lesbian of color and a Jew, this has meant affirming various parts of their identities that are devalued by society. The women in "Wonderful Older Women" challenged themselves and each other to see themselves as individuals and to stand up for their rights.

By challenging the devaluation of women in our society, feminism enables us to value ourselves and other women. For many of us who had previously seen our mothers through the prism of the patriarchal family, feminism allowed us to see the older women in our families in a new light and to appreciate their ingenuity and persistence in the midst of oppressive situations. Past generations of women bequeath a legacy of strength, which can provide sustenance and hope. In "Dear Mama," Sonia Sanchez recognized in retrospect her mother's steady support for her daughter's "right to be different." From responding to situations of harassment to facing an alienating work situation, women have called upon their ingenuity to maintain their humanity. For example, after interviewing female Puerto Rican garment workers in New York City who courageously pushed against the limits they encountered, Blanca Vázquez concludes, "if we are to survive, we need to be like our mothers in fundamental ways." By reevaluating their mother's lives, women have found nourishment for their own developing identities and talents.

As we affirm our right to grow and change as individuals, we are contesting traditions that assume the centrality of women's relationships with men and the insignificance of women's friendships with each other. In several selections, women describe the exhilaration of knowing that other women share their experience and of being able to support each other's efforts to grow and change. Female friends have helped women survive the effects of sexism in our relationships and in our society. Support groups, such as the one described by Terry Dezzo, have been crucial in ending women's feelings of isolation and enabling women to help each other through difficult times. Rejecting the prevailing notion that it is the individual's responsibility to solve what are often viewed as individual problems, the women in the selections reached out to each other to offer comfort, support, and insights about their shared experience.

Our society glorifies the nuclear family and disparages people, particularly women, who live outside it. Feminists believe that women should be able to choose how and with whom they live. Since one can choose freely only if a variety of lifestyles are considered legitimate, feminists seek to expand women's options, recognizing that different women will choose different ways to live and love. For example, Mary Helen Washington points out that being single can strengthen a woman's sense of self.

Feminists dispute the very notion that heterosexual intercourse is the best and most natural form of sexual expression. Pointing out that our sexuality is socially constructed, feminists have challenged the taboos against women loving women and championed lesbians' right to build lives with each other. This alternative is not always easy, given the homophobia in our society. In the selections, lesbians discuss the difficulty of being honest with themselves and others in the process of coming out, and the necessity of overcoming their heterosexist training in order to acknowledge their emotions. While some women feel sexual toward other women all of their lives, others, like the woman interviewed by Anne Koedt, had been heterosexual and became involved in lesbian relationships after fighting "through that initial wall of undefined fears" and falling in love with a woman. For several women, sexual and emotional relationships with other women enriched their lives and enhanced their self-confidence.

Many women are building relationships with men based on reciprocity and respect rather than dominance and submission, which is not easy in a society that reinforces traditional roles. Literary and cultural images of male and female sexuality have had negative effects on women's views of heterosexual relationships, as Marge Piercy points out. She describes the sharing of work, laughter, sensuality, and intimacy in a long-term relationship as the basis of a passionate and satisfying sex life. Some women have found that only by being very intentional and formal about roles and responsibilities have they been able to change the sexual inequalities that creep into daily life. The results of these efforts, however, can be relationships of freedom and love.

Feminists insist that the nuclear family is not the only viable form in which to build lasting relationships and raise children. For feminists, a broadened definition of family includes any living arrangement in which people share time and space, contribute to the physical and psychological tasks of making a household function, share common history and ritual, and make a commitment to stay together over time. Members are not necessarily tied by biology or by the sanction of the state or church or by living in the same house all the time. Feminists work toward building families in which all members both give and receive support and love and have space to grow as autonomous individuals.

By supporting their families and maintaining nurturing homes, single mothers like Barbara Omalade are defying the notion that children don't stand a chance in life because their father isn't present. Lesbian parents have struggled to affirm the validity of their families, even though they are different from others. Some women have created cooperative living arrangements in which they share household and parenting responsibilities. Whatever the form our living together takes, feminists hope to create democratic, cooperative living arrangements in which responsibility, power, and love are shared and in which women can find both freedom and love. Personal experiences in equitable communities and relationships will help us envision and create similar communities of care in our society at large.

As the writings in Part VII make clear, many of these ways of living and loving are not supported by the institutions that structure our society. Changing institutions, therefore, is essential in order for women to have the power to shape their lives. Part VIII will describe the ways women are working together to reshape the contours of social, economic, and political life in the United States.

Growing Strong: Alone and Together

The selections that follow describe some of the many forms that women's struggle for self-determination can take. These examples provide inspiration for other women attempting to change their lives. In the poems, you will recognize the emotional sources of the writers' developing strength.

The woman in Sonia Sanchez's poem draws on her own ingenuity and a tradition of female resistance to maintain her self-respect. For some women, survival itself is an act of strength and resilience, as Maureen Ismay portrays in her poem. It is difficult, however, to take pride in who we are when aspects of our identity are disparaged by others. Discovering our strengths is a process that often involves challenging prevailing norms and values, as both Anne Waters' and Ruth Dreamdigger's pieces describe.

Women sometimes testify to the legacy of their mothers when they identify sources of strength. The creativity, courage, pain, and love of mothers and grandmothers often provide both a grounding and inspiration for reshaping women's lives. The unconditional love of Sonia Sanchez's mother and the powerful memories of her mothers's friends is the focus of her piece, "Dear Mama." Blanca Vázquez' interviews with Puerto Rican garment workers depict how the perseverance and combativeness of women can be a source of inspiration to daughters in an effort "to fight in countless ways to resist the lack of dignity in our lives."

While social norms have devalued women's friendships, these alliances have provided crucial support to women. Friendship can cross ethnic and class lines, as Linda Hogan and Terry Dezzo describe in their pieces.

99

style no. 1

SONIA SANCHEZ

i come from a long line of rough mamas.

so here i was walking down market street. coming out of a city hall meeting. night wind at my back, dressed in my finest. black cashmere coat caressing the rim of my gray suede boots. hat sitting acey duecy. anointing the avenue with my black smell.

and this old dude. red as his car inching its way on the sidewalk. honked his horn. slid his body almost out of his skin. toward me. psst. psst. hey. let's you and me have some fun. psst. psst. c'mon babe. don't you want some of this?

and he pulled his penis out of his pants. held the temporal wonder of men in his hands.

i stopped. looked at him. a memory from deep in the eye. a memory of saturday afternoon moviehouses where knowledge comes with a tremulous cry. old white men. spiderlike. spinning their webs towards young girls legs and out budabbot and loucostello smiles melted. and we moved in the high noon walk of black girls. smelling the breath of an old undertow.

and i saw mama Dixon, dancing on his head.
mama Dixon. big loud friend of the family. who
stunned us with her curses and liquor. being herself.
whose skin breathed hilarious breaths. and i greased
my words on her tongue. and she gave them back to
me like newly tasted wine.

motha fucka. you even offend the night i said.
you look like an old mole coming out of its hole. take
yo slimy sat ole ass home. fo you get what's coming
to you. and yo generation. ask yo mama to skin you.
that is if you have had one cuz anybody ugly as you
couldna been born.

and i turned my eyes eastward. toward the garage. waking up the incipient night with my steps.
ready for the short days. the wind singing in my
veins.   [1987]

 100

Surviving

MAUREEN ISMAY

Surviving
Just surviving
Keeping it all at bay
and just having enough to pay
just enough to eat
just surviving on the little pay
and sending the kids to school
    Where will the money come from?

Just surviving
    an yu cyaan see thru yu yeye
fa yu just surviving . . .
on the little
when you haven't any strength
    left in you body—
                just surviving

Dem a seh you lazy
            when yu jus surviving
on the little
Dem seh dis
            an dem seh dat
    when yu jus surviving

when they take more than they give
And yu sick
            yu sick so
and struggling, struggling
Just surviving . . .   [1988]

 101

Journeys of the Mind

ANNE WATERS

You cannot
extricate
my Indianness
my Jewishness
my Lesbianness.
You cannot
reach in and
exorcise that
pain, or joy.

You can take
me to your schools
but you cannot
take my mind
because
Indians and Jews
and Lesbians
don't forget
we don't forget
we remember—always
because we can't
forget.

You can dress me
in your clothes
cut my hair
make up my face
put heeled shoes
on my feet
and force me
to paint
a smile on
my face.
But I won't forget.

I remember.
Because Indians
and Jews and
Lesbians
don't forget.

In the first cycle
I absorb
all that is
about me.
what said
what seen
what heard
what I learn
as a small child
—someone places a
cowboy hat and gun
on my body
I pulling   I tugging
      off
   throwing to the floor
run in silence to
my mother's arms.
We never forget
this first cycle.

In the second cycle
I am taught contradictory
values—schooled in
white ways my father but
not my mother trusted—
forced to assimilate
made forgetful
placed on a path not
of my own choosing
I am dosed with
amnesia for years
and years and years.
I become the light-skinned
terror of my own dreams—
chased by everyone.
I become outside
the frame of the
picture.

The third cycle
begins with
alienated confusion

as the amnesia of
childhood breaks
I dig into my own
I crawl out of lies and
into my mother's life.
I look at her with
new eyes   new sight
and new ears that
demand she re-tell
the stories of old
because *she*
has *not* forgotten.
In the third cycle
I try to sort out
what is
and what is not
mine.

After five months
of not holding down
my food
after reclaiming
re-knowing
re-membering
I pick up the pieces.
and finding myself
I emerge
no longer a victim
of my own self-destruction.
I am a Lesbian of color
who refuses
to be
washed out.   [1988]

 102

Wonderful Older Women

RUTH DREAMDIGGER

Wonderful, Wonderful Older Women
(To the tune, "Wonderful, Wonderful
Copenhagen")

Wonderful, wonderful older women,
Wonderful women are we.

And we're here to say that we're on our way
Breaking chains and flying free.

We are the women who've borne the children,
Cooked and cleaned and cried.
But we're learning how to be changing now,
And we're wonderful women, wonderful women,
Wonderful women, we're WOW!!

The young person yells, "Go to it, grandma!" as I ride my bicycle along the city street. "But you're too old to wear your hair that way," says the precocious four-year-old, squinting at my straight, grey hair, cut in a buster-brown style. "You look so young," says the well-meaning friend.

To all of them I feel like shouting, "No! No! No! Stop the stereotyping! Stop the categorizing! Stop the patronizing! And stop devaluing the years of my life!" For these are some of the ways in which people, confused by societal myths, try to smother me in my 57 years.

With 28 years of mothering behind me (loving, thinking, planning for others), I figure that I have about 28 years of dream-digging ahead of me. (I chose the name Dreamdigger because it tells me who I am, just as names were originally meant to do. I am a dreamer in two ways: I try to understand my sleeping dreams, and I also have a life-long dream of a loving society. I am a digger into my own personality, into whatever work I do, and also into the earth.) I don't relish society dragging me down by loading old patterns on me. Realistically I know that the fight to be myself—not "grandma," not "mother," not "little old lady in tennis shoes" will take up much of the energy of those 28 years.

History (or herstory, as I say now) is powerfully against me. Down through the centuries older women have been stereotyped and persecuted just as have been Blacks and Jews. As termagants, gossips, witches, they have been dunked, burned, stoned. As mothers to grown men, grandmas to young people, ancient aunts, sweet old ladies, they have been deposited in rocking chairs, kept in upstairs rooms, patronized and driven to depression and alcoholism. (I heard on the radio just today: "Grandmothers don't have to do anything. They just have to be there.") They have been feared for their power and ridiculed for their ineptitude. Oc-

casionally they have been revered as Wise Old Women.

The rising tide of expectations has caught up older women just as it has caught up other oppressed groups. A mind-boggling thought has entered our heads: "*We don't have to take the roles assigned to us!*" Freed from the straight-jacket in which motherhood held many of us, we are looking warily at the new garment which society holds out to us. No, thank you kindly, we are not going to be little old ladies!

So, what are we going to be then? We are going to be artists, workers, musicians, scholars, revolutionaries, speakers, organizers, travelers, lovers, gardeners, writers. In short, we will do everything that everybody else does (except that maybe we won't do quite so much laundry, house-cleaning, and child-care!).

How will we do it? First of all, we will search for ourselves beneath the layers that have been laid upon us as children, as adolescents, as wives and mothers, as single women. We will use for that purpose every tool that seems right for us—consciousness raising, professional counseling (warily), peer counseling, dream groups, and whatever else our fertile brains discover.

Secondly, we will band together for support, for the exchange of ideas, and for **empowerment.** I write that in bold letters because it is hard for me to think of having power—in my own life, in the world of ideas, in the effort to shake up the patriarchal structure—but **empowerment** is what I work toward, not *in spite of* being an older woman, but *because* I am an older woman with the variety of strengths I have acquired in my life struggle.

In the Movement for a New Society,* that band-

---

*The Movement for a New Society (1971–1988) was a nationwide network of small groups working for basic social change. Although non-religious, it had a strong Quaker influence.

MNS members believed that the process of achieving a goal was as important as the goal itself, and that the personal and the political were closely entwined. Most members lived communally and did their political work in small groups known as collectives. Although many non-violent actions were carried out (e.g., blockade of arms shipments to Pakistan; opposition to Limerick nuclear plant), MNS was best known for its training sessions, which were attended by

ing together has come about through a collective known as WOW (Wonderful Older Women). As I think back to those first rather sporadic meetings, I am amazed at the number of ways in which we showed our lack of confidence in ourselves and in each other. But we persevered, knowing that we did have it within ourselves to be supportive of each other. As we taped our herstories in those early days, I noted that one woman spoke only about her family, not one word about herself. We brainstormed the negative ideas that we feel other people have of us, and then we brainstormed the qualities that we know we have as vibrant, caring, thoughtful human beings. We discussed papers that had been written by other members of the MNS community. We planned a picnic together.

But I think the event that either marked or evoked the change in us from a collection of frightened and frustrated individuals to a collective of women who saw themselves as a potential force in the community was a weekend retreat after we had been meeting for several months. Here was a group of women who had spent almost all of their lives nourishing and supporting other people. Here we were all together, without any children to nourish and support, without any men to nourish and support, and we did an amazing job of nourishing and supporting each other. When we drove back together, we knew that a change had occurred. Although we didn't become *officially* an MNS collective until many months later, we ourselves knew from that weekend that we were indeed a collective of Wonderful Older Women.

We decided to set ourselves the task of writing. Most of us have tremendous blocks about seeing ourselves as writers. But by using a process of group writing developed by some people within the MNS community, we are getting over that hurdle. Our paper will be about social change from our felt needs

as older women. We have brainstormed our herstories, our struggles, our oppressions, and we have started to talk and listen in small groups, which will then give us encouragement as each puts together the thoughts that have emerged. When we have completed the writing on these three sections, we will work together on strategy.

In the fall the Continental Walk for Disarmament and Social Justice came through Philadelphia. One of our members was on the organizing committee and asked WOW to lead the singing. We felt a little uneasy, but not undone, to find that we were preceded by professional singers! But it was soon apparent that we were a hit. With our arms around each other, supporting each other both physically and psychologically, we sang with such thorough enjoyment of this new experience that everyone caught our enthusiasm. It was our vitality that carried the occasion, vitality that has much more to do with lack of fear than with age.

Our most recent challenge was a speak-out to MNS women about the ways in which we have to deal with discrimination even in this revolutionary community. (In a speak-out, the members of an oppressed group speak their feelings freely without response by the listeners. After the speak-out, the listeners can meet in small groups to express their feelings out of hearing of the speak-out members.) We often feel invisible, are not taken seriously. We have difficulty in joining communal households. The struggles of our lives are not acknowledged, our efforts to rid ourselves of old survival patterns are unappreciated, our achievements are unrecognized. And in ways more subtle than in the world at large, we are still stereotyped, categorized, patronized, and the years of our lives treated like a disease. But the younger MNS women did hear us and did begin to understand the importance of coming to terms with us, with their own mothers, and with the fact that they, too, will sometime be older (The MNS community has been the best growing place we have seen for older women, but, in the words of the feminist song, "We still ain't satisfied.")

Our next effort will be responsibility for the Orientation Weekend, which Philadelphia MNS schedules every month. People who share in this experience learn a little about MNS analysis, vision and

---

people from all over the world. Several people who were MNS members continue to focus on that activity.

MNS members tended to be prolific writers. Probably the most widely read book is *Resource Manual for a Living Revolution* (fondly nicknamed *The Monster Manual*). A spin-off of MNS, New Society Publishers, P.O. Box 582, Santa Cruz, CA 95061-0582, continues to publish books related to nonviolent social change.

strategy, living in community, macro-analysis, training and action. It is the first time that we have worked together as organizers of more than an evening meeting.

These are the visible actions we are taking, but the psychological strength we have received from each other since the retreat is most important of all. Older women often support and comfort each other in times of trial. It is less often that they have supported each other to be assertive in getting what they want, need and deserve. We remain individuals and rejoice in our individuality. This is important because society tends to lump all older women together in one big blob of a stereotype. We encourage each other to stand up for our rights, to be different when we want to be, to try new jobs, to travel, to lead workshops.

We constantly remind each other that the phrase "personal is political" is particularly relevant for us. Each time we show that our old age is a fine time of life, we give a younger woman hope and energy. Each time we disprove a myth about older women, we are performing a political act. For myths about the way groups of people *should* be are glue that holds together society when it is not truly functional. Each time we refuse to be "mother" to a grown person, we are undermining the structure that imprisons women and maintains men in false responsibility patterns. Mothers can be considered one of the classes of people on whom capitalism depends. Men who carry huge amounts of responsibility (and in a patriarchal system, almost every man feels that he does) must have someone to take care of them, someone with whom they can be little boys. Each time we refuse to absorb the tensions of dog-eat-dog economy, we throw a monkey wrench into the capitalist society, which, with its emphasis on competition, is certain to create tremendous pressures. When women refuse to take the mother role, the system will have to change to accommodate reasonable sharing of responsibility. The secretary on the job and the wife or mother at home are the ones who soften life for those who function within it, whether they be a busy executive, ambitious young man, or worker bedevilled by his foreman. It is hard for us as older women to stop being absorbers because we have done it for so long, and because it is so closely associated with love. But as we see more clearly how we are used, we can say "No."

Today while I waited for the trolley, I sang this little ditty to myself. Maybe it will feel good to you, as it did to me.

I'm gonna free myself to sing about myself
Sing about myself, sing about myself,
I'm gonna free myself to sing about myself,
For singing is what I need for me.

I also decided that I needed to cry, dance, think, shout and laugh about myself. How about you?

SUGGESTIONS FOR OURSELVES AS OLDER WOMEN

Affirm our past and plan our future.
Take care of our bodies.
Respect our capacity for clear thinking.
Recognize the unique beauty of older women.
Form a support-action group with older women, but form friendships in a wide age spectrum.
Expect to be taken seriously.
Be ready for new ideas and new loyalties.
Expect sexual and sensual pleasure.
Undertake some structure or discipline in which personal growth will take place.
Look for new areas of competence.
Please ourselves in clothing, habits and life styles even if (especially if) our choices do not fit the usual image of the older woman.   [1977]

 103

Dear Mama

SONIA SANCHEZ

It is Christmas eve and the year is passing away with calloused feet. My father, your son and I decorate the night with words. Sit ceremoniously in human song. Watch our blue sapphire words eclipse the night. We have come to this simplicity from afar.

He stirs, pulls from his pocket a faded picture of you. Blackwoman. Sitting in frigid peace. All of your biography preserved in your face. And my eyes draw up short as he says, "her name was Elizabeth but we used to call her Lizzie." And I hold your picture in my hands. But I know your name by heart. It's Mama. I hold you in my hands and let time pass over my face: "Let my baby be. She ain't like the others. She rough. She'll stumble on gentleness later on."

Ah Mama. Gentleness ain't never been no stranger to my genes. But I did like the roughness of running and swallowing the wind, diving in rivers I could barely swim, jumping from second story windows into a saving backyard bush. I did love you for loving me so hard until I slid inside your veins and sailed your blood to an uncrucified shore.

And I remember Saturday afternoons at our house. The old sister deaconesses sitting in sacred pain. Black cadavers burning with lost aromas. And I crawled behind the couch and listened to breaths I had never breathed. Tasted their enormous martyrdom. Lives spent on so many things. Heard their laughter at Sister Smith's latest performance in church—her purse sailing toward Brother Thomas's head again. And I hugged the laughter round my knees. Draped it round my shoulder like a Spanish shawl.

And history began once again. I received it and let it circulate in my blood. I learned on those Saturday afternoons about women rooted in themselves, raising themselves in dark America, discharging their pain without ever stopping. I learned about women fighting men back when they hit them: "Don't never let no mens hit you mo than once girl." I learned about "womens waking up they mens" in the nite with pans of hot grease and the compromises reached after the smell of hot grease had penetrated their sleepy brains. I learned about loose women walking their abandoned walk down front in church, crossing their legs instead of their hands to God. And I crept into my eyes. Alone with my daydreams of being woman. Adult. Powerful. Loving. Like them. Allowing nobody to rule me if I didn't want to be.

And when they left. When those old bodies had gathered up their sovereign smells. After they had kissed and packed up beans snapped and cakes cooked and laughter bagged. After they had called out their last goodbyes, I crawled out of my place. Surveyed the room. Then walked over to the couch where some had sat for hours and bent my head and smelled their evening smells. I screamed out loud, "oooweeee! Ain't that stinky!" and I laughed laughter from a thousand corridors. And you turned Mama, closed the door, chased me round the room until I crawled into a corner where your large body could not reach me. But your laughter pierced the little alcove where I sat laughing at the night. And your humming sprinkled my small space. Your humming about your Jesus and how one day he was gonna take you home . . .

Because you died when I was six Mama, I never laughed like that again. Because you died without warning Mama, my sister and I moved from family to stepmother to friend of the family. I never felt your warmth again.

But I knew corners and alcoves and closets where I was pushed when some mad woman went out of control. Where I sat for days while some woman raved in rhymes about unwanted children. And work. And not enough money. Or love. And I sat out my childhood with stutters and poems gathered in my head like some winter storm. And the poems erased the stutters and pain. And the words loved me and I loved them in return.

My first real poem was about you Mama and death. My first real poem recited an alphabet of spit splattering a white bus driver's face after he tried to push cousin Lucille off a bus and she left Birmingham under the cover of darkness. Forever. My first real poem was about your Charleswhite arms holding me up against death.

My life flows from you Mama. My style comes from a long line of Louises who picked me up in the nite to keep me from wetting the bed. A long line of Sarahs who fed me and my sister and fourteen other children from watery soups and beans and a lot of imagination. A long line of Lizzies who made me understand love. Sharing. Holding a child up to the stars. Holding your tribe in a grip of love. A long line of Black people holding each other up against silence.

I still hear your humming Mama. The color of your song calls me home. The color of your words saying, "Let her be. She got a right to be different. She gonna stumble on herself one of these days. Just let the child be."

And I be Mama.   [1987]

 104

The Stories Our Mothers Tell: Projections of Self in the Stories of Puerto Rican Women Garment Workers

BLANCA VÁZQUEZ

This excerpt is part of a larger manuscript entitled "Stories to Live By: Continuity and Change in Three Generations of Puerto Rican Women Garment Workers," written by Celia Alvarez, Rina Benmayor, Ana Juarbe and Blanca Vázquez, Center for Puerto Rican Studies, Hunter College, City University of New York. Founded as a result of the student and community movements of the 1960s and 70s, the Center has been documenting the Puerto Rican migration and the development of Puerto Rican community life in the U.S. since 1973. This work was undertaken in the mid-1980s as part of the Centro's "Voices of the Migration Project, An Oral History of the Puerto Rican Migration." We turned to oral histories because much of the history of Puerto Ricans in the United States resided in the memories and lived experiences of the overwhelmingly working-class Puerto Rican migrants. In the first phase of the project, we gathered the life histories of *pioneros,* pioneer migrants who had migrated in the 1920s and 30s. Many of those whom we in-

terviewed had been active in creating organizations such as the Liga Puertorriqueña e Hispana (1926) and hometown clubs.

Because women were central to the world of work, family and the re-creation of community life, in the second phase of the project, we concentrated on the experiences of Puerto Rican women within the migration. We chose garment production as the most representative work experience of Puerto Rican women. For the most part, the research team was composed of first generation daughters of garment workers, and this close affinity to the work conditioned our interpretation of the life stories, as well as the *telling.* The stories contained accounts of hard work and pain as well as laughter, celebration and joy. In relaying their life experiences to a younger generation of listeners, the women were imparting lessons to us about perseverance, survival and success against the constraints imposed by the class, racial and gender discrimination they faced in the new environment.

The women whose life histories I am examining are now in their fifties and sixties. They grew up in Puerto Rico, for the most part, . . . in the midst of the Great Depression, a time of tremendous social upheaval and economic reorganization in Puerto Rico. They came from rural areas, still tied to declining agricultural sectors such as tobacco or coffee, or to wage labor in the cities and towns. My mother, for example, was born in Mayagüez to a very poor family. At the age of eight she helped her mother do home needlework. Shortly afterwards her mother died and she was then raised by her grandmother who took in laundry for a living and was also a midwife. My great-grandmother started her own life story by saying that she had been born in 1875, two years after slavery was abolished in Puerto Rico. The significance of this is that her mother had been a slave and that she herself had escaped this fate. Thus, the lives of these . . . women reflect the changes in Puerto Rico's social, political and economic reorganization under Spanish and U.S. rule.

Poverty and hardship characterize the early lives of the women. By the 1930s, the world-wide crises in capitalism had left the Puerto Rican economy in shambles. All the women worked as children to help support their families. They were also pulled from school because of this economic necessity. Education was out of the question for most of the poor, and especially for female children who in addition to being paid and most often unpaid workers, also helped cook, clean and care for their brothers and sisters while their mothers worked. . . . The women recount the experience of being pulled from school as a lost opportunity in their lives, the pain still evident in the *telling*. Out of this longing came the commitment to give to their children the education they had so missed in their lives. Education was the only escape from poverty, the only way to get off the land and out of the kitchens and *talleres*.

In looking across the board at the stories Puerto Rican women were telling, convergences began to emerge in the self-images of the women. These projections-of-self were powerful and offer an alternative view of working-class women: they convey a sense of women as strong, resourceful, ingenious and determined to overcome the obstacles they face day to day in the world of work. These images resonate from women I knew personally as well as from women I had had no prior contact with. The ways in which the women project themselves and what they have struggled against is indicative of a common historical experience and speaks to a convergence of individual and collective history.

The stories of María R., drawn from the world of work, the arena in which she has been able to assert her selfhood despite oppressive conditions, illustrate these self-images. [At the time, María was] a 55-year-old garment worker and mother of seven children who migrated to New York from a rural area of Puerto Rico in 1948. Married at a very young age, she had two daughters when she and her husband decided they could not raise a family on the land and "progress." First her husband, then María and finally her two small daughters migrated to New York. The first story explains how María learned to sew on a machine.

Well, I continued working with the intention of looking for something better, but every time I went out to find a job, all the jobs available were for sewing machine operators and I said to myself, "My God, I have to learn to sew." I told [my husband] that we had to find a school so I could learn to sew. Then I went to a school on 14th Street and Union Square and I signed up for three classes. They

charged $25 and the only thing they really taught us was to sew a straight seam.

But I took the classes . . . and I went to look for work as an operator. I didn't really know how to sew. I only knew how to start the machine although I had some knowledge of the machine because my mother had a small manual one in Puerto Rico. I used to watch my grandmother sew on that machine and I thought I could do it.

Well, I went to look for work, and oh, my God, wherever I went, whenever I sat down at the machine and touched the pedal, the machine seemed to run by itself! I was thrown out of a number of factories but five minutes here, fifteen minutes there, I kept getting more and more practice.

Then, I said to myself, "I'm going to see what kind of machines they have and if I see a Singer machine I'm going to say that I don't know how to sew on that particular machine." I went to a factory at 380 Broome Street and I noticed that they had Mero machines and no Singer machines. Now, since I had failed so many times I told the man that I knew how to sew but not on the machine they had. I told him I knew how to sew on a Singer. Blanca, because of that lie they showed me how to sew on the Mero. The man said to me, "If you can sew on a Singer, this one is easier." Then I said to him, "How is that possible with all those spools of thread?" He said, "Well, I'll show you." He sat me down and calmly showed me how to thread the machine, how to tie up the thread when a spool ran low, not to let it run out, and that's where I started working on chenille robes.

This first story María tells in her animated way of speaking illustrates her ingenuity and resourcefulness. First she goes to school to learn to sew on a machine, then after repeated rejections at various factories because she doesn't sew well enough, María strategizes to get the job. She takes advantage of these "trial" periods to improve her sewing skills, then she tells one foreman that she knows how to sew but not on that particular machine. The foreman assures her that if she can sew on a Singer, she can learn to sew on a Mero and proceeds to give her the orientation she needs.

This story is typical of other stories María tells. She conveys that she has never been one to give up regardless of the objective problems she encounters. She doesn't downplay the disadvantages she faces, her lack of sewing skills or ability to speak English.

In fact, she highlights these things in her stories, setting us up for a sort of punch line. The obstacles she faces are precisely the things she will operate against and overcome. The constraints are clear and that she will find a way around them, through them or over them is an inevitable outcome of her stories. In this first story it is her determination, willingness to face rejection and ultimately a clever little lie that will see her through to her goal—a better paying job so she can help to educate and feed her children.

The second story María tells takes place a few years later. Here we begin to see a change in her strategy, a different sense of her value as a worker and of her options in life. She starts the story by saying, "I was very important on the job."

> I went to another place making panties. Then I learned another machine, the zig zag machine. At that time I was earning about $40 a week. Only two people know how to work on that machine, an American guy and I. We used to start the garment and then we would give it to the other operators. So that meant that any day that we missed these other people doesn't have no work to do and they had to send them home. So I was very important on the job.
>
> Every time that a garment was new and it took me longer, I had to fight for the price. So at one point [a new garment] came in and this work was very hard. I cannot make enough money for the hours . . . and I said, "No, I am not doing this." He gave me a little more money but I said, "No, no, I can't do this job at this price," and so he fired me. I never was fired in my life from no job. He told me if you don't want to do the work just go home, but at this time I had the protection of the union. So I said, "O.K., I go home." I got up, took my pocketbook, then my coat and left but I [didn't] come here. I went to the union place and I report him. [The agent] said, "Don't worry about it. I'll be there tomorrow." I'll never forget, it was a Friday. On Monday he came up with me and . . . he talked to the boss and said, "You're going to time her with a clock and you are going to see how long she takes with the garment and you're going to pay her accordingly."
>
> He did that and it came out to be more money. So he paid me but inside of me I was mad because he had fired me, *embarrassed* me in front of 50 people. And I say, "You are going to pay me one of these days." I was very rebellious in that.
>
> And I waited . . . that particular day, the work was piled up to the ceiling, work that only I and this man we have to work first. I waited for that moment [when] this fellow was sick. I worked two days, I'll never forget. I worked Monday and Tuesday and on Wednesday I didn't report to work. I went next door and I [found] another job, this time in bathing suits. They paid me about 75 cents a garment which at that time, this was in 1956, was good money.
>
> So on Friday when I was supposed to collect my money for the days I worked, the secretary told me that Al [wanted] to talk to me. So he came over and he told me, "María, you can't do this to me. You know that we don't have nobody to operate that machine. How much you want?" I said, "I don't want nothing. I don't want to work for you no more." He said, "You can't do that to me, you know I was paying good money." I said, "I don't care for your money." He said, "You don't find no job." I said, "I already have another job and I'll give you the address. I now work in Julia Sportswear." He knew that place paid good money.

Now María displays a different set of skills and strategies. At the beginning of the story she defines her status and worth as a worker with marketable skills. As the story progresses, she makes clear that being a union member confers rights that she will exercise and she can now fight in English as well as in Spanish. Not only does María still not fear rejection, she invites it by challenging her boss on what she feels is an unjust and exploitative price. He fires her for her defiance and she gets even by leaving the job precisely at a time when he needs her. Because of the relative ease of finding work in the boom era of the 1950s and 60s, María had the option as other women did—to go from factory to factory, to "shop" for better salaries and working conditions. Ultimately, it is this structural reality of garment production that allows María a wider range of strategies. In a subsequent story, María collectivizes her combativeness when as a chairlady in another factory, she stops the machines over an unfair piecework rate and calls in the union representative to back up the workers.

What then are the features of these stories? In the first place, they tell us that María is a very resourceful person and that she relies on her own ingenuity to overcome the obstacles in her life. This resourcefulness is a constant feature of her stories and appears in the narrations of other garment workers. As María's life story unfolds, she returns to school in order to enroll in a Manpower Training program in the 1970s and becomes a clerical worker in a public hospital.

The most striking pattern in María's stories and that of other garment workers I interviewed was one of omission. Missing from these stories was a sense of victimization. In spite of the hardships and discrimination these women have faced, there was little sense of resignation or defeat.

The women were projecting to us images of strength and combat in the face of the obstacles and constraints in their lives. The constraints are real and shared as a community, as measured by all the indices of poverty and disadvantage. The constraints are also ideological, and herein is the strength of these stories. In telling us these stories, the women impart values to us that will guide younger generations in what we have to do to survive in this country. In that sense, these stories can be said to have real intended meaning; they contain purpose and plan. Embedded in the stories are positive images and real strategies for women, for their children and for all who would listen.

The fact that these are stories of struggle and "success" is significant. I believe that on a symbolic level, these stories are the key to how we have survived as a people. We may not know the historical "facts," what really happened in those factory exchanges with the boss, how it would play back if we could recapture what actually happened. We are not looking at behavior which can be measured objectively. We are listening to how people relate their lives—*what is of value to them*. What we do know is that these stories "as is" and on face value have meaning for us as insiders; that they reveal a felt need to convey to younger generations what kind of people we are and need to be. The images and projections we get *as* women *from* women is that women struggle, wheel and deal, maneuver and confront and do whatever they have to do to accomplish their goals. The message we get from these stories is that if we are to survive, we need to be like our mothers in fundamental ways.

The lessons embedded in the stories differ and change over time. At times the confrontation with those who have power over us is direct; at times it is necessary to circumvent. At times the mechanism to cope is simply humor, to be able to take a difficult situation and put it into perspective by making it lighter for ourselves. . . .

The stories of garment workers . . . do what the larger society does not: they validate our experience and affirm our worth. The Centro's Oral History project has provided a space for our common experiences to be recognized. The stories we have collected allow us to give our mothers credit for being garment workers, for taking care of our families, for struggling in the community and at the workplace and for doing that with courage and commitment and at times, at great personal cost. Ultimately, underlying what our parents are saying is that they have not wholly internalized or accepted the terms of class and race that are meted out in this country. The underlying message we get, then, is one of resistance and rebellion.

We have learned a renewed respect for the struggles of garment workers, for their steadfastness, ingenuity and resolve in the midst of an alienating, oppressive and often hostile environment. If these stories prepare us, a younger generation of listeners, for anything, it is to understand how we survive as a people: through persistence, perseverance, combativeness, creativity and hard work. If we are to go further collectively we must internalize these lessons, drawn from the everyday lives of common people, and struggle together across ethnic, racial, language and national lines to create true opportunity and equality. To ensure that better future for our children that compelled our mothers and fathers to go to work each day, we, too, must fight in countless ways to resist the lack of dignity in our lives. For me, that is the value and the legacy contained in these stories.   [1987]

🌿 105

Friday Night

LINDA HOGAN

Sometimes I see a light in her kitchen
that almost touches mine,
and her shadow falls straight
through trees and peppermint
and lies down at my door
like it wants to come in.

Never mind that on Friday nights
she slumps out her own torn screen
and lies down crying on the stoop.
And don't ask about the reasons;
she pays her penalties for weeping.
Emergency Room:
Eighty dollars to knock a woman out.
And there are laughing red-faced neighbor men
who put down their hammers
to phone the county.
Her crying tries them all.
Don't ask for reasons
why they do not collapse
outside their own tight jawbones
or the rooms they build
a tooth and nail at a time.

Never mind she's Mexican
and I'm Indian
and we have both replaced the words
to the national anthem with our own.
Or that her house smells of fried tortillas
and mine of Itchko and sassafras.

Tonight she was weeping in the safety of moonlight
and red maples.
I took her a cup of peppermint tea,
and honey,
it was fine blue china
with marigolds growing inside the curves.
In the dark, under the praying mimosa
we sat smoking little caves of tobacco light,
me and the *Señora of Hysteria*, who said
Peppermint is every bit as good as the ambulance.
And I said, Yes. It is home grown.   [1985]

🌿 106

Help from the Mothers' Group

TERRY DEZZO

Terry: I first met Nancy when she came to pick me up
and give me a ride, the first time I went to a meeting
of the Mothers' Group. That was in '68. My family was living in a condemned convent for a few
months, because our house had been gutted by fire.

Nancy's husband is at the university and her family
had just moved into the area. I went to the Mothers'
Group from then up until some time in '71, when it
got to be too difficult with studying and then I was
working afternoons. But it was really important to
me for those years.

Nancy: The group actually started the year before I
came to Storrs in some homes in Eagleville where
a lot of low-income people are concentrated. Betty
Heiss and Betty Jane Bennett, whose husbands are
also on the faculty at the University of Connecticut,
were really responsible for getting it started. Then
other middle-income women got involved, and
more and more low-income women from other
parts of town and the trailer parks.

Terry: I hate to think how my life might have been
without the Mothers' Group. It was like an oasis because it was a place to go and get some kind of relief,
and some kind of enjoyment and knowledge. It was
something that directed me to the things I needed
and helped me to find things I didn't even know
about. Also I hate to think what would have happened if I'd have gone on feeling completely friend-
less, because at that point I don't think I had a
friend, except for the public health nurse. She
couldn't have been a greater help, but it was almost
like a therapy session and I needed something relax-
ing, too. So both kind of complemented each other.

Nancy: That was one of the things that was important
to many of us about the group—the possibilities it
had for individuals. The first thing was trying to
break down the kind of isolation women live in
when they have small children, no day care centers,
no transportation and no money. Every solution
you find has to be your own personal solution. In
general, it was a way to help people find ways to
kind of come back in control of their own lives,
rather than feeling like victims in life. I don't know
that we succeeded in that very well in a group sense,
but I think that has happened for some individuals.
And now there's a network of people who can be
called on for emergencies and things like that.

Terry: The feeling of being alone and not being able to
handle a situation is almost defeating itself. I think
everybody who went to the Mothers' Group really
needed each other. The whole week started to focus around that Tuesday. I remember so many
times when we had to end the meeting because the
kids were coming home from school, but we just
couldn't end it. Sometimes you had something
worrying you and it took a longer time to get it out.
But if you were able to talk about it, you just felt
that much better and you'd go home really lifted.

With my divorce, the personal contact there gave me a great deal of support. I was beginning to give up on ever having any kind of peaceful relationship by that time, but I didn't know how to go about certain things, and I needed help in just thinking it out. People like Nancy, especially Nancy, would act like a sounding board for me a lot of times. And she didn't only say things to make me feel I was right and I should just leave. She was really good at seeing both sides of it and helping me understand what was going on. I think that was one of the big reasons why I came through it and could function from then on. I finally felt I'd done everything I possibly could, so I was able to just shut the door on the past.

Nancy: Besides helping each other personally and developing really rewarding relationships, we tried to do things that were useful in a concrete way too.

Terry: I think the first year was the community garden and then we started a kind of nursery school in the church where we met, and then dieting.

Nancy: There were several women who wanted to lose weight, which was pretty impossible on the diets their budgets forced them on. We also talked about how to get the most out of surplus foods, and we had cooking and baking demonstrations.

Terry: It was about then we started the buying club too. We went to visit other people who had them in nearby areas and we wrote and got literature from different places around the country. Then we set it up the way we wanted. We decided to keep it simple, just a few items we could really get a good buy on, and not get into complicated bookkeeping. We decided we really wanted meat, that was the biggest thing, but we also have produce. On some items you save maybe 5 or 10 percent, but it varies a lot. Sometimes it's much more. It just means that you have to put a little away and plan ahead, but if you're on welfare, it really makes a difference.

Nancy: Almost every week we had speakers. One was an insurance man, a professor, and that was really important. I think what made us most sharply aware of it was that one of the mother's sons had been killed while he was delivering newspapers. He was struck by a car. When they went to the funeral director, the first thing he said was, "Well, where's your money?" Here they were, just wiped out with grief, and he was saying, "I want my money first and then you can bury your son." Always the same kind of problem for poor people, which the middle class almost never has.

Well, that made people who were poor feel it was almost imperative to carry that many more kinds of insurance, just in case. And there's quite a difference in types of insurance policies and what you pay, what kind of rights you have within that. I didn't know you could really shop around for insurance like that either. So this man came, and we tried to have other speakers who would have some kind of input into what were really concrete problems for people.

Terry: We had marriage counselors, too, and a psychologist who talked about sex education for kids. I think everybody was trying to figure out where they were at. It was the kind of thing where you wanted to do right by your kids and you were worrying about all kinds of things.

Nancy: I think that really helped people to open up a lot. Maybe it's because a number of us had teenaged kids at the time, but that was an area we really wanted to talk about and rarely do with anybody else, especially not in a whole room full of people. There was a lot of worry about young girls—are they going to get pregnant, what's the relationship between young men and women? And adults, too, some real feelings of defensiveness about it, that it was men who made the decisions about sex. And maybe women felt powerless, not knowing how to cope with it, but worried about it. So the sex education and marriage counseling were very helpful.

Terry: One of the biggest things that happened to me in the Mothers' Group was getting involved with the Montessori School. I remember Edie Carey had just come back from England and she was setting up her nursery school again, and someone mentioned that anybody with a three-year-old child who was interested should talk to her about getting a scholarship. That's how the whole thing really started. Michelle, my second youngest, went to the nursery school there and then I read in the paper about there being a Montessori course, and it seemed like the kind of teaching I would like. But there again, I needed a little encouragement.

That was the transition year, when my husband left. I went to the Montessori School the last day to pick up Michelle. They were cleaning up, trying to pack up to move to another church, and I thought I really should try to help with the kids, especially since Michelle had gotten this scholarship. While I was there I talked with some of the teachers about the school and then, about two weeks later, Edie called me and asked if I wanted to work there in the fall.

In the meantime, the Mothers' Group was starting on developing a day care center too. It took about a year or more to get it going, and I had applied for a teacher's aide job. I thought I could work there as a start and then eventually maybe go to school. But it all happened much faster. Things have a way of happening to me, bang, bang, bang! So when Edie offered me the job, I said I really didn't know because I'd already put in an application to the day care center and I was really involved with it at that point. That was my first love. I was on the board for a few years, and I was the first secretary of the board. But I decided to take the job at the Montessori School and gradually I kind of broke away from the day care center. Then I took the Montessori course in the summer of '70, my first course since high school, and I really got into it.

Nancy: We spent a lot of our energies getting that day care center started. We also started looking at a lot of other problems—like housing, for instance—which we never got very far on. There's a big housing debate going on in town now because low-income people have been consistently squeezed out. The university controls land prices here and we've seen the pressure and what it does to people.

Then health care in general is still . . . people get to the doctor when it's an emergency and there just aren't enough doctors to go around. The same is true with dentists. We found out there was only one dentist in town who was kind of known as the welfare dentist. He wouldn't take a child under eight and I guess he's a real butcher. But the dentists felt they had made a reasonable solution by saying, "Well, everybody who's poor can go there."

The dentists claimed there were too many problems with the welfare office, too many forms, and that welfare patients were unreliable. Well, we began to put pressure on them and finally we did get them to agree to take people who were on welfare. But you still have to really be willing to fight for your rights if you're poor, and if you have any feelings of insecurity, that's really difficult.

Terry: I was only on welfare for a year and a half all together. My family helped me a little, and then what I did was I started a nursery school in my home so I could get off of it. This is where a lot of people in the Mothers' Group and with the Montessori School were really great, especially one woman who was a teacher there. She called people she knew at the university who had small children, and I gather she got the people to donate to a fund for scholarships for low-income children to come to my school. I thought that was really incredible.

[1976]

Ways of Living

The ability to make conscious choices about personal relationships is central to women's freedom. Because such choice is integral to feminism, this section presents a wide variety of alternatives for living and loving.

Women who are single or celibate are often stigmatized in our society. Yet some women have found the experience of living with oneself to be satisfying and liberating. In her poem, Paulette Childress White uses the metaphor of a tree alone to describe the freedom of being single. Similarly, Mary Helen Washington and Adrienne Rich speak to the strength they find in living on their own.

Many women choose to build sexual and emotional relationships with men. In an effort to make their relationships equitable and loving, women have often reshaped traditional forms of female-male partnership. Marge Piercy speaks to the issue of sexual fulfillment in relationships in "The Turn On." Including children in a male-female relationship brings challenges as well as rewards. Alix Kates Shulman describes the agreement that she and her husband made in their attempt to bring equity to parenting. While it may appear mechanical and extreme, it reflects the resolve and intentionality many parents find necessary to change gendered social roles and patterns in the family.

Patricia Hill Collins speaks to the unique struggles of African-American women who are building relationships with African-American men. The "love and trouble tradition" reflects the reality that these relationships can be simultaneously good and bad. The "tradition" reflects the tensions and conflicts, as well as intimacy, in relationships between African-American women and men.

Some women have affirmed themselves and taken control of their lives by choosing to build sexual and emotional relationships with other women. The pieces by Ann Koedt and Jewelle Gomez describe how they overcame societal taboos and trusted themselves to reach out to other women. "Coming out" to relatives and friends can be a particularly difficult part of the process of identifying oneself as a lesbian.

Feminists have redefined the institution of the family to make it more inclusive of various women's lives. The final group of writers in this section describe their experiences in one of a variety of types of families. Barbara Omolade explores the myths about black single mothers. She describes how the Sisterhood of Black Single Mothers serves as an extended family to black women working to build loving relationships with each other and their children. Audre Lorde speaks to the challenge and satisfaction of raising children as a lesbian in a homophobic society. For Ellen Davidson, living collectively brings benefits to both adults and children.

🌿 107

A Tree Alone

PAULETTE CHILDRESS WHITE

Apart from the forest
have you seen
that a tree alone
will often take inventive form . . .

that apart from the forest
a single tree
will sometimes grow awry
in brave and extraordinary search
for its own shape.

One single tree can make
the beauty of the forest plain.

Who has not seen
the rare and awesome beauty
that a tree alone can be.

🌿 108

Working at Single Bliss

MARY HELEN WASHINGTON

I

Apart from the forest
have you seen
that a tree alone
will often take inventive form . . .

—Paulette Childress White
"A Tree Alone"

She who has chosen her Self, who defines her Self, by
choice, neither in relation to children nor men; who is Self-
identified, is a Spinster, a whirling dervish spinning in a
new time/space.

—Mary Daly
Gyn/Ecology (Beacon Press)

Last year I was asked to be on the "Tom Cottle
Show," a syndicated television program that origi-
nates here in Boston. The psychiatrist-host wanted
to interview six single women about their singleness.

I hesitated only a moment before refusing. Six single
women discussing the significance of their lives?
No, I instinctively knew that the interview would
end up being an interrogation of six unmarrieds (a
pejorative, like coloreds)—women trying to rationalize lives of loss. Losers at the marriage game. *Les
femmes manqués.*

I watched the program they put together without
me, and sure enough, Cottle asked a few perfunctory questions about singleness and freedom, and
then moved on rapidly to the real killer questions. I
found it painful to watch these very fine women
trapped in the net he'd laid. "Don't you ever come
home from these glamorous lives of freedom [read
selfishness] and sit down to dinner alone and just
cry?" "What about sex?" "What about children?"
The women struggled to answer these insulting
questions with dignity and humor, but clearly the
game was rigged against them. Imagine the inter-
viewer lining up six couples and asking them the
same kinds of questions: "Well, what about your
sex lives?" "Why don't you have any children?" (or
"Why do you have so many?") "Don't you ever
come home at night, sit down to dinner, and wonder
why you ever married the person on the other side
of the table?" Of course, this interview would never
take place—the normal restraint and politeness that
are reserved for people whose positions are socially
acceptable assure married folks some measure of
protection and, at least, common decency.

"You're so lucky, footloose and fancy-free, with
no responsibilities," a friend with two children once
said to me. Ostensibly that's a compliment, or at
least, it's supposed to be. But underneath it is really
a critique of single people, implying that their lives
do not have the moral stature of a life with "responsibilities." It's a comment that used to leave me feeling a little like a kid, a failed adult; for what's an adult
with no responsibilities? A kid. I have had to learn
to recognize and reject the veiled contempt in this
statement because, of course, single people do have
responsibilities.

At age 40, I have been a single adult for 20 years.
No, I am neither widowed nor divorced. I am single
in the pristine sense of that word—which unleashes
that basic fear in all of us, "What will I do if I'm left
by myself?" As I have more or less successfully dealt
with that fear over the years, I am somewhat indig-

nant at being cast as an irresponsible gadfly, unencumbered by the problems of Big People. I have earned a living and "kept myself," and I have done that without being either male or white in a world dominated by men and corroded by racism. I've sat up nights with students' papers and even later with their problems. Without any of the social props married people have, I have given many memorable parties. Like my aunts before me, I've celebrated the births, birthdays, first communions, graduations, football games, and track meets of my 10 nephews. And not a hair on my mother's head changes color without my noticing it.

As Zora Hurston's Janie says, "Two things everybody's got tuh do fuh theyselves. They got tuh go tuh God, and they got tuh find out about livin' fuh theyselves." If anything, a single person may be more aware of the responsibility to discover and create meaning in her life, to find community, to honor her creativity, to live out her values, than the person whose life is circumferenced by an immediate and intimate family life.

II

To be single and busy—nothing bad in that. Such people do much good.

—Elizabeth Hardwick
Sleepless Nights (Random House)

To some extent my adolescent imagination was bewitched by the myth that marriage is *the* vertical choice in a woman's life—one that raises her status, completes her life, fulfills her dreams, and makes her a valid person in society. In the 1950s, all the movies, all the songs directed us to this one choice: to find our worldly prince and go two by two into the ark. Nothing else was supposed to matter quite as much and it was a surprise to discover that something else matters just as much, sometimes more.

But in spite of the romance-marriage-motherhood bombardment, I grew up in a kind of war-free zone where I heard the bombs and artillery all around me but was spared from a direct attack. I was raised in two very separate but mutually supportive communities—one black, one Catholic, both of which taught me that a woman could be her own person in the world.

In the all-women's Catholic high school and college in Cleveland, Ohio, where I put in eight formative years, we were required to think of ourselves as women with destinies, women whose achievements mattered—whether we chose marriage or religious life or, as it was called then, a life of "single blessedness." In fact, marriage and the single life seemed to my convent-honed ninth-grade mind to have a clearly equal status: they were both inferior to the intrinsically superior religious life.

The program of spiritual, intellectual, social, and physical development the nuns demanded of us allowed an involvement with myself I craved even in the ninth grade. *Some* dating was encouraged at Notre Dame Academy (ninth through twelfth grades)—not as a consuming emotional involvement but as part of a "normal social development." Boys had their place—on the periphery of one's life. (A girl who came to school with her boyfriend's taped class ring on her finger was subject to expulsion.) You were expected to be the central, dominant figure in the fabric of your own life.

The nuns themselves were vivid illustrations of that principle. For me they were the most powerful images of women imaginable—not ladies-in-waiting, not submissive homebodies, not domestic drudges, not deviants. They ran these women-dominated universes with aplomb and authority. Even if "Father" appeared on Monday morning for our weekly religious lesson, his appearance was tolerated as a kind of necessary token of the male hierarchy, and, when he left, the waters ran back together, leaving no noticeable trace of his presence.

Nuns were the busiest people I knew then. No matter how graceful and dignified the pace, they always seemed to be hurrying up and down the corridors of Notre Dame planning something important and exciting. Sister Wilbur directed dramatics and went to New York occasionally to see the latest Off-Broadway productions. Sister Kathryn Ann wrote poetry and went to teach in Africa. Another sister coached debate and took our winning teams to state championships in Columbus. Though technically nuns are not single, they do not have that affiliation with a male figure to establish their status. (After Mary Daly it should not be necessary to point out that God is not a man.) They also have to ward off the same stigma of being different from the norm as single people do. So it's only a little ironic that I got some of my sense of how a woman could be complete and autonomous and comfortable in the world—*sans* marriage—from the Sisters of Notre Dame.

The message I got from the black community about single life was equally forceful. So many black girls heard these words, they might have been programmed tapes: "Girl, get yourself an education, you can't count on a man to take care of you." "An education is something no one can take from you." "Any fool can get married, but not everyone can go to school."

I didn't know it then, but this was my feminist primer. Aim high, they said, because that is the only way a black girl can claim a place in this world. Marriage was a chancy thing, not dependable like diplomas: my mother and aunts and uncles said that even if you married a Somebody—a doctor or a lawyer—there was no assurance that he'd have a good heart or treat you right. They thought that the worst thing a woman could do was to get into financial dependency with a man—and it was not that they hated or distrusted men so much as they distrusted any situation that made an already vulnerable woman more powerless.

There was such reverence in my mother's voice for women of achievement that I never connected their social status with anything as mundane as marriage. The first black woman with a Ph.D., the first black woman school principal, the first woman doctor—I knew their names by heart and wanted to be one of them and do important things.

My third-grade teacher, the first black teacher at Parkwood Elementary in Cleveland, Ohio, was a single woman in her thirties. At age nine, I saw her as a tall, majestic creature who wore earrings, drove her own car, and made school pure joy. To my family and the neighborhood, Miss Hilliard was like a totem of our tribe's good fortune: an independent, self-sufficient, educated woman bringing her treasures back to their children. She was a part of that tradition of 19th-century black women whose desire for "race uplift" sent them to teach in the South and to schools like Dunbar High in Washington, D.C., and the School for Colored Youth in Philadelphia. Though many of these women were married, the majority of them were widowed for a great many years and those were often the years of achievement for them.

One of these 19th-century stellar examples, Anna Julia Cooper, dismissed the question of marriage as a false issue. The question should not be "How shall I so cramp, stunt, simplify, and nullify myself as to make me eligible for the horror of being swallowed up into some little man," but how shall a generation of women demand of themselves and of men "the noblest, the grandest and the best" in their capacities.

III

In the places of their childhoods, the troubles they had getting grown, the tales of men they told among themselves as we sat unnoted at their feet, we saw some image of a past and future self. The world had loved them even less than their men but this did not keep them from scheming on its favor.

—Sherley Anne Williams
Some One Sweet Angel Chile (William Morrow)

I learned early about being single from my five aunts. By the time I was old enough to notice, four were widowed and one divorced, so from my 12-year-old perspective, they were single women for a good part of their lives. They ran their own households, cooked, entertained, searched for spirituality, helped my mother to raise eight children, traveled some, went to work, cared for the sick, planned picnics. In short, they made up their lives by themselves, inventing the forms that satisfied them. And in the course of their "scheming" they passed on to me something about the rituals and liturgy of single life.

The eldest of these aunts, Aunt Bessie, lived as a single woman for 26 years. Her husband of 40 years died when she was 60 and she began to live alone for the first time since she was 18. She bought a huge old house, painted, decorated, and furnished every room with Oriental rugs and secondhand furniture purchased at estate sales. (Black people discovered this bonanza in the 1940s long before it became a middle-class fad.) She put in a new lawn, grew African violets, and started a whole new life for herself on Ashbury Avenue.

Aunt Bessie was secretly proud of how well she

was doing on her own, and she used to tell me slyly how many of these changes she could not have made as a married woman: "Uncle wouldn't have bought this house, baby; he wouldn't have wanted this much space. He wouldn't have changed neighborhoods." She was finally doing exactly what pleased her, and the shape of her life as she had designed it in her singularity was much more varied, dynamic, and daring. What I learned from her is symbolized by that multilevel house on Ashbury Avenue. She had three bedrooms—she needed them for guests; on the third floor she made hats, which she sold for a living; the huge old basement was for her tools and lawn work. All this room was essential to the amount of living she planned to do.

Since she willed all of her furniture to me, my own flat resembles that house in many ways, and her spirit came with the furnishings: I have the sense of inhabiting every corner of my life just as she lived in all 10 rooms of her house. Even my overstocked refrigerator is a reflection of something I learned from her about taking care of your life. Another aunt, Hazel, died only a few years after she was widowed, and I remember Aunt Bessie's explanation of her untimely death as a warning about the perils of not taking your life seriously. "Hazel stopped cooking for herself after her husband died, just ate snacks and junk food instead of making a proper dinner for herself. And she got that cancer and died." The message was clear to me—even at age 12—that single life could be difficult at times and that living it well required some effort, but you were not supposed to let it kill you.

IV

[Friendship] is a profound experience which calls forth our humanness and shapes our being. . . . This is true for all persons, but it has a special significance for single persons. For it is in the context of friendship that most single persons experience the intimacy and immediacy of others.

—Francine Cardman
"On Being Single"

Girded up with all of this psychological armament from my past, I still entered adult life without the powerful and sustaining myths and rituals that could provide respect and support for single life. Terms like "old maid" and "spinster," not yet redefined by a feminist consciousness, could still be used to belittle and oppress single women. By the time I was 35, I had participated in scores of marriage ceremonies, and even had begun sending anniversary cards to my married friends. But never once did I think of celebrating the anniversary of a friendship—even one that was by then 25 years old. (Aren't you entitled to gifts of silver at that milestone?)

Once, about 10 years ago, five of us single women from Cleveland took a trip to Mexico together. (Actually only four of the group were single; the fifth, Ernestine, was married and three months pregnant.) I remember that trip as seven days and eight nights of adventure, laughter, discovery, and closeness.

We were such typical tourists—taking snapshots of ancient ruins, posing in front of cathedrals, paying exorbitant sums to see the cliff divers (whose entire act took about 20 seconds), floating down debris-filled waterways to see some totally unnoteworthy sights, learning the hard way that in the hot Acapulco sun even us "killer browns" could get a sunburn. We stayed up at night talking about our lives, our dreams, our careers, our men, and laughing so hard in these late-night sessions that we hardly had the energy for the next morning's tour.

It was the laughter and the good talk (remember Toni Cade Bambara's short story "The Johnson Girls") that made the trip seem so complete. It was so perfect that even in the midst of the experience I knew it was to be a precious memory. Years later I asked my friend, Ponchita, why she thought the five of us never planned another trip like that, why we let such good times drift out of our lives without an attempt to recapture them. "Because," she said, "it wasn't enough. It was fun, stimulating, warm, exciting, but it wasn't 'The Thing That Made Life Complete,' and it wasn't leading us in that direction; I guess it was a little like 'recess.'" We wanted nests, not excitement. We wanted domestic bliss, not lives lived at random, no matter how thrilling, how wonderful. So there was the potential—those "dependable and immediate supports" existed. But without the dependable myths to accompany them, we couldn't seriously invest ourselves in those experiences.

When my friend Meg suggested we celebrate

Mother's Day this year with a brunch for all our single, childless women friends, and bring pictures of the nieces and nephews we dote on, I recognized immediately the psychic value in honoring our own form of caretaking. We were establishing rituals by which we could ceremonially acknowledge our particular social identities.

My oldest friend Ponchita and I did exchange gifts last year on the twenty-fifth anniversary of our friendship, and never again will the form "anniversary" mean only a rite (right) of the married. My journey through the single life was beginning to have its own milestones and to be guided by its own cartography.

V

A life of pure decision, of thoughtful calculations, every inclination honored. They go about on their own, nicely accompanied in their singularity by the companion of possibility.

—Elizabeth Hardwick
Sleepless Nights

Our Mexico trip was in 1971. In the next 10 years, I earned a Ph.D., became director of black studies at the University of Detroit, edited two anthologies, threw out my makeshift bricks-and-board furniture, began to think about buying a house and adopting a child, and in the process, decided that my life was no longer "on hold." These deliberate choices made me begin to regard my single status as an honorable estate. But you know, when I look back at that checklist of accomplishments and serious life plans, I feel resentful that I had to work so hard for the honor that naturally accompanies the married state. Overcompensation, however, sometimes has its rewards: I had established a reputation in my profession that brought the prospect of a fellowship year at Radcliffe and a new job in Boston.

When I was leaving Detroit, I was acutely aware of my single status. What kind of life was it, I wondered, if you could start all over again in a new city with nothing to show for your past except your furniture and your diplomas? I didn't even have a cat. Where were the signs and symbols of a coherent, meaningful life that others could recognize? What was I doing living at *random* like this? I had made this "pure" decision and was honoring my inclination to live in another city, to take a job that offered

excitement and challenge. As I packed boxes alone, signed contracts with moving companies, and said good-bye at numerous dinners and going-away parties to all the friends I had made over 10 years, I felt not so very different from a friend who was moving after separating from his wife: "like a rhinoceros being cut loose from the herd."

I think it was the wide-open, netless freedom of it all that scared me, because I was truly *not* alone. I moved into a triple-decker in Cambridge where I live in a kind of semi-cooperative with two other families. Here, I feel secure, but independent and private. The journalist on the second floor and I read each other's work, and I exchange ideas about teaching methods with the three other professors in the house. We all share meals occasionally; we've met one another's extended families; and we celebrate one another's assorted triumphs. I have put together another network of friends whose lives I feel intimately involved in, and who, like me, are interested in making single life work—not disappear.

But I do not yet have the solid sense of belonging to a community that I had in Cleveland and Detroit, and sometimes I am unsettled by the variousness and unpredictableness of my single life. This simply means that I still have some choices to make—about deepening friendships, about having children (possibly adopting them), about establishing closer ties with the black community in Boston. If and when I do adopt a child, she or he will have a selection of godparents and aunts and uncles as large and varied as I had. That is one of the surest signs of the richness of my single life.

VI

You're wondering if I'm lonely:
OK then, yes, I'm lonely
as a plane rides lonely and level
on its radio beam, aiming
across the Rockies
for the blue-strung aisles
of an airfield on the ocean

—Adrienne Rich
"Song" from *Diving into the Wreck* (Norton)

Last year Elizabeth Stone wrote an article in the *Village Voice* called "A Married Woman" in which she discussed how much her life had changed since she married at the age of 33. Somewhat boastfully, she remarked at the end that she had hardly made any reference in the whole article to her husband. But if a single woman describes her life without reference to romance—no matter how rich and satisfying her life may be, no matter what she says about wonderful friends, exciting work, cultural and intellectual accomplishments—in fact, the *more* she says about these things—the more skeptical people's reactions will be. That one fact—her romantic involvement—if it is not acceptable can cancel out all the rest. This is how society keeps the single woman feeling perilous about her sense of personal success.

Still, everybody wants and needs some kind of special alliance(s) in her life. Some people have alliances called marriage. (I like that word alliance: it keeps marriage in its proper—horizontal—place.) I'd like an alliance with a man who could be a comrade and kindred spirit, and I've had such alliances in the past. Even with the hassles, they were enriching and enjoyable experiences for me, but I have never wanted to forsake my singularity for this kind of emotional involvement. Whatever psychic forces drive me have always steered me toward autonomy and independence, out toward the ocean's expanse and away from the shore.

I don't want to sound so smooth and glib and clear-eyed about it all, because it has taken me more than a decade to get this sense of balance and control. A lot of rosaries and perpetual candles and expensive long-distance calls have gotten me through the hard times when I would have chosen the holy cloister over another day of "single blessedness." The truth is that those hard times were not caused by being single. They were part of every woman's struggle to find commitment and contentment for herself. Singleness does not define me, is not an essential characteristic of me. I simply wish to have it acknowledged as a legitimate way to be in the world. After all, we started using Ms. instead of Mrs. or Miss because *none* of us wanted to be defined by the presence or absence of a man.

VII
Apart from the forest
a single tree will sometimes grow awry
in brave and extraordinary search
for its own shape

—Paulette Childress White
"A Tree Alone"

When I first started running in 1972, I ran regularly with a man. As long as I had this male companion, the other men passing by either ignored me or gave me slight nods to show their approval of my supervised state. Eventually I got up the nerve to run alone around Detroit's Palmer Park, and then the men came out of the trees to make comments—usually to tell me what I was doing wrong ("Lift your legs higher" or "Stop waving your arms"), or to flirt ("Can I run with you, baby?" was by far the most common remark, though others were nastier).

Once a carload of black teenagers who were parked in the lot at the end of my run started making comments about my physical anatomy, which I started to dismiss as just a dumb teenage ritual. But on this particular day, something made me stop my run, walk over to the car, and say, "You know, when you see a sister out trying to get some exercise, as hard as that is for us, you ought to be trying to support her, because she needs all the help she can get." I didn't know how they would respond, so I was surprised when they apologized, and somewhat shamefaced, one of them said: "Go on, sister; we're with you."

Now, that incident occurred because I was alone, and the image has become part of my self-definition: I am a woman in the world—single and powerful and astonished at my ability to create my own security, "in brave and extraordinary search for my own shape."   [1982]

 109

Song

ADRIENNE RICH

You're wondering if I'm lonely:
OK then, yes, I'm lonely
as a plane rides lonely and level
on its radio beam, aiming
across the Rockies
for the blue-strung aisles
of an airfield on the ocean

You want to ask, am I lonely?
Well, of course, lonely

as a woman driving across country
day after day, leaving behind
mile after mile
little towns she might have stopped
and lived and died in, lonely

If I'm lonely
it must be the loneliness
of waking first, of breathing
dawn's first cold breath on the city
of being the one awake
in a house wrapped in sleep

If I'm lonely
it's with the rowboat ice-fast on the shore
in the last red light of the year
that knows what it is, that knows it's neither
ice nor mud nor winter light
but wood, with a gift for burning   [1973]

 110

Loving Another Woman

ANNE KOEDT

The following is from a taped interview with a woman who talked about her love relationship with another woman. Both of these women, who requested anonymity, had previously had only heterosexual relationships; both are feminists. The interview was conducted by Anne Koedt.

Question: You said you had been friends for a while before you realized you were attracted to each other. How did you become aware of it?

Answer: I wasn't conscious of it until one evening when we were together and it all just sort of exploded. But, looking back, there are always signs, only one represses seeing them.

For example, I remember one evening—we are in the same feminist group together—and we were all talking very abstractly about love. All of a sudden, even though the group was carrying on the conversation in a theoretical way, we were having a personal conversation. We were starting to tell each other that we liked each other. Of course one of the things we discussed was: What is the thin line between friendship and love?

Or, there were times when we were very aware of having "accidentally" touched each other. And

Jennie told me later that when we first met she remembered thinking, "abstractly" again, that if she were ever to get involved with a woman, she'd like to get involved with someone like me.

The mind-blowing thing is that you aren't at all conscious of what you are feeling; rather, you subconsciously, and systematically, refuse to deal with the implications of what's coming out. You just let it hang there because you're too scared to let it continue and see what it means.

Q: What did you do when you became aware of your mutual attraction?

A: We'd been seeing a lot of each other, and I was at her house for dinner. During the evening—we were having a nice time, but I remember also feeling uncomfortable—I became very aware of her as we were sitting together looking at something. There was an unusual kind of tension throughout the whole evening.

It was quite late by the time we broke up, so she asked me whether I wanted to stay over and sleep on her couch. And I remember really being very uptight—something I certainly wouldn't have felt in any other situation with a friend. Yet, even when I was uptight and felt that in some way by staying I would get myself into something, I wasn't quite sure what—something new and dangerous—I decided to stay anyway.

It wasn't really until I tried to fall asleep, and couldn't, that all of a sudden I became very, very aware. I was flooded with a tremendous attraction for her. And I wanted to tell her, I wanted to sleep with her, I wanted to let her know what I was feeling. At the same time I was totally bewildered, because here I was—not only did I want to tell her, but I was having a hard time just facing up to what was coming out in myself. My mind was working overtime trying to deal with this new thing.

She was awake too, and so we sat and talked. It took me about two hours to build up the courage to even bring up the subject. I think it is probably one of the most difficult things I ever had to do. To say—to in any way whatsoever open up the subject—to say anything was just so hard.

When I did bring it up in an oblique way and told her that I was attracted to her, she replied somewhat generally that she felt the same way. You see, she was as scared as I was, but I didn't know it. I thought she seemed very cool, so I wasn't even sure if she was interested. Although I think subconsciously I knew, because otherwise I wouldn't have asked her—I think I would have been too scared of rejection.

But when I finally did bring it up, and she said she felt the same way, well, at that point there was really no space left for anything in your mind. So we agreed to just drop it and let things happen as they would at a later time. My main, immediate worry was that maybe I had blown a good friendship which I really valued. Also, even if she did feel the same way, would we know what to do with it?

Q: When you first realized that you were possibly getting involved with a woman, were you afraid or upset?

A: No. The strange thing is that the next morning, after I left, I felt a fantastic high. I was bouncing down the street and the sun was shining and I felt tremendously good. My mind was on a super high.

When I got home I couldn't do any kind of work. My mind kept operating on this emergency speed, trying to deal with my new feelings for her. So I sat down and wrote a letter to myself. Just wrote it free association—didn't try to work it out in any kind of theory—and as I was writing I was learning from myself what I was feeling. Unexpectedly I wasn't feeling guilty or worried. I felt great.

Q: When did you start sleeping with each other?

A: The next time we were together. Again, we really wanted each other, but to finally make the move, the same move that with a man would have been automatic, was tremendously difficult . . . and exhilarating. Although we did sleep together, it wasn't sexual; just affectionate and very sensual. After that evening we started sleeping together sexually as well.

I guess it was also a surprise to find that you weren't struck down by God in a final shaft of lightning. That once you fight through that initial wall of undefined fears (built to protect those taboos), they wither rapidly, and leave you to operate freely in a new self-defined circle of what's natural. You have a new sense of boldness, of daring, about yourself.

Q: Was it different from what you had thought a relationship with a woman would be like?

A: Generally, no. Most of the things that I had thought intellectually in fact turned out to be true in my experience. One thing, however, was different. Like, I'd really felt that very possibly a relationship with a woman might not be terribly physical. That it would be for the most part warm and affectionate. I think I probably thought this because with men sex is so frequently confused with conquest. Men have applied a symbolic value to sex, where the penis equals dominance and the vagina equals submission. Since sensuality has no specific sex and is rather a general expression of mutual affection, its symbolic value, power-wise, is nil. So sex with a man is usually genitally oriented.

Perhaps I wasn't quite sure what would happen to sexuality once it was removed from its conventional context. But one of the things I discovered was that when you really like somebody, there's a perfectly natural connection between affection and love and sensuality and sexuality. That sexuality is a natural part of sensuality.

Q: How is sex different with a woman?

A: One of the really mind-blowing things about all this has been that it added a whole new dimension to my own sexuality. You can have good sex, technically, with a woman or a man. But at this point in time I think women have a much broader sense of sensuality. Since she and I both brought our experiences as women to sexuality, it was quite something.

Another aspect of sexuality is your feelings. Again, this is of course an area that has been delegated to women; we are supposed to provide the love and affection. It is one of our duties in a male-female relationship. Though it has been very oppressive in the context that we've been allowed it, the *ability* to show affection and love for someone else is, I think, a fine thing—which men should develop more in themselves, as a matter of fact. Love and affection are a necessary aspect of full sexuality. And one of the things I really enjoy with Jennie is this uninhibited ability to show our feelings.

Q: Is the physical aspect of loving women really as satisfying as sex with a man?

A: Yes.

Q: You've been together a while now. What's your relationship like?

A: Once we got over the initial week or so of just getting used to this entirely new thing, it very quickly became natural—natural is really the word I'd use for it. It was like adding another dimension to what we'd already been feeling for each other. It is quite a combination to fall in love with your friend.

We don't have any plans, any desire, to live together, although we do see a great deal of each other. We both like our own apartments, our own space.

I think one of the good things we did in the beginning was to say: Let's just see where it will go. We didn't say that we loved each other, just that we liked each other. We didn't immediately proclaim it a "relationship," as one is accustomed to do with a man—you know, making mental plans for the next ten years. So each new feeling was often surprising, and very intensely experienced.

Q: What would you say is the difference between this relationship and those you have had with men?

A: Well, one of the biggest differences is that for the first time I haven't felt those knots-in-the-stomach undercurrents of trying to figure out what's *really* happening under what you *think* is happening.

I think it all boils down to an absence of role-playing; I haven't felt with Jen that we've fallen into that. Both of us are equally strong persons. I mean, you can ask yourself the question, if there were going to be roles, who'd play what? Well, I certainly won't play "the female," and I won't play "the male," and it's just as absurd to imagine her in either one of them. So in fact what we have is much more like what one gets in a friendship, which is more equalized. It's a more above-board feeling.

I don't find the traditional contradictions. If I do something strong and self-assertive, she doesn't find that a conflict with her having a relationship with me. I don't get reminded that I might be making myself "less womanly." And along with that there's less *self*-censorship, too. There's a mutual, unqualified, support for daring to try new things that I have never quite known before.

As a result, my old sense of limits is changing. For example, for the first time in my life I'm beginning to feel that I don't have a weak body, that my body isn't some kind of passive baggage. The other day I gritted my teeth and slid down a fireman's pole at a park playground. It may sound ordinary, but it was something I had never dared before, and I felt a very private victory.

Q: Given the social disapproval and legal restrictions against lesbianism, what are some of the external problems you have faced?

A: One thing is that I hesitate to show my affection for her in public. If you're walking down the street and you want to put your arm around someone or give them a kiss—the kind of thing you do without thinking if it is a man—well, that's hardly considered romantic by most people if it's done with someone of your own sex. I know that if I were to express my feelings in public with Jennie, there would be a lot of social intrusion that I would have to deal with. Somehow, people would assume a license to intrude upon your privacy in public; their hostile comments, hostile attitudes, would ruin the whole experience. So you're sort of caught in a bind. But we have in fact begun to do it more and more, because it bothers me that I can't express my feeling as I see fit, without hostile interference.

Q: What made you fall in love with a woman?

A: Well, that's a hard question. I think maybe it's even a bit misleading the way you phrased it. Because I didn't fall in love with "a woman," I fell in love with Jen—which is not exactly the same thing. A better way to ask the question is: How were you able to *overcome* the fact that it was a woman? In other words, how was I able to overcome my heterosexual training and allow my feelings for her to come out?

Certainly in my case it would never have happened without the existence of the women's movement. My own awareness of "maleness" and "femaleness" had become acute, and I was really probing what it meant. You see, I think in a sense I never wanted to be either male *or* female. Even when I was quite little and in many ways seemed feminine and "passive"—deep down, I never felt at home with the kinds of things women were supposed to be. On the other hand, I didn't particularly want to be a man either, so I didn't develop a male identity. Before I even got involved with the women's movement, I was already wanting something new. But the movement brought it out into the open for me.

Another thing the movement helped me with was shedding the notion that, however independent my life was, I must have a man; that somehow, no matter what I did myself, there was something that needed that magical element of male approval. Without confronting this I could never have allowed myself to fall in love with Jennie. In a way, I am like an addict who has kicked the habit.

But most important of all, I like her. In fact I think she's the healthiest person I have ever been involved with. See, I think we were lucky, because it happened spontaneously and unexpectedly from both sides. We didn't do it because we felt compelled to put our ideological beliefs into reality.

Many feminists are now beginning to at least theoretically consider the fact that there's no reason why one shouldn't love a woman. But I think that a certain kind of experimentation going on now with lesbianism can be really bad. Because even if you do ideologically think that it is perfectly fine—well, that's a *political* position; but being able to love somebody is a very personal and private thing as well, and even if you remove political barriers, well, then you are left with finding an individual who particularly fits *you*.

So I guess I'm saying that I don't think women who are beginning to think about lesbianism should get involved with anyone until they are really attracted to somebody. And that includes refusing to be seduced by lesbians who play the male seduction game and tell you, "you don't love women," and "you are oppressing us" if you don't jump into bed with them. It's terrible to try to seduce someone on ideological grounds.

Q: Do you now look at women in a more sexual way?
A: You mean, do I now eye all women as potential bed partners? No. Nor did I ever see men that way. As a matter of fact, I've never found myself being attracted to a man just because, for example, he had a good physique. I had a sexual relationship with whatever boyfriend I had, but I related to most other men pretty asexually. It's no different with women. My female friends—well, I still see them as friends, because that's what they are. I don't sit around and have secret fantasies of being in bed with them.

But there's a real question here: What is the source, the impetus, for one's sexuality? Is it affection and love, or is it essentially conquest in bed? If it's sex as conquest in bed, then the question you just asked is relevant, for adding the category of women to those you sleep with would mean that every woman—who's attractive enough to be a prize worth conquering, of course—could arouse your sexuality. But if the sexual source lies in affection and love, then the question becomes absurd. For one obviously does not immediately fall in love with every woman one meets simply because one is *able* to sleep with women.

Also, one thing that really turns me off about this whole business of viewing women as potential bedmates is the implied possessiveness of it. It has taken me this long just to figure out how men are treating women sexually; now when I see some lesbians doing precisely the same kinds of things, I'm supposed to have instant amnesia in the name of sisterhood. I have heard some lesbians say things like, "I see all men as my rivals," or have heard them proudly discuss how they intimidated a heterosexual couple publicly to "teach the woman a political lesson." This brings out in me the same kind of intense rage that I get when, for example, I hear white men discussing how black men are "taking their women" (or vice versa). Who the hell says we belong to anyone?

Q: Do you think that you would have difficulty relating to a man again if this relationship broke up? That is, can you "go back" to men after having had a relationship with a woman?
A: It's an interesting thing that when people ask that question, most often what they're really asking is, are you "lost" to the world of what's "natural"? Sometimes I find myself not wanting to answer the question at all just because they're starting out by assuming that something's wrong with having a relationship with a woman. That's usually what's meant by "go back to men"—like you've been off someplace wild and crazy and, most of all, unsafe, and can you find your way home to papa, or something. So first of all it wouldn't be "going back."

And since I didn't become involved with a woman in order to make a political statement, by the same token I wouldn't make the converse statement. So, sure I could have a relationship with a man if he were the right kind of person and if he had rejected playing "the man" with me—that leaves out a lot of men here, I must add. But if a man had the right combination of qualities, I see no reason why I shouldn't be able to love him as much as I now love her.

At a certain point, I think, you realize that the final qualification is not being male or female, but whether they've joined the middle. That is— whether they have started from the male or the female side—they've gone toward the center where they are working toward combining the healthy aspects of so-called male and female characteristics. That's where I want to go and that's what I'm beginning to realize I respond to in other people.

Q: Now that you've gotten involved with a woman, what is your attitude toward gay and lesbian groups?
A: I have really mixed feelings about them. To some extent, for example, there has been a healthy interplay between the gay movement and the feminist movement. Feminists have had a very good influence on the gay movement because women's liberation challenges the very nature of the sex role system, not just whether one may be allowed to make transfers within it. On the other hand, the gay movement has helped open up the question of

women loving other women. Though some of this was beginning to happen by itself, lesbians made a point of pressing the issue and therefore speeded up the process.

But there is a problem to me with focusing on sexual choice, as the gay movement does. Sleeping with another woman is not *necessarily* a healthy thing by itself. It does not mean—or prove, for that matter—that you therefore love women. It doesn't mean that you have avoided bad "male" or "female" behavior. It doesn't guarantee you anything. If you think about it, it can be the same game with new partners: On the one hand, male roles are learned, not genetic; women can ape them too. On the other, the feminine role can be comfortably carried into lesbianism, except now instead of a woman being passive with a man, she's passive with another woman. Which is all very familiar and is all going nowhere.

The confusing of sexual *partners* with sexual *roles* has also led to a really bizarre situation where some lesbians insist that you aren't really a radical feminist if you are not in bed with a woman. Which is wrong politically and outrageous personally.

Q: Did the fact that lesbians pushed the issue in the women's movement have a major effect upon your own decision to have a relationship with a woman?

A: It's hard to know. I think that the lesbian movement has escalated the thinking in the women's movement, and to that extent it probably escalated mine.

But at the same time I know I was slowly getting there myself anyway. I'd been thinking about it for a long time. Because it is a natural question; if you want to remove sexual roles, and if you say that men and women are equal human beings, well, the next question is: Why should you only love men? I remember asking myself that question, and I remember it being discussed in many workshops I was in—what is it that makes us assume that you can only receive and give love to a man?   [1973]

🦎 111

I Lost It at the Movies

JEWELLE GOMEZ

My grandmother, Lydia, and my mother, Dolores, were both talking to me from their bathroom stalls in the Times Square movie theater. I was washing butter from my hands at the sink and didn't think it at all odd. The people in my family are always talking; conversation is a life force in our existence. My great-grandmother, Grace, would narrate her life story from 7:00 A.M. until we went to bed at night. The only break was when we were reading or the reverential periods when we sat looking out of our tenement windows, observing the neighborhood, which we naturally talked about later.

So it was not odd that Lydia and Dolores talked non-stop from their stalls, oblivious to everyone except us. I hadn't expected it to happen there, though. I hadn't really expected an "it" to happen at all. To be a lesbian was part of who I was, like being left-handed—even when I'd slept with men. When my great-grandmother asked me in the last days of her life if I would be marrying my college boyfriend I said yes, knowing I would not, knowing I was a lesbian.

It seemed a fact that needed no expression. Even my first encounter with the word "bulldagger" was not charged with emotional conflict. As a teen in the 1960s my grandmother told a story about a particular building in our Boston neighborhood that had gone to seed. She described the building's past through the experience of a party she'd attended there thirty years before. The best part of the evening had been a woman she'd met and danced with. Lydia had been a professional dancer and singer on the black theater circuit; to dance with women was who she was. They'd danced, then the woman walked her home and asked her out. I heard the delicacy my grandmother searched for even in her re-telling of how she'd explained to the "bulldagger," as she called her, that she liked her fine but she was more interested in men. I was struck with how careful my grandmother had been to make it clear to that woman (and in effect to me) that there was no offense taken in her attentions, that she just didn't "go that way," as they used to say. I was so happy at thirteen to have a word for what I knew myself to be. The word was mysterious and curious, as if from a new language that used some other alphabet which left nothing to cling to when touching its curves and crevices. But still a word existed and my grandmother was not flinching in using it. In fact she'd smiled at the good heart and good looks of the bulldagger who'd asked her.

Once I had the knowledge of a word and a sense

of its importance to me, I didn't feel the need to explain, confess, or define my identity as a lesbian. The process of reclaiming my ethnic identity in this country was already all-consuming. Later, of course, in moments of glorious self-righteousness, I did make declarations. But they were not usually ones I had to make. Mostly they were a testing of the waters. A preparation for the rest of the world which, unlike my grandmother, might not have a grounding in what true love is about. My first lover, the woman who'd been in my bed once a week most of our high school years, finally married. I told her with my poems that I was a lesbian. She was not afraid to ask if what she'd read was about her, about my love for her. So there, amidst her growing children, errant husband, and bowling trophies I said yes, the poems were about her and my love for her, a love I'd always regret relinquishing to her reflexive obeisance to tradition. She did not flinch either. We still get drunk together when I go home to Boston.

During the 1970s I focused less on career than on how to eat and be creative at the same time. Graduate school and a string of non-traditional jobs (stage manager, mid-town messenger, etc.) left me so busy I had no time to think about my identity. It was a long time before I made the connection between my desire, my isolation, and the difficulty I had with my writing. I thought of myself as a lesbian between girlfriends—except the between had lasted five years. After some anxiety and frustration I deliberately set about meeting women. Actually, I knew many women, including my closest friend at the time, another black woman also in the theatre. She became uncharacteristically obtuse when I tried to open up and explain my frustration at going to the many parties we attended and being too afraid to approach women I was attracted to, certain I would be rejected either because the women were straight and horrified or gay and terrified of being exposed. For my friend theoretical homosexuality was acceptable, even trendy. Any uncomfortable experience was irrelevant to her. She was impatient and unsympathetic. I drifted away from her in pursuit of the women's community, a phrase that was not in my vocabulary yet, but I knew it was something more than just "women." I fell into that community by connecting with other women writers, and that helped me to focus on my writing and on my social life as a lesbian.

Still, none of my experiences demanded that I bare my soul. I remained honest but not explicit. Expediency, diplomacy, discretion, are all words that come to mind now. At that time I knew no political framework through which to filter my experience. I was more preoccupied with the Attica riots than with Stonewall. The media helped to focus our attentions within a proscribed spectrum and obscure the connections between the issues. I worried about who would shelter Angela Davis, but the concept of sexual politics was remote and theoretical.

I'm not certain exactly when and where the theory and reality converged.

Being a black woman and a lesbian unexpectedly blended like that famous scene in Ingmar Bergman's film *Persona*. The different faces came together as one, and my desire became part of my heritage, my skin, my perspective, my politics, and my future. And I felt sure that it had been my past that helped make the future possible. The women in my family had acted as if their lives were meaningful. Their lives were art. To be a lesbian among them was to be an artist. Perhaps the convergence came when I saw the faces of my great-grandmother, grandmother, and mother in those of the community of women I finally connected with. There was the same adventurous glint in their eyes; the same determined step; the penchant for breaking into song and for not waiting for anyone to take care of them.

I need not pretend to be other than who I was with any of these women. But did I need to declare it? During the holidays when I brought home best friends or lovers my family always welcomed us warmly, clasping us to their magnificent bosoms. Yet there was always an element of silence in our neighborhood, and surprisingly enough in our family, that was disturbing to me. Among the regulars in my father, Duke's, bar, was Maurice. He was eccentric, flamboyant, and still ordinary. He was accorded the same respect by neighborhood children as every other adult. His indiscretions took their place comfortably among the cyclical, Saturday night, man/woman scandals of our neighborhood. I regret never having asked my father how Maurice and he had become friends.

Soon I felt the discomforting silence pressing against my life more persistently. During visits home to Boston it no longer sufficed that Lydia and Dolores were loving and kind to the "friend" I brought home. Maybe it was just my getting older. Living in New York City at the age of thirty in 1980, there was little I kept deliberately hidden from anyone. The genteel silence that hovered around me when I entered our home was palpable but I was unsure whether it was already there when I arrived or if I carried it home within myself. It cut me off from what I knew was a kind of fulfillment available only from my family. The lifeline from Grace, to Lydia, to Dolores, to Jewelle was a strong one. We were bound by so many things, not the least of which was looking so much alike. I was not willing to be orphaned by silence.

If the idea of cathedral weddings and station wagons held no appeal for me, the concept of an extended family was certainly important. But my efforts were stunted by our inability to talk about the life I was creating for myself, for all of us. It felt all the more foolish because I thought I knew how my family would react. I was confident they would respond with their customary aplomb just as they had when I'd first had my hair cut as an Afro (which they hated) or when I brought home friends who were vegetarians (which they found curious). While we had disagreed over some issues, like the fight my mother and I had over Vietnam when I was nineteen, always when the deal went down we sided with each other. Somewhere deep inside I think I believed that neither my grandmother nor my mother would ever censure my choices. Neither had actually raised me; my great-grandmother had done that, and she had been a steely barricade against any encroachment on our personal freedoms and she'd never disapproved out loud of anything I'd done.

But it was not enough to have an unabashed admiration for these women. It is one thing to have pride in how they'd so graciously survived in spite of the odds against them. It was something else to be standing in a Times Square movie theater faced with the chance to say "it" out loud and risk the loss of their brilliant and benevolent smiles.

My mother had started reading the graffiti written on the wall of the bathroom stall. We hooted at each of her dramatic renderings. Then she said (not breaking her rhythm since we all know timing is everything), "Here's one I haven't seen before— 'DYKES UNITE'." There was that profound si-

lence again, as if the frames of my life had ground to a halt. We were in a freeze-frame and options played themselves out in my head in rapid succession: Say nothing? Say something? Say what?

I laughed and said, "Yeah, but have you seen the rubber stamp on my desk at home?"

"No," said my mother with a slight bit of puzzlement. "What does it say?"

"I saw it," my grandmother called out from her stall. "It says: 'Lesbian Money!'"

"What?"

"*Lesbian Money*," Lydia repeated.

"I just stamp it on my big bills," I said tentatively, and we all screamed with laughter. The other woman at the sinks tried to pretend we didn't exist.

Since then there has been little discussion. There have been some moments of awkwardness, usually in social situations where they feel uncertain. Although we have not explored the "it," the shift in our relationship is clear. When I go home it is with my lover and she is received as such. I was lucky. My family was as relieved as I to finally know who I was.   [1990]

🌿 112

The Turn On

MARGE PIERCY

Fantasies are sex in the head. I have often observed that what turns me on in thinking about sex is not at all what turns me on in real time. My erotic fantasies and my sexual reality are quite distinct. My fantasies run to the exotic: a great many of them occur in other times and even in other worlds.

When I was younger, this distinction was not so sharp to me as it is now. In my blue and spiky youth, I was under the spell of various literary incubi; what attracted me was what had been programmed into me as attractive, for purposes far from my own. I was taught to choose men who tried to reduce my autonomy and who attempted to control me in ways that would have prevented me from doing any useful work of my own. Very negative human qualities had been programmed into me by literary and popular culture as triggers to sexual response: male self-pity, sullenness, posing, narcissism, self-dramatization, being or pretending to be violent. I responded to several sorts of men, none of them suitable—but I am not at all persuaded there existed then the sort of men I find attractive now.

Besides the Heathcliff mood-monsters, I was sometimes attracted to men who told me they were geniuses, generally scientists, since that was one field in which I could in no way contest their assertions. I was moved by these contorted, bright types who seemed to yearn for the land of the emotions as for some lush jungle that they could not penetrate. I would of course be their guide.

I imagined that some store of warmth was hidden in these oysters, a pearl of great price and a love that would be worth the incredible work of trying to open a shell not by force but by persuasion and passion. I believe this tendency could probably be better satisfied by that fad of a few years ago, the Pet Rock.

What turns me on not in the head, not in theory, not on paper, but in daily life? Truthfully, my most passionate moments have never been brief encounters. I have given a lot of rope to my sexual curiosity over the years and it has led me into many adventures and strange encounters; but none of them offered the pure sexual pleasure of being in my own bed with someone I trust and love. In my adventures, my omnivorous curiosity was always far better satisfied than my sexuality.

I do not find orgasm easy with a new sexual partner. A woman never quite knows what she is going to find when someone takes off his clothes. Often the polite social mask falls with the pants and she may find a passionate animal, or a four-year-old who wants to make mud pies and scream at mommy, or a machine freak who wants to program her the way he programs his personal computer.

A woman is never quite sure what she has got herself into, and she is generally committed to it, no matter how rough the ride, at least for the duration of the evening or night. Sex with someone new is exciting in the head, but to me tense with anxiety in reality. Even if the new partner's manner is wholly benign, there is anxiety over whether your own body

will please. Unless you are plastic perfect, your body reflects the life you have lived. It has its scars, its stretch marks, its wounds of pleasure or pain, its signs of hard use or soft living. You are offering up your skin, your flesh, and there is always that element of suffering oneself to be judged.

There is also the awkwardness of finding out what each other likes and dislikes once the relationship has been established. Our sexual preference may be quite different with different partners. Some men are never any good at oral sex so it is pointless to try to tell them how you like to be eaten. They approach the vagina with such fear and loathing you might as well give up. Hardly any man nowadays goes about saying how sex disgusts him, so you only find out that cold naysaying hatred after you've already climbed into bed. Some men with the best will in the world are simply incompetent. I have never been able to decide if this is real or feigned incompetence. It reminds me of the old trick of volunteering to do the dishes and being sure to do them so badly that you will not be asked to do them again.

Unless you are overprogrammed in your pleasures, clearly what you enjoy most with one partner may be different from what you enjoy most with another. All those small adjustments and explanations and verbal or nonverbal requests occur over a period of time. In a good sexual relationship you don't ever quite stop making them, but they occur after a while in a context of permission and ease.

Once that ease is created, often I find situations of working together on a common household project or job erotic. I don't necessarily mean something intellectual. That doesn't seem to work nearly as well as something physical. It could be planting beans or building a grape arbor or laying flagstones. The context of working together for a common good that is tangible acts directly on my sexual center.

I do not respond to the skinny icons of our culture. They speak of me of control, anxiety, mistrust of the flesh and of our animal natures. I like a fair amount of flesh and I also appreciate muscles: the kind that ordinary women and men develop when they do physical work. I do not like bodies that appear carved out of plastic resin. I like some belly and some bounce to snuggle against. My partner working outside with me looks good to me, in filthy jeans and an old shirt, as we carry around bags of bone meal and manure. In warmer weather, working in the garden tends to turn us both on, but in truth there is little fine sensual pleasure in attempting to copulate among the rows of cabbages while trying not to crush any, and the bugs do bite bare flesh. It is nicer to take the turned-on feeling inside. I am a great one for enjoying the out-of-doors and then going in for good food, good wine, and a comfortable bed.

Shared laughter is erotic too. Sometimes we are passionate and grunty in our sex, but sometimes we are silly, and silliness can be just as delightful. The permission to play in bed is something that perhaps only people who are fully at ease with each other can signal. It is permission to take on roles, to make noises, to try out spontaneous gestures and notions.

My sexuality is close to my sensuality. I find the common link in our culture between sex and violence peculiar, as if others around me were whipped into a frenzy of desire by the sight of a traffic light or the smell of wet wool. The difference between pleasure and pain is a sharply marked boundary to me. Whatever pleases me tends to express itself in sex eventually.

Sex is one of the few times, at its best, when the conscious mind ceases to be aware of its own machinations. We become our feelings, our sensations, our appetite, without all the quibbling and second-guessing and motive-scouring that normally goes on. While I value, perhaps even overvalue, my own intellect and honed consciousness, I seek those moments of respite from the constant chatter of evaluation. My cats soothe me by their animal presence; my garden soothes me as it requires my hard work and my attention. Sex is the ultimate cave, short of sleep and the sinking of the mind into the body. Sleep and sex are connected as animal functions: when I have trouble with one, I may well have trouble with the other. Insomnia and difficulty in orgasm are both warning signs of something wrong at the core, a problem that has to be dealt with.

When I have good sex with someone, I put up with more and am infinitely more motivated to work out problems. When someone withdraws sexually —a great way to manipulate a partner who likes sex—then already part of the motivation for getting

through the muck is diminished. It's all part of the same whole. If you feel closer, the sex tends to be better; if you feel more distant, then the sex tends to be weaker.

I am not someone who is turned on by jealousy. That kind of competition and insecurity makes me ill at ease with my own sexuality. One of my prerequisites for sexual response is that I have a sense that the other person also finds me attractive— though our relationship doesn't have to be sexually exclusive.

That may seem contradictory, but it isn't. I require being able to trust my sexual partner, to feel sure that my partner is willing to offer real intimacy and love. Without that trust, I can never approach full sexual response. Women have such a range of pleasure, anyhow, from little bitty orgasms that are like buzzes and blips to orgasms that pick you up and carry you off and drop you after what feels like miles and years of intensity. I like sex pretty often and have never required that ecstasy be presented to me. I figure it's a mutual responsibility. But there are prerequisites to letting go that have to be there.

To be afraid of a partner, unable to speak my mind or lose my temper or express my will, would dampen my sexuality. Under the gross inequality that has existed between almost all men and women, I think few women can flourish sexually. To be defined as a sexual receptacle for someone else means to be negated as the one who desires.

For some in our culture, sex is possessing. For some, sex is conquering. For some, sex is doing something to someone before they can do it to you. For me, it is primarily knowing, both the other and oneself. In sex I know my body in an immediate way, from deep within it.

In good sex, my partner opens to me his full vulnerability, his capacity for pleasure, tenderness, and passion. We are communicating directly skin on skin. We are communicating through pressure and smell and taste and little sounds, far more than in the occasional words that may be spoken.

If I say that talk is erotic to me, I don't mean spatting and I don't mean those where-were-you-last-night? ordeals. I have had lovers who seemed turned on by fighting, and relationships in which a kind of tearing and gouging and screaming seemed essential, and might end up with fairly heated sex; but those relationships were with basically inarticulate men who needed a fair amount of shouting and banging around to feel in touch. I find I often do want to make love after a fight, but not because I am aroused. It is simply to affirm that the relationship continues.

No, the talking that is most erotic to me is simply conversation at its own pace, a combination of the intense and the casual, the free association of two people who know each other well but who always have something new to report, to question, to discuss. When we are talking that way, I feel caressed.

Since my partner and I both write at home computers and raise much of our food organically, we are always sharing new skills—whether about the construction of a pitched roof or the recovery of some inadvertently erased data. Bringing to each other new glittering bits of knowledge in our hot beaks is surely part of our mating dance. We like to admire each other, as I think most people in egalitarian couples do.

On such occasions, we often feel especially close. I think it is feeling intimate that produces the best sex—not a great surprise, finally. The more trips we take together, whether by car or by computer or by walking in the dunes, the more opportunities we give each other to explore the rich variables of each other's mind and body. The best sex for me arises out of such an intimacy, constantly stimulated and renewed. [1984]

 113

A Marriage Agreement

ALIX KATES SHULMAN

When my husband and I were first married, a decade ago, keeping house was less a burden than a game. We both worked full-time in New York City, so our small apartment stayed empty most of the day and taking care of it was very little trouble. Twice a month we'd spend Saturday cleaning and doing our laundry at the laundromat. We shopped for food together after work, and though I usually did the cooking, my husband was happy to help. Since our meals were simple and casual, there were few dishes to wash. We occasionally had dinner out and usually ate breakfast at a diner near our offices. We spent most of our free time doing things we enjoyed together, such as taking long walks in the evenings and spending weekends in Central Park. Our domestic life was beautifully uncomplicated.

When our son was born, our domestic life suddenly became *quite* complicated; and two years later, when our daughter was born, it became impossible. We automatically accepted the traditional sex roles that society assigns. My husband worked all day in an office; I left my job and stayed at home, taking on almost all the burdens of housekeeping and child raising.

When I was working I had grown used to seeing people during the day, to having a life outside the home. But now I was restricted to the company of two demanding preschoolers and to the four walls of an apartment. It seemed unfair that while my husband's life had changed little when the children were born, domestic life had become the only life I had.

I tried to cope with the demands of my new situation, assuming that other women were able to handle even larger families with ease and still find time for themselves. I couldn't seem to do that.

We had to move to another apartment to accommodate our larger family, and because of the children, keeping it reasonably neat took several hours a day. I prepared half a dozen meals every day for from one to four people at a time—and everyone ate different food. Shopping for this brood—or even just running out for a quart of milk—meant putting on snowsuits, boots and mittens; getting strollers or carriages up and down the stairs; and scheduling the trip so it would not interfere with one of the children's feeding or nap or illness or some other domestic job. Laundry was now a daily chore. I seemed to be working every minute of the day—and still there were dishes in the sink; still there wasn't time enough to do everything.

Even more burdensome than the physical work of housekeeping was the relentless responsibility I had for my children. I loved them, but they seemed to be taking over my life. There was nothing I could do, or even contemplate, without first considering how they would be affected. As they grew older, just answering their constant questions ruled out even a private mental life. I had once enjoyed reading, but now if there was a moment free, instead of reading for myself, I read to them. I wanted to work on my own writing, but there simply weren't enough hours in the day. I had no time for myself; the children were always *there*.

As my husband's job began keeping him at work later and later—and sometimes taking him out of town—I missed his help and companionship. I wished he would come home at six o'clock and spend time with the children so they could know him better. I continued to buy food with him in mind and dutifully set his place at the table. Yet sometimes whole weeks would go by without his having dinner with us. When he did get home the children often were asleep, and we both were too tired ourselves to do anything but sleep.

We accepted the demands of his work as unavoidable. Like most couples, we assumed that the wife must accommodate to the husband's schedule, since it is his work that brings in the money.

As the children grew older I began free-lance editing at home. I felt I had to squeeze it into my "free" time and not allow it to interfere with my domestic duties or the time I owed my husband—just as he felt he had to squeeze in time for the children during weekends. We were both chronically dissatisfied, but we knew no solutions.

After I had been home with the children for six years I began to attend meetings of the newly formed Women's Liberation Movement in New York City. At these meetings I began to see that my situation was not uncommon; other women too felt drained and frustrated as housewives and mothers. When we started to talk about how we would have chosen to arrange our lives, most of us agreed that even though we might have preferred something different, we had never felt we had a choice in the matter. We realized that we had slipped into full domestic responsibility simply as a matter of course, and it seemed unfair.

When I added them up, the chores I was responsible for amounted to a hectic 6 A.M.–9 P.M. (often later) job, without salary, breaks or vacation. No employer would be able to demand these hours legally, but most mothers take them for granted—as I did until I became a feminist.

For years mothers like me have acquiesced to the strain of the preschool years and endless household maintenance without any real choice. Why, I asked myself, should a couple's decision to have a family mean that the woman must immerse years of her life in their children? And why should men like my husband miss caring for and knowing their children?

Eventually, after an arduous examination of our situation, my husband and I decided that we no longer had to accept the sex roles that had turned us into a lame family. Out of equal parts love for each other and desperation at our situation, we decided to re-examine the patterns we had been living by, and starting again from scratch, to define our roles for ourselves.

We began by agreeing to share completely all responsibility for raising our children (by then aged five and seven) and caring for our household. If this new arrangement meant that my husband would have to change his job or that I would have to do more free-lance work or that we would have to live on a different scale, then we would. It would be worth it if it could make us once again equal, independent and loving as we had been when we were first married.

Simply agreeing verbally to share domestic duties didn't work, despite our best intentions. And when we tried to divide them "spontaneously," we ended up following the traditional patterns. Our old habits were too deep-rooted. So we sat down and drew up a formal agreement, acceptable to both of us, that clearly defined the responsibilities we each had.

It may sound a bit formal, but it has worked for us. Here it is:

MARRIAGE AGREEMENT

I. Principles

We reject the notion that the work which brings in more money is more valuable. The ability to earn more money is a privilege which must not be compounded by enabling the larger earner to buy out of his/her duties and put the burden either on the partner who earns less or on another person hired from outside.

We believe that each partner <u>has an equal right to his/her own time, work, value, choices.</u> As long as all duties are performed, each of us may use his/her extra time any way he/she chooses. If he/she wants to use it making money, fine. If he/she wants to spend it with spouse, fine. If not, fine.

As parents we believe <u>we must share all responsibility for taking care of our children and home</u>—not only the work but also the responsibility. At least during the first year of this agreement, *sharing responsibility* shall mean dividing the *jobs* and dividing the *time*.

In principle, jobs should be shared equally, 50-50, but deals may be made by mutual agreement. If jobs and schedule are divided on any other than a 50-50 basis, then at any time either party may call for a re-examination and redistribution of jobs or a revision of the schedule. Any deviation from 50-50 must be for the convenience of both parties. If one party works overtime in any domestic job, he/she must be compensated by equal extra work by the other. The schedule may be flexible, but changes must be formally agreed upon. The terms of this agreement are rights and duties, not privileges and favors.

II. Job Breakdown and Schedule

(A) Children

1. Mornings: Waking children; getting their clothes out; making their lunches; seeing that they have notes, homework, money, bus passes, books; brushing their hair; giving them breakfast (making coffee for us). Every other week each parent does all.

2. Transportation: Getting children to and from lessons, doctors, dentists (including making appointments), friends' houses, park, parties, movies, libraries. Parts occurring between 3 and 6 P.M. fall to wife. She must be compensated by extra work from husband (see 10 below). Husband does all weekend transportation and pick-ups after 6.

3. Help: Helping with homework, personal problems, projects like cooking, making gifts, ex-

periments, planting; answering questions; explaining things. Parts occurring between 3 and 6 P.M. fall to wife. After 6 P.M. husband does Tuesday, Thursday and Sunday; wife does Monday, Wednesday and Saturday. Friday is free for whoever has done extra work during the week.

4. Nighttime (after 6 P.M.): Getting children to take baths, brush their teeth, put away their toys and clothes, go to bed; reading with them; tucking them in and having nighttime talks; handling if they wake or call in the night. Husband does Tuesday, Thursday and Sunday. Wife does Monday, Wednesday and Saturday. Friday is split according to who has done extra work during the week.

5. Baby sitters: Getting baby sitters (which sometimes takes an hour of phoning). Baby sitters must be called by the parent the sitter is to replace. If no sitter turns up, that parent must stay home.

6. Sick care: Calling doctors; checking symptoms; getting prescriptions filled; remembering to give medicine; taking days off to stay home with sick child; providing special activities. This must still be worked out equally, since now wife seems to do it all. (The same goes for the now frequently declared school closings for so-called political protests, whereby the mayor gets credit at the expense of the mothers of young children. The mayor closes only the schools, not the places of business or the government offices.) In any case, wife must be compensated (see 10 below).

7. Weekends: All usual child care, plus special activities (beach, park, zoo). Split equally. Husband is free all Saturday, wife is free all Sunday.

(B) Housework

8. Cooking: Breakfast; dinner (children, parents, guests). Breakfasts during the week are divided equally; husband does all weekend breakfasts (including shopping for them and dishes). Wife does all dinners except Sunday nights. Husband does Sunday dinner and any other dinners on his nights of responsibility if

wife isn't home. Whoever invites guests does shopping, cooking and dishes; if both invite them, split work.

9. Shopping: Food for all meals, housewares, clothing and supplies for children. Divide by convenience. Generally, wife does local daily food shopping; husband does special shopping for supplies and children's things.

10. Cleaning: Dishes daily; apartment weekly, biweekly or monthly. Husband does dishes Tuesday, Thursday and Sunday. Wife does Monday, Wednesday and Saturday. Friday is split according to who has done extra work during week. Husband does all the house cleaning in exchange for wife's extra child care (3 to 6 daily) and sick care.

11. Laundry: Home laundry, making beds, dry cleaning (take and pick up). Wife does home laundry. Husband does dry-cleaning delivery and pickup. Wife strips beds, husband remakes them.

Our agreement changed our lives. Surprisingly, once we had written it down, we had to refer to it only two or three times. But we still had to work to keep the old habits from intruding. If it was my husband's night to take care of the children, I had to be careful not to check up on how he was managing. And if the baby sitter didn't show up for him, I would have to remember it was *his* problem.

Eventually the agreement entered our heads, and now, after two successful years of following it, we find that our new roles come to us as readily as the old ones had. I willingly help my husband clean the apartment (knowing it is his responsibility) and he often helps me with the laundry or the meals. We work together and trade off duties with ease now that the responsibilities are truly shared. We each have less work, more hours together and less resentment.

Before we made our agreement I had never been able to find the time to finish even one book. Over the past two years I've written three children's books, a biography and a novel and edited a collection of writings (all will have been published by spring of 1972). Without our agreement I would never have been able to do this.

At present my husband works a regular 40-hour week, and I write at home during the six hours the children are in school. He earns more money now than I do, so his salary covers more of our expenses than the money I make with my free-lance work. But if either of us should change jobs, working hours or income, we would probably adjust our agreement.

Perhaps the best testimonial of all to our marriage agreement is the change that has taken place in our family life. One day after it had been in effect for only four months our daughter said to my husband, "You know, Daddy, I used to love Mommy more than you, but now I love you both the same."

[1971]

ꕤ 114

Sexual Politics and Black Women's Relationships

PATRICIA HILL COLLINS

In her ground-breaking essay, "On the Issue of Roles," Toni Cade Bambara remarks, "now it doesn't take any particular expertise to observe that one of the most characteristic features of our community is the antagonism between our men and our women" (Bambara 1970, 106). Exploring the tensions between African-American men and women has been a long-standing theme in Black feminist thought. In an 1833 speech, Maria Stewart boldly challenged what she saw as Black men's lackluster response to racism: "Talk, without effort, is nothing; you are abundantly capable, gentlemen, of making yourselves men of distinction; and this gross neglect, on your part, causes my blood to boil within me" (Richardson 1987, 58). Ma Rainey, Bessie Smith, and other classic Black women blues singers offer rich advice to Black women on how to deal with unfaithful and unreliable men (Harrison 1978, 1988; Lieb 1981; Russell 1982). More recently, Black women's troubles with Black men have generated anger and, from that anger, self-reflection: "We have been and are angry sometimes," suggests Bonnie Daniels, "not for what men have done, but for what we've allowed ourselves to become, again and again in my past, in my mother's past, in my centuries of womanhood passed over, for the 'sake' of men, whose manhood we've helped undermine" (1979, 62).

Another long-standing theme in Black feminist thought is the great love Black women feel for Black men. African-American slave narratives contain countless examples of newly emancipated slaves who spent years trying to locate their lost loved ones (Gutman 1976). Love poems written to Black men characterize much of Black women's poetry (Stetson 1981). Black women's music is similarly replete with love songs. Whether the playful voice of Alberta Hunter proclaiming that her "man is a handy man," the mournful cries of Billie Holiday singing "My Man," the sadness Nina Simone evokes in "I Loves You Porgy" at being forced to leave her man, or the powerful voice of Jennifer Holliday, who cries out, "you're gonna love me," Black vocalists identify Black women's relationships with Black men as a source of strength, support, and sustenance (Harrison 1978, 1988; Russell 1982). Black activist Fannie Lou Hamer succinctly captures what a good relationship between a Black woman and man can be: "You know, I'm not hung up on this about liberating myself from the black man, I'm not going to try that thing. I got a black husband, six feet three, two hundred and forty pounds, with a 14 shoe, that I don't *want* to be liberated from" (Lerner 1972, 612).

African-American women have long commented on this "love and trouble" tradition in Black women's relationships with Black men. Novelist Gayl Jones explains: "The relationships between the men and the women I'm dealing with are blues relationships. So they're out of a tradition of 'love and trouble.' . . . Blues talks about the simultaneity of good and bad, as feeling, as something felt. . . . Blues acknowledges all different kinds of feelings at once" (Harper 1979, 360). Both the tensions between African-American women and men and the strong attachment that we feel for one another represent the both/and conceptual stance in Black feminist thought.

Understanding this love and trouble tradition requires assessing the influence of Eurocentric gender ideology—particularly its emphasis on oppositional dichotomous sex roles—on the work and family experiences of African-Americans. Definitions of appropriate gender behavior for Black women, Black men, white women, and white men not only affect social institutions such as schools and labor markets, they also simultaneously shape daily interactions among and within each group. Analyses claiming that African-Americans would be "just like whites" if offered comparable opportunities implicitly support the prevailing sex/gender hierarchy and offer the allegedly "normal" gender ideology of white male and female sex roles as alternatives for putatively "deviant" Afrocentric ones. Similarly, those proclaiming that Black men experience more severe oppression than Black women and that Black women must unquestioningly support Black male sexism rarely challenge the overarching gender ideology that confines both whites and Blacks (see, e.g., Staples 1979). As Audre Lorde queries, "if society ascribes roles to black men which they are not allowed to fulfill, is it black women who must bend and alter our lives to compensate, or is it society that needs changing?" (1984, 61). Bonnie Daniels provides an answer: "I've learned . . . that being less than what I am capable of being to boost someone else's ego *does not help either of us* for real" (1979, 61).

Black women intellectuals directly challenge not only that portion of Eurocentric gender ideology applied to African-Americans—for example, the controlling images of mammy, the matriarch, the welfare mother, and Jezebel—but often base this rejection on a more general critique of Eurocentric gender ideology itself. Sojourner Truth's 1851 query, "I could work as much and eat as much as a man—when I could get it—and bear the lash as well! And ain't I a woman?" confronts the premises of the cult of true womanhood that "real" women were fragile and ornamental. Toni Cade Bambara contends that Eurocentric sex roles are not only troublesome for African-Americans but damaging: "I have always, I think, opposed the stereotypical definitions of 'masculine' and 'feminine,' . . . because I always found the either/or implicit in those definitions antithetical to what I was all about—and what revolution for self is all about—the whole person" (Bambara 1970, 101). Black activist Frances Beale echoes Bambara by identifying the negative effects that sexism within the Black community had on Black political activism in the 1960s:

> Unfortunately, there seems to be some confusion in the Movement today as to who has been oppressing whom. Since the advent of Black power, the Black male has exerted a more prominent leadership role in our struggle for justice in this country. He sees the system for what it really is for the most part, but where he rejects its values and mores on many issues, when it comes to women, he seems to take his guidelines from the pages of the *Ladies' Home Journal.* (Beale 1970, 92)

While some African-American women criticize Eurocentric gender ideology, even fewer have directly challenged Black men who accept externally defined notions of both Black and white masculinity (Sizemore 1973; Wallace 1978). The blues tradition provides the most consistent and long-standing text of Black women who demand that Black men reject stereotypical sex roles and "change their ways." Songs often encourage Black men to define new types of relationships. In "Do Right Woman—Do Right Man," when Aretha Franklin (1967) sings that a woman is only human and is not a plaything but is flesh and blood just like a man, she echoes Sojourner Truth's claim that women and men are equally human. Aretha sings about knowing that she's living in a "man's world" but she encourages her man not to "prove" that he's a man by using or abusing her. As long as she and her man are together, she wants him to show some "respect" for her. Her position is clear—if he wants a "do right, all night woman," he's got to be a "do right, all night man." Aretha challenges African-American men to reject Eurocentric gender ideology that posits "it's a man's world" in order to be a "do right man." By showing Black women respect and being an "all night" man—one who is faithful, financially reliable, and sexually expressive—Black men can have a relationship with a "do right woman." [1990]

REFERENCES

Bambara, Toni Cade. 1970. "On the Issue of Roles." In *The Black Woman: An Anthology,* edited by Toni Cade (Bambara), 101–10. New York: Signet.

Beale, Frances. 1970. "Double Jeopardy: To Be Black and Female." In *The Black Woman: An Anthology,* edited by Toni Cade (Bambara), 90–100. New York: Signet.

Daniels, Bonnie. 1979. "For Colored Girls . . . A Catharsis." *Black Scholar* 10(8–9): 61–61.

Franklin, Aretha. 1967. *I Never Loved a Man the Way I Love You.* Atlantic Recording Corp.

Gutman, Herbert. 1976. *The Black Family in Slavery and Freedom, 1750–1925.* New York: Random House.

Harper, Michael S. 1979. "Gayl Jones: An Interview." In *Chant of Saints: A Gathering of Afro-American Literature, Art, and Scholarship,* edited by Michael S. Harper and Robert B. Stepto, 352–75. Urbana: University of Illinois Press.

Harrison, Daphne Duval. 1978. "Black Women in the Blues Tradition." In *The Afro-American Woman: Struggles and Images,* edited by Sharon Harley and Rosalyn Terborg-Penn, 58–73. Port Washington, NY: Kennikat Press.

———. 1988. *Black Pearls: Blues Queens of the 1920s.* New Brunswick, NJ: Rutgers University Press.

Lerner, Gerda, ed. 1972. *Black Women in White America: A Documentary History.* New York: Vintage.

Lieb, Sandra. 1981. *Mother of the Blues: A Study of Ma Rainey.* Amherst: University of Massachusetts Press.

Lorde, Audre. 1984. *Sister Outsider.* Trumansberg, NY: The Crossing Press.

Richardson, Marilyn, ed. 1987. *Maria W. Stewart, America's First Black Woman Political Writer.* Bloomington: Indiana University Press.

Russell, Michele. 1982. "Slave Codes and Liner Notes." In *But Some of Us Are Brave,* edited by Gloria T. Hull, Patricia Bell Scott, and Barbara Smith, 129–40. Old Westbury, NY: Feminist Press.

Sizemore, Barbara A. 1973. "Sexism and the Black Male." *Black Scholar* 4(6–7): 2–11.

Staples, Robert. 1979. "The Myth of Black Macho: A Response to Angry Black Feminist." *Black Scholar* 10(6): 24–33.

Stetson, Erlene, ed. 1981. *Black Sister: Poetry by Black American Women, 1746–1980.* Bloomington: Indiana University Press.

Wallace, Michele. 1978. *Black Macho and the Myth of the Superwoman.* New York: Dial Press.

🌿 115

It's a Family Affair: The Real Lives of Black Single Mothers

BARBARA OMOLADE

No family survives without resources and support. Black single mothers, like Black families generally, rely heavily on relatives and friends for help in raising the children and managing a household. When I became a single parent, one of the first people who helped me was another Black single mother who daily encouraged me to look for work. The Black woman principal of a private preschool allowed me to work part-time to offset the school fees of my three children. Black male friends and white female co-workers did child care and helped me shop. My aunts and uncles stood by in case I needed money or babysitting. And most important, my children's father continued his relationship with them.

These new networks and the traditional kinship ties of Black families are the most useful support systems for Black single mothers. Though many believe that they're disintegrating, they remain vital and effective. It is when they are weak or problematic because loved ones are dead, ill, or far away that Black women and their families go into crisis and must rely on the church or social service agencies. Growing numbers of women in central Brooklyn now supplement or replace these supports with help from the Sisterhood of Black Single Mothers, a 12-year-old self-help organization founded and built by Daphne Busby, herself a single parent.

I found out about the Sisterhood while working on my master's degree, when I was still married. I was immediately impressed with the positive attitude of the women in it. A few years later a friend invited me to a conference sponsored by the Sisterhood where men conducted workshops on money, pornography, and relationships for participants of both sexes. I volunteered to help the group and was asked to participate in their Big Sister program for teenage mothers. In 1982, I coordinated a successful 13-week Black women's history series for the Sisterhood. Though I've used its services only informally, I know how well it helps Black single mothers survive.

The Sisterhood's first step in empowering a Black single mother is to encourage her to name her own reality, rejecting negative labels like "unwed," "illegitimate," and "teenage mother" (this last a code for saying you will have a lifetime of misery and trouble). The organization then offers practical support: every day women come in or phone for help with welfare, housing, protection from violence, health and education problems. It is truly a sisterhood, not a social work agency with paid advocates, who are often distanced from the problems and possibilities of Black women and their families. Daphne and her two-person staff regard other Black single mothers as sisters and peers. Their philosophy is rooted in our past, when Black women supported each other in day-to-day living as well as helping each other through crisis and celebration.

Daphne's greatest success as an organizer has been with teenage mothers. In 1979, the Sisterhood launched its Big Sister program with a Ford Foundation grant. The big sisters modeled successful mothering, encouraging the little sisters to stay in school, develop healthy parenting practices and self-respect, and maintain good relations with the fathers and their own families. The grant ended, but the spirit of the project has continued throughout the Sisterhood's work. Many organizations with much larger budgets and staffs have tried to duplicate the model, but have failed because of their moralism and disdain for the teenage mother's condition; they feel she will never amount to much and can't help showing it. The Sisterhood's staff, in contrast, knows that support for teenagers before, during, and after pregnancy will allow parents, children, and their families to build more successful lives.

The Sisterhood does not try to keep women in isolation from the rest of the community, but actively supports Black fatherhood. Each Father's Day, the Sisterhood sponsors a program featuring men who best exemplify positive fatherhood: married and single fathers, nonresident fathers, teenagers, and men active in the community. Black men have always been part of the counseling and other activities of the Sisterhood; recently it started a fathers' self-help group.

It's clear that Black single mothers need to influence and shape public policy on welfare, child custody, education, health care, and housing, and the Sisterhood is a natural center for campaigns on such issues. For years Daphne Busby has been speaking about Black single mothers and the Black family and has now joined the New York State Governor's Advisory Committee on Black Affairs and the New York State Commission on Child Support. Black single mothers across the country have expressed a growing interest in affiliating with the Sisterhood because no similar group exists in their area.

In fact, any group of Black single mothers composed of at least two or three sisters who care about each other can break the isolation and help each other survive with successful family experiences. The Sisterhood of Black Single Mothers is based on a model of self-help and self-definition which asserts that sisters who are experiencing single motherhood are best able to help and support each other in their parenting, professional, and private lives. A new group can work on common material needs such as obtaining child support, housing, and child care which can involve agencies, advocacy, and information sharing; or they can work on common personal needs such as loneliness, stress and self-doubt which call for sharing experiences and concerns. The sisters could also plan social events for themselves and their friends such as picnics, theatre parties, and pot luck dinners. Single parent fathers, older and younger women, and guest speakers could be invited to small meetings to share information with and give support to the members of the group. One of the most rewarding experiences of a single mothers' support group can be planning activities for the children such as holiday parties, camping trips, and sports.

The Sisterhood's concerns are not only relevant to Black people. White families have always been held up as the model Black families had to follow. Yet now, as Robert Hill noted, "White families, especially since more white women have entered the labor force, are increasingly adopting coping patterns that historically were used by Blacks."

We know that all families are in trouble: it's hard rearing children in a country burdened with a narrow puritan moralism, racial and sexual stratification, poverty and oppression obscured by selective social visions of national success and material wealth. Focusing solely on the problems of Black single mothers only deflects our attention from the real crisis in the family—the nation's lack of commitment to children's welfare and progressive social policies; the conflicts between men and women, adults and children, that prevent loving relationships.

The scapegoating of Black single mothers makes it hard to honestly discuss the families of poor and working-class Black people. If we criticize the welfare system, we give ammunition to an administration bent on dismantling welfare. If we attack Black male chauvinism, our remarks add to the undermining of young and working-class Black men. If we criticize Black women's participation in their own "sweet suffering," we reinforce those who deny the reality of Black female oppression or disparage Black women's competence. If we speak in public, we are accused of adding to white racist self-fulfilling prophesies of Black failure. Yet if we are silent about the weaknesses in Black families, keeping Black male violence and failure in the closet, we risk further abuse of Black women and children.

Many Black spokespeople would rather lament the increase of Black single mothers than seek to understand its causes; they would rather be alarmed about Black teenage pregnancy than do something concrete for Black teenagers and speak out firmly against the sexual abuse of young women. Since few of the social scientists, public officials, and media commentators of either race who purport to analyze and judge our lives understand the real strengths or difficulties of Black single mothers and their families, their suggestions for solving the "crisis of the Black family" are paternalistic and impractical.

Many, assuming that the major cause of the rise in Black female-headed households is Black male unemployment, propose that job training and employment programs focus mainly on Black men. This idea not only condones job discrimination against Black women but ignores the chauvinism that so often causes Black women to leave their relationships in the first place. Appeals to Black men to find their manhood in employment so as to reassert their dominance over Black women can only increase the number of Black single mothers. Many Black men are overcoming their sexist attitudes and seeking loving and equitable relationships with their spouses and children; Black women are also beginning to explore their own weaknesses and problems in establishing positive relationships with Black men. Yet dreams of patriarchal restoration have continued to permeate the Black family debate. If this is to change, Black women must speak truthfully, naming our own reality and vision of the Black family.

The families of Black single women are hardly immune to trouble and failure, and from their perspective on the edge of a new frontier in family living, Black women are conscious not only of the family's possibilities, but of its limits. In a racist and patriarchal system our sons will never truly be their own men and our daughters will be taught to despise all that is wonderful about Black womanhood. We worry that street violence and drugs will claim our male children. We realize that our daughters, like those in two-parent households, are drawn into motherhood and wifelike loyalties to men far too early in their lives.

But in their struggle against those limits—weathering changes from within and without, pitting themselves against social agencies and public opinion—Black single mothers and their families have something to offer us all. By daily demonstrating that they can survive and succeed without marriage, that they may even be better off without it, they challenge the basic patriarchal ideal. My children and other children of Black single mothers are better people because they do not have to live in families where violence, sexual abuse, and emotional estrangement are the daily, hidden reality. They are not burdened by violent sexist nightmares that block their strength and sensibilities at the core of where they live. They know that fathers and mothers are only men and women, not infallible tyrants or gods. They have choices and a voice. In a society where men are taught to dominate and women to follow, we all have a lot to overcome in learning to build relationships, with each other and with our children, based on love and justice. For many Black single mothers, this is what the struggle is about. [1986]

 116

Turning the Beat Around: Lesbian Parenting 1986

AUDRE LORDE

These days it seems like everywhere I turn somebody is either having a baby or talking about having a baby, and on one level that feels quite benign because I love babies. At the same time, I can't help asking myself what it means in terms of where we are as a country, as well as where we are as people of Color within a white racist system. And when infants begin to appear with noticeable regularity within the Gay and Lesbian community, I find this occurrence even more worthy of close and unsentimental scrutiny.

We are Lesbians and Gays of Color surviving in a country that defines human—when it concerns itself with the question at all—as straight and white. We are Gays and Lesbians of Color at a time in that country's history when its domestic and international policies, as well as its posture toward those developing nations with which we share heritage, are so reactionary that self-preservation demands we involve ourselves actively in those policies and postures. And we must have some input and effect upon those policies if we are ever to take a responsible place within the international community of peoples of Color, a human community which includes two-thirds of the world's population. It is a time when the increase in conservatism upon every front affecting our lives as people of Color is oppressively obvious, from the recent appointment of a Supreme Court Chief Justice in flagrant disregard of his history of racial intolerance, to the largely unprotested rise in racial stereotypes and demeaning images saturating our popular media—radio, television, videos, movies, music.

We are Gays and Lesbians of Color at a time when the advent of a new and uncontrolled disease has carved wrenching inroads into the ranks of our comrades, our lovers, our friends. And the connection between these two facts—the rise in social and political conservatism and the appearance of what has become known in the general public's mind as the *gay* disease, AIDS—has not been sufficiently scrutinized. But we certainly see their unholy wedding in the increase of sanctioned and self-righteous acts of heterosexism and homophobia, from queer-bashing in our streets to the legal invasion of our bedrooms. Should we miss these connections between racism and homophobia, we are also asked to believe that this monstrously convenient disease—and I use *convenient* here in the sense of *convenient for extermination*—originated spontaneously and mysteriously in Africa. Yet, for all the public hysteria surrounding AIDS, almost nothing is heard of the growing incidence of CAIDS—along the Mexican border, in the Near East and in the other areas of industrial imperialism. Chemically Acquired Immune Deficiency Syndrome is an industrial disease caused by prolonged exposure to trichloroethylene. TCE is a chemical in wholesale use in the electronic sweatshops of the world, where workers are primarily people of Color, in Malaysia, Sri Lanka, the Philippines, and Mexico.

It is a time when we, Lesbians and Gays of Color, cannot ignore our position as citizens of a country that stands on the wrong side of every liberation struggle on this globe; a country that publicly condones and connives with the most vicious and systematic program for genocide since Nazi Germany—apartheid South Africa.

How do we raise children to deal with these realities? For if we do not, we only disarm them, send them out into the jaws of the dragon unprepared. If we raise our children in the absence of an accurate picture of the world as we know it, then we blunt their most effective weapons for survival and growth, as well as their motivation for social change.

We are Gays and Lesbians of Color in a time when race-war is being fought in a small Idaho town, Coeur D'Alene. It is a time when the lynching of two Black people in California within twenty miles of each other is called nonracial and coincidental by the local media. One of the two victims was a Black Gay man, Timothy Lee; the other was a Black woman reporter investigating his death, Jacqueline Peters.

It is a time when local and national funds for day care and other programs which offer help to poor and working-class families are being cut, a time when even the definition of family is growing more and more restrictive.

But we are having babies! And I say, thank the goddess. As members of ethnic and racial communities historically under siege, every Gay and Lesbian of Color knows deep down inside that the question of children is not merely an academic one, nor do our children represent a theoretical hold upon some vague immortality. Our parents are examples of survival as a living pursuit, and no matter how different from them we may now find ourselves, we have built their example into our definitions of self—which is why we can be here tonight, naming ourselves. We know that all our work upon this planet is not going to be done in our lifetimes, and

maybe not even in our children's lifetimes. But if we do what we came to do, our children will carry it on through their own living. And if we can keep this earth spinning and remain upon it long enough, the future belongs to us and our children because we are fashioning it with a vision rooted in human possibility and growth, a vision that does not shrivel before adversity.

There are those who say the urge to have children is a reaction to encroaching despair, a last desperate outcry before the leap into the void. I disagree. I believe that raising children is one way of participating in the future, in social change. On the other hand, it would be dangerous as well as sentimental to think that childrearing alone is enough to bring about a liveable future in the absence of any definition of that future. For unless we develop some cohesive vision of that world in which we hope these children will participate, and some sense of our own responsibilities in the shaping of that world, we will only raise new performers in the master's sorry drama.

So what does this all have to do with Lesbian parenting? Well, when I talk about mothering, I do so with an urgency born of my consciousness as a Lesbian and a Black African Caribbean american woman staked out in white racist sexist homophobic america.

I gave birth to two children. I have a daughter and a son. The memory of their childhood years, storms and all, remains a joy to me. Those years were the most chaotic as well as the most creative of my life. Raising two children together with my lover, Frances, balancing the intricacies of relationship within that four-person interracial family, taught me invaluable measurements for my self, my capacities, my real agendas. It gave me tangible and sometimes painful lessons about difference, about power, and about purpose.

We were a Black and a white Lesbian in our forties, raising two Black children. Making do was not going to be a safe way to live our lives, nor was pretense, nor euphemism. *Lesbian* is a name for women who love each other. *Black* means of African ancestry. Our lives would never be simple. We had to learn and to teach what works when we lived, always, with a cautionary awareness of the social forces aligned against us—at the same time there was laundry to be done, dental appointments to be kept, and no you can't watch cartoons because we think they rot your feelings and we pay the electricity.

I knew, for example, that the rage I felt and kept carefully under lock and key would one day be matched by a similar rage in my children: the rage of Black survival within the daily trivializations of white racism. I had to discover ways to own and use that rage if I was to teach them how to own and use theirs, so that we did not wind up torturing ourselves by turning our rage against each other. It was not restraint I had to learn, but ways to use my rage to fuel actions, actions that could alter the very circumstances of oppression feeding my rage.

Screaming at my daughter's childish banter instead of standing up to a racist bus driver was misplacing my anger, making her its innocent victim. Getting a migraine headache instead of injecting my Black woman's voice into the smug whiteness of a Women's Studies meeting was swallowing that anger, turning it against myself. Neither one of these actions offered solutions I wanted to give my children for dealing with relationships or racism. Learning to recognize and label my angers, and to put them where they belonged in some effective way, became crucial—not only for my own survival, but also for my children's. So that when I was justifiably angry with one of them—and no one short of sainthood can live around growing children and not get angry at one time or another—I could express the anger appropriate to the situation and not have that anger magnified and distorted by all my other unexpressed and unused furies. I was not always successful in achieving that distinction, but trying kept me conscious of the difference.

If I could not learn to handle my anger, how could I expect the children to learn to handle theirs in some constructive way—not deny it or hide it or self-destruct upon it? As a Black Lesbian mother I came to realize I could not afford the energy drains of denial and still be open to my own growth. And if we do not grow with our children, they cannot learn.

That was a long and sometimes arduous journey toward self-possession. And that journey was sweetened by an increasing ability to stretch far beyond what I had previously thought possible—in understanding, in seeing common events in a new per-

spective, in trusting my own perceptions. It was an exciting journey, sweetened also by the sounds of their laughter in the street and the endearing beauty of the bodies of children sleeping. My daughter and my son made issues of survival daily questions, the answers to which had to be scrutinized as well as practiced. And what our children learned about using their own power and difference within our family, I hope they will someday use to save the world. I can hope for no less. I know that I am constantly learning from them. Still.

Like getting used to looking up instead of down. How looking up all the time gives you a slight ache in the back of the neck. Jonathan, at seventeen, asking, "Hey, Ma, how come you never hit us until we were bigger'n you?" At that moment realizing I guess I never hit my kids when they were little for the same reason my father never hit me: because we were afraid that our rage at the world in which we lived might leak out to contaminate and destroy someone we loved. But my father never learned to express his anger beyond imaginary conversations behind closed doors. Instead, he stoppered it, denying me his image, and he died of inchoate rage at fifty-one. My mother, on the other hand, would beat me until she wept from weariness. But it was not me, the overly rambunctious child, who sold her rotting food and spat upon her and her children in the street.

Frances and I wanted the children to know who we were and who they were, and that we were proud of them and of ourselves, and we hoped they would be proud of themselves and of us, too. But I remember Beth's fifteen-year-old angry coolness: "You think just because you're lesbians you're so different from the rest of them, but you're not, you're just like all the other parents. . . ." Then she launched into a fairly accurate record of our disciplines, our demands, our errors.

What I remember most of all now is that we were not just like all the other parents. Our family was not just like all the other families. That did not keep us from being a family any more than our being Lesbians kept Frances and me from being parents. But we did not have to be just like all the rest in order to be valid. We were an interracial Lesbian family with radical parents in the most conservative borough of New York City. Exploring the meaning of those differences kept us all stretching and learning, and we used that exploration to get us from Friday to Thursday, from toothache through homework to who was going to babysit when we both worked late and did Frances go to PTA meetings.

There are certain basic requirements of any child—food, clothing, shelter, love. So what makes our children different? We do. Gays and Lesbians of Color are different because we are embattled by reason of our sexuality and our Color, and if there is any lesson we must teach our children, it is that difference is a creative force for change, that survival and struggle for the future is not a theoretical issue. It is the very texture of our lives, just as revolution is the texture of the lives of the children who stuff their pockets with stones in Soweto and quickstep all the way to Johannesburg to fall in the streets from tear gas and rubber bullets in front of Anglo-American Corporation. Those children did not choose to die little heroes. They did not ask their mothers and fathers for permission to run in the streets and die. They do it because somewhere their parents gave them an example of what can be paid for survival, and these children carry on the same work by redefining their roles in an inhuman environment.

The children of Lesbians of Color did not choose their Color nor their mamas. But these are the facts of their lives, and the power as well as the peril of these realities must not be hidden from them as they seek self-definition.

And yes, sometimes our daughter and son did pay a price for our insisting upon the articulation of our differences—political, racial, sexual. That is difficult for me to say, because it hurts to raise your children knowing they may be sacrificed to your vision, your beliefs. But as children of Color, Lesbian parents or no, our children are programmed to be sacrifices to the vision of white racist profit-oriented sexist homophobic america, and that we cannot allow. So if we must raise our children to be warriors rather than cannon fodder, at least let us be very clear in what war we are fighting and what inevitable shape victory will wear. Then our children will choose their own battles.

Lesbians and Gays of Color and the children of Lesbians and Gays of Color are in the forefront of every struggle for human dignity in this country to-day, and that is not by accident. At the same time, we must remember when they are children that they are children, and need love, protection, and direction. From the beginning, Frances and I tried to teach the children that they each had a right to define herself and himself and to feel his own and her own feelings. They also had to take responsibility for the actions which arose out of those feelings. In order to do this teaching, we had to make sure that Beth and Jonathan had access to information from which to form those definitions—true information, no matter how uncomfortable it might be for us. We also had to provide them with sufficient space within which to feel anger, fear, rebellion, joy.

We were very lucky to have the love and support of other Lesbians, most of whom did not have children of their own, but who loved us and our son and daughter. That support was particularly important at those times when some apparently insurmountable breach left us feeling isolated and alone as Lesbian parents. Another source of support and connection came from other Black women who were raising children alone. Even so, there were times when it seemed to Frances and me that we would not survive neighborhood disapproval, a double case of chickenpox, or escalating teen-age rebellion. It is really scary when your children take what they have learned about self-assertion and nonviolent power and decide to test it in confrontations with you. But that is a necessary part of learning themselves, and the primary question is, have they learned to use it well?

Our daughter and son are in their twenties now. They are both warriors, and the battlefields shift: the war is the same. It stretches from the brothels of Southeast Asia to the blood-ridden alleys of Capetown to the incinerated Lesbian in Berlin to Michael Stewart's purloined eyes and grandmother Eleanor Bumpurs shot dead in the projects of New York. It stretches from the classroom where our daughter teaches Black and Latino third graders to chant, "I am somebody beautiful," to the college campus where our son replaced the Stars and Stripes with the flag of South Africa to protest his school's refusal to divest. They are in the process of choosing their own weapons, and no doubt some of those weapons will feel completely alien to me. Yet I trust them, deeply, because they were raised to be their own woman, their own man, in struggle, and in the service of all of our futures.   [1987]

🌿 117

Communal Living

ELLEN DAVIDSON

As I write this, Alan is sitting on my lap. He's typing with great determination and delight, adding his own thoughts to this piece. My 1½-year-old daughter is at a sitter's house in order to let me write in peace, and here I am working with my 1½-year-old housemate as my helper. While this makes writing difficult, it also embodies a piece of the essence of communal living, a perfect example to keep in mind as I write.

Living in a communal house is unpredictable. You can't have an orderly life in which you control what happens. It's hard to find the salad servers when you want them. The measuring cup is never in the place that seems obvious. You can finally get your laundry sorted, and, when you head down to the basement, someone else is doing laundry and has four loads piled up and waiting. When you're in a hurry, there are inevitably two cars behind yours in the driveway. Communal living can also mean coming home and smelling homemade warm brownies, available right then and there for an afternoon snack. Or coming home and finding a housemate has made cedar plant shelves for the backyard. Or finding our 4-year-old in our housemates' bed for a morning cuddle because we were out of ours when she came looking. Or having fascinating conversations at all hours, conversations that stretch my thinking and imagination. There is something wonderfully companionable about brushing your teeth with another four or five people at the sink.

My husband and I have lived communally for 5½ years. For several years, there were eight adults and two children living here. For a while, there were four women and four men and then, for several years, five women and three men. When two of the adults

moved out at the time two babies were being born, we decided space was tight and didn't replace those two adults. For the last year and a half, we have had the same group of two women, four men, and four children. We are two couples with two children each and two single people.

What does it mean to be a feminist living communally? It means that, in many ways, I can live out my values more easily and raise my children in an environment that is richer and more diverse.

For me, one of the most important values of feminism is affirmation of diversity. In a house with many other adults and children, we all experience, in deep and immediate personal ways, a range of values, beliefs, and lifestyles. My daughters are part of the lives of women and men who stay home and women and men who have jobs outside the home. Our housemates have friends in many circles. Our children meet people of different races and different values as extended family members rather than strangers. "Looking different" is not something our children will have to learn to understand later. For four years we had housemates who were actively involved in a New England dance community. There were meetings at our house. Dancing and music surrounded us. Now one of our housemates is active in the local Haitian community and in Haitian politics. There is a ten-foot cardboard boat in our basement from a demonstration against the deportation of Haitian refugees. Watching and participating in its creation on our front porch allowed all of us to learn more about Haiti and more about sails.

To me, being a feminist also means working toward a society that allows access to and affirmation for a wide range of work choices. Linda, the only other woman in the house, chooses to stay home full-time with her toddler while her husband works full-time. Both Jim and I work part-time and take care of our children part-time. One of the other two men in the house works full-time and the other part-time.

Our house is in a very diverse neighborhood. At the foot of our hill, you can go to a series of small markets: Haitian, Indian, Japanese/Korean, Guatemalan. At our neighborhood school, 50% of the children come from non-English-speaking homes. Hannah, our daughter, plays with a group of friends ranging in age from 3 to 8, consisting of both girls and boys and containing a mix of ethnicities and races. This is easy in a multiethnic neighborhood. We bring Channukah cookies, in the shapes of dreidels, menorahs, or six-pointed stars, to our Chinese neighbors, and they invite us over to celebrate the Chinese New Year. Every day, we have to work much harder to live in a house with diverse values and beliefs. At holidays, it is delightful to experience each other's customs and traditions. The older children love having more celebrations, doing more projects, hearing more stories. But it also creates tension with my husband's parents who, as Jews, have struggled to fight societal forces of assimilation and find it difficult to visit our house when Christian holidays are celebrated as part of our children's home lives.

As parents we aren't responsible for all of the daily modeling for our daughters. All of the men in our house cook comfortably and regularly. They are not Sunday morning brunch chefs. One of our male roommates could as frequently be found making his own clothes as replacing our bathroom floor, making eggroll filling in a five-gallon bucket as building recycling bins for the back porch—all with great enjoyment and expertise. More importantly than the way chores are divided, gender is rarely the determinant of how people think or feel—of nurturance, of emotional expression, of political perspective. In many ways, the gender roles in our house are so nontraditional that I can't fully keep in my consciousness what is daily life for so many people in this country.

In weighing life choices and making decisions to continue or not with this lifestyle, I find myself thinking about the advantages and disadvantages for our family. There is a very clear financial advantage. Living communally is much less expensive. On our income we couldn't possibly own a home in the Boston area any other way. Living communally means that we have enough money so that daily expenses are not a problem. It means that Jim and I can each work part-time and thus have more time together, more time with our children, and more time for other activities. We can have jobs we love and work at them a reasonable, rather than an excessive, amount of time.

It also means that less time is devoted to daily chores. We share these in a rather haphazard way, which works more or less efficiently depending on people's standards and how busy we each are. It does, however, consistently mean less work and more time to spend in other ways. Each of us is responsible for cooking less than one night a week, but we get full, delicious home-cooked meals five nights a week. We eat together at a table with cloth napkins and lit candles.

This time saving is one of the ways that makes it easier to live more ecologically—an important feminist value in my mind. The saving of time and energy from daily chores can go toward growing a prolific vegetable garden and doing complex recycling. Weather-proofing the house and buying energy-efficient light bulbs are chores that are chosen by interested people. We have the advantage of having the convenience of appliances but not having to own as many of them: a washing machine among all of us rather than having a washing machine for a family of four, two refrigerators, and two phones. We don't use a dishwasher because we all help clean up after dinner, carrying dinnertime conversations into the kitchen. In fact, those are often the best conversations, as it's hard to focus at the dinner table with three children all under 5 years old. But after dinner, during cleanup, the children have drifted off to jump on the sofa, draw pictures, climb on their climbing structure . . . so we can talk more peacefully and often in more depth.

In spite of the chaos at dinner, dinnertime is still one of the best advantages of living communally, offering time to think and learn more about the world. Usually at least a few people have read the newspaper or heard some interesting tidbit on National Public Radio they want to discuss. We share ideas from conversations with other friends and colleagues. Often someone has been to a rally or picked up flyers around town. Dinnertime is when I learn more about the world, challenge my assumptions, get answers to my questions.

A big piece of my work is to supervise student teachers, and I need to be well informed about whatever they are teaching so I can ask useful questions and understand their lessons. At home, I have easy access to much of this information. I can describe lessons to my scientist housemates and check them for accuracy. I can learn more myself about whatever topic is being taught and thus ask better questions. So, while I never expected to learn about the metabolic activity of Haitian pigs, I am quite fascinated to have this information. When thermometers in different temperatures of water didn't behave as I, or my student, expected, I can go home and improve my own understanding of this situation.

Aaron, Jim, and I worked on a major curriculum project last spring; we wrote the teachers' guide for the PBS children's geography quiz show, "Where in the World Is Carmen Sandiego?" While we could have done a collaborative writing project even when not living communally, doing it this way meant we could work in small spurts as well as large chunks, have inspirations and discuss them at 11 P.M. or 7 A.M., and share resources easily. Elizabeth, now 12, has been our curriculum consultant for years. She plays all the games designed by my mathematics methods students and helps me critique them. We interview her to demonstrate understanding children's thinking. She gives us feedback on lessons we design.

There are many ways in which living communally makes child care easier. For regular weekly child care, we hire a sitter. But for time to talk on the phone, have conferences, run out to the store, put in a load of laundry, go to meetings, or go out to dinner, we can exchange with each other. We don't keep track. We don't trade hours. We simply ask if someone is home and willing to take care of our children. We are sensitive to each other's needs and may well hire a sitter for an evening out if our housemates have been doing a lot of child care for us lately. But this certainly gives us more mobility—it is easier, faster, cheaper, and more convenient than relying only on paid babysitters.

Our children have special relationships with different adults. Aaron is a wonderful companion for walks, a lover of plants, fish, and bugs. When Jim and I were called to be substitutes at Hannah's nursery school and were both busy working, Patrick went in for us. The children were thrilled to have a real veterinarian to talk with. When I am gone late at work, Aviva is perfectly delighted to nurse from Linda. Before dinner, Glen sometimes takes the three younger children out to a nearby park to run. Our house is named Tkanye, the Russian word for weaving, a name we chose as we are weaving our

lives together. A few years ago Jim and I wove bags for all of our housemates. We had the same warp for all the bags and varied the weft according to each person's style and our sense of their preferences in color and texture.

When Hannah was born 4½ years ago, she came into the world as our first child but with a doting big sister. Elizabeth, at 7 years old, was delighted to have a new baby in the house. For her, Hannah provided all the benefits of a baby sister with few of the disadvantages. Hannah giggled and bounced when Elizabeth entered a room, followed her around, tried to do everything she did—but Elizabeth didn't have to share her parents' love or attention. What a deal! When Elizabeth decided we were being too lackadaisical about toilet training Hannah, she took over putting Hannah on the potty. Hannah was thrilled to be becoming a big girl and to be wearing Elizabeth's old panties. Hannah and her friends play dress-up for hours with Elizabeth's outgrown party clothes. Last summer, Elizabeth went on a five-day vacation with us to a farm. Jim and I and the girls loved her company; having an older child along enriched the whole experience. Elizabeth loved getting to go on an extra vacation when her parents weren't available.

For Aviva, living communally has provided her a twin without the total exhaustion I would expect must be the case for parents of twins. Three weeks after she was born, Linda and Glen had Alan. Aviva wakes up in the morning looking for Alan. They share toys and fight over toys. They chase each other around the house. Occasionally they wear matching outfits.

Sometimes this feels to me like being back in a college dormitory or a sleepaway summer camp, both experiences I loved. Linda and I can share clothes with each other, something many of us give up if we get married to a man and live just as a couple. We both like reading feminist mysteries and trade these back and forth. As I go about my day and have experiences at work or in the community, I'm aware of thinking about what stories to tell Linda when I get home, stories she will enjoy because she is a woman. Linda is home during the day and reads the newspaper much more diligently than I do. I can count on her to point out articles I shouldn't miss. She and I often do small shopping errands for each other, not keeping track or charging the other, assuming it will all even out. When one of us finds a wonderfully cute baby outfit in a catalogue or in a store, we sometimes buy two of them, one for each baby. We give these for no occasion and with no record keeping.

This summer the house participated in a citywide community circus, one of whose most impressive events is stilting. Hannah, at 4½, was originally considered too young to stilt. However, she insisted, so Jim and Elizabeth made her some stilts and, with both their help, was able to learn. The rest of us became intrigued with stilting. Soon, the whole house had stilts, courtesy of our master stilt-maker, Glen. I made stilting dresses for Hannah and me, and worked with Jim to make stilting pants for him. Elizabeth and I worked together to make her a stilting kimono, 2½ feet taller than her actual height. Linda rigged up a bridal dress for Hannah and a neighbor friend of Elizabeth's for the stilting fashion show. Since Alan and Aviva thought they were in the circus and often wandered across the stage, I made them both clown costumes to formalize their roles. Jim and Elizabeth worked on pompons and trim. Patrick, our 6-foot 4-inch housemate, looked particularly impressive on Jim's 2½-foot stilts. A real community effort.

Communal living also has disadvantages. I'm not sure how these disadvantages relate to feminism, but they are decidedly central to my thinking about this choice. In many ways, Jim and I end up feeling like we are "married" to a whole group of people, a group we don't necessarily love and didn't know very well before living with them. This is true for others we talk with who live communally, for many of the same reasons. Because people's life situations change, there are times when housemates move on. For economic reasons, it is usually necessary to fill the spots. For us, on one occasion, Aaron, an old, close friend of ours, was eager to move in. However, on other occasions, we have had to look farther afield, choosing among strangers and friends of friends.

But even when you do know someone well, you can't necessarily know what they'll be like to live with. While we usually know much about our life-partner's style and habits from having spent nights and extensive time together before committing ourselves to a long-term arrangement, it is highly un-

likely to know all that about even close friends before deciding to live together. Many of the issues that you have to work out in a marriage—money, housekeeping, child raising—come up again and again living in a group. These are both easier and harder to resolve with people you don't love and with whom you don't have a long-term commitment. On the one hand, differences may not matter so much—a housemate's choices still don't affect us as deeply as our partner's choices. But in spite of having a baseline agreement of "generosity of spirit," housemates sometimes still make judgments about each other's daily choices, and this can lead to tension.

There are daily adjustments to be made in what we can do. Every time there is hope for a thunderstorm, Hannah has been desperately wanting to make "Thunder Cake," a recipe in a book we often read aloud. If we lived just as a nuclear family, we could stop cooking dinner at the first sound of a storm, get out all those ingredients, and bake. When living with others, it's not as easy or fair to disrupt the dinner process. Living communally you have to choose your issues. One of our housemates insisted, for several months, on keeping his nonfunctioning car in the driveway. This took away space that the children could have used for biking, stilting, and roller skating. This was an issue worth raising, worth talking about, but not one to get into a major fight about. Other issues we choose to ignore rather than live with constant negotiation.

Maintaining outside friendships is different when you live communally. Sometimes our friends don't like or enjoy all of our housemates. That makes it less fun to have them over to visit. Sometimes our friends like our housemates but find that visiting, when the house starts with ten people at the dinner table, is overwhelming. Sometimes we try to have company on weekends when there are no official house meals, but that may or may not mean the kitchen and dining room are all ours.

There is a level of chaos inherent in having so many people in one house. The noise and activity feel never-ending. When Alan and Aviva are fighting, it is hard to determine how to discipline a child who isn't yours.

Though these problems are real, in balance, this choice seems right for us for now.

I'm aware how fascinating our house is to my colleagues, students, and others who visit us. When I had one of my classes over for classwork and dinner, I told them the rooms they could work in for their small groups. I made a comment that people who wanted to get a look at the whole house should choose the guest room on the third floor, as they could then peek in all the other rooms on the way. Four people immediately said, "We'll go up there," and ran off.

A friend of Patrick's from Kenya was here visiting with a friend of his. He explained to his friend how the men in this house were all brothers living here with their wives and children. He seemed delighted that we had made a choice so like the choices made in his country. Our next-door neighbors are Chinese. We have spent several years figuring out their relationship with each other, as they seem to

have done with us. They, too, seem to have decided on one of the men as their "head of household" and all the rest of them as family.

For me, an important part of feminism is modeling alternative choices. As people visit and talk with us, they can begin to think more freely and broadly about options for living arrangements other than a traditional nuclear family. There are days when I think of this lifestyle as being completely different from what life would be like if Jim, Hannah, Aviva, and I had our own house. I envision that choice as making my daily life feel altogether different. Then there are other times when I can't even imagine why people ask so many questions because it doesn't feel different at all. We simply live together, as more than just roommates, in a loosely bonded extended family.   [1992]

PART VIII

Changing Our World

While changing the position of women in our society can seem like an overwhelming task, women have, in fact, made significant progress when we have organized. The feminist movement has been crucial because it has critiqued male domination and demanded the inclusion of women in social and political life. By thus changing the environment, organized feminism has stimulated women to work on their own behalf wherever they are. Part VIII begins with a brief survey of what historians often refer to as the first and second waves of feminism in the U.S. Both these movements had profound effects on society and culture. In this discussion we examine both the strengths and the weaknesses of these movements, so that knowledge of the past can inform our efforts to improve the position of women in the present.

The first wave of feminism, which emerged in the 1840s, began with a wide-ranging critique of women's social, political, and economic position in society as expressed by the Resolutions of the Seneca Falls Women's Rights Convention. Much of this initial breadth, however, was lost as the movement narrowed to focus on achieving the right to vote. The second wave of feminism, emerging in the 1960s, revived many of these issues and developed a critique of the politics of personal life through a process that came to be called consciousness raising, as described in Kathie Sarachild's essay. While the analysis that emerged from these discussions was often presented as applicable to all women, it reflected the experience of the women in the early consciousness-raising groups, most of whom were white and middle class. Women in the Black Liberation and Chicano movements of the late 1960s and 1970s were questioning sexism within their own movements, often encountering resistance from movement men. While some of the ideas being articulated by white feminists resonated in the lives of women of color, others were alien to their experience. As Barbara Smith, Alma Garcia, and Kate Shanley describe, women of color generated feminist analysis that spoke to their experience and recognized the simultaneity of oppression.

While the achievements of the feminist movement are impressive, the goal of creating a society in which women are able to participate fully in all aspects of social and political life is still unrealized. In the midst of the process of approaching this goal, however, a multilayered assault against feminism was launched. In the 1980s, the "new right," a coalition of conservative and religious organizations, mounted an offensive against women's rights and has succeeded in restricting women's reproductive freedom, diluting affirmative action programs, and preventing the passage of the Equal Rights Amendment. Most people in the U.S. favor equal rights and reproductive freedom for women, but they are not sufficiently organized to prevent the erosion of many of the accomplishments of the previous decades. While there is still a great deal of support for the general goals of feminism, many women have not identified themselves with the feminist movement. "I'm not a feminist but"—a refrain of the 1980s—represented the success of a media attack on feminism that Susan Faludi exposes in the excerpt from her best-selling book, *Backlash: The Undeclared War Against American Women.*

Nevertheless, feminism has not disappeared; it continues to grow, taking new forms as it tackles new problems. During the last ten years, a global feminist movement has developed, bringing women together from all parts of the world. Western feminists meeting with women in Africa, Asia, and Latin America have realized that feminism must encompass survival issues, such as access to food and water, in order to support women's struggle for self-determination. This expanding global consciousness raises challenging issues for feminists in the U.S. Charlotte Bunch urges us to examine the impact of our country's policies on the daily lives of women around the world. She suggests that one of the most useful things we can do for women elsewhere is to "make changes in the U.S. and in how it exercises power in the world." In the past five years, feminists seeking to connect women of various countries have established organizations, sponsored international conferences, and promoted education about women's issues in various parts of the world. Such networks increase the possibility of cooperative action across national boundaries. A global feminist movement can challenge what Charlotte Bunch calls the "dynamic of domination embedded in male violence" by working against militarism, racism, and sexism wherever they exist.

In the 1990s, there are signs of another revival of feminist energy in the United States. A renewed reproductive rights movement has arisen in response to the anti-abortion decisions of the Supreme Court. Women are running for office with money from feminist fund-raising efforts, and young women are beginning to talk about a "third wave" of American feminism. The massive increase in wage-earning mothers during the past two decades is heightening our awareness of the need for public policy changes that will support women and their families.

One of the strengths of contemporary feminism is its multi-issue approach. As women confront sexism in different situations, new issues emerge, and our understanding of women's experience deepens. The final section includes descriptions of women organizing in various contexts from the 1970s to the 1990s. The writers tell stories of women who, inspired by the growing legitimacy of feminist concerns, refused to accept unfair treatment or who perceived a problem and decided to do something about it. In all of these organizing efforts, consciousness raising was a crucial ingredient—women needed to talk to each other about their experience in order to develop strategy. In some situations, such as women dealing with AIDS in prison, breaking the silence in itself makes an enormous difference. These stories demonstrate that, despite the media proclamations, feminism did not die in the 1980s; it continued to live in the many efforts of women organizing around specific issues on both national and local levels.

The final selections address the activism of the 1990s. They include a reproductive rights agenda that approaches the full breadth of the issue. Learning from the mistakes of the past, Kathryn Kolbert argues for a strategy to address all women's right to make decisions about childbearing, sexuality, and parenting. This agenda provides a model for conceptualizing other women's issues in a comprehensive way, such as violence against women, equality in the workplace, and family policy. As women develop strategies and tactics to address these issues, they are reviving such methods as civil disobedience and developing new approaches to change. Because young women grew up in a world in which feminist ideas and language were an integral part of our culture, they bring a fresh perspective to feminism.

Feminism as a Social Movement

We have discussed feminist *ideas* earlier in this book, but we turn in this section to a consideration of <u>feminism</u> as a *social movement*. While women have worked in a variety of settings to improve their lives, an organized movement whose central focus is eliminating the subordination of women has been crucial in making social, political, and cultural change. This section begins with a brief history of the feminist movement in the United States, followed by documents that emerged from these movements. "The Declaration of Sentiments" and "Resolutions" were adopted by a convention in 1848 at Seneca Falls, New York, which initiated the nineteenth-century women's rights movement. Kathie Sarachild's essay was written in the early days of the second wave of feminism. It describes the evolution of consciousness raising as a technique for understanding women's oppression, an important source of insight for women's liberation activists in the 1960s and 1970s.

Women of color cannot separate their oppression as women from the racism they encounter in their daily lives. They have developed a body of feminist theory that emerges from their particular experiences and considers the interaction between racism and sexism. The three selections that describe this theory all address the many forms of oppression that women of color experience and the necessity of working against all forms simultaneously. This effort involves struggling with men against racism while challenging their sexism, a process that is often painful.

The feminism of women of color draws on the day-to-day heroism of mothers and grandmothers, which is embodied for Barbara Smith in Alice Walker's definition of "womanist." Chicana feminists, Alma Garcia explains, have had to struggle against sexist traditions deeply embedded in their culture. Kate Shanley points out, however, that American Indian feminists seek to retain the alternative family forms and communal values of tribal life. As all these articles point out, coalitions among different groups of women can only be meaningful if each group has had a chance to develop its own agenda.

Like any movement that challenges established hierarchies and cherished beliefs, the feminist movement has encountered ridicule and opposition. In her best-selling book *Backlash: The Undeclared War Against American Women,* Susan Faludi exposes the media assault on feminism during the 1980s. Faludi argues that the press, television, movies, and the fashion industry have tried to convince women to relinquish the struggle for equality and respect by proclaiming that although women have won all the rights they need, it only makes them miserable. In fact, equality has not been achieved, and women are struggling to combine work and family without institutional supports.

Despite the backlash, women throughout the world continue to organize against violence, discrimination, and exploitation. One of the most exciting developments of the 1980s was the networking among women from around the world. Many international organizations have emerged that address violence against women, the role of women in development, and the effect of war on women's lives, and seek to increase women's political and economic power around the world. The final essay in this section describes the effect of this movement on the perspective of a participant from the United States.

🌿 118

A History of Feminist Movements in the U.S.

AMY KESSELMAN

The history of feminism is a story of ebb and flow. There have been periods when women's issues were on everyone's lips. Laws changed, barriers toppled, and a world where women and men participated equally in all aspects of life seemed to be around the corner. Such periods were often followed by periods of reaction in which feminism was labeled evil and socially destructive, and efforts to achieve equality for women stagnated.

While women have worked to improve their lives throughout history in a variety of ways, historians often describe the organized women's movements of the United States as two waves of feminism. These waves pushed women's issues to the forefront of national politics. The first and second waves of U.S. feminism were both born in periods of cultural upheaval, when many people were engaged in questioning social, cultural, and political norms. The first wave of feminism emerged among women who were active in the reform movements of the 1840s and 1850s. In particular, the antislavery movement nurtured female organizing efforts and stimulated thinking about the meaning of human rights for women. In 1848, a group of women who had been involved in Quaker and antislavery activities organized a convention at Seneca Falls, New York, to "discuss the social, civil and religious rights of women" (Flexner, 1970, p. 74). About 300 people gathered and adopted a series of resolutions drafted by Elizabeth Cady Stanton, calling for an end to the subordination of women in all areas of life. While both women and men attended this convention, the

speeches and resolutions made it clear, in the words of Stanton, "that woman herself must do this work; for woman alone can understand the height, the depth, the length and the breadth of her degradation" (Flexner, 1970, p. 77). After the Seneca Falls convention, women's rights conventions were held yearly, and women all over the country engaged in efforts to change unjust laws, improve the education of women, and eliminate the barriers to women's participation in public life.

While the leadership of the women's rights movement was predominantly white, there were several prominent African-American women who worked for the emancipation of both African Americans and women. Maria Stewart of Boston was one of the first women to speak in public to groups of women and men, urging African-American women to become economically independent. Sojourner Truth, a spell-binding orator, spoke at women's rights and antislavery meetings of the connection between freedom for women and emancipation of enslaved African Americans. After the Civil War, Mary Ann Shadd Cary argued that black women were eligible to vote under the Fourteenth Amendment, and she successfully registered to vote in 1871. Frances Ellen Watkins Harpur, a poet and lecturer, spoke frequently at women's rights conventions as a voice for black women (Giddings, 1984).

Obtaining the right to vote was just one of the many goals of the women's rights movement at first, but by the end of the Civil War, it became the primary focus of the movement. Women's rights activists believed that winning suffrage was a necessary tool for achieving all other aspects of women's emancipation. Women worked state by state to obtain the right to vote, and by 1900, they had gained suffrage in several western states. After the turn of the century, a new generation of women suffragists renewed the effort to pass an amendment to the Constitution granting women the right to vote.

The focus on suffrage had advantages and disadvantages. It was a concrete reform that could be used to mobilize women, and it symbolized, perhaps more than anything else, the participation of women as individuals in public life (Du Bois, 1978). On the other hand, winning the right to vote required gaining the approval of male voters and politicians. Women suffragists often adopted whatever arguments they felt were necessary to persuade those in power that it was in their interest to grant women the right to vote. They often invoked traditional gender roles as they campaigned for the vote, urging, for example, that women would "sew the seams and cook the meals; to vote won't take us long" (Knight & Julty, 1958).

Suffragist pragmatism also intensified the racism, nativism, and class bias of the white, native-born leadership of the major suffrage organizations (Kraditor, 1981). In the late nineteenth and early twentieth centuries, immigrants poured into the United States, radically changing the social, economic, and political landscape. The rhetoric of women's suffrage leadership often reflected the bias of white, native-born citizens against these new Americans. Carrie Chapman Catt, for example, who became president of the National American Woman's Suffrage Association, warned against the danger of "the ignorant foreign vote which was sought to be brought up by each party . . ." (Catt, 1894, p. 125). Urging literacy requirements, she concluded that the best solution would be to "cut off the vote of the slums and give it to the women . . ." (Catt, 1894, p. 125).

Similarly, southern white suffragists were willing to invoke racism to further their cause, arguing that the enfranchisement of white women would help sustain white supremacy in the South. When the NAWSA voted in 1903 to allow state chapters to determine their own membership, it gave tacit approval to southern racism. Southern clubs excluded African-American women and often argued that suffrage be granted only to those who met property or literacy requirements.

Despite the racism of white women's suffrage organizations, African-American women were actively involved in efforts to gain the right to vote in the early twentieth century by organizing black women's suffrage clubs throughout the U.S. "If white women needed the vote to acquire advantages and protection of their rights, then black women needed the vote even more so" argued Adella Hunt Logan, a member of the Tuskegee Woman's Club (Giddings, 1984, p. 121). The NAWSA, however, was engaged in efforts to get the women's suffrage amendment passed by a U.S. Senate dominated by white southern men. As a result, they were less than hospitable to African-American women's groups who wanted to affiliate, arguing that they should resubmit their application after the vote was won.

While the women's suffrage movement focused on the single issue of winning the right to vote, the late nineteenth and early twentieth centuries saw the flowering of many different efforts by women to improve their lives and the lives of others. A movement to make birth control legal and available to all women was led by Margaret Sanger, Emma Goldman, and others. A crusade against lynching was initiated by Ida B. Wells. Black and white women educators worked to improve women's educational opportunities, and women labor activists organized to improve the wages and working conditions of the wage-earning women who worked in factories, stores, and offices.

Attitudes toward women's capabilities began to shift, and the image of the "new woman" of the early twentieth century embodied self-reliance and involvement with the world. During this period, the word "feminism" was introduced by women who believed women's emancipation required deeper changes than the right to vote. They argued for the full integration of women into social, political, and economic life. While suffragists often argued for the right to vote in the name of women's traditional roles, claiming that women's propensity for nurturance and housekeeping would be useful in the public world, feminists renounced self-sacrifice in favor of self-development (Cott, 1987). African-American activists like Anna Cooper argued for a women's movement that challenged all forms of domination and made alliances with all oppressed peoples. Socialists like Charlotte Perkins Gilman suggested that women's emancipation required the elimination of private housekeeping in favor of community kitchens and child-care centers.

After 72 years of work, the women's suffrage amendment was ratified by the states in 1920. In the decades that followed, the women's movement shrank in numbers and influence, and those women who remained active were divided about the best way to improve women's lives. While the Constitution now gave all citizens the right to vote, African Americans of both sexes had been disenfranchised in the South by racist violence and state laws. While magazines and newspapers often proclaimed that women's equality had been achieved, the barriers to their full participation in the workplace, in politics, and in cultural and social life remained intact. Feminism fell into disrepute, conjuring up images of fanatic women out to spoil men's fun. When the Great Depression of the 1930s created massive unemployment, female wage earners were regarded with suspicion, further intensifying antifeminist sentiment. By the post–World War II era, a resurgence of the cult of domesticity denigrated female ambition, even though large numbers of women were working for wages. In the 1960s, when women again began to rebel against their subordinate status, the first wave of feminism was a distant memory, and recovering its history was an important ingredient in developing a new movement.

What lessons can we learn from the rise and fall of the first wave of American feminism? Winning the right to vote, a seemingly basic democratic right, took almost a century to accomplish and required an enormous amount of brilliant organizing, writing, and speaking. The benefit of hindsight, however, enables us to see that a great deal was sacrificed to achieve this goal. The capitulation of the suffrage movement to racism and prejudice against immigrants meant that it spoke for a narrow segment of women. Its failure to challenge the division between men's and women's worlds meant that when it won the right to vote, many forms of sexism remained. The suffrage movement demonstrates the perils of focusing exclusively on one goal, deferring others until it is achieved.

The second wave of feminism developed among different groups of women whose combined resources and insights augmented its power. The equal rights segment of the movement originated among women working within government agencies who were frustrated with the slow pace of change. They founded the National Organization for Women (NOW) in 1966 to work for equality in work, education, and politics. One of NOW's founders, Betty Friedan, wrote the influential best seller, *The Feminine Mystique*. This book described the frustrations of college-educated suburban housewives and argued that women should be encouraged to pursue careers as well as motherhood (Friedan, 1964).

The tensions that were building in the lives of women during the 1950s and 1960s, however, went beyond the need for work outside the home; they had to do with the devaluation of women in everyday life, sexual objectification, the violence against women that permeated society, and the socialization of women to meet the needs of men (Evans, 1979). These aspects of sexism were so tightly woven into the fabric of American culture that they were taken for granted and rarely discussed. Young women who had been involved in the social movements for peace and justice in the 1960s were able to bring these issues into the open. Accustomed to being on the fringes of respectability, they were willing to talk about subjects that were previously hidden and analyze their own lives for insights about the nature of women's oppression. "Consciousness raising," the reexamination of one's life through feminist lenses, was a tool for understanding women's experience. As women began to talk about their childhoods, their sexual lives, their feelings about being female, their work and school experiences, and their experience of male violence, the contours of feminist theory emerged. These young women called their movement "women's liberation," and argued for radical changes in the political, social, and economic institutions of our country.

The interaction between these two groups strengthened the feminist movement. NOW broadened its agenda to include the issues raised by women's liberation, recognizing that the achievement of equality would require deep systemic changes in the relationship between home and family, the concepts of "femininity" and "masculinity," and the educational and political systems. While women's liberation groups were generating analysis and challenging long-held assumptions, NOW provided concrete strategies for implementing these ideas, such as litigation against discriminatory corporations and efforts to change laws governing rape, violence, and divorce.

As different groups of women developed feminist analysis to address their experience, feminism grew deeper and broader. The process was not always without friction, as groups who felt their needs were being ignored confronted the leaders of feminist organizations. After several stormy meetings, NOW included the protection of lesbian rights in its agenda. Women of color reshaped feminist analysis to address their experience, and challenged feminist organizations to work against racism and develop an "all-inclusive sisterhood" (Dill, 1983).

Feminists accomplished a great deal in a short period of time. Ridiculed at first by the media, they quickly changed public consciousness about a host of issues, from rape to employment discrimination. Feminists worked in a variety of ways to change laws, attitudes, practices, and institutions. NOW and other equal rights groups challenged sex-segregated want ads, sued hundreds of major corporations for sex discrimination, and lobbied in state legislatures to change laws about rape, domestic violence, divorce, and employment. Women working outside the system established battered women's shelters, rape crisis centers, and feminist health clinics. Feminists inside universities created women's studies programs and engaged in research about women in various disciplines. Throughout the 1970s and 1980s, countless women made changes in their individual lives: going back to school or to a job, leaving oppressive marriages, developing emotional and sexual relationships with other women, working to develop relationships of mutuality and respect with men.

Because reproductive freedom was clearly central to women's efforts to participate fully and equally in society, feminists throughout the country united in efforts to repeal abortion laws, reinvigorating an abortion reform movement that had been active throughout the 1960s. While a few states legalized abortion in the early 1970s, most state legislatures were resistant to efforts to decriminalize abortion, so women throughout the country filed suits against state laws that made abortion illegal. The suit against the Texas laws, *Roe v. Wade,* made its way to the Supreme Court, which legalized abortion in its landmark decision in 1973.

Many feminists felt that the effort to end sex discrimination would be substantially enhanced by a federal amendment guaranteeing equal rights to women. In 1972, an Equal Rights Amendment was passed by the U.S. Congress, proclaiming that "equality of rights under the laws shall not be denied or abridged by the U.S. or by any State on account of sex" (Hoff-Wilson, 1986, p. 125). The amendment was then sent on to be ratified by the states and

was quickly approved in the legislatures of 34 of the 38 states required for final passage. It stalled, however, in 14 states in which a new coalition of conservative organizations had mobilized to defeat it. Charging that the Equal Rights Amendment and the feminist revolution that it came to symbolize would undermine traditional values and deprive women of the protections they have as wives and mothers, opponents of the ERA enlisted women in their anti-ERA campaign. Mormon and evangelical religious organizations poured resources into efforts to defeat the ERA. Their rhetoric tapped into anxiety about changes in the division of labor, sexuality, and the family and galvanized a new antifeminist coalition that opposed the ERA, the legalization of abortion, and other feminist reforms. When the deadline arrived in 1982, the ERA had not passed in enough states for ratification.

The ascendancy of the right wing in the Republican Party in the 1980s further enhanced the power of the new right assault, and many of the gains of the 1970s were seriously threatened. The second wave of feminism, however, left an indelible imprint on American society. While the momentum may have slowed, millions of women's lives have been changed, and cherished assumptions about gender, sexuality, work, and family have been deeply shaken. Although women remain a minority in positions of political power, their voices are being heard more clearly on public policy issues. Integrating feminist approaches to these issues into public policy will require continued pressure on the centers of political power.

REFERENCES

Catt, C. C. (1894). *The Woman's Journal*, Dec. 15, as quoted in A. Kraditor, *The Ideas of the Woman's Suffrage Movement, 1890–1920*. New York: Norton, 1981, p. 125.

Cott, N. F. (1987). *Grounding of Modern Feminism*. New Haven, CT: Yale Univserity Press.

Dill, B. T. (1983). "Race, Class, and Gender: Prospects for an All-Inclusive Sisterhood." *Feminist Studies* 9(1), pp. 131–50.

Du Bois, E. C. (1978). *Feminism and Suffrage: The Emergence of an Independent Women's Movement in America 1848–69*. Ithaca, NY: Cornell University Press.

Evans, S. M. (1979). *Personal Politics: The Roots of Women's Liberation in the Civil Rights Movement and the New Left*. New York: Knopf.

Flexner, E. (1970). *Century of Struggle*. Cambridge, MA: Harvard University Press.

Friedan, B. (1964). *The Feminine Mystique*. New York: Dell.

Giddings, P. (1984). *When and Where I Enter*. New York: Morrow.

Hoff-Wilson, J. (Ed.) (1986). *Rights of Passage: The Past and Future of the Equal Rights Amendment.* Bloomington, IN: Indiana University Press, p. 125.

Knight, E., & Julty, S. (1958). "Getting Out the Vote," in *Songs of the Suffragettes* (Phonograph Record No. FH5281), Folkways.

Kraditor, A. (1981). *The Ideas of the Women's Suffrage Movement, 1890–1920.* New York: Norton.   [1992]

❧ 119

1848

The Seneca Falls Women's Rights Convention

"DECLARATION OF SENTIMENTS"

When, in the course of human events, it becomes necessary for one portion of the family of man to assume among the people of the earth a position different from that which they have hitherto occupied, but one to which the laws of nature and of nature's God entitle them, a decent respect to the opinions of mankind requires that they should declare the causes that impel them to such a course.

We hold these truths to be self-evident: that all men and women are created equal; that they are endowed by their Creator with certain inalienable rights; that among these are life, liberty, and the pursuit of happiness; that to secure these rights governments are instituted, deriving their just powers from the consent of the governed. Whenever any form of government becomes destructive of these ends, it is the right of those who suffer from it to refuse allegiance to it, and to insist upon the institution of a new government, laying its foundation on such principles, and organizing its powers in such form, as to them shall seem most likely to effect their safety and happiness. Prudence indeed, will dictate that governments long established should not be changed for light and transient causes; and accordingly all experience hath shown that mankind are more disposed to suffer, while evils are sufferable, than to right themselves by abolishing the forms to which they were accustomed. But when a long train of abuses and usurpations, pursuing invariably the same object evinces a design to reduce them under absolute despotism, it is their duty to throw off such government, and to provide new guards for their future security. Such has been the patient sufferance of the women under this government, and such is now the necessity which constrains them to demand the equal station to which they are entitled.

The history of mankind is a history of repeated injuries and usurpations on the part of man toward woman, having in direct object the establishment of an absolute tyranny over her. To prove this, let facts be submitted to a candid world.

He has never permitted her to exercise her inalienable right to the elective franchise.

He has compelled her to submit to laws, in the formation of which she had no voice.

He has withheld from her rights which are given to the most ignorant and degraded men—both natives and foreigners.

Having deprived her of this first right of a citizen, the elective franchise, thereby leaving her without representation in the halls of legislation, he has oppressed her on all sides.

He has made her, if married, in the eye of the law, civilly dead.

He has taken from her all right in property, even to the wages she earns.

He has made her, morally, an irresponsible being, as she can commit many crimes with impunity, provided they be done in the presence of her husband. In the covenant of marriage, she is compelled to promise obedience to her husband, he becoming, to all intents and purposes, her master—the law giving him power to deprive her of her liberty, and to administer chastisement.

He has so framed the laws of divorce, as to what shall be the proper causes, and in case of separation, to whom the guardianship of the children shall be given, as to be wholly regardless of the happiness of women—the law, in all cases, going upon a false supposition of the supremacy of man, and giving all power into his hands.

After depriving her of all rights as a married woman, if single, and the owner of property, he has taxed her to support a government which recognizes her only when her property can be made profitable to it.

He has monopolized nearly all the profitable employments, and from those she is permitted to follow, she receives but a scanty remuneration. He closes against her all the avenues to wealth and distinction which he considers most honorable to himself. As a teacher of theology, medicine, or law, she is not known.

He has denied her the facilities for obtaining a thorough education, all colleges being closed against her.

He allows her in Church, as well as State, but a subordinate position, claiming Apostolic authority for her exclusion from the ministry, and, with some exceptions, from any public participation in the affairs of the Church.

He has created a false public sentiment by giving to the world a different code of morals for men and women, by which moral delinquencies which exclude women from society, are not only tolerated, but deemed of little account in man.

He has usurped the prerogative of Jehovah himself, claiming it as his right to assign for her a sphere of action, when that belongs to her conscience and to her God.

He has endeavored, in every way that he could, to destroy her confidence in her own powers, to lessen her self-respect, and to make her willing to lead a dependent and abject life.

Now, in view of this entire disfranchisement of one-half the people of this country, their social and religious degradation—in view of the unjust laws above mentioned, and because women do feel themselves aggrieved, oppressed, and fraudulently deprived of their most sacred rights, we insist that they have immediate admission to all the rights and privileges which belong to them as citizens of the United States.

In entering upon the great work before us, we anticipate no small amount of misconception, misrepresentation, and ridicule; but we shall use every instrumentality within our power to effect our object. We shall employ agents, circulate tracts, petition the State and National legislatures, and endeavor to enlist the pulpit and the press in our behalf. We hope this Convention will be followed by a series of Conventions embracing every part of the country.

SENECA FALLS RESOLUTIONS

Whereas, The great precept of nature is conceded to be, that "man shall pursue his own true and substantial happiness." Blackstone in his Commentaries remarks, that this law of Nature being coeval with mankind, and dictated by God himself, is of course superior in obligation to any other. It is binding over all the globe, in all countries and at all times; no human laws are of any validity if contrary to this, and such of them as are valid, derive all their force, and all their validity, and all their authority, mediately and immediately, from this original; therefore;

Resolved, That such laws as conflict, in any way, with the true and substantial happiness of woman, are contrary to the great precept of nature and of no validity, for this is "superior in obligation to any other."

Resolved, That all laws which prevent woman from occupying such a station in society as her conscience shall dictate, or which place her in a position inferior to that of man, are contrary to the great precept of nature, and therefore of no force or authority.

Resolved, That woman is man's equal—was intended to be so by the Creator, and the highest good of the race demands that she should be recognized as such.

Resolved, That the women of this country ought to be enlightened in regard to the laws under which they live, that they may no longer publish their degradation by declaring themselves satisfied with their present position, nor their ignorance, by asserting that they have all the rights they want.

Resolved, That inasmuch as man, while claiming for himself intellectual superiority, does accord to woman moral superiority, it is pre-eminently his duty to encourage her to speak and teach, as she has an opportunity, in all religious assemblies.

Resolved, That the same amount of virtue, delicacy, and refinement of behavior that is required of woman in the social state, should also be required of man, and the same transgressions should be visited with equal severity on both man and woman.

Resolved, That the objection of indelicacy and impropriety, which is so often brought against woman when she addresses a public audience, comes with a very ill-grace from those who encourage, by their attendance, her appearance on the stage, in the concert, or in feats of the circus.

Resolved, That woman has too long rested satisfied in the circumscribed limits which corrupt customs and a perverted application of the Scriptures have marked out for her, and that it is time she should move in the enlarged sphere which her great Creator has assigned her.

Resolved, That it is the duty of the women of this country to secure to themselves their sacred right to the elective franchise.

Resolved, That the equality of human rights results necessarily from the fact of the identity of the race in capabilities and responsibilities.

Resolved, therefore, That, being invested by the Creator with the same capabilities, and the same consciousness of responsibility for their exercise, it is demonstrably the right and duty of woman, equally with man, to promote every righteous cause by every righteous means; and especially in regard to the great subjects of morals and religion, it is self-evidently her right to participate with her brother in teaching them, both in private and in public, by writing and by speaking, by any instrumentalities proper to be used, and in any assemblies proper to be held; and this being a self-evident truth growing out of the divinely implanted principles of human nature, any custom or authority adverse to it, whether modern or wearing the hoary sanction of antiquity, is to be regarded as a self-evident falsehood, and at war with mankind.

Resolved, That the speedy success of our cause depends upon the zealous and untiring efforts of both men and women, for the overthrow of the monopoly of the pulpit, and for the securing to women an equal participation with men in the various trades, professions, and commerce.   [1848]

🌿 120

Consciousness Raising: A Radical Weapon

KATHIE SARACHILD

From a talk given to the First National Conference of Stewardesses for Women's Rights in New York City, March 12, 1973.

To be able to understand what feminist consciousness-raising is all about, it is important to remember that it began as a program among women who all considered themselves radicals.

Before we go any further, let's examine the word "radical." It is a word that is often used to suggest extremist, but actually it doesn't mean that. The dictionary says radical means root, coming from the Latin word for root. And that is what we meant by calling ourselves radicals. We were interested in getting to the roots of problems in society. You might say we wanted to pull up weeds in the garden by their roots, not just pick off the leaves at the top to make things momentarily look good. Women's Liberation was started by women who considered themselves radicals in this sense.

Our aim in forming a women's liberation group was to start a *mass movement of women* to put an end to the barriers of segregation and discrimination based on sex. We knew radical thinking and radical action would be necessary to do this. We also believed it necessary to form Women's Liberation groups which excluded men from their meetings.

In order to have a radical approach, to get to the root, it seemed logical that we had to study the situation of women, not just take random action. How best to do this came up in the women's liberation group I was in—New York Radical Women, one of the first in the country—shortly after the group had formed. We were planning our first public action and wandered into a discussion about what to do next. One woman in the group, Ann Forer, spoke up: "I think we have a lot more to do just in the area of raising our consciousness," she said. "Raising consciousness?" I wondered what she meant by that. I'd never heard it applied to women before.

"I've only begun thinking about women as an oppressed group," she continued, "and each day, I'm still learning more about it—my consciousness gets higher."

Now I didn't consider that I had just started thinking about the oppression of women. In fact, I thought of myself as having done lots of thinking about it for quite a while, and lots of reading, too. But then Ann went on to give an example of something she'd noticed that turned out to be a deeper way of seeing it for me, too.

"I think a lot about being attractive," Ann said. "People don't find the real self of a woman attractive." And then she went on to give some examples. And I just sat there listening to her describe all the false ways women have to act: playing dumb, always being agreeable, always being nice, not to mention what we had to do to our bodies with the clothes and shoes we wore, the diets we had to go through, going blind not wearing glasses, all because men didn't find our real selves, our human freedom, our basic humanity "attractive." And I realized I still could learn a lot about how to understand and describe the particular oppression of women in ways that could reach other women in the way this had just reached me. The whole group was moved as I was, and we decided on the spot that what we needed—in the words Ann used—was to "raise our consciousness some more."

At the next meeting there was an argument in the group about how to do this. One woman—Peggy Dobbins—said that what she wanted to do was make a very intensive study of all the literature on the question of whether there really were any biological differences between men and women. I found myself angered by that idea.

"I think it would be a waste of time," I said. "For every scientific study we quote, the opposition can find their scientific studies to quote. Besides, the question is what *we* want to be, what we think we are, not what some authorities in the name of science are arguing over what we are. It is scientifically impossible to tell what the biological differences are between men and women—if there are any besides the obvious physical ones—until all the social and political factors applying to men and women are equal. Everything we have to know, have to prove, we can get from the realities of our own lives. For instance, on the subject of women's intelligence. We know from our own experience that women play dumb for men because, if we're too smart, men won't like us. I know, because I've done it. We've all done it. Therefore, we can simply deduce that women are smarter than men are aware of, and smarter than all those people who make studies are aware of, and that there are a lot of women around who are a lot smarter than they look and smarter than anybody but themselves and maybe a few of their friends know."

In the end the group decided to raise its consciousness by studying women's lives by topics like childhood, jobs, motherhood, etc. We'd do any outside reading we wanted to and thought was important. But our starting point for discussion, as well as our test of the accuracy of what any of the books said, would be the actual experience we had in these areas.

One of the questions, suggested by Ann Forer, we would bring at all times to our studies would be—who and what has an *interest* in maintaining the oppression in our lives. The kind of actions the group should engage in, at this point, we decided—acting on an idea of Carol Hanisch, another woman in the group—would be consciousness-raising actions . . . actions brought to the public for the specific purpose of challenging old ideas and raising new ones, the very same issues of feminism we were studying ourselves. Our role was not to be a "service organization," we decided, nor a large "membership organization." What we were talking about being was, in effect, Carol explained, a "zap" action, political agitation and education group something like what the Student Non-Violent Coordinating Committee (S.N.C.C.) had been. We would be the first to dare to say and do the undareable, what women really felt and wanted. The first job now was to raise awareness and understanding, our own and others— awareness that would prompt people to organize and to act on a mass scale.

The decision to emphasize our own feelings and experiences as women and to test all generalizations and reading we did by our own experience was actually the scientific method of research. We were in effect repeating the 17th century challenge of science to scholasticism: "study nature, not books," and put all theories to the test of living practice and action. It was also a method of radical organizing tested by other revolutions. We were applying to women and to ourselves as women's liberation organizers the practice a number of us had learned as organizers in the civil rights movement in the South in the early 1960's.

Consciousness-raising—studying the whole gamut of women's lives, starting with the full reality of one's own—would also be a way of keeping the movement radical by preventing it from getting sidetracked into single issue reforms and single issue organizing. It would be a way of carrying theory about women further than it had ever been carried before, as the groundwork for achieving a radical solution for women as yet attained nowhere.

It seemed clear that knowing how our own lives related to the general condition of women would make us better fighters on behalf of women as a whole. We felt that all women would have to see the fight of women as their own, not as something just to help "other women," that they would have to see this truth about their own lives before they would fight in a radical way for anyone. "Go fight your own oppressors," Stokely Carmichael had said to the white civil rights workers when the black power movement began. "You don't get radicalized fighting other people's battles," as Beverly Jones, author of the pioneering essay, "Toward a Female Liberation Movement," put it.   [1973]

121

Introduction to Home Girls: A Black Feminist Anthology

BARBARA SMITH

Black women as a group have never been fools. We couldn't afford to be. Yet in the last two decades many of us have been deterred from identifying with a liberation struggle which might say significant things to women like ourselves, women who believe that we were put here for a purpose in our own right, women who are usually not afraid to struggle.

Although our involvement has increased considerably in recent years, there are countless reasons why Black and other Third World women have not identified with contemporary feminism in large numbers.[1] The racism of white women in the women's movement has certainly been a major factor. The powers-that-be are also aware that a movement of progressive Third World women in this country would alter life as we know it. As a result there has been a concerted effort to keep women of color from organizing autonomously and from organizing with other women around women's political issues. Third World men, desiring to maintain power over "their women" at all costs, have been among the most willing reinforcers of the fears and myths about the women's movement, attempting to scare us away from figuring things out for ourselves.

It is fascinating to look at various kinds of media from the late 1960s and early 1970s, when feminism was making its great initial impact, in order to see what Black men, Native American men, Asian American men, Latino men, and white men were saying about the irrelevance of "women's lib" to women of color. White men and Third World men, ranging from conservatives to radicals, pointed to the seeming lack of participation of women of color in the movement in order to discredit it and to undermine the efforts of the movement as a whole. All kinds of men were running scared because they knew that if the women in their midst were changing, they were going to have to change too. In 1976 I wrote:

> Feminism is potentially the most threatening of movements to Black and other Third World people because it makes it absolutely essential that we examine the way we live, how we treat each other, and what we believe. It calls into question the most basic assumption about our existence and this is the idea that biological, i.e., sexual identity determines all, that it is the rationale for power relationships as well as for all other levels of human identity and action. An irony is that among Third World people biological determinism is rejected and fought against when it is applied to race, but generally unquestioned when it applies to sex.[2]

In reaction to the "threat" of such change, Black men, with the collaboration of some Black women, developed a set of myths to divert Black women from our own freedom.

MYTHS

Myth No. 1: The Black woman is already liberated. This myth confuses liberation with the fact that Black women have had to take on responsibilities that our oppression gives us no choice but to handle. This is an insidious, but widespread myth that many Black women have believed themselves. Heading families, working outside the home, not building lives or expectations dependent on males, seldom being sheltered or pampered as women, Black women have known that their lives in some ways incorporated goals that white middle-class women were striving for, but race and class privilege, of course, reshaped the meaning of those goals profoundly. As W.E.B. DuBois said so long ago about Black women: ". . . our women in black had freedom contemptuously thrust upon them."[3] Of all the people here, women of color generally have the fewest choices about the circumstances of their lives. An ability to cope under the worst conditions is not liberation, although our spiritual capacities have often made it look like a life. Black men didn't say anything about how poverty, unequal pay, no childcare, violence of every kind including battering, rape, and sterilization abuse, translated into "liberation."

Underlying this myth is the assumption that Black women are towers of strength who neither feel nor need what other human beings do, either emotionally or materially. White male social scientists, particularly Daniel P. Moynihan with his "matriarchy theory," further reinforce distortions concerning Black women's actual status. A song inspired by their mothers and sung by Sweet Honey in the Rock, "Oughta Be A Woman," lyrics by June Jordan and music by Bernice Johnson Reagon, responds succinctly to the insensitivity of the myth that Black women are already liberated and illustrates the home-based concerns of Black feminism:

Oughta Be A Woman

Washing the floors to send you to college
Staying at home so you can feel safe
What do you think is the soul of her knowledge
What do you think that makes her feel safe

Biting her lips and lowering her eyes
To make sure there's food on the table
What do you think would be her surprise
If the world was as willing as she's able

Hugging herself in an old kitchen chair
She listens to your hurt and your rage
What do you think she knows of despair
What is the aching of age

The fathers, the children, the brothers
Turn to her and everybody white turns to her
What about her turning around
Alone in the everyday light

There oughta be a woman can break
Down, sit down, break down, sit down
Like everybody else call it quits on Mondays
Blues on Tuesdays, sleep until Sunday
Down, sit down, break down, sit down

A way outa no way is flesh outa flesh
Courage that cries out at night

A way outa no way is flesh outa flesh
Bravery kept outa sight
A way outa no way is too much to ask
Too much of a task for any one woman[4]

Myth No. 2: Racism is the primary (or only) oppression Black women have to confront. (Once we get that taken care of, then Black women, men, and children will all flourish. Or as Ms. Luisah Teish writes, we can look forward to being "the property of powerful men.")[5]

This myth goes hand in hand with the one that the Black woman is already liberated. The notion that struggling against or eliminating racism will completely alleviate Black women's problems does not take into account the way that sexual oppression cuts across all racial, nationality, age, religious, ethnic, and class groupings. Afro-Americans are no exception.

It also does not take into account how oppression operates. Every generation of Black people, up until now, has had to face the reality that no matter how hard we work we will probably not see the end of racism in our lifetimes. Yet many of us keep faith and try to do all we can to make change now. If we have to wait for racism to be obliterated *before* we can begin to address sexism, we will be waiting for a long time. Denying that sexual oppression exists or requiring that we wait to bring it up until racism, or in some cases capitalism, is toppled, is a bankrupt position. A Black feminist perspective has no use for ranking oppressions, but instead demonstrates the simultaneity of oppressions as they affect Third World women's lives.

Myth No. 3: Feminism is nothing but man-hating. (And men have never done anything that would legitimately inspire hatred.)

It is important to make a distinction between attacking institutionalized, systematic oppression (the goal of any serious progressive movement) and attacking men as individuals. Unfortunately, some of the most widely distributed writing about Black women's issues has not made this distinction sufficiently clear. Our issues have not been concisely defined in these writings, causing much adverse reaction and confusion about what Black feminism really is.[6]

This myth is one of the silliest and at the same

time one of the most dangerous. Anti-feminists are incapable of making a distinction between being critically opposed to sexual oppression and simply hating men. Women's desire for fairness and safety in our lives does not necessitate hating men. Trying to educate and inform men about how their feet are planted on our necks doesn't translate into hatred either. Centuries of anti-racist struggle by various people of color are not reduced, except by racists, to our merely hating white people. If anything it seems that the opposite is true. People of color know that white people have abused us unmercifully and it is only sane for us to try to change that treatment by every means possible.

Likewise the bodies of murdered women are strewn across the landscape of this country. Rape is a national pastime, a form of torture visited upon all girls and women, from babies to the aged. One out of three women in the U.S. will be raped during her lifetime. Battering and incest, those home-based crimes, are pandemic. Murder, of course, is men's ultimate violent "solution." And if you're thinking as you read this that I'm exaggerating, please go get today's newspaper and verify the facts. If anything is going down here it's woman-hatred, not man-hatred, a war against women. But wanting to end this war still doesn't equal man-hating. The feminist movement and the anti-racist movement have in common trying to ensure decent human life. Opposition to either movement aligns one with the most reactionary elements in American society.

Myth No. 4: Women's issues are narrow, apolitical concerns. People of color need to deal with the "larger struggle." This myth once again characterizes women's oppression as not particularly serious, and by no means a matter of life and death. I have often wished I could spread the word that a movement committed to fighting sexual, racial, economic, and heterosexist oppression, not to mention one which opposes imperialism, anti-Semitism, the oppressions visited upon the physically disabled, the old and the young, at the same time that it challenges militarism and imminent nuclear destruction is the very opposite of narrow. All segments of the women's movement have not dealt with all of these issues, but neither have all segments of Black people. This myth is plausible when the women's movement is equated only with its most bourgeois and reformist elements. The most progressive sectors of the feminist movement, which includes some radical white women, have taken the above issues, and many more, quite seriously. Third World women have been the most consistent in defining our politics broadly. Why is it that feminism is considered "white-minded" and "narrow" while socialism or Marxism, from verifiably white origins, is legitimately embraced by Third World male politicos, without their having their identity credentials questioned for a minute?

Myth No. 5: Those feminists are nothing but Lesbians. This may be the most pernicious myth of all and it is essential to understand that the distortion lies in the phrase "nothing but" and not in the identification Lesbian. "Nothing but" reduces Lesbians to a category of beings deserving of only the most violent attack, a category totally alien from "decent" Black folks, i.e., not your sisters, mothers, daughters, aunts, and cousins, but bizarre outsiders like no one you know or *ever* knew.

Many of the most committed and outspoken feminists of color have been and are Lesbians. Since many of us are also radicals, our politics, as indicated by the issues merely outlined above, encompass all people. We're also as Black as we ever were. (I always find it fascinating, for example, that many of the Black Lesbian-feminists I know still wear their hair natural, indicating that for us it was more than a "style.") Black feminism and Black Lesbianism are not interchangeable. Feminism is a political movement and many Lesbians are not feminists. Although it is also true that many Black feminists are not Lesbians, this myth has acted as an accusation and a deterrent to keep non-Lesbian Black feminists from manifesting themselves, for fear it will be hurled against them.

Fortunately this is changing. Personally, I have seen increasing evidence that many Black women of whatever sexual preference are more concerned with exploring and ending our oppression than they are committed to being either homophobic or sexually separatist. Direct historical precedent exists for such commitments. In 1957, Black playwright and activist Lorraine Hansberry wrote the following in a letter to *The Ladder,* an early Lesbian periodical:

I think it is about time that equipped women began to take on some of the ethical questions which a male-dominated culture has produced and dissect and analyze them quite to pieces in a serious fashion. It is time that "half the human race" had something to say about the nature of its existence. Otherwise—without revised basic thinking—the woman intellectual is likely to find herself trying to draw conclusions—moral conclusions—based on acceptance of a social moral superstructure which has never admitted to the equality of women and is therefore immoral itself. As per marriage, as per sexual practices, as per the rearing of children, etc. In this kind of work there may be women to emerge who will be able to formulate a new and possible concept that homosexual persecution and condemnation has at its roots not only social ignorance, but a philosophically active anti-feminist dogma.[7]

I would like a lot more people to be aware that Lorraine Hansberry, one of our most respected artists and thinkers, was asking in a Lesbian context some of the same questions we are asking today, and for which we have been so maligned.

Black heterosexuals' panic about the existence of both Black Lesbians and Black gay men is a problem that they have to deal with themselves. A first step would be for them to better understand their own heterosexuality, which need not be defined by attacking everybody who is not heterosexual.

HOME TRUTHS

Above are some of the myths that have plagued Black feminism. The truth is that there is a vital movement of women of color in this country. Despite continual resistance to women of color defining our specific issues and organizing around them, it is safe to say in 1982 that we have a movement of our own. I have been involved in building that movement since 1973. It has been a struggle every step of the way and I feel we are still in just the beginning stages of developing a workable politics and practice. Yet the feminism of women of color, particularly of Afro-American women, has wrought many changes during these years, has had both obvious and unrecognized impact upon the development of other political groupings and upon the lives and hopes of countless women.

The very nature of radical thought and action is that it has exponentially far-reaching results. But because all forms of media ignore Black women, in particular Black feminists, and because we have no widely distributed communication mechanisms of our own, few know the details of what we have accomplished. One of the purposes of *Home Girls* is to get the word out about Black feminism to the people who need it most: Black people in the U.S., the Caribbean, Latin America, Africa—everywhere. It is not possible for a single introduction or a single book to encompass all of what Black feminism is, but there is basic information I want every reader to have about the meaning of Black feminism as I have lived and understood it.

In 1977, a Black feminist organization in Boston of which I was a member from its founding in 1974, the Combahee River Collective, drafted a political statement for our own use and for inclusion in Zillah Eisenstein's anthology, *Capitalist Patriarchy and the Case for Socialist Feminism*. In our opening paragraph we wrote:

> The most general statement of our politics at the present time would be that we are actively committed to struggling against racial, sexual, heterosexual, and class oppression and see as our particular task the development of integrated analysis and practice based upon the fact that the major systems of oppression are interlocking. The synthesis of these oppressions creates the conditions of our lives. As Black women we see Black feminism as the logical political movement to combat the manifold and simultaneous oppressions that all women of color face.

The concept of the simultaneity of oppression is still the crux of a Black feminist understanding of political reality and, I believe, one of the most significant ideological contributions of Black feminist thought.

We examined our own lives and found that everything out there was kicking our behinds—race, class, sex, and homophobia. We saw no reason to rank oppressions, or, as many forces in the Black community would have us do, to pretend that sexism, among all the "isms," was not happening to us. Black feminists' efforts to comprehend the complexity of our situation as it was actually occurring, almost immediately began to deflate some of the cherished myths about Black womanhood, for example, that we are "castrating matriarchs" or that we are more economically privileged than Black men. Although we made use of the insights of other political ideologies, such as socialism, we added an element that has often been missing from the theory of others: what oppression is comprised of on a day-to-day basis, or as Black feminist musician Linda Tillery sings, ". . . what it's really like/To live this life of triple jeopardy."[8]

This multi-issued approach to politics has probably been most often used by other women of color who face very similar dynamics, at least as far as institutionalized oppression is concerned. It has also altered the women's movement as a whole. As a result of Third World feminist organizing, the women's movement now takes much more seriously the necessity for a multi-issued strategy for challenging women's oppression. The more progressive elements of the left have also begun to recognize that the promotion of sexism and homophobia within their ranks, besides being ethically unconscionable, ultimately undermines their ability to organize. Even a few Third World organizations have begun to include the challenging of women's and gay oppression on their public agendas.

Approaching politics with a comprehension of the simultaneity of oppressions has helped to create a political atmosphere particularly conducive to coalition building. Among all feminists, Third World women have undoubtedly felt most viscerally the need for linking struggles and have also been most capable of forging such coalitions. A commitment to principled coalitions, based not upon expediency, but upon our actual need for each other is a second major contribution of Black feminist struggle. Many contributors to *Home Girls* write out of a sense of our ultimate interdependence. Bernice Johnson Reagon's essay, "Coalition Politics: Turning the Century," should be particularly noted. She writes:

> You don't go into coalition because you just *like* it. The only reason you would consider trying to team up with somebody who could possibly kill you, is because that's the only way you can figure you can stay alive. . . . Most of the time you feel threatened to the core and if you don't you're not really doing no coalescing.

The necessity for coalitions has pushed many groups to rigorously examine the attitudes and ignorance within themselves which prevent coalitions from succeeding. Most notably, there has been the commitment of some white feminists to make racism a priority issue within the women's movement, to take responsibility for their racism as individuals, and to do antiracist organizing in coalition with other groups. Because I have written and spoken about racism during my entire involvement as a feminist and have also presented workshops on racism for white women's organizations for several years during the 1970s, I have not only seen that there are white women who are fully committed to eradicating racism, but that new understandings of racial politics have evolved from feminism, which other progressive people would do well to comprehend.[9]

Having begun my political life in the Civil Rights movement and having seen the Black liberation movement virtually destroyed by the white power structure, I have been encouraged in recent years that women can be a significant force for bringing about racial change in a way that unites oppressions instead of isolating them. At the same time the percentage of white feminists who are concerned about racism is still a minority of the movement, and even within this minority those who are personally sensitive and completely serious about formulating an *activist* challenge to racism are fewer still. Because I have usually worked with politically radical feminists, I know that there are indeed white women worth building coalitions with, at the same time that there are apolitical, even reactionary, women who take the name of feminism in vain.

One of the greatest gifts of Black feminism to ourselves has been to make it a little easier simply to *be* Black and female. A Black feminist analysis has enabled us to understand that we are not hated and abused because there is something wrong with us, but because our status and treatment is absolutely prescribed by the racist, misogynistic system under which we live. There is not a Black woman in this country who has not, at some time, internalized and been deeply scarred by the hateful propaganda about us. There is not a Black woman in America who has not felt, at least once, like "the mule of the world," to use Zora Neale Hurston's still apt phrase.[10] Until Black feminism, very few people besides Black women actually cared about or took seriously the demoralization of being female *and* colored *and* poor *and* hated.

When I was growing up, despite my family's efforts to explain, or at least describe, attitudes prevalent in the outside world, I often thought that there was something fundamentally wrong with me because it was obvious that me and everybody like me was held in such contempt. The cold eyes of certain white teachers in school, the Black men who yelled from cars as Beverly and I stood waiting for the bus, convinced me that I must have done something horrible. How was I to know that racism and sexism had formed a blueprint for my mistreatment long before I had ever arrived here? As with most Black women, others' hatred of me became self-hatred, which has diminished over the years, but has by no means disappeared. Black feminism has, for me and for so many others, given us the tools to finally comprehend that it is not something we have done that has heaped this psychic violence and material abuse upon us, but the very fact that, because of who we are, we are multiply oppressed. Unlike any other movement, Black feminism provides the theory that clarifies the nature of Black women's experience, makes possible positive support from other Black women, and encourages political action that will change the very system that has put us down.

NOTES

1. The terms Third World women and women of color are used here to designate Native American, Asian American, Latina, and Afro-American women in the U.S. and the indigenous peoples of Third World countries wherever they may live. Both the terms Third World women and women of color apply to Black American women. At times in the introduction Black women are specifically designated as Black or Afro-American and at other times the terms women of color and Third World women are used to refer to women of color as a whole.

2. Smith, Barbara. "Notes for Yet Another Paper on Black Feminism, Or Will the Real Enemy Please Stand Up?" in *Conditions: Five, The Black Women's Issue,* eds. Bethel & Smith. Vol. 2, No. 2 (Autumn, 1979), p. 124.

3. DuBois, W.E.B. *Darkwater, Voices from Within the Veil,* New York: AMS Press, 1969, p. 185.

4. Jordan, June & Bernice Johnson Reagon. "Oughta Be A Woman," *Good News,* Chicago: Flying Fish Records, 1981, Songtalk Publishing Co. Quoted by permission.

5. Teish, Luisah. "Women's Spirituality: A Household Act," in *Home Girls,* ed. Smith. Watertown: Persephone Press, Inc., 1983. All subsequent references to work in *Home Girls* will not be cited.

6. See Linda C. Powell's review of Michele Wallace's *Black Macho and the Myth of the Super Woman* ("Black Macho and Black Feminism") in this volume and my review of Bell Hooks' (Gloria Watkins) *Ain't I A Woman: Black Women and Feminism* in *The New Women's Times Feminist Review,* Vol. 9, no. 24 (November, 1982), pp. 10, 11, 18, 19 & 20 and in *The Black Scholar,* Vol. 14, No. 1 (January/February 1983), pp. 38–45.

7. Quoted from *Gay American History: Lesbians and Gay Men in the U.S.A.,* ed. Jonathan Katz. New York: T. Y. Crowell, 1976, p. 425. Also see Adrienne Rich's "The Problem with Lorraine Hansberry," in "Lorraine Hansberry: Art of Thunder, Vision of Light," *Freedomways,* Vol. 19, No. 4, 1979, pp. 247–255 for more material about her woman-identification.

8. Tillery, Linda. "Freedom Time," *Linda Tillery,* Oakland: Olivia Records, 1977, Tuizer Music.

9. Some useful articles on racism by white feminists are Elly Bulkin's "Racism and Writing: Some Implications for White Lesbian Critics." *Sinister Wisdom* 13 (Spring, 1980), pp. 3–22; Minnie Bruce Pratt's "Rebellion." *Feminary,* Vol. 11, Nos. 1 & 2, (1980), pp. 6–20; and Adrienne Rich's "Disloyal to Civilization: Feminism, Racism, Gynephobia." *On Lies, Secrets and Silence: Selected Prose* 1966–1978. New York: W. W. Norton, 1979, pp. 275–310.

10. Hurston, Zora Neale. *Their Eyes Were Watching God.* Urbana: University of Illinois, 1937, 1978, p. 29.   [1983]

 122

The Development of Chicana Feminist Discourse

ALMA M. GARCIA

Between 1970 and 1980, a Chicana feminist movement developed in the United States that addressed the specific issues that affected Chicanas as women of color. The growth of the Chicana feminist movement can be traced in the speeches, essays, letters, and articles published in Chicano and Chicana newspapers, journals, newsletters, and other printed materials.

During the sixties, American society witnessed the development of the Chicano movement, a social movement characterized by a politics of protest (Barrera 1974; Muñoz 1974; Navarro 1974). The Chicano movement focused on a wide range of issues: social justice, equality, educational reforms, and political and economic self-determination for Chicano communities in the United States. Various struggles evolved within this movement: the United Farmworkers unionization efforts (Dunne 1967; Kushner 1975; Matthiesen 1969; Nelson 1966); the New Mexico Land Grant Movement (Nabokov 1969); the Colorado-based Crusade for Justice (Castro 1974; Meier and Rivera 1972); the Chicano student movement (Garcia and de la Garza 1977); and the Raza Unida Party (Shockley 1974).

Chicanas participated actively in each of these struggles. By the end of the sixties, Chicanas began to assess the rewards and limits of their participation. The 1970s witnessed the development of Chicana feminists whose activities, organizations, and writings can be analyzed in terms of a feminist movement by women of color in American society. Chicana feminists outlined a cluster of ideas that crystallized into an emergent Chicana feminist debate. In the same way that Chicano males were reinterpreting the historical and contemporary experience of Chicanos in the United States, Chicanas began to investigate the forces shaping their own experiences as women of color.

The Chicana feminist movement emerged primarily as a result of the dynamics within the Chicano movement. In the 1960s and 1970s, the American political scene witnessed far-reaching social protest movements whose political courses often paralleled and at times exerted influence over each other (Freeman 1983; Piven and Cloward 1979). The development of feminist movements has been explained by the participation of women in larger social movements. Macias (1982), for example, links the early development of the Mexican feminist movement to the participation of women in the Mexican Revolution. Similarly, Freeman's (1984) analysis of the white feminist movement points out that many white feminists who were active in the early years of its development had previously been involved in the new left and civil rights movements. It was in these movements that white feminists experienced the constraints of male domination. Black feminists have similarly traced the development of a Black feminist movement during the 1960s and 1970s to their experiences with sexism in the larger Black movement (Davis 1983; Dill 1983; Hooks 1981, 1984; Joseph and Lewis 1981; White 1984). In this way, then, the origins of Chicana feminism parallel those of other feminist movements.

ORIGINS OF CHICANA FEMINISM

Rowbotham (1974) argues that women may develop a feminist consciousness as a result of their experiences with sexism in revolutionary struggles or mass social movements. To the extent that such movements are male dominated, women are likely to develop a feminist consciousness. Chicana feminists began the search for a "room of their own" by assessing their participation within the Chicano movement. Their feminist consciousness emerged from a struggle for equality with Chicano men and from a reassessment of the role of the family as a means of resistance to oppressive societal conditions.

Historically, as well as during the 1960s and 1970s, the Chicano family represented a source of cultural and political resistance to the various types of discrimination experienced in American society (Zinn 1975). At the cultural level, the Chicano movement emphasized the need to safeguard the value of family loyalty. At the political level, the Chicano movement used the family as a strategic organizational tool for protest activities.

Dramatic changes in the structure of Chicano families occurred as they participated in the Chicano movement. Specifically, women began to question their traditional female roles (Zinn 1975a). Thus, a Chicana feminist movement originated from the nationalist Chicano struggle. Rowbotham (1974, p. 206) refers to such a feminist movement as "a colony within a colony." But as the Chicano movement developed during the 1970s, Chicana feminists began to draw their own political agenda and raised a series of questions to assess their role within the Chicano movement. They entered into a dialogue with each other that explicitly reflected their struggles to secure a room of their own within the Chicano movement.

DEFINING FEMINISM FOR WOMEN OF COLOR

A central question of feminist discourse is the definition of feminism. The lack of consensus reflects different political ideologies and divergent social-class bases. In the United States, Chicana feminists shared the task of defining their ideology and movement with white, Black, and Asian American feminists. Like Black and Asian American feminists, Chicana feminists struggled to gain social equality and end sexist and racist oppression. Like them, Chicana feminists recognized that the nature of social inequality for women of color was multidimensional

(Cheng 1984; Chow 1987; Hooks 1981). Like Black and Asian American feminists, Chicana feminists struggled to gain equal status in the male-dominated nationalist movements and also in American society. To them, feminism represented a movement to end sexist oppression within a broader social protest movement. Again, like Black and Asian American feminists, Chicana feminists fought for social equality in the 1970s. They understood that their movement needed to go beyond women's rights and include the men of their group, who also faced racial subordination (Hooks 1981). Chicanas believed that feminism involved more than an analysis of gender because, as women of color, they were affected by both race and class in their everyday lives. Thus, Chicana feminism, as a social movement to improve the position of Chicanas in American society, represented a struggle that was both nationalist and feminist.

Chicana, Black, and Asian American feminists were all confronted with the issue of engaging in a feminist struggle to end sexist oppression within a broader nationalist struggle to end racist oppression. All experienced male domination in their own communities as well as in the larger society. Chow (1987) identifies gender stereotypes of Asian American women and the patriarchal family structure as major sources of women's oppression. Cultural, political, and economic constraints have, according to Chow (1987), limited the full development of a feminist consciousness and movement among Asian American women. The cross-pressures resulting from the demands of a nationalist and a feminist struggle led some Asian American women to organize feminist organizations that, however, continued to address broader issues affecting the Asian American community.

Black women were also faced with addressing feminist issues within a nationalist movement. According to Dill (1983), Black women played a major historical role in Black resistance movements and, in addition, brought a feminist component to these movements (Davis 1983; Dill 1983). Black women have struggled with Black men in nationalist movements but have also recognized and fought against the sexism in such political movements in the Black community (Hooks 1984). Although they wrote

and spoke as Black feminists, they did not organize separately from Black men.

Among the major ideological questions facing all three groups of feminists were the relationship between feminism and the ideology of cultural nationalism or racial pride, feminism and feminist baiting within the larger movements, and the relationship between their feminist movements and the white feminist movement.

CHICANA FEMINISM AND CULTURAL NATIONALISM

Throughout the seventies and now, in the eighties, Chicana feminists have been forced to respond to the criticism that cultural nationalism and feminism are irreconcilable. In the first issue of the newspaper, *Hijas de Cuauhtemoc*, Anna Nieto Gomez (1971) stated that a major issue facing Chicanas active in the Chicano movement was the need to organize to improve their status as women within the larger social movement. Francisca Flores (1971b, p. i), another leading Chicana feminist, stated:

> [Chicanas] can no longer remain in a subservient role or as auxiliary forces in the [Chicano] movement. They must be included in the front line of communication, leadership and organizational responsibility. . . . The issue of equality, freedom and self-determination of the Chicana—like the right of self-determination, equality, and liberation of the Mexican [Chicano] community—is not negotiable. Anyone opposing the right of women to organize into their own form of organization has no place in the leadership of the movement.

Supporting this position, Bernice Rincon (1971) argued that a Chicana feminist movement that sought equality and justice for Chicanas would strengthen the Chicano movement. Yet in the process, Chicana feminists challenged traditional gender roles because they limited their participation and acceptance within the Chicano movement.

Throughout the seventies, Chicana feminists viewed the struggle against sexism within the Chicano movement and the struggle against racism in the larger society as integral parts of Chicana feminism. As Gomez (1976, p. 10) said:

> Chicana feminism is in various stages of development. However, in general, Chicana feminism is the

recognition that women are oppressed as a group and are exploited as part of *la Raza* people. It is a direction to be responsible to identify and act upon the issues and needs of Chicana women. Chicana feminists are involved in understanding the nature of women's oppression.

Cultural nationalism represented a major ideological component of the Chicano movement. Its emphasis on Chicano cultural pride and cultural survival within an Anglo-dominated society gave significant political direction to the Chicano movement. One source of ideological disagreement between Chicana feminism and this cultural nationalist ideology was cultural survival. Many Chicana feminists believed that a focus on cultural survival did not acknowledge the need to alter male-female relations within Chicano communities. For example, Chicana feminists criticized the notion of the "ideal Chicana" that glorified Chicanas as strong, long-suffering women who had endured and kept Chicano culture and the family intact. To Chicana feminists, this concept represented an obstacle to the redefinition of gender roles. Nieto (1975, p. 4) stated:

> Some Chicanas are praised as they emulate the sanctified example set by [the Virgin] Mary. The woman *par excellence* is mother and wife. She is to love and support her husband and to nurture and teach her children. Thus, may she gain fulfillment as a woman. For a Chicana bent upon fulfillment of her personhood, this restricted perspective of her role as a woman is not only inadequate but crippling.

Chicana feminists were also skeptical about the cultural nationalist interpretation of machismo. Such an interpretation viewed machismo as an ideological tool used by the dominant Anglo society to justify the inequalities experienced by Chicanos. According to this interpretation, the relationship between Chicanos and the larger society was that of an internal colony dominated and exploited by the capitalist economy (Almaguer 1974; Barrera 1979). Machismo, like other cultural traits, was blamed by Anglos for blocking Chicanos from succeeding in American society. In reality, the economic structure and colony-like exploitation were to blame. . . .

Chicana feminists called for a focus on the uni-versal aspects of sexism that shape gender relations in both Anglo and Chicano culture. While they acknowledged the economic exploitation of all Chicanos, Chicana feminists outlined the double exploitation experienced by Chicanas. Riddell (1974, p. 159) concluded: "It was when Chicanas began to seek work outside the family groups that sexism became a key factor of oppression along with racism." Francisca Flores (1971a, p. 4) summarized some of the consequences of sexism:

> It is not surprising that more and more Chicanas are forced to go to work in order to supplement the family income. The children are farmed out to a relative to baby-sit with them, and since these women are employed in the lower income jobs, the extra pressure placed on them can become unbearable.

Thus, while the Chicano movement was addressing the issue of racial oppression facing all Chicanos, Chicana feminists argued that it lacked an analysis of sexism. Similarly, Black and Asian American women stressed the interconnectedness of race and gender oppression. Hooks (1984, p. 52) analyzes racism and sexism in terms of their "intersecting, complementary nature." She also emphasizes that one struggle should not take priority over the other. White (1984) criticizes Black men whose nationalism limited discussions of Black women's experiences with sexist oppression. The writings of other Black feminists criticized a Black cultural nationalist ideology that overlooked the consequences of sexist oppression (Beale 1975; Cade 1970; Davis 1971; Joseph and Lewis 1981). Many Asian American women were also critical of the Asian American movement whose focus on racism ignored the impact of sexism on the daily lives of women. The participation of Asian American women in various community struggles increased their encounters with sexism (Chow 1987). As a result, some Asian American women developed a feminist consciousness and organized as women around feminist issues.

CHICANA FEMINISM AND FEMINIST BAITING

The systematic analysis by Chicana feminists of the impact of racism and sexism on Chicanas in American society and, above all, within the Chicano movement was often misunderstood as a threat to the political unity of the Chicano movement. As Marta Cotera (1977, p. 9), a leading voice of Chicana feminism pointed out:

> The aggregate cultural values we [Chicanas] share can also work to our benefit if we choose to scrutinize our cultural traditions, isolate the positive attributes and interpret them for the benefit of women. It's unreal that *Hispanas* have been browbeaten for so long about our so-called conservative (meaning reactionary) culture. It's also unreal that we have let men interpret culture only as those practices and attitudes that determine who does the dishes around the house. We as women also have the right to interpret and define the philosophical and religious traditions beneficial to us within our culture, and which we have inherited as our tradition. To do this, we must become both conversant with our history and philosophical evolution, and analytical about the institutional and behavioral manifestations of the same.

Such Chicana feminists were attacked for developing a "divisive ideology"—a feminist ideology that was frequently viewed as a threat to the Chicano movement as a whole. As Chicana feminists examined their roles as women activists within the Chicano movement, an ideological split developed. One group active in the Chicano movement saw themselves as "loyalists" who believed that the Chicano movement did not have to deal with sexual inequities since Chicano men as well as Chicano women experienced racial oppression. According to Gomez (1973, p. 35), who was not a loyalist, their view was that if men oppress women, it is not the men's fault but rather that of the system.

Even if such a problem existed, and they did not believe that it did, the loyalists maintained that such a matter would best be resolved internally within the Chicano movement. They denounced the formation of a separate Chicana feminist movement on the grounds that it was a politically dangerous strategy, perhaps Anglo inspired. Such a movement would undermine the unity of the Chicano movement by raising an issue that was not seen as a central one. Loyalists viewed racism as the most important issue within the Chicano movement. . . .

Chicana feminist lesbians experienced even stronger attacks from those who viewed feminism as a divisive ideology. In a political climate that already viewed feminist ideology with suspicion, lesbianism as a sexual lifestyle and political ideology came under even more attack. Clearly, a cultural nationalist ideology that perpetuated such stereotypical images of Chicanas as "good wives and good mothers" found it difficult to accept a Chicana feminist lesbian movement.

Cherríe Moraga's writings during the 1970s reflect the struggles of Chicana feminist lesbians who, together with other Chicana feminists, were finding the sexism evident within the Chicano movement intolerable. Just as Chicana feminists analyzed their life circumstances as members of an ethnic minority and as women, Chicana feminist lesbians addressed themselves to the oppression they experienced as lesbians. As Moraga (1981, p. 28) stated:

> My lesbianism is the avenue through which I have learned the most about silence and oppression. . . . In this country, lesbianism is a poverty—as is being brown, as is being a woman, as is being just plain poor. The danger lies in ranking the oppressions. The danger lies in failing to acknowledge the specificity of the oppression.

Chicana, Black, and Asian American feminists experienced similar cross-pressures of feminist-baiting and lesbian-baiting attacks. As they organized around feminist struggles, these women of color encountered criticism from both male and female cultural nationalists who often viewed feminism as little more than an "anti-male" ideology. Lesbianism was identified as an extreme derivation of feminism. A direct connection was frequently made that viewed feminism and lesbianism as synonymous. Attacks against feminists—Chicanas, Blacks, and Asian Americans—derived from the existence of homophobia within each of these communities. As lesbian women of color published their writings, attacks against them increased (Moraga 1983).

Responses to such attacks varied within and between the feminist movements of women of color. Some groups tried one strategy and later adopted another. Some lesbians pursued a separatist strategy within their own racial and ethnic communities (Moraga and Anzaldua 1981; White 1984). Others attempted to form lesbian coalitions across racial and ethnic lines. Both strategies represented a response to the marginalization of lesbians produced by recurrent waves of homophobic sentiments in Chicano, Black, and Asian American communities (Moraga and Anzaldua 1981). A third response consisted of working within the broader nationalist movements in these communities and the feminist movements within them in order to challenge their heterosexual biases and resultant homophobia. As early as 1974, the "Black Feminist Statement" written by a Boston-based feminist group—the Combahee River Collective—stated (1981, p. 213): "We struggle together with Black men against racism, while we also struggle with Black men against sexism." Similarly, Moraga (1981) challenged the white feminist movement to examine its racist tendencies; the Chicano movement, its sexist tendencies; and both, their homophobic tendencies. In this way, Moraga (1981) argued that such movements to end oppression would begin to respect diversity within their own ranks. . . .

Chicana feminists responded quickly and often vehemently to such charges. Flores (1971a, p. 1) answered these antifeminist attacks in an editorial in which she argued that birth control, abortion, and sex education were not merely "white issues." In response to the accusation that feminists were responsible for the "betrayal of [Chicano] culture and heritage," Flores said, "Our culture hell"—a phrase that became a dramatic slogan of the Chicana feminist movement.

Chicana feminists' defense throughout the 1970s against those claiming that a feminist movement was divisive for the Chicano movement was to reassess their roles within the Chicano movement and to call for an end to male domination. Their challenges of traditional gender roles represented a means to achieve equality (Longeaux y Vasquez 1969a, 1969b). In order to increase the participation of and opportunities for women in the Chicano movement, feminists agreed that both Chicanos and Chicanas had to address the issue of gender inequality (Chapa 1973; Chavez 1971; Del Castillo 1974; Cotera 1977; Moreno 1979). Furthermore, Chicana feminists argued that the resistance that they encountered reflected the existence of sexism on the part of Chicano males and the antifeminist attitudes of the Chicana loyalists. Gomez (1973, p. 31), re-

viewing the experiences of Chicana feminists in the Chicano movement, concluded that Chicanas "involved in discussing and applying the women's question have been ostracized, isolated and ignored." She argued that "in organizations where cultural nationalism is extremely strong, Chicana feminists experience intense harassment and ostracism" (1973, p. 38).

Black and Asian American women also faced severe criticism as they pursued feminist issues in their own communities. Indeed, as their participation in collective efforts to end racial oppression increased, so did their confrontations with sexism (Chow 1987; Hooks 1984; White 1984). . . .

CHICANA FEMINISTS AND WHITE FEMINISTS

It is difficult to determine the extent to which Chicana feminists sympathized with the white feminist movement. A 1976 study at the University of San Diego that examined the attitudes of Chicanas regarding the white feminist movement found that the majority of Chicanas surveyed believed that the movement had affected their lives. In addition, they identified with such key issues as the right to legal abortions on demand and access to low-cost birth control. Nevertheless, the survey found that "even though the majority of Chicanas . . . could relate to certain issues of the women's movement, for the most part they saw it as being an elitist movement comprised of white middle-class women who [saw] the oppressor as the males of this country" (Orozco 1976, p. 12).

Nevertheless, some Chicana feminists considered the possibility of forming coalitions with white feminists as their attempts to work within the Chicano movement were suppressed. Since white feminists were themselves struggling against sexism, building coalitions with them was seen as an alternative strategy for Chicana feminists (Rincon 1971). Almost immediately, however, Chicana feminists recognized the problems involved in adopting this political strategy. As Longeaux y Vasquez (1971, p. 11) acknowledged, "Some of our own Chicanas may be attracted to the white woman's liberation movement, but we really don't feel comfortable there. We want to be a Chicana *primero* [first]." For other Chicanas, the demands of white women were "irrelevant to the Chicana movement" (Hernandez 1971, p. 9).

Several issues made such coalition building difficult. First, Chicana feminists criticized what they considered to be a cornerstone of white feminist thought, an emphasis on gender oppression to explain the life circumstances of women. Chicana feminists believed that the white feminist movement overlooked the effects of racial oppression experienced by Chicanas and other women of color. Thus, Del Castillo (1974, p. 8) maintained that the Chicana feminist movement was "different primarily because we are [racially] oppressed people." In addition, Chicana feminists criticized white feminists who believed that a general women's movement would be able to overcome racial differences among women. Chicanas interpreted this as a failure by the white feminist movement to deal with the issue of racism. Without the incorporation of an analysis of racial oppression to explain the experiences of Chicanas as well as of other women of color, Chicana feminists believed that a coalition with white feminists would be highly unlikely (Chapa 1973; Cotera 1977; Gomez 1973; Longeaux y Vasquez 1971). As Longeaux y Vasquez (1971, p. 11) concluded: "We must have a clearer vision of our plight and certainly we cannot blame our men for the oppression of the women."

In the 1970s, Chicana feminists reconciled their demands for an end to sexism within the Chicano movement and their rejection of the saliency of gender oppression by separating the two issues. They clearly identified the struggle against sexism in the Chicano movement as a major issue, arguing that sexism prevented their full participation (Fallis 1974; Gomez 1976). They also arranged that sexist behavior and ideology on the part of both Chicano males and Anglos represented the key to understanding women's oppression. However, they remained critical of an analysis of women's experiences that focused exclusively on gender oppression.

Chicana feminists adopted an analysis that began with race as a critical variable in interpreting the experiences of Chicano communities in the United States. They expanded this analysis by identifying gender as a variable interconnected with race in ana-

lyzing the specific daily life circumstances of Chicanas as women in Chicano communities. Chicana feminists did not view women's struggles as secondary to the nationalist movement but argued instead for an analysis of race and gender as multiple sources of oppression (Cotera 1977). Thus, Chicana feminism went beyond the limits of an exclusively racial theory of oppression that tended to overlook gender and also went beyond the limits of a theory of oppression based exclusively on gender that tended to overlook race.

A second factor preventing an alliance between Chicana feminists and white feminists was the middle-class orientation of white feminists. While some Chicana feminists recognized the legitimacy of the demands made by white feminists and even admitted sharing some of these demands, they argued that "it is not our business as Chicanas to identify with the white women's liberation movement as a home base for working for our people" (Longeaux y Vasquez 1971, p. 11).

Throughout the 1970s, Chicana feminists viewed the white feminist movement as a middle-class movement (Chapa 1973; Cotera 1980; Longeaux y Vasquez 1970; Martinez 1972; Nieto 1974; Orozco 1976). In contrast, Chicana feminists analyzed the Chicano movement in general as a working-class movement. They repeatedly made reference to such differences, and many Chicana feminists began their writings with a section that disassociated themselves from the "women's liberation movement." Chicana feminists as activists in the broader Chicano movement identified as major struggles the farmworkers movement, welfare rights, undocumented workers, and prison rights. Such issues were seen as far removed from the demands of the white feminist movement, and Chicana feminists could not get white feminist organizations to deal with them (Cotera 1980).

Similar concerns regarding the white feminist movement were raised by Black and Asian American feminists. Black feminists have documented the historical and contemporary schisms between Black feminists and white feminists, emphasizing the socioeconomic and political differences (Davis 1971, 1983; Dill 1983; LaRue 1970). More specifically, Black feminists have been critical of the white feminists who advocate a female solidarity that cuts across racial, ethnic, and social class lines. As Dill (1983, p. 131) states:

> The cry "Sisterhood is powerful!" has engaged only a few segments of the female population in the United States. Black, Hispanic, Native American, and Asian American women of all classes, as well as many working-class women, have not readily identified themselves as sisters of the white middle-class women who have been in the forefront of the movement.

Like Black feminists, Asian American feminists have also had strong reservations regarding the white feminist movement. For many Asian Americans, white feminism has primarily focused on gender as an analytical category and has thus lacked a systematic analysis of race and class (Chow 1987; Fong 1978; Wong 1980; Woo 1971).

White feminist organizations were also accused of being exclusionary, patronizing, or racist in their dealings with Chicanas and other women of color. Cotera (1980, p. 227) states:

> Minority women could fill volumes with examples of put-down, put-ons, and out-and-out racism shown to them by the leadership in the [white feminist] movement. There are three major problem areas in the minority-majority relationship in the movement: (1) paternalism or materialism, (2) extremely limited opportunities for minority women . . . , (3) outright discrimination against minority women in the movement.

Although Chicana feminists continued to be critical of building coalitions with white feminists toward the end of the seventies, they acknowledged the diversity of ideologies within the white feminist movement. Chicana feminists sympathetic to radical socialist feminism because of its anticapitalist framework wrote of working-class oppression that cut across racial and ethnic lines. Their later writings discussed the possibility of joining with white working-class women, but strategies for forming such political coalitions were not made explicit (Cotera 1977: Marquez and Ramirez 1977).

Instead, Del Castillo and other Chicana feminists favored coalitions between Chicanas and other women of color while keeping their respective au-

tonomous organizations. Such coalitions would recognize the inherent racial oppression of capitalism rather than universal gender oppression. When Longeaux y Vasquez (1971) stated that she was "Chicana *primero*," she was stressing the saliency of race over gender in explaining the oppression experienced by Chicanas. The word *Chicana* however, simultaneously expresses a woman's race and gender. Not until later—in the 1980s—would Chicana feminist ideology call for an analysis that stressed the interrelationship of race, class, and gender in explaining the conditions of Chicanas in American society (Cordova et al. 1986; Zinn 1982), just as Black and Asian American feminists have done.

Chicana feminists continued to stress the importance of developing autonomous feminist organizations that would address the struggles of Chicanas as members of an ethnic minority and as women. Rather than attempt to overcome the obstacles to coalition building between Chicana feminists and white feminists, Chicanas called for autonomous feminist organizations for all women of color (Cotera 1977; Gonzalez 1980; Nieto 1975). Chicana feminists believed that sisterhood was indeed powerful but only to the extent that racial and class differences were understood and, above all, respected. As Nieto (1974, p. 4) concludes:

> The Chicana must demand that dignity and respect within the women's rights movement which allows her to practice feminism within the context of her own culture. . . . Her approaches to feminism must be drawn from her own world.

AN UPDATE: THE 1980S TO THE PRESENT

During the 1980s, Chicana feminists raised critical issues concerning the nature of the oppression experienced by Chicanas and other women of color. Chicana feminists, like African American, Asian American, and Native American feminists, examined the consequences of the intersection of race, class, and gender in the daily lives of women in American society. Chicana feminists have adopted the theoretical perspective which emphasizes the simultaneous impact of these critical variables for women of color (Anzaldua 1987, 1990; Garcia 1986; Hooks 1984, 1989; Moraga 1983; Moraga and Anzaldua 1981).

Chicana feminists have emphasized that Chicanas have made few gains in comparison to white men and women as well as Chicano men in terms of their labor force participation, income, education levels, rates of poverty, and other socioeconomic status indicators. Over the last forty years, Chicanas have made only small occupational moves from low-pay unskilled jobs to higher-pay skilled or semi-professional employment. Studies indicate that about 66% of Chicanas remain occupationally segregated in such low-pay jobs as sales, clerical, service, and factory work. Furthermore, Chicanas experience major social-structural constraints which limit their upward social mobility (Romero 1992; Segura 1989). Less than 15% of all Chicanas have entered the occupational ranks of professionals, educational administrators, and business managers. In addition Chicano families had approximately two-thirds of the family income of non-Hispanic families. This is approximately the same ratio as ten years ago. In addition, about 46% of families headed by Chicanas had incomes which fell below the poverty level.

Chicana feminists are also concerned with educational attainment levels for Chicanas. The persistently low levels of educational attainment for Chicanas illustrates the role of race, class, and gender stratification in reinforcing and perpetuating inequalities. Chicanas, as well as all Latinas, have shockingly high dropout rates. Not surprisingly, Chicanas are vastly underrepresented at all levels of higher education (Orozco 1986; Segura 1986; Sierra 1986). According to one of the few studies on Chicanas in higher education, "Mexican American females are the poorest and most underrepresented of all population groups in higher education" (Chacon, 1982).

Despite the limited numbers of Chicana academics, Chicana feminist discourse has developed within the academy as Chicana feminists have entered into specific dialogues with other feminists. Such dialogues have focused on critical differences among feminists regarding feminist theory and women's studies. Although various issues are shaping Chicana feminist thought, one overarching theme involves the origins, nature, and consequences of exclusionary practices directed at Chicanas and other women of color within feminist theory and feminist scholarship in general. Chicanas have criticized feminist scholarship for the exclusionary practices which have resulted from the discipline's limited attention to differences among women regarding race, ethnicity, class, and sexual preference (Baca Zinn et al. 1986). Interestingly, Chicana feminists are also critical of Chicano studies and ethnic studies scholarship which have too often lacked a systematic gender analysis (Alarcon 1991; Garcia 1992; Mujeres en Marcha 1983; Orozco 1986). As a result, Chicana feminist discourse is integrating the experiences of Chicanas within these academic disciplines. Chicana feminist scholars advocate restructuring the academy in order to integrate what Scott (1988) has called the "new knowledge" about women, in this case, Chicanas.

Chicana feminist discourse, therefore, has been evolving by focusing on (1) the persistent sources of inequality which shape the daily life circumstances of Chicanas, and (2) the need to identify sources of exclusionary practices within feminist theory as well as women's studies, Chicano studies, and ethnic studies. Baca Zinn et al. suggest that "to build a more diverse women's studies and an integrated feminist theory," universities need to hire more women of color faculty members (1986, p. 300). Also, feminist publications need to place more women of color on their editorial boards in order to better assure that their publications will represent a diversity of feminist scholarship. Lastly, Chicana feminists continue to engage in frank, often painful, debates with other feminists in order to develop a more inclusionary feminist discourse. The decade of the 1990s will be one in which feminist movements develop as feminists' agendas continue to address the complexities of gender inequality for women from a diversity of backgrounds.

REFERENCES

Alarcon, Norma. 1991. "The Theoretical Subject(s) of *This Bridge Called My Back* and Anglo American Feminism," in Hector Calderon and Jose David Saldivar, eds., *Criticism in the Borderlands: Studies in Chicano Literature, Culture, and Ideology* (Durham: Duke University): 28–39.

Almaguer, Tomas. 1974. "Historical Notes on Chicano Oppression." *Aztlan* 5:27–56.

Anzaldua, Gloria. 1987. *Borderlands/La Frontera: The New Mestiza* (San Francisco: Aunt Lute Press).

Anzaldua, Gloria, ed. 1990. *Making Faces, Making Soul—*

Haciendo Caras: Creative and Critical Perspectives by Women of Color (San Francisco: Aunt Lute Press).

Baca Zinn, Maxine et al. 1986. "The Cost of Exclusionary Practices in Women's Studies," *Signs: Journal of Women in Culture and Society* 11:290–302.

Barrera, Mario. 1974. "The Study of Politics and the Chicano." *Aztlan* 5:9–26.

———. 1979. *Race and Class in the Southwest* (Notre Dame, IN: University of Notre Dame Press).

Beale, Frances. 1975. "Slave of a Slave No More: Black Women in Struggle." *Black Scholar* 6:2–10.

Cade, Toni. 1970. *The Black Woman* (New York: Signet).

Castro, Tony. 1974. *Chicano Power* (New York: Saturday Review Press).

Chacon, Maria. 1982. *Chicanas in Post Secondary Education* (Stanford: Stanford University Press).

Chapa, Evey. 1973. "Report from the National Women's Political Caucus." *Magazin* 11:37–39.

Chavez, Henri. 1971. "The Chicanas." *Regeneracion* 1:14.

Cheng, Lucie. 1984. "Asian American Women and Feminism." *Sojourner* 10:11–12.

Chow, Esther Ngan-Ling. 1987. "The Development of Feminist Consciousness Among Asian American Women." *Gender and Society* 1:284–99.

Combahee River Collective. 1981. "A Black Feminist Statement." in *This Bridge Called My Back: Writings by Radical Women of Color,* edited by Cherrie Moraga and Gloria Anzaldua (Watertown, MA: Persephone): 210–18.

Cordova, Teresa, et al. 1986. *Chicana Voices: Intersection of Class, Race and Gender* (Austin, TX: Center for Mexican American Studies).

Cotera, Marta. 1973. "La Mujer Mexicana: Mexicano Feminism." *Magazin* 1:30–32.

———. 1977. *The Chicana Feminist* (Austin, TX: Austin Information Systems Development).

———. 1980. "Feminism: The Chicana and Anglo Versions: An Historical Analysis," in *Twice a Minority: Mexican American Women,* edited by Margarita Melville (St. Louis, MO: C. V. Mosby): 217–32.

Davis, Angela. 1971. "Reflections on Black Women's Role in the Community of Slaves." *Black Scholar* 3:3–13.

———. 1983. *Women, Race and Class* (New York: Random House).

Del Castillo, Adelaida. 1974. "La Vision Chicana." *La Gente* 8.

Dill, Bonnie Thornton. 1983. "Race, Class, and Gender: Prospects for an All-Inclusive Sisterhood." *Feminist Studies* 9:131–50.

Dunne, John. 1967. *Delano: The Story of the California Grape Strike* (New York: Strauss).

Fallis, Guadalupe Valdes. 1974. "The Liberated Chicana—A Struggle Against Tradition." *Women: A Journal of Liberation* 3:20.

Flores, Francisca. 1971a. "Conference of Mexican Women: Un Remolino. *Regeneracion* 1(1): 1–4.

———. 1971b. "El Mundo Femenil Mexicana." *Regeneracion* 1(10): 1.

Fong, Katheryn M. 1978. "Feminism is Fine, But What's It Done for Asian America?" in *This Bridge Called My Back: Writings by Radical Women of Color,* edited by Cherrie Moraga and Gloria Anzaldua (Watertown, MA: Persephone) 6:21–22.

Freeman, Jo, ed. 1983. "On the Origins of Social Movements," in *Social Movements of the Sixties and Seventies* (New York: Longman): 8–30.

———, ed. 1984. "The Women's Liberation Movement: Its Origins, Structure, Activities, and Ideas," in *Women: A Feminist Perspective* (Palo Alto, CA: Mayfield): 543–56.

Garcia, Alma M. 1986. "Studying Chicanas: Bringing Women in to the Frame of Chicano Studies," in *Chicana Voices: Intersections of Class, Race, and Gender,* edited by Teresa Cordova et al. (Austin, TX: Center for Mexican American Studies): 19–29.

———. 1992. "Chicano Studies and 'La Chicana' Courses: Curriculum Options and Reforms," in Mary Romero and Cordelia Candelaria, eds., *Community Empowerment and Chicano Scholarship* (Berkeley: Selected Proceedings of the National Association for Chicano Studies): 53–60.

Garcia, F. Chris, and Rudolpho O. de la Garza. 1977. *The Chicano Political Experience* (North Scituate, MA: Duxbury).

Gomez, Anna Nieto. 1971. "Chicanas Identify." *Hijas de Cuahtemoc* (April): 9.

———. 1973. "La Feminista." *Encuentro Femenil* 1:34–47.

———. 1976. "Sexism in the Movement." *La Gente* 6(4): 10.

Gonzalez, Sylvia. 1980. "Toward a Feminist Pedagogy for Chicana Self-Actualization." *Frontiers* 5:48–51.

Hernandez, Carmen. 1971. "Carmen Speaks Out." *Papel Chicano* (June 12): 8–9.

Hooks, Bell. 1981. *Ain't I a Woman: Black Women and Feminism* (Boston: South End Press).

———. 1984. *Feminist Theory: From Margin to Center* (Boston: South End Press).

———. 1989. *Talking Back: Thinking Feminist: Thinking Black* (Boston: South End Press).

Joseph, Gloria, and Jill Lewis. 1981. *Common Differences: Conflicts in Black and White Feminist Perspectives* (Garden City, NY: Doubleday).

Kushner, Sam. 1975. *Long Road to Delano* (New York: International).

LaRue, Linda. 1970. "The Black Movement and Women's Liberation." *Black Scholar* 1:36–42.

Longeaux y Vasquez, Enriqueta. 1969a. "The Woman of La Raza." *El Grito del Norte* 2 (November): 11.

———. 1969b. "La Chicana: Let's Build a New Life." *El Grito del Norte* 2 (November): 11.

———. 1970. "The Mexican-American Woman." *Sisterhood Is Powerful,* edited by Robin Morgan (New York: Vintage): 379–84.

———. 1971. "Soy Chicana Primero." *El Grito del Norte* 4 (April 26): 11.

Macias, Anna. 1982. *Against All Odds* (Westport, CT: Greenwood).

Marquez, Evelina, and Margarita Ramirez. 1977. "Women's Task Is to Gain Liberation." *Essay on La Mujer,* edited by Rosaura Sanches and Rosa Martinez Cruz (Los Angeles: UCLA Chicano Studies Center): 188–94.

Martinez, Elizabeth. 1972. "The Chicana." *Ideal* 44:1–3.

Matthiesen, Peter. 1969. *Sal Si Puedes: Cesar Chavez and the New American Revolution* (New York: Random House).

Meier, Matt, and Feliciano Rivera. 1972. *The Chicanos* (New York: Hill & Wang).

Moraga, Cherrie. 1981. "La Guerra." in *This Bridge Called My Back: Writings by Radical Women of Color,* edited by Cherrie Moraga and Gloria Anzaldua (Watertown, MA: Persephone): 27–34.

———. 1983. *Loving in the War Years: Lo que nunca paso por sus labios* (Boston: South End Press).

Moraga, Cherrie, and Gloria Anzaldua, eds. 1981. *This Bridge Called My Back: Writings by Radical Women of Color* (Watertown, MA: Persephone).

Moreno, Dorinda. 1979. "The Image of the Chicana and the La Raza Woman." *Caracol* 2:14–15.

Mujeres en Marcha. 1983. *Chicanas in the 1980's: Unsettled Issues* (Berkeley, CA: Chicano Studies Publication Unit).

Muñoz, Carlos, Jr. 1974. "The Politics of Protest and Liberation: A Case Study of Repression and Cooptation." *Aztlan* 5:119–41.

Nabokov, Peter. 1969. *Tijerina and the Courthouse Raid.* (Albuquerque, NM: University of New Mexico Press).

Navarro, Armando. 1974. "The Evolution of Chicano Politics." *Aztlan* 5:57–84.

Nelson, Eugene. 1966. *Huelga: The First 100 Days* (Delano, CA: Farm Workers Press).

Nieto, Consuelo. 1974. "The Chicana and the Women's Rights Movement." *La Luz* 3 (September): 10–11, 32.

———. 1975. "Consuelo Nieto on the Women's Movement." *Interracial Books for Children Bulletin* 5:4.

Orozco, Cynthia. 1986. "Sexism in Chicano Studies and the Community," in Teresa Cordova et al., eds. *Chicana Voices: Intersections of Class, Race, and Gender* (Austin, TX: Center for Mexican American Studies): 11–18.

Orozco, Yolanda. 1976. "La Chicana and 'Women's Liberation.'" *Voz Fronteriza* (January 5): 6, 12.

Piven, Frances Fox, and Richard A. Cloward. 1979. *Poor People's Movements: Why They Succeed, How They Fail* (New York: Vintage).

Riddell, Adalijiza Sosa. 1974. "Chicanas en el Movimiento." *Aztlan* 5:155–65.

Rincon, Bernice. 1971. "La Chicana: Her Role in the Past and Her Search for a New Role in the Future." *Regeneracion* 1(10): 15–17.

Romero, Mary. 1992. *Maid in the U.S.A.* (New York: Routledge).

Rowbotham, Sheila. 1974. *Women, Resistance and Revolution: A History of Women and Revolution in the Modern World* (New York: Vintage).

Scott, Joan Wallach. 1988. *Gender and Politics of History* (New York: Columbia University Press).

Segura, Denise. 1986. "Chicanas and Triple Oppression in the Labor Force," in Teresa Cordova et al., eds. *Chicana Voices: Intersections of Class, Race and Gender* (Austin, TX: Center for Mexican American Studies): 47–65.

———. 1989. "Chicana and Mexican Immigrant Women at Work: The Impact of Class, Race, and Gender on Occupational Mobility." *Gender & Society* (3): 37–52.

Shockley, John. 1974. *Chicano Revolt in a Texas Town* (South Bend, IN: University of Notre Dame Press).

Sierra, Christine Marie. 1986. "The University Setting Reinforces Inequality," in Teresa Cordova et al., eds. *Chicana Voices: Intersections of Class, Race, and Gender* (Austin, TX: Center for Mexican American Studies): 5–7.

White, Frances. 1984. "Listening to the Voices of Black Feminism." *Radical America* 18:7–25.

Wong, Germaine Q. 1980. "Impediments to Asian-Pacific-American Women Organizing," in *The Conference on the Educational and Occupational Needs of Asian Pacific Women* (Washington, D.C.: National Institute of Education): 89–103.

Woo, Margaret. 1971. "Women + Man = Political Unity," in *Asian Women,* edited by Editorial Staff (Berkeley, CA: University of California Press): 15–16.

Zinn, Maxine Baca. 1975. "Political Familism: Toward Sex Role Equality in Chicano Families." *Aztlan* 6:13–27.

———. 1982. "Mexican-American Women in the Social Sciences." *Signs: Journal of Women in Culture and Society* 8: 259–72.   [1992]

🌿 123

Thoughts on Indian Feminism

KATE SHANLEY

Attending the Ohoyo conference in Grand Forks, North Dakota was a returning home for me in a spiritual sense—taking my place beside other Indian women, and an actual sense—being with my relatives and loved ones after finally finishing my pre-doctoral requirements at the university. Although I have been a full-time student for the past six years, I brought to the academic experience many years in the workaday world as a mother, registered nurse, volunteer tutor, social worker aide, and high school outreach worker. What I am offering in this article are my thoughts as an Indian woman on feminism. Mine is a political perspective that seeks to re-view the real-life positions of women in relation to the theories that attempt to address the needs of those women.

Issues such as equal pay for equal work, child health and welfare, and a woman's right to make her own choices regarding contraceptive use, sterilization and abortion—key issues to the majority women's movement—affect Indian women as well; however, equality *per se,* may have a different meaning for Indian women and Indian people. That difference begins with personal and tribal sovereignty— the right to be legally recognized as peoples empowered to determine our own destinies. Thus, the Indian women's movement seeks equality in two ways that do not concern mainstream women: (1) on the individual level, the Indian woman struggles to promote the survival of a social structure whose organizational principles represent notions of family different from those of the mainstream; and (2) on the societal level, the People seek sovereignty as a people in order to maintain a vital legal and spiritual connection to the land, in order to *survive* as a people.

The nuclear family has little relevance to Indian women; in fact, in many ways, mainstream feminists now are striving to redefine family and community in a way that Indian women have long known. The American lifestyle from which white middle-class women are fighting to free themselves, has not taken hold in Indian communities. Tribal and communal values have survived after four hundred years of colonial oppression.

It may be that the desire on the part of mainstream feminists to include Indian women, however sincere, represents tokenism just now, because too often Indian people, by being thought of as spiritual "mascots" to the American endeavor, are seen more as artifacts than a real people able to speak for ourselves. Given the public's general ignorance about Indian people, in other words, it is possible that Indian people's real-life concerns are not relevant to the mainstream feminist movement in a way that constitutes anything more than a "representative" facade. Charges against the women's movement of heterosexism and racism abound these days; it is not my intention to add to them except to stress that we must all be vigilant in examining the underlying assumptions that motivate us. Internalization of negative (that is, sexist and racist) attitudes towards ourselves and others can and quite often does result from colonialist (white patriarchal) oppression. It is more useful to attack the systems that keep us ignorant of each other's histories.

The other way in which the Indian women's movement differs in emphasis from the majority women's movement, lies in the importance Indian people place on tribal sovereignty—it is the single most pressing political issue in Indian country today. For Indian people to survive culturally as well as materially, many battles must be fought and won in the courts of law, precisely because it is the legal recognition that enables Indian people to govern ourselves according to our own world view—a world view that is antithetical to the *wasicu* (the Lakota term for "takers of the fat") definition of progress. Equality for Indian women within tribal communities, therefore, holds more significance than equality in terms of the general rubric "American."

Up to now I have been referring to the women's movement as though it were a single, well-defined organization. It is not. Perhaps in many ways socialist feminists hold views similar to the views of many Indian people regarding private property and the nuclear family. Certainly, there are some Indian people who are capitalistic. The point I would like to stress, however, is that rather than seeing differences according to a hierarchy of oppressions (white over Indian, male over female), we must practice a politics that allows for diversity in cultural identity as well as in sexual identity.

The word "feminism" has special meanings to Indian women, including the idea of promoting the continuity of tradition, and consequently, pursuing the recognition of tribal sovereignty. Even so, Indian feminists are united with mainstream feminists in outrage against woman and child battering, sexist employment and educational practices, and in many other social concerns. Just as sovereignty cannot be granted but *must be recognized* as an inherent right to self-determination, so Indian feminism must also be recognized as powerful in its own terms, in its own right.

Feminism becomes an incredibly powerful term when it incorporates diversity—not as a superficial political position, but as a practice. The women's movement and the Indian movement for sovereignty suffer similar trivialization, because narrow factions turn ignorance to their own benefit so that they can exploit human beings and the lands they live on for corporate profit. The time has come for Indian women and Indian people to be known on our own terms. This nuclear age demands new terms of communication for all people. Our survival depends on it. Peace.   [1984]

 124

Blame It on Feminism

SUSAN FALUDI

To be a woman in America at the close of the 20th century—what good fortune. That's what we keep hearing, anyway. The barricades have fallen, politicians assure us. Women have "made it," Madison Avenue cheers. Women's fight for equality has "largely been won," *Time* magazine announces. Enroll at any university, join any law firm, apply for credit at any bank. Women have so many opportunities now, corporate leaders say, that we don't really need equal opportunity policies. Women are so equal now, lawmakers say, that we no longer need an Equal Rights Amendment. Women have "so much," former President Ronald Reagan says, that the White House no longer needs to appoint them to higher office. Even American Express ads are saluting a woman's freedom to charge it. At last, women have received their full citizenship papers.

And yet . . .

Behind this celebration of the American woman's victory, behind the news, cheerfully and endlessly repeated, that the struggle for women's rights is won, another message flashes. You may be free and equal now, it says to women, but you have never been more miserable.

This bulletin of despair is posted everywhere—at the newsstand, on the TV set, at the movies, in advertisements and doctors' offices and academic journals. Professional women are suffering "burnout" and succumbing to an "infertility epidemic." Single women are grieving from a "man shortage." The *New York Times* reports: Childless women are "depressed and confused" and their ranks are swelling. *Newsweek* says: Unwed women are "hysterical" and crumbling under a "profound crisis of confidence." The health advice manuals inform: High-powered career women are stricken with unprecedented outbreaks of "stress-induced disorders," hair loss, bad nerves, alcoholism, and even heart attacks. The psychology books advise: Independent women's loneliness represents "a major mental health problem today." Even founding feminist Betty Friedan has been spreading the word: she warns that women now suffer from a new identity crisis and "new 'problems that have no name.'"

How can American women be in so much trouble at the same time that they are supposed to be so blessed? If the status of women has never been higher, why is their emotional state so low? If women got what they asked for, what could possibly be the matter now?

The prevailing wisdom of the past decade has supported one, and only one, answer to this riddle: it must be all that equality that's causing all that pain. Women are unhappy precisely *because* they are free. Women are enslaved by their own liberation. They have grabbed at the gold ring of independence, only to miss the one ring that really matters. They have gained control of their fertility, only to destroy it. They have pursued their own professional dreams—and lost out on the greatest female adventure. The women's movement, as we are told time and again, has proved women's own worst enemy.

"In dispensing its spoils, women's liberation has given my generation high incomes, our own cigarette, the option of single parenthood, rape crisis centers, personal lines of credit, free love, and female gynecologists," Mona Charen, a young law student, writes in the *National Review,* in an article titled "The Feminist Mistake." "In return it has effectively robbed us of one thing upon which the happiness of most women rests—men." The *National Review* is a conservative publication, but such charges against the women's movement are not confined to its pages. "Our generation was the human sacrifice" to the women's movement, *Los Angeles Times* feature writer Elizabeth Mehren contends in a *Time* cover story. Baby-boom women like her, she says, have been duped by feminism: "We believed the rhetoric." In *Newsweek,* writer Kay Ebeling dubs feminism "the Great Experiment That Failed" and asserts "women in my generation, its perpetrators, are the casualties." Even the beauty magazines are saying it: *Harper's Bazaar* accuses the women's movement of having "lost us [women] ground instead of gaining it."

In the last decade, publications from the *New York Times* to *Vanity Fair* to the *Nation* have issued a steady stream of indictments against the women's movement, with such headlines as WHEN FEMINISM FAILED or THE AWFUL TRUTH ABOUT WOMEN'S LIB. They hold the campaign for women's equality responsible for nearly every woe besetting women, from mental depression to meager savings accounts, from teenage suicides to eating disorders to bad complexions. The "Today" show says women's liberation is to blame for bag ladies. A guest columnist in the *Baltimore Sun* even proposes that feminists produced the rise in slasher movies. By making the "violence" of abortion more acceptable, the author reasons, women's rights activists made it all right to show graphic murders on screen.

At the same time, other outlets of popular culture have been forging the same connection: in Hollywood films, of which *Fatal Attraction* is only the most famous, emancipated women with condominiums of their own slink wild-eyed between bare walls, paying for their liberty with an empty bed, a barren womb. "My biological clock is ticking so loud it keeps me awake at night," Sally Field cries in the film *Surrender,* as, in an all too common transformation in the cinema of the '80s, an actress who once played scrappy working heroines is now showcased groveling for a groom. In prime-time television shows, from "thirtysomething" to "Family Man," single, professional, and feminist women are humiliated, turned into harpies, or hit by nervous breakdowns; the wise ones recant their independent ways by the closing sequence. In popular novels, from Gail Parent's *A Sign of the Eighties* to Stephen King's *Misery,* unwed women shrink to sniveling spinsters or inflate to fire-breathing she-devils; renouncing all aspirations but marriage, they beg for wedding bands from strangers or swing axes at reluctant bachelors. We "blew it by waiting," a typically remorseful careerist sobs in Freda Bright's *Singular Women;* she and her sister professionals are "condemned to be childless forever." Even Erica Jong's high-flying independent heroine literally crashes by the end of the decade, as the author supplants *Fear of Flying*'s saucy Isadora Wing, a symbol of female sexual emancipation in the '70s, with an embittered careerist-turned-recovering-"co-dependent" in *Any Woman's Blues*—a book that is intended, as the narrator bluntly states, "to demonstrate what a deadend the so-called sexual revolution had become, and how desperate so-called free women were in the last few years of our decadent epoch."

Popular psychology manuals peddle the same diagnosis for contemporary female distress. "Feminism, having promised her a stronger sense of her own identity, has given her little more than an identity *crisis,*" the best-selling advice manual *Being a Woman* asserts. The authors of the era's self-help classic *Smart Women/Foolish Choices* proclaim that women's distress was "an unfortunate consequence of feminism," because "it created a myth among women that the apex of self-realization could be achieved only through autonomy, independence, and career."

In the Reagan and Bush years, government officials have needed no prompting to endorse this thesis. Reagan spokeswoman Faith Whittlesey declared feminism a "straitjacket" for women, in the White House's only policy speech on the status of the American female population—entitled "Radical Feminism in Retreat." Law enforcement officers and judges, too, have pointed a damning finger at feminism, claiming that they can chart a path from rising female independence to rising female pathology. As a California sheriff explained it to the press, "Women are enjoying a lot more freedom now, and as a result, they are committing more crimes." The U.S. Attorney General's Commission on Pornography even proposed that women's professional advancement might be responsible for rising rape rates. With more women in college and at work now, the commission members reasoned in their report, women just have more opportunities to be raped.

Some academics have signed on to the consensus, too—and they are the "experts" who have enjoyed the highest profiles on the media circuit. On network news and talk shows, they have advised millions of women that feminism has condemned them to "a lesser life." Legal scholars have railed against "the equality trap." Sociologists have claimed that "feminist-inspired" legislative reforms have stripped women of special "protections." Economists have argued that well-paid working women have created "a less stable American family." And demographers, with greatest fanfare, have legitimated the prevailing wisdom with so-called neutral data on sex ratios and fertility trends; they say they actually have the numbers to prove that equality doesn't mix with marriage and motherhood.

Finally, some "liberated" women themselves have joined the lamentations. In confessional accounts, works that invariably receive a hearty greeting from the publishing industry, "recovering Superwomen" tell all. In *The Cost of Loving: Women and the New Fear of Intimacy,* Megan Marshall, a Harvard-pedigreed writer, asserts that the feminist "Myth of Independence" has turned her generation into unloved and unhappy fast-trackers, "dehumanized" by careers and "uncertain of their gender identity." Other diaries of mad Superwomen charge that "the hard-core feminist viewpoint," as one of them puts it, has relegated educated executive achievers to solitary nights of frozen dinners and closet drinking. The triumph of equality, they report, has merely given women hives, stomach cramps, eye-twitching disorders, even comas.

But what "equality" are all these authorities talking about?

If American women are so equal, why do they represent two-thirds of all poor adults? Why are more than 80 percent of full-time working women making less than $20,000 a year, nearly double the male rate? Why are they still far more likely than men to live in poor housing and receive no health insurance, and twice as likely to draw no pension? Why does the average working woman's salary still lag as far behind the average man's as it did twenty years ago? Why does the average female college graduate today earn less than a man with no more than a high school diploma (just as she did in the '50s)—and why does the average female high school graduate today earn less than a male high school dropout? Why do American women, in fact, face the worst gender-based pay gap in the developed world?

If women have "made it," then why are nearly 80 percent of working women still stuck in traditional "female" jobs—as secretaries, administrative "support" workers and salesclerks? And, conversely, why are they less than 8 percent of all federal and state judges, less than 6 percent of all law partners, and less than one half of 1 percent of top corporate managers? Why are there only three female state governors, two female U.S. senators, and two Fortune 500 chief executives? Why are only nineteen of the four thousand corporate officers and directors women—and why do more than half the boards of Fortune companies still lack even one female member?

If women "have it all," then why don't they have the most basic requirements to achieve equality in the work force? Unlike virtually all other industrialized nations, the U.S. government still has no family-leave and child care programs—and more than 99 percent of American private employers don't offer child care either. Though business leaders say they are aware of and deplore sex discrimination, corporate America has yet to make an honest effort toward eradicating it. In a 1990 national poll of chief executives at Fortune 1000 companies, more than 80 percent acknowledged that discrimination impedes female employees' progress—yet, less than 1 percent of these same companies regarded *remedying* sex discrimination as a goal that their personnel departments should pursue. In fact, when the companies' human resource officers were asked to rate their department's priorities, women's advancement ranked last.

If women are so "free," why are their reproductive freedoms in greater jeopardy today than a decade earlier? Why do women who want to postpone childbearing now have fewer options than ten years ago? The availability of different forms of contraception has declined, research for new birth control has virtually halted, new laws restricting abortion—or even *information* about abortion—for young and poor women have been passed, and the U.S. Supreme Court has shown little ardor in defending the right it granted in 1973.

Nor is women's struggle for equal education over; as a 1989 study found, three-fourths of all high schools still violate the federal law banning sex discrimination in education. In colleges, undergraduate women receive only 70 percent of the aid undergraduate men get in grants and work-study jobs—and women's sports programs receive a pittance compared with men's. A review of state equal-education laws in the late '80s found that only thirteen states had adopted the minimum provisions required by the federal Title IX law—and only seven states had anti-discrimination regulations that covered all education levels.

Nor do women enjoy equality in their own homes, where they still shoulder 70 percent of the household duties—and the only major change in the last fifteen years is that now middle-class men *think* they do more around the house. (In fact, a national poll finds the ranks of women saying their husbands share equally in child care shrunk to 31 percent in 1987 from 40 percent three years earlier.) Furthermore, in thirty states, it is still generally legal for husbands to rape their wives; and only ten states have laws mandating arrest for domestic violence—even though battering was the leading cause of injury of women in the late '80s. Women who have no other option but to flee find that isn't much of an alternative either. Federal funding for battered women's shelters has been withheld and one third of the 1 million battered women who seek emergency shelter each year can find none. Blows from men contributed far more to the rising numbers of "bag ladies" than the ill effects of feminism. In the '80s, almost half of all homeless women (the fastest growing segment of the homeless) were refugees of domestic violence.

The word may be that women have been "liberated," but women themselves seem to feel otherwise. Repeatedly in national surveys, majorities of women say they are still far from equality. Nearly 70 percent of women polled by the *New York Times* in 1989 said the movement for women's rights had only just begun. Most women in the 1990 Virginia Slims opinion poll agreed with the statement that conditions for their sex in American society had improved "a little, not a lot." In poll after poll in the decade, overwhelming majorities of women said they needed equal pay and equal job opportunities, they needed an Equal Rights Amendment, they needed the right to an abortion without government interference, they needed a federal law guaranteeing maternity leave, they needed decent child care services. They have none of these. So how exactly have we "won" the war for women's rights?

Seen against this background, the much ballyhooed claim that feminism is responsible for making women miserable becomes absurd—and irrelevant. The afflictions ascribed to feminism are all myths. From "the man shortage" to "the infertility epidemic" to "female burnout" to "toxic day care," these so-called female crises have had their origins not in the actual conditions of women's lives but rather in a closed system that starts and ends in the media, popular culture, and advertising—an endless feedback loop that perpetuates and exaggerates its own false images of womanhood.

Women themselves don't single out the women's movement as the source of their misery. To the contrary, in national surveys 75 to 95 percent of women credit the feminist campaign with *improving* their lives, and a similar proportion say that the women's movement should keep pushing for change. Less than 8 percent think the women's movement might have actually made their lot worse.

* * *

What actually is troubling the American female population, then? If the many ponderers of the Woman Question really wanted to know, they might have asked their subjects. In public opinion surveys, women consistently rank their own *inequality,* at work and at home, among their most urgent concerns. Over and over, women complain to pollsters about a lack of economic, not marital, opportunities; they protest that working men, not working women, fail to spend time in the nursery and the kitchen. The Roper Organization's survey analysts find that men's opposition to equality is "a major cause of resentment and stress" and "a major irritant for most women today." It is justice for their gender, not wedding rings and bassinets, that women believe to be in desperately short supply. When the *New York Times* polled women in 1989 about "the most important problem facing women today," job discrimination was the overwhelming winner; none of the crises the media and popular culture had so assiduously promoted even made the charts. In the 1990 Virginia Slims poll, women were most upset by their lack of money, followed by the refusal of their men to shoulder child care and domestic duties. By contrast, when the women were asked where the quest for a husband or the desire to hold a "less pressured" job or to stay at home ranked on their list of concerns, they placed them at the bottom.

As the last decade ran its course, women's unhappiness with inequality only mounted. In national polls, the ranks of women protesting discriminatory treatment in business, political, and personal life climbed sharply. The proportion of women complaining of unequal employment opportunities jumped more than ten points from the '70s, and the number of women complaining of unequal barriers to job advancement climbed even higher. By the end of the decade, 80 percent to 95 percent of women said they suffered from job discrimination and unequal pay. Sex discrimination charges filed with the Equal Employment Opportunity Commission rose nearly 25 percent in the Reagan years, and charges of general harassment directed at working women climbed 208 percent. In the decade, complaints of sexual harassment jumped 70 percent. At home, a much increased proportion of women complained to pollsters of male mistreatment, unequal relationships, and male efforts to, in the words of the Virginia Slims poll, "keep women down." The share of women in the Roper surveys who agreed that men were "basically kind, gentle, and thoughtful" fell from almost 70 percent in 1970 to 50 percent by 1990. And outside their homes, women felt more threatened, too: in the 1990 Virginia Slims poll, 72 percent of women said they felt "more afraid and uneasy on the streets today" than they did a few years ago. Lest this be attributed only to a general rise in criminal activity, by contrast only 49 percent of men felt this way.

While the women's movement has certainly made women more cognizant of their own inequality, the rising chorus of female protest shouldn't be written off as feminist-induced "oversensitivity." The monitors that serve to track slippage in women's status have been working overtime since the early '80s. Government and private surveys are showing that women's already vast representation in the lowliest occupations is rising, their tiny presence in higher-paying trade and craft jobs stalled or backsliding, their minuscule representation in upper management posts stagnant or falling, and their pay dropping in the very occupations where they have made the most "progress." The status of women lowest on the income ladder has plunged most perilously; government budget cuts in the first four years of the Reagan administration alone pushed nearly 2 million female-headed families and nearly 5 million women below the poverty line. And the prime target of government rollbacks has been one sex only: one-third of the Reagan budget cuts, for example, came out of programs that predominantly serve women—even more extraordinary when one considers that all these programs combined represent only 10 percent of the federal budget.

The alarms aren't just going off in the work force. In national politics, the already small numbers of women in both elective posts and political appointments fell during the '80s. In private life, the average amount that a divorced man paid in child support fell by about 25 percent from the late '70s to the mid-'80s (to a mere $140 a month). Domestic-violence shelters recorded a more than 100 percent increase in the numbers of women taking refuge in their quarters between 1983 and 1987. And government records chronicled a spectacular rise in sexual violence against women. Reported rapes more than doubled from the early '70s—at nearly twice the rate of all other violent crimes and four times the overall crime rate in the United States. While the homicide rate declined, sex-related murders rose 160 percent between 1976 and 1984. And these murders weren't simply the random, impersonal byproduct of a violent society; at least one-third of the women were killed by their husbands or boyfriends, and the majority of that group were murdered just after declaring their independence in the most intimate manner—by filing for divorce and leaving home.

By the end of the decade, women were starting to tell pollsters that they feared their sex's social status was once again beginning to slip. They believed they were facing an "erosion of respect," as the 1990 Virginia Slims poll summed up the sentiment. After years in which an increasing percentage of women had said their status had improved from a decade earlier, the proportion suddenly shrunk by 5 percent in the last half of the '80s, the Roper Organization reported. And it fell most sharply among women in their thirties—the age group most targeted by the media and advertisers—dropping about ten percentage points between 1985 and 1990.

Some women began to piece the picture together. In the 1989 *New York Times* poll, more than half of black women and one-fourth of white women put it into words. They told pollsters they believed men were now trying to retract the gains women had made in the last twenty years. "I wanted more autonomy," was how one woman, a thirty-seven-year-old nurse, put it. And her estranged husband "wanted to take it away."

The truth is that the last decade has seen a powerful counter-assault on women's rights, a backlash, an attempt to retract the handful of small and hard-won victories that the feminist movement did manage to win for women. This counterassault is largely insidious: in a kind of pop-culture version of the Big Lie, it stands the truth boldly on its head and proclaims that the very steps that have elevated women's position have actually led to their downfall.

The backlash is at once sophisticated and banal,

deceptively "progressive" and proudly backward. It deploys both the "new" findings of "scientific research" and the dime-store moralism of yesteryear; it turns into media sound bites both the glib pronouncements of pop-psych trend-watchers and the frenzied rhetoric of New Right preachers. The backlash has succeeded in framing virtually the whole issue of women's rights in its own language. Just as Reaganism shifted political discourse far to the right and demonized liberalism, so the backlash convinced the public that women's "liberation" was the true contemporary American scourge—the source of an endless laundry list of personal, social, and economic problems.

But what has made women unhappy in the last decade is not their "equality"—which they don't yet have—but the rising pressure to halt, and even reverse, women's quest for that equality. The "man shortage" and the "infertility epidemic" are not the price of liberation; in fact, they do not even exist. But these chimeras are the chisels of a society-wide backlash. They are part of a relentless whittling-down process—much of it amounting to outright propaganda—that has served to stir women's private anxieties and break their political wills. Identifying feminism as women's enemy only furthers the ends of a backlash against women's equality, simultaneously deflecting attention from the backlash's central role and recruiting women to attack their own cause.

Some social observers may well ask whether the current pressures on women actually constitute a backlash—or just a continuation of American society's long-standing resistance to women's rights. Certainly hostility to female independence has always been with us. But if fear and loathing of feminism is a sort of perpetual viral condition in our culture, it is not always in an acute stage; its symptoms subside and resurface periodically. And it is these episodes of resurgence, such as the one we face now, that can accurately be termed "backlashes" to women's advancement. If we trace these occurrences in American history, we find such flare-ups are hardly random; they have always been triggered by the perception—accurate or not—that women are making great strides. These outbreaks are backlashes because they have always arisen in reaction to women's "progress," caused not simply by a bedrock of mi-

sogyny but by the specific efforts of contemporary women to improve their status, efforts that have been interpreted time and again by men—especially men grappling with real threats to their economic and social well-being on other fronts—as spelling their own masculine doom.

The most recent round of backlash first surfaced in the late '70s on the fringes, among the evangelical right. By the early '80s, the fundamentalist ideology had shouldered its way into the White House. By the mid-'80s, as resistance to women's rights acquired political and social acceptability, it passed into the popular culture. And in every case, the timing coincided with signs that women were believed to be on the verge of breakthrough.

Just when women's quest for equal rights seemed closest to achieving its objectives, the backlash struck it down. Just when a "gender gap" at the voting booth surfaced in 1980, and women in politics began to talk of capitalizing on it, the Republican party elevated Ronald Reagan and both political parties began to shunt women's rights off their platforms. Just when support for feminism and the Equal Rights Amendment reached a record high in 1981, the amendment was defeated the following year. Just when women were starting to mobilize against battering and sexual assaults, the federal government stalled funding for battered-women's programs, defeated bills to fund shelters, and shut down its Office of Domestic Violence—only two years after opening it in 1979. Just when record numbers of younger women were supporting feminist goals in the mid-'80s (more of them, in fact, than older women) and a majority of all women were calling themselves feminists, the media declared the advent of a younger "postfeminist generation" that supposedly reviled the women's movement. Just when women racked up their largest percentage ever supporting the right to abortion, the U.S. Supreme Court moved toward reconsidering it.

In other words, the antifeminist backlash has been set off not by women's achievement of full equality but by the increased possibility that they might win it. It is a preemptive strike that stops women long before they reach the finish line. "A backlash may be an indication that women really have had an effect," feminist psychiatrist Dr. Jean Baker Miller has written, "but backlashes occur when advances have been small, before changes are sufficient to help many people. . . . It is almost as if the leaders of backlashes use the fear of change as a threat before major change has occurred." In the last decade, some women did make substantial advances before the backlash hit, but millions of others were left behind, stranded. Some women now enjoy the right to legal abortion—but not the 44 million women, from the indigent to the military work force, who depend on the federal government for their medical care. Some women can now walk into high-paying professional careers—but not the more than 19 million still in the typing pools or behind the department store sales counters. (Contrary to popular myth about the "have-it-all" baby-boom women, the largest percentage of women in this generation remain typists and clerks.)

As the backlash has gathered force, it has cut off the few from the many—and the few women who have advanced seek to prove, as a social survival tactic, that they aren't so interested in advancement after all. Some of them parade their defection from the women's movement, while their working-class peers founder and cling to the splintered remains of the feminist cause. While a very few affluent and celebrity women who are showcased in news articles boast about having "found my niche as Mrs. Andy Mill" and going home to "bake bread," the many working-class women appeal for their economic rights—flocking to unions in record numbers, striking on their own for pay equity and establishing their own fledgling groups for working women's rights. In 1986, while 41 percent of upper-income women were claiming in the Gallup poll that they were not feminists, only 26 percent of low-income women were making the same claim.

* * *

Women's advances and retreats are generally described in military terms: battles won, battles lost, points and territory gained and surrendered. The metaphor of combat is not without its merits in this context and, clearly, the same sort of martial accounting and vocabulary is already surfacing here. But by imagining the conflict as two battalions neatly arrayed on either side of the line, we miss the entangled nature, the locked embrace, of a "war" between women and the male culture they inhabit.

We miss the reactive nature of a backlash, which, by definition, can exist only in response to another force.

In times when feminism is at a low ebb, women assume the reactive role—privately and most often covertly struggling to assert themselves against the dominant cultural tide. But when feminism itself becomes the tide, the opposition doesn't simply go along with the reversal: it digs in its heels, brandishes its fists, builds walls and dams. And its resistance creates countercurrents and treacherous undertows.

The force and furor of the backlash churn beneath the surface, largely invisible to the public eye. On occasion in the last decade, they have burst into view. We have seen New Right politicians condemn women's independence, antiabortion protesters firebomb women's clinics, fundamentalist preachers damn feminists as "whores" and "witches." Other signs of the backlash's wrath, by their sheer brutality, can push their way into public consciousness for a time—the sharp increase in rape, for example, or the rise in pornography that depicts extreme violence against women.

More subtle indicators in popular culture may receive momentary, and often bemused, media notice, then quickly slip from social awareness: A report, for instance, that the image of women on prime-time TV shows has suddenly degenerated. A survey of mystery fiction finding the numbers of female characters tortured and mutilated mysteriously multiplying. The puzzling news that, as one commentator put it, "So many hit songs have the B-word [bitch] to refer to women that some rap music seems to be veering toward rape music." The ascendancy of virulently misogynist comics like Andrew Dice Clay—who called women "pigs" and "sluts" and strutted in films in which women were beaten, tortured, and blown up—or radio hosts like Rush Limbaugh, whose broadsides against "femi-Nazi" feminists made his syndicated program the most popular radio talk show in the nation. Or word that in 1987, the American Women in Radio & Television couldn't award its annual prize for ads that feature women positively: it could find no ad that qualified.

These phenomena are all related, but that doesn't mean they are somehow coordinated. The backlash is not a conspiracy, with a council dispatching agents from some central control room, nor are the people who serve its ends often aware of their role; some even consider themselves feminists. For the most part, its workings are encoded and internalized, diffuse and chameleonic. Not all of the manifestations of the backlash are of equal weight or significance either; some are mere ephemera, generated by a culture machine that is always scrounging for a "fresh" angle. Taken as a whole, however, these codes and cajolings, these whispers and threats and myths, move overwhelmingly in one direction: they try to push women back into their "acceptable" roles—whether as Daddy's girl or fluttery romantic, active nester or passive love object.

Although the backlash is not an organized movement, that doesn't make it any less destructive. In fact, the lack of orchestration, the absence of a single string-puller, only makes it harder to see—and perhaps more effective. A backlash against women's rights succeeds to the degree that it appears *not* to be political, that it appears not to be a struggle at all. It is most powerful when it goes private, when it lodges inside a woman's mind and turns her vision inward, until she imagines the pressure is all in her head, until she begins to enforce the backlash, too—on herself.

In the last decade, the backlash has moved through the culture's secret chambers, traveling through passageways of flattery and fear. Along the way, it has adopted disguises: a mask of mild derision or the painted face of deep "concern." Its lips profess pity for any woman who won't fit the mold, while it tries to clamp the mold around her ears. It pursues a divide-and-conquer strategy: single versus married women, working women versus homemakers, middle- versus working-class. It manipulates a system of rewards and punishments, elevating women who follow its rules, isolating those who don't. The backlash remarkets old myths about women as new facts and ignores all appeals to reason. Cornered, it denies its own existence, points an accusatory finger at feminism, and burrows deeper underground.

Backlash happens to be the title of a 1947 Hollywood movie in which a man frames his wife for a murder he's committed. The backlash against women's rights works in much the same way: its rhetoric charges feminists with all the crimes it perpetrates.

The backlash line blames the women's movement for the "feminization of poverty"—while the backlash's own instigators in Washington pushed through the budget cuts that helped impoverish millions of women, fought pay equity proposals, and undermined equal opportunity laws. The backlash line claims the women's movement cares nothing for children's rights—while its own representatives in the capital and state legislatures have blocked one bill after another to improve child care, slashed billions of dollars in federal aid for children, and relaxed state licensing standards for day care centers. The backlash line accuses the women's movement of creating a generation of unhappy single and childless women—but its purveyors in the media are the ones guilty of making single and childless women feel like circus freaks.

To blame feminism for women's "lesser life" is to miss entirely the point of feminism, which is to win women a wider range of experience. Feminism remains a pretty simple concept, despite repeated—and enormously effective—efforts to dress it up in greasepaint and turn its proponents into gargoyles. As Rebecca West wrote sardonically in 1913, "I myself have never been able to find out precisely what feminism is: I only know that people call me a feminist whenever I express sentiments that differentiate me from a doormat."

The meaning of the word "feminist" has not really changed since it first appeared in a book review in the *Athenaeum* of April 27, 1895, describing a woman who "has in her the capacity of fighting her way back to independence." It is the basic proposition that, as Nora put it in Ibsen's *A Doll's House* a century ago, "Before everything else I'm a human being." It is the simply worded sign hoisted by a little girl in the 1970 Women's Strike for Equality: I AM NOT A BARBIE DOLL. Feminism asks the world to recognize at long last that women aren't decorative ornaments, worthy vessels, members of a "special-interest group." They are half (in fact, now more than half) of the national population, and just as deserving of rights and opportunities, just as capable of participating in the world's events, as the other half. Feminism's agenda is basic: It asks that women not be forced to "choose" between public justice and private happiness. It asks that women be free to define themselves—instead of having their identity defined for them, time and again, by their culture and their men.

The fact that these are still such incendiary notions should tell us that American women have a way to go before they enter the promised land of equality.

NOTES

418   Women's fight for . . . : Nancy Gibbs, "The Dreams of Youth," *Time,* Special Issue: "Women: The Road Ahead," Fall 1990, p. 12.

418   Women have "so much" . . . : Eleanor Smeal, *Why and How Women Will Elect the Next President* (New York: Harper & Row, 1984), p. 56.

418   The *New York Times* reports . . . : Georgia Dullea, "Women Reconsider Childbearing Over 30," *New York Times,* Feb. 25, 1982, p. C1.

418   *Newsweek* says: Unwed women . . . : Eloise Salholz, "The Marriage Crunch," *Newsweek,* June 2, 1986, p. 55.

418   The health advice manuals . . . : See, for example, Dr. Herbert J. Freudenberger and Gail North, *Women's Burnout* (New York: Viking Penguin, 1985); Marjorie Hansen Shaevitz, *The Superwoman Syndrome* (New York: Warner Books, 1984); Harriet Braiker, *The Type E Woman* (New York: Dodd, Mead, 1986); Donald Morse and M. Lawrence Furst, *Women Under Stress* (New York: Van Nostrand Reinhold Co., 1982); Georgia Witkin-Lanoil, *The Female Stress Syndrome* (New York: Newmarket Press, 1984).

418   The psychology books . . . : Dr. Stephen and Susan Price, *No More Lonely Nights: Overcoming the Hidden Fears That Keep You from Getting Married* (New York: G. P. Putnam's Sons, 1988), p. 19.

418   Even founding feminist Betty Friedan . . . : Betty Friedan, *The Second Stage* (New York: Summit Books, 1981), p. 9.

418   "In dispensing its spoils . . .": Mona Charen, "The Feminist Mistake," *National Review,* March 23, 1984, p. 24.

418   "Our generation was the human sacrifice . . .": Claudia Wallis, "Women Face the '90s," *Time,* Dec. 4, 1989, p. 82.

418   In *Newsweek,* writer . . . : Kay Ebeling, "The Failure of Feminism," *Newsweek,* Nov. 19, 1990, p. 9.

418   Even the beauty magazines . . . : Marilyn Webb, "His Fault Divorce," *Harper's Bazaar,* Aug. 1988, p. 156.

418   In the last decade . . . : Mary Anne Dolan, "When Feminism Failed," *The New York Times Magazine,* June 26, 1988, p. 21; Erica Jong, "The Awful Truth About Women's Liberation," *Vanity Fair,* April 1986, p. 92.

418   The "Today" show . . . : Jane Birnbaum, "The Dark Side of Women's Liberation," *Los Angeles Herald Examiner,* May 24, 1986.

418   A guest columnist . . . : Robert J. Hooper, "Slasher Movies Owe Success to Abortion" (originally printed in the *Baltimore Sun*), *Minneapolis Star Tribune,* Feb. 1, 1990, p. 17A.

419   In popular novels . . . : Gail Parent, *A Sign of the Eighties* (New York: G. P. Putnam's Sons, 1987); Stephen King, *Misery* (New York: Viking, 1987).

419   We "blew it by . . .": Freda Bright, *Singular Women* (New York: Bantam Books, 1988), p. 12.

419   Even Erica Jong's . . . : Erica Jong, *Any Woman's Blues* (New York: Harper & Row, 1989) pp. 2–3. A new generation of young "post-feminist" female writers, such as Mary Gaitskill and Susan Minot, also produced a bumper crop of grim-faced unwed heroines. These passive and masochistic "girls" wandered the city zombie-like; they came alive and took action only in seeking out male abuse. For a good analysis of this genre, see James Wolcott, "The Good-Bad Girls," *Vanity Fair,* Dec. 1988, p. 43.

419   "Feminism, having promised her . . .": Dr. Toni Grant, *Being a Woman: Fulfilling Your Femininity and Finding Love* (New York: Random House, 1988), p. 25.

419   The authors of . . . : Dr. Connell Cowan and Dr. Melvyn Kinder, *Smart Women/Foolish Choices* (New York: New American Library, 1985) p. 16.

419   Reagan spokeswoman Faith . . . : Faith Whittlesey, "Radical Feminism in Retreat," Dec. 8, 1984, speech at the Center for the Study of the Presidency, 15th Annual Leadership Conference, St. Louis, Mo., p. 7.

419   As a California sheriff . . . : Don Martinez, "More Women Ending Up in Prisons," *San Francisco Examiner,* Sept. 4, 1990, p. A1. Judges have blamed women's increasing economic independence for increasing *male* crime, too: "What do we do [about crowded prisons]?" Texas District Judge John McKellips asked, rhetorically. "Well, we can start in our homes. Mothers can stay home and raise their children during the formative years." See "For the Record," *Ms.,* May 1988, p. 69.

419   The U.S. Attorney General's . . . : Attorney General's Commission on Pornography, Final Report, July 1986, p. 144. The commissioner's report goes on to undermine its own logic, conceding that since women raped by acquaintances are the least likely to report the crime, it might be difficult to attribute a rise in reported rape rates to them, after all.

419   On network news . . . : Sylvia Ann Hewlett, *A Lesser Life: The Myth of Women's Liberation in America* (New York: William Morrow, 1986).

419   Legal scholars have . . . : Mary Ann Mason, *The Equality Trap* (New York: Simon and Schuster, 1988).

419   Economists have argued . . . : James P. Smith and Michael Ward, "Women in the Labor Market and in the Family," *The Journal of Economic Perspectives,* Winter 1989, 3, no. 1: 9–23.

419   In *The Cost of Loving* . . . : Megan Marshall, *The Cost of Loving: Women and the New Fear of Intimacy* (New York: G. P. Putnam's Sons, 1984), p. 218.

420   Other diaries of . . . : Hilary Cosell, *Woman on a Seesaw: The Ups and Downs of Making It* (New York: G. P. Putnam's Sons, 1985); Deborah Fallows, *A Mother's Work* (Boston: Houghton Mifflin, 1985); Carol Orsborn, *Enough is Enough* (New York: Pocket Books, 1986); Susan Bakos, *This Wasn't Supposed to Happen* (New York: Continuum, 1985). Even when the women aren't really renouncing their liberation, their publishers promote the texts as if they were. Mary Kay Blakely's *Wake Me When It's Over* (New York: Random House, 1989), an account of the author's diabetes-induced coma, is billed on the dust jacket as "a chilling memoir in which a working supermom exceeds her limit and discovers the

thin line between sanity and lunacy and between life and death."

420   If American women are so equal . . . : "Money, Income and Poverty Status in the U.S.," 1989, Current Population Reports, U.S. Bureau of the Census, Department of Commerce, Series P-60, #168.

420   Why are nearly 75 percent . . . : Margaret W. Newton, "Women and Pension Coverage," *The American Woman 1988–89: A Status Report,* ed. by Sara E. Rix (New York: W. W. Norton & Co., 1989) p. 268.

420   Why are they still . . . : Cushing N. Dolbeare and Anne J. Stone, "Women and Affordable Housing," *The American Woman 1990–91: A Status Report,* ed. by Sara E. Rix (W. W. Norton & Co., 1990) p. 106; Newton, "Pension Coverage," p. 268; "1990 Profile," 9 to 5/National Association of Working Women; Salaried and Professional Women's Commission Report, 1989, p. 2.

420   Why does the average . . . : "Briefing Paper on the Wage Gap," National Committee on Pay Equity, p. 3; "Average Earnings of Year-Round, Full-Time Workers by Sex and Educational Attainment," 1987, U.S. Bureau of the Census, February 1989, cited in *The American Woman 1990–91,* p. 392.

420   If women have "made it," then . . . : Susanna Downie, "Decade of Achievement, 1977–1987," The National Women's Conference Center, May 1988, p. 35; statistics from 9 to 5/National Association of Working Women.

420   And, conversely . . . : Statistics from Women's Research & Education Institute, U.S. Bureau of the Census, U.S. Bureau of Labor Statistics, Catalyst, Center for the American Woman and Politics. See also *The American Woman 1990–91,* p. 359; Deborah L. Rhode, "Perspectives on Professional Women," *Stanford Law Review,* 40, no. 5 (May 1988): 1178–79; Anne Jardim and Margaret Hennig, "The Last Barrier," *Working Woman,* Nov. 1990, p. 130; Jaclyn Fierman, "Why Women Still Don't Hit the Top," *Fortune,* July 30, 1990, p. 40.

420   Unlike virtually . . . : "1990 Profile," 9 to 5/National Association of Working Women; Bureau of Labor Statistics, 1987 survey of nation's employers. See also "Who Gives and Who Gets," *American Demographics,* May 1988, p. 16; "Children and Families: Public Policies and Outcomes, A Fact Sheet of International Comparisons," U.S. House of Representatives, Select Committee on Children, Youth and Families.

420   In a 1990 national poll . . . : "Women in Corporate Management," national poll of Fortune 1000 companies by Catalyst, 1990.

420   Why do women who want . . . : Data from Alan Guttmacher Institute.

420   Nor is women's struggle for equal education . . . : *The American Woman 1990–91,* p. 63; "Feminization of Power Campaign Extends to the Campus," Eleanor Smeal Report, 6, no. 1, Aug. 31, 1988; Project on Equal Education Rights, National Organization for Women's Legal Defense and Education Fund, 1987.

420   Nor do women . . . : Rhode, "Professional Women," p. 1183; Mark Clements Research Inc.'s Annual Study of Women's Attitudes, 1987; Arlie Hochschild, *The Second Shift: Working Parents and the Revolution at Home* (New York: Viking, 1989), p. 227. In fact, Hochschild's twelve-year survey, from 1976 to 1988, found that the men who said they were helping tended to be the ones who did the least.

420   Furthermore, in three-fourths of the states . . . : Statistics from National Center on Women and Family Law, 1987; National Woman Abuse Prevention Project; Cynthia Diehm and Margo Ross, "Battered Women," *The American Woman 1988–89,* p. 292.

421   Federal funding . . . : "Unlocking the Door: An Action Program for Meeting the Housing Needs of Women," Women and Housing Task Force, 1988, National Low-Income Housing Coalition, pp. 6, 8.

421   In the '80s, almost half of all homeless . . . : Katha Pollitt, "Georgie Porgie Is a Bully," *Time,* Fall 1990, Special Issue, p. 24. A survey in New York City found as many as 40 percent of all homeless people are battered women: "Understanding Domestic Violence Fact Sheets," National Woman Abuse Prevention Project.

421   Nearly 70 percent . . . : E. J. Dionne, Jr., "Struggle for Work and Family Fueling Women's Movement," *New York Times,* Aug. 22, 1989, p. A1. The Yankelovich Clancy Shulman poll (Oct. 23–25, 1989, for *Time*/CNN) and the 1990 Virginia Slims Opinion Poll (The Roper Organization Inc., 1990) found similarly large majorities of women who said that they needed a strong women's movement to keep pushing for change.

421   Most women in the . . . : The 1990 Virginia Slims Opinion Poll, The Roper Organization, Inc., pp. 8, 18.

421   In poll after . . . : The Louis Harris poll, 1984, found 64 percent of women wanted the Equal Rights Amendment and 65 percent favored affirmative action. Similar results emerged from the national *Woman's Day* poll (Feb. 17, 1984) by *Woman's Day* and Wellesley College Center for Research on Women, which emphasized middle-American conventional women (80 percent were mothers and 30 percent were full-time homemakers). The *Woman's Day* poll found a majority of women, from all economic classes, seeking a wide range of women's rights. For instance, 68 percent of the women said they wanted the ERA, 79 percent supported a woman's right to choose an abortion, and 61 percent favored a federally subsidized national child-care program. Mark Clements Research Inc.'s Annual Study of Women's Attitudes found in 1987 that 87 percent of women wanted a federal law guaranteeing maternity leave and about 94 percent said that more child care should be available. (In addition, 86 percent wanted a federal law enforcing the payment of child support.) The Louis Harris Poll found 80 percent of women calling for the creation of more day-care centers. See *The Eleanor Smeal Report,* June 28, 1984, p. 3; Warren T. Brookes, "Day Care: Is It a Real Crisis or a War Over Political Turf?" *San Francisco Chronicle,* April 27, 1988, p. 6; Louis Harris, *Inside America* (New York: Vintage Books, 1987), p. 96.

421   To the contrary . . . : In the 1989 *Time*/CNN poll, 94 percent of women polled said the movement made them more independent; 82 percent said it is still improving women's lives. Only 8 percent said it may have made their lives worse. A 1986 *Newsweek* Gallup poll found that 56 percent of women identified themselves as "feminists," and only 4 percent described themselves as "anti-feminists."

421   In public opinion . . . : In the Annual Study of Women's Attitudes (1988, Mark Clements Research), when

women were asked, "What makes you angry?" they picked three items as their top concerns: poverty, crime, and their own inequality. In the 1989 *New York Times* Poll, when women were asked what was the most important problem facing women today, job inequality ranked first.

421   The Roper Organization's . . . : Bickley Townsend and Kathleen O'Neil, "American Women Get Mad," *American Demographics,* Aug. 1990, p. 26.

421   When the *New York Times* . . . : Dionne, "Struggle for Work and Family," p. A14.

421   In the 1990 . . . : 1990 Virginia Slims Opinion Poll, pp. 29–30, 32.

421   In national polls . . . : Data from Roper Organization and Louis Harris polls. The 1990 Roper survey found most women reporting that things had "gotten worse" in the home and that men were more eager "to keep women down": See 1990 Virginia Slims Opinion Poll, pp. 18, 21, 54. The Gallup Organization polls charted an 8 percent increase in job discrimination complaints from women between 1975 and 1982. Mark Clements Research's 1987 Women's Views Survey (commissioned by *Glamour* magazine) found that on the matter of women's inequality, "more women feel there is a problem today." Reports of wage discrimination, the survey noted, had jumped from 76 percent in 1982 to 85 percent in 1988. (See "How Women's Minds Have Changed in the Last Five Years," *Glamour,* Jan. 1987, p. 168.) The annual surveys by Mark Clements Research also find huge and increasing majorities of women complaining of unequal treatment in hiring, advancement, and opportunities in both corporate and political life. (In 1987, only 30 percent of women believed they got equal treatment with men when being considered for financial credit.) A *Time* 1989 poll found 94 percent of women complaining of unequal pay, 82 percent of job discrimination.

421   Sex discrimination charges . . . : Statistics from U.S. Equal Employment Opportunity Commission, "National Database: Charge Receipt Listing," 1982–88; "Sexual Harassment," 1981–89.

422   At home, a much increased . . . : Townsend and O'Neil, "American Women Get Mad," p. 28.

422   And outside their . . . : 1990 Virginia Slims Opinion Poll, p. 38.

422   Government and private surveys . . . : Economic trends from U.S. Bureau of Labor Statistics, U.S. Equal Employment Opportunity Commission, Office of Federal Contract Compliance, National Committee on Pay Equity, National Commission on Working Women. . .

422   The status of women . . . : In the first six years of the Reagan administration, $50 billion was cut from these social programs, while at the same time defense spending rose $142 billion. See "Inequality of Sacrifice: The Impact of the Reagan Budget on Women," Coalition on Women and the Budget, Washington, D.C., 1986, pp. 5, 7; Sara E. Rix and Anne J. Stone, "Reductions and Realities: How the Federal Budget Affects Women," Women's Research and Education Institute, Washington, D.C., 1983, pp. 4–5.

422   In national politics . . . : Data from Center for the American Woman and Politics, Eagleton Institute of Politics. See Chapter 9 on women in politics.

422   In private life, the average . . . : Philip Robins, "Why Are Child Support Award Amounts Declining?" June

1989, Institute for Research on Poverty Discussion Paper No. 885–89, pp. 6–7.

422   Domestic-violence shelters . . . : "Unlocking the Door," p. 8.

422   Reported rapes more than . . . : Statistics are from the U.S. Department of Justice's Bureau of Justice Statistics; the Sourcebook of Criminal Justice Statistics, 1984, p. 380; Uniform Crime Reports, FBI, "Crime in the United States," 1986; "Sexual Assault: An Overview," National Victims Resource Center, Nov. 1987, p. 1. While rape rates between 1960 and 1970 rose 95 percent, this increase—unlike that of the '80s—was part of a 126 percent increase in violent crime in that era. (Crime statisticians have widely rejected the argument that the increase in the '80s might simply be the result of an increasing tendency for women to report sexual assaults. The National Crime Survey found no significant change in the percentage of rapes reported to police in the periods between 1973–77 and 1978–82.) Scattered indicators suggest a sharp rise in the rate of rapes committed by young men, too. Between 1983 and 1987, rape arrests of boys under 18 years old rose 15 percent. In New York City between 1987 and 1989, according to data from the district attorney's office, rape arrests of boys under the age of 13 rose 200 percent. In Alaska, according to the state Division of Youth and Family Services, sexual abuse and assaults from young men increased ninefold in the course of the '80s, the fastest growing juvenile problem in the state. See Larry Campbell, "Sexually Abusive Juveniles," *Anchorage Daily News,* Jan. 9, 1981, p. 1.

422   They believed they were facing . . . : 1990 Virginia Slims Opinion Poll, p. 16.

422   In the 1989 *New York Times* . . . : Lisa Belkin, "Bars to Equality of Sexes Seen as Eroding, Slowly," *New York Times,* Aug. 20, 1989, p. 16.

423   Just when women . . . : "Inequality of Sacrifice," p. 23.

423   Just when record numbers . . . : A 1986 Gallup poll conducted for *Newsweek* found a majority of women described themselves as feminists and only 4 percent said they were "antifeminists." While large majorities of women throughout the '80s kept on favoring the full feminist agenda (from the ERA to legal abortion), the proportion of women who were willing publicly to call themselves feminists dropped off suddenly in the late '80s, after the mass media declared feminism the "F-word." By 1989, only one in three women were calling themselves feminists in the polls. Nonetheless, the pattern of younger women espousing the most pro-feminist sentiments continued throughout the decade. In the 1989 Yankelovich poll for *Time*/CNN, for example, 76 percent of women in their teens and 71 percent of women in their twenties said they believed feminists spoke for the average American woman, compared with 59 percent of women in their thirties. Asked the same question about the National Organization for Women, the gap appeared again: 83 percent of women in their teens and 72 percent of women in their twenties said NOW was in touch with the average woman, compared with 65 percent of women in their thirties. See Downie, "Decade of Achievement," p. 1; 1986 Gallup/*Newsweek* poll; 1989 Yankelovich/*Time*/CNN poll.

423   "A backlash may be an indication that . . .": Dr. Jean Baker Miller, *Toward a New Psychology of Women* (Boston: Beacon Press, 1976), pp. xv–xvi.

424 Some women now . . . : Kate Michelman, "20 Years Defending Choice, 1969–1988," National Abortion Rights Action League, p. 4.

424 Some women can now . . . : "Employment and Earnings," Current Population Survey, Table 22, Bureau of Labor Statistics, U.S. Department of Labor.

424 (Contrary to popular myth . . .): Cheryl Russell, *100 Predictions for the Baby Boom* (New York: Plenum Press, 1987), p. 64.

424 While a very few . . . : "A New Kind of Love Match," *Newsweek*, Sept. 4, 1989, p. 73; Barbara Hetzer, "Superwoman Goes Home," *Fortune*, Aug. 18, 1986, p. 20; "Facts on Working Women," Aug. 1989, Women's Bureau, U.S. Department of Labor, no. 89—2; and data from the Coalition of Labor Union Women and Amalgamated Clothing and Textile Workers Union. The surge of women joining unions in the late '80s was so great that it single-handedly halted the ten-year decline in union membership. Black women joined unions at the greatest rate. Women led strikes around the country, from the Yale University administrative staffs to the Daughters of Mother Jones in Virginia (who were instrumental in the Pittston coal labor battle) to the Delta Pride catfish plant processors in Mississippi (where women organized the largest strike by black workers ever in the state, lodging a protest against a plant that paid its mostly female employees poverty wages, punished them if they skinned less than 24,000 fish a day, and limited them to six timed bathroom breaks a week). See Tony Freemantle, "Weary Strikers Hold Out in Battle of Pay Principle," *Houston Chronicle*, Dec. 2, 1990, p. 1A; Peter T. Kilborn, "Labor Fight on a Catfish 'Plantation,'" *The News and Observer*, Dec. 16, 1990, p. J2.

424 In 1986, while . . . : 1986 Gallup Poll; Barbara Ehrenreich, "The Next Wave," *Ms.*, July/August 1987, p. 166; Sarah Harder, "Flourishing in the Mainstream: The U.S. Women's Movement Today," *The American Woman 1990–91*, p. 281. Also see 1989 Yankelovich Poll: 71 percent of black women said feminists have been helpful to women, compared with 61 percent of white women. A 1987 poll by the National Women's Conference Commission found that 65 percent of black women called themselves feminists, compared with 56 percent of white women.

424 Other signs of . . . : For increase in violent pornography, see, for example, April 1986 study in the Attorney General's Commission on Pornography, Final Report, pp. 1402–3.

424 More subtle indicators . . . : Sally Steenland, "Women Out of View: An Analysis of Female Characters on 1987–88 TV Programs," National Commission on Working Women, November 1987. Mystery fiction survey was conducted by Sisters In Crime and presented at the 1988 Mystery Writers of America conference; additional information comes from personal interview in May 1988 with the group's director, mystery writer Sara Paretsky. On popular music: Alice Kahn, "Macho—the Second Wave," *San Francisco Chronicle*, Sept. 16, 1990, Sunday Punch section, p. 2. On Andrew Dice Clay: Craig MacInnis, "Comedians Only a Mother Could Love," *Toronto Star*, May 20, 1990, p. C6; Valerie Scher, "Clay's Idea of a Punch Line Is a Belch After a Beer," *San Diego Union and Tribune*, Aug. 17, 1990, p. C1. On Rush Limbaugh: Dave Matheny, "Morning Rush Is a Gas," *San Francisco Examiner*, Jan. 2, 1991, p. C1. On American Women in Radio & TV: Betsy Sharkey, "The Invisible Woman," *Adweek*, July 6, 1987, p. 4.

425 The backlash line claims . . . : Data from Children's Defense Fund. See also Ellen Wojahm, "Who's Minding the Kids?" *Savvy*, Oct. 1987, p. 16; "Child Care: The Time is Now," Children's Defense Fund, 1987, pp. 8–10.

425 "I myself . . .": Rebecca West, *The Clarion*, Nov. 14, 1913, cited in Cheris Kramarae and Paula A. Treichler, *A Feminist Dictionary* (London: Pandora Press, 1985) p. 160.

425 The meaning of the word "feminist" . . . : *The Feminist Papers: From Adams to de Beauvoir,* ed. by Alice S. Rossi (New York: Bantam Books, 1973), p. xiii. For discussion of historical origins of term feminism, see Karen Offen, "Defining Feminism: A Comparative Historical Approach," in *Signs: Journal of Women in Culture and Society*, 1988, 14, no. 1, pp. 119–57.

425 I AM NOT A BARBIE DOLL . . . : Carol Hymowitz and Michaele Weissman, *A History of Women in America* (New York: Bantam Books, 1978), p. 341.   [1991]

 125

Bringing The Global Home

CHARLOTTE BUNCH

One of the most exciting world developments today is the emergence of feminism all over the globe. Women of almost every culture, color, and class are claiming feminism for themselves. Indigenous movements are developing that address the specific regional concerns of women's lives and that expand the definition of what feminism means and can do in the future.

This growth of feminism provides both the challenge and the opportunity for a truly global women's movement to emerge in the 1980s. But a global movement involves more than just the separate development of feminism in each region, as exciting and important as that is. Global feminism also requires that we learn from each other and develop a global perspective within each of our movements. It means expansion of our understandings of feminism and changes in our work, as we respond to the ideas and challenges of women with different perspectives. It means discovering what other perspectives and movements mean to our own local setting. Any struggle for change in the late-twentieth century must have a global consciousness since the world operates and controls our lives internationally already. The strength of feminism has been and still is in its decentralized grass-roots nature, but for that strength to be most effective, we must base our local and national actions on a world view that incorporates the global context of our lives. This is the challenge of bringing the global home.

A global feminist perspective on patriarchy worldwide also illustrates how issues are interconnected, not separate isolated phenomena competing for our attention. This involves connections among each aspect of women's oppression and of that subordination to the socioeconomic conditions of society, as well as between local problems and global realities.

To develop global feminism today is not a luxury—it requires going to the heart of the problems in our world and looking at nothing less than the threats to the very survival of the planet. We are standing on a precipice facing such possibilities as nuclear destruction, worldwide famine and depletion of our natural resources, industrial contamination, and death in many forms. These are the fruits of a world ruled by the patriarchal mode—of what I call the "dynamic of domination," in which profits and property have priority over people, and where fear and hatred of differences have prevented a celebration of and learning from our diversity.

Feminists are part of a world struggle that is taking place today over the direction that the future will take. Crucial choices are being made about the very possibilities for life in the twenty-first century—from macro-level decisions about control over resources and weapons to micro-level decisions about control over individual reproduction and sexuality. At this juncture in history, feminism is perhaps the most important force for change that can begin to reverse the dynamic of patriarchal domination by challenging and transforming the way in which humans look at ourselves in relation to each other and to the world. . . .

A GLOBAL VIEW OF FEMINISM

The excitement and urgency of issues of global feminism were brought home to me at a Workshop on Feminist Ideology and Structures sponsored by the Asian and Pacific Centre for Women and Development in Bangkok in 1979. Women from each

region presented what they were doing in relation to the themes of the UN Decade for Women. In doing this, we realized the importance of the international male-dominated media in influencing what we knew and thought about each other before we came to Bangkok.

We saw how the media has made the women's movement and feminism appear trivial, silly, selfish, naïve, and/or crazy in the industrialized countries while practically denying its existence in the Third World. Western feminists have been portrayed as concerned only with burning bras, having sex, hating men, and/or getting to be head of General Motors. Such stereotypes ignore the work of most feminists and distort even the few activities the media do report. So, for example, basic political points that women have tried to communicate—about what it means to love ourselves in a woman-hating society—get twisted into a focus on "hating" men. Or those demonstrations that did discard high-heeled shoes, makeup, or bras, as symbolic of male control over women's self-definition and mobility, have been stripped of their political content.

Thus, women who feel that their priorities are survival issues of food or housing are led to think that Western feminists are not concerned with these matters. Similarly, media attempts to portray all feminists as a privileged elite within each country seek to isolate us from other women. The real strength of feminism can be seen best in the fact that more and more women come to embrace it in spite of the overwhelming effort that has gone into distorting it and trying to keep women away.

By acknowledging the power of the media's distortion of feminism at the Bangkok workshop, we were able to see the importance of defining it clearly for ourselves. Our definition brought together the right of every woman to equity, dignity, and freedom of choice through the power to control her own life and the removal of all forms of inequalities and oppression in society. We saw feminism as a world view that has an impact on all aspects of life, and affirmed the broad context of the assertion that the "personal is political." This is to say that the individual aspects of oppression and change are not separate from the need for political and institutional change.

Through our discussion, we were able to agree on the use of this concept of feminism to describe women's struggles. While some had reservations about using the word "feminism," we chose not to allow media or government distortions to scare us away from it. As one Asian pointed out, if we shied away from the term, we would simply be attacked or ridiculed for other actions or words, since those who opposed us were against what we sought for women and the world and not really concerned with our language.

In Copenhagen at the 1980 NGO Forum, the conference newspaper came out with a quote-of-the-day from a Western feminist that read: "To talk feminism to a woman who has no water, no home, and no food is to talk nonsense." Many of us felt that the quote posed a crucial challenge to feminists. We passed out a leaflet, "What Is Feminism?," describing it as a perspective on the world that would address such issues, and we invited women to a special session on the topic. Over three hundred women from diverse regions gathered to debate what feminism really means to us and how that has been distorted by the media and even within our own movements.

The second challenge we saw in the quote was that if it were true and feminists did not speak to such issues, then we would indeed be irrelevant to many women. We therefore discussed the importance of a feminist approach to development—one that both addresses how to make home, food, and water available to all and extends beyond equating "development" with industrialization. Terms like "developing nations" are suspect and patronizing. While we need to look at the real material needs of all people from a feminist perspective, we can hardly call any countries "developed." For this reason, while I find all labels that generalize about diverse parts of the world problematic, I use "Western" or "industrialized" and "Third World," rather than "developing" and "developed."

Recently at a meeting in New York, I saw another example of confusion about the meaning of feminism. Two women who had just engaged in civil disobedience against nuclear weapons were discussing feminism as the motivating force behind their actions, when a man jumped up impatiently objecting, "But I thought this meeting was about disarmament, not feminism." It was the equivalent of "to talk feminism in the face of nuclear destruction is to talk nonsense." Such attitudes portray feminism as

a luxury of secondary concern and thus both dismiss female experience as unimportant and limit our politics. They fundamentally misconstrue feminism as about "women's issues" rather than as a political perspective on life.

Seeing feminism as a transformational view is crucial to a global perspective. But to adopt a global outlook does not mean, as some feminists fear and male politicos often demand, that we abandon working on the "women's issues" that we fought to put on the political agenda. Nor does it imply setting aside our analysis of sexual politics. Rather it requires that we take what we have learned about sexual politics and use feminist theory to expose the connections between the "women's issues" and other world questions. In this way, we demonstrate our point that all issues are women's issues and need feminist analysis. For example, we must show how a society that tacitly sanctions male violence against women and children, whether incest and battery at home, rape on the streets, or sexual harassment on the job, is bound to produce people who are militaristic and believe in their right to dominate others on the basis of other differences such as skin color or nationality. Or we can point out how the heterosexist assumption that every "good" woman wants to and eventually will be supported by a man fuels the economic policies that have produced the feminization of poverty worldwide. This refusal to accept a woman who lives without a man as fully human thus allows policy makers to propose such ideas as keeping welfare payments or even job opportunities for single mothers limited since they "contribute to the destruction of the family."

The examples are endless. The task is not one of changing our issues but of expanding the frameworks from which we understand our work. It means taking what we have learned in working on "women's issues" and relating that to other areas, demanding that these not be seen as competing but as enabling us to bring about more profound change. To use the illustration above, to seek to end militarism without also ending the dynamic of domination embedded in male violence at home would be futile. And so, too, the reverse: we will never fully end male violence against individual women unless we also stop celebrating the organized violence of war as manly and appropriate behavior.

MAKING CONNECTIONS

The interconnectedness of the economic and sexual exploitation of women with militarism and racism is well illustrated in the area of forced prostitution and female sexual slavery. It is impossible to work on one aspect of this issue without confronting the whole socioeconomic context of women's lives. For example, females in India who are forced into prostitution are often either sold by poverty-stricken families for whom a girl child is considered a liability, or they have sought to escape arranged marriages they find intolerable. In the United States, many girls led into forced prostitution are teenage runaways who were victims of sexual or physical abuse at home, and for whom there are no jobs, services, or safe places to live.

In parts of Southeast Asia, many women face the limited economic options of rural poverty; joining assembly lines that pay poorly, destroy eyesight, and often discard workers over thirty; or of entering the "entertainment industry." In Thailand and the Philippines, national economies dependent on prostitution resulted from U.S. military brothels during the Vietnam War. When that demand decreased, prostitution was channeled into sex tourism—the organized multimillion-dollar transnational business of systematically selling women's bodies as part of packaged tours, which feeds numerous middlemen and brings foreign capital into the country. In all these situations, the patriarchal beliefs that men have the right to women's bodies, and that "other" races or "lower" classes are subhuman, underlie the abuse women endure.

Feminists organizing against these practices must link their various aspects. Thus, for example, women have simultaneously protested against sex tourism and militarism, created refuges for individual victims who escape, and sought to help women develop skills in order to gain more control over their lives. Japanese businesses pioneered the development of sex tourism. Feminists in Japan pioneered the opposition to this traffic. They work with Southeast Asian women to expose and shame the Japanese government and the businesses involved in an effort to cut down on the trade from their end.

On the international level, it is clear that female sexual slavery, forced prostitution, and violence against women operate across national boundaries and are political and human rights abuses of great magnitude. Yet, the male-defined human rights community by-and-large refuses to see any but the most narrowly defined cases of slavery or "political" torture as their domain. We must ask what is it when a woman faces death at the hands of her family to save its honor because she was raped? What is it when two young lesbians commit suicide together rather than be forced into unwanted marriages? What is it when a woman trafficked out of her country does not try to escape because she knows she will be returned by the police and beaten or deported? An understanding of sexual politics reveals all these and many more situations to be political human-rights violations deserving asylum, refugee status, and the help that other political victims are granted. As limited as human rights are in our world, we must demand at least that basic recognition for such women, while we seek to expand concern for human rights generally.

In these areas as well as others, feminists are creating new interpretations and approaches—to human rights, to development, to community and family, to conflict resolution, and so on. From local to global interaction, we must create alternative visions of how we can live in the world based on women's experiences and needs in the here-and-now.

LEARNING FROM DIVERSITY

In sharing experiences and visions across national and cultural lines, feminists are inspired by what others are doing. But we are also confronted with the real differences among us. On the one hand, our diversity is our strength. It makes it possible for us to imagine more possibilities and to draw upon a wider range of women's experiences. On the other hand, differences can also divide us if we do not take seriously the variations on female oppression that women suffer according to race, class, ethnicity, religion, sexual preference, age, nationality, physical disability, and so on. These are not simply added onto the oppression of women by sex, but shape the forms by which we experience that subordination. Thus, we cannot simply add up the types of oppression that a woman suffers one-by-one as independent factors but must look at how they are interrelated.

If we take this approach, we should be more capable of breaking down the ways in which difference itself separates people. Patriarchal society is constructed on a model of domination by which each group is assigned a place in the hierarchy according to various differences, and then allocated power or privileges based on that position. In this way, difference becomes threatening because it involves winning or losing one's position/privileges. If we eliminated the assignment of power and privilege according to difference, we could perhaps begin to enjoy real choices of style and variations of culture as offering more creative possibilities in life.

The world has been torn apart by various male divisions and conflicts for thousands of years and we should not assume that women can overcome and solve in a short time what patriarchy has so intricately conceived. The oppressions, resentments, fears, and patterns of behavior that have developed due to racism, classism, nationalism, and sexism, are very deep. We cannot just wish them away with our desire for women to transcend differences. Above all, we do not overcome differences by denying them or downplaying their effects on us—especially when the one denying is in the position of privilege.

A white woman can only legitimately talk about overcoming differences of race if she struggles to understand racism both as it affects her personally and as she affects it politically. A heterosexual can get beyond the divisions of sexual preference only by learning about both the oppression of lesbians and by acknowledging the insights that come from that orientation. A U.S. American must understand the effects of colonialism before she can hope for unity with women beyond national boundaries. Too often the call to transcend differences has been a call to ignore them at the expense of the oppressed. This cannot be the route of global feminism. We can only hope to chart a path beyond male divisions by walking through them and taking seriously their detrimental effects on us as women. This examination of and effort to eliminate other aspects of oppression does not come before or after working on sexism—it is simultaneous.

A crucial part of this process is understanding that reality does not look the same from different people's perspectives. It is not surprising that one way that feminists have come to understand about differences has been through the love of a person from another culture or race. It takes persistence

and motivation—which love often engenders—to get beyond one's ethnocentric assumptions and really learn about other perspectives. In this process and while seeking to eliminate oppression, we also discover new possibilities and insights that come from the experience and survival of other peoples.

In considering what diversity means for a global movement, one of the most difficult areas for feminists is culture. In general, we affirm cultural diversity and the variety it brings to our lives. Yet, almost all existing cultures today are male-dominated. We know the horrors male powers have wrought over the centuries in imposing one cultural standard over another. Popular opposition to such imposition has often included affirmation of traditional cultures. Certainly none of our cultures can claim to have the answers to women's liberation since we are oppressed in all of them.

We must face the fact that in some instances male powers are justifying the continuation or advocating the adoption of practices oppressive to women by labeling them "cultural" and/or "resistance to Western influence." Feminists must refuse to accept *any* forms of domination of women—whether in the name of tradition or in the name of modernization. This is just the same as refusing to accept racial discrimination in the name of "culture," whether in the South of the USA or in South Africa. Feminists are seeking new models for society that allow for diversity while not accepting the domination of any group. For this, women in each culture must sort out what is best from their own culture and what is oppressive. Through our contact with each other, we can then challenge ethnocentric biases and move beyond the unconscious cultural assumptions inherent in our thinking.

In taking into account and challenging the various forms of domination in the world, we do not necessarily accept existing male theories about or solutions to them. We must always have a woman-identified approach—that is, one of seeking to identify with women's situations rather than accepting male definitions of reality. Such a process enables us to distinguish what is useful from male theories and to see where feminist approaches are being or need to be applied to issues such as race, class, and culture. Further, in a world so saturated with woman-hating, it is through woman-identification, which involves profoundly learning to love women and to listen for women's authentic perspectives, that we can make breakthroughs in these areas.

We confront a similar dilemma when examining nationalism. From a feminist perspective, I see nationalism as the ultimate expression of the patriarchal dynamic of domination—where groups battle for control over geographic territory, and justify violence and aggression in the name of national security. Therefore I prefer the term "global" to "international" because I see feminism as a movement among peoples beyond national boundaries and not among nation-states. Yet, nationalism has also symbolized the struggle of oppressed peoples against the control of other nations. And many attempts to go beyond nationalism have simply been supranational empire-building, such as the idea of turning Africans into "Frenchmen." Further, in the context of increasing global control over us all by transnational corporations, many see nationalism as a form of resistance. In seeking to be global, feminists must therefore find ways to transcend patriarchal nationalism without demanding sameness, and while still preserving means of identity and culture that are not based on domination.

THINK GLOBALLY, ACT LOCALLY

A major obstacle that feminists face in seeking to be global is our lack of control over the resources necessary for maintaining greater contact worldwide. It takes time and money as well as energy and commitment to overcome the problems of distance, language, and culture. Feminists have little control over existing institutions with global networks, such as the media, churches, universities, and the state, but sometimes we must utilize such networks even as we try to set up our own.

Since feminists have limited resources for global travel and communication, it is vital that we learn how to be global in consciousness while taking action locally. For this, we must resist the tendency to separate "international" work into a specialized category of political activity that is often viewed as inaccessible to most women. This tendency reflects a hierarchical mode in which the "world level" is viewed as above the "local level." For those whose work focuses primarily on the global aspects of issues, the challenge is not to lose touch with the local arena on which any effective movement is based.

For those whose work is focused locally, the challenge is to develop a global perspective that informs local work. For all of us, the central question is to understand how the issues of women all over the world are interrelated and to discern what that means specifically in each setting.

Global interaction is not something that we choose to do or not to do. It is something in which we are already participating. All we choose is whether to be aware of it or not, whether to try to understand it and how that affects our actions. For citizens of the U.S., we begin our global consciousness with awareness of the impact that our country's policies have on other people's daily lives. I learned in the antiwar movement that often the most useful thing that we can do for people elsewhere is to make changes in the U.S. and in how it exercises power in the world.

There are many well-known issues such as military aggression, foreign aid and trade policies, or the possibility of worldwide destruction through nuclear weapons or chemical contamination that we see as global. But there are numerous less obvious illustrations of global interrelatedness, from the present world economy where women are manipulated as an international cheap labor pool to the traffic in women's bodies for forced prostitution. Therefore, any attempt we make to deal with the needs of women in the U.S., such as employment, must examine the global context of the problem. In this instance, that means understanding how multinational corporations move their plants from country to country or state to state, exploiting female poverty and discouraging unionization by threatening to move again. We must use global strategies, such as that proposed by one group on the Texas-Mexico border advocating an international bill of rights for women workers as a way to organize together for basic standards for all. In a world where global forces affect us daily, it is neither possible nor conscionable to achieve a feminist utopia in one country alone. . . .

A MATTER OF PERSPECTIVE

Beyond techniques and information, the primary task remains one of attitude, approach, and perspective. The point is not that we necessarily change the focus of our work but that we make connections that help to bring its global aspects to consciousness—in our programs, our slogans, our publications, and our conversations with other women. It is when we try to make a hierarchy of issues, keeping them separate and denying the importance of some in order to address others, that we are all defeated.

To use a previous example, if I cannot develop an analysis and discuss openly the ways in which heterosexism supports the international feminization of poverty, without having some women's homophobia prevent them from utilizing this insight, or without having some lesbians fear that I have abandoned "their issue" by working more on global poverty, then work in both areas is diminished. I believe that the path to effective global feminist theory and action is not through denial of any issue or analysis but through listening, questioning, struggling, and seeking to make connections among them.

To work locally with a global perspective does require stretching feminism, not to abandon its insights but to shed its cultural biases, and thus to expand its capacity to reach all people. In this process, we risk what seems certain at home by taking it into the world and having it change through interaction with other realities and perceptions. It can be frightening. But if we have confidence in ourselves and in the feminist process, it can also be exciting. It can mean the growth of a more effective feminism with a greater ability to address the world and to bring change. If we fail to take these risks and ignore the global dimensions of our lives, we lose possibilities for individual growth and we doom feminism to a less effective role in the world struggle over the direction of the twenty-first century.

My visions of global feminism are grand, perhaps even grandiose. But the state of the world today demands that women become less modest and dream/plan/act/risk on a larger scale. At the same time, the realization of global visions can only be achieved through the everyday lives and action of women locally. It depends on women deciding to shape their own destiny, claiming their right to the world, and exercising their responsibility to make it in some way, large or small, a better place for all. As more women do this with a growing world perspective and sense of connection to others, we can say that feminism is meeting the challenge of bringing the global home.   [1987]

Women Organizing: Many Issues, Many Voices

The ideas of feminism have influenced countless women, changing our ideas about ourselves and expectations of our future. But ending women's subordination requires more than consciousness. It requires working together to challenge sexist practices and institutions and creating organizations that embody a vision of a more humane and just society. How do people move from a consciousness of injustice to political involvement? The essay by Rebecca Walker, a recent graduate of Yale University, describes the process by which she commits herself to working politically for women's freedom. Written immediately after the U.S. Senate confirmation hearings of Clarence Thomas, the Supreme Court Justice, after he had been accused of sexual harassment by Anita Hill, a former employee, Walker's essay echoes the outrage of many women at what they saw as a vivid enactment of women's political powerlessness.

The rebirth of feminism in the 1970s quickly spawned a women's health movement that educated women about their bodies, challenged sexist bias in health care institutions, and created feminist clinics that provided health care to women in a supportive and respectful environment. In her historical survey of the women's health movement, Helen Rodriguez-Trias describes the ways the movement broadened and deepened as it incorporated the concerns and perspectives of different groups of women. There have been some improvements in women's health care since this essay was written, and many more women have entered the medical profession. But medical research and health care institutions continue to ignore women's needs. Organizations such as the National Women's Health Network are pressuring the medical establishment to pay more attention to women's health issues.

Feminism cannot be located in one central organization. Rather, it exists in the myriad groups and organizing projects that women form when they encounter injustice or seek to address unmet needs. We present here three examples of women organizing in the various arenas in which they found themselves. In each situation, the first step was breaking the silence about women's experience and naming the problems they faced. The ideas and activities of each group reflect their particular needs and perspectives. The feminism that develops in the workplace by the women in "Nine to Five," for example, is different from the community-based feminism of the National Congress of Neighborhood Women. Both groups were organized in the 1970s and have changed somewhat as the environment has changed, but they still exist today, organizing around the problems that still confront women in the neighborhood and in the office. The women in "Voices" created an organization for women with AIDS in prison during the late 1980s. Their organization was able to make institutional changes while meeting the needs of female prisoners.

A new wave of activism is developing in the 1990s among women of all ages and backgrounds. As we confront the issues of the 1990s, it is important to develop strategies that address the needs of all women. The agenda designed by Kathryn Kolbert, a lawyer active in the defense of women's right to choose, conceives of reproductive rights broadly. She emphasizes not only the legality of abortion but access to abortion, birth control, and other reproductive health services. Kolbert's agenda also recognizes that for women to make reproductive choices, we must have economic equality and sexual freedom.

One of the tactics women and other oppressed groups have used in the past is civil disobedience. As Barbara Yoshida describes, this tactic is reappearing in response to women's loss of reproductive freedom. In her book *Feminist Fatale*, Paula Kamen interviewed young feminists about their lives and describes some of the many feminist activities that young women are engaged in today.

❦ 126

Becoming the Third Wave

REBECCA WALKER

I am not one of the people who sat transfixed before the television, watching the Senate hearings. I had classes to go to, papers to write, and frankly, the whole thing was too painful. A black man grilled by a panel of white men about his sexual deviance. A black woman claiming harassment and being discredited by other women. . . . I could not bring myself to watch that sensationalized assault [on] the human spirit.

To me, the hearings were not about determining whether or not Clarence Thomas did in fact harass Anita Hill. They were about checking and redefining the extent of women's credibility and power.

Can a woman's experience undermine a man's career? Can a woman's voice, a woman's sense of self-worth and injustice, challenge a structure predicated upon the subjugation of our gender? Anita Hill's testimony threatened to do that and more. If Thomas had not been confirmed, every man in the United States would be at risk. For how many senators never told a sexist joke? How many men have not used their protected male privilege to thwart in some way the influence or ideas of a woman colleague, friend, or relative?

For those whose sense of power is so obviously connected to the health and vigor of the penis, it would have been a metaphoric castration. Of course this is too great a threat.

While some may laud the whole spectacle for the consciousness it raised around sexual harassment, its very real outcome is more informative. He was promoted. She was repudiated. Men were assured of the inviolability of their penis/power. Women were admonished to keep their experiences to themselves.

The backlash against U.S. women is real. As the misconception of equality between the sexes becomes more ubiquitous, so does the attempt to restrict the boundaries of women's personal and political power. Thomas's confirmation, the ultimate rally of support for the male paradigm of harassment, sends a clear message to women: "Shut up! Even if you speak, we will not listen."

I will not be silenced.

I acknowledge the fact that we live under siege. I intend to fight back. I have uncovered and unleashed more repressed anger than I thought possible. For the umpteenth time in my 22 years, I have been radicalized, politicized, shaken awake. I have come to voice again, and this time my voice is not conciliatory.

The night after Thomas' confirmation I ask the man I am intimate with what he thinks of the whole mess. His concern is primarily with Thomas' propensity to demolish civil rights and opportunities for people of color. I launch into a tirade. "When will progressive black men prioritize my rights and well-being? When will they stop talking so damn much about 'the race' as if it revolved exclusively around them?" He tells me I wear my emotions on my sleeve. I scream "I need to know, are you with me or are you going to help them try to destroy me?"

A week later I am on a train to New York. A beautiful mother and daughter, both wearing green outfits, sit across the aisle from me. The little girl has tightly plaited braids. Her brown skin is glowing and smooth, her eyes bright as she chatters happily while looking out the window. Two men get on the train and sit directly behind me, shaking my seat as they thud into place. I bury myself in *The Sound and the Fury*. Loudly they begin to talk about women. "Man, I fucked that bitch all night and then I never called her again." "Man, there's lots of girlies over there, you know that ho, live over there by Tyrone? Well, I snatched that shit up."

The mother moves closer to her now quiet daughter. Looking at her small back I can see that she is listening to the men. I am thinking of how I can transform the situation, of all the people in the car whose silence makes us complicit.

Another large man gets on the train. After exchanging loud greetings with the two men, he sits next to me. He tells them he is going to Philadelphia to visit his wife and child. I am suckered into thinking that he is different. Then, "Man, there's a ton of females in Philly, just waitin' for you to give 'em some." I turn my head and allow the fire in my eyes to burn into him. He takes up two seats and has hands with huge swollen knuckles. I imagine the gold rings on his fingers slamming into my face. He senses something, "What's your name, sweetheart?" The other men lean forward over the seat.

A torrent explodes: "I ain't your sweetheart, I ain't your bitch, I ain't your baby. How dare you have the nerve to sit up here and talk about women that way, and then try to speak to me." The woman/mother chimes in to the beat with claps of sisterhood. The men are momentarily stunned. Then the comeback: "Aw, bitch, don't play that woman shit over here 'cause that's bullshit." He slaps the back of one hand against the palm of the other. I refuse to back down. Words fly.

My instinct kicks in, telling me to get out. "Since I see you all are not going to move, I will." I move to the first car. I am so angry that thoughts of murder, of physically retaliating against them, of separatism, engulf me. I am almost out of body, just shy of being pure force. I am sick of the way women are negated, violated, devalued, ignored. I am livid, unrelenting in my anger at those who invade my space, who wish to take away my rights, who refuse to hear my voice.

As the days pass, I push myself to figure out what it means to be a part of the Third Wave of feminism. I begin to realize that I owe it to myself, to my little sister on the train, to all of the daughters yet to be born, to push beyond my rage and articulate an agenda. After battling with ideas of separatism and militancy, I connect with my own feelings of powerlessness. I realize that I must undergo a transformation if I am truly committed to women's empowerment. My involvement must reach beyond my own voice in discussion, beyond voting, beyond reading feminist theory. My anger and awareness must translate into tangible action.

I am ready to decide, as my mother decided before me, to devote much of my energy to the history, health, and healing of women. Each of my choices will have to hold to my feminist standard of justice. To be a feminist is to integrate an ideology of equality and female empowerment into the very fiber of my life. It is to search for personal clarity in the midst of systemic destruction, to join in sisterhood with women when often we are divided, to understand power structures with the intention of challenging them.

While this may sound simple, it is exactly the kind of stand that many of my peers are unwilling to take. So I write this as a plea to all women, especially the women of my generation: Let Thomas' confirmation serve to remind you, as it did me, that the fight is far from over. Let this dismissal of a woman's experience move you to anger. Turn that outrage into political power. Do not vote for them unless they work for us. Do not have sex with them, do not break bread with them, do not nurture them if they don't prioritize our freedom to control our bodies and our lives.

I am not a postfeminism feminist. I am the Third Wave.   [1992]

127

The Women's Health Movement: Women Take Power

HELEN RODRIGUEZ-TRIAS

Out of scattered small groups meeting in each other's homes, women forged a women's health movement of national dimensions in less than two decades. Though its effect on specific health issues was profound, the movement's main contribution was a new feminist consciousness. Feminist vision expanded beyond the concerns of women in relation to doctors to concerns of *people* in relation to the socioeconomic realities of the health care *system*. Its proponents were and still are primarily white, well-educated middle-class young women who had to confront their ideas on race, class, and sex privilege as they built coalitions for what became known in the 1980s as reproductive rights. In their effort to organize, they came into conflict with working-class Third World* women organizing for welfare and health rights in the community. From these clashes among women of different class and ethnic origin, with different concerns and priorities, came a unified view that brought major advances. Nowhere was this more apparent than in the movements for abortion rights and against sterilization abuse.

BEGINNINGS

In the consciousness-raising groups of the sixties, women became more aware of their concerns and dissatisfactions with much of their health care. More and more tales of discomfort, humiliation, and abuse at the hands of professionals emerged. A distrust of medical technology grew, along with a suspicion that much of it answered the needs of profit rather than of patients. Reports of unnecessary surgery, particularly on women, led to more questions, as did the medicalization of childbirth, menstrua-

tion, and menopause. As patriarchy in the family was questioned, so was patriarchy in the doctor-patient relationship.[1]

Women began to realize that they were by far the most frequent users of health services for themselves, their children, or other dependent family members. A women's consumer movement emerged. Its evolution was typified by a group of women in Boston who met in 1969 to discuss their concerns about their bodies, their sexuality, and their health. Soon their activities expanded into educational seminars for women in their homes, day care centers, nurseries, schools, and churches. From these discussions came the first mimeographed edition of *Our Bodies, Ourselves,* which in less than ten years was to reach around the world.[2]

Women continued to discuss, expose, publicize, organize. They wrote newsletters, magazine articles, and pamphlets. They read and studied important critiques such as Ehrenreich and English's *Witches, Midwives, and Nurses* and *Complaints and Disorders,* which stated that health care had once been primarily in the hands of women.[3] In less than a century it was usurped by men who organized medicine to exclude not only white women but also black people and people from the working class.

The feminist viewpoint was that women's reproductive functions, which are normal life events, were turned into "medical conditions" and were commercialized by men. Some feminists, going further, placed blame on a corporate establishment that put profits first and exploited illness, both real and that created by the medical world itself.

Although many who joined the women's health movement participated in broader health care reforms for community centers, worker organization, free clinics, and such, they focused on specific women's health issues. For example, some created the self-help movement on the premise that women could learn about their bodies and provide routine gynecological care for themselves and others. Many who had organized storefront clinics later organized self-help clinics along similar egalitarian patterns.

A narrower focus permitted the concentration in several key areas: contraceptives and experimentation on women, gynecological and obstetrical care, the use of dangerous drugs, particularly of diethyl-

---

*Editor's note: "Third World" was used to describe women of color in the U.S. at the time this article was written.

stilbestrol (DES), women in the health professions, and reproductive freedom.

While predominately white middle-class women organized a health movement around their concerns, putting emphasis on changing their relationship to doctors and controlling their own bodies, working-class and Third World women were clamoring for day care, welfare rights, entry-level jobs in the health care system, and the establishment of community health centers. White women concentrated on *health care,* women of color and of the working class on *health status* with a gut understanding of its socioeconomic determinants. The two points of departure initially made for parallel movements, which nevertheless converged with great effect in the arena of reproductive rights. Before this convergence and the lessons it produced are described, a brief sketch of the problems and progress in the other key areas of work will serve to provide an overview of the women's health movement today.

CONTRACEPTIVES AND EXPERIMENTATION ON WOMEN

Barbara Seaman's widely read book, *The Doctors' Case against the Pill,* published in 1969, and later exposés revealed that women were experimented on with oral contraceptives.[4] Furthermore, there was evidence that manufacturers concealed hazards and that the Food and Drug Administration did not conduct or require adequate tests. The original study of the pill—in Puerto Rico, in the 1950s—included only 132 women and left uninvestigated two or three suspicious deaths as well as using doses of estrogen considered prohibitive by U.S. standards.[5]

Third World women in the United States were frequent subjects of unethical experiments, such as one pill test in 1970 in which 76 Mexican-American women were given placebos without their consent. Ten became pregnant! Doctors did not even censure the investigators; on the contrary, the paper presenting the results of the experiment was well received. When questioned on methodology, the investigator replied, "If you think you can explain a placebo test to women like these, you have never met Mrs. Gomez from the West Side."[6]

Depo-Provera, an injectable, long-acting contraceptive, carcinogenic in animal testing, became another source of bitter controversy. The drug companies have continued an effort to obtain FDA approval while members of the consumer movement have continued to the present to oppose it as unsafe.

Intrauterine devices had proliferated greatly without demonstrations of safety. By 1974, some 2 million women had the Dalkon shield in their uteri and another million had other devices—all virtually untested for their long-term safety.

As the reports of deadly complications of pills and IUDs grew, so did women's anger at being used. Women exchanged information through newsletters and other publications, organized, participated in hearings, and initiated lawsuits. The National Women's Health Network, founded in 1975 by Barbara Seaman, Phyllis Chester, Belita Cowan, Mary Howell, and Alice Wolfson, quickly became involved in pressuring the FDA for safety standards.[7]

After a lengthy court battle on pill information, a victory was won in 1978. Manufacturers are now required to include information on hazards in packages of estrogen-containing pills. Another victory was a court mandate that the FDA "regulate medical devices, including IUDs and clips, rings, and bands for sterilization—products over which the agency previously had no clear statutory jurisdiction. Devices already on the market are now required to apply for approval and submit evidence of safety and effectiveness."[8]

The battle over Depo-Provera rages on as manufacturers in the United States continue to press for FDA approval for wide-scale use. Through several conduits, including the federal Agency for International Development (AID) and the International Planned Parenthood Federation (IPPF), large amounts of Depo have been exported and injected into 5 million women in countries as disparate and far removed as Thailand, the Philippines, Egypt, and Chile—in fact, in a total of seventy countries![9] Today many people in the health movement condemn these practices, thus taking the side of others who expose and deplore them.[10]

GYNECOLOGICAL AND OBSTETRICAL CARE

Women's contentions that gynecological care was perfunctory, impersonal, and generally demeaning in the hands of most gynecologists seemed well substantiated by their experience. Moreover, the frequency of gynecological surgery in the United States far surpassed that in other countries. In the seventies, hysterectomy became one of the most frequently performed major operations—over 400,000 per year. Audits suggested that perhaps one-third were unnecessary.

The self-help movement, revolutionary in its concept that women could provide gynecological care for themselves and each other, challenged the control of gynecologists. Begun by Carol Downer and other West Coast women in 1971, the movement grew rapidly as thousands of women trained themselves in the use of the speculum, in menstrual extraction, and in simple remedies for common vaginal infections. When Carol Downer and Coleen Wilson were arrested in 1972 and charged with practicing medicine without a license, women across the country rose in support. Margaret Mead, who was among the supporters, observed that "men began taking over obstetrics and they invented a tool that allowed them to look inside women. You could call this progress, except that when women tried to look inside themselves, this was called practicing medicine without a license."[11]

After her acquittal, Carol Downer continued as the recognized leader of self-help, aiding in the creation of thousands of clinics. Although the movement challenged doctors and hospital hierarchy, it remained small and peripheral enough to be ultimately nonthreatening to the establishment as a whole.

Women's experiences with childbirth practices were no happier than with gynecological care. Any delivery of an infant in a hospital was an elaborate, frequently traumatic procedure, fraught with the discomfort of monitors, extensive laboratory tests, intravenous medications, analgesia, anesthesia, episiotomies, and other questionable, if not downright dangerous, routines. The risk of a Caesarean section was increasing, with rates from 20 to 30 percent becoming common.[12]

Nurse-midwifery programs were virtually nonexistent. It was practically impossible to obtain any but the most interventionist forms of childbirth services. Only a few elite clinics even practiced natural childbirth.

The International Childbirth Association, whose outspoken president, Doris Haire, is one of the foremost exponents of spontaneous birth in homelike environments, and many others had campaigned for decades.[13] Hospitals that catered to a middle-class, educated clientele finally put their anesthesia machines, monitors, oxygen tanks, and the like out of sight, decked birthing rooms with curtains and other amenities, allowed fathers to participate, and permitted babies to remain with their mothers from birth. Some even brought midwives to deliver infants in their traditional, supportive, noninterventionist ways.

Still, today, the vast majority of women and infants are subjected to the trauma of unprepared childbirth among strangers. Hospitals have numerous routines that interfere with mother-child bonding, family participation, and breast feeding. The alarming rise in the rate of Caesarean sections continues.[14] Doctors offer innumerable justifications for their increasing use of surgery, the most frequent being their fear of malpractice suits if a baby is "less than perfect" after vaginal birth.

Women exert little or no control over institutional practices that entrap them once they are in the hospital. In her article entitled "The Caesarean Epidemic," Gena Corea uses the story of Laurie Olsen.[15] Laurie is the daughter of Tillie, the feminist writer, and Jack, a teacher of labor history; she is also the sister of three feminists, and herself a policy researcher and writer. Laurie's labor in an Oakland, California, hospital went from one procedure to another in a choreographed sequence from the rupture of membranes, which occurred before her arrival, to the electronic fetal monitor, to the induction by Pitocin and the Caesarean section, when the Pitocin did not seem to work. Laurie herself later commented that natural childbirth and other reforms had remained marginal to institutional practices.[16]

DES

Diethylstilbestrol (DES), a synthetic estrogen, was in the news in early 1971. At Harvard, Dr. Arthur Herbst discovered that a rare and frequently fatal form of vaginal cancer attacking girls in their teens could be traced to DES given to their mothers while the girls were in utero.[17]

DES was given to an estimated 6 million pregnant women between 1943 and 1959, thus exposing at least 3 million children to its toxicity.[18] The drug was originally popularized in the forties for the prevention of miscarriage and later used widely to stimulate "better placental function and hence bigger and healthier babies."[19] Even after Dr. Herbst's discovery had become widely publicized and despite pressure from the Cancer Control Bureau of the New York State Department of Health and numerous investigators that the FDA ban the use of synthetic estrogen in pregnancy, no action was taken for nearly a year. It was only under pressure from DES mothers urging Congress that the FDA finally acted. Its delay exposed an estimated additional 60,000 children to DES, now known to also cause genital abnormalities in boys.[20]

As women learned about the resistance of the public health agencies and doctors to the gathering and sharing of information that would lead to earlier detection, they became incensed. DES lawsuits were initiated in almost every state. In Michigan and Massachusetts, women organized to bring class action suits that would make Eli Lilly and the other manufacturers pay damages for the treatment of DES daughters and sons. Others followed. After several years of agitation spearheaded by DES mothers in New York, California, and other states, a national action group on DES was formed in 1976.

Their campaign to educate the public, physicians, and health officials resulted in screening programs in most states and in an increasingly vocal, educated public. Nonetheless, DES is still widely used today as the "morning after" pill to avoid conception, for the prevention of breast engorgement in women who do not breastfeed their newborn infants, as replacement therapy for women in menopause, and most of all in cattle feed to stimulate greater weight gain. Women are therefore continuing to wage the struggle against this widespread prescription of a proven carcinogen.

WOMEN IN HEALTH PROFESSIONS

Women, who compose over 70 percent of the health work force, are notoriously absent from the higher professional echelons of doctors and administrators. In 1970 the situation was even worse: only 8 percent of all doctors were women, and women made up only 3 percent of all obstetrician-gynecologists.

Partly owing to the distrust of professionals and partly to its community bases, which were outside of institutions, women's health organizations were not particularly concerned with the increased entry of women into medical school or into obstetrics and gynecology. Their thrust was more toward educating women to choose doctors wisely, self-help, and development of referral services. Nevertheless, the women's movement did generate sufficient pressure that, from 1970 to 1980, admissions of women into medical school rose from less than 10 percent to nearly 30 percent. A perhaps more important effect of the women's movement is on the women applicants themselves. Few are untouched by its activism and affirmation of women's rights. Before they attended medical school, many had already been advocates on health or women's issues. They bring organizational experience, which they put to good use in providing supportive networks for each other.

In some medical schools women students have successfully petitioned for the removal of lecturers whose remarks were particularly offensive and for the inclusion of research studies by women on women's health issues in the curriculum. Because of the efforts of sensitive educators, teaching by trained patients who became teaching assistants has become established in several medical schools. The teaching assistants are articulate in their guidance of students as these learn to perform pelvic and breast examinations on them. Students report that their sensitivity to patients' reactions increased on a par with their interviewing and physical-examination skills.

Despite increased admissions of women, several areas of concern remain. Minority admissions are now hitting a new low,[21] and it seems that the gains by women are coming at the expense of setbacks for black, Hispanic, and Native American men. The stage is set for destructive competition. In addition the admission of women has not resulted in any increase in status for women faculty in medical schools.

REPRODUCTIVE FREEDOM: CASE STUDIES IN ABORTION RIGHTS, STERILIZATION ABUSE, AND POPULATION CONTROL

Beginning in the 1800s, legislation restricting abortion services to all but the few sanctioned by teams of doctors in medical centers existed in all states, despite the grim reality of women sick and dying from illegal abortions.[22] Sometimes the very same doctors from the medical centers performed highly illegal but profitable abortions at other sites.

The abortion rights movement, which began taking shape in the 1960s with advocates among the professionals—the American Law Institute (1959) and the Association for the Study of Abortion (1964)—soon received a major impetus from feminist groups. Although not in complete agreement, women were increasingly advocating repeal rather than reform of the laws governing abortions. The second National Organization for Women convention, in 1967, demanded access to contraceptive information and repeal of restrictive abortion legislation.

By 1970, laws in Hawaii, Alaska, and New York had been repealed, albeit with some qualifications regarding residency status, dates beyond which an abortion could not be performed, requirement of spouse or parental consent, and performance in a hospital.

Feminists had organized the NOW Task Force on Reproduction and Its Control, New Yorkers for Abortion Law Repeal, and the Women's National Abortion Action Coalition (WONAAC). These were joined by other abortion rights groups, such as the Association to Repeal Abortion Laws (ARAL) and the National Association for Repeal of Abortion Laws (NARAL).[23]

Dramatic demonstrations and hearings were held in major cities. Women, dressed in mourning, disrupted hearings, invaded rallies against abortion reform, and demonstrated at the AMA convention in Chicago in 1970. Feminists organized and joined others in the underground abortion referral network, which consisted mainly of out-of-state physicians and unfortunately usually entailed an expensive package inaccessible to poor women. Some groups broadened their direct services, and in Chicago the Women's Liberation Union organized a service group that performed 11,000 abortions in four years at the low cost of $50. No one was denied an abortion for lack of funds, and no one died.

In 1973, the millions of signators, thousands of marchers, hundreds of organizers, and dozens who had laid their personal freedom on the line risking prosecution were elated—the U.S. Supreme Court decided in *Roe* v. *Wade* and *Doe* v. *Bolton* that during the first three months of pregnancy, abortion was to be a free choice to be negotiated between a woman and her physician.[24]

Women were unprepared for the mushrooming of abortion programs that followed. Some, more experienced than others, were able to organize their own clinics; others acted as referral sources or as workers in the clinics. Their vast experience as patients (often humiliating), as advocates, and as counselors (revealing) brought a new consciousness of the economics and politics of the health care system to the most advanced groups. The focus became quality care, although even nominally safe abortion services were still far from available for millions of women who lacked money and were in communities that failed to provide them.

Through the years 1973–77, as safe abortion services became more accessible to white, middle-class, urban women, who made up the backbone of the abortion rights movement, a certain complacency took hold. The movement generally failed to address charges by Third World women that they were sometimes pressured into having abortions at welfare centers or by low-income women that they were being forced to accept "package deals" of abortion and sterilization at the medical centers that had abortion programs.[25] Planned Parenthood Federation and others in the forefront of the abortion rights struggles also supported government programs for birth control, which were considered suspect by blacks and members of other minority groups.[26]

As this complacency was growing, the forces of reaction were gathering strength under the slogan "Right to Life." Rushed by those forces, the Hyde amendment passed in 1977 and each year after that effectively cut off Medicaid funding for abortion in all cases except those in which pregnancy would endanger the life of the mother or in which it had been caused by rape or incest. In June of 1980 the Supreme Court ruled it constitutional.

The abortion rights movement, now known as Pro-Choice, still reeling from the blows dealt by an increasingly strident, violent, and well-funded "Right-to-Life" movement, was forced to begin to reevaluate its partial neglect of the concerns of low-income women.

Rosie Jimenez, a Mexican-American Texan, was the first documented victim of the Hyde amendment.[27] She died following an illegal abortion performed in Mexico, her Medicaid card in her purse. Increasingly, black and Hispanic women spoke more loudly at rallies. Welfare rights, the Black United Front, the Third World Women's Alliance (now known as the Alliance against Women's Oppression), and other organizations representing poor and Third World women became more involved in the struggle to maintain women's right to choose. The seeds of unity were sown. Soon even the most elitist Pro-Choice organizations were modifying their messages on the "need to reduce welfare rolls." Today, as Congress debates a constitutional amendment granting full civil rights to the fertilized ovum, which might well make abortion a capital offense, women once more march, petition, demonstrate, and get arrested. As the threat to reproductive freedom grows, the coalitions grow broader.

If the weaknesses of the abortion rights movement could largely be attributed to its failure to address the concerns of black, Hispanic, native American, and other working-class women from its beginning, the strength of the movement against sterilization abuse certainly came precisely from its roots among these same disenfranchised groups. It quickly developed a constituency among these very same groups, whose members were able to confront members of the women's health movement about their racism and attitudes of class superiority.[28]

THE MOVEMENT TO END STERILIZATION ABUSE

By the early seventies, numerous community organizations, particularly National Welfare Rights, had become alarmed at reports of the forced sterilization of women on welfare and of those receiving care in city, county, and other government hospitals. *Relf v. Weinberger* (1973) brought on behalf of two black, allegedly retarded girls, aged twelve and fourteen, who had been sterilized without their knowledge or consent in a federally funded program in Alabama, rocked the conscience of many sectors.[29] Civil libertarians, newspaper editors, jurists, politicians, journalists, and civil rights activists gave wide publicity to the case. The resultant pressure prompted the Department of Health, Education, and Welfare to promulgate, in April 1974, guidelines to curb sterilization abuse. The regulations, which included a moratorium on the sterilization of incompetent people and those under twenty-one, were largely ineffective and unknown or ignored by providers of sterilization services, even a year or two later.[30]

Simultaneously the number of sterilizations was rising at a rapid rate, particularly after 1973.[31] From the Los Angeles County Hospital staff came information that Mexican women were being sterilized in large numbers, in many cases without properly obtained informed consent. Interviews showed that abuses were widespread. They consisted of waving consent forms before a laboring woman's eyes, requesting the signature of forms in English from patients who spoke only Spanish, and operating without consent.[32] In New York sterilization rates in city hospitals serving Hispanic and black communities had risen alarmingly.[33]

Several women's organizations united around the issues raised by forced sterilization. The Committee against Forced Sterilization, on the West Coast, and the Committee to End Sterilization Abuse (CESA), in New York City, were representative of groups that carried out community education, publicizing and campaigning against the excesses of doctors and hospitals.

In several cities that contained major academic medical centers the presence of Programs for International Education in Gynecology and Obstetrics was exposed. These programs train gynecologists from Third World countries to sterilize women using the laparoscope and send them back to work in AID-supported programs in their nations. Women's health organizations in California and New York developed coalitions promulgating guidelines to promote informed consent and thus protect women from abuses. In California the focus was on guidelines to be approved and implemented by the state department of health. In New York, the Health and Hospitals Corporation (HHC), which has the administrative responsibility for the city hospitals, was targeted for pressure.

The Committee to End Sterilization Abuse (CESA) was organized at a showing of "Blood of the Condor," a film exposing AID sterilization of Bolivian Quechua Indians. In the ensuing discussion several people in the audience revealed personal experiences or friends' experiences with forced sterilization and agreed to organize. Although its original focus was the exposure of population control programs as a means of continuing the exploitation of people, the committee became more and more involved in sterilization abuse as an infringement of individual rights.

In its activities in the community, members approached Puerto Rican and black organizations— at community centers, churches, political headquarters, and schools, for the opportunity to speak. They quickly gathered story after story of abuses similar to those in the rest of the country. The Advisory Committee on Sterilization Guidelines for New York City Hospitals undertook the task of developing more effective regulations for hospitals. A broad representation of hospital community boards, health advocacy groups, health care professionals, consumers, civil rights, legal rights, and Third World community groups brought their viewpoints to the discussions. The representation of such diverse groups as the National Black Feminist Organization, the Lower East Side Neighborhood Health Center, Healthright, Health-PAC, CESA, the Center for Constitutional Rights, the Family Planning Division of the Human Resources Administration, the Puerto Rican Socialist Party, *Ms.* magazine, and the National Organization for Women ensured the sharing of many experiences, opinions, and positions. It quickly became evident that the issue of sterilization abuse could mobilize much broader segments than could that of abortion rights.

This coalition drafted the following guidelines for performing sterilizations: a thirty-day waiting period; an interdiction of consent at times of delivery, abortion, or hospitalization for any major illness or procedure; the requirement that full counseling on birth control be available so that alternatives are offered; the stipulation that the idea of sterilization not originate with the doctor; and the provision that informational materials be in the language best understood by the woman.

The guidelines also stated that if she wished, the woman could bring a patient advocate of her choosing to participate at any stage of the process. She could also have a witness of her choice sign the consent form. Perhaps the most important point was that a woman should express in her own words, in writing on the consent form, her understanding

of what the sterilization entailed, particularly its permanence.[34] . . .

The HHC Advisory Committee was unprepared for the furor that greeted its initial position paper. The ferocity of the opposition was vented in letters, articles, meetings, and ultimately, in September 1975, a suit against the guidelines.

Typical of the power conflict over who makes the rules or who regulates whom was the suit by the six professors of obstetrics and gynecology, alleging that the guidelines infringed [on] their right to free speech, since doctors were mandated to discuss sterilization only in the context of other methods of birth control.[35] Their suit, eventually dropped, was against *all* guidelines, including those of HEW, the state, and of course HHC. It made patent their unwillingness to abide by any regulations except their own. Some physicians had already expressed the fear that one set of regulations would lead to another and that they would soon be told when and how to perform surgery.

A related conflict emerged over the right of a consumer group, albeit one functioning within a corporate structure accountable to the public, to develop regulations by which the hospitals must abide. This incursion into the institutions called for advocacy, counseling, interpreters, and educational and other services as requisite for the process of obtaining informed consent. The structure of institutions was being altered.

As the groups opposing sterilization abuse continued their work, more and more conflicts with and within the women's health movement surfaced. Typical responses occurred at the 1975 Women's Health Conference held in Boston, where members of the nearly all-white audience challenged the four panelists who spoke on population control. After the speakers presented critiques of U.S. government sponsorship of population control programs in Latin American and other countries, some members of the audience objected to the views presented. A few defended the need for population control programs as a means of maintaining the environment or promoting peace or furthering economic development. Others defended the compulsory sterilization of mentally retarded individuals on the grounds that they are unfit for parenthood. Most women who took exception to the guidelines or legislation did so on the basis of personal experience. In the past they had been denied their request for sterilization because of their status (unmarried) or the number of their children (usually the doctor thought they had too few). They therefore opposed a waiting period or any other regulation that they interpreted as limiting access.

It became clear once more that personal experiences made for divergent viewpoints. While young white middle-class women were denied their requests for sterilization, low-income women or women of certain ethnicity were misled or coerced into them. The ensuing debate, like many others that followed over the years, had a healthful effect. Several organizations, including the Boston Women's Health Book Collective, made the issue of sterilization abuse their own, initiating campaigns to combat it.

In New York City the organizations took to the streets as the successful movement for HHC guidelines grew to one for city council legislation. The elevation to the public level created conditions favorable for new coalitions, including the prestigious National Council of Churches, which through its project called Interreligious Foundations for Community Organization (IFCO) sponsored the National Conference on Sterilization Abuse in Washington, D.C., in September 1979. Over eighty people, half of whom were from ethnic minorities and one-tenth of whom were men, met to present testimony. Representatives from civil rights groups, women's groups, and church organizations denounced U.S. government policies promoting the sterilization of minority women. Mary Ann Bear—from Lame Deer, Montana—moved the conference when she presented testimony on the massive sterilization of Indian women. Such action "threatens our survival, tampers with basic religious values and human rights to reproduce," she said, adding, "As a minority we native Americans do not have to limit our numbers."

The growth of these new coalitions not only ensured the success of the legislation in New York City but also generated sufficient pressure on a national level on HEW that in 1978 it promulgated new, stronger guidelines patterned after the New York City law (Public Law 37). In HEW's ten regions, its officials heard hundreds of people testify in favor of more stringent guidelines and stronger enforcement than those of 1973 provided.[36]

Sterilization abuse, formerly recognized only by those who had been its direct targets, became a generally acknowledged problem that could no longer be denied. Third World women and their allies had made their point; they had succeeded in escalating the struggle for guidelines to legislation, from local to national arenas. The existence of the HEW guidelines gives substance to the current work in monitoring that the National Women's Health Network now spearheads.[37]

POPULATION CONTROL

The work on sterilization abuse catalyzed a change in yet another realm from national to international perspectives. Puerto Rican women described the events in Puerto Rico, where over a period of thirty-five years privately funded foundations based in the United States and the Puerto Rican government, with U.S. government funds, had by 1968 sterilized over one-third of the women of childbearing age.[38] In the forties, just when women were joining the work force in large numbers as industrialization opened up job opportunities, sterilizations were provided at minimal or no cost. Women suffered from lack of safe, legal abortion services, alternative methods of contraception, day care services, and general health services, yet they were offered sterilizations. Large numbers of those sterilized believed that it was temporary.

Through this example from Puerto Rico, many women in the women's health movement came to understand that the nature of the colonial relations between Puerto Rico and the United States made coercion possible through a population control program.

Black women spoke of the increased sterilization in the South, the use of hysterectomy as a way of sterilizing young black women, and the move in at least ten states to pass laws permitting the compulsory sterilization of welfare recipients.[39] At the same time, they noted the presence of AID population control programs in Africa, Latin America, and Asia.

Native American women and men exposed the unprecedented number of sterilizations on reservations without evidence of informed consent,[40] while they showed the efforts of several corporations to deprive them of their land, particularly that which contained uranium.[41] Mexican women told of increasing sterilization programs just across the U.S. border, in Juarez and other border cities where U.S. industries have established plants employing thousands of women.

As the picture emerged, the militancy against the U.S. corporations and the government-supported agencies involved in population control programs overseas increased.

A new development among women workers in U.S. industry in 1979 raised additional concerns for health and safety on the job. In that year, some women employed by the American Cyanamid Company in West Virginia charged that the company had threatened to fire them from the lead pigments division of the plant unless they underwent sterilizations. Lead exposure is harmful to all workers, but this is especially so for unborn children. The company feared the possibility of pregnancies.

In public forums, women debated representatives of the Association for Voluntary Sterilization, Zero Population Growth, International Planned Parenthood Federation, and other organizations involved in population control. The activities of U.S. government agencies were exposed in a vast network of newsletters, journals, and magazines, as well as in a prolific output of scholarly books. Information on sterilization abuse and its complex connections to U.S. corporate interests was widely disseminated.[42]

THE PAST AND THE PROMISE

The women's health movement, to its credit, challenged one of the largest industries in the country. Its greatest challenge was to professional authority in its demand for control of women's bodies. The struggle for control took many forms: legislation pertaining to women, the participation of women in their own health care, the marketing of products. To a lesser degree, women's demands altered the childbirth and abortion practices in hospitals, the admission of women to medical schools and their curricula, and the organization of services such as self-help clinics. But there has been almost no impact on surgery on women, particularly Caesarean sections and hysterectomies, on the prescription

and exporting of dangerous drugs and contraceptive techniques, or on the relationship of patients to health care institutions. Moreover, the movement affected only a relatively small number of women and not the many who because of education, age, or geographic or other circumstances were beyond the reach of organizing efforts.

The most serious weaknesses of the movement remain its failure to cement alliances with working-class women and women from ethnic minorities. When women in the movement posed utopian solutions such as filling health needs through self-help, they alienated women who struggled to bring medical care into their communities. The frequently expressed, narrow feminist view that men were the enemy further alienated potential allies among men and some progressive organizations.

In addition, the women's health movement did not seek to understand or expose the poor working conditions in the health industry itself or to link the concerns of women health workers with those of consumers. Often the thrust was individualistic and at best reformist; as if being in the "know" and shopping for better care were the goals. Ultimately, its greatest weakness was its overall failure to address the need for power within the institutions where most of the abuses were taking place.

However, the tremendous importance and potential of the movement lies in its ability to catalyze revolutionary changes in its participants. The structure and models it created also have lasting value. The Boston Women's Health Book Collective spoke of this process of transformation of women's consciousness: "We are white, middle class women, and as such can describe only what life has been for us. But we do realize that poor women and nonwhite women have suffered far more from the kinds of misinformation and mistreatment that we are describing in this book. In some ways learning about our womanhood from the inside out has allowed us to cross over the socially created barriers of race, color, income, and class, and to feel a sense of identity with all women in the experience of being female."[43]

In a similar way, thousands of women were moved—their self-concepts changed. Those who had for too long submitted passively, though internally raging at the patronizing, poor care they received from their doctors, felt validated in the consciousness-raising process and became empowered by education, organizing experience, carrying out struggles, and winning victories. They will never be the same.

Those who came with a perspective other than the direct feminist one, who were involved in Third World liberation struggles, found a forum in the women's health movement. And if sometimes the debates were painful because of the ignorance or insensitivity they revealed, they were always fundamental because they exposed the most divisive of ideological constraints—attitudes of superiority based on race or class. We were forced to grapple with each other's prejudices and eventually by sharing experiences to understand our different positions and reach unity.

Bringing organized women into direct conflict with the holders of power in the medical establishment radicalized many. Some moved beyond reform and came to advocate revolutionary changes in the health care system and in American society itself.

Its thrusts into medical schools and other health institutions placed more women in positions of increased power. These women in turn are providing support for others who enter now.

Women who have been advocates, counselors, providers, administrators, and community organizers of health care institutions can act as links between their communities and these institutions. It is now possible to develop consumer projects in which health services are monitored. For example, the National Women's Health Network has published a guide for monitoring the HEW guidelines on sterilization in order to help community organizations develop activities to prevent abuses.[44] It may provide a model for penetrating the institutional structures themselves.

A massive body of literature attests to the prolific writings of women scholars on health, but what is most impressive is the national recognition that many have gained. The unquestionable stature of women researchers is sufficiently evident that funding sources have taken note. A recent example is provided by Helen Marieskind, who conducted the study on Caesarean sections at the request of HEW.

Women's research findings and pertinent health information are broadly distributed to hundreds of thousands via the network of organizations.

It is precisely in the creation of organizations of national scope, such as the National Women's Health Network and the Reproductive Rights National Network, that the women's health movement has made a unique contribution.

A promising recent initiative has been the joining of forces with trade unions and the occupational health movement in the Coalition for the Reproductive Rights of Workers, which is concerned with the effects of chemicals, radiation, and other hazards on the reproductive systems of both women and men.

The movement showed that it could ultimately cut across class and ethnic lines when it focused on what was happening to the majority of women.

Where it will go, no one can predict. The danger of co-optation, ever present in this society, is great. Women may be satisfied to testify, impel legislation, influence those in power to grant abortion services and better contraceptives, assume more places in the medical hierarchy, and hold well-paying positions in foundations, federations, and the like. Or they may overcome their racism and their own comfortable class positions sufficiently to join workers, Third World people, and other progressive forces in the health industry and the general society for a sweeping restructuring that will empower the workers and patients.

The author wishes to thank the many sisters and brothers who participated in the struggles for women's, and ultimately people's, liberation; they make the history that is the subject of this [article].

For many years, the collective Committee to End Sterilization Abuse (CESA) was my political home. Thanks, compañeras and compañeros, for deepening my understanding of reproductive-rights issues. The countless members of the National Women's Health Network and Center on Constitutional Rights, the Committee for Abortion Rights and Against Sterilization Abuse (CARASA), and the Reproductive Rights National Network (R_2N_2) continue to lead the way.

My friends Esta Armstrong, Rhonda Copelon, Adisa Douglas, Carola Greengard, Eddie Gonzalez, Linda Tschirhart Sanford, Susan Schechter, Barbara Seaman, Amy Schwartz, Karen Stamm, Nancy Stearns, and Nora Zamidow, and my daughters Laura and Jo Ellen Brainin all took time from their own valuable work to review and make helpful suggestions.

I give special thanks to Sheryl Burt Ruzek for her excellent analytical history *The Women's Health Movement* and to Sue Davis for her wise support and generous sharing of her writing skills. And finally, in memoriam, thanks to my dear friend Joan Kelly—feminist historian—for having been my friend and counselor.

NOTES

1. Sheryl Burt Ruzek, *The Women's Health Movement: Feminist Alternatives to Medical Control* (New York: Praeger, 1979).
2. The Boston Women's Health Book Collective, *Our Bodies, Ourselves* (Boston: New England Free Press, 1969).
3. Barbara Ehrenreich and Deirdre English, *Witches, Midwives, and Nurses: A History of Women Healers*, Glass Mountain Pamphlet, no. 1 (Old Westbury, N.Y.: Feminist Press, 1972); idem, *Complaints and Disorders: The Sexual Politics of Sickness* (Old Westbury, N.Y.: Feminist Press, 1973).
4. Barbara Seaman, *The Doctors' Case against the Pill* (New York: Avon, 1969).
5. Barbara Seaman and Gideon Seaman, *Women and the Crisis in Sex Hormones* (New York: Rawson Associates, 1977), 60–149.
6. Barbara Seaman, *Free and Female* (New York: Fawcett, 1972), 180–81.
7. Belita Cowan, "Going to Washington: The Women's Health Lobby," *Health Right* 2, no. 3 (1976): 4, 8.
8. Ruzek, *Women's Health Movement*, 44.
9. Barbara Ehrenreich, Mark Dowie, and Stephen Minkin, "The Charge: Gynocide; The Accused: The U.S. Government," *Mother Jones*, November 1979.
10. Stephen Minkin, "Depo-Provera: A Critical Analysis" *Women and Health* 5 (Summer 1980).
11. Ruzek, *Women's Health Movement*, 58.
12. Helen Marieskind, *An Evaluation of Caesarean Section in the United States* (Washington, D.C., DHEW, 1979).
13. Ruzek, *Women's Health Movement*, 48.
14. Gena Corea, "The Caesarean Epidemic," *Mother Jones*, July 1980.
15. Ibid.
16. Laurie Olsen, Letter to Editor, in *Mother Jones*, August 1980.
17. Seaman, *Doctors' Case against the Pill*, 14.
18. Ibid., 20.
19. Ibid., 6.
20. Ibid., 16.
21. Hal Strelnick and Richard Younge, *Double Indemnity: The Poverty and Mythology of Affirmative Action in the Health Professional Schools* (New York: Health-PAC, 1980).
22. Helen Rodriguez-Trias, "Tragedies We Hope Never to Be Repeated," *Response* 14, no. 8 (1982): 22. (Cincinnati: General Board of Global Ministries, United Methodist Church).
23. Ruzek, *Women's Health Movement*, 22.
24. Ibid., 25.
25. Robert E. McGarraugh, Jr., *Sterilization without Consent: Teaching Hospital Violations of HEW Regulations: A Report by Public Citizens' Health Research Group* (Washington, D.C.: Public Citizens' Health Research Group, 1975).
26. James E. Allen, "An Appearance of Genocide: A Review of Governmental Family-Planning Program Policies," *Perspectives in Biology and Medicine* 20 (1977): 300–306; Allen Chase, *The Legacy of Malthus: The Social Costs of the New Scientific Racism* (New York: Knopf, 1977).
27. *Morbidity and Mortality Weekly Report*, November 4, 1977.
28. Helen Rodriguez-Trias, "Sterilization Abuse" (Reid Memorial Lecture, Barnard Women's Center, 1978).
29. Relf v. Weinberger, 372 F. Supp. 1196. 1199 (D.D.C. 1974).
30. McGarraugh, *Sterilization without Consent*; Elissa Krauss, "Hospital Survey on Sterilization Policies: Reproductive Freedom Project," *American Civil Liberties Union Reports*, March, 1975.
31. New York City Health and Hospitals Corporation, *Why Sterilization Guidelines Are Needed* (New York: Office of Quality Assurance, 1975).
32. Claudia Dreifus, "Sterilizing the Poor," *The Progressive*, December 1975, p. 13; Joan Kelly, "Sterilization and Civil Rights," *Rights* 23 (September, 1977): 9–11 (New York: National Emergency Civil Liberties Committee).
33. "Why Sterilization Guidelines Are Needed."
34. New York City Health and Hospitals Corporation, *Guidelines on Sterilization Procedures* (New York: Office of Quality Assurance, 1975).
35. Gordon W. Douglas et al. and John L. S. Holloman et al., Civil Action File no. 76, CW6 U.S. District Court, January 5, 1976.
36. Department of Health, Education, and Welfare, Regional Hearings on Guidelines on Sterilization, unpublished testimony, 1978.
37. *Sterilization Abuse: What It Is and How It Can Be Controlled* (Washington, D.C.: National Women's Health Network, 1981).
38. José Vázquez-Calzada, "La esterilizacion femenina en Puerto Rico," *Revista de Ciencias Sociales* 17 (1973): 281–308.
39. Allen, "Appearance of Genocide."
40. General Accounting Office, Report to Hon. James G. Abourezk, Report no. B 16403(5), November 1976, p. 3.
41. "Uri Charges I.H.S. with Genocide Policy," *Hospital Tribune*, no. 13, August 1977.
42. Bonnie Mass, *Population Target* (Toronto: Latin American Working Group, 1976); Terry L. McCoy et al., *The Dynamics of Population Policy in Latin America* (Cambridge, Mass.: Ballinger, 1974).
43. *Our Bodies, Ourselves*, 1973 edition, p. 2.
44. *Sterilization Abuse.*   [1984]

128

National Congress of Neighborhood Women

LINDSY VAN GELDER

I grew up in the kind of house where if someone mentioned the Seven Sisters, they were referring to the family down the street, not to the likes of Vassar and Mount Holyoke. Maybe that's partly why I felt instant delight the first time I walked into the headquarters of the National Congress of Neighborhood Women in Brooklyn, New York. Imagine a rally for the Equal Rights Amendment in the parish social hall with scores of Edith Bunkers crossed with Wonder Womans, and you begin to get an idea of the NCNW's unique vitality.

"There's a stereotype of the working-class woman as being passive and inarticulate and incapable of thinking about the 'larger' issues outside her home," says Christine Noschese, NCNW staff director. "There's another myth that says the Women's Movement is antifamily, antichurch, antineighborhood." Noschese—who has a thicket of street-urchin ringlets and the kind of passionate, hand-waving energy that makes you think she could probably jolly Marabel Morgan into founding a child-care center—believes that traditional values and feminist activism are not never-the-twain-shall-meet opposites. On the contrary, the NCNW operates on the premise "that sisterhood *begins* in the family."

Before the founding of the NCNW four years ago, "class" was a bit of a scare-word in the Women's Movement. Precisely because we did focus on everyday matters like who did the dishes—instead of traditional leftist abstractions about the "proletariat"—we were branded early on in the press as a "middle-class movement." (The press then compounded its judgment by seeking out only our most colorful or "presentable" spokeswomen—thus feeding a self-fulfilling prophecy.) Many feminists reacted by simply denying that a class problem existed. (Or a race problem, or a sexual preference or age problem, or any of the other divide-and-conquer complexities that threatened what we knew

to be true—that feminism offers the potential to change *all* women's lives.)

But the truth is that a disproportionate amount of early feminist energy came (not surprisingly) from those white, college-educated women in their twenties who had been encouraged by their parents and teachers to develop their talents—at least up to a point. NCNW President Laura Scanlon—who grew up behind her immigrant parents' delicatessen and now holds a Ph.D. in education—notes that such encouragement is quite different from the experience of a lower-middle-class girl whose parents' reaction to her desire to be a doctor might be "Who do you think *you* are?" Nor were working-class women always comfortable with burgeoning feminist styles and structures. Consciousness-raising comes easier to a middle-class woman who's been in group therapy than to a woman brought up to believe that you should never wash your dirty laundry in public; equal pay for equal work is a luxury concept for women who can't get work at all.

Enter the NCNW. The concept for the organization grew out of a 1974 meeting in Washington, D.C., attended by Barbara Mikulski (then a Baltimore city councilwoman, now Democratic Congressional Representative) and some 150 other women active in ethnic and community groups across the country. One of them was Jan Peterson, then director of an antipoverty agency in the Williamsburg section of Brooklyn. Several months earlier, Peterson had organized an open meeting for Williamsburg women to talk about the problems they shared as women and how a new women's organization might solve them.

At the original meeting, two of the most pressing concerns expressed were the need for jobs and the desire for more education. Using her antipoverty contacts and know-how, Peterson then proceeded to wangle federal money to set up the first NCNW staff as well as community-based jobs for 25 women in senior-citizen centers and schools.

This revolution-by-subsidy structure and the NCNW's continued emphasis on bread-and-butter concerns put the group in sharp contrast to the "typical" Movement organizations formed around issues or consciousness-raising and powered by volunteer labor. "We're not too big on abstract theory," explained Christine Noschese. "Our main concern is providing direct services—helping women get education, jobs, better child care, health care, and setting up battered women's shelters." The NCNW has also been active in causes which at first glance don't seem classically "feminist"—badgering the city not to shut down a local firehouse, for instance. Thus, the organization functions day-to-day much more like a community center than does the average Movement group whose membership is only peripherally related to geographic closeness.

There are now more than 100 active "members" in the NCNW, which has successively moved from a storefront to a factory loft to its new floor-through headquarters (in what used to be a Catholic high school) on a street of small manufacturing companies and neat one- and two-family homes.

The women who use the center are Italian, Polish, black, and Hispanic, of all ages. And while most of them are married and mothers, there are also single, divorced, and lesbian women. ("The gay issue isn't an issue here," joked one woman. "At Polish and Italian parties, the women have *always* danced with each other.") Most are women from the neighborhood whose previous political experience was in churches and block associations; others—like Scanlon, Noschese, and Peterson—returned to their working-class roots after managing to get a college education and becoming active in the Women's Movement.

Politically, the group has more variety than a vacant lot has weeds—ranging from various stripes of feminists (five of whom were New York State delegates to the National Women's Conference in Houston) to women who hold conservative views on abortion, plus a hefty sprinkling of others who tend to start discussions with the phrase, "I'm not a feminist, *but*. . . ." The one thing everyone accepts is her sister's right to call herself whatever the hell she pleases and to focus on the issues that most touch her life.

Such unity is often baffling to middle-class feminists outside the group. Several years ago, one NCNW activist voted against the New York State ERA and gave interviews to several newspaper reporters, charging that middle-class ERA supporters had failed to think through the implications of alimony-loss and other possible legislative changes for her and women like her. It was the kind of difference of opinion that would easily have caused a schism in another feminist group; but while there *was* plenty of loud arguing around the NCNW where most of the women worked hard for the Amendment, no one questioned the fact that the woman had voted out of her own perception of what was best for women.

Laura Scanlon believes that the NCNW women also come from backgrounds that uniquely equip them to manage such conflicts—that you wouldn't for instance, disown your mother or sister because she disagreed with you on abortion. "I like to think that those of us who grew up in these traditional families and neighborhoods have certain skills—like how to form an ongoing emotional support system or how to mobilize your community," she said. "If these skills are transferable, I think we can make some really important contributions to the rest of the Women's Movement in the next few years."

For those of us who tend to mistrust institutions like church and family as historic oppressors of women, the NCNW-brand of feminism can indeed seem controversial. At second glance, however, the group's concerns look startlingly akin to the who-does-the-dishes immediate gut-issues that originally characterized us as a "middle-class" movement. Several NCNW members, for instance, recently shook up an Italian-American conference by demanding that the men who were present schedule a discussion about sexism in Italian-American male culture.

The "traditional" NCNW has also managed—more than many "radical" groups—to create and nurture alternative feminist structures. The group helped to open a shelter for battered women, established a credit union branch, and have made plans for a legal services center concentrating on women's problems. Last year the NCNW organized Project Open Doors, a 38-group New York City women's coalition, which successfully negotiated with the government for $2.6 million in job slots under the Comprehensive Employment and Training Act (CETA). The grant has provided jobs for 200 feminists in dozens of projects—a self-defense school for single mothers and their children, a program to monitor local hospital compliance with sterilization guidelines, a carpentry class for East Harlem women, research into the lives and works of early

American women poets, job counseling for women in blue-collar trades, a film about battered women, and more. Alice Quinn, project director of Open Doors, coordinates and administers the various CETA projects out of the Brooklyn headquarters.

Another extraordinary NCNW success story was the establishment (through foundation grants) of an accredited, tuition-free NCNW junior college, also operated on the Brooklyn premises. "After the first meeting, it was obvious that a lot of women really wanted more education," recalled Christine Noschese; but many were unwilling or unable to leave the neighborhood to take advantage of existing opportunities. Furthermore, added Laura Scanlon, many felt alienated by the attitude that "a working-class person only goes to college to break *out* of the working class. The women here wanted the kind of education that helps you give something back to your community." Curriculum thus evolved in keeping with NCNW's overall amalgam of hard-nosed pragmatism and misty-eyed group pride: economics students analyze the New York City budget cuts that affect the neighborhood, and writing students produce essays on such topics as "My Italian Grandmother, Theresa."

One current student is 50-year-old Ida Collazo, who wears an enormous button on her blouse that says: YOU CAN DO IT. It was a gift from one of her daughters, who said that she "ought to be able to do college after ten kids." Collazo is almost high on her newfound knowledge: "I used to hate math. Now—metrics, probabilities, standard deviations—ask me anything. Thanks to the NCNW, God bless them!" But without the NCNW's "buddy system"—a flying squad of sisterly support that mobilizes at the drop of discouragement and operates as the exact reverse of the competition for grades found at most other schools—Collazo admits she'd be back home with the children: "In the beginning, I cried. I almost quit, *write that down*, it might make somebody who reads it take hope." Several dozen women have already earned degrees, and the NCNW is now in the process of setting up two similar college programs in other Brooklyn neighborhoods.

The group has also begun forming a nationwide information-sharing network with dozens of senior citizen, neighborhood, ethnic, and women's organizations across the country, all of which have become official NCNW affiliates for the nominal fee of $5 a year. In the future, the affiliates may band together to lobby for federal laws and programs affecting localities or low-income women in particular. (The NCNW, for instance, is critical of various federal income eligibility requirements that are limited to the very poor, leaving working-class families in a no-woman's-land where they can't, say, afford private child care but can't get into public child care either.)

"I don't think everybody has to be a card-carrying ERA/abortion-rights/gay-rights/women-candidates kind of feminist to advance women's rights," said Jan Peterson. "We're the ones who are reaching the traditional woman who cares a lot about, for example, the poor public transportation in her community and how that affects her safety and her job options." Just because they address such everyday community-survival issues, she added, the NCNW and groups like it may be "the only answer to the right-wing movement in this country today."

[1979]

🌿 129

Nine to Five

ELLEN CASSIDY and KAREN NUSSBAUM

A company once tried to sell office equipment by advertising "This machine is just like your secretary: silent, efficient, and easily manipulable." Those days are over. There is a new spirit in the office.

A movement is afoot. All over the country, women office workers are demanding equal pay, fair promotion opportunity, decent working conditions, and respect. What is happening? How did it all begin?

For us, it began when we were twenty years old and clerk-typists at Harvard University. One day Karen was staggering down the hall carrying a load of doctoral dissertations. "Why aren't you smiling, dear?" asked a passing professor with a wink. Another day Ellen's boss ceremoniously placed a note on her desk before disappearing back into his office. "Please remove calendar from my wall," it said.

Ellen went to his office, unstuck two pieces of masking tape from the calendar, and put it on his desk. Why had he wasted his time ordering her to do something that he could have done himself in ten seconds?

Then one afternoon a young male student came into our office. Standing in front of Karen and looking directly at her, he asked, "Isn't anyone here?" At that moment, we realized what it was that our working lives lacked. It was respect. The lack of respect was as commonplace as paper clips. So routine, in fact, that we wondered if there was something wrong with *us* in finding such treatment objectionable.

It wasn't long before we discovered that our own experience was very similar to that of other women office workers. In 1972 we attended a weekend workshop for office workers at the YWCA. As the conference got rolling, the problems poured out. Whatever the industry or the size of the office, women faced a lack of respect, low pay, limited advancement opportunity, and little say over working conditions.

Ellen's story about the calendar was matched and topped by story after story about women required to perform favors for their bosses, cover for them, do their work. One woman complained that her years of experience seemed to be standing in the way of advancement rather than helping her get ahead. Another said she'd gone to college but found that her education hadn't helped her get a better job.

Many complained that they performed duties that were far outside their job descriptions, to which others responded that they wished they *had* job descriptions. An insurance worker said she was doing the same work as the men in her office but was being paid less. Several women said they had trained men to be their own supervisors.

For others, the problems weren't particularly dramatic. They just worked 35 or 40 hours a week, and worked hard, but didn't bring home enough money. A teller said she didn't make enough to get a loan from the bank she worked for. A clerk in a hospital couldn't afford to get sick; a university secretary couldn't afford to send her children to college.

For a few of us, an office job was a way to make a living temporarily, until marriage or until we went back to school. But for most, office work was a life-time career. And it wasn't necessarily the jobs themselves that we wanted changed. For the most part, we liked our jobs. We liked the variety, the contact with people. We liked being at the hub of the company and knowing what was going on. We liked communicating by phone, in writing, in person. We liked using our initiative, judgment, and diplomatic skills. We were proud of our work. What we didn't like was the way we were treated and how little we were paid.

A consensus grew in our little seminar: We were being taken advantage of, and it was time to put a stop to it. Ten of us got together after the workshop and printed a short newsletter about the issues that frustrated us most. Before work, we stood at subway exits and in front of Boston's biggest office buildings and distributed it to the women hurrying to their jobs. The response was overwhelming. We received dozens of letters and phone calls, and soon held a meeting attended by 300 women, all bursting with grievances about their work situations.

A few months later, in November 1973, we formed an association of working women and called it 9 to 5, after the usual hours of the business day. And if we had thought there was a crying need for such an organization, we became even more convinced when we went to the library for statistics to back up our claims of unfair working conditions.

The situation was much worse than we'd realized. According to the Department of Labor, clerical workers earned less on the average than every kind of blue-collar worker. Women workers earned only a fraction of men's pay in every occupation, and worse yet, that fraction had diminished over the past generation. Within the realm of office work, we averaged $5,000 less per year than men.

We were also surprised to find out from the Department of Labor that office workers were—and are—the largest and fastest-growing sector of the work force. When most people are asked to picture the typical American worker, a man with a lunch pail comes to mind. Yet in fact the typical American worker is a woman at a keyboard. There are nearly 20 million of us, accounting for more than one out of every five workers. Office industries are growing and thriving, and the demand for our labor is healthy. All these conditions increase our chances of winning better treatment.

The movement began to grow. When a business journal carried a brief mention of the organization, we were flooded with over 3,000 calls and letters from secretaries all over the country. Some spoke in whispers; one woman said her boss had threatened to fire her if she joined. ("So I *had* to call," she explained.) We learned of women taking action all over the country, in the smallest, most out-of-the-way places. Eight bank workers in a tiny, conservative Midwestern town went on strike for eighteen long, cold months after the bank president told them, "We're not all equal, you know." Their story became national news. We were contacted by a woman in a small Southern town who had overheard a young man boasting that his salary exceeded hers. She and her coworkers filed charges and won the largest back-pay settlement in the state's civil rights history.

We joined forces with women workers organizing in other cities. We answered letters about job problems and held workshops on how to ask for a raise, plan for retirement, and organize to win better treatment. The news of victories began to roll in. Women reported that they had asked for raises for the first time in their lives—and gotten them. Petitions were circulated. Groups of women met with their bosses to demand policy changes. Women rewrote their job descriptions to make them more accurate, and stopped making coffee. Women in the publishing, insurance, and banking industries filed discrimination charges and won millions of dollars in back pay as well as new promotion and training programs.

National Secretaries' Week, established in 1952 by the U.S. Department of Commerce, underwent a radical transformation. The last full week in April had been a time when bosses were supposed to present their secretaries with a bouquet of roses or a box of candy in thanks for a year of hard work. Now secretaries used the occasion both to reflect with pride on their contributions and to ask whether they were being fairly compensated. "Raises, not roses" became a nationwide rallying cry.

Office workers began to be visible. Representatives of 9 to 5 were even invited to speak at management conferences. Managers suddenly wanted to know what office workers were thinking. Some began to overhaul their employment policies and make much-needed changes.

To be sure, many bosses dragged their feet and fought back outright when asked to treat office workers better. The Chamber of Commerce of one Southern city even sent out a letter to all its members, inviting them to a training session on how to respond to office workers' demands for grievance procedures and higher pay. But the mailing backfired. Secretaries themselves opened the mail for their bosses, read the letter, and deluged the local 9 to 5 office with applications for membership.

The labor movement became interested in office workers. In 1981, 9 to 5 and the Service Employees International Union jointly established District 925, a nationwide union for office workers. Progress was made in our organizing efforts from Washington, D.C., to Washington State, and office workers from all over the country called for information on organizing a union. . . .*

Today 9 to 5 is a national association of working women. Women call every day to ask how to join or how to form a local chapter. Some are individuals; others are members of groups that have been meeting for months at a local church or company cafeteria. Our national newsletter is read by typists, administrative assistants, tellers, editors, word-processing operators, secretaries, clerks.

The outlook for women office workers is now vastly different from what it was a decade ago. It is true that the majority of the nation's 42 million working women are still employed in so-called women's jobs. But what has changed dramatically is our ability to win respect and fair treatment. Public opinion is now on our side. We no longer have to spend our time convincing others that discrimination exists, or that women deserve equal pay, fair promotion opportunities, and respect. Along with this new climate, our growing numbers give us strength, and our urgent economic needs give us a compelling reason to take action. And finally, women have realized that we will have to organize to achieve the rights and respect we deserve.   [1983]

---

*Editor's note: 9 to 5 is now in Milwaukee; the phone number is (414) 272-7795.

130

Voices

WOMEN OF ACE (AIDS COUNSELING
AND EDUCATION), BEDFORD HILLS
CORRECTIONAL FACILITY

*The authors of this essay are Kathy Boudin, July Clark, "D,"
Katrina Haslip, Maria D. L. Hernandez, Suzanne Kessler,
Sonia Perez, Deborah Plunkett, Aida Rivera, Doris Romeo,
Carmen Royster, Cathy Salce, Renee Scott, Jenny Serrano, and
Pearl Ward.*

INTRODUCTION

We are writing about ACE because we feel that it
has made a tremendous difference in this prison
and could make a difference in other prisons. ACE
stands for AIDS Counseling and Education. It is a
collective effort by women in Bedford Hills Correctional Facility. This article will reflect that collec-
tivity by being a patchwork quilt of many women's
voices.

ACE was started by inmates in 1988 because of
the crisis that AIDS was creating in our community.
According to a blind study done in the Fall-Winter
of 1987–88, almost 20 percent of the women entering the New York state prison system were HIV infected.[1] It is likely to be higher today. In addition,
women here have family members who are sick and
friends who are dying. People have intense fears of
transmission through casual contact because we live
so closely together. Women are worried about their
children and about having safe sex. All this need and
energy led to the creation of ACE.

BEFORE ACE

Prior to the formation of ACE, Bedford was an environment of fear, stigma, lack of information, and
evasion. AIDS was a word that was whispered.
People had no forum in which to talk about their
fears. The doctors and nurses showed their biases. They preferred to just give advice, and many
wouldn't touch people because of their own fears.
There were several deaths. This inflamed people's
fear more. People didn't want to look at their own
vulnerability—their IV drug use and unsafe sex.

I felt very negative about people who I knew were
sick. To save face, I spoke to them from afar. I felt
that they all should be put into a building by themselves because I heard that people who were healthy
could make them sick and so they should get specific care. I figured that I have more time (on my
sentence); why should I be isolated? They should
be. I felt very negative and it came a lot from fear.[2]

Women at Bedford who are sick are housed in a
hospital unit called In Patient Care (IPC). ACE
members remember what IPC was like before ACE:

The IPC area—the infirmary—was horrible before, a place where nobody wanted to be. It was a
place to go to die. Before ACE people started going
there, it looked like a dungeon. It was unsanitary.
Just the look of it made people feel like they were
going to die. That was the end.

There was no support system for women who
wanted to take the HIV-antibody test:

I had a friend who tested positive. The doctor told
her, you are HIV positive, but that doesn't mean you
have AIDS. You shouldn't have sex, or have a baby,
and you should avoid stress. Period. No information
was given to her. No counseling and support. She
freaked out.

THE BEGINNING OF ACE:
BREAKING THE SILENCE

Some of us sensed that people needed to talk, but
no one would break the silence. Finally, five women
got together, and made a proposal to the superintendent:

We said that we ourselves had to help ourselves. We
believed that as peers we would be the most effective in education, counseling, and building a community of support. We stated four main goals: to
save lives through preventing the spread of HIV; to
create more humane conditions for those who are
HIV positive; to give support and education to
women with fears, questions, and needs related to
AIDS; to act as a bridge to community groups
to help women as they reenter the community.

The superintendent accepted the proposal. Each of
the five women sought out other women in the
population who they believed were sensitive and
would be interested in breaking the silence. When

they reached 35, they stopped and a meeting was called.

BREAKING THE SILENCE CHANGED US: WE BEGAN TO BUILD A COMMUNITY

At that first meeting a sigh of relief was felt and it rippled out. There was a need from so many directions. People went around the table and said why they were there. About the fourth or fifth woman said, "I'm here because I have AIDS." There was an intense silence. It was the first time anyone had said that aloud in a group. By the end of the meeting, several more women had said that they were HIV positive. Breaking the silence, the faith that it took, and the trust it built was really how ACE started.

BREAKING THE SILENCE MEANT SOMETHING SPECIAL TO PWAS

I often ask myself how it is that I came to be open about my status. For me, AIDS had been one of my best kept secrets. It took me approximately 15 months to discuss this issue openly. As if not saying it aloud would make it go away. I watched other people with AIDS (PWAs), who were much more open than I was at the time, reveal to audiences their status/their vulnerability, while sharing from a distance, from silence, every word that was being uttered by them. I wanted to be a part of what they were building, what they were doing, their statement, "I am a PWA," because I was. It was a relief when I said it. I could stop going on with the lie. I could be me. People were supportive and they didn't shun me. And now I can go anywhere and be myself.

SUPPORTING PWAS

PWAs and HIV-positive women are at the heart of our work. ACE believes that everyone facing HIV-related illness is confronting issues of life and death and struggling to survive and thrive.

We had to have some place for PWAs to share their experiences with each other. There have been numerous support groups which allowed us to express things that hadn't been verbalized but that had been on our minds. It was interesting to see that we had similar issues: how to tell significant others, our own vulnerability about being open, living with AIDS. My first group was a mixture of people. Some were recently diagnosed and others had been diagnosed

for two years. It was informative and it was emotional. Sometimes we would just come to a meeting and cry. Or we might come there and not even talk about the issue of AIDS and just have a humor session because we are just tired of AIDS.

One of the first things that ACE ever did was to work in IPC.

ACE started going to IPC. We painted, cleaned up, made it look so good that now the women want to stay there. We take care of the girls who are sick, making them feel comfortable and alive. Now, women there know they have a friend. They feel free, they talk, and look forward to visits. They know they're not there to die, not like before.

BEING A BUDDY

I have been involved in ACE for about three years. About a year ago I started visiting the women in IPC. I was really afraid at first. Not afraid of getting sick, but of becoming emotionally involved and then have the women die. At first, I tried to keep my feelings and friendship at a minimum. The more I went, the more I lost this fear. There is one woman I have gotten closer to than the rest. She has been in IPC since I first started going there. We are buddies. For me to be her buddy means unconditionally loving her and accepting her decisions. I go almost every night to IPC. Some nights we just sit there and say nothing. But there is comfort in my presence. She had a stroke before I met her. So there is a lot she cannot do for herself. There are times when I bathe and dress her. Iron her clothes. I do not think of any of these things as chores. Soon she will be going home. I am overjoyed, but I'm also saddened knowing that I will not see her again. I will miss her hugs, her complaining, and her love. But I would do it all over again and I probably will with someone else.

MEDICAL ADVOCACY

It is obviously a matter of life or death for anyone who is HIV infected to get good medical care and have a good relationship with her health providers. Medical facilities in prisons start out understaffed and ill equipped, and the AIDS crisis escalated these problems enormously. In the 1970s women prisoners here instituted a class action suit, *Todaro v. Ward*, to demand better medical care. Because of that case, the medical facilities and care at Bedford are monitored for the court by an outside expert.

That expert issued a report criticizing all aspects of the medical department for being inadequately prepared to meet women's AIDS-related medical needs, and the prison faced a court hearing and possible contempt charges. Under that pressure the state agreed to numerous changes that brought new medical staff and resources, including a full-time medical director, a part-time infectious disease specialist, and more nurses. ACE was able to institute a medical advocacy plan that allowed ACE members to accompany women to their doctor's consultation visit to ensure that nothing was missed. Afterward, there can be a private discussion between the patient and the advocate to clarify matters for the woman, to explore possibilities of treatment, or just to allow the person to express whatever emotions she experienced when she received the news from the doctor.

PEER EDUCATION

Our approach is *peer* education, which we believe is best suited for the task of enabling a community to mobilize itself to deal with AIDS. The people doing the training clearly have a personal stake in the community. The education is for all, in the interests of all. This is communicated from the beginning by the women doing the teaching.

Our peer education takes a problem-posing approach. We present issues as problems facing all of us, problems to be examined by drawing on the knowledge and experience of the women being trained. What are the issues between a man and a woman, for example, that make it hard for a woman to demand that her man use a condom? Will distributing free needles or advocating bleach kits stop the spread of AIDS among IV drug users?

Our educational work is holistic. Education is not solely a presentation of facts, although that is an important part of the trainers' responsibilities. But what impact do feelings and attitudes have on how people deal with facts? Why would a person who knows that you cannot get AIDS by eating from a PWA's plate still act occasionally as if you could? Why would a person who knows that sex without a condom could be inviting death, not use a condom? For education to be a deep process, it involves understanding the whole person; for education to take root within a community, it means thinking about things on a community, social level.

Coming to prison, living under these conditions, was scary, and AIDS made it even scarier. I was part of a society that made judgments and had preconceived ideas about the women in prison.

EDUCATING OURSELVES

Workshops

To become members of ACE, women must be educated through a series of eight workshops. We look at how stigma and blame have been associated with diseases throughout history, and how the sexism of this society impacts on women in the AIDS epidemic. We teach about the nature of the virus, strategies for treatment, and holistic approaches. After the eight weeks, we ask who would like to become involved, and then there is a screening process. The Superintendent has final approval. The workshops are followed by more intensive training of women who become members.

Orientation

When women enter the New York state prison system, they must come first to Bedford Hills, where they either stay or move on after several weeks to one of several other women's prisons. ACE members talk with the women when they first arrive.

We do orientations of 10 to 35 women. We explain to them how you can and cannot get AIDS, about testing and about ACE. Sometimes the crowd is very boisterous and rude. I say "AIDS" and they don't want to hear about it. But those are the ones I try to reach. After orientation is over, the main ones that didn't want to hear about AIDS are the ones who want to talk more and I feel good about that. A lot of times, their loudness is a defense because they are afraid of their own vulnerability. They know that they are at risk for HIV infection because of previous behaviors. After I finish doing orientation, I have a sense of warmth, because I know I made a difference in some of their lives.

Seminars

One of the main ways we interact with our sisters is through seminars. We talk about AIDS issues with groups of women on living units, in classrooms, and in some of the other prison programs such as family violence, drug treatment, and Children's Center.

The four back buildings are dormitories, each holding 100 women with double bunked beds. We from ACE gather right after count, with our easel and newsprint and magic markers and our three-by-five cards with the information on whatever presentation we're making. We move in twos and threes through the connecting tunnels to the building. When we arrive some of the women are sitting in the rec room, but many others are in their cubicles/cells. They ask why we're here. We look like a traveling troupe—and we've felt like it, not knowing what to expect. Some women are excited that we're going to talk about AIDS. Others say, "forget it," or "fuck you, I've heard enough about it, it's depressing."

But we begin, and people slowly gather.

We ask the women to help us role-play a situation such as a woman going home from prison, trying to convince her man, who has been taking care of her while she's inside, to use a condom. Then the role-play is analyzed. What problems are encountered and how do we deal with those problems? We try to come up with suggestions that we can see ourselves using in that situation. We talk about the risk of violence.

One of the most immediate problems people have is whether or not to take the HIV-antibody test. We do not push testing. We explain what the test is and have a group discussion of things the women need to consider. A woman may be inclined to get tested, but she needs to know that she is likely to be transferred upstate before the results come back from the lab. The choice is up to her. Toward the end of the seminar, PWAs talk about their experiences living with AIDS.

When they speak, they bring together everything that we have said. Not only that, but they let people know that living with AIDS is not instant death. It makes people realize why the struggles, working together, and being as one are so important. When I hear the women who are PWAs speak, it makes me realize that I could have been in their shoes, or I could still be, if they hadn't been willing to talk about their risk behaviors and what has happened to them. It gives me the courage to realize that it's not all about me. It's actually about us.

We end each seminar with all the women standing with our arms around each other or holding hands—without any fear of casual contact—singing our theme song, "Sister."[3] We sing, having come to a new place where we are for each other, unified. We all feel some sense of relief and some sense of hope. Talking about AIDS openly has changed how we live. We leave the seminar with the knowledge that we can talk about AIDS and that we're going to be okay. . . .

Counseling

When we conduct the seminars and orientation sessions, women come up to us afterward with personal questions and problems. It could be they are HIV positive, or they are thinking of taking the test, or they have a family member who is sick, or they are thinking about getting involved with someone in a relationship. Sometimes they raise one issue, but underlying it are a lot of other issues they're not yet ready to talk about. Because women know we're in ACE, we're approached in our housing units, at school, on the job, in the mess hall, as we walk from one place to another. Women stop us, needing to talk. We're a haven for women because they know ACE has a principle of confidentiality. Women can trust us not to abuse the information they are sharing with us.

Peer counseling. I'm just impressed that we can do it. I didn't know what kind of potential we'd have as peers. We talk the language that each of us understands. Even if it's silent, even if it's with our eyes, it's something that each of us seems to understand. I know I wouldn't want someone from the Department of Health who hasn't even taken a Valium to try to educate me about IV drug use. How could they give me helpful hints? I would feel that they are so out of tune with reality that I wouldn't be able to hear them.

A CRISIS AND OPPORTUNITY FOR OUR COMMUNITY

We are a small community and we are so isolated you can feel it—the suffering, the losses, the fears, the anxiety. Out in the street you don't have a community of women affected and living together facing a problem in this same way. We can draw on the particular strengths that women bring: nurturance, caring, and personal openness. So many women prisoners have worked in nursing and old age homes. Yet when they did, they were never given respect. Here these same activities are valued, and the women are told "thank you," and that creates initiative and feelings of self-worth. And ACE helps us to be more self-conscious about a culture of caring that as women we tend to create in our daily lives.

> For the first time in prison I was part of a group that cared about other prisoners in prison. What did that feel like? It felt like I wasn't alone in caring about people, because in this type of setting I was beginning to wonder about people caring.

OUR IMPACT ON WOMEN

We know that we have played a role in communicating information about what is safe and what is not safe in sexual behavior—both between a man and woman and between two women—and we have certainly been able to create open and relaxed discussions about all this. But we know that actually changing behaviors is another leap ahead of us. We are learning that it's not a one-shot deal, that information doesn't equal behavior change, and it's not just an individual thing. Social norms have to change, and this takes time. And when you talk about women having to initiate change you're up against the fact that women don't have that kind of empowerment in this society. Women who have been influenced by ACE have experienced a change in attitude, but it is unclear whether this will translate into behavior change once they leave the prison.

> When I first started taking the workshops I was 100 percent against using condoms. And yet I like anal sex. But now my views are different. We're the bosses of our own bodies. You know, a lot of people say it's a man's world. Well, I can't completely agree.

OUR DIVERSITY IS A STRENGTH

We are a diverse community of women: Black, Latin, and white, and also from countries throughout the world. In ACE there was at first a tendency to deny the differences, maybe out of fear of disunity. Now there is a more explicit consciousness growing that we can affirm our diversity and our commonality because both are important. In the last workshop on women, we broke for a while into three groups—Black, Latina, and white women—to explore the ways AIDS impacted on our particular

culture and communities. We are doing more of those kinds of discussions and developing materials that address concerns of specific communities. The Hispanic Sector of ACE is particularly active, conducting seminars in Spanish and holding open meetings for the population to foster Hispanic awareness of AIDS issues.

> The workshops didn't deal enough with different ethnic areas, and being Puerto Rican and half-Indian, some things seemed ridiculous in terms of the Hispanic family. Some of the ways people were talking about sex wouldn't work in a traditional Hispanic family. For example, you can't just tell your husband that he has to wear a condom. Or say to him, "You have to take responsibility." These approaches could lead to marital rape or abuse. The empowerment of Hispanic women means making sure that their children are brought up.

WORKING IN A PRISON

We have a unique situation at Bedford Hills. We have a prison administration that is supportive of inmates developing a peer-based program to deal with AIDS. However, because we are in a prison there are a lot of constraints and frustrations. Before we had staff persons to supervise us, we could not work out of an office space. That meant that we couldn't see women who wanted to talk on an individual level unless we ran into them in the yard or rec room.

You could be helping someone in IPC take her daily shower; it's taking longer than usual because she is in a lot of pain or she needs to talk, but that's not taken into consideration when the officer tells you that you have to leave immediately because it's "count-time." You could be in the rec room, a large room with a bunch of card tables, loud music, and an officer overseeing groups of women sitting on broken-down chairs. You're talking to a woman in crisis who needs comforting. You reach out to give her a hug and the C.O. may come over to admonish you, "No physical contact, ladies." Or maybe a woman has just tested positive. She's taken her first tentative steps to reach out by talking to someone from ACE and joining a support group. Days after her first meeting, she is transferred to another prison.

It's been difficult to be able to call ourselves counselors and have our work formally acknowl-

"Sister"

CRIS WILLIAMSON

Born of the earth
Child of God
Just one among the family
And you can count on me
To share the load
And I will always help you
Hold burdens
And I will be the one
To help you ease your pain

Lean on me, I am your sister
Believe on me, I am your friend

I will fold you in my arms
Like a white wing dove
Shine in your soul
Your spirit is crying

Born of the earth
Child of God
Just one among the family
And you can count on me
To share the load
And I will always help you
Hold burdens
And I will be the one
To help you ease your pain

Lean on me, I am your sister
Believe on me, I am your friend
Lean on me, I am your sister
Believe on me, I am your friend

edged by the administration. Counseling is usually done by professionals in here because it carries such liability and responsibility. We're struggling for the legitimacy of peer counseling. The reality is that we've been doing it in our daily lives here through informal dialogue. We now have civilian staff to supervise us, and Columbia University will be conducting a certification training program to justify the title "peer counselor."

After working over two years on our own, we are now being funded by a grant from the New York State AIDS Institute, coordinated by Columbia University School of Public Health and by Women and AIDS Resource Network (WARN). The money has allowed hiring staff to work with ACE. ACE began as a totally volunteer inmate organization with no office or materials, operating on a shoestring and scrambling for every meeting. Now we have an office in a prime location of the prison, computers, and a civilian staff responsible for making certain that there is something to show for their salaries. Inmates who used to work whenever they could find the time are now paid 73 cents a day as staff officially assigned to the ACE Center. The crises are no longer centered around the problems of being inside a prison, but more on how to sustain momentum and a real grassroots initiative in the context of a prison. This is a problem faced by many other community organizations when they move past the initial momentum and become more established institutions.

BUILDING A CULTURE OF SURVIVAL

When, in the spring of 1987, we said, "Let's make quilt squares for our sisters who have died," there were more than 15 names. Over the next year we made more and more quilt squares. The deaths took a toll not just on those who knew the women but on all of us. Too many women were dying among us. And, for those who were HIV positive or worried that they might be, each death heightened their own vulnerabilities and fears. We have had to develop ways to let people who are sick know that if they die, their lives will be remembered, they will be honored and celebrated, and they will stay in our hearts.

> I remember our first memorial. Several hundred women contributed money—25 cents, 50 cents, a dollar—for flowers. Both Spanish and Black women sang and in the beginning everyone held hands and sang "That's What Friends Are For," and in the end we sang "Sister." People spoke about what Ro meant to them. Ro had died and we couldn't change that. But we didn't just feel terrible. We felt love and caring and that together we could survive the sadness and loss.
>
> In the streets, funerals were so plastic, but here, people knew that it could be them. It's not just to pay respect. When we sang "Sister," there was a charge between us. Our hands were extended to each other. There was a need for ACE and we could feel it in the air.

It was out of that same need that ACE was formed. It will be out of that same need that ACE will continue to strive to build community and an environment of trust and support. We are all we have—ourselves. If we do not latch on to this hope that has strengthened us and this drive that has broken our silence, we too will suffer and we will remain stigmatized and isolated. Feel our drive in our determination to make changes, and think "community," and make a difference.

NOTES

1. Perry F. Smith et al., *Infection Among Women Entering the New York State Correctional System* (1990), unpublished manuscript.
2. All quotations are from the authors' conversations with prisoners at Bedford Hills.
3. By Cris Williamson, from the album *The Changer and the Changed,* Olivia Records, 1975.   [1990]

 131

Developing a Reproductive Rights Agenda for the 1990s

KATHRYN KOLBERT

This is a call for a reproductive rights agenda for the 1990s. It suggests a process for developing a comprehensive approach to reproductive rights issues and outlines an agenda that can serve as a starting point for further discussions. Defining our goals is essential to achieving them. By taking the time now to articulate our vision of the future and grapple with the many hard questions that surround reproduction—questions about sexuality, childbearing, and parenting—we can develop and build a consensus about the basic premises of our work. We will then be better able to set priorities and develop collective strategies to achieve our goals.

1. FREEDOM AND LEGAL RIGHTS TO MAKE VOLUNTARY DECISIONS

Our law[s] and social institutions must enable women to make voluntary, thoughtful, and deliberate choices about their own sexuality, childbearing, and parenting and must respect the decisions that women make for themselves and their families.

All persons must have the legal right to make voluntary and informed decisions. Our legal system cannot be used to deprive women of equal access to a full range of reproductive options. Nor can it be used to coerce women's reproductive behavior or choices, regardless of age, ancestry, creed, disability, economic status, marital status, national origin, parental status, race, sex, or sexual orientation.

2. COMPREHENSIVE, QUALITY, AND AFFORDABLE HEALTH CARE AND HUMAN SERVICES

A. A Full Range of Reproductive Options

Women must have access to existing methods of safe, quality birth control, and medical research must develop better, safer methods. Men as well as women must assume responsibility for birth control, and technologies must be developed that will enable them to do so.

Women who find themselves pregnant must have access to quality counseling to determine their reproductive choices. If they choose to terminate their pregnancies, they must have access to safe and affordable abortion services at or near their homes or jobs.

Women who choose to carry a pregnancy to term must have access to quality prenatal care, genetic screening and counseling, childbirth and postpartum care, and pediatric care for their children.

Pregnant women, especially poor women and women in Black, Hispanic, and Native American communities who are experiencing a crisis of drug and alcohol abuse, must be provided reproductive health and maternity services in an environment that is supportive and free of stigma. They must be fully informed of the risks to themselves and their infants in a way that is caring and nonpunitive and that helps them to deal with additional problems of poverty, poor housing, and male violence.

All women must have access to confidential and quality care for sexually transmitted diseases. Women who are HIV positive or at risk for AIDS who are or may become pregnant have the same right to noncoercive counseling and choice as women with other disabilities or possible fetal impairments. AIDS testing, like prenatal diagnosis, should be offered on an anonymous or confidential and voluntary basis and within a program of counseling and education that respects all persons' rights to express their sexuality.

B. Comprehensive Care

Because reproductive choice includes the ability to care for as well as bear children, comprehensive health care and human services must be available to all families. Whether offered through the Medicaid program, private insurance, or a national health plan, the services must be physically accessible—to disabled and rural women, to those dependent on public transportation, to those who work nights—and must be affordable to all.

C. Safe and Quality Care

Health and human services including all reproductive health services should focus on health, wellness, and the prevention of problems, as well as on the cure and amelioration of problems, and should be provided in a culturally supportive manner, in an environment that is free from violence, deception, and fraud. Women should define their own needs and be enabled through the use of these services to make positive changes in their lives.

Medical practitioners must not adopt unnecessary or invasive practices that endanger women's lives or health and must not use their power or authority to coerce reproductive decisions. For example, procedures such as sterilization, hysterectomy, amniocentesis, ultrasound, Caesarean section, or electronic fetal monitoring should be used only when medically appropriate. To prevent further medical abuse, the crisis in malpractice and liability insurance which has forced medical practitioners to adopt unnecessary or invasive practices in order to protect against legal liability must be addressed without leaving women unprotected.

D. Informed Consent and Informed Refusal

Principles of informed consent and informed refusal must be an intrinsic part of the decision making process and must be backed up by supportive counseling. Only when women have full knowledge about the ramifications of accepting or rejecting a particular health option, including explanations of medical procedures and their risks and benefits in understandable terms in the woman's own language, can decisions be voluntary. At the same time, women must have the option of refusing particular types of information—e.g., the sex of the child after amniocentesis. In addition, informed consent must not become a pretext for harassment or discouragement of a particular reproductive choice, such as abortion or sterilization.

3. SEXUALITY, REPRODUCTIVE, AND LIFE SKILL EDUCATION

Women, particularly teenage women, often become pregnant because they lack essential knowledge about sex, pregnancy, and contraception. Persons of all ages must have sufficient information about their sexuality and reproductive health to make intelligent decisions about sexuality, childbearing, and parenting. Information about how their bodies work, varied forms of sexuality, contraceptives, and sexually transmitted diseases must be provided to all persons at accessible locations, in a manner that is understandable and age-appropriate. Men as well as women must be taught that they have equal responsibility to be well informed about and to participate fully in choices related to sexual behavior, reproduction, and parenting.

As society grows increasingly concerned about the transmission of AIDS, women and men should be fully informed about the risks and pathology of AIDS and the necessity of using condoms or other "safe sex" practices. Public education campaigns to prevent AIDS should be administered in a context that respects all persons' needs to express their sexuality, both inside and outside the traditional framework of marriage and heterosexuality.

But education about sexuality and reproduction is only a part of the solution. Women, especially young women, often choose to become mothers because they have no realistic possibilities of advancement in society. Our educational system must provide women with the opportunity to set ambitious goals for their future, and the background to make these goals a reality, enabling women to choose motherhood when it is the best choice for them.

4. FREEDOM TO EXPRESS ONE'S SEXUALITY, AND TO ADOPT VARIED FAMILY ARRANGEMENTS OR LIFESTYLES

If women and men are coerced or socialized into heterosexual relationships, or if childbearing or childrearing is permissible only within heterosexual relationships, then people's ability to make intimate decisions about reproduction, as well as about sexuality and parenting, is constrained. Society must not discriminate against, stigmatize, or penalize persons on the basis of their sexuality or sexual preference. Moreover, varied forms of sexual expression including heterosexuality, bisexuality, and homosexuality must be accepted as normal human responses, with positive meaning and value.

Women must be free to say no to sexuality, childbearing, and parenting as they are to choose these options. Women must be free to express their sexuality in whatever noncoercive forms they choose, without recriminations, without effect on their value in our society or their self-esteem, and without fear of becoming pregnant if they do not wish to be so.

Varied forms of family and living arrangements must be acceptable choices. When women choose to parent outside of marriage, or to live collectively or inter-generationally, these choices must be respected. The legal barriers to and social stigma of unwed parenthood, inter-racial childbearing, or lesbian motherhood must be eliminated if true reproductive choice for all women is to be an option. Moreover, since pressure to have children is often brought about because there are few other acceptable adult-child relationships, we must encourage alternative forms of adult-child interaction.

5. ECONOMIC EQUITY AND REPRODUCTION

In order that all persons have equal opportunity to become parents, they must have the means to do so. The economic barriers to alternative forms of reproduction, such as the cost of adoption, donor insemination, in vitro fertilization, or embryo transfer must be lessened for low-income women through fee reduction or subsidies.

If we want a society in which children are truly an option, women must have the economic means to raise their children—to provide adequate food, clothing, and shelter and quality child care and education. We must work to eliminate the feminization of poverty that today so limits women's reproductive options and work to create jobs and a welfare system that afford dignity to all. Without an economy and social services that support women, women are unable to support their children and families; responsible parenting is possible only in a society that provides the necessary resources for parents.

Public policies must be enacted that will ease the burdens of working parents, caught between responsibilities of job and home. In addition to quality, affordable child care services, a reproductive rights agenda requires gender-neutral pregnancy and child care leave provisions and flexible work schedules available without penalty to fathers as well as mothers. To make these provisions available to all working parents and not just the most privileged, leave time must be paid. Corporate and governmental employers should be encouraged to initiate internal education programs, similar to those currently underway regarding sexual harassment, to change employee attitudes about male and same-sex partner participation in prenatal and child care tasks.

6. FREEDOM FROM VIOLENCE

Because fear of violence by a spouse or partner and fear of sexual assault limit everyone's ability to make intimate decisions, all persons must be free to choose whether, when, and with whom they have sex and have children, and to raise their children without fear of sexual assault, abuse, violence, or harassment in their homes, on the streets, or at their jobs.

7. FREEDOM FROM REPRODUCTIVE HAZARDS

All persons must be free from reproductive hazards within the environment, in their homes, and at their workplaces. Rather than attempting to repair the effects of reproductive hazards by treating infertility or disease or by banning fertile women from hazardous worksites (and consequently from higher paying jobs), we must eliminate the hazards.

8. FAMILY LAW AND SERVICES

In order to enable all persons to freely form the arrangements in which they parent, they must be able to establish and terminate these arrangements without economic and social penalty. Fair and equitable divorce, child support, and child custody laws must be available and enforceable by women whose marriage or other family arrangements have dissolved or proven inadequate. In the event of the death or disability of both of a child's parents, governmental and community resources must provide for the well-being of the child. In the event of child abuse or neglect, governmental and community resources must provide necessary medical, social, and legal services to keep families together.

9. POLITICAL PARTICIPATION

All persons must have the full right to express their views and, through organized, collective, and non-violent action, to work actively for positive, systematic changes that will guarantee reproductive choice. Women must have the opportunity to be involved at all levels of the political process and within all political parties and be encouraged to take positions of leadership.   [1988]

🌿 132

Taking It Lying Down . . . In the Street!

BARBARA YOSHIDA

It was 2:30 on a hot afternoon in July. The apartment was packed with people sitting on the floor, with barely enough room to move. If there was air conditioning, we couldn't feel it. Some of us were fanning ourselves, and we were all trying to keep from talking. People wanted to talk because they were nervous, and some were just plain scared. The noise level would rise in a wave, someone would plead for quiet, and a few moments later another wave of voices would rise. We wanted to get moving. It was almost impossible to sit quietly. For several weeks now the tension has been building, and here we were, within a stone's throw of the Holland Tunnel. Only we weren't here to throw stones. All we wanted to do was sit down in the street.

For several weeks, in anticipation by the Supreme Court on the Casey decision, pro-choice activists had been planning a massive civil disobedience action: to shut down the Tunnel on the eve of the July 4th weekend. There was really never a doubt in my mind that I would participate. I did wonder about all those flyers, though. They were wheatpasted all over downtown Manhattan. Seemed risky to me, to flaunt the action publicly like that.

This was the perfect action for my first civil disobedience, though, because I feel more strongly about it than any other issue. It concerns women's rights, women's health, and civil rights in general.

We knew that whatever decision the Supreme Court made, it would chip away at *Roe v. Wade,* and if they wanted us to take it lying down, we'd take it lying down in the street! They can't acknowledge our rights to make decisions about our own bodies and then take that right away—not even a little bit.

So on July 1st I left the WAC (Women's Action Coalition) meeting with Marilyn Minter and we headed over to the Gay & Lesbian Center on West 13th Street. We found out that we couldn't actually meet at the Center. The Court had slapped an injunction on us, a very widesweeping one: no one could walk down any street even *leading* to Port Authority property, from now 'til the end of time, and we couldn't meet at the Center. Because the Center was named in the injunction, we knew for sure that cops had been at our meetings. We grouped together down the street, were told to go to a second location, and from there went to a third address where we met on the roof.

It was a fine night for a bunch of bad girls to get together. OK, there were some bad boys, too. The thing that really impressed me was that the women were organizing this and the men were there to show support. I've never been to an Act-Up meeting. I've heard that the men pretty much run things. It seems to me, though, that a transference of knowledge has taken place there from men to women that has not occurred in the heterosexual world. Gay men have shared the power. Or maybe lesbian women have just taken it—they are even more marginalized in our society than gay men or heterosexual women, they have learned how the gay men take power, and they know they can do the same thing. Three or four women took the responsibility to organize this action and see it through, injunction and all. And it was extremely well organized. Our legal team was headed by three women: Mary Dorman, Lori Cohen, and Joan Gibbs. Many training sessions, conducted by women, had led to this rooftop meeting.

At first, the dark rooftop was only back-lit by the streetlights far below, which made it a bit romantic. We discussed the ramifications of violating the injunction—the possibility of more charges being given than the usual "dis con" (disorderly conduct) and "resisting arrest" charges, being kept in jail longer, more people being "put through the system," maybe even fines. People were urged to reconsider, and leave if they wanted. Some left. I am sure that the group would have been twice as large if it hadn't been for the injunction. Personally, it made me even more committed—it made my blood boil. Someone hooked up a light, and we put down the phone number of a person to be contacted if we were kept in jail too long, and any special information, such as medication we might need. This information would be kept at "Central." Before leaving, everyone received a slip of paper with an address and time on it for the next day, July 2nd. We were told to memorize it and talk to no one.

The next afternoon, the group found itself divided among several different locations within walking distance of the Tunnel. An hour later we left those locations in groups of three, each of us memorizing part of yet another address. We were not to stop anywhere along the way, ensuring that no one would make a phone call to tip off the police. Walking to this final destination, we felt the thrill of being part of a covert operation. The police were all over the place, and we were walking down Varick, right in the middle of them. There were plenty of paddy wagons, too.

Now we were packed in this space, two hundred hot, edgy people. Many of us were doing civil disobedience for the first time. Finally we got the word to start filing down the stairs, which would open right on Watts Street. It was relief to start moving. Within minutes we heard that the first people were already being arrested! We had to run down the stairs, still trying to hold hands. We rushed out to Varick Street and sat down. Another group ran up Varick to block a second entrance to the Tunnel. The first arrests were rougher than necessary. We all chanted "No violence!" I looked at a cop standing right in·front of me, and his fists were clenched in anger. I looked right into his eyes and said "No violence!" until I saw his fists relax. Soon the arrests became slow-paced and methodical. We continued to chant, "Abortion is health care, health care is a right!" as each person's turn came to be arrested.

I must say that I took pride in being arrested for something that meant so much to me. I was never politically active before, and now that another wave of feminism is building, I have a chance to jump on that wave and hang ten! Women often have difficulty taking action, doing things for themselves. Becoming an activist is one of the most empowering things I've ever done for myself. Civil disobedience is a particularly effective tool for social change, and it's *especially* good for women.

I'll never forget that feeling. Forcing the police to lift me into the van because I would not help them, I felt in control, and I kept shouting "No choice, no peace!" It became a litany, a personal affirmation of everything I believed. The quality of my voice began to change. I felt a deep growl from somewhere down in my gut erupting into this rhythmic chant. I was speaking to the entire world, I was part of something much bigger than myself, bigger than this one action. I almost didn't recognize my own voice. I felt charged and powerful. I have never been more sure of myself, more sure that what I was doing was right.   [1992]

🦎 133

The Activists

PAULA KAMEN

ACQUAINTANCE RAPE BATTLES

Students are organizing on an individual campus level to combat another intensely disputed and personal issue: acquaintance rape. While acquaintance rape happens everywhere, college activists have made strides to bring it to the forefront of public debate.

Some of the most strenuous attempts are to make universities responsive with a variety of treatment and prevention measures including setting up counseling services, rape crisis hot lines and a centralized visible office; publicizing these services; conducting surveys to document the extent of the problem on campus; and more consistently, systematically and strictly prosecuting cases.

One challenge for activists is that unlike with reproductive rights, there is not as yet a well-known national network specifically for people fighting acquaintance rape, as of this writing. (Some networks fighting many types of rape with a large component

on acquaintance-rape prevention are the National Coalition Against Sexual Assault in Washington, D.C., the National Network for Victims of Sexual Assault in Arlington, Virginia, and the Men's Anti-Rape Resource Center in Washington, D.C.) This can mean that they are inventing their own strategies and are isolated in their struggles. At the 1991 NOW First Young Feminist Conference, I witnessed rape-prevention activists from dozens of campuses meeting each other and acknowledging their common experiences for the first time.

A frequent complaint was a lack of concern, commitment or funding for programs. In a speech, Susan Denevan told about her personal battles with the administration of the University of Minnesota, which was representative of other schools, and how her political career had begun. She had been a counselor on campus for the sexual violence program, which suddenly was being threatened.

"[The program] was funded in 1985 because the university was very concerned about image, because one of its high-profile basketball players had been brought up on rape charges twice, so in order to look good, the university started a program. And four years later when they thought no one was looking, they tried to take away the peer-counseling element and crisis line," she said.

"I became involved with others in a political battle to restore the sexual-violence program, and it resulted in my being arrested along with twelve other people in a series of demonstrations last February," she said, referring to 1990.

"A result of the actions is that the university has increased the budget for more people on staff and will increase the services and program development."

This was one of the few stories with a happy ending. Organizers from the University of Florida, Gainesville, told me how their two counseling programs, among the most advanced and acclaimed in the country, had been under siege. The first, the Sexual Assault Recovery Services, gives counseling to victims, and the second, the student-run Campus Organized Against Rape, delivers education.

In recent years, Dr. Claire Walsh, the founder of both programs, has become an unofficial national expert on campus organizing around this issue. Walsh and COAR representatives have appeared on at least a dozen national television talk shows and shared their knowledge with about 500 universities and media organizations.

Supporters of these programs say that administrative changes have crippled the first program and threatened the second. An Associated Press report from November 1990 lists activists' claims that administrators have harassed activists, cut financial support, fired their employees and severed the relationship between the two programs. Administrators and the student-body president countered by saying the programs have been financially mismanaged and have been guilty of political advocacy.

The controversy prompted student protest rallies, a supporting petition signed by 1,500 students and a flurry of letters to the editor of the University of Florida student newspaper. Walsh later resigned, citing differences with the administration.

Betty Campbell, twenty-seven, program coordinator for COAR, and others from the campus said that administrators are "trying to put rape back in the closet" and protect an image. She contends administrators aren't educated enough about the problem of acquaintance rape, which has only been in public dialogue for about five years. However, one more recognized incentive for all administrators is to avoid bad publicity with prevention of these crimes or to avoid a civil law suit from a victim claiming the university was negligent in not taking any preventive measures.

Campbell, who had been recently fired and re-hired, explained why she has fought hard for the program.

"I think that it gives life back to folks," she said. "It gives victims a chance to feel that there is somebody in this world who cares about them. These programs give them power, whereas sexual assault, it makes people feel like they don't have power."

Campbell stressed that COAR is unique in the country because it helps shift the focus of rape prevention to men. COAR conducts programs for both male and female students, uses male peer counselors and has a male president.

But even in cases when relations with the administration are smoother, the basic education battles are universal. Rape-prevention educators are also struggling with their fellow students to change attitudes and challenge myths.

FIGHTING POVERTY

Other young feminists have taken to the streets to promote social change following their own unique visions and philosophies. Some fight grass-roots battles against poverty that have otherwise been abandoned as hopeless or not worth the effort.

Among them, Elise Mann is innovating new partnerships and coalitions. Here, at her gritty third-floor loft office on the South Side of Chicago, is the cutting edge of feminism. Outside the building other offices have been abandoned, with their windows boarded and insides burnt out.

Mann explained that she feels the future of the women's movement is to "jump start" interested groups with its foundation of knowledge and resources. She is the executive director of Women United for a Better Chicago, founded in 1983, which has brought the strength of the women's movement into the inner city as an advocacy and organizing tool. It has specifically reached out to some of the most disempowered and stigmatized: the city's public-housing residents.

"I think that there's a real fear around poverty that permeates the society, whether it's by the feminists or archconservatives or what have you," said Mann. "I think it really boils down to recognizing people's dignity, self-respect."

Women United, a historically multiracial group, has helped public-housing residents set up their own action group CHARTA, or Chicago Housing Authority Residents Taking Action. The group, which emerged from a Women United public-housing conference in 1987, empowers women by providing information about housing and city policies, and giving them more of a voice and feeling of control in their lives.

"That's a whole area, a whole population of women, that hasn't been touched or reached out to during the women's movement," said Mann. "There are 150,000 that live in public-housing developments in Chicago. I'm talking the vast majority, 80 percent, are single heads of households. There is always the stigma around people living in public housing, and not a lot of attention paid to working together."

Mann, who is white, comes from the mixed lower and middle-class South Side neighborhood of Hyde

Park and grew up with a strong role model. Her father, a state representative, was instrumental in dialogues between the Jewish and black communities in the 1960s and 1970s, and was an early ally of the late Chicago mayor Harold Washington, a progressive African American.

Now Mann has followed his lead and is further applying her feminist principles to empower others. The board of Women United hired her in 1988 right after she graduated from Northwestern University in Evanston, Illinois.

"They took a chance on someone like me who had a history of student activism but no experience in the nonprofit sector," she said.

Since, Mann and her board have helped CHARTA with the basics: acting as fiscal agent to get it grants, teaching how to prepare for and run a meeting, and sharing their office space.

Alberta McCain, fifty-five, who is black and the president of CHARTA, explained that her group's independence has determined its effectiveness in meeting its own needs. Now CHARTA is almost a completely separate entity.

"They gave suggestions," said McCain, "but [they didn't] say, 'If you don't follow my way you won't have it or it won't be right.' They gave us freedom, and I think that's a credit to them as well as to us."

One of the first organizing efforts was to make the housing developments' tenant advisory councils more accountable to residents. They had become self-serving through the years and were not responsive to the tenants. Mann says the elections were corrupt, done through petitions, to which only a privileged handful of people had access. CHARTA started a secret ballot election, which brought some of the members to formal leadership.

"That is really participatory democracy, what I think feminism is all about," said Mann.

CHARTA has also helped make the housing developments more true to their original purpose of temporary housing. It helped implement a freeze on rent when someone gets a job, to allow them a period to save and get back on their feet.

McCain said the power comes through information. One example is a flier published that outlines the often overlooked "repair and deduct" clause in the lease that covers minor repairs. She also holds workshops about "empowerment," from developing leadership skills to holding forums for candidates to tell how they will help residents.

Mann recognizes that conflicts exist between Women United organizers and CHARTA residents, who often have different ideas of how things should be run. CHARTA is also challenged in confronting such a mammoth and entrenched system. It has a limited budget and resources, and can make only a minimal difference in the realm of the larger-scale reform that is much needed.

But Mann said one great achievement is realizing the true meaning of diversity for feminist groups. She said it comes with outreach that includes addressing the issues of those who most need empowerment.

"I think that some of the problems that I've seen with some of the groups is they are wanting to have diversity, but they are not really wanting to know what that means, in the fullest sense of the word," said Mann. "They are always wanting to invite people in, and not wanting to go out."

LABOR ORGANIZING

Like public-housing residents, other women organizing across the country have the same motivation: survival. They are people who haven't chosen to take the life path of activists; it just happened that way. Many are struggling across the country to improve labor conditions in low-paying fields in order to improve their lives.

One effort is to institutionalize a voice and leverage for workers, or form unions, in traditional women's fields, such as the service industries. Organizing labor is one of the most recognized strategies for raising the wages of women in low-income jobs.

Chrystl Bridgeforth, twenty-six, who works in the national office of the Coalition of Labor Union Women in New York, said unions provide needed security for the growing numbers of women entering the work force. "If you go to work, the employer is getting a service from you, and you are getting paid by the employer. But if you are a union member, you are getting something more. You have a relationship with the employer."

She also emphasized protection from injury, especially in nontraditional work. "We don't all have easy jobs. There's people who have to go out there and work on an assembly line, to work with things hazardous to their health. What if there isn't something to check how much lead is in there? That means anyone could bring anything in, and you have to accept it because you need the paycheck."

More than 30 percent of workers (twenty-eight million) earn a less-than-adequate or low wage, generally defined as $5.30 an hour or less. But among unionized workers, only 13 percent earn low wages. Almost half of these workers in this category live in households with children.

At each wage level, unionized workers are more likely to be covered by their employers' health insurance. They also have more leverage to negotiate benefits, such as child care and parental leave.

But union organizers are stressing a special need for women to unite in new frontiers, traditionally female careers. They want to take the battle from the automobile plant to the typing pool. The largest women's occupational category is secretarial and clerical workers, with women making up 80 percent of the 142 million full-time workers, according to 1990 statistics from Institute for Women's Policy Research.

While these workers' wages are central to family income, salaries are low. The median weekly salary for full-time nonsupervisory secretaries and clericals is $300. But full-time unionized workers in these occupations earn an additional $56 a week more than those not covered by a union contract. Only 13 percent of workers in these fields are unionized, according to the Institute.

Donene Williams, twenty-seven, the president of the Harvard University local of clerical workers, has witnessed firsthand the changes and the challenges. When she started work at Harvard in 1987 as a secretary, clericals were in the last leg of an arduous drive that had started when she was ten years old. In her basement office, rows of black-and-white pictures of different stages in organizing, leading up to the victory campaign, hang on a beam of the low ceiling.

Now the unionization of the 3,400 support-staff workers stands as a model for other clericals at both public and private universities.

Williams first got involved as an "activist" whose main job was to go out and talk to co-workers one on one. She said while it was intimidating at first, this practice was their greatest weapon. When she and about eighty others finally got to the negotiating table, they were able to document the workers' problems with story after story.

"[Administrators] really had a misconception of what our lives were like," Williams said, speaking with the same serious and straightforward tone she likely used at that table. "We said for our people, the American dream isn't to own our own home. It's to live in an apartment without roommates."

The gains were dramatic in the first three-year contract. They negotiated an average of a 32 percent increase in salaries, a pension improvement and a pool of $50,000 for child care and $25,000 for education, to be set aside each year.

Williams said organizers unwittingly innovated their own effective feminist negotiating skills, which she describes as a "less combative, a less competitive style.

"It forces the employer to work on our terms. They aren't used to this. As you can imagine, Harvard is a bastion of white maleness. They're used to fighting hard and doing things the best and coming out on top.

"And we're forcing them to work in the manner in which we want to work: 'You sit down and you figure out what are all the parts of the problem, and figure out what is the best thing to do, and do the right thing.'"

Organizers also were successful in looking after the interests of everyone in the group, not just their own. Williams, who was head of the negotiating team for health benefits, explained. "It's single-minded as a young person to say I only care about child care and education benefits. 'I won't retire for thirty years, so it's not important to me.'"

She described the end goal: "It's developing a community at Harvard. It's finding people working in isolated parts of the campus and bringing them together and finding a sense of common ground."

Most of the people in the union fit Williams's demographic group: young women in their twenties. As a result, these clericals had difficulty in visualizing themselves as union members, who are traditionally white males in industrial fields, such as in welding or carpentry. Williams certainly does not fit the burly macho stereotype, with her small thin build and short blond hair.

"Most of us have never been in a union or don't come from a background with family members in unions," said Williams, who attended California State University and was raised in a household supported by public aid. "I knew basically that unions helped people get higher wages and that they had to go on strike sometimes. That's what I knew about unions."

She stressed why both women's image of themselves in unions and unions' reception of women have to change. "It's not a part of [women's] culture because unions have been traditionally populated by men and run by men. That's not necessarily true anymore because of the way the American work force is changing. More and more women are working, and more and more women are the sole income providers for their families."

CONCLUSION

The first expressly feminist piece of writing I ever read was "Diving into the Wreck," a poem by Adrienne Rich, which has come to my mind while writing this book and thinking about the future. Freshman year of college, I first examined, in a paper, the meaning of some of the imagery, which is as relevant now as it was when the words were written in 1972.

The narrator of the poem is on a treacherous and unguided journey: "I came to explore the wreck," she says. She is bravely diving into the ocean to investigate an old and deteriorating ship. Her equipment is a knife, perhaps for fighting; a camera, for recording what she finds; and a "book of myths," as a journal.

To get a clear view, she has to struggle to get deep, deep, deep, beyond the surface of the water:

I go down
Rung after rung and still
the oxygen immerses me
the blue light
the clear atoms
of our human air.
I go down.
My flippers cripple me,

I crawl like an insect down the ladder
and there is no one
to tell me when the ocean
will begin

In my paper, I said Rich was taking the initiative to inspect the tired and unneeded parts of society, exposing its myths. A central source of the myths seemed to be sexism, which has kept women from achieving their potential.

Now younger feminists are calling for women and men to embark on another difficult mission: a continued exploration of these myths—and others—that still requires plunging way beneath the surface.

The great payoff, the still elusive treasure waiting to be plundered, is based on the original radical feminist vision of "sisterhood," which was a more popular topic of discussion at the time the poem was written. As Bell Hooks has said, sisterhood is essential for a mass-based political movement and real change and improvements to occur. Sisterhood is still possible, and also powerful. But, for too many people, the word has become as outdated as other concepts from the Seventies, joining the ranks of disco and the leisure suit.

In researching this book, it has become clear that everyone has to take different paths and shatter their own myths. But I have also observed some general patterns of thinking that could provide useful approaches for different groups.

First, for many nonactivists, a basic myth that seems yet to be overcome is the rigid stereotype of what a feminist or an activist is. As I have written, feminism is not to gender what communism is to class. It does not mean wiping out all distinctions between the sexes and dismantling all traditions. But it does mean asking questions about them.

Besides, those interviewed who call themselves feminists have themselves illustrated that there is no one way to be a feminist. They espouse no one mode of thinking, of being, of dressing, of talking, of strategizing. A diversity of opinions and ideas defining feminism keeps it fluid, vigilant, growing and responsive to people's needs.

One danger of the feminist stereotype is that it divides women instead of uniting them. It discourages them from looking beyond the surface of what feminism is and keeps them "in their place," not recognizing their own present convictions. You can't make waves if you're afraid to even dive into the water. Yet it seems that after just a little bit of thought, people overcome this block and realize that they support some of feminism's most basic principles.

The potential of those who don't consider themselves feminists is tremendous to support a mass-based political movement. They can give organizers new strength just by acting on what they believe in.

"People have to know that activists are not a rare breed," said Jamie Lee Evans. "They are just like you. They are just like me. They are just like everyone. They come from all classes, all colors, all religions."

"It's easier for people not to do anything when they see that there is a certain breed of warriors who were born that way, who are supposed to do the work, and that's not true."

Second, for older feminists and others, there seems to be a need to shatter myths about younger people being too apathetic, too young or inexperienced to be politicized, not naturally inclined to politics. To take part in the feminist movement, young women need confidence and space to express their needs and assume real leadership roles. This should not just be done to be considerate to younger women. It is a question of survival for the torch to be passed and remain burning.

Next, to men: In joining the civil rights struggle for empowerment of women, many have realized that seeing their stake in the issues and becoming aware of sexism is the first step. But it is only the beginning. More need to do an in-depth housecleaning of their own attitudes. With this effort, they can become an essential component in a mass-based women's movement and also empower themselves.

But many men do not seem to have undertaken even the most basic thinking to break down their own stereotypes of the "feminist man" as a feminine, castrated, overly sensitive doormat of women. Often, this is a more rigid stereotype than that of feminist women, and discourages men's thought and investigation into feminism.

Finally, to all women: While committed feminist men work to think about their dominance, women must also contemplate their own contribution to the current system. One of the most difficult feminist battles is internal: to fight the myths about other women. Activists have called for a new stage of consciousness-raising about race and class and homophobia and anti-Semitism—any force that makes someone feared as "the other."

With this work, differences can be transformed from barriers into launching pads.

Yet, for all, in addition to addressing myths, the greatest key to feminism in the Nineties is perhaps the neglected element of social consciousness. It involves making a commitment to women—a most basic and fundamental principle of feminism.

This transforms feminism from an exclusive, self-centered, individualist struggle to one for women. It also acts as an insurance policy for the movement to survive and develop. People know the work isn't done when their own personal goals have been realized.

But in writing this book, I have noticed a schism in social consciousness among two distinct groups: the activists and nonactivists. The nonactivists seemed mainly to name concerns of the white and middle class and did not seem to focus beyond to people of color or those with low incomes. For example, keeping abortion legal was named, while access to abortion for the poor or younger women was not.

In contrast, the activists seemed to miss the white middle class, which is a significant power and constituency. In "progressive" and bohemian circles, even the white middle class did not seem to want to associate itself with the white middle class. Radical feminists also must not forget the bread-and-butter issues of family—child care, parental leave, making the workplace more flexible, violence against women—which affect everyone. The white middle class—which is slowly, economically, becoming the white lower class—has some important and urgent issues that should not be trivialized or scorned.

The period of pronounced activism of the 1960s can still provide some powerful lessons. Then, social consciousness was a part of popular dialogue, and people seemed to cultivate more confidence in their abilities to effect change for themselves and for others.

The 1960s also seemed to encompass more of a collective vision. I agree that individual battles are

essential, such as in becoming a teacher or a social worker, being philanthropic, volunteering. But
while working in one's niche, the feminist must also
keep an eye on the big picture. This means being a
watchdog of social policy and voting according to
one's beliefs.

Young women must also do their own revision
of some 1960s concepts. They need to temper
grand, idealistic visions with some realism and cau-
tiousness. Those activists and feminists interviewed
seemed to realize that activists in the Sixties almost collapsed under the weight of their own ambition. Social-justice activists seemed to run a long-
distance race to achieve the Utopian Society with
the drive and speed of sprinters. But the runners appeared spent after the first lap.

I'll paraphrase the outlook that several activists
related to me. In the Nineties, feminists have to pace
themselves and keep their eyes down to see barriers
that must be confronted. Meanwhile, they must also
always be looking far enough ahead to see the finish line.

Making this commitment is difficult because it
goes against the way young people have generally
been socialized. Especially for white middle-class
people, it requires a special effort to look beyond
one's own experience. This involves initiative in
learning about others and the risk of journeying into
the unknown, being awkward and hitting snags.

Obliterating all these myths and building this social consciousness and sisterhood sounds like a lot
of work. Is it worth the struggle? Why don't we just
call ourselves humanists and abandon the feminist
critiques? Why do we want to continue the women's
movement?

The reason to break all these myths? I can summarize it in one word: power.

Feminism is one model for empowering the individual and then harnessing that collective energy
for change. For the movement, more people acting
on their beliefs can mean new life. This common
goal of power for all women can give dialogue new
freshness and drive. In political terms, a result is to
stop and reverse the feminization of poverty, and ac-
celerate and transform the feminization of power.

The motivation for power was most forcefully
demonstrated by Anna Padia, director of human
rights for the Newspaper Guild. A thunderous

speaker, she drew rapt attention at an ambitious
conference in October of 1990, planned by young
women and the Institute for Women's Policy Research in Washington, D.C., with the following:

> The reason for a diverse East Coast network—
> why? The answer is power. Both the individual
> power and the collective power to make the changes
> you want personally, professionally on the job, in
> the community and in every institution that you are
> now in or will be involved in during the future.
>
> This is not to underestimate the power of one
> individual, for surely we know of individuals who
> have accomplished great things. Nor is this view to
> underestimate the tremendous power that already
> exists and that each of you now possesses, whether
> you know it or not.
>
> But take your one hand, make that into a fist.
> Take that fist and magnify that a thousand fold and
> you have a very different kind of power. If you take
> that single one articulate voice of yours and you add
> it to a choir of a million, you have power.
>
> Send that one postcard to that president, or the
> Congress, or the manufacturer that makes products
> that are not healthy to your life . . . and you will be
> heard.
>
> You will persuade. You will compel the attention
> to effect and implement the policies, the programs,
> and the very important young women's perspectives
> that only you can define.

To get at that power, women must visualize
themselves as having the right to it. Susan Denevan,
twenty-three, the 1990–1991 student body president at the University of Minnesota, said that sexism—both in self-image and in how women are
treated—keeps women from achieving power. In
this realm, women still basically have the myth of
themselves as "the second sex."

"Due to sexism, the system of power distribution
has made women not want to be involved with the
process of policy-making. When we include classism, sexism, ableism and heterosexism, we see how
many people have been locked out of decision-
making and our reluctance grows even greater," she
said, speaking at NOW's First Young Feminist Conference in 1991.

Denevan also stressed that through traditional
and available channels, women can invent the future
and transform institutions. "What kind of power do
we as women bring to traditional politics? We bring

an emphasis on community and interdependence. And not on hierarchy or self-promotion. What does this mean? It means that we see how our survival is linked with the survival of others and of our environment."

But, she added, survival is not enough, and the real source of power must be self-determination, a basic feminist goal.

"Self-determination for all peoples will only be achieved when our current system of power distribution is overthrown. Overthrown does not necessarily mean violent revolution, but it does mean directly confronting the assumptions and actions that disenfranchise all but those conforming to the white male model of leadership."

This myth-breaking of all types of sexism and stereotypes is a weighty, unsettling challenge. It involves unraveling countless assumptions about oneself and about others. It involves confrontation, feeling uncomfortable, taking risks.

But these tremendous challenges also make feminism thrilling. This is groundbreaking work! Nothing could be more revolutionary than breaking down these barriers and empowering ourselves and others. In this country, in a growing multicultural society, looking at issues of diversity is the road to future success in every area: economic, social, in personal relationships. Now feminists are at the forefront of this struggle and are pioneering concepts of understanding and overcoming and celebrating difference.

The waters seem to be at just the right temperature for entry. In traveling across the country, I have noticed a phenomenon of people becoming more aware and concerned about women's rights and other social issues. In unison, people are telling me the same ideas, using almost the same language to describe how they are feeling. Different professors of women's studies across the country have told me that they sense the pendulum swinging back slightly from the right and students becoming more committed to working for others.

Everyone's help is needed to turn any current trends into serious dialogue to propel a movement.

These feelings have the potential to result in more than just influencing the looks of the new spring fashions. Instead of continuing to look back to the beat of the Sixties with nostalgia, young people can take their energies and build on past work and make something they can be proud of. The innovative work of the activists profiled gives proof that young people can bring about change.

This work can also teach outsiders a lesson in defining a feminist. In building solidarity, feminists can transcend the popular myth that they are part of a fringe group.

The issue is not just who opens the door for women.

The issue is opening the doors of opportunity and empowering all people—certainly not a trivial matter.   [1991]

🌿 134

Like a Mountain

NAOMI LITTLEBEAR

Nobody can push back an ocean
It's gonna rise back up in waves.
And nobody can stop the wind from blowin',
Stop a mind from growin'.

Somebody may stop my voice from singing
But the song will live on and on.

You can't kill the spirit
It's like a mountain,
Old and strong; it lives on and on.

Nobody can stop a woman from feelin'
That she has to rise up like the sun
Somebody may change the words we're sayin'
But the truth will live on and on.

You can't kill the spirit
It's like a mountain,
Old and strong; it lives on and on.   [c. 1970]

We hope that the many different voices in *Women: Images and Realities* have spoken to you and deepened your understanding of women's experience. While you may not have agreed with everything you read, we hope the book has stimulated your thinking. We have tried in this anthology to do several things: to demonstrate the commonalities and differences among women, to emphasize the power of women talking and working together, to stimulate your thinking about the ways women of different backgrounds can work together effectively, and to encourage you to participate in the process of improving women's lives. Although this book has concluded, we hope your involvement with feminism continues.

For Further Reading and Research

PART I: *WHAT IS WOMEN'S STUDIES?*

All the Women Are White, All the Blacks Are Men, But Some of Us Are Brave. Gloria Hull, Patricia Bell Scott, and Barbara Smith. Feminist Press, Old Westbury, NY, 1982.

Changing Our Minds: Feminist Transformation of Knowledge. Susan Aiken, Karen Anderson, Myra Dinnerstein, Judy Note Lensink, and Patricia Mac Corquodale, eds. SUNY Press, Albany, NY, 1988.

Feminist Education: A Special Topic Issue of the Journal of Thought. Barbara Hillyer Davis. College of Education, University of Oklahoma, Norman, 1985.

"Feminist Pedagogies and Differences in the Classroom," Parts I and II. Pam Annas and Frinde Maher, eds. *Radical Teacher, 41* and *42,* March 1992.

Feminist Pedagogy, An Update. Frinde Maher and Nancy Schniedewind, eds. *Women's Studies Quarterly,* Fall/Winter 1993.

Feminist Perspective in the Academy: The Difference It Makes. A. E. Langland and W. Grove, eds. University of Chicago Press, Chicago, 1983.

Feminist Scholarship: Kindling in the Groves of Academe. Ellen Carol Dubois, Gail Paradise Kelly, Elizabeth Lapovsky Kennedy, Carolyn W. Korsmeyer, and Lillian S. Robinson, eds. University of Illinois Press, Chicago, 1985.

Foundations for a Feminist Restructuring of the Academic Disciplines. Michele A. Paludi and Gertrude A. Steuernagel, eds. Harrington Park Press, New York, 1990.

Gendered Subjects: The Dynamics of Feminist Teaching. Margo Culley and Catherine Protuges, eds. Routledge & Kegan Paul, New York, 1985.

The Impact of Feminist Research in the Academy. Christie Farnham, ed. Indiana University Press, Indianapolis, 1987.

Learning About Women: Gender, Politics, and Power. Jill K. Conway, Susan C. Bourque, and Joan W. Scott, eds. University of Michigan Press, Ann Arbor, 1989.

Learning Our Way: Essays in Feminist Education. Charlotte Bunch and Sandra Pollack, eds. The Crossing Press, Trumansburg, NY, 1983.

Lesbian Studies: Present and Future. Margaret Cruikshank, ed. Feminist Press, Old Westbury, NY, 1982.

Men's Studies Modified: The Impact of Feminism on the Academic Disciplines. D. Spender, ed. Pergamon Press, Elmsford, NY, 1981.

Myths of Gender, Biological Theories about Women and Men. Anne Fausto-Sterling. Basic Books, New York, 1992.

Science and Gender: A Critique of Biology and Its Theories on Women. Ruth Bleier. Pergamon Press, New York, 1984.

Sexual Stratification: A Cross-Cultural View. Alice Schlegel, ed. Columbia University Press, New York, 1977.

Talking Back: Thinking Feminist, Thinking Black. bell hooks. South End Press, Boston, 1989.

Theories of Women's Studies. Gloria Bowles and Renate Duelli Klein, eds. Routledge & Kegan Paul, New York, 1983.

Transforming the Curriculum: Ethnic Studies and Women's Studies. Johnella Butler and John Walter. SUNY Press, Albany, NY, 1991.

Woman: Culture and Society. Michelle Zimbalist Rosaldo and Louise Lamphere, eds. Stanford University Press, Stanford, CA, 1974.

Women's Studies International. Aruna Rao, ed. Feminist Press, New York, 1991.

Women's Studies in the South. Rhoda E. Barge Johnson, ed. Kendall/Hunt, Dubuque, IA, 1991.

PART II: BECOMING A WOMAN IN OUR SOCIETY

Dominant Ideas About Women

The Church and the Second Sex. Mary Daly. Beacon Press, Boston, 1985.

Daughters of Sorrow: Attitudes Towards Black Women 1880–1920. Beverly Guy-Sheftell. Carlsen, Brooklyn, NY, 1990.

Disfigured Images: The Historical Assault on Afro-American Women. Patricia Morton. Greenwood Press, New York, 1991.

Images of Women in Literature. Mary Anne Ferguson. Houghton Mifflin, Boston, 1977.

Visions of Women: Being a Fascinating Anthology with Analysis of Philosophers' Views of Women from Ancient to Modern Times. Linda Bell, ed. Humana Press, Clifton, NJ, 1983.

Women in Western Political Thought. Susan Moller Okin. Princeton University Press, Princeton, NJ, 1979.

Learning Sexism

Body Politics: Power, Sex and Non-Verbal Communication. Nancy Henley. Prentice-Hall, Englewood Cliffs, NJ, 1977.

"The Classroom Climate: A Chilly One for Women." Roberta Hall and Bernice Sandler. Project on the Status and Education of Women, Association of American Colleges, Washington, DC, 1982.

Educated in Romance: Women, Achievement and College Culture. Dorothy Holland. University of Chicago Press, Chicago, 1990.

From Reverence to Rape: The Treatment of Women in the Movies. Molly Haskell. University of Chicago Press, Chicago, 1987.

Gender Advertisements. Irving Goffman. Harvard University Press, Cambridge, MA, 1979.

Gender Influences in Classroom Interaction. Louise Wilkinson. Academic Press, Orlando, FL, 1985.

Gender and Non-Verbal Behavior. Nancy Henley and Clara Mayo. Springer-Verlag, New York, 1981.

How Schools Shortchange Girls. American Association of University Women, Washington, DC, 1992.

Language, Gender, and Society. Nancy Henley, Charise Kramarae, and Barrie Thorne, eds. Newbury House, Rowley, MA, 1983.

Man Made Language. Dale Spender. Routledge & Kegan Paul, Boston, 1985.

"Missing Voices: Women in the U.S. News Media." Special issue of *Extra,* New York, 1982.

Putting on Appearances: Gender and Advertising. Diane Barthel. Temple University Press, Philadelphia, 1988.

"Redesigning Women." Special issue of *Media and Values,* 49, Winter 1989.

"Secrets in Public: Sexual Harassment in Our Schools." Nan Stein, Nancy Marshall, and Linda Tropp, eds. Center for Research on Women, Wellesley, MA, 1993.

Sex Equity Handbook for Schools. Myra Sadker and David Sadker. Longman, New York, 1983.

What's Wrong with This Picture? The Status of Women on Screen and Behind the Camera in Entertainment TV. Sally Steenland. National Commission on Working Women of Wider Opportunities for Women, Los Angeles, 1990.

Woman Warrior. Maxine Hong Kingston. Vintage Books, New York, 1977.

PART III: GENDER AND WOMEN'S BODIES

The Female Body

Beauty Bound. Rita Jackaway Freedman. Lexington Books, Lexington, MA, 1985.

The Beauty Myth: How Images of Beauty Are Used Against Women. Naomi Wolf. Morrow, New York, 1991.

Beauty Secrets: Women and the Politics of Appearance. Wendy Chapkis. South End Press, Boston, 1986.

The Bluest Eye. Toni Morrison. Random House, New York, 1970.

Face Value: The Politics of Beauty. Robin Tolmach Lakoff and Raquel Scherr. Routledge & Kegan Paul, London, 1984.

Femininity. Susan Brownmiller. Simon & Schuster, New York, 1984.

"The Media and Blacks—Selling It Like It Isn't." Gloria Joseph, in *Common Differences, Conflicts in Black and White Feminist Perspectives.* Gloria Joseph and Jill Lewis, eds. South End Press, Boston, 1986.

The Psychology of the Female Body. Jane M. Ussher. Routledge & Kegan Paul, London, 1989.

Sexuality

All Things are Possible. Yvonne A. Duffy. A. J. Gavin, Ann Arbor, MI, 1981.

Closer to Home: Bisexuality and Feminism. Elizabeth Reba Weise. Seal Press, Seattle, WA, 1992.

Dangerous Passage: The Social Control of Sexuality in Women's Adolescence. Constance A. Nathanson. Temple University Press, Philadelphia, 1991.

The Eternal Garden: Seasons of Our Sexuality. Sally Wendkos Olds. Times Books, New York, 1985.

"The Everyday Life of Black Lesbians' Sexuality." Cheryl Clarke, in B. Worland, ed. *Inversions.* Press Gang Publishers, Vancouver, B.C., Canada, 1991.

The Hite Report: A Nationwide Study of Female Sexuality. Shere Hite. Dell, New York, 1976.

Lesbian Sex. JoAnn Loulan. Spinster/Aunt Lute, San Francisco, 1987.

"The Myth of the Erotic Exotic." Elaine Louie. *Village Voice,* New York, April 1973.

Pleasure and Danger: Exploring Female Sexuality. Carole S. Vance. Routledge & Kegan Paul, Boston, 1984.

Powers of Desire: The Politics of Sexuality. Ann Barr Snitow, Christine Stansell, and Sharon Thompson, eds. Monthly Review Press, New York, 1983.

Re-making Love: The Feminization of Sex. Barbara Ehrenreich, Elizabeth Hess, and Gloria Jacobs. Anchor Press/Doubleday, Garden City, NY, 1986.

PART IV: INSTITUTIONS THAT SHAPE WOMEN'S LIVES

The Legal System

Alchemy of Race and Rights. Patricia J. Williams. Harvard University Press, Cambridge, MA, 1991.

The Female Body and The Law. Zillah R. Eisenstein. University of California Press, Berkeley, 1988.

Feminism and the Power of Law. Carol Smart. Routledge & Kegan Paul, New York, 1989.

Feminism Unmodified: Discourses on Life and Law. Catharine A. MacKinnon. Harvard University Press, Cambridge, MA, 1987.

Feminist Legal Theory: Readings in Law and Gender. Katharine T. Bartlett and Rosanne Kennedy, eds. Westview Press, Boulder, CO, 1991.

Law, Gender, and Injustice: A Legal History of U.S. Women. Joan Hoff. New York University Press, New York, 1991.

Work

Black Women in the Labor Force. Phyllis Wallace with Linda Datcher and Julianne Malveaux. MIT Press, Cambridge, MA, 1980.

Between Feminism and Labor: The Significance of the Comparable Worth Movement. Linda Blum. University of California Press, Berkeley, 1991.

Black Women in the Workplace: Impacts of Structural Change in the Economy. Bette Woody. Greenwood Press, New York, 1992.

For Crying Out Loud: Women and Poverty in the U.S. Rochelle Lefkowitz and Ann Withorn, eds. Pilgrim Press, New York, 1986.

The Economic Emergence of Women. Barbara Bergmann. Basic Books, New York, 1986.

The Endless Day: The Political Economy of Women and Work. Bettina Berch. Harcourt Brace Jovanovich, New York, 1982.

"Fact Sheet on Women and Work." National Commission on Working Women of Wider Opportunities for Women. Washington, DC, 1989.

Hard-Hatted Women: Stories of Struggle and Success in the Trades. Molly Martin, ed. Seal Press, Seattle, WA, 1989.

International Migration: The Female Experience. Rita James Simon and Caroline B. Brettell, eds. Rowman and Allanheld, Totowa, NJ, 1986.

Issei, Nissei, War Bride: Three Generations of Japanese American Women in Domestic Service. Evelyn Nakano Glenn. Temple University Press, Philadelphia, 1986.

Ivory Power: Sexual Harassment on Campus. Michelle Paludi. SUNY Press, Albany, NY, 1990.

Lives on the Edge: Single Mothers and Their Children in the Other America. Valerie Polokow, University of Chicago Press, Chicago, 1993.

Men and Women of the Corporation. Rosabeth Moss Kanter. Basic Books, New York, 1977.

Mexicanas at Work in the United States. Margarita Melville, ed. Mexican American Studies Program, University of Houston, Houston, TX, 1988.

Never Done: A History of American Housework. Susan Strasser. Pantheon, New York, 1982.

Race, Gender and Work: A Multicultural Economic History of Women in the United States. Theresa Amott and Julie Matthaei. South End Press, Boston, 1991.

Sex Work: Writings by Women in the Sex Industry. Frederique De Lo Costa and Priscilla Alexander, eds. Cleis Press, Pittsburgh, PA, 1987.

Tyranny of Kindness: Dismantling the Welfare System to End Poverty in America. Theresa Funiciello. Atlantic Monthly Press, New York, 1993.

When No Means No: A Guide to Sexual Harassment. Cheryl Gomez-Preston with Randi Reisfel. Carol Publishing Group, Secaucus, NJ, 1993.

With Silk Wings: Asian American Women at Work. Elain Kim and Janice Otani. Asian Women United of California, Oakland, CA, 1983.

Women Changing Work. Patricia W. Lunneborg. Bergin and Garvey, New York, 1990.

Women and Children Last: The Plight of Poor Women in Affluent America. Ruth Sidel. Viking, New York, 1988.

Women Workers and Global Restructuring. Kathryn Ward, ed. I.L.R. Press, Ithaca, NY, 1990.

"Women's Unpaid Labor: Home and Community." Sarah Fenstermaker Berk, in *Women Working,* Ann Stromberg and Shirley Harkess, eds. Mayfield, Mountain View, CA, 1988.

Women's Work, Women's Lives: A Comparative Economic Perspective. Francine Blau. National Bureau of Economic Research, Cambridge, MA, 1990.

The Family

Balancing Acts: On Being a Mother. Katherine Gieve. Virago, London, 1989.

Black Mothers and Daughters: Their Roles and Functions in American Society. Gloria Joseph. Doubleday, New York, 1981.

The Joy Luck Club. Amy Tan. Putnam, New York, 1989.

Mothering: Essays in Feminist Theory. Joyce Trebilcot. Rowman & Allanheld, Totowa, NJ, 1983.

Of Woman Born: Motherhood as Experience and Institution. Adrienne Rich. Norton, New York, 1986.

Ourselves and Our Children: A Book By and For Parents. Boston Women's Health Book Collective. Random House, New York, 1987.

"Out of the Stream: An Essay on Unconventional Motherhood." Shirley Glubka. *Feminist Studies, 9,* 2, Summer 1983.

Recreating Motherhood: Ideology and Technology in a Patriarchal Society. Barbara Katz Rothman. Norton, New York, 1989.

Rethinking the Family: Some Feminist Questions. Barrie Thorne and Marilyn Yalom, eds. Northeastern University Press, Boston, 1992.

Ties That Bind: Essays on Mothering and Patriarchy. Jean F. O'Barr, Deborah Pope, and Mary Wyer, eds. University of Chicago Press, Chicago, 1990.

"Why I Want a Wife." Judy Syfers, in *Radical Feminism,* Anne Koedt and Ellen Levine, eds. Quadrangle, New York, 1980.

Health Care

Alive and Well: A Lesbian Health Guide. Circe Hepburn. Crossing Press, Freedom, CA, 1988.

The Black Women's Health Book: Speaking for Ourselves. Evelyn C. White, ed. Seal Press, Seattle, WA, 1990.

The Cancer Journals. Audre Lorde. Spinsters Ink, Argyles, NY, 1980.

Double Exposure: Women's Health Hazards on the Job and at Home. Wendy Chavkin. Monthly Review Press, New York, NY, 1984.

Every Woman's Health: The Complete Guide to Body and Mind. June Jackson Christmas and Douglass S. Thompson. Doubleday, Garden City, NY, 1985.

The New Our Bodies, Ourselves: A Book By and For Women. Boston Women's Health Book Collective. Simon & Schuster, New York, 1992.

The Psychology of Women's Health and Health Care. Paula Nicolson, Jane M. Ussher, and Jo Campling. Macmillan, New York, 1992.

River of Tears: The Politics of Black Women's Health. Delores S. Aldridge and La Frances Rodgers-Rose. Traces Publishing, Newark, NJ, 1993.

Seizing Our Bodies: The Politics of Women's Health. Claudia Dreifus, Vintage Books, New York, 1977.

Women and Madness. Phyllis Chesler. Doubleday, Garden City, NY, 1972.

PART V: THE DIFFERENCES AMONG US: DIVISIONS AND CONNECTIONS

All American Women: Lines That Divide, Ties That Bind. Johnetta Cole, ed. Free Press, New York, 1986.

American Indian Women, Telling Their Lives. Gretchen M. Bataille and Kathleen Mullen Sand. University of Nebraska Press, Lincoln, 1984.

Asian and Pacific American Experiences: Women's Perspectives. Nobuya Tsuchida, Linda Mealey, and Gail Thoen, eds. Asian/Pacific American Learning Resource Center and General College, University of Minnesota, Minneapolis, 1982.

Bodies of Water. Michelle Cliff. Dutton, New York, 1990.

Borderlands/La Frontera. Gloria Anzaldua. Spinsters/Aunt Lute, San Francisco, 1987.

Calling Home: Working Class Women's Writings: An Anthology. Janet Zandy, ed. Rutgers University Press, New Brunswick, NJ, 1990.

Changing Our Power: An Introduction to Women's Studies. Jo Whitehorse Chochran, Donna Langston, Carolyn Woodward, eds. Kendall/Hunt, Dubuque, IA, 1991.

Common Differences: Conflicts in Black and White Feminist Perspectives. Gloria Joseph and Jill Lewis, eds. South End Press, Boston, 1986.

Daughter of Earth. Agnes Smedley. Feminist Press, Old Westbury, NY, 1973.

The Forbidden Stitch: An Asian American Women's Anthology. Shirley Geok-lum, Mauyumi Tsutakawa, and Margarita Donnely, eds. Calyx Books, Corvalis, OR, 1989.

Homophobia: A Weapon of Sexism. Suzanne Pharr. Chardon Press, Little Rock, AR, 1988.

I Am Your Sister: Black Women Organizing Across Sexualities. Audre Lorde. Kitchen Table Press, Latham, NY, 1986.

Loving in the War Years. Cherrie Moraga. South End Press, Boston, 1983.

Making Face, Making Soul, Creative and Critical Perspectives by Women of Color. Gloria Anzaldua, ed. Aunt Lute, San Francisco, 1990.

Making Waves: An Anthology of Writings By and About Asian American Women. Asian Women United, ed. Beacon Press, Boston, 1989.

Nice Jewish Girls: A Lesbian Anthology. Evelyn Torton Beck, ed. Beacon Press, Boston, 1989.

Nobody Speaks for Me: Self-Portraits of American Working Class Women. Nancy Seifer. Simon & Schuster, New York, 1976.

The Sacred Hoop: Recovering the Feminine in American Indian Tradition. Paula Gunn Allen. Beacon Press, Boston, 1986.

Sister Outsider. Audre Lorde. Crossing Press, Trumansburg, NY, 1984.

That's What She Said: Contemporary Poetry and Fiction by Native American Women. Rayna Green, ed. Indiana University Press, Bloomington, 1984.

The Things That Divide Us. Faith Conlon, ed. Seal Press, Seattle, WA, 1985.

This Bridge Called My Back: Writings by Radical Women of Color. Cherrie Moraga and Gloria Anzaldua, eds. Kitchen Table Press, Latham, NY, 1983.

The Tribe of Dina: A Jewish Women's Anthology. Melanie Kaye-Kantrowitz and Irena Klepfisz, eds. Beacon Press, Boston, 1986.

Yours in Struggle: Three Feminist Perspectives on Anti-Semitism and Racism. Elly Bulkin, Minnie Bruce Pratt, and Barbara Smith. Long Haul Press, New York, 1984.

Women, Race and Class. Angela Davis. Vintage Books, New York, 1982.

With Wings: An Anthology of Literature By and About Women with Disabilities. Marsha Saxton and Florence Howe, eds. Feminist Press, Old Westbury, NY, 1987.

PART VI: THE CONSEQUENCES OF SEXISM: CURRENT ISSUES

Aging

Growing Older, Getting Better. Jane Porcino. Addison-Wesley, Reading, MA, 1983.

Korean Elderly Women in America: Everyday Life, Health, and Illness. Keum Young Chung Pang. AMS Press, New York, 1991.

Look Me in the Eye: Old Women, Aging, and Ageism. Barbara Macdonald and Cynthia Rich. Spinsters Ink, San Francisco, 1983.

"Management." Margaret Lamb, in *Solo: Women on Women Alone,* L. and L. Hammelian, eds. Dell, New York, 1977.

Ourselves, Growing Older: Women Aging with Knowledge and Power. Paula Doress, Diana Laskin Siegal, Midlife and Older Women Book Project, and Boston Women's Health Book Collective. Simon & Schuster, New York, 1987.

Tish Sommers, Activist, and the Founding of the Older Women's League. Patricia Huckle and Tish Sommers. University of Tennessee Press, Knoxville, 1991.

When I Am an Old Woman I Shall Wear Purple. Sandra Martz. Papier-Mache Press, Manhattan Beach, CA, 1987.

Rights and Choices: Reproductive Health

The Choices We Made: 25 Women and Men Speak Out About Abortion. Angela Bonavoglia. Random House, New York, 1991.

Our Right to Choose: Toward a New Ethic of Abortion. Beverly W. Harrison. Beacon Press, Boston, 1983.

A Question of Choice. Sarah Weddington. Putnam, New York, 1992.

Reproductive Rights and Wrongs: The Global Politics of Population Control and Contraceptive Choice. Betsy Hartmann. Harper & Row, New York, 1987.

Roe v. Wade, cite as 93 s.ct. 705 (1973). Jane Roe, et al., appellants, v. Henry Wade, no. 70-18. Argued Dec. 13, 1971. Reargued Oct. 11, 1972. Decided Jan. 22, 1973. Supreme Court reporter.

Taking Chances: Abortion and the Decision Not to Contracept. Kristin Luker. University of California Press, Berkeley, 1975.

Violence Against Women in Intimate Relationships

Battered Wives. Del Martin. Glide Publications, San Francisco, 1976.

Chain, Chain, Change: For Black Women Dealing with Physical and Emotional Abuse. Evelyn C. White. Seal Press, Seattle, WA, 1985.

For the Latina in an Abusive Relationship. Myrna Zambrano. Seal Press, Seattle, WA, 1983.

Getting Free: A Handbook for Women in Abusive Relationships. Ginny Nicarthy. Seal Press, Seattle, WA, 1986.

Heroes of Their Own Lives: The Politics and History of Family Violence, Boston, 1880–1960. Linda Gordon. Viking, New York, 1988.

Rape and Sexual Abuse

Acquaintance Rape: The Hidden Crime. Andrea Parrot and Laurie Bechhofer. Wiley, New York, 1991.

Against Our Will: Men, Women, and Rape. Susan Brownmiller. Simon & Schuster, New York, 1975.

Bastard Out of Carolina. Dorothy Allison. Dutton, New York, 1992.

The Courage to Heal. Ellen Bass and Laura Davis. Harper & Row, New York, 1988.

Female Sexual Slavery. Kathleen Barry. Avon, New York, 1979.

Fraternity Gang Rape. Peggy Sanday. New York University Press, New York, 1990.

I Know Why the Caged Bird Sings. Maya Angelou. Random House, New York, 1969.

I Never Called It Rape. Robin Warshaw and Mary P. Koss. Harper & Row, New York, 1988.

Rape: The Politics of Consciousness. Susan Griffin. Harper & Row, San Francisco, 1986.

Secret Survivors: Uncovering Incest and Its Aftereffects in Women. Sue E. Blume. Wiley, New York, 1990.

Sexual Assault on Campus: The Problem and the Solution. Carol Bohmer and Andrea Parrot. Lexington Books, New York, 1993.

Voices in the Night: Women Speaking About Incest. Toni A. H. McNaron and Yarrow Margan. Cleis Press, Minneapolis, MN, 1982.

PART VII: CHANGING OUR LIVES

Coming Home Alive. Aurora Levina Morales and Rosario Morales. Firebrand Books, Ithaca, NY, 1986.

Composing a Life. Mary Catherine Bateson. New American Library, New York, 1990.

Considering Parenthood: A Workbook for Lesbians. Stacey Pies. Spinsters Ink, San Francisco, 1985.

A Family Affair: The Real Lives of Black Single Mothers. Barbara Omolade. Kitchen Table: Women of Color Press, Albany, NY, 1986.

Farewell to Manzanar. Jeanne Wakatsuki Houston. Bantam, New York, 1974.

A Habit of Survival: Five Extraordinary Women Share the Conflicts and Struggles That Define Their Lives as Black Women in America. Kesho Yvonne Scott. Ballantine, New York, 1991.

In the Company of My Sisters. Julia Boyd. Dutton, New York, 1993.

In Search of Our Mothers' Gardens. Alice Walker. Harcourt Brace Jovanovich, New York, 1983.

Lesbian Nuns: Breaking the Silence. Rosemary Curb and Nancy Manahan. Naiad Press, Tallahassee, FL, 1985.

Mama Day. Gloria Naylor. Ticknor & Fields, New York, 1988.

A Passion for Friends: Toward a Philosophy of Female Affection. Janice Raymond. Beacon Press, Boston, 1986.

Politics of the Heart: A Lesbian Parenting Anthology. Sandra Pollack and Jeanne Vaughn, eds. Firebrand Books, Ithaca, NY, 1987.

Sisters of the Yam: Black Women and Self Recovery. bell hooks. South End Press, Boston, 1993.

Solving Women's Problems. Hoagie Wycoff. Grove Press, New York, 1977.

Toward a New Psychology of Women. Jean Baker Miller. Beacon Press, Boston, 1986.

Women and Stepfamilies: Voices of Anger and Love. Nan Bauer Maglin and Nancy Schniedewind, eds. Temple University Press, Philadelphia, 1989.

PART VIII: CHANGING OUR WORLD

Feminism as a Social Movement

Ain't I a Woman: Black Women and Feminism. bell hooks. South End Press, Boston, 1981.

American Feminist Thought. Linda Kauffman, ed. Blackwell, New York, 1993.

"A Black Feminist Statement." Combahee River Collective, in *But Some of Us Are Brave,* Gloria Hull, Patricia Bell Scott, and Barbara Smith, eds. Feminist Press, Old Westbury, NY, 1982.

Black Feminist Thought: Knowledge, Consciousness and the Politics of Empowerment. Patricia Hill Collins. Unwin Hyman, Boston, 1990.

The Black Woman. Tony Cade Bambara, ed. New American Library, New York, 1970.

Century of Struggle. Eleanor Flexner. Atheneum, New York, 1972.

The Chicana Feminist. Martha Cotera. Informations Systems Development, Austin, TX, 1976.

Contemporary Feminist Thought. Hester Eisenstein. G. K. Hall, Boston, 1983.

The Feminist Papers from Adams to De Beauvoir. Alice Rossi. Northeastern University Press, Boston, 1973.

Feminist Theory: The Intellectual Traditions of American Feminism. Josephine Donovan. F. Unger, New York, 1985.

Freedom from Violence: Women's Strategies from Around the World. Margaret Schuler, ed. OEF International Unifem, New York, 1992.

From Margin to Center. bell hooks. South End Press, Boston, 1984.

Gather Your Strength, Sisters: The Emerging Role of Chinese Women Community Workers. Stacey G. H. Yap. (Immigrant Communities and Ethnic Minorities in the U.S. and Canada Series: No. 24.) 1987.

Home Girls: A Black Feminist Anthology. Barbara Smith, ed. Kitchen Table Press, Latham, NY, 1983.

Moving the Mountain: The Women's Movement in America Since 1960. Flora Davis. Simon & Schuster, New York, 1991.

On Account of Sex: The Politics of Women's Issues, 1945–1968. Cynthia Harrison. University of California Press, Berkeley, 1988.

Ours By Right: Women's Rights as Human Rights. Joanna Kerr, ed. Zed Books, New York, 1993.

Sisterhood Is Global: The First Anthology of Writings from the International Women's Movement. Robin Morgan, ed. Doubleday, Garden City, NY, 1984.

Third World, 2nd Sex, Vol. II. Miranda Davies, ed. Zed Books, Atlantic Highlands, NJ, 1987.

Third World Women and the Politics of Feminism. Chandra Mohanty, Ann Russo and Lourdes Torres, eds. Indiana University Press, Bloomington, 1991.

What Is Feminism? Juliet Mitchell and Ann Oakley, eds. Pantheon, New York, 1986.

When and Where I Enter. The Impact of Black Women on Race and Sex in America. Paula Giddings. Morrow, New York, 1984.

Women Organizing: Many Issues, Many Voices

Abortion Without Apology: Radical History for the 1990s. Ninia Baehr. South End Press, Boston, 1990.

Abortion and the Politics of Motherhood. Kristin Luker. University of California Press, Berkeley, 1984.

Back Off: How to Confront and Stop Sexual Harassment. Martha Langelan. Fireside Books, New York, 1993.

"Breathing Life into Ourselves: The Evolution of the National Black Women's Health Project." Byllye Avery, in *The Black Woman's Health Book,* Evelyn White, ed. Seal Press, Seattle, WA, 1990.

Bridges of Power: Women's Multicultural Alliances. Lisa Albrecht and Rose Brewer. New Society Publishers, Philadelphia, 1990.

Feminist Fatale. Paula Kamen. Donald Fine Publishers, New York, 1991.

From Abortion to Reproductive Freedom: Transforming a Movement. Marlene Fried, ed. South End Press, Boston, 1990.

Guide to Combatting Sexual Harassment: Candid from 9 to 5, The National Association of Working Women. Ellen Bravo and Ellen Cassidy. Wiley, New York, 1992.

"La Mujer Puertorriquena, Su Cuerpo, y Su Lucha por la Vida: Experiences with Empowerment in Hartford Connecticut." Candida Flores, Lani Davison, Enid Mercedes Rey, Migdalia Rivera, and Maria Serrano, in *From Abortion to Reproductive Freedom: Transforming a Movement,* Marlene Gerber Fried, ed. South End Press, Boston, 1990.

Passionate Politics. Charlotte Bunch. St. Martin's Press, New York, 1987.

Vaginal Politics. Ellen Frankfort. Quadrangle Books, New York, 1972.

Women, AIDS, and Activism. Act Up/NY, Women and Aids Book Group. South End Press, Boston, 1990.

Women and Male Violence: The Visions and Struggles of the Battered Women's Movement. Susan Schechter, South End Press, Boston, 1982.

Women and the Politics of Empowerment. Ann Bookman and Sandra Morgan. Temple University Press, Philadelphia, 1988.

"Working Together, Growing Together: A Brief History of the Boston Women's Health Book Collective." Wendy Coppedge Sanford. *Heresies,* 2, (3), 1979.

You Can't Kill the Spirit. Pam McAllister. New Society Publishers, Philadelphia, 1992.

Credits

Article 1: Reprinted from *Talking Back: Thinking Feminism, Thinking Black* by bell hooks with permission of South End Press, 116 Saint Botolph St., Boston, MA 02115.

Article 2: Reprinted from *On Lies, Secrets and Silence: Selected Prose 1966–1978,* by Adrienne Rich by permission of W. W. Norton & Company, Inc. Copyright © 1979 by W. W. Norton & Company, Inc.

Article 3: "Definition of 'Womanist'" from *In Search of Our Mothers' Gardens: Womanist Prose.* Copyright © 1983 by Alice Walker, reprinted by permission of Harcourt Brace, Inc.

Article 4: "Learning Women's Studies" by Taly Rutenberg from *Theories of Women's Studies,* Gloria Bowles and Renate Duelli Klein, eds. Reprinted by permission of Routledge.

Article 5: Copyright © 1992 by Stacey G. H. Yap. Reprinted by permission of the author.

Article 6: Copyright © 1991 by Danista Hunte. Reprinted by permission of the author.

Article 7: Copyright © 1992 by Luana Ferreira. Reprinted by permission of the author.

Article 8: Copyright © 1992 by Lucita Woodis. Reprinted by permission of the author.

Article 9: Copyright © 1992 by Deborah Halstead Lennon. Reprinted by permission of the author.

Article 10: From *The Politics of Women's Biology* by Ruth Hubbard. Copyright © 1990 by Rutgers, The State University. Reprinted by permission of Rutgers.

Article 11: Copyright © 1992 by Meredith L. Brown. Reprinted by permission of the author.

Article 12: Reminiscences by Frances D. Gage of Sojourner Truth at the Akron Convention, Akron, Ohio, May 28–29, 1851.

Article 13: Reprinted from *The Feminine Mystique* by Betty Friedan, by permission of W. W. Norton & Company, Inc. Copyright © 1974, 1963 by Betty Friedan. Copyright renewed 1991.

Article 14: From *Circles on the Water* by Marge Piercy. Copyright © 1982 by Marge Piercy. Reprinted by permission of Alfred A. Knopf, Inc.

Article 15: From *Borderlands/La Frontera, The New Mestiza.* Copyright © 1987 by Gloria Anzaldua. Reprinted by permission of Aunt Lute Books.

Article 16: From *Watchers and Seekers,* Rhonda Cobham and Merle Collins, eds., first published by The Women's Press Ltd., 1987, 34 Great Sutton Street, London EC1V ODX.

Article 17: Reprinted from *Lilith* magazine. Copyright © 1987. Subscriptions to *Lilith,* the nation's only independent Jewish women's magazine, are $16.00 per year, avail-able from *Lilith,* dept. WIR-90, 250 West 57th Street, #2432, New York, NY 10107.

Article 18: Reprinted from *With Wings: An Anthology of Literature by and about Women with Disabilities,* Marshal Saxton and Florence Howe, eds., pp. 82–83. Copyright © 1987 by Debra Kent.

Article 19: Copyright © 1992 by Folami Harris-Gray. Reprinted by permission of the author.

Article 20: Copyright © 1969 by Naomi Weisstein. (Abridged and edited by Virginia Blaisdell.) Reprinted by permission of the author.

Article 21: "The Gift" reprinted with permission of the author. Copyright © Murielle Minard.

Article 22: "Growing" by Helena María Viramontes. Reprinted from *Cuentos: Stories by Latinas,* Alma Gomez, Cherrie Morago, Mariana Romo-Carmona, eds. Kitchen Table Press, P.O. Box 908, Latham, NY 12110.

Article 23: Reprinted from *Journal for the Education of the Gifted.* Vol. XII, No. 2, 1989, pp. 118–130. Copyright © 1989 The Association for the Gifted (edited). Revised for this volume by the author in 1992.

Article 24: Reprinted with permission from *Psychology Today Magazine.* Copyright © 1985 Sussex Publishers, Inc.

Article 25: Reprinted from *Women: A Feminist Perspective.* Jo Freeman, ed. Copyright © 1979, 1975 by Jo Freeman, copyright 1985, 1989 by Mayfield Publishing Company.

Article 26: Reprinted with permission of National Commission on Working Women, Wider Opportunities for Women.

Article 27: Reprinted from *Ms.,* vol. 1, no. 6, December 1972. Copyright © 1978 Lois Gould. Reprinted by permission of The Charlotte Sheedy Literary Agency.

Article 28: Copyright © 1986 by Wendy Chapkis. Reprinted by permission of the author.

Article 29: From *This Bridge Called My Back: Writings by Radical Women of Color,* Cherrie Moraga and Gloria Anzaldua, eds. Copyright © 1981 by Nellie Wong. Reprinted with permission of the author.

Article 30: From *The Third Women,* Dexter Fisher, ed., copyright © 1980 by Houghton-Mifflin Co. Reprinted by permission of the author.

Article 31: From *The Tribe of Dina: A Jewish Women's Anthology,* Melanie Kaye/Kantrowitz. Copyright © 1986 by Aishe Berger. Reprinted by permission of the author.

Article 32: Reprinted by permission of Curtis Brown, Ltd. Copyright © 1980 by Lucille Clifton.

Article 33: "Bra One" by Vickie Sears from *Simple Songs* by Vickie Sears, published by Firebrand Books, Ithaca, New York.

© 1984 by Lindsy Van Gelder. Reprinted by permission of the author.

Article 76: From *Chicana Lesbians*, Carla Trujillo, ed. Third Woman Press, 1991. Reprinted by permission of the author.

Article 77: An earlier version of "Identity: Skin Blood Heart" by Minnie Bruce Pratt in *Rebellion Essays 1980–1991*, Firebrand Books, Ithaca, New York. Copyright © 1991 by Minnie Bruce Pratt.

Article 78: Copyright © 1988 by Peggy McIntosh. Excerpted from "White Privilege and Male Privilege: A Personal Account of Coming to See Correspondences Through Work in Women's Studies," Working Paper #189, Wellesley College Center for Research on Women, Wellesley, MA 02181. Longer version available. *Permission to reprint must be obtained from Peggy McIntosh at (617) 283-2520.*

Article 79: From *A Burst of Light* by Audre Lorde. Copyright © 1988 by Audre Lorde. Permission granted by Firebrand Books, Ithaca, New York.

Article 80: Reprinted with permission from Older Women's League.

Article 81: From *Look Me in the Eye: Old Women, Aging, and Ageism,* Expanded Edition, by Barbara Macdonald with Cynthia Rich, 76–87. Minneapolis: Spinsters Ink, 1983. Available from: Spinsters Ink, P.O. Box 300170, Minneapolis, MN 55403. $8.95.

Article 82: From *Number Our Days* by Barbara Meyerhoff. Copyright © 1978 by Barbara Meyerhoff. Used by permission of the publisher, Dutton, an imprint of New American Library, a division of Penguin Books USA Inc.

Article 83: From *Every Other Path,* Arcadio Morales, Jr. and Brian Martinez, eds. Permission granted by Francisco A. Lomeli.

Article 84: Originally published in *The Village Voice.* Reprinted from *Beginning to See the Light.* Copyright © 1992 by Ellen Willis, Wesleyan University Press. Reprinted by permission of University Press of New England.

Article 85: Copyright © 1992 by Laura Wells. Reprinted by permission of the author.

Article 86: From *The Black Women's Health Book,* Evelyn C. White, ed. Reprinted with permission of the publisher, Seal Press, Seattle, 1990.

Article 87: Copyright © 1990 by the Feminist Majority Foundation, 1600 Wilson Blvd., #801, Arlington, VA 22209.

Article 88: Testimony of William Bell (on Raised Bill #5447) Connecticut State Legislature, Hartford, Connecticut. Delivered March 2, 1990.

Article 89: Reprinted with permission from NOW Legal Defense and Education Fund, Fact Sheet #3, 1989.

Article 90: First printed in *Sojourner: The Women's Forum,* October 1990, vol. 16, No. 2, pp. 16–18. Reprinted by permission of the author.

Article 91: From *Battered Wives,* by Del Martin, Pocket Books. Copyright © 1983 by Del Martin. Reprinted by permission of the author.

Article 92: From *The Forbidden Stitch: An Asian American Women's Anthology,* Shirley Geok-lin Lim et al., eds.

CALYX Books. Copyright © 1989. Reprinted by permission of the publisher.

Article 93: Reprinted with the permission of Macmillan Publishing Company from *Thinking About Women: Sociological Perspectives on Sex and Gender,* Second edition, by Margaret L. Anderson. Copyright © 1988 by Macmillan Publishing Company.

Article 94: From *For the Latina in an Abusive Relationship,* by Myrna Zambrano, published by Seal Press. Copyright © 1985. Reprinted by permission of the publisher.

Article 95: Reprinted from *Ramparts,* Vol. 10, No. 3, September 1971, by permission of the author.

Article 96: From *Nappy Edges* by Ntozake Shange. Copyright © 1972, 1974, 1975, 1976, 1977, 1978 by Ntozake Shange. Reprinted with permission from St. Martin's Press, Inc., New York.

Article 97: From *I Never Called it Rape* by Robin Warshaw and Mary P. Koss. Copyright © 1988 by the *Ms.* Foundation for Education and Communication, Inc. Reprinted by permission of HarperCollins, Publishers, Inc.

Article 98: From *Voices in the Night: Women Speaking About Incest,* Roni A. H. McNaron and Yarrow Morgan, eds., 1982. Reprinted by permission of Cleis Press.

Article 99: From *Under a Soprano Sky* by Sonia Sanchez, Africa World Press, Trenton, NJ. Reprinted by permission of the author.

Article 100: From *Watchers and Seekers: Creative Writing by Black Women,* Rhonda Cobham and Merle Collins, eds., Harper & Row, 1988.

Article 101: From *Living the Spirit,* Will Roscoe, ed. St. Martin's, 1988.

Article 102: Reprinted by permission of the author.

Article 103: From *Voices in the Night: Women Speaking About Incest.* Roni A. H. McNaron and Yarrow Morgan, eds., 1982. Reprinted by permission of Cleis Press.

Article 104: From a working paper by Center for Puerto Rican Studies, Hunter College, New York.

Article 105: From *Seeing Through the Sun,* University of Massachusetts Press, 1985. Reprinted by permission of the author.

Article 106: From *Nobody Speaks for Me* by Nancy Seifer. Copyright © 1976 by Nancy Seifer. Reprinted by permission of Simon & Schuster, Inc.

Article 107: Reprinted by permission of the author.

Article 108: From *Ms.* magazine, 1982. Reprinted by permission of the author.

Article 109: Reprinted from *The Fact of a Doorframe, Poems Selected and New, 1950–1984* by Adrienne Rich, by permission of the author and W. W. Norton & Company, Inc. Copyright © 1984 by Adrienne Rich. Copyright © 1975, 1978 by W. W. Norton & Company, Inc. Copyright © 1981 by Adrienne Rich.

Article 110: From *Radical Feminism,* Anne Koedt, Ellen Levine and Anita Rapone, eds., NY Times/Quadrangle, 1973. Copyright © 1971 by Anne Koedt. This article first appeared in *Notes From the Third Year.* Reprinted by permission of the author.

Article 111: From *Forty-Three Septembers* by Jewelle Gomez,

Firebrand Books, Ithaca, NY. Reprinted by permission of the author.

Article 112: Reprinted by permission of the Wallace Literary Agency, Inc. First appeared in *Ms.* Copyright © 1984 by Marge Piercy and Middlemarsh, Inc.

Article 113: From *Redbook,* August 1971. Copyright © 1970, 1971 by Alix Kates Shulman. Reprinted by permission of the author.

Article 114: Reprinted from *Black Feminist Thought* by Patricia Hill Collins by permission of Routledge, New York, and the author. Copyright © 1990 by Patricia Hill Collins.

Article 115: From *It's a Family Affair: The Real Lives of Black Single Mothers* by Barbara Omolade. Copyright © 1986 by Barbara Omolade. Used with permission of the author and Kitchen Table: Women of Color Press, P.O. Box 908, Latham, NY 12110.

Article 116: Reprinted from *A Burst of Light* by Audre Lorde, by permission of Firebrand Books, Ithaca, New York. Copyright © 1988 by Audre Lorde.

Article 117: Copyright © 1992 by Ellen Davidson. Reprinted by permission of the author.

Article 118: Copyright © 1992 by Amy Kesselman.

Article 119: The Seneca Falls Woman's Rights Convention, Seneca Falls, New York, July 10 and 20, 1848.

Article 120: Excerpt from "Consciousness-Raising: A Radical Weapon," by Kathie Sarachild. From *Feminist Revolution,* edited by Redstockings (New York: Redstockings, 1975; abridged ed. with additional writings, New York: Random House, 1978). Available from Redstockings Women's Liberation Archives Distribution Project, P.O. Box 2625, Gainesville, FL 32602-2625. Redstockings can be reached directly at P.O. Box 744 Stuyvesant Station, New York, NY 10009-0744. Please enclose a self-addressed stamped envelope with inquiries.

Article 121: From *Home Girls: A Black Feminist Anthology* by Barbara Smith. Copyright © 1983 by Barbara Smith. Used with permission of the author and Kitchen Table: Women of Color Press, P.O. Box 908, Latham, NY 12110.

Article 122: From *Gender and Society,* June 1989. Reprinted by permission of the author.

Article 123: From *A Gathering of the Spirit: Writing and Art by North American Women,* edited by Beth Brant, Sinister Wisdom Books, 1984.

Article 124: From *Backlash* by Susan Faludi. Copyright © 1991 by Susan Faludi. Reprinted by permission of Crown Publishers, Inc.

Article 125: Edited version from *Passionate Politics,* St. Martin's Press, 1987. Reprinted by permission of the author.

Article 126: From *Ms.,* January/February 1992. Reprinted with permission of the author.

Article 127: From *Reforming Medicine: Lessons of the Last Quarter Century* by Victor W. Sidel and Ruth Sidel. Copyright © 1984 by Random House, Inc. Reprinted by permission of Pantheon Books, a division of Random House, Inc.

Article 128: From *Ms.,* February 1979. Copyright © 1979 by Lindsy Van Gelder. Reprinted by permission of the author.

Article 129: Reprinted by permission of 9 to 5: National Association of Working Women. Copyright © 1983 by 9 to 5, National Association of Working Women.

Article 130: From *Women, AIDS and Activism.* ACT UP/NY Women and AIDS Book Group, 1990, South End Press. Reprinted with permission of publisher.

Article 131: Reprinted with permission from *Reproductive Laws for the 1990s, A Briefing Handbook.* Women's Rights Litigation Clinic, Rutgers University.

Article 132: Reprinted from *New Directions for Women,* September/October 1992. 108 W. Palisade Ave., Englewood, NJ 07631. (201) 568-0226.

Article 133: From *Feminist Fatale* by Paula Kamen. Reprinted by permission of Donald Fine, Inc.

Box p. 47: "JAP: The New Antisemitic Code Word" reprinted from *Lilith* magazine, copyright © 1987. Subscriptions to *Lilith,* the nation's only independent Jewish women's magazine, are $16.00 per year, available from *Lilith,* Dept. WIR-93, 250 West 57th Street, New York, NY 10107.

Box p. 68: "Checklist for Inclusive Teaching" from *Cross-Cultural Perspectives on the Curriculum,* Deborah Rosenfelt. Reprinted by permission of the author.

Box p. 81: "Lesbian Invisibility in the Media" by Karin Schwartz. Reprinted from FAIR's journal *EXTRA!,* March/April 1991. FAIR (Fairness & Accuracy in Reporting), 130 West 25th Street, New York, NY 10001.

Box p. 128: "Demanding a Condom" by Kat Doud. Reprinted from *Women, AIDS & Activism,* South End Press, 1990. Copyright © 1990 by the ACT UP/New York Women and AIDS Book Group.

Box pp. 166 and 167: "Going Public" and "Factory Harassment" reprinted with permission from *Equal Means: Women Organizing Economic Solutions* (Vol. 1, No. 2, Spring 1992), a tri-annual journal published by the Ms. Foundation for Women. Subscriptions available for $24/4 issues from: *Equal Means,* 2512 Ninth St., #3, Berkeley, CA 94710. (510) 549-9931.

Box p. 169: "Office Double Standards" reprinted by permission of *Ms.* magazine. Copyright © 1990.

Box p. 216: "Ann so enjoys these little Gyno-to-Lesbo chats" by permission of Making Waves Greeting Cards. Cartoon by Valerie Young.

Box p. 245: "Breaking Chains and Encouraging Life" from *In Search of Our Mothers' Gardens: Womanist Prose,* copyright © 1983 by Alice Walker. Reprinted by permission of Harcourt Brace, Inc.

Box p. 460: "Sisters." Words by Cris Williamson. Copyright © 1975 Bird Ankles Music (BMI). Used by permission. All rights reserved.